Volume 1 of *The Cambridge History of British Theatre* begins in Roman Britain and ends with Charles II's restoration to the throne imminent. The four essays in Part I treat pre-Elizabethan theatre, the eight in Part II focus on the riches of the Elizabethan era, and the seven in Part III on theatrical developments during and after the reigns of James I and Charles I. The essays are written for the general reader by leading British and American scholars, who combine an interest in the written drama with an understanding of the material conditions of the evolving professional theatre which the drama helped to sustain, often enough against formidable odds. The volume unfolds a story of enterprise, innovation and, sometimes, of desperate survival over years in which theatre and drama were necessarily embroiled in the politics of everyday life: a vivid subject vividly presented.

JANE MILLING is Lecturer in Drama at the University of Exeter. She has written on Restoration performers and female dramatists. Her work in the modern period includes co-authorship with Graham Ley of *Modern Theories of Performance: From Stanislavski to Boal* (2001).

PETER THOMSON is Emeritus Professor of Drama at the University of Exeter. His books include *Shakespeare's Theatre* (1992), *Brecht: Mother Courage and Her Children* (Cambridge, 1997), *Shakespeare's Professional Career* (Cambridge, 1992, 1999) and *On Actors and Acting* (2000).

THE CAMBRIDGE HISTORY OF

BRITISH THEATRE

General Editor
PETER THOMSON, *University of Exeter*

The Cambridge History of British Theatre provides a uniquely authoritative account of the turbulent and often troublesome public life of performance in Britain. Whilst making full use of new research in a subject that is at the centre of current concern, the essays are designed for the general reader as well as for the specialist. Each volume is fully illustrated. Together, they offer a comprehensive and comprehensible history of theatre, of which plays are a part but by no means the whole.

The Cambridge History of British Theatre, Volume 1: Origins to 1660
EDITED BY JANE MILLING AND PETER THOMSON

The Cambridge History of British Theatre, Volume 2: 1660 to 1895
EDITED BY JOSEPH DONOHUE

The Cambridge History of British Theatre, Volume 3: Since 1895
EDITED BY BAZ KERSHAW

THE CAMBRIDGE
HISTORY OF
BRITISH THEATRE

*

VOLUME I
Origins to 1660

*

Edited by
JANE MILLING
and
PETER THOMSON

CAMBRIDGE
UNIVERSITY PRESS

PUBLISHED BY THE PRESS SYNDICATE OF THE UNIVERSITY OF CAMBRIDGE
The Pitt Building, Trumpington Street, Cambridge CB2 1RP, United Kingdom

CAMBRIDGE UNIVERSITY PRESS
The Edinburgh Building, Cambridge, CB2 2RU, UK
40 West 20th Street, New York, NY 10011–4211, USA
477 Williamstown Road, Port Melbourne, VIC 3207, Australia
Ruiz de Alarcón 13, 28014 Madrid, Spain
Dock House, The Waterfront, Cape Town 8001, South Africa

http://www.cambridge.org

First published 2004

Printed in the United Kingdom at the University Press, Cambridge

Typeface Dante 10.5/13 pt.   *System* LaTeX 2$_\varepsilon$ [TB]

A catalogue record for this book is available from the British Library

ISBN 0 521 65040 2 hardback

Volume 2: 1660 to 1895
ISBN: 0 521 65068 2

Volume 3: Since 1895
ISBN: 0 521 65132 8

Three volume set:
ISBN: 0 521 82790 6

Contents

Contents

Illustrations

Notes on contributors

MARTIN BUTLER is Professor of English Renaissance Drama at the University of Leeds. His books include *Theatre and Crisis, 1632–1642* (1984) and (as editor) *Re-Presenting Ben Jonson* (1999). His edition of *Cymbeline* is shortly to appear in the New Cambridge Shakespeare, and he is general editor of the Cambridge edition of the *Works of Ben Jonson*, to be published in 2005.

DOUGLAS BRUSTER is Professor at the University of Texas, Austin. His books include *Drama and the Market in the Age of Shakespeare* (1992), *Quoting Shakespeare: Form and Culture in Early Modern Drama* (2000) and he is the editor of Thomas Middleton and William Rowley's *The Changeling* for *The Collected Works of Thomas Middleton* (2000). He has just finished *Shakespeare and the Question of Culture* (2003).

RICHARD ALLEN CAVE is Professor of Drama and Theatre Arts at Royal Holloway, University of London. He has written extensively on aspects of Renaissance drama (especially Jonson and Webster), nineteenth-century and modern theatre, Anglo-Irish drama, forms of dance theatre and the study of the body as a medium of expression. He has edited several works by the Irish novelist George Moore and the plays of Yeats and Wilde. While general editor of *Theatre in Focus*, he contributed monographs on Terence Gray and Charles Ricketts to the series.

JANET CLARE is Senior Lecturer at the Department of English, University College Dublin. Her books include *'Art Made Tongue-tied by Authority': Elizabethan and Jacobean Dramatic Censorship* (1990 and 1999) and *Drama of the English Republic, 1649–1660* (2002). She has written extensively on Renaissance drama and censorship, including chapters and articles in *Marlowe Studies* (2000), *Constructing Christopher Marlowe* (2000), *Essays on Marston* (2001) and *Literature and Censorship in Renaissance England* (2001).

JOHN C. COLDEWEY is Professor of English at the University of Washington. He has published widely in the area of medieval and Renaissance drama. He is the editor of *REED: Nottinghamshire* (forthcoming), *Early English Drama* (1993), with W. R. Streitberger, of *Drama: Classical to Contemporary* (1998), with Brian Copenhaver, of two volumes of *Renaissance Latin Drama in England* (1984, 1991) and, with Marianne Briscoe, of *Contexts for Early English Drama* (1989).

JANETTE DILLON is Professor of Drama at the University of Nottingham. She has published widely on medieval and Renaissance literature and performance, and her recent publications include *Language and Stage in Medieval and Renaissance England* (1998), *Theatre, Court and City 1595–1610: Drama and Social Space in London* (2000) and *Performance and Spectacle in Hall's Chronicle* (2002). She is currently continuing to work on aspects of spectacle.

RICHARD DUTTON is Professor of English at Ohio State University. From 1974 to 2003 he taught at Lancaster University. His research centres on the culture of early modern England, with particular interests in matters of censorship and textual editing. His monographs include *William Shakespeare: a Literary Life* (1989; in the Palgrave Literary Lives series, of which he is general editor), *Ben Jonson: Authority: Criticism* (1996) and *Licensing, Censorship and Authorship in Early Modern England: Buggeswords* (2000). His scholarly editions include *Women Beware Women and Other Plays by Thomas Middleton* (1999) and Jonson's *Epicene* (2003, in the Revels Plays series, of which he is a general editor) and *Volpone* (forthcoming in the Cambridge *Ben Jonson*).

PETER H. GREENFIELD is Professor of English at the University of Puget Sound. He is the editor of *Research Opportunities in Renaissance Drama* and author of many articles and chapters on regional performance, including in *A New History of Early English Drama* (1997), *Carnival and the Carnivalesque* (1998) and *Blackwell Companion to Renaissance Drama* (2002). He is the editor, with Audrey Douglas, of *REED: Cumberland, Westmorland and Gloucestershire* (1986) and *Drama in Hampshire before 1642*, with Jane Cowling (forthcoming). He is currently editing *REED: Hampshire, Hertfordshire, Bedfordshire*.

ANDREW GURR is Emeritus Professor of English at the University of Reading and, until recently, Director of Globe Research at the Shakespeare Globe Centre, London. His publications include *The Shakespearean Stage, 1574–1642* (1970, 1980 and 1992), *Writers in Exile* (1981), *Playgoing in Shakespeare's London* (1987 and 1997), with John Orrell, *Rebuilding Shakespeare's Globe* (1989), with J. R. Mulryne and Margaret Shewring, *Shakespeare's Globe Rebuilt* (1997), *The Shakespearian Playing Companies* (1996) and, with Mariko Ichikawa, *Staging in Shakespeare's Theatres* (2001). He has edited several Renaissance plays, including *Richard II* and *Henry V* for the New Cambridge Shakespeare, and the Quarto *Henry V* for the Cambridge Quarto series. He has written extensively about the design, the archaeology and the sociology of the London theatres of Shakespeare's time.

PETER HAPPÉ is a Visiting Fellow in the English Department of the University of Southampton. He has published widely on the drama of the Middle Ages and the early modern period, his most recent books being *English Drama before Shakespeare* (1999), an edition of Jonson's *The Magnetic Lady* (2000) and a co-edition, with Clifford Davidson, of *The World and the Child* (1999). He has just finished a book on Cycle Plays and is a contributing editor to the Cambridge *Ben Jonson*, working on *A Tale of a Tub*.

DIANA E. HENDERSON is Associate Professor of Literature at MIT. She is the author of *Passion Made Public: Elizabethan Lyric, Gender and Performance* (1995) and numerous articles on early modern drama, poetry and culture, as well as Shakespeare on film and in the modern world. Her current book project is entitled *Uneasy Collaborations: Working with Shakespeare across Time and Media.*

ROSLYN L. KNUTSON is Professor of English at the University of Arkansas at Little Rock. She is the author of *Playing Companies and Commerce in Shakespeare's Time* (2001) and *The Repertory of Shakespeare's Company, 1594–1613* (1991). She has published in journals, annuals and anthologies including *Shakespeare Survey, Shakespeare Quarterly, English Literary Renaissance, Medieval and Renaissance Literature in English* and *A New History of Early English Drama.*

DAVID LINDLEY is Professor of Renaissance Literature at the University of Leeds. He has published widely on the court masque, including an edited collection of essays in 1984 and an edition of selected masques for Oxford's World's Classics in 1995. Other major publications include a study of *Thomas Campion* (1986), *The Trials of Frances Howard* (1993), exploring one of the major scandals of the Jacobean court, and an edition of *The Tempest* for the New Cambridge Shakespeare (2002).

JOHN J. McGAVIN has just finished a stint as Head of English and Assistant Dean at the University of Southampton, where he is involved in the Wessex Medieval Centre. He is the author of *Chaucer and Dissimilarity* (2000) and of various articles on rhetoric and English and Scottish Drama. He is editing *Records of Early Drama: Scotland* in association with the University of Toronto's Records of Early English Drama series.

JANE MILLING is a lecturer at the Drama Department of the University of Exeter. She has written articles on Restoration drama, gender and politics and contributed to the new *Dictionary of National Biography.* She is the author, with Graham Ley, of *Modern Theories of Performance* (2001) and a contributing series editor of Theatre and Performance Practices (Palgrave). Her current book project is entitled *Susanna Centlivre: Theatre and Cultural Politics in the Early Eighteenth Century.*

PETER THOMSON is Emeritus Professor of Drama at the University of Exeter. He is the author of *Shakespeare's Theatre* (1984 and 1992), *Shakespeare's Professional Career* (1992), *On Actors and Acting* (2000) and three books on Bertolt Brecht. He is an associate editor of the forthcoming *New Dictionary of National Biography.*

SUZANNE WESTFALL is Professor of English and Theatre at Lafayette College. She is the author of *Patrons and Performance: Early Tudor Household Revels* (1990) and editor of *Shakespeare and Theatrical Patronage in Early Modern England* (2002). She has contributed to the *Blackwell Companion to Renaissance Drama* (2002) and *A New History of Early English Drama* (1997). At present, she is working on the court revels of Edward VI and a survey of internet sites for Early Modern Theatre for the journal *Early Theatre.* She also directs plays.

MARTIN WHITE is Professor of Drama at the University of Bristol. He has written extensively on Elizabethan and Jacobean drama and Renaissance performance. Recent books include *Renaissance Drama in Action* (1998) and *Middleton and Tourneur* (1992). His research into Renaissance performance practice has been guided by his direction of authentic revivals of plays of the period.

PAUL WHITFIELD WHITE is Associate Professor of English, specialising in Renaissance Drama and Literature and Medieval Drama, at Purdue University. Among his publications are *Theatre and Reformation: Protestantism, Patronage, and Playing in Tudor England* (1993), *Marlowe, History, and Sexuality: New Critical Essays on Christopher Marlowe* (1998) and, with Suzanne Westfall, *Shakespeare and Theatrical Patronage in Early Modern England* (2002). He has contributed to books and journals including *A New History of Early English Drama* (1997), *Shakespeare Studies* and *Journal of Medieval and Early Modern Studies*.

General preface

It is not the aim of the three-volume *Cambridge History of British Theatre* to construct theatrical history as a seamless narrative, not least because such seamlessness would be a distortion of the stop / start / try-again, often opportunistic, truth. Chronology has guided, but not bullied, us. The editorial privilege has been to assemble a team of international scholars able to speak with authority on their assigned (or sometimes chosen) topics. The binding subject is theatre, to which drama is a major, but not the only, contributor.

Each of the volumes includes some essays which are broad surveys, some which treat specific themes or episodes, some which are socio-theatrical 'snapshots' of single years and some which offer case studies of particular performance events. There is, of course, an underlying assertion: that a nation's theatre is necessarily and importantly expressive of, even when resistant to, the values that predominate at the time, but the choice of what to emphasise and what, however regretfully, to omit has rested with the volume's editor or editors. The aim has been to provide a comprehensive 'history' that makes no vain pretence to all-inclusiveness. The character of the volumes is the character of their contributors, and those contributors have been more often asked to use a searchlight than a floodlight in order to illuminate the past.

It is in the nature of 'histories' to be superseded. These volumes, though, may hope to stand as a millennial record of scholarship on a cultural enterprise – the British theatre whose uniqueness is still valued. They are addressed to a readership that ranges from students to sheer enthusiasts. A 'history' is not the place for scholars to talk in secret to other scholars. If we have ever erred in that direction, it has been without the sanction of Victoria Cooper, who has shepherded these volumes through to publication with the generosity that is well known to all the authors who have worked with her.

Peter Thomson

Chronology

	Theatrical events	**Political events**
1540	Lindsay's *Satire of the Three Estates* acted before the Scottish court at Linlithgow.	Fall and execution of Thomas Cromwell. Henry VIII marries Ann of Cleves (marriage annulled); marries Katherine Howard.
1542		War with Scotland (until 1560); Katherine Howard executed; James V dies, Mary Queen of Scots born and succeeds to Scottish throne. Founding of the Roman Inquisition.
1543	Act of Parliament forbids plays meddling with religious doctrine.	Henry VIII marries Katherine Parr; Act 'for the Advancement of True Religion' against unauthorised translations of the Bible. Copernicus's *De revolutionibus* published.
1544		Henry VIII at war with France. Boulogne captured. John Bale's *Brief Chronicle concerning Sir John Oldcastle* published.
1545	First full-time post of Master of the Revels.	Council of Trent meets to reform Catholic church.
1546		War with France ends. Luther dies.
1547	Anti-Catholic plays mark Edward VI's coronation. Act of 1543	Henry VIII dies. Edward VI succeeds to the throne. Henry

repealed. Sebastian Westcott becomes master of Paul's Boys.

Howard, Earl of Surrey, executed and Somerset becomes Protector. Chantries suppressed.

1549 Kett's rebellion supported by audience for annual play at Wymondham near Norwich. All English plays banned for two months.

War with France (until 1550). Kett's rebellion. Act of Uniformity, Catholic mass illegal. First *Book of Common Prayer*.

1550

Catholic bishops removed in England.

1551 Royal proclamation requires all professional acting companies to be licensed.

1552 *Troas*, first of Seneca's plays acted in England at Trinity College, Cambridge.

Somerset executed. Second Act of Uniformity. Second *Book of Common Prayer*.

1553 Bale's anti-Catholic trilogy (*God's Promises, John the Baptist's Preaching, Temptation of our Lord*) acted at Kilkenny. Renewal of ban on doctrinal plays.

Forty-Two Articles. Edward VI dies. Mary I succeeds to the throne.

1554 Version of Lindsay's *Satire of the Three Estates* acted at Carlton Hill, Edinburgh, before Marie de Guise.

Sir Thomas Wyatt's rebellion. Lady Jane Grey executed. Mary marries Philip of Spain. England reconciled with Rome. Knox meets Calvin at Geneva. Reginald Pole made Cardinal Legate in England.

1555 Nicholas Udall headmaster of Westminster School. Worcester's Men become active.

Latimer and Ridley burned. Religious peace of Augsburg.

1556 Seditious plays against Mary and Philip performed by Sir Francis Leke's company.

Cranmer burned. Charles V, Holy Roman emperor, abdicates. His son (Mary I's consort) Philip II crowned King of Spain.

1557 Seditious plays in Kent.

War with France (to 1559). Pole's legatine commission withdrawn.

1558		Loss of Calais. Mary dies. Elizabeth I succeeds to the throne. Knox's *First Blast of the Trumpet against the Monstrous Regiment of Women* published.
1559	Renewed governmental prohibition of plays of religious controversy. Warwick's Men become active.	Knox's return to Scotland sparks religious revolt. Third Act of Uniformity and Act of Supremacy. Matthew Parker appointed Archbishop of Canterbury. England and Spain make peace with France.
1560	Westcott begins regular court performances with Paul's Boys.	Treaty of Edinburgh. French expelled from Scotland.
1561	Thomas Ashton becomes headmaster of Shrewsbury School and begins annual open-air religious plays.	O'Neill's rebellion in Ireland.
1562	*Gorboduc* first performed at Inner Temple, later at court before Elizabeth I.	Civil war in France.
1563	Derby's Men become active.	Thirty-Nine Articles of Religion define Anglican theology. First Poor Law. Foxe's *Acts and Monuments* published.
1564	Elizabeth I sees Plautus's *Aulularia*, Haliwell's *Dido* and Udall's *Ezechias* at King's College Chapel, Cambridge. Rich's Men become active.	Calvin dies.
1566	Elizabeth I sees *Marcus Geminus*, Calfhill's *Progne* and Edwards's *Palamon and Arcite* at Christ Church hall, Oxford. Richard Farrant begins annual court play with Windsor Chapel Children.	Revolt in the Netherlands.

1567	John Brayne builds Red Lion playhouse in Stepney, east of London.	Duke of Alva in the Netherlands. The 'council of Blood'.
1568		Mary Queen of Scots flees to England.
1569	Last performance of York miracle cycle. Sussex's Men become active.	Rising in the north against Elizabeth.
1570		Elizabeth excommunicated by Pope Pius V.
1571		Ridolfi plot. Elizabeth breaks off diplomatic relations with Spain.
1572	Act for the Punishment of Vagabonds (includes unlicensed travelling players). Richard Mulcaster begins annual court play with Merchant Taylors' boys.	Massacre of St Bartholomew. Knox dies.
1573	Italian players (including women) allowed to act in London by command of the Privy Council. Leicester's Men active.	Diplomatic relations with Spain resumed.
1574	Elizabeth grants patent to Earl of Leicester's company.	Persecution of Catholics in England.
1575	Earl of Leicester entertains Elizabeth I at Kenilworth with shows. Mayor of Chester summoned for permitting performance of miracle cycle. Westcott using part of St Paul's school property for 'private theatre' performances.	New Poor Law. Anabaptists burned in England.
1576	James Burbage and John Brayne build The Theatre in Shoreditch, London. Richard Farrant takes over Chapel Royal plays and sets up Blackfriars 'private' theatre.	Edmund Grindal appointed Archbishop of Canterbury. Frobisher's voyage begins.

1577	Strange's Men active. Curtain playhouse opens? Newington Butts playhouse built about this time.	Drake sets off around the world.
1579	Edmond Tilney appointed Master of the Revels.	Proposed marriage of Elizabeth I and Duke of Anjou. Military involvement supporting Dutch rebellion against Spain.
1580	Oxford's Men active.	
1582	Chamberlain's Men active.	
1583	Queen's Men formed. Oxford's Boys perform at Blackfriars.	Whitgift made Archbishop of Canterbury. Throckmorton plot.
1584		Ralegh fails in Virginia. Oath of Association to defend Elizabeth.
1585	Admiral's Men active.	
1586	Will Kemp at Frederick II's court in Elsinore.	Battle of Zutphen. Babbington plot to free Mary Queen of Scots; her trial. Star Chamber forbids publications without ecclesiastical approval.
1587	Rose playhouse built.	Pope declares crusade against England. Mary Queen of Scots executed. Drake at Cadiz.
1588	Tarlton dies.	The Spanish Armada fails.
1589		James VI of Scotland marries Anne of Denmark.
1590	Paul's Boys cease playing.	
1592	Plague closes the playhouses for two years. Pembroke's Men on tour.	
1593		Non-attendance at church punishable by banishment.
1594	Admiral's Men and Chamberlain's Men begin playing.	
1595		Ralegh in Guiana. Drake and Hawkins die in West Indies. Tyrone rebellion in Ireland.

1596	Second Blackfriars playhouse built.	Essex attacks Cadiz.
1597		Second Armada fails.
1598	Playing in London restricted to Admiral's and Chamberlain's Men.	Philip II of Spain dies. Poor Law revised.
1599	Globe playhouse built. Paul's Boys resurrected.	Essex as general in Ireland: recalled and imprisoned.
1600	Fortune playhouse built. Chapel Boys active again.	East India Company founded. Prince Charles (later Charles I) born to James VI of Scotland. Gowrie plot against James.
1601		Essex rebellion and execution.
1603	Admiral's Men become Prince Henry's Men, Chamberlain's Men become King's Men.	Death of Elizabeth. Accession of James VI of Scotland as James I of England. Surrender of Earl of Tyrone, end of Irish rebellion.
1604	Worcester's Men become Queen Anne's Men. Children of the Queen's Revels formed.	
1605	Red Bull built.	James inaugurates campaign against recusants. Gunpowder plot discovered.
1606	Whitefriars playhouse built.	
1607	King's Revels boy company at Whitefriars.	Robert Carr, James's Scottish favourite, knighted. Francis Bacon appointed solicitor-general.
1608	King's Men lease Blackfriars.	Robert Cecil, Earl of Salisbury, appointed lord treasurer.
1609	Cockpit (Phoenix) built.	
1610	George Buc becomes Master of Revels.	Plantation of Ulster. In Holland Olden Barneveldt and Grotius espouse Arminian views.
1611	Lady Elizabeth's Men active.	George Abbot appointed Archbishop of Canterbury. Carr made Viscount Rochester. Sale of baronetcies at £1,095 a piece.

1612	Prince's Men active. Thomas Heywood's *Apology for Actors* published.	Prince Henry dies. Lancashire witches hanged.
1613	Prince Henry's Men become Palsgrave's Men. Globe burns down. Children of the Revels and Lady Elizabeth's Men amalgamate.	Princess Elizabeth marries Frederick, the Elector Palatine. The Essex divorce – the Countess of Essex marries Robert Carr, later Earl of Somerset. Death of Thomas Overbury. Sarmiento (Count of Gondomar) appointed Spanish ambassador.
1614	Second Globe playhouse built. Hope playhouse built.	'Addled' Parliament.
1615	Porter's Hall playhouse built. Cockpit/Phoenix used as theatre.	Trial of Earl and Countess of Somerset for Overbury's murder. Sale of peerages.
1616	Ben Jonson's *Works* published in Folio, and he receives a life pension from James I. Death of Shakespeare.	Ralegh's expedition to Guiana. First Congregational church founded in England.
1617	Shrove Tuesday riots damage the Phoenix playhouse.	James I's journey to Scotland.
1618	Ralegh's execution arranged for same day (29 October) as Lord Mayor's show.	Beginning of the Thirty Years' War.
1619	Remnants of Queen Anne's company become Red Bull (Revels) company. Inigo Jones begins work on Banqueting House (completed 1622).	Death of Queen Anne. Execution of Olden Barneveldt.
1620		Spanish invasion of Palatinate. King Frederick of Bohemia expelled from kingdom. Pilgrim Fathers found New Plymouth, Massachusetts.
1621	Fortune Theatre burns down.	Parliament attacks monopolies and patents and impeaches Bacon for taking bribes. Hostility between king and Commons.

1622	John Astley briefly Master of the Revels.	
1623	New Fortune Theatre opened. Henry Herbert becomes Master of the Revels.	Massacre at Amboyna. Prince Charles and Duke of Buckingham on match-making visit to infanta in Spain. Elector Frederick expelled from Palatinate by imperial troops.
1624	*A Game at Chess* performed at Globe. Actors and author called before Privy Council.	War with Spain. Richelieu becomes first minister of France.
1625	London playhouses close at death of James (27 March). Plague keeps them closed until November/December, when Queen Henrietta's Men become active.	Death of James I and accession of Charles I. Marriage to Henrietta Maria of France. Plague in London.
1626	Remnants of Prince's Men form Red Bull company. Queen Henrietta Maria and ladies perform French play at Somerset House. Riot in Fortune Theatre.	Opposition between king and Commons over forced loan.
1627		England declares war on France. Siege of La Rochelle.
1628		Charles accepts Petition of Right condemning extra-parliamentary taxation. Murder of the Duke of Buckingham.
1629	Salisbury Court playhouse built. Visiting French troupe, including actresses, meet a hostile reception at Blackfriars. Also perform at Red Bull and Fortune.	Charles I dissolves third parliament: beginning of eleven years' personal rule. Imprisonment of Sir John Eliot and rebellious MPs. Peace with France.
1630	Plague closes theatres for seven months. Cockpit-in-Court opened.	Birth of future Charles II.

1631	Prince Charles's Men become active. Plague closures in early part of year.	
1632	Cockpit-in-Court converted.	
1633	Queen performs in Montague's *The Shepherd's Paradise* at Somerset House.	
1634	Spanish actors at court. William Prynne pilloried and imprisoned for *Histrio-Mastix*.	Charles visits Scotland. Death of Wallenstein. William Laud appointed Archbishop of Canterbury. Birth of future James II.
1635	French actors in London.	
1636	Plague closures from 12 May to 2 October 1637. August / September – troupes play before king at Oxford.	Charles I and Laud visit Oxford.
1637	Brief reopening of theatres in February. Beeston's Boys formed. Queen's Men active. Ogilby's Men active in Dublin. Werburgh Street Theatre built there.	Ship money controversy. Scots ordered to accept English Prayer Book.
1638	New Masquing House at Whitehall.	Star Chamber ruling that 'Rex is Lex'. Solemn League and Covenant.
1639	Red Bull actors summoned by Privy Council for libellous *The Whore New Vamped*. Lord Mayor's shows stopped.	First Bishops' War. Strafford becomes king's chief counsellor.
1640	Beeston imprisoned for Beeston's Boys' play at Cockpit. William Davenant replaces him to run company until 1641. September / November – plague closures.	The 'Short' Parliament (13 April – 5 May). Second Bishops' War. 'Long' Parliament summoned. Laud and Strafford arrested. Citizens bring 'Root and Branch' petition to Commons proposing abolition of bishops.
1641	August / November – plague closures. *The Stage-Player's*	Execution of Strafford. Star Chamber and Court of High

Complaint published. Davenant, Suckling and Jermyn flee after army plot uncovered.

Commission abolished. Root and Branch bill and Grand Remonstrance. Irish rebellion.

1642 Parliamentary debates on suppression of plays: 2 September – Parliament orders closure of theatres.

Attempted arrest of five MPs. Charles takes refuge in York. 22 August – Royal standard raised at Nottingham. 23 October – battle of Edgehill. Charles I establishes headquarters in Oxford.

1643 *The Actors' Remonstrance*. Some players at Oxford throughout the war. Raid on illicit performance at Fortune.

Parliament accepts Scottish alliance and Solemn League and Covenant. Death of John Hampden, John Pym and Louis XIII.

1644 Interior of Globe playhouse dismantled.

2 July – battle of Marston Moor.

1645 Masquing House at Whitehall 'pulled down'.

Prayer Book abolished. Laud executed. New Model Army formed under Cromwell and Fairfax. 14 June battle of Naseby.

1646 King's players petition and win salary arrears from House of Lords. Davenant in Paris.

Presbyterianism made state religion. King takes refuge with Scots. Oxford surrenders.

1647 Players act publicly at Salisbury Court, Cockpit and Fortune. 16 July – parliamentary order against playing. 22 October – further parliamentary order against playing. Beaumont and Fletcher Folio published.

King handed over to parliament in London, seized by army on 4 June, escapes to Isle of Wight. Putney debates between Levellers and army generals.

1648 Players at Cockpit and Red Bull. 9 February – ordinance to suppress players. June and July ordinances for suppression passed. Surreptitious performances continue.

Second Civil War. Defeat of Scottish royal army at Preston. 6–7 December Pride's Purge. End of Thirty Years' War with Treaty of Westphalia.

1649	Interiors of Fortune, Cockpit and Salisbury Court dismantled. Red Bull continues performances.	King's trial and execution on 30 January. Rump Parliament abolishes House of Lords and monarchy. Commonwealth proclaimed. Levellers capture Burford. Cromwell crushes Irish rebellion.
1650	'Humble Petition' of impoverished actors to Parliament. Raid on Red Bull. Beeston repairs Cockpit and sets up a boy's training company.	Charles II in Scotland accepts Covenant.
1651		Charles II crowned at Scone. Battle of Worcester and Charles's escape. Royalist estates confiscated.
1652	Beeston buys lease of Salisbury Court.	End of Irish War.
1653	Robert Cox performs at Red Bull. Gibbon's Tennis Court used for performances. Raid on performance of Killigrew's *Claracilla*. John Rowe, in *Tragi-Comoedia*, implies illicit provincial performance.	Parliament expelled by Cromwell. 'Barebones' parliament sits July – December. Instrument of Government establishes Protectorate. Trial and acquittal of John Lilburne.
1654	Attempts to suppress playing. Raid on *Wit Without Money* at Red Bull.	Peace with Holland. First protectorate parliament.
1655	Plays at Red Bull, raided on 14 September. Blackfriars playhouse 'pulled down'. Lord Mayor's shows resume.	Proclamation on religious liberty. War with Spain. Treaty with France.
1656	Davenant apparently using Gibbon's Tennis Court, Cockpit and Apothecaries' Hall for performance. May – performances at Rutland House. Hope Theatre 'pulled down'.	Second protectorate parliament. Naval victories in war with Spain.

1657		Cromwell declines kingship.
1658	Davenant's performances at Cockpit.	Parliament dissolved. Death of Oliver Cromwell on 3 September. Richard Cromwell appointed Lord Protector.
1659	Performances at Red Bull. Davenant imprisoned for part in royalist plot. *Siege of Rhodes* acted at Cockpit. Actors arrested for performing at Red Bull.	End of Protectorate. Rump Parliament recalled. Monck leads army from Scotland.
1660	Theatre patents granted to Killigrew and Davenant.	Monck recalls MPs excluded since 1648, who vote for dissolution of parliament. Declaration of Breda. New Parliament recalls Charles II, who enters London on 29 May. Founding of Royal Society.

PART I

*

PRE-ELIZABETHAN THEATRE

From Roman to Renaissance in drama and theatre

JOHN C. COLDEWEY

Roman remains: the Phantom limb

phantom limb, the sensation that an amputated limb is still present, often associated with painful paresthesia. (Syn. *stump hallucination*)
(*Stedman's Medical Dictionary*, 26th edition)

Patients recovering from amputations often report that during post-operative healing – in some cases long after convalescence is over – they feel twinges of pain or itching from the lost limb, an odd misfiring in the central nervous system and cerebral cortex indicating that life continues to haunt what is now clearly empty space. This phenomenon, a medical condition commonly known as a 'phantom limb', compounds the body's wistful remembrance with something less than material fact. It may be a useful condition to keep in mind as we approach the Roman theatrical tradition in Britain from a place and time as far removed as the present. Like a phantom limb, Roman drama in Britain continues to send signals of its once vital life long after all but stony remnants of its presence have disappeared, long after the vast civilisation that spawned and nurtured it passed on into history. Our experience of the Roman theatrical tradition, poignant, incomplete, perhaps suspicious, has its roots in that vibrant, vanished, phantom culture.

Today, in the early dawn of the twenty-first century, the rise and fall of the phantom Roman empire and its cultural dominion, spanning five hundred years of British history over two millennia ago, seem far-off events in a sequence hard to imagine, hard to suggest as even tangentially important to a modern history of British theatre. The past is passed by so easily. With the single blink of an eye, a contemporary theatre aficionado with interests in scripts, stages and costumes might quickly bypass whole centuries of Roman invasion, occupation and cultural colonialism. Worse, the fragmentary nature or sheer lack of historical evidence ensures that even when the tremendous project of Roman colonisation and its later collapse come under close scrutiny, the difficulties of detail prove almost impossible to catalogue. And how relevant might such ancient events be, in any case, to our understanding of current theatrical practices? And yet, whatever modern misgivings may come into play, clearly in those unimaginably distant days, sponsored by that astonishing Roman civilisation, the first true performances of drama in Britain took place, the first true theatres were built, and the heritage of the modern stage began. For us it represents a necessary starting point, the first seeds of a future that continue to flower today.

As usual when we are discussing plays and performances, whatever we know about early practices is necessarily linked to a larger story, since the genre of drama always functions not only as a literary archetype but as a social artifact as well. The meanings and impulses of staged events depend not only upon texts but also upon cultural contexts. For our purposes – tracing the earliest theatrical traditions in the country – this generic feature of drama proves a mercy, for we lack any playtexts specific to the Roman province of Britannia. We can, however, still explore collateral kinds of evidence to derive some sense of what the beginnings of drama here may have entailed. Mercifully too, although many details are in dispute, the main contours of the larger story of Roman occupation and withdrawal are relatively well known and easily related. Those chronologically distant Roman traditions, combined with architectural ruins from Roman times and other physical evidence from antiquity, can provide us with oblique but suggestive contemporary testimony about early British theatrical habits.

First, the familiar story. During the middle of the first century before Christ, in 55 BC, a Roman expeditionary force of some 10,000 foot soldiers and 500 cavalry under the command of Julius Caesar arrived in Britain. It took only a few successful skirmishes to impress resident Celtic tribal inhabitants with the ruthlessness and efficiency of Roman military power, and then Caesar and his reconnaissance troops sailed back to Gaul. The Romans, for their part, seem to have been impressed with the possibility of an easy conquest, for a year later they returned with an even larger military contingent: 25,000 legionaries and 2,000 cavalry. This time, although the Celtic tribes offered fiercer resistance, once again they proved unequal to the seasoned and disciplined Roman troops. Having conquered the most powerful regional tribe, the Catuvellauni, Caesar forged a convenient peace with its leaders, arranging for regular tribute to be paid to Rome. Then the Romans disappeared from Britain again for nearly a century. Back in Rome the government was in tumult, and civil war threatened to break down the republic itself, so for generations in Britain a succession of tribal representatives maintained trade with the empire and the Romans ruled loosely, *in absentia*. Celtic tribes in the south and east of Britain seem to have struggled amongst themselves for power, and early minted coins – one of the few kinds of evidence surviving from this period – suggest a sequence of Celtic rulers. Tribal fighting finally led to fully consolidated rule in those areas the Romans had conquered, and during the course of time, Britain (or a large part of it) became established as a client state of Rome. For the time being tribes managed to retain their Celtic identities, maintaining an only partially Romanised culture. But this situation would soon change.

Nearly midway through the following century, by about AD 40, a renewal of violent tribal clashes in Britain turned Rome's attention once more in that direction. The famously unbalanced emperor Caligula contemplated invasion, though in the end seems to have lost interest and called the project off. After he was murdered, his successor Claudius moved the plan forward once again, and in AD 43 a force of some 40,000 men arrived in Britain, overwhelming any opposition. The new emperor, in need of the popularity that a military conquest might bring at home, quickly made his way across the channel to appear in full martial splendour – including, memorably, his fighting elephants – impressing the locals and celebrating victory before returning triumphantly to Rome a few weeks later. Claudius left behind his commander, Plautius, to serve as governor and to extend and consolidate colonial rule. Clearly, this time the Romans had come to stay. Within two generations legionary expeditions vigorously extended their military presence and pushed the edges of occupied territory into the south-west as far as Exeter, west into Wales, and north to the Scottish lowlands. Better equipped and trained, the Romans were facing essentially bronze-age enemies, and victory was in many senses foreordained. The experienced troops quashed tribal revolts and uprisings handily, often brutally. With the exception of the uprising of Boudicca, queen of the Iceni, who joined with the Trinovantes in a nearly successful bloody revolt in AD 60, the script of Roman conquest was reenacted across the countryside, setting the scene for commercial exploitation and the spread of the Roman way of life. Colonisation came fast on the heels of conquest. Roman troops were quickly joined by Roman bureaucrats buttressed by Roman workers and artisans. Together they brought new fiscal policies, trade, social discipline and order to the conquered land, conveniently adapting local customs to their own practices.

As they secured the frontiers of the new province of Britannia, the Romans established towns in strategic locations: places like Colchester (Camulodunum), where a group of veterans set up the first *colonia*, or chartered town, in AD 49, extending the legionary fortress which had itself been built across from the former capitol of the once powerful Trinovantes tribe. The settlement soon became an elaborate regional centre for Roman citizens, complete with a temple and a forum, public buildings, tessellated walkways, and, according to Tacitus, a theatre. Urban planning and architecture were patterned on Roman models here as in other early towns. These were established at St Albans (Verulamium, former capitol of the Catuvellauni tribe), at the three *coloniae* of Lincoln (Lindum), York (Eboracum) and Gloucester (Glevum), at trading communities like London (Londinium), Canterbury (Durovernum), Silchester (Calleva) and a host of other places. The Roman military forces spread scores of fortified settlements thickly across the countryside, many of which eventually developed and flourished as major population centres with local markets and governments. All these centres, and most military sites as well, were linked by the ongoing construction of more than 5,000 miles of skilfully engineered roads, completed in the main by the end of the first century (see figure 1).

Within two or three generations the Romans had successfully imported an elaborate network of institutions to serve colonial Britannia: not only military but social, political, economic, religious and ceremonial, signalling utter change in every arena of life. They developed markets, farms, villas, baths, vineyards, systems of transportation and communication, and they brought a new rule of law. They introduced a true money economy and other economic structures profoundly different from the tribal practices of the indigenous Celtic peoples. However remote and provincial Britannia may have seemed from the centre of action, in a surprisingly short time it had taken on much of the colouring of the bustling Roman empire. And over time the conquered people not only took part in the advanced material culture, they also came to share Roman habits of mind, ideologies, pleasures and pastimes. Tacitus, son-in-law to Agricola, the distinguished Roman general and governor of Britannia from AD 77–84, saw this cultural imperialism as a kind of cruel colonising trick. Writing just after the end of the first century AD, he noted that

> . . . they who lately disdained the tongue of Rome now coveted its eloquence. Hence, too, a liking sprang up for our style of dress, and the 'toga' became fashionable. Step by step they were led to things which dispose to vice, the lounge, the bath, the elegant banquet. All this in their ignorance, they called civilisation, when it was but a part of their servitude.[1]

1 Tacitus, *The Complete Works*, 21.

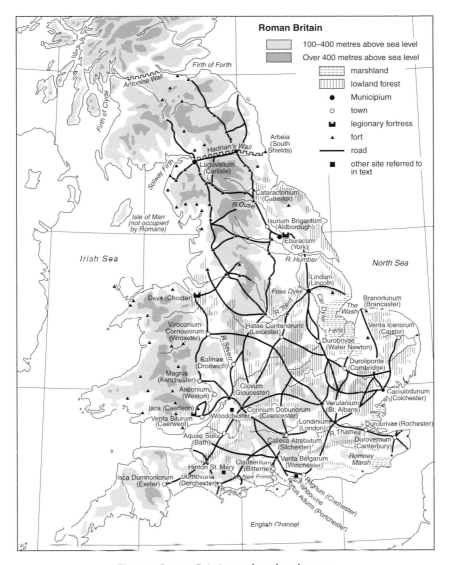

Figure 1 Roman Britain, roads and settlements

But by then the project had such enormous momentum that it could hardly be slowed. In the year 130 Hadrian had completed his stupendous eighty-mile fortified wall running sea to sea in the north of the country, from the Tyne to the Solway. Within the next twenty years his successor put up the turf-and-ditch Antonine wall even further north, along the Forth–Clyde line. Occasional breaches of these fortified boundaries occurred, but Hadrian's wall proved most durable, and Romanisation continued within the protected territory to the south at an astonishing pace. Turning back raids from Scotland and Wales and the south-west, legionary troops forced the borders of occupation outwards, and for generations the growth and development of the burgeoning society under Roman military rule went on virtually free from serious challenge.

And so time passed, a good deal of it, centuries. It would be hard to overestimate the transformative power and importance of Romanisation during this era. Now a distinct province of Rome, Britannia prospered while the phenomenal growth of the empire itself continued unabated, apparently invincible, inevitable, expanding across most of the known worlds of Europe and the near east. And in Britannia, through all of the four centuries of Roman glory, generations flourished, increasing in number and wealth. The population then is estimated to have reached between three and four million people, about as great a number as were alive before the Black Death struck in the fourteenth century.[2] And clearly the powerful Roman culture put down deep roots during the time it ruled Britain. As new towns and villas were founded, older communities settled in for the long haul, consolidating, spreading, investing in public amenities, building and rebuilding civic structures central to the Roman way of life: temples, basilicas, forums, baths, amphitheatres and theatres.

During the second and third centuries, Roman domination tamed the landscape of Britain. Over six hundred villas arose in rural settings – some of them, like Chedworth in Gloucestershire, or the palatial quarters at Fishbourne, quite spectacular – marking the homes of successful chieftains, or centres of large agricultural holdings, sometimes acting as regional leisure retreats. But the main thrust of Romanisation was felt in urban development. Towns were platted along the recognisable Roman grid system, and they thrived within other fully articulated systems of protection, support, transport and trade. The positioning of these towns did not, of course, occur by happenstance. From the beginning, they were situated about a day's march apart, along an increasingly developed network of roads radiating out from London – a settlement that had evolved early on as the main commercial centre for the province. These roads, with post and relay stations along the way, acted not only as a means of military transport, but as the main arteries for trade and information, for such foreign goods as wine, pottery, bronzeware and glass. Smooth, strongly built and well maintained, the roads offered easy access to every corner of the land.

---

2 See Jones, *The End of Roman Britain*, 13–14.

The three main routes out of London extended to Lincoln, York and the north, to Chester and up to Carlisle, and to Gloucester, Wales and the south-west. Facilitated by these conduits, the final quarter of the first century saw a surge of public building and development in such centres as Verulamium, Silchester, Cirencester, Winchester, Canterbury, Chichester and Exeter.

As early as the second century, Christianity slowly began to make inroads in the culture, though it was not until after Constantine was hailed as the Augustus of the west in 312 that the entire Roman empire would become nominally Christian. In Britannia certainly no overnight conversion occurred, though some Christian liturgical remains from the second and third centuries testify to its vitality. During these same centuries, however, a serious political storm was in the making for the empire and for Britannia. In the third and fourth centuries, Roman military expansion in Europe shaded imperceptibly into over-extension, while in Rome itself power corrupted the social order and the privilege of citizenship was regularly abused. Ultimately the centre could no longer hold. By the fifth century – certainly by the year AD 400 – the long golden afternoon of empire had faded, though there was no sign of the utter darkness that lay ahead. As imperial energy drained, all forward movement ceased. In the northern and western European provinces, local resistance to the Roman legions became more successful: tough Germanic tribes – themselves pushed by pitiless nomadic raiders coming out of the Asian steppes – presented strong military challenges. Tasting success, the Germanic tribes went on the offensive and began to storm the empire itself. The conflict increased over two or three generations until at last a fatally weakened Rome fell before triumphant but ignorant Visigoths. The rough barbarians wrested control and booty from the helpless centre of the empire, and by AD 463, Rome had been sacked twice. Almost overnight its far-reaching accomplishments became merely history. In AD 467 the last of the Roman emperors died, and the civilisation that once stretched from far northern and western Europe to the far east collapsed utterly before the invaders. Only the eastern part of the empire, the prosperous Byzantine world centred in Constantinople, remained intact. The crude conquerors of the western Roman world made poor governors, and in succeeding decades they greedily proceeded simply to dismember the empire and to pick clean the bones of the classical world. The gutted remnants, clearly spectacular even today, can still be seen in widespread ruins familiar to us mainly as tourist attractions: bleached pillars of temples, impressive stretches of aqueducts, suggestive shapes of amphitheatres, public baths, forums, and a host of other public and private buildings scattered across the face of two continents.

Through this whole time of development, expansion, over-extension and collapse, we know that theatrical practices of all kinds were a mainstay in Roman culture. In Rome, the heart of the empire, theatre ruled. Plays and farces filled the stages, mimes and acrobats roamed the streets, and wildly popular sporting events jammed the amphitheatres. Public spectacle attended events large and small: military triumphs, political victories, milestones in emperors' personal lives, the many feast days associated with gods. It is hard for us, at this remove, to imagine just how thoroughly performance permeated the Roman world. And not only in Rome did one do as the Romans, but in the provinces too. The almost numberless ruins of buildings dedicated to performance, found wherever the Romans set up a town of any size, provide ocular proof of their love and cultivation of spectacle.

For our project of tracing the history of theatre in Britain, these last three or four centuries are both too easy and too hard to generalise about as a local phenomenon, given the real dearth of evidence. We can say little about the lives of individuals in the more than fifteen or twenty generations of people who lived and died during the course of those years. We know that the Romans transformed material and imaginative landscapes in ways that archaeologists and cultural historians are still trying to reconstruct. Of the plays, shows and spectacles performed in Britain over this long span of time, no texts or scripts survive other than those more generally associated with Roman theatre proper. Today only oblique witnesses to the nature of the performances are available: a few historical references, some mosaics, inscriptions, a mask or two, and the mute remains of stone theatres and amphitheatres found in a number of Roman towns whose skeletal forms still dot the countryside. In one way or another, however, it is certain that the history of the empire, of Britannia, and of individual communities was played out in the theatres of this province. And we know too that theatre played an important part in the social lives of its earliest practitioners.

We might begin to develop some picture of the place of theatre in Roman life by picking over one of those ruins ourselves. Within an easy day's journey north out of London, following Watling Street to where it passed along the banks of the meandering river Ver, lay the first true administrative capital of the province, Verulamium (now St Albans). Here the Romans established one of their earliest settlements, making it a *municipium* in Claudian times. Let us pay it a visit now, since Verulamium also happens to be one of the few sites in Roman Britain where a public theatre is known to have been built; indeed, its ruins have survived for our inspection. Other theatres existed elsewhere, without doubt: Colchester apparently had two of them, one within the town and one at the nearby temple complex of Gosbecks Farm; and traces of a large theatre have survived at Canterbury. At Brough-on-Humber an inscription suggests that a theatre may well have existed there, although no remains have been located. In Verulamium, by contrast, the remnants of the building itself can still be seen, offering real evidence about just how elaborate such structures were, and about what might have gone on inside their walls. We should note in passing that many Roman towns in Britain sported amphitheatres, those architectural kissing cousins of theatres. Possible remains have been identified in at least fifteen sites.[3] But there is no indication that amphitheatres were used for anything but spectacle: races, sporting events, gladiatorial contests and the like.

The theatre in Verulamium was only one architectural feature of a highly sophisticated town, and theatrical events were no doubt linked to a thriving civic culture. Today an extensive complex of well-preserved ruins attests to the early development of the site. Founded as a fortified town in Claudian times, it had a forum, a basilica, houses and timber-framed shops, some of which seem to have been engaged in the manufacture of metalwork. In spite of its walled fortifications, Verulamium was overrun by Boudicca's forces in AD 60, its entire population was slaughtered and its buildings burnt to the ground. The town would spend the next two generations recovering, rebuilding. An inscription tells us that a new forum was dedicated by Agricola in AD 79, and by the end of the century the renewal plans seem to have succeeded spectacularly, creating the largest forum and basilica complex north of the Alps. At its centre stretched an enormous forum piazza, over 90 metres long and 60 metres wide, surrounded by a colonnaded walkway. Clustered around that was a massive group of imposing buildings (see figure 2): on the south-west side, running the entire length of the forum, a civic hall housed administrative offices and a council chamber, probably, in large rooms with tessellated floors and plastered walls; on the north-east side, between the forum and Watling Street, stood a tremendous basilica, some 120 metres long and reaching a height of perhaps 30 metres, with an elaborate façade on the main road and other entrances facing the forum. To the north-west was a range of shops, and immediately west of those, a temple. Across Watling Street from the basilica was the *macellum*, or market hall, enclosing shops of all kinds. The town also had public baths and that certain badge of importance, a mint. The second century continued the building boom in Verulamium, although some time around AD 155 a disastrous

3 In addition to St Albans, the sites are Caerwent, Caister-by-Norwich, Carmarthen, Chichester, Cirencester, Colchester, Dorchester, Leicester, London, Sarmizagethusa, Silchester, Trier, Wroxeter and York.

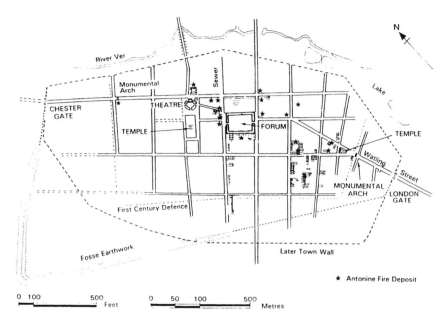

Figure 2 Plan of late Antonine Verulamium

fire swept through the town from end to end, and the process of rebuilding had to begin again. It was at this time, or perhaps slightly before, that the theatre was erected.

Were we to visit Verulamium in the late second or early third century, then, following Watling Street up from London, we would enter through a gateway, past an ancient temple complex and shops – workshops, perhaps, smithies and cookshops and houses on our left, and through a monumental arch (see right side of figure 2). A hundred or so metres ahead would loom the walls of the forum, where Watling Street, the main road, turned. Following it, we would skirt the end of the basilica towering high above. Not much further along Watling Street we would travel past the elaborate façade of the basilica itself – no doubt decorated with carvings, statues, and inscriptions. Beyond the basilica the main road to Colchester led off to the right, down a hill and across the river Ver, but Watling Street continued straight ahead towards a monumental arch marking the far end of town. Before reaching that arch, just before coming to the road leading right towards Colchester, stood a large covered market building, or *macellum*, on the right-hand corner; and there on the left, its flat back facing the intersection, lay the D-shaped theatre (see figure 3).

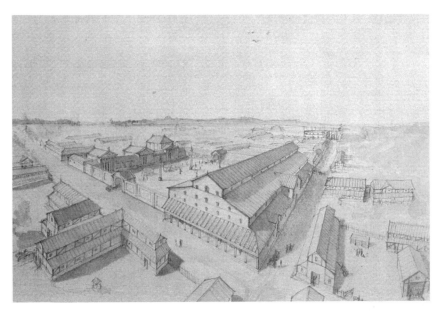

Figure 3 Reconstruction of Verulamium looking north; note theatre above basilica

Figure 4 Remains of the theatre at Verulamium

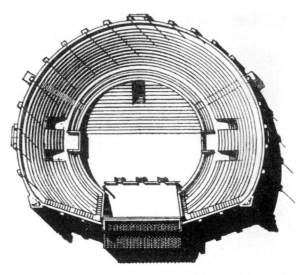

Figure 5 Verulamium theatre in the late second century

Today the remnants of that building form a large and impressive horseshoe, a foundation of stone and turf. It is the only completely exposed theatrical ruins in Britain (see figure 4). First discovered in 1847, the site was not excavated until 1930–5. Archaeological evidence suggests that the original building was built in the mid second century and altered twice, once at the end of the century and again at the end of the third. Even from the plan of the building (see figure 5) we can easily discern a startlingly contemporary outdoor playhouse, with features no less sophisticated than those found in Elizabethan structures. In its heyday, the theatre at Verulamium may have looked something like the modern rendering by Alan Sorrell, based on the stone and earthen remains (see figure 6). The aerial view in this depiction looks north-east, towards the intersection of Watling Street and the road to Colchester; the theatre stood with its flat back to Watling Street.

The theatre's functional familiarity is perhaps as astonishing to the modern eye as is the reconstruction of Verulamium itself. The first thing to notice is its size and amenities. Although small in comparison with some theatres and amphitheatres found in Rome proper or with some of the other structures erected by the Romans for entertainment elsewhere in the empire – the elaborate theatre at Orange in modern-day France, for example – the theatre at Verulamium was still very large indeed, easily accommodating an audience of several thousand people. The enclosed steeply banked seating arrangement created superior acoustics and sightlines, while the stage offered a platform

Figure 6 Modern reconstruction of the theatre at Verulamium, an aerial view, from a painting by Alan Sorrell

that dominated one end entirely. When the stage was redesigned and rebuilt during the second and third centuries, the main changes were a remodelling of the entrances and a consolidation of the playing area. The stage itself was extended into the orchestra space, as was the tiered seating immediately opposite; later the orchestra was cleared again. In front of the stage, hidden by a butt wall, was a metre-deep trench into which a drop curtain seems to have been lowered – a Roman invention.[4] At performance time the crowd entered via gates flanked by seats directly opposite and to the right and left of the stage. The stage itself, made of wood, was covered overhead with a decorated roofed structure supported by five columns (see figure 7).

On our imagined late second-century trip to Verulamium, then, we could enter into that theatre, its stage already widened and deepened, its interior accessible through arched doorways and covered aisles. We could sit in the new tier of seats facing the raised stage across the remaining open space of the orchestra. The green plastered walls surrounding the yard would lead our eye beyond the butt wall and curtain slot to the stage itself, decorated above with

4 For a fuller account, see Liversidge, *Britain in the Roman Empire*, 368–71.

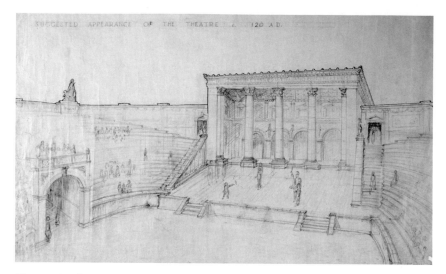

Figure 7 Modern reconstruction of the theatre at Verulamium, interior, from a rendering by A. G. W. Lowther

yellow cornices, and set off with carved rows of red and orange Acanthus leaves along its top.[5] With the curtain retracted, we could see the line of columns further upstage, surmounted by elaborate Corinthian capitals, architecturally framing the scenes to be performed. Since the tiers of seats extended beyond the semicircular, past both edges of the stage, we would be surrounded on nearly three sides by other spectators. This design feature allowed the orchestra, as well as the stage, to act as a focal centre for the assembled audience. It also enabled the theatrical space to accommodate entertainments and spectacles of many kinds – plays, mimes, music and dance could be performed on the stage proper, while other kinds of spectacular or ritual events could be performed in the orchestra.

What might we have seen there, had we sat down in that crowded theatre so very long ago? No one knows. The possibilities range from classical comedy and tragedy, with masks and robes and the sung dialogue characteristic of Roman theatrical traditions, to miming or music, performed perhaps by itinerant troupes, to more physically orientated circus-like events, including acrobats, wrestlers, jugglers, or games with wild beasts and gladiators. Whether we might see an improvisational or a scripted performance while we sat there is also unclear; both are mentioned from time to time in a number of ways and

5 Fragments of these decorations have survived. See ibid., 369–71.

in a number of places formerly under Roman rule. For their theatrical tradition proper, the Romans had followed the lead of the Greek dramatists, whom they both admired and seemed to find intimidating. Playwrights like Plautus and Terence typically coarsened domestic comedy and made it more physical, while Seneca closeted and rhetoricised tragedy, making it more grandiloquent. It is hard to know if such fare regularly reached provinces like Britannia or not. But classically comic or tragic or not, scripted or not, even acted or not – as opposed to declaimed, danced, sung, or fought with sword and shield, trident and net – the vigour of performance and the importance of theatrical spectacle as the main habit of entertainment throughout the empire is undisputed. By the fourth century, according to the Roman calendar that set certain dates for such entertainment, 101 days were allotted each year to the theatre, and another ten to the amphitheatre. Whatever we saw and heard, sitting there in the theatre in Verulamium, chances are that we would have been part of an avid and experienced audience, and like many modern audiences would have vowed to return another day. As would be true for other theatres in Britannia and the empire, then, the theatre in Verulamium would have offered frequent performances of varying sophistication or vulgarity throughout the course of the year in a surprisingly familiar space.

A bird's-eye view looking down at us sitting there in the tiers of the second-century theatre in Verulamium would reveal a second thing worth noting about the building: it was sited precisely midway between the market hall (*macellum*) located immediately across Watling Street to the north, and the temple complex located immediately to the south. Today this siting acts as a convenient geographical reminder of the material significance that spectacular performance played in civic life, while suggesting also the dovetailing of theatrical spectacle and ancient religion. Certainly the building of theatres in other towns like Canterbury and Colchester, along with the clear popularity of amphitheatres in towns all over the country during these times, implies something of the central role that entertainment played in provincial society. It also provides testimony to social mixing and to the existence of a relatively luxurious life for many in Britannia. By the year 350, after all, the province had been part of the Roman empire for over 300 years, and much of its culture followed the lead of imperial tastes. Public buildings and private villas alike sported central heating from hypocausts, had tessellated floors, tile roofs, marble veneers, decorative frescoes and mosaics. Surviving domestic items like fine glass and tableware, personal jewellery with gold-plated beads and carved gemstones, speak for active trade with other parts of the empire, for sophisticated tastes and imported comforts. Taken together, the rich, even sumptuous, material surroundings, furnishings and adornments found in Britannia unmistakably convey a world of fine living enjoyed by those of substance among the provincial population. Some items, like the oversized ceramic theatrical mask found in Baldock, Hertfordshire, or the shallow green-glass 'gladiator vase' from Colchester showing eight named gladiators, or the mosaics depicting chariot-racing in Horkstow, Lincolnshire, reinforce the picture of a Romanised culture and a society that sponsored and valued performative arts of all kinds – just as in the imperial centre of culture, Rome.

Theatres in the towns of Britannia like Verulamium provided sites for entertaining the well-to-do crowd, to be sure, and they also provided a home for communal gatherings of all kinds. Today we tend to think of theatrical performances mainly as plays, but we know too that the line dividing ritual and theatricality has always been a shifting one, difficult to differentiate, and the close connection between drama and religion is familiar to us from as far back as Classical Greece. In ancient Rome and its provinces, theatres were used for a number of purposes, some of the earliest ones clearly religious. Given the large number of Roman deities and the popularity of imperial cults, it is little wonder that rites and processions, choral singing and ritualised celebrations for a whole range of gods proliferated over time. Theatres were natural and suitable sites for such elaborate public veneration, and it was common for them to be situated contiguous to a temple, as they were at Verulamium, at Gosbecks and Colchester, and at Catterick on the north bank of the river Swale. When temples were built they were not intended to house whole congregations of worshippers, but acted in essence as monuments to the deities, often attesting to the honour of particular gods. They served as symbols of the community, housed the image of the god, and sheltered the votive gifts of people and state. Public ceremony and worship were conducted in the forecourt of the temples, usually in the open air. Thus, theatres built in those forecourts and adjacent to temples maintained a strong religious aura about them, and they were certainly used – either primarily or secondarily – for religiously approved activities. All these activities were sanctioned and supported, in Verulamium and elsewhere, for the duration of the empire.

The periodic rebuilding of the theatre at Verulamium suggests that it was used regularly during its lifetime, but some time during the later fourth century it fell into disuse, ending up as a rubbish-tip for the stalls in the market just across Watling Street. Its decline followed a trend common in the late empire against theatrical activity. In Britannia as elsewhere, one of the reasons for this decline was the unchanging nature of public performance and the changing cultural horizons of expectations. Comedy had come to rely almost entirely upon grotesque farce and lewd pantomime, while in the amphitheatres bloody contests of men and beasts predominated. But over the course of time public taste for such fare seems to have been diminishing; in the fourth century the change coincided with a turn toward Christianity and against the whole array of religious ceremonies and ritual performances associated with the large pantheon of Roman deities. The diminished public taste for spectacle may well reflect the shift in religious sensibilities that had been occurring gradually, culminating in the widespread adoption of Christianity in 313 after Emperor Constantine's conversion. By the end of the century (393) Theodosius I had made the profession of any religion other than Christianity unlawful. This newly state-sanctioned religion, so unlike the numerous non-exclusive religious sects followed by the Romans for so long, allowed for no 'false' gods. Also, surely in part because of bloody public shows involving Christian victims, the church now reacted, suppressing buildings connected with pagan cults and opposing spectacular performances of almost every kind. Thus the theatres, so often built next to pagan temples and intimately involved with ritual practices, suffered wide destruction and neglect. Not only is the rise of popular Roman theatrical displays linked to the surrounding religious culture, then, but their fall as well. In a fitting twist of fate, Verulamium in provincial Britannia would ultimately become St Albans, named after the earliest Christian martyr in Britain. Alban, an early inhabitant of Roman Verulamium, refused to take part in official sacrifices after his conversion to Christianity, and is reputed to have been executed near where St Albans Abbey now stands. The Christian monument to St Alban would, in years to come, draw thousands in pious ritual to a site not far from where the old temple and theatre complex had provided an earlier brand of ritual performance to a different audience.

The Christian society was not sympathetic to theatrical performance. Some sense of the Christian antagonism towards such things as they were staged in the late Roman world can be gleaned from the writings of Tertullian (c. AD 150–c. 220) and St Augustine. Tertullian objected to Roman shows in his *De Spectaculis*, written about the year 200. In it, he condemned everything that was fabricated as corrupt, sinful, part of a demonic plot to cloud mankind's vision. 'Demons', he claimed, 'with the purpose of attracting many away from his Lord and binding him to their own service, achieved their purpose by granting him the artistic talents required by the shows.'[6] A play's falsification of God's world was wrong, and an actor's fabrication of a new identity in particular, whether of a good or an evil character, constituted a sin. In doing so, evil was imitated

---

6 See the essay 'On the spectacles' in Thelwell's translation of *The Writings of Septimus Florens Tertullianus*.

and good was mocked. Playing female characters – which pantomimes did as a specialty – mocked nature itself and broke God's law, Tertullian claimed, and Christians should avoid all such spectacles as diabolical snares for the gullible:

> Christians are forbidden the theatre . . . where . . . the best path to God's favour is the vileness of the Atellan gestures or the buffoon in woman's clothing . . . in His law it is stated that a man is cursed who attires himself in female garments; what then must be his judgment on the pantomime, who is trained up to play the woman!

Augustine, writing two centuries later, voiced essentially the same condemnation; though he himself had frequented theatres in his youth and taken part in performances. Perhaps because of this, his understanding of the theatre was more intellectually complicated than Tertullian's, and he often used acting as a metaphor for the self-aware life.

In any case, by the end of the fourth century the abandonment of Roman theatres was the least of the problems Britannia had to endure, for the empire itself was tottering. In 395 it formally split into two parts, the eastern ruled from Constantinople and the more besieged western from Rome. In provincial Britannia, news was grim in every direction. In the north of the country Hadrian's wall failed before the repeated attacks from the Picts and Scots; on the west, Irish raiders continued to make predations; and on the east and along the channel coasts the Saxons from northern Europe were pushing hard by sea. In 401, Roman troops in Britannia were sent back across the channel to defend Italy against the Visigoths led by Alaric, and by 406 the last remnants of the army were withdrawn from Britain, never to return. Increasingly desperate and defenceless now, in 410 the Britons appealed for help to Emperor Honorius, who informed them they would have to take care of themselves, signalling that Roman protection of Britannia was a thing of the past. Alaric had in fact at last entered Rome. In any case, the year 410 effectively marked the end of direct Roman rule in Britannia. And thus began the long slide.

Roman troop-withdrawal from Britain affected far more than the country's ability to defend itself. As Rosalind Niblett points out, its entire economic base disintegrated completely.

> The economy was based on gold, silver and bronze coins, produced by the central government to pay the army, but which percolated through the whole of provincial society. By the fourth century households up and down the country relied on factories for supplies of pottery, glassware, brick and tile, together with any food or goods not produced locally. All these were purchased with money gained from the sale of surplus local produce. Thus the whole system

depended not only on good communications, but also on the maintenance of a money based economy, which in turn depended on the presence of the Roman army.[7]

The severe economic disruption foreshadowed a breakdown of the Roman social order that had evolved over hundreds of years. With the supply of new coins cut off, the use of current coins – increasingly worn – gradually declined over the next two decades until, by 430, barter had replaced it. Within two generations without a money economy, the agricultural system dependent upon organised crop production by Roman villas fell apart utterly, with landlords, tenants and labourers at odds. Industries producing such things as ironwork and pottery for a national market collapsed, and local markets centred in towns followed suit. A few towns lasted as settlements or as walled havens from marauders until later in the fifth century, but as institutions, as centres of cultural continuity, most of the towns had stopped functioning by 450.

With its economy destroyed, its social order shattered, its land no longer productive, Britain drifted into the dark, murky future like so many other regions once under Roman control. Perishing along with the social constructs of the Roman world were its material constructions: the widespread fortifications, towering city walls, and buildings that housed its former life – piazzas and forums, basilicas, temples, market-places and theatres. These structures deteriorated and eventually fell into ruin, their stonework pulled apart and used for more mundane forms of shelter. In Verulamium, as Roman cultural habits and social pastimes and cults disappeared, so too did theatrical performances, public displays, spectacles and ritual observances. The theatre itself seems to have been dismantled over the course of the next century, stone by stone down to its foundations, until it disappeared entirely back into the earth. Uncovered again today, the silent emptiness of the theatrical space still testifies eloquently to its own history, its former space and structure. It still signals like a phantom limb at some of the possibilities of its former life. But its circumstances also point toward the future. Building materials from the theatre are thought to have been used in the construction of St Albans Abbey some centuries later, an ironic transposition of elements from a public showplace to a private prayer space. But that carrying away and redeployment of material from a public theatre to a holy church also suggests that, however deeply buried, the seeds of performance might eventually spring to life again. As if alive with a kind of theatrical charge that could affect the buildings they were used in, the stones themselves would house another metamorphosis of

---

7 Niblett, *Roman Hertfordshire*, 213.

theatrical activity in Britain, one that would occur centuries in the future. The next stage was a kind of reversal, where church liturgy became transformed into staged event. Ultimately, of course, staged event was to find its way back into the theatre.

Liturgical drama: shall these bones live?

Shall these bones live? shall these
Bones live?....
Under a juniper-tree the bones sang, scattered and shining...
Forgetting themselves and each other, united
In the quiet of the desert. This is the land which ye
Shall divide by lot. And neither division nor unity
Matters. This is the land. We have our inheritance.

(T. S. Eliot, *Ash Wednesday*)

When T. S. Eliot wrote *Ash Wednesday*, the first of his unabashedly confessional, religiously inspired compositions, he was at a turning-point in his own life, struggling to negotiate a balance between the private need for spiritual experience, found close by in familiar ritual forms, and the public power that poetic form conferred upon a wide range of cultic phenomena, including eastern beliefs and the magic of words themselves to resonate in the human heart. Eliot exploited this cultic property of language so as to suggest a world of mystical truth available through faith. Paradoxically, his poetry came to represent an alternative quasi-religious experience divorced from liturgy or dogma. His accomplishment was to render the reader a participant, through the force of poetic expression, in an inner world that moved from denial to supplication, from loss to fulfilment, from hopelessness to communion, from turmoil to peace. Twenty-first-century theatre historians face a similar challenge in dealing with medieval drama at a time in history when religious faith is suspect in public ceremony and certainly abandoned on stage. As will become apparent, coming to terms with liturgical plays and their relatives, Latin music-dramas, will require a shift of sensibility, a new understanding of context, an appreciation of ritual and of the lyric power rooted in religious art.

We might profitably begin by tracing some of the historical developments that led away from the Romans and towards the Roman church, noting along the way how completely theatrical performance was eclipsed before it could rise again. As we trace the history of drama through these times, perhaps the key words to remember are 'spectacle' and 'communal context'. Spectacle had in fact already overshadowed any serious drama in the theatre during the late Roman empire. Centuries later, long after any memory of dramatic practices had disappeared, spectacle would become the means to usher in its return. In Rome – and thus elsewhere in the empire, of course – plays had degenerated into mere public display and sports; the staging of events like chariot races, gladiatorial contests, and beast fights in amphitheatres, all of which proved far more popular than theatrical ventures. Pantomime was the exception, but even it became increasingly racy. The world of Roman public entertainment thus turned crass, spectacular in the worst sense of the word. Still, even pure spectacle required a modicum of organisation, structure and scheduling, and even pantomime required a relatively cultivated audience that might appreciate the finer points of dance and choral music. But when the empire vanished, even such meagre theatrical fare disappeared along with any audience at all.

By the time that Justinian was crowned emperor in Constantinople, in 527, the western part of the Roman empire had been lost for good. Justinian made some attempts to reinscribe old borders and maintain some integrity in the disintegrating realm, but these met with minimal success. For better or worse, Visigoths had won the day, as would the Lombards later in the century. A fragmented tribal rule replaced the unified Roman imperial model. Meanwhile, in the east the Byzantine empire grew stronger and more powerful than ever. As a kind of emblem of the times, we might remember that Justinian was the last Roman emperor to speak Latin rather than Greek. His long and busy reign (527–68) consolidated power and brought a legal halt to any non-Christian religious practices. The legacy of his building programme included the spectacular Hagia Sophia, and his cultural legacy included a legal code that was to become the foundation of much modern jurisprudence. Around 528 Justinian married Theodora, an actress or a dancer, but clearly a performer of some kind. Her father had been the bearkeeper at the Hippodrome, and her mother a professional dancer and an actress as well. The new emperor and empress ruled together successfully until her death from cancer some twenty years later. Theodora's background as performer merits our attention here, for it clearly indicates that in the east professional performance traditions were still alive during the sixth century. In the west, whatever remained of popular theatre perished as the empire collapsed. There, nothing survives from these times – no actresses' names or nuptial announcements, no contemporary references, architectural ruins or theatrical artifacts – to suggest that the theatre had any life left in it at all.

In what had been Roman Britannia, that lush and temperate outpost far from classical ground zero, the process of social disintegration was already far advanced by the time of Justinian's wedding in 528. From the moment the Roman troops were recalled – signalling the final breakdown of the social order – it would take nearly three centuries, from the fifth until the eighth, simply to establish stable political rule. During these centuries, continuing raids and wholesale immigration by the Saxons changed Britain's racial make-up and culture utterly. The new society that slowly emerged in the wake of Roman abandonment was by all accounts and every measure of surviving evidence a cruder one, certainly no place for anything like the drama that had been practised when the empire had flourished. Except for a few late performances by mimes, jugglers, tumblers, rope-walkers, stilt-walkers, strong men and the like, who made their way across the countryside from time to time, the door to the vital world of Roman theatricality was shut forever. Folk celebrations no doubt existed, but the towns and villages had been rendered exposed, vulnerable, and the act of travelling itself was now dangerous, tedious, slow. As a sign of these times it may be useful to remember that for virtually a thousand years after the Romans left Britannia, the best roads in the country remained the ones they had built, even after centuries of chronic neglect and decay.

In the short term the Saxon settlements provided rough forms of shelter and protection, similar perhaps to the chilly Nordic world figured forth in Anglo-Saxon poems like *Beowulf*, where tribal affiliations and family fiefdoms structured all aspects of life, and the high-gabled mead hall acted as the centre of regional power. And so from the ruins of the former Roman empire a sequence of narrow cultures slowly firmed up over the course of the next few centuries. Augustine, sent by Pope Gregory the Great, brought literacy in the service of Christianity to the shores of Britain and to its Anglo-Saxon kings in the late sixth century. The religion took root, ultimately replacing Teutonic pagan gods. Generations passed as a new cultural identity conformed itself to Christian worship, and while shifting political kingdoms shook off the pitiless, frighteningly successful Viking raids – predations that would end only with the Norman conquest of 1066. Performance within this society was limited to the singing and chanting of bards and minstrels before a liege lord and feasting thanes. Studies have shown that, however complex the weaving of narrative threads in such compositions, the performative circumstances remained crude, consisting in the main of minstrels or a bardic *scop* strumming a harp and declaiming. No specific references to any other kind of performances survive, except in occasional ecclesiastical prohibitions directed mainly against mimes.[8] For an idea of what constituted mimetic activities we can turn to some elegiac

---

8 For a representative sampling of these prohibitions, see Chambers, *The Mediaeval Stage*, I, 290–306.

lines surviving from Carolingian times, which purport to be the epitaph of a mime named Vitalis:

> I used to mimic the face, manner and words of those talking,
> So that you would think many people spoke from one mouth.
> The subject, presented with a twin image of himself before his eyes,
> Would tremble to see a more real self existing in my faces.
> Oh, how often a lady saw herself in my performance,
> And blushed for shame, horribly embarrassed.
> Thus, as many human forms as were seen in my body
> Were snatched away with me by the dismal day of death.[9]

In late Roman times the church had been cruelly satirised in pantomime and song, and it had ever opposed performances requiring impersonation. Such warnings were now regularly repeated. In 789, for example, a church law threatened corporal punishment and exile to any player who counterfeited a priest, and from the seventh century onwards clerics were repeatedly forbidden ever to participate in such entertainments. Whether the prohibitions recorded at this time should be considered as evidence for actual mimetic activities requiring sanction, or whether they were simply reprocessing old anxieties harboured by an overly sensitive ecclesiastical hierarchy, must remain unknown.

Meanwhile, perhaps it is unfair to characterise life so bleakly during these centuries when dramatic practices had fallen by the way, for the Anglo-Saxons developed reasonably sophisticated political and social structures, set up courts of law and established a substantial central bureaucracy and a flourishing government at the local level. If they accomplished little new in the way of building (with the notable exception of Offa's Dyke, built to separate England from Wales in the eighth century), they managed at least to maintain the physical infrastructure of roads, bridges and fortifications inherited from the Romans. The West Saxon kings worked out a strong military network of mercenary soldiers in select households of great lay and ecclesiastical magnates in the realm, and King Alfred the Great (871–99) built up a large navy with newly designed ships, deployed as part of a strategy coordinating land and sea operations with the defensive use of burghs.

The military achievements of Alfred's reign coincided with the establishment of a great number of religious houses, as Anglo-Saxon culture evolved into a more zealous Christian community. Indeed, by the beginning of the ninth century the church had come to wield immense spiritual and temporal

---

9 Quoted from Axton, *European Drama of the Early Middle Ages*, 17.

power throughout all of western Europe, and its political aspirations came to rival those of kings. In the year 800, with Charlemagne crowned by the pope as its head, the newly created Holy Roman empire assumed formal existence, uniting church and state, marrying religion to politics for centuries to come. With a monopoly on literacy and learning, the Christian church now bridged the gulf between heaven and earth, mediating and preserving the shreds of thought that had survived the passing of the classical world. It shaped new learning to conform to its teaching, achieving an enormous and pervasive presence nearly impossible to imagine today.

Into this culture in 1066 the Norman conquest introduced a stunning moment of consolidation and redirection. During the latter part of the Middle Ages, from the eleventh until the fourteenth centuries, the forces of Christendom mounted the great crusades against the infidels who occupied the Holy Land. The crusades demonstrated how effectively the spiritual and temporal missions of the church might be galvanised and turned outwards with a territorial imperative. As a massive reclamation project with clear expansionist impulses, the crusades mark the end of political impotence for western Christendom; they display all too well the gathering force of a military fist in the Christian glove. The turbulent times can best be described in terms of polar opposites: politically chaotic yet spiritually disciplined, intellectually high-minded but psychologically obtuse, privately sentimental and publicly brutal, technologically backward but philosophically advanced, obsessively pious and ostentatiously materialistic.

Over the longer term, then, in Britain as in much of western Europe, the rule of Roman law had been replaced gradually by two forces: first, the social rule of feudalism, a code built on the concept of loyalty to a liege lord, whose military and political power protected the community that served him; and, second, the universal rule of Christian conduct promulgated by the Christian church, with its emergent hierarchy of popes and bishops and priests. Christianity spawned cathedrals and monasteries and churches as sites of spiritual and temporal power, while feudalism resided in castles and manors, places where many toiled to benefit a privileged few. Thus the famous 'three estates', or classes, of the Middle Ages came to exist side by side: the warrior class (knights and kings), the priestly class (those with ecclesiastical rank) and the peasant class. In time, all three would be implicated in the emergence of new kinds of drama.

The first new kind of drama to develop was liturgical drama, and it appeared within the services of the Christian church. Its appearance carries a certain ironic edge, given the long tradition of religious fulmination against most kinds of theatrical representation. But as time had passed in the early Middle Ages, in the absence of anything but transitory political organisation, Christianity and its rites flourished, emerging by default as the main site not only for sacred, but for social and secular activity. Its central coherence of doctrine and ceremony had come to serve as a primary, widely shared cultural structure stretching across Europe. However far abroad the church might spread, it maintained a certain unity of ritual expression through its liturgy – that is, its elaborate model of worship, conducted in Latin. The Latin liturgy in fact provided a detailed organising principle for passing the entire year in the service of God, season by season, week by week, feast day by feast day, canonical hour by canonical hour. Included in the liturgy were prayers for every occasion and event, with specific directions for sacred rites and sacramental practices, including incantations, dialogue, music and dress. Given the long relationship between ritual and theatrical practice, we need hardly wonder that the codified liturgy of the church might now act as the site for the earliest kind of medieval drama.

In the monasteries and abbeys that were springing up like mushrooms across the European landscape, Christian liturgy inspired new forms of dramatic practices. In at least one place, the close gathering of a holy community seems to have inspired a notable theatrical experiment. During the tenth century, a nun named Hrotsvitha at the abbey of Gandersheim in Germany wrote six Latin plays, modelled on the works of the Roman comedian Terence. Her compositions stand as the earliest surviving formal drama experiments during the era. The plots of her plays revolve, predictably, around issues of morality and chastity and sainthood. In one of her plays, for example, *Dulcitius*, the unsavory advances of a lustful governor, Dulcitius, upon a chaste group of virgins are foiled by divine intervention, which makes him mistake kitchen pots and pans for women and grapple comically with them. Ultimately the holy virgins are martyred, and they embrace death willingly. Meant as saintly instruction for the other nuns in her abbey, Hrotsvitha's compositions may never have enjoyed performance beyond recitation. In any case, they were never copied or distributed, and hence remain unique specimens of an apparently anomalous talent.

At about the same time, another kind of dramatic performance was spreading in other monastic settings, based on musical embellishments of the liturgy known as tropes, or significant phrases extended musically for emphasis. Liturgical dramas, in turn, extended the musical phrases one step further, enacting biblical stories referred to in the liturgy. Their purpose, clearly, was to heighten the religious experience of the ritual practices. The best-known example of such liturgical embellishment is the *quem quaeritis* trope, which dramatises the Easter morning biblical episode in which the three Marys

(Mary Magdalene, Mary Jacobus and Mary Salome, as in Mark, 16:1) approach the sepulchre where Jesus was buried. Asked by the angel guarding the tomb, '*Quem quaeritis?*' [Whom do you seek?], they respond that they are seeking Jesus, and the angel informs them that Christ has risen. In the directions for performing this service, clerics are instructed to dress for the parts and to sing the dialogue antiphonally – in answering voices – using the holy space of the church as their stage. Such an arrangement was characteristic of liturgical drama. However detailed they became, the dialogues remained brief and the action short. But with this musical enactment of a charged moment in the liturgy, the clerical participants turned the corner from ritual to theatre. In its own way, drama thus survived the end of the Roman era and the crude temper of Saxon times by going underground, and now it had begun to resurface, inspired and fostered by ritual practices at the heart of the Christian church, an institution that formerly had shunned it.

But even elaborate dramatic rituals are not plays in any modern sense of the word, and since they rarely spread beyond the monastic setting, they may appear as a theatrical cul-de-sac. Yet we need to take them seriously, since they acted as harbingers and incubators of the theatre of the future. The ritual elaborations seem to have been created initially as spurs to meditation, and as such they succeeded splendidly – or so the evidence of their widespread usage would attest. Their popularity rested upon concerns relatively foreign to us, but crucial to consider. Viewed from the perspective of the early twenty-first century they may seem odd ducks out of water, incomplete, with a rootedness in ritual and a seriousness of purpose unfamiliar as a source of entertainment. And it is true that the power of these plays, telegraphed through music and gesture, requires special effort on the part of a modern audience to appreciate. Yet they deserve and repay close attention.

To help understand their effects, we will need to recall the intense spiritual processes that monastic institutions facilitated, and we should try not thinking of liturgical drama in modern theatrical terms. As is true with all medieval drama, the spectacle of performance needs to be mediated two ways: historically, with an appreciation of its cultural context and sponsoring agent – the Christian church in a monastic setting; and aesthetically, with an appreciation of the ways that liturgy gave expression to deeply held communal beliefs. We might pause for a moment, then, to explore one of the simplest and oldest embellishments of the liturgy – the *quem quaeritis* ceremony of the *Visitatio Sepulchri* (Visit to the Sepulchre), as it was recorded in Winchester in the tenth century. With more or less elaboration, a version of this ceremony was enacted for centuries on Easter morning, not only in monasteries in Britain but throughout western Europe. What might it have meant to those whose lives were so completely steeped in Christian ritual, and what can it mean to us? The formal instructions for the ceremony are succinct enough to quote in full:

> While the third lesson is being recited, let four brethren dress themselves; of whom let one, dressed in an alb, enter as if for some other reason, and let him approach the place of the sepulchre unobserved, and there, holding a palm in his hand, let him sit down quietly. While the third responsory is being sung, let the remaining three follow, all of them dressed in copes, and carrying in their hands censers filled with incense; and haltingly, in the manner of seeking something, let them come before the place of the sepulchre. These things are done in imitation of the angel seated on the monument, and of the women coming with spices to anoint the body of Jesus. When therefore the seated one shall see the three approaching him, wandering about as if seeking something, let him begin to sing in a sweet and modulated voice: Quem Quaeritis? When this has been sung to its end, the three shall answer, with one voice, Jhesum Nazarenum [Jesus of Nazareth]. The former shall respond: Non est hic. Surrexit sicut praedixerat. Ite, nuntiate quia surrexit a mortuis [He is not here; he has risen, just as he foretold; go, announce that he has risen from the dead]. At this command let the three turn toward the choir, saying: Alleluia. Resurrexit Dominus [Alleluia, the Lord has risen]. When this is said, let the one seated, as if calling the others back, say the antiphon: Venite et videte locum [Come and look at the place]. Then let him rise and lift the veil and show them the place, bare of the cross but with only the linen in which the cross was wrapped; at this sight let them set down their censers in that same sepulchre, and take up the linen and hold it before the clergy and, as if showing that the Lord has risen and is no longer wrapped in it, let them sing this antiphon: Surrexit Dominus de sepulcro [The Lord has risen from the sepulchre], and let them then lay the linen on the altar. When the antiphon is finished, let the Prior, rejoicing with them at the triumph of our king – in that he arose having conquered death – begin the hymn: Te Deum laudamus [We praise thee, O God]. This begun, the bells all chime out together.[10]

For much of the twentieth century the opinion of theatre historians was that such liturgical services did not, strictly speaking, constitute drama. Karl Young, the most ardent twentieth-century collector and editor of liturgical drama, states the case baldly for the *quem quaeritis* elaboration: 'The dramatic features of this service... may have contributed suggestions as to the possibility of inventing drama, and may, indirectly, have encouraged it; but the liturgy itself, in its ordinary observances, remained always merely worship.'[11] What Young did not credit was that the embedded features of these extensions of Christian

---

10 From the *Regularis Concordia* (AD 965–75) of Ethelwold, Bishop of Winchester, designed for use by English Benedictines. It is here presented in the version published in Young, *Drama of the Mediaeval Church*, I, 249–50.

11 Ibid., I, 85.

liturgy led one way or the other towards theatrical representation. That is, the exegetical cross-referencing of character and action, the conscious use of symbolic costume, the familiar scripting of sung dialogue, the action blocked out on the stage-like arena representing another place, and above all the use of impersonation, clearly cross the line from ritual to drama, albeit drama of a special kind.

One of the first to understand and point out the powerful symbiotic relationship between Christian rites and drama was O. B. Hardison, Jr, whose *Christian Rite and Christian Drama in the Middle Ages* pushed early drama studies in new directions. Hardison points out, first of all, that, despite Young's reservations, the celebration of Christian mass itself offered real drama:

> the 'dramatic instinct' of European man did not 'die out' during the earlier Middle Ages, as historians of drama have asserted. Instead, it found expression in the central ceremony of Christian worship, the Mass. This being the case, an understanding of the medieval interpretation of the Mass should illuminate many hitherto obscure aspects of the history of European drama...Just as the Mass is a sacred drama encompassing all history and embodying in its structure the central pattern of Christian life on which all Christian drama must draw, the celebration of the Mass contains all elements necessary to secular performance.[12]

And while the mass lies at the heart of Hardison's concern, just as it lies at the centre of the Roman liturgy, the performative possibilities of the mass are merely a beginning. Other liturgical moments offered more, even richer, bases for theatrical scripting, as the embellished *quem quaeritis* ceremony excerpted above amply illustrates. Hardison demonstrated how the Christian rites might constitute drama, but he was less interested in how and why such compositions came to arise. That question needs to be addressed before we can deal with the ceremony itself. Part of the answer to the question can be found in the historical development of the liturgy.

During the ninth and tenth centuries, when the ecclesiastical authority in Rome was vigorously extending its power and control, the Latin liturgy changed drastically. From the outset, local ritual practices throughout the Christian world had regularly been appropriated, adapted and normalised, but not thoroughly codified. One of the best modern scholars of liturgical drama, the late C. Clifford Flanigan, notes that by the end of the eighth century two main lines of liturgical practice had emerged in western Europe, the Gallican and the Roman rites. The Gallican rite was characterised by often poetically

---

12 Hardison, *Christian Rite and Christian Drama*, 41 and 79.

lush prayers and effusive incantations celebrating the *mysterium tremendens* of the Christian faith. Although followed widely, it was actively discouraged in the ninth and tenth centuries as part of larger Carolingian reform efforts in favour of the Roman service – a flatter, far less self-dramatising set of rituals. Precisely at this time and place, the embellishment of liturgical tropes first appeared; Flanigan suggests that the two processes are not unrelated.[13] The musical and dramatic embellishments, in structural terms, filled in where a more poetic and imaginative set of liturgical rites had previously held sway. Dramatic enactment and ritual thus combined, offering some familiar pay-offs even (or perhaps especially) for the most devout monastic audience.

Another part of the answer can be found, as might be expected, in human agency, the conscious actions of individuals who worked to change the nature of sacred ritual. A figure whose name surfaces early in this regard is Amalarius (*c.* 780–850), the ninth-century Bishop of Metz, prominent at the court of Charlemagne, who sought to enhance public worship by allegorising through word and gesture the dramatic conflicts embedded in the mass. Amalarius saw that at some times in the service the officiating priest represents Christ – betrayed, suffering on the cross, resurrected – and at other times he represents the high priest of the temple, or Nicodemus assisting in the burial of Christ's body. The deacons and congregation correspondingly represent at various moments the sleeping disciples or Jews witnessing Christ's agonies or other crowds involved in the biblical events commemorated by the mass. The altar comes to act as Christ's sepulchre. In 814 Amalarius wrote his *Pastoral Dialogues on the Roman Rite* and a few years later the *Book of the Service*, which proved highly influential. His objective was to show how Christ's Passion was implicit in the service of the mass, and how the celebrating priest might reflect the Passion with an outward show of joy or sorrow or anguish in movement and gesture. The practices urged by Amalarius proved wildly popular among clergy and congregations alike – a fact we know in part by the ecclesiastical resistance they elicited, including condemnation as heresy at the council of Quiercy in 838.[14] The main point to make here is that these histrionic renditions of the mass clearly signal a heightened understanding regarding liturgical services themselves: namely, that their words and actions are more than symbolic, that they are charged with meaning, that they can sanctify the participants in special ways when translated into dialogue and gesture. During the next two centuries in monastic life in western Europe, this heightened understanding

---

13 Flanigan's numerous essays all broke new ground; for this analysis see 'The liturgical context of the *Quem Queritis* trope', *Comparative Drama* 8 (1974), 45–72.
14 For details, see Harris, *Medieval Theatre in Context*, 26.

of dramatic ritual led to widespread acceptance of the mass and of ceremonial enhancements of the liturgy well beyond the mass. The enhancements spread naturally to those times in the church calendar when crucial events in Christian history were celebrated, times like Christmas and Easter, the seasons of Advent and Passion Week. Clearly, ritual mimesis had now come of age within the church itself.

Certainly by the tenth century, after the Gallican rite had been superseded by the Roman rite, and as ceremonies like those initiated by Amalarius circulated through much of western Europe, a deep understanding of the larger power of the liturgy circulated as well. The seamless dovetailing in it of past and present, public and private, symbol and allegory, promoted an enhanced piety, and a new enthusiasm for piety. During virtually any Easter week, then, in this or the next century, and in literally hundreds of monastic settings, the *Visitatio Sepulchri* assumed particular importance on Easter morning. And it formed but one part of an even larger set of liturgical enactments of events surrounding Christ's passion, death, burial and resurrection. As we circle back to the text of that embellished service now, we should keep in mind that the actions and gestures and dialogue the ceremony contains had become saturated with meaning, and we should note too that the service acted as the culmination of an entire week of intense liturgical activity.

The ordinary design of the monastic church in which this liturgical activity took place was long and narrow to accommodate processions (as opposed to the shorter, squarer, post-Reformation sounding-box plan with an imposing pulpit). At the eastern end, centred in the semi-circular apse, was the altar with a cross or crucifix on it. The apse had not yet been separated from the choir by a communion rail; indeed, members of the choir were seated in two tiers all around the semi-circle, divided in half by an elevated prior's seat or bishop's throne in the middle. As we envision this arrangement at the east end of the monastic church, where semi-circular tiered seating focuses on a centrally placed raised platform – the altar – around and upon which the action occurs, we might also recognise the startlingly familiar mirror image of a theatre, as it has existed from ancient to modern times.

Starting on Passion Sunday two weeks before Easter, the church was gradually darkened, its effigies and ornaments shrouded. On Holy Thursday, typically, three separate hosts were consecrated: one for that day's commemoration of the Last Supper, one for Good Friday when Christ was crucified, and one for Easter Sunday to celebrate the resurrection. The consecrated hosts were stored in a tower-shaped chalice or enclosure on the altar. On Good Friday, just after the time of the Crucifixion, the brethren enacted the deposition from the cross and Christ's burial, taking the cross or crucifix from the altar, wrapping it with a veil – used to represent Christ's shroud – and placing it in a nearby likeness of a sepulchre – usually a curtained structure to one side of the altar. As this was taking place an actual burial service was pronounced; then two or three brethren were chosen to represent the soldiers guarding the tomb, chanting psalms and standing watch at the sepulchre, through the night and through the whole of the next day until Easter. For Easter Saturday services, when Christ was in the tomb, no host was consecrated and no communion given. The only light in the church during this Easter vigil was cast by the great Paschal candle, tall and thick enough to burn until the Ascension.

This sequence of ritual reenactments of Christ's Passion, death and burial set the scene for the *Visitatio Sepulchri* on Easter morning. Then the rubrics for the ceremony quoted above make clear what follows: one of the brethren dressed in white, assuming the role of the Angel, slips into the curtained 'tomb' early on, unremarked by the congregation if possible. Three other brethren impersonating the Marys then approach. The curtains open and the famous 'Whom do you seek?' dialogue is sung. When the Angel has announced the resurrection and provided the Marys with ocular proof of the empty tomb, they sing extended Alleluias, and the prior leads everyone in *'Te Deum Laudamus'*, a hymn of praise signalling the conclusion of the ceremony (see figure 8). The joyful ringing of the church bells brings the action to a close.

The *Visitatio Sepulchri*, with its liturgical ceremony involving the *quem quaeritis*, clearly could not function like any play performed in a theatre today, however familiar its use of costume and props, its imagined setting on a stage-like platform, or its use of gesture and dialogue and apparent impersonation. It functioned, rather, as a cultic phenomenon in which both the actors and spectators were in fact participants. The action of the ceremony, while it seems to have a beginning (the approach of the Marys), a middle (the central exchange with the revelation regarding Christ's resurrection) and an end (songs of joy accompanied by church bells), is not a self-contained drama; it is part of the Easter nocturnes, surrounded by a responsary and versicle, a culminating moment in a sequence of sacred events leading up to the central mystery of the Christian faith. As the 'stone' is rolled back from the tomb, time itself is rolled back, so those present may receive the blessings of the Saviour, now transcendently invisible, absent yet present. The ceremony quoted above, from the famous Winchester Troper, was used in Benedictine monasteries in Britain. But in all the monasteries across Europe where this and similar services were so widely enacted for so long, the ceremony held particular meaning. To understand, we need only recall that the ordinary meaning of *quaerere* ('to seek'), when it

Figure 8 The Three Marys and the Angel at the sepulchre. Ivory plaque from Cologne, second half of twelfth century. Note the liturgical censer

appears in the Vulgate, was always seen to refer to the seeking out of Christ, of divine truth – a commonplace for the very kind of seeking at the heart of the monastic life. Taken together, the entire action of the Easter nocturne service suggests that seeking Christ and finding an empty tomb is a cause for exaltation, and not only an exaltation of Christ but of all mankind in Christ. In theology, this signal event – the discovery of Christ's resurrection – is central: it marks the end of the human quest for the divine.

The larger currents informing the *Visitatio Sepulchri* ceremony and its contemporary meaning for a monastic audience are the kinds of feature that sometimes make medieval liturgical plays difficult for us to appreciate, distant as they are in time and sensibility. Their power clearly depended in part on a whole range of liturgical services and ritual celebrations that extended well beyond Easter itself, beyond Easter week, to the entire ecclesiastical year in which Easter acted as the principal feast. And over time, other feast days like Christmas, or the Ascension, or Epiphany, also came to have dramatic liturgical ceremonies associated with their celebration. Such ritual traditions, once begun, tended to persist for centuries. The main point to grasp here is that the liturgical dramas which were attached to ritual moments in the Christian year enhanced those moments by supercharging them for the community of spectators. Their very theatricality acted as a lightning-rod for cultic experience. They were not incidentally theatrical, and their performances played out in ways that depended upon ritual context and upon communal participation, much more than is possible for modern plays. No play today can be performed within so sacred a cultural space – or one as saturated with pious expectations – as a monastery, and at such charged moments in a sequence of ritual practices, and with spectators so eager to play their holy parts in ritual reenactments. These ritual contexts for liturgical plays helped bring holy history into the present for whole communities of worshippers.

Mircea Eliade has suggested that a common feature of all ritual is its commemoration of sacred events that took place in a mythic time; however, a unique quality of Christian ritual is its *recovery* of historical time: 'the sacred calendar indefinitely rehearses the same events of the existence of Christ'.[15] And while 'the liturgy is precisely a commemoration of the life and Passion of the Saviour.... this commemoration is in fact a reactualization of those days'.[16] If Eliade is right, the performance of liturgical plays thus collapsed time itself like a telescope, so that what was past – those chosen moments of sacred history commemorated annually in the ecclesiastical calendar – could actually be made to happen again and again for entire communities that participated in the ritual process. This much seems clear for a monastic audience contemporary with the plays, for whom participation was natural, encouraged, expected.

But what are we to do, a thousand years later? Is it possible that these plays might live again at all for unbelievers outside a monastery? Or must they remain musty set-pieces, trotted out from time to time to illustrate the history of representation in another time and place, the dry bones of a pious corpse? The answer will not be found in the liturgy or ritual embedded in the plays,

15 Eliade, *The Sacred and the Profane*, 23.
16 Eliade, *Cosmos and History*, 23.

though it would be easy to extend the description of ritual action beyond the *Visitatio Sepulchri* to include similar ceremonies connected with other ecclesiastical feasts. The actions of all of them share the flavour of this one, and they depend upon many of the same attributes, the same sacred contexts. While it may be important to appreciate such contexts to understand the depth of spiritual investment in liturgical plays, to gain a sense of their performative power we must turn elsewhere, to the matter of spectacle, to that quality of theatre which easily transcends belief, the suspension of disbelief, and time itself.

The most obvious performative quality of these plays, one that has hardly been explored except in the most recent criticism, is that of music. It may seem odd that this aspect has been ignored, since these liturgical plays are all by definition music-dramas, ordinarily transcribed with full musical notation in the manuscript (see figure 9). But earlier scholarly interests seem to have focused independently on theology or liturgy or music, much as medieval manuscript editors have ignored how illuminations enhance the text while art historians have ignored the text. Here, in these plays, the 'dialogue' in fact was always sung, so that hovering over all the ritual action, however rich, music sounded – plainsong (Gregorian) chant, sung antiphonally from side to side of the altar. We should imagine it accompanying the simple text, surging and dipping, offering meditations on the movements and words of the figures, interpreting their significance for salvation history. We should remember too that from the beginning, in terms of spectacle, musical troping had trumped language altogether. Those musical embellishments often took minutes to sound a single syllable of the word 'Alleluia', for example, developing into *longissimae melodiae* (greatly extended melodies).[17] In time, tropes evolved into sequences, which shared the same performative emphasis on music; these in turn carried forward into the linguistically lusher terrain of liturgical drama, where our interest lies. For these compositions, as for their predecessors, theatrical effect depended tremendously on music. The ceremonies functioned not only as literary but also as musical expansions of liturgical and non-liturgical text and action alike, opening up the meaning for participants. But chant provided more than simple accompaniment for texts. The liquid intonation of the notes, rising and falling, questioning and answering in antiphonal dialogue, offered an austere beauty, and the flowing monotonic voices echoed the holy and solitary ethos of monastic life itself.

By a quirky turn of popular culture, Gregorian chant has again become chic, and today monastic choirs are paid tidy sums to make recordings of the

---

17 For further discussion, see Smoldon, *The Music of the Medieval Church Dramas*, 51ff.

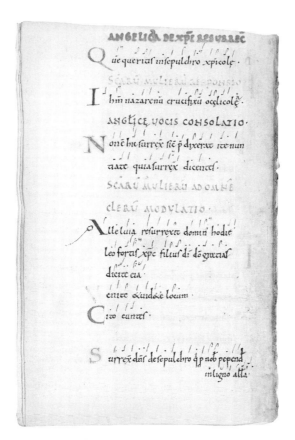

Figure 9 *Visitatio Sepulchri*: an eleventh-century copy of the Winchester Troper
(*c.* AD 980). The music is shown in Anglo-Saxon neumes

mass and of liturgical services connected to sacred holidays like Christmas
and Easter. In assessing the affective power of this music in performance, it
may be of some interest that modern scientific investigations show that chant
actually boosts the production of alpha waves in the brain, inducing a mood
of calmness and peace. We can reasonably conclude that the spare beauty of
these rhythmic cadences affects modern spectators in much the same way it
always affected participants from earlier times, promoting a mood that enabled
contemplation and uplifted the heart.

Thus liturgical plays in performance offered audiences in the past – and
perhaps in the present – a theatrical experience rich and rare, one dependent
on music. Originally used as a means to promote belief rather than to suspend disbelief, the music of the plays offers stunning affective power. The

musicologist William Smoldon is probably close to the mark when he suggests that we should view medieval music-drama much as we would modern opera.[18] Today in our own world, the power of operatic masters like Verdi or Puccini depends on a different kind of faith in a different kind of culture, but, as in early liturgical plays, music does more than reinforce the action. Opera plots depend upon a near-religious faith in human love, in all its transcendent and darker manifestations. It celebrates or laments these human bonds carried beyond death; it depicts unreasoning jealousies, thoughtless betrayals, triumphant unions. And, keyed to the relatively simple plot lines of operas like *La Bohème*, *La Traviata*, *Madame Butterfly*, are melodies of ravishing beauty, haunting arias whose melodies alone can bring figures like Mimi or Carmen back from death, songs that forever offer Madame Butterfly the hope of love and the pain of its failure. And so it is with the music in the liturgical plays, on a different scale and in a different range. As in opera, music was always integral to their performance; it wrapped into their meaning, filled their outward ceremony with a yearning and seeking for divine love, for grace and a vision of salvation. In the *Visitatio Sepulchri* this seeking is for the body of Christ in the empty tomb, which itself paradoxically betokens Christ's absence and continuing presence. For the three Marys as for the medieval audience, the resurrection has occurred before anyone but the Angel arrived at the scene, and that central action remains as invisible as the salvation newly available for all mankind, for each participant in the play, for every spectator. The salvific triumph can be heard distinctly in the accompanying chants and in the concluding *Te Deum Laudamus*. In the *Visitatio Sepulchri*, as in other liturgical ceremonies, the psalms sung during the service were themselves parts of an ancient and ongoing exegetical tradition concerning Christ's life and resurrection and the Paschal season, and for the faithful and informed believer the celebrants' movements as the psalms are sung had special cultic meaning. But even for the uninformed and for the non-believer we should note that the mere performance of the service offers vicarious spiritual experience. Empowered by its music, liturgical drama promoted meditation and it telegraphed essential truths at Easter, Christmas and other ecclesiastical feasts. Whenever its ceremonies commemorated holy events, it reenacted and reactualised them for all who might hear, all who might understand with their heart that sacred actions in the past might lead to present glorification.

In England, Ethelwold's *Regularis Concordia* (*c.* 970) and the eleventh-century Winchester Troper represent the earliest surviving examples of acted *quem*

18 See Smoldon, 'The origins of the *quem quaeritis* trope and the Easter sepulchre music-drama', in Sticca (ed.), *The Medieval Drama*, 123.

quaeritis dialogue, but so little evidence for liturgical drama survived the devastation of manuscripts at the Reformation that it is difficult to know if the elaborate musical embellishments practised so widely on the continent took place in this country. After the Norman conquest in 1066 and extending forward for perhaps four hundred years, references in a few extant service books and inventories testify to performances in the great cathedral churches of York, Lincoln, Lichfield and Norwich. And if we were to return again to the town of St Albans during the twelfth century, we would find, gratifyingly, that liturgical plays formed part of both Christmas and Easter ceremonies at the great monastery there. The actual text of an Easter play has survived from Barking Abbey, where the Benedictine nuns instituted a *Visitatio* ceremony along with a symbolic enactment of the Harrowing of Hell in the late fourteenth century. The play includes not only the visit of the Marys – here played by women – but also a version of Mary Magdalene meeting up with the disciples Peter and John. The Harrowing of Hell involves processionals and the singing of the antiphon *tollite portas* ('open the gates') as the officiating priest beats on the doors of hell. The entire convent then joins in processions to the sepulchre, and the resurrection is celebrated by displaying a consecrated host in a monstrance during the singing of *'Christus resurgens'*. Here at Barking, as elsewhere, actions are suited to the music, and both join to enhance the affective power of the liturgical service.

One last feature of liturgical drama, as obvious and unremarked as its music, deserves to be mentioned: its language, Latin. Like music, the Latin of these plays is crucial to their proper performance. From well before medieval times until well afterwards, Latin remained the universal language of ordinary communication for the Christian church, so it was only natural that nascent plays would use it. But all those trained to speak Latin as part of day-to-day ecclesiastical matters also knew that it had higher functions, that it was the language of doctrine, of ritual, of Jerome's Bible itself. The Vulgate tongue resonated in clerical circles, then, but more importantly it functioned as part of a larger sacred Christian discourse, an ongoing conversation with God. Over the centuries Latin phrases, even whole passages from the Bible and from the mass and liturgical services became familiar, as easy to quote or parody, to mimic, echo or intone, as a Hamlet soliloquy is today. Indeed, an even better analogue might be the many passages and phrases from the King James version of the Bible so widely recognised throughout the English-speaking world. In Christian ritual services from the earliest days Latin had thus acquired a sanctity, an incantatory quality, a kind of charged music of its own. To appreciate this aspect of liturgical plays we might follow the lead of opera again, noting simply that operatic works are most effectively performed in their original languages – Verdi's Italian or Mozart's German, for example – whatever the language of the audience might be. Like the languages of opera, the Latin of liturgical plays functioned well beyond its use as dialogue in commemorated events. As sacred sound, as an instrument of divine conversation, Latin gestured beyond the sense of the words towards a transcendent cultic meaning. So the liturgical services that surrounded and occasioned these music-dramas were embellished by the language itself in ways that deepened their mystery rather than explained it. The language, like the music, was more and less familiar, more and less known, and it helped push the performative edge of the reenactments back into the realm of ritual. The resulting cultic power of liturgical plays thus draws on the symbiotic dependence between ritual and theatre, between surface representations – visual and aural – and deeper mysteries, reinforcing religious beliefs regarding the spiritual efficacy of historical action on present participants. The plays weave back and forth between liturgy and drama, out of the ritual into the representational, and back again. Cynthia Bourgeault has suggested that liturgical drama in fact triangulates theatre, music and liturgy to achieve a kind of 'dramatic modality',[19] and that the back-and-forth opening to liturgy and drama represents 'the basic breathing' of this kind of drama.

Considering this interplay between ritual and theatricality in liturgical drama is like viewing the famous Escher print that depicts black birds flying from right to left defined by white birds flying from left to right. And focusing on the rise of theatrical practices embedded in liturgical services has been like focusing on the path and trajectory of only the black birds. It is time now to turn briefly to their white counterparts. The freshest voice to sound on this matter in the last generation has been that of Johann Drumbl, who effectively reverses the fields of enquiry. Rather than seeing liturgical drama as an extension of sacred functions, Drumbl insists that such dramatic activity in reality represents repeated attempts by the church to rationalise unruly dramatic impulses arising outside ecclesiastical auspices. The great number of ceremonies and services incorporating sung antiphonal exchanges – which never exceeded even ten lines of dialogue in the *quem quaeritis* compositions – do not, Drumbl suggests,

> help us to study the development of medieval dramatic writing, but are, on the contrary, documents of its lack of success. The real medieval dramatic

19 See Bourgeault, 'Liturgical dramaturgy and modern production', in Campbell and David-son (eds.), *The Fleury Playbook*, 145.

tradition...can often be traced not in these documents, which show us 'adapted' (i.e. liturgically oriented) versions, but in the space that the re-formers, who transmitted these 'liturgical' versions of medieval drama to us, consciously left aside.[20]

It is in that space 'consciously left aside' where we might profitably look for other, more recognisable theatrical representations.

By now it should be clear that even if liturgical music-dramas had been the only theatrical achievements to survive the early Middle Ages in Britain and Europe, we might still count ourselves fortunate, given their undoubted cultic power. But in fact there was more, as Drumbl intimates. By the late eleventh and early twelfth centuries, following the Norman conquest, Latin music-dramas with little connection to liturgical services other than sharing the feast day of a saint or holy event began to spring up on the continent, and surely in Britain as well. In France, the most spectacular early examples of non-liturgical drama are to be found in the *Fleury Playbook*. This self-contained gathering of ten plays is not a service book in any sense of the word, although many of the plays clearly resemble dramatic rituals in liturgical manuscripts. Included in the *Playbook* are a *Visitatio Sepulchri* play, one of Herod (*Ordo ad Repraesentandum Herodem*) and one of the Slaughter of the Innocents (*Ad Interfectionem Puerorum*). Others deal with some St Nicholas miracles, including a play of his rescue of *Tres Filiae* (three poverty-stricken young women) and of his resuscitation of *Tres Clerici* (three murdered students). Further biblical stories are dramatised in plays of the Conversion of St Paul, the Raising of Lazarus, and others.

Although the Fleury plays are partially constructed out of pre-existing bits of liturgical text and music, the *Playbook* has no intrinsic relationship with any set of liturgical books or the cultic life of a specific community. Indeed, the musical composition of the plays reflects nearly every important form of religious music, from plainsong through rhymed, strophic verse. Some of the plays call for rather large casts and include a chorus. Their imaginative accomplishments as theatrical pieces – with varying sophistication from play to play – demonstrate a clear grasp of stage action and characterisation. In the Herod play, for example, when Herod slips into his famous rage, his own son comes forward to pacify him. Their following exchange suggests a motive of filial love at play, coupled with anxiety about inheriting the father's throne, allegorically referencing God the Father and the newly born Son of God. The play draws on three Christmas antiphons: '*Bethlehem, non es minima*', '*O regem*

20 Drumbl, *Quem Quaeritis? Teatro sacro dell'alto medioevo*, 366.

caeli' and '*O admirabile commercium'*, though it was more likely to have been performed on the feast of the Epiphany (6 January), which commemorates the coming of the Three Kings. The play, that is, might easily have been acted and sung on a feast day other than the one whose events it commemorates. Indeed, immediately following the Herod play in the Fleury manuscript appears the play of the Slaughter of the Innocents, whose feast day (28 December) preceded the Epiphany. The main point to make here is simple: with the music-dramas in the Fleury *Playbook*, musical and theatrical considerations regularly trump liturgical ones, even as the plays borrow from the liturgy with processionals, prayers and proclamations, paraphrase and innuendo.

Another example of a play that successfully triangulates musical, theatrical and liturgical vectors is the Beauvois *Play of Daniel*, one of the best-known and frequently performed early music-dramas. It provides a good illustration of how rich the twelfth-century theatrical tradition had grown within ecclesiastical auspices. Although composed and scored independently from the liturgy, this long and spectacular play certainly worked as an extension of a large liturgical cursus on the Feast of the Circumcision (1 January), when it was probably performed as part of Christmastide celebrations in the cathedral church of Beauvois. The *Ludus Danielis* requires elaborate staging, props and costumes, including a magnificent palace for Darius and a lions' den with 'live' lions. The action includes processionals and the spectacle of lions devouring those thrown into their den. The score, as modern performances confirm, offers some of the finest music to have survived from medieval times. The stage directions specify that the singers be accompanied by instruments – harps, zithers and drums – and that in addition to its eight festive processions of singers and musicians, ritual dances should form part of the performance.

In the Fleury *Playbook* and the Beauvois *Play of Daniel*, the interweaving of musical, theatrical and liturgical forces thus achieves striking dramatic power. These two examples might be multiplied with an array of other independent twelfth-century Latin music-dramas from all over Europe: Hildegard of Bingen's *Ordo Virtutem* and the Benediktbeuern *Christmas Play*, *Passion Play* and *Resurrection Play* (parts of the *Carmina Burana* manuscript) in Germany; the Montecassino *Passion Play* in Italy; the *Daniel* and *Lazarus* plays by Abelard's student Hilarius (who may have been English), and others.[21] What should be abundantly clear by now, however, is that the monastic traditions of late medieval music-drama harnessed forces of performance that fed and underpinned the development of British theatre. Yet we should also note that the

---

21 These and other texts are variously anthologised in Bevington, *Medieval Drama* and Dronke (ed. and trans.), *Nine Medieval Latin Plays*.

monastic setting for these plays ensured a monastic audience, and that the purposes of the plays remained more sacred than recreational.

Were we to return yet again to St Albans in 1119, we would encounter their new abbot, a monk by the name of Geoffrey, who, we learn, had already dabbled in drama. In the *Gesta Abbatum S. Albani*, the chronicler tells us in an aside that when Geoffrey had been a young schoolmaster in Dunstable he had attempted to stage a 'play of St Catherine' (*ludus de sancta Katerina*), but disaster ensued. He had borrowed copes from the monastery for the performance and a fire had broken out, destroying the splendid vestments. As a token of his penance Geoffrey offered to become a monk. We do not know if the fire occurred before or after the performance, but the play of St Catherine was clearly intended for a clerical audience, and doubtless resembled the other independent Latin music-dramas we have glanced at here. That is, it would have been composed for serious pedagogical, rhetorical, literary, poetical, scholastic, religious and hymnographical reasons. Like the others it would have been a closed production, limited to a pious audience relatively rich in learning, one used to musical complexity and reasonably fluent in Latin. This tradition of Latin music-dramas composed outside official liturgical ceremonies lasted for a long time in Britain and Europe, continuing for two or three more centuries alongside plays more rooted in liturgy and ritual practice. In England the practice did not perish until the monasteries that had spawned and sponsored it were dissolved in the sixteenth century.

One last crucial step yet to be considered for early medieval British theatrical traditions is the apparent move of this essentially elite form of Latin music-drama into the popular vernacular culture. Such a shift proved key to the rise of a widespread theatrical tradition, one performed under civic rather than ecclesiastical auspices. It was this vernacular tradition that cracked open the doors leading to the future, and that is where we must now turn.

Later medieval drama: the inheritance

> And now this is 'an inheritance' –
> Upright, rudimentary, unshiftably planked
> In the long ago, yet willable forward
>
> Again and again and again, cargoed with
> Its own dumb, tongue-and-groove worthiness
> And un-get-roundable weight.
> (Seamus Heaney, 'The Settle Bed', lines
> 13–18, *Seeing Things*, New York: 1991)

Although the surviving evidence is slim, we know that from the twelfth until the fourteenth century, theatrical practices burgeoned and multiplied in Europe and England. Initially produced as part of the 'twelfth-century renaissance' – a period rich in scholastic thought and intellectual fermentation – the innovations in drama spun forward into later times. The age saw great universities founded in a number of cities like Paris, Salamanca and, closer to home, Oxford and Cambridge. A vast classical store of philosophical, theological and scientific works – including virtually all of Aristotle – which had been lost to the west for half a millennium, in fact survived in Arabic texts and was now discovered among the holdings of Moorish libraries that were overrun by victorious crusaders. As the texts were translated into Latin they precipitated a new age of learning and thought, a relearning of the rudiments of faith and rationality, a shift of European intellectual culture from the monasteries to the universities.

The emphasis on the serious and accomplished Latin music-dramas above may have suggested that the work of theatrical composition was a fairly sombre matter, loaded with purely pious purpose. But such is never the whole story in theatre, then or now. Indeed, a number of bawdy Latin comedies also survives from these centuries. The plays betray knowledge of classical traditions and texts – of Plautus and Terence, perhaps Menander, and certainly of Ovid. Evidently written as academic exercises, they required a learned audience to achieve their full effects, but they were far from pious. The list of such plays includes the anonymous *Pamphilus* and *Babio*, *Geta* and *Aulularia* by Vitalis of Blois, *Alda* by William of Blois, *Lidia* by Arnulf of Orléans[22] and *Milo* by Matthew of Vendôme. Many of the playwrights whose names we know came from the Loire valley in France, although the author of the quite licentious *Babio* may well have been an Englishman, since four of the five surviving manuscripts are from England, as are the only contemporary references to it.

It is worth remarking that a rare twelfth-century illustrated manuscript of the comedies of Terence belonged to the abbey of St Albans – the very same abbey, we may recall, that could well have been constructed with bricks salvaged from the ancient Roman theatre there. Now, in the twelfth century, after centuries of theatrical amnesia, the bricks of St Albans seem oddly counterpointed by its manuscript holdings. In the manuscript appear 139 detailed illustrations of Terence's plays, showing actors wearing Roman masks. Although they were drawn in the twelfth century, these illustrations clearly derive from a much older Carolingian manuscript tradition of illustrating Terence, and that,

22 For the texts of these six plays, see Elliott (ed. and trans.), *Seven Medieval Latin Comedies*.

Figure 10 Twelfth-century illustration of a cabinet of Roman masks associated with the plays of Terence. From a manuscript of the comedies of Terence in the monastic library at St Albans

in turn, dates back to the late days of classical theatre. Typically the drawings depict scenes from Terence's plays with the characters labelled, and one shows thirteen of the masks arranged in a storage cabinet, suggesting something of the range of available characters and facial expressions used in classical – and perhaps medieval – performances (see figure 10).

At the same time, alongside the ongoing performances of Latin music-drama, Latin classical comedy and lurid Latin farce, another tradition of drama was developing during the twelfth century as well, a vernacular tradition. One of the finest of these vernacular plays is the Anglo-Norman *Adam*, which dates from around 1160. Variously known as *Le Mystère d'Adam, Le Jeu d'Adam* or *Ordo Repraesentationis Adae*, it was probably the work of a monk or a secular canon in England. The play clearly demonstrates the signal shift from sung to spoken drama, with vernacular dialogue replacing musical verse as the main source of poetic impact. The Anglo-Norman *Adam* mixes traditions freely, drawing upon liturgical passages and apocryphal sources, spoken interchanges and sung choral pieces, ecclesiastical formalism and popular diction, vernacular dialogue and Latin stage directions. Its characters include God, Adam and Eve, their children Cain and Abel, a group of prophets and patriarchs, and Satan and his band of Devils. The performance follows eight passages from Genesis used in the *Liber Responsalis*, or Book of Responses for Sexagesima, and these provide the backbone of the action – from the creation and fall of Adam and Eve to Abel's murder. At the end, a parade of patriarchal prophets makes explicit connections between Old Testament stories and the coming of Christ, first in Latin and then paraphrased in the vernacular. The performers fall into three categories: singers, speakers and mimes, and elaborate stage directions describe the lush garden of Paradise, the smoking Hell of the devils' kitchen, the earthly field where Cain and Abel and the biblical patriarchs appear. The stage directions also instruct Adam and the other actors how to perform their parts, and these sound almost contemporary:

> *Adam shall be well trained not to answer too quickly nor too slowly, when he has to answer. Not only Adam but all the actors shall be instructed to control their speech and to make their actions appropriate to the matter they speak of; and, in speaking the verse, not to add a syllable, nor to take one away, but to enunciate everything distinctly, and to say everything in the order laid down. When anyone shall speak of Paradise, he shall look towards it and point it out with his hand.*[23]

We should note, too, that the Anglo-Norman *Adam* was staged outside rather than inside the church. The porch, or perhaps the steps immediately outside the entrance, probably represented earth, with a hell stage – including devils – placed at the bottom of the steps; the prophets could then process into the church itself as a representation of heaven. It is hard to imagine a more emblematic location than the church steps, which enabled the play to be acted half in and half out of the church itself, to demonstrate how theatrical activity now took part in paired ecclesiastical and secular worlds, sacred and profane spaces, learned and colloquial discourses, high and low art.

The Anglo-Norman *Adam* was hardly a lonely representative of vernacular drama in its time. Other plays of the twelfth century like the Anglo-Norman *Le Seinte Resureccion* (c. 1175; surviving in manuscripts of both English and French provenance), the Old Castilian *Auto de los Reyes Magos* (c. 1155) and Jean Bodel's *Jeu de Saint-Nicholas* (c. 1200) offer ample evidence that the vernacular theatrical

---

23 For commentary on the play, see Muir, *Liturgy and Drama in the Anglo-Norman Adam* and Noonen, *Le Jeu d'Adam*. An English translation is in Bevington, *Medieval Drama*.

tradition was thriving, and that it enriched and expanded the stock of sacred, learned Latin drama.

The thirteenth century carried these accomplishments forward and added more, and we will turn in due course to these. But because the drama of the time was intimately connected to larger religious issues, we need to pay some brief attention to the rich ecclesiastical background, where an increasingly powerful hierarchy had begun to play out its theological anxieties in sometimes violent ways. By the end of the twelfth century, disputations over the nature of sin, confession and penance had hardened into heresies like those of the Waldenses and Albigenses, whose followers preached poverty and practised strict living, publicly opposing the lurid self-indulgence and corruption often seen among those higher up the ecclesiastical ladder. Such heretics challenged papal authority so relentlessly and with such ferocity that in 1209 Pope Innocent III initiated the savage Albigensian crusade, a pitiless campaign resulting in widespread and fearful slaughter. The ecclesiastical anxiety over such heresies as the Albigensian ultimately led to the founding of the Inquisition in 1233 by Gregory IX.

It is no accident that the Franciscan and Benedictine orders were founded in the early thirteenth century by St Francis of Assisi and St Benedict, who professed similar goals of self-purification, and who required vows of poverty, chastity and obedience. Adding to these ecclesiastical excitements, the Fourth Lateran Council met in Rome in 1215, and, after decades of doctrinal debate regarding the nature of sin and confession, instituted the sacrament of Penance. Defining this new sacrament meant redefining sin itself and promulgating rules of behaviour to a largely illiterate population. The process produced an obsessive concern with the nature of sin and its punishment, and a guilt-ridden self-consciousness began to permeate every kind of public or private ecclesiastical matter for the rest of the thirteenth century and beyond. The newly constituted Franciscan and Benedictine orders preached widely, offering the sacrament of Penance to the population at large, and became instrumental in promulgating doctrinal rules regarding sin and repentance. Popular devotional treatises and works written for lay people also began to circulate, like the Middle English *Cursor Mundi* (late thirteenth century) and Robert Mannyng of Brunne's *Handlyng Synne* (early fourteenth century), as did collections of sermons and other forms of public religious instruction.[24] It is against this background of theological debate and heresy, of piety and ostentation, of lay devotion and instruction, that we need to place the establishment of a new feast

24 For thoughtful commentary, see Harris, *Medieval Theatre in Context*, 81–9.

day, one that offered fresh theatrical possibilities to an enormous audience, particularly in England.

In a proclamation of 1264, Pope Urban IV announced the need for a new feast to celebrate the body of Christ in all its real and allegorical glory, and to reaffirm its form in the consecrated host. Urban died before his plan could be implemented, and nearly fifty years passed before the feast of Corpus Christi was officially established by Pope Clement V in 1311. Corpus Christi was to be celebrated on the Thursday after Trinity Sunday, eleven days after Whitsunday (Pentecost). The date was tied to the movable feast of Easter and occupied a relatively uneventful time in the church calendar. As it occurred between 23 May and 24 June (modern 4 June and 6 July) it enjoyed the likelihood of good weather, a fact that seems to have encouraged outdoor public processions and displays of the consecrated host. The occasion and timing of the feast of Corpus Christi thus proved popular from the time it was incorporated in the early fourteenth century, and in succeeding years the commemorative ceremonies became more and more elaborate. In cities and towns, villages and parishes, processional celebrations developed, involving entire local communities – the temporal wing of the body of Christ. And so the stage was set for a new kind of drama to emerge, one that would be, predictably, communal; one that relied upon spectacular processions; one that celebrated the whole body of Christ on earth, one that involved the entire community of Christians.

Within two generations – by the mid fourteenth century – elaborate Corpus Christi processions were commonplace, coexisting in Europe and Britain alongside liturgical and Latin theatrical traditions, all underwritten in one way or another by the church. But now everything was about to change utterly, for waiting in the wings was the Black Death. The advent of the bubonic plague wracked medieval society from top to bottom, and, along with everything else, theatrical practices underwent a radical shift. The Black Death, transmitted either by fleas carried by rats or pneumonically by humans, swept across Europe in 1348, reaching Britain as an epidemic in 1349. Its immediate impact was devastating, and the disease became endemic for the next 300 years, erupting without warning, bringing hideous suffering and often grotesque disfigurement before death – which would frequently be greeted as a mercy.

It is now generally agreed that more than one-third of the European population perished in the plague, and its survivors faced an altered world. Labour became scarce and expensive, translating into opportunity for the poorer ranks, giving them new social and geographical mobility. In Britain, agricultural workers left the countryside for the towns, whose populations actually grew during the late fourteenth century despite the precipitous drop in the general population. Under demographic and social stress, craftsmen and tradesmen in towns began to consolidate their power by forming craft guilds, organisations that functioned to preserve the quality of goods and services for a town in exchange for monopoly control. Guilds also operated as fraternal organisations, frequently providing workers a stake in the burgeoning mercantile culture and also a kind of life insurance for when they died.[25] Meanwhile, in society at large, the Black Death had other far-reaching consequences. It shattered earlier spiritual and philosophical certainties, giving rise to new religious sects, new forms of penitential abasement and affective piety. The complex algebra of class and social rank, too, altered forever in the wake of the plague's destruction, as the ravages of the disease began to ring the long death-knell for the established hierarchy of the feudal order. In combination, the extreme demographic change, the concomitant growth of towns and the founding of guilds provided motive and opportunity for a new kind of medieval drama in the vernacular culture. And the feast of Corpus Christi offered an old and new occasion.

During these late Middle Ages in the north of England and in the midlands, towns like York and Coventry, Lincoln and Chester came into their own as wealthy regional power centres. The formation of craft guilds in such larger towns produced self-regulating working conditions for individual craftsmen, and over the years more authority, prominence and power accrued to the guilds as their social stock rose within their communities. Soon enough prominent guild members were included in ruling oligarchies of towns, made brethren of town councils, and the guilds themselves were situated to take part in their civic cultures, in devising and enabling community entertainment. Not surprisingly, in town after town civic pageantry now flourished, often with guild support. Celebrations included outdoor perambulations of civic and ecclesiastical boundaries, sumptuous processions featuring town officials and public dignitaries, guild leaders and members, parades with spectacular displays, public markets and fairs, and musical entertainments. On the ecclesiastically sanctioned feasts of Corpus Christi and Whitsunday, the pure display of processions gave way to more organised shows with *tableaux vivants*, and eventually to guild-sponsored plays. Ordinary and extraordinary citizens became actors and the city itself became the stage. In England, in an astonishing number of places, towns coordinated and directed guilds to perform that most widely known form of medieval drama, the great mystery cycles.

25 See Coldewey, 'Some economic aspects of the late medieval drama', in Briscoe and Coldewey (eds.), *Contexts for Early English Drama*, 77–101.

The mystery cycles (from the French *mystère* [craft]) portray Christian history from the creation of the world until the Last Judgment, dramatising stories from biblical and apocryphal sources. Characteristically, cycle plays were sponsored by civic corporations, with a town official coordinating the plays, which were ordinarily performed by craft or religious guilds. The long drama of biblical history was broken up into short pageants – dramatised episodes produced by individual guilds. Tremendously popular, the mystery cycles flourished from the last quarter of the fourteenth century to the mid sixteenth century, when they fell victim to reformed sensibilities. Manuscripts of complete cycles have survived from York (with about 48 pageants), Chester (with 24 pageants), and, perhaps, Wakefield (with 32 pageants).[26] The text of a fourth cycle, known as the N-Town plays (with 42 pageants), derives from East Anglia, though its composition and history of performance remain obscure.[27] The N-Town plays may have been a travelling text, or a collection of playtexts belonging to a travelling company, or perhaps a flexible sequence of plays deriving from a sponsoring monastic institution. A few individual pageants that were once parts of cycles in other places have survived as well, and they attest to the vigour of the cycle-play tradition in towns like Coventry, Newcastle, Beverley and Norwich. Taken together, a total of about 150 cycle pageants have been preserved in one form or another. In addition, references to plays in the local records of many other towns suggest that cycle plays were a familiar cultural activity right up to the time of the Reformation.

The cycle plays thus form a substantial body of theatrical material, one which has attracted the lion's share of critical attention paid to late medieval drama. This is so in part because of its sheer bulk, but it is also true because the interpretative task is so daunting. Many scholarly and critical issues need to be negotiated before we can understand the cycle plays in context. Vexed matters of textual transmission, of interactions between cycles and individual pageants, of the voluminous civic and ecclesiastical records pertinent to performance histories, of past and present performance possibilities, all call for attention. And although their subjects were ostensibly religious, these plays registered contemporary political, doctrinal, ideological, economic and aesthetic concerns as well, so that larger cultural perspectives are helpful.

It might be useful to point to an example. One of the most highly regarded pageants from a play cycle is the *Second Shepherds' Play*, written by the

---

26 There is renewed doubt about the likelihood of Wakefield's hosting the plays traditionally ascribed to it.

27 For useful commentaries on the four surviving cycles, see Beadle (ed.), *The Cambridge Companion to Medieval English Theatre*.

so-called 'Wakefield Master', who composed or revised at least half a dozen of the pageants in the Wakefield cycle. The play – the second of two shepherds' plays in the cycle – braids three plot lines together sequentially. The first concerns three shepherds tending their sheep on the moors; their dissatisfactions with the weather, personal troubles and social conditions are soon complicated when one of their sheep is stolen by Mak, a devilish rogue married to a shrew of a wife, Gill. After Mak's crime is discovered and he is treated with charity instead of punishment, an Angel appears and invites the shepherds to visit the newborn Christ child, to whom they bring symbolic gifts. Most striking about the play is its apparently effortless overlaying of symbol and character. The shepherds come to represent humanity as they travel together from woe towards joyful news of the incarnation, the divine epiphany affecting all generations to come. The dialogue seems effortlessly natural and includes a southern accent for Mak; throughout the play the Wakefield Master maintains his signature nine-line stanza (or, according to the most recent editor of the cycle, a thirteen-line stanza),[28] one of the most formally complicated metres to be found in any work of the fifteenth century. The final tableau of the play, a Christmas crèche scene focused on the baby Jesus, is counterpointed and previewed by the earlier domestic scene of discovery at Mak and Gill's cottage, where the sheep had been disguised as a swaddled infant. Humour and poignancy, charity and divine fulfilment mix freely here, even as the pageant voices social criticism. Comic and serious at once, it gives contemporary human faces to representative New Testament figures.

The Wakefield plays were performed with 'place and scaffold' staging, using a scaffold stage or stages located next to a playing 'place'. This constituted one common configuration of the medieval stage, but some cycles employed a quite different technique, using 'pageant wagons' – carts with decorated superstructures to accommodate the action, drawn from site to site within a town for multiple performances. Whichever method was used, the general circumstances of cycle-play production and performance can be sketched out fairly easily. Individual pageants were the responsibility of craft or trade guilds to put on, usually with the oversight and coordination of civic authorities. The town council normally would decide on the venue, and then each guild had to arrange for the financing of its pageant, assemble the cast, secure props and costumes, erect and decorate stages or pageant wagons, arrange for rehearsals and, finally, mount the play. Few towns put their cycles on annually,

---

28 See Stevens, *Four Middle English Mystery Cycles*, and compare the Early English Text Society edition of the Wakefield cycle.

but they were performed often enough for the guilds to establish routines. Sometimes, as at York and Chester, pageant wagons followed a set course through the town, stopping at several stations to perform; in other places the plays were apparently mounted in a single location after a procession through main streets. Songs were a common feature of many pageants, and town musicians frequently accompanied the performances. A cycle might be performed in one day, although a two- or three-day performance was also common, particularly if mounting the plays was part of a larger civic festival, as at Coventry and York. In one way or another a sizeable segment of the community participated in the productions, acting as managers, players, supporting cast or stage hands. The audience was large and diverse, made up of virtually every level of provincial society; often including people from other communities within travelling distance. Practically speaking, it would have been very difficult for any single spectator to see an entire cycle in any given year, but over the course of a lifetime repeated exposure might well familiarise one with all its episodes. The cycles quite literally made the stories from the Bible come alive to audiences who relished them and took them to heart.

Importantly, that urge to instruct as well as delight, so readily apparent in the mystery cycle texts, has important consequences for the theatrical success of these plays. From the point of view of performance, individual pageants have individual strengths, and each might be approached independently by a sponsoring guild. But in conception and in performance the cycle plays were constructed to be a single process, a unified sequence of episodes whose pious intent dictated form and content and mode of production. So not only characters, but also motifs and themes carry from pageant to pageant, establishing a unique character for each cycle, freighting each with special resonance. For all the cycle plays, the doctrinal core remained Roman Catholic, no matter how earnestly they may have been revised during their later careers in Protestant times; a fact that worked against them in the mid sixteenth century, when they were at last fully suppressed. The ingrained instructional impulse that governed their composition originally provided a source of real popularity within sponsoring communities, who were proud to display their piety along with their power, but ultimately this feature of the cycle plays brought trouble in communities with reformed leaders.

The instructional impulse beating at the heart of the cycle plays also carries aesthetic implications. As acting scripts they might be dull safely, without having to pay that ultimate consequence of dull plays in later ages: financial failure. Today, when measured by the yardstick of doctrinal instruction, the cycle plays never fail, even in cases where their value as compelling theatrical performance seems forced in modern productions. Of course, when we highlight the performances of the Wakefield Master's work, or of his counterpart in York, the 'York Realist', the theatrical power of their creations may seem undisputed. But for many other pageants that power is not as apparent. Although the cycle plays seem always to have been vigorously performed, nothing in their mode of production ensured entertainment or even spectacle – nothing, that is, beyond the traditional flamboyance of biblical or apocryphal characters and enthusiastic rhetorical flourishes. The success and survival of these plays, that is to say, depended more upon the institutional traditions and community machinery in which they played a part, rather than upon theatrical excellence. Yet in another form of medieval drama theatricality played a more substantial role, as central a role as profit.

Despite the scale of the cycle plays and the elaborate social understandings they promoted in urban settings, the most common kind of medieval drama performed during the late Middle Ages was a different sort of enterprise altogether, often for obvious material reasons. Ordinary communities were simply too small to have in place the municipal, financial and social structures necessary to mount such enormous undertakings as cycle plays. Instead, towns and villages often shared governance between the parish church and the locally elected or appointed leaders, that is, between priests and community representatives. As it turns out, they seem to have handled the job remarkably well. In number, frequency of performance and geographical distribution, the plays not associated with cycles – the non-cycle plays – were the theatrical mainstay for literally hundreds of communities in Britain from the late fifteenth until the mid sixteenth century. In East Anglia, where small towns and villages formed a dense matrix of networked communities, these plays were especially popular, although their performances were by no means limited to this part of the country.[29] Almost everywhere, it seems – and as performance records now show – non-cycle play productions became an astonishingly popular source of entertainment, instruction and profit.

Generally speaking, non-cycle plays fall into three categories: saint plays, morality plays and biblical or secular history plays. Saint plays dramatise the lives, the conversions, the miracles and sometimes the grisly deaths of saints, and records indicate that they were performed in parishes to celebrate feast days of patron saints, although there is some difficulty distinguishing actual plays from celebrations involving sporting contests and games. Hundreds of

29 There is additional information about East Anglian performance patterns in Gibson, *The Theater of Devotion* and Coldewey, 'The non-cycle plays and the East Anglian tradition', in Beadle (ed.), *The Cambridge Companion to Medieval English Theatre*, 189–210.

references to saint plays exist in local records from the fifteenth and sixteenth centuries, but terms like 'play' and 'game' and 'ludus' often clearly refer to other kinds of festive ceremonies, and hardly any examples of the plays themselves survived the Reformation.[30] In England, only the Digby plays of *The Conversion of St Paul* and of *Mary Magdalene* represent the genre. In Cornwall, which itself had an elaborate tradition of outdoor theatre in the round, a play of *St Meriasek* is still extant. The Digby plays offer spectacle of the first order, with Paul's conversion on the road to Damascus accompanied by stage pyrotechnics, lightning and thunder, and the intrusion of two garrulous, howling devils, Belial and Mercury. The Digby *Mary Magdalene*, over 2,100 lines long, includes many of the well-known though often apocryphal episodes of the saint's life: her childhood days with Martha and Lazarus, her sinful times in the tavern world, her conversion and repentance, her trip to Marseilles and preaching to the Pagan King and Queen there, her last years alone in the desert. The staging of the play requires perhaps two dozen scaffold stages and special effects like a boat 'sailing' around the playing space, burning temples, collapsing heathen statues and angelic deliveries from clouds. To this day the play presents performance challenges to anyone willing to put it on. Yet the staged spectacle inherent in saint plays like the Digby *Conversion of St Paul* and *Mary Magdalene* offers a striking contrast to many less theatrically demanding pageants in the cycle plays. One obvious reason is that, like the non-cycle plays, they often had to pay their own way, to turn a profit for the sponsoring institution.

In both literary and theatrical terms, morality plays were even more ambitious compositions than saint plays, and several elaborate examples survive. These plays present allegorical figures that baldly represent the forces of evil or temptation in battle with the forces of good. The vices and virtues stage an inner war of the soul, or *psychomachia*, a form inherited from Prudentius a thousand years earlier. Characteristically, morality plays promote the path of righteousness and demonise the morally wrong paths a Christian might take in the familiar journey through life. In all, five morality plays have survived, three of them in the same manuscript (the Macro manuscript, now at the Folger Shakespeare Library in Washington). One of the earliest English vernacular plays was in fact a morality: the fourteenth-century *The Pride of Life*, which depicts the prideful King of Life, who foolishly decides to do battle with Death, and proceeds to learn the price of folly. The longest and most elaborate of the moralities, *The Castle of Perseverance*, includes a drawing of its stage plan along with its text (see figure 11). It includes some thirty-five speaking parts

---

30 See Davidson, *The Saint Play in Medieval Europe*.

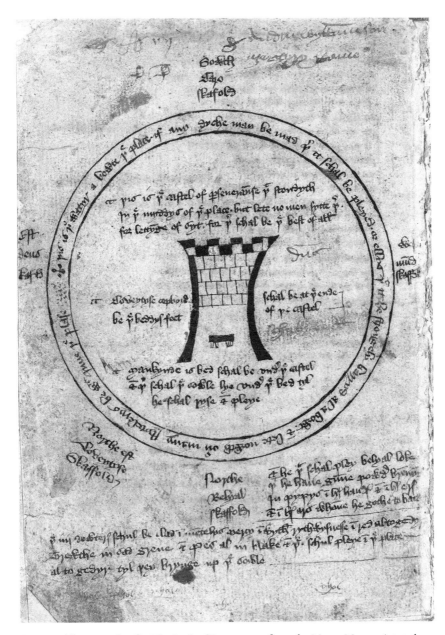

Figure 11 The stage plan for *The Castle of Perseverance*, from the Macro Manuscript at the Folger Shakespeare Library, offering a rare glimpse of medieval stage specifications and management

matched into opposing camps, including Good and Bad Angels, the seven Cardinal Virtues and the seven Deadly Sins. The climax involves storming the great stage castle of virtuous perseverance that stands in the centre of the large round playing space. In the balance hangs the soul of its main character, Humanum Genus (Humankind), whose temptation-ridden journey through life forms the spine of the play. Yet another morality play, *Wisdom*, offers rich pageantry while drawing upon esoteric Christian writings and wisdom literature to portray Christ the King battling with Lucifer over the human soul of Anima. The antithesis of *Wisdom* is *Mankind*, which joins together learned and earthy language, scatological humour and sombre admonition. Its eponymous main character, beset by Vice figures under the command of Mischief, is defended by Mercy, and the play is interrupted by the appearance of the devil Titivillus, a folk-play character with a satchel and net and an enormous head, for whom a collection, or *quête*, is made.

The last of the five surviving English morality plays, *Everyman*, is unlike any other medieval play in a number of important respects. First of all, it is the only printed play to come out of the Middle Ages: that is, it has existed in printed form from its earliest appearance in the first decade of the sixteenth century. This fact implies a reading audience as well as a spectating one. Second, the play is a translation, an English version of the Dutch *Elckerlijc*, which it follows very closely. It is thus part of a European theatrical tradition rather than a purely English one. The Dutch *Elckerlijc* (1485) is one of hundreds of surviving anonymous Rederijkers' (rhetoricians') plays, which were encouraged and supported in the low countries by local chambers of rhetoric from the second quarter of the fifteenth century until the beginning of the seventeenth. These chambers were made up of leading burgesses in their communities, bent on instilling morality, piety and culture locally through the entertaining medium of drama. The translation of *Everyman* may have been made because the Dutch play was already so well regarded in its own country.

Despite this anomalous ancestry, *Everyman* has earned a reputation as the quintessential morality play, and indeed it represents the genre in its most distilled form. Its use of allegory depicts outer and inner characteristics common to everyone; its main character, Everyman, operates both as a sombre, rigidly conceived static figure, and as a dynamic one, who by the end of the play has learned faster and better than the audience itself. Accosted by Death but given a brief reprieve, he attempts to convince the characters Fellowship, Kindred, Cousin and Goods to accompany him. Then he tries to coax Beauty, Strength, Discretion and Five Wits. In the end, only Good Deeds travels with him to the grave. The inner action demonstrates the typical – and typically painful – movement from sinful state to recognition to redemptive action, offering the moral pattern for which morality plays are famous.

Every detail of *Everyman* contributes to its very considerable impact: its spare conceptions of representative allegorical character types, its insistent, unrelenting sequence of loss, its through-line of action that carries directly toward the inevitable conclusion, its unadorned language and sombre tone, its unblinking depiction of the psychological and physiological processes of dying and its religious earnestness. The poetic resonance of the play gathers as it progresses, aided by the repeated pattern of hope and disappointment, and in this regard it has a distinctively modern feel, however dated its doctrine. Despite the fact that the play is a translation – or perhaps because of that fact – it displays a verbal tightness and a sense of play with language that link it comfortably with later Tudor interludes and early Elizabethan fare.

Missing from *Everyman* are the antics and high spirits often associated with Vice figures common to the other morality plays. There is little sugar-coating on the moral pill this play presents to its main character and to its audience. Hardly any spectacle – or even lively action – marks its performance. Still, from the theatrical point of view *Everyman* offers ample scope for awe and wonder, not least by means of the commanding figure of Death at the beginning and the yawning grave into which Everyman presumably descends at the end. Everyman himself changes from a naive and desperate simpleton to a figure of gravity, grace and courage during the course of the play, and it is the contemplation of how he might die (or, the play would imply, how the rest of us might live) that produces this shift. The other characters are, of course, more impersonal abstractions of external and internal human qualities, and the action of the play is to strip them away one by one, echoing at once the last minutes and the whole life of every human being. The Messenger who speaks the prologue and the Doctor who speaks the epilogue both mediate the audience's psychological entry into and out of this long meditation – this self-confessed 'treatise ... in maner of a moral play', as it is called on the title page. Deceptively simple on or off the stage, *Everyman* offers one of the most memorable and powerful late medieval parables to haunt the modern imagination, and, however it represents the morality-play tradition, its stature as a literary and theatrical masterpiece is undisputed.

Biblical or secular history plays, which reenact strange, violent or otherwise compelling plots on the stage, form yet another kind of non-cycle drama. Good examples of these are the fourteenth-century *Dux Moraud*, the fifteenth-century Digby *Killing of the Children*, the Brome *Abraham and Isaac* and the Croxton *Play of the Sacrament*. The action of *Dux Moraud* is clear, though only one actor's part (Dux) has survived. It features incest between the chief character and his daughter, the murder of a bastard baby and a drastic repentance. *The Killing of the Children* likewise offers dark and violent fare, as the biblical slaughter of the innocents takes place onstage, jokingly overseen by a swaggering coward named Watkyn.

But of all the non-cycle plays, the Croxton *Play of the Sacrament* tops the list of what might be called the medieval theatre of curiosity. A hybrid of legend, conversion play and folk play, it portrays the relatively common story of Jews gaining possession of a consecrated host and testing it by torture. In these stories the host comes to life to provide convincing proof of transubstantiation – the doctrine that Jesus was physically present in consecrated bread and wine. In the Croxton play the torture scenes parody a mass service, and at the centre of the play occurs an interpolated episode featuring a quack folk doctor, Master Brundiche of Brabant, whose arrival on the scene is introduced by his irreverent servant Colle. Brundiche (a scatological pun on 'Brown Ditch') boasts that he can heal the hand of Jonathas the Jew, which had been pulled off in a previous frantic scene. He fails, predictably, and his failure contrasts with the true ministrations of Jesus, whose figure now appears in spectacular fashion emerging out of an exploding oven. The characters and sequence of action in this interpolated episode derive from the English folk-play tradition, in particular mummer plays where a boastful doctor attempts fruitlessly to heal a fallen figure. Although the earliest surviving copies of these folk plays were not written down until the eighteenth century, they are clearly ancient compositions, including exotic and grotesque characters like 'Big Head' and 'Turkey Snipe' (or 'Turkish Knight') who has typically, and literally, lost his head or otherwise been slain in a fight and is in need of repair.

The energy and vitality of that folk tradition thus inform the *Play of the Sacrament*, not only in the exuberance of the Doctor episode, but also in the treatment of the host and in the clownish loss of the hand of Jonathas. All the antics lead to the Jews' conversion and baptism (rather than to their slaughter, as happens in a contemporary French analogue) and by the end of the play the tone shifts to one of thanksgiving and praise. The conditions of performance for the Croxton play are unknown. It was composed after 1461, the date given at the close of the play as when the enacted events were supposed to have taken place. Its language and the place names mentioned in it point towards an East Anglian origin. A note in the manuscript tells us that 'nine may play yt at ease', suggesting that the play enjoyed a stage career on the road as part of a travelling company, or even that the script itself travelled for different local productions. In any event, it provides one more splendid example of how fast-moving, rich and inventive non-cycle plays tended to be.

The characteristically lively treatment of subject matter, of character types and action found in non-cycle plays should make clear how much more they relied upon theatrical spectacle than did the mystery plays. Then as now, spectacle translated itself into profit for the sponsoring institution, whether it was the local parish or the town council. Late medieval records indicate that a common purpose for such plays was to raise money to support town or parish projects, and the presence of this early commercial motive renders the theatrical enterprises more recognisable and modern. It ought to come as no surprise that the non-cycle plays form a tangible link between medieval and Renaissance dramatic fare. Yet these plays are far more than simple, histori-cally interesting attempts to do what the Elizabethan theatre might accomplish more fully at a later date. A more useful – and more accurate – way to charac-terise them is as remarkable celebrations of late medieval English theatricality, typical of a popular culture that reached a climax during the fifteenth and sixteenth centuries. Even Shakespeare's plays, which excelled verbally, were constrained by relatively limited space, costumes and machinery. As spectacle, they never actually surpassed the sumptuous and spirited productions of the earlier popular theatre. Indeed, not until the theatrical extravaganzas of the nineteenth and twentieth centuries was dramatic spectacle exploited so freely and effectively as it was in late medieval times.

It would be hard to say which of the kinds of medieval plays made for the most effective theatre. Certainly all the non-cycle plays rely enormously upon spectacle. Many employ music as part of the show; all abound in special effects and colourful characters, and all go well beyond the pat Horatian formula to delight and instruct. In the past, this theatricality has been little explored by literary critics or theatre historians, partly because of an unfamiliarity with the playtexts, and also because more serious questions have only recently been posed about how theatrical elements enhance verbal meaning and how texts signify in performance. Technically speaking, all medieval plays are comedies that amply demonstrate Christianity's salvific vision in highly accomplished theatrical ways – we have only to remember the howling, suffering, smoking devils, or farcical routines in which vice characters are foiled, or the broad scatological humour so often mined by the plays. Yet we must be wary of construing them simply as examples of naive high jinks or circus-like chambers of horror, to fasten only on possibilities for spirited performance. Darker visions and more serious voices in late medieval culture find expression here as well, and many of the main conflicts in the plays still trouble humanity. The tension between human love and higher love and the difficulty of squaring common sense and ethical behaviour, for example, are not issues limited to the fifteenth or sixteenth centuries. Likewise, psychological themes worked out in the morality plays, like the consequences of guilt and retribution, or the puzzle and pathos of a good life gone bad, along with the spectre of death's certain oblivion – individual and shared – are issues still conjured with today. And even when distanced by humour, scenes of torture remain viscerally affecting, perpetually hateful, perpetually familiar.

Thus, whenever the bogeymen and spooks of the medieval imagination show up in these plays displaying their stage antics, shtiks and gags, it should be recognised that their theatrical power, while often broadly comic, is regularly countered by a thematic and equally dramatic emphasis on human sorrow and loss, on the ugly power of hatred and rancour, on the baffling banality of evil, on the individual character's place in a sombre earthbound scheme of Christian suffering. The unexpected reversals of fortune that catapult such representative figures as Everyman, or Mankind in his play, or Humanum Genus in *The Castle of Perseverance*, into salvific history remain simply that: the final movement in a complex orchestration of preordained justice and mercy. In these plays, hope shrinks fearfully before the certainty of dark justice, and virtually all the plays point towards the concluding act of a human pilgrimage through an earthly vale of tears.

In the meantime, although we should be wary of the extravagant out-pourings of evil characters in these plays – the famous ranting of Herod, the exultant shrieks and private calculations of devils and vices, the pomping and boasting of worldly kings – we should also be suspicious of similar excesses emanating from the idealised, often allegorised characters aligned on the side of good. Their blatantly pious speeches and tedious explanations of doctrinal niceties offer something of a tip-off. The pure goodness of such otherwise human figures, along with the extempore moralising of interpreters in pro-logues, epilogues and running commentaries, have all too often been taken at face value in modern criticism and played straight in modern performances. They should not be. What we are faced with in these plays is not the use of the profane to prove the sacred, nor do we find its opposite, the systematic subversion of sacred truths or moral and ethical themes by virtue of the sheer power of theatrical representation. In the poetic experience peculiar to the late medieval theatre, primal elements of both good and evil seem oddly, in-extricably, bound together by overstated theatricality. The plays horrify and amuse and comfort all at once. They pander to extreme tastes for violence and grotesque action onstage, while offering rationalisations and nostalgia all in the same texts. Theatrical exuberance forces this amalgam of ancient text and popular cultural forms, allowing the plays to reach forward towards a timeless present. Ultimately, in the non-cycle plays especially, however far back their original stories may stretch, the use of costume, accent and gesture under-scores a real sense that actions of the distant past permeate the present, just as present actions determine the future. By all accounts these dramatic texts resonated in their original theatrical space much as they resonate today, and in them can be found touching explorations of recurrent conflicts and univer-sal themes, surprising strategies, ideological face-offs, and fictive, simplified, affecting examples of men and women caught at the extremities of Christian life.

No more cake, no more ales: the end of communal festive drama

> For thei beleve on a cake – me thynk yt ys onkynd.
> And all they seye how the prest dothe yt bynd
> (Jonathas the Jew, in the Croxton *Play of the*
> *Sacrament*, lines 200–1)

> Dost thou think, because thou art virtuous, there shall be no more
> cakes and ale? (Malvolio, in *Twelfth Night*, 2.3.116–17)

As we have seen, for an astonishingly large number of towns and villages, churches and town halls, inns and other public venues in the late fifteenth and early sixteenth centuries, early English plays both embodied and reflected the milieu that produced them. As the cultural anthropologist Clifford Geertz might have it, they acted out, for their own culture, stories it told itself about itself.[31] Communities were instructed and entertained by the plays, and the plays offered material proof of a community's piety and substance. Certainly the civic corporations sponsoring cycle plays knew that the performances translated into more than entertainment, and it is clear that biblical stories in particular reinforced social and ecclesiastical authority, often by challenging it. In Old Testament plays like the *Creation*, the *Fall of Adam* or the *Killing of Abel*, and in those involving howling devils or temptation scenes, norms of order were regularly challenged, often inverted, only to be reasserted – one of the central functions of carnival, according to Bakhtin.[32] The carnivalesque inversion and reassertion of order, so apparent early on in folk rituals, in

---

31 Geertz elaborates this notion in *The Interpretation of Cultures*.
32 Central texts on carnival are Bakhtin, *The Dialogic Imagination* and Bristol, *Carnival and Theatre*.

boy-bishop routines, in mummings, parish ales and other related activities, were adroitly appropriated by cycle and non-cycle plays alike, and it may be useful to recall that, whatever serious issues early English plays attempted to negotiate in their own day, they were ordinarily tied to festive occasions of one kind or another, publicly marking moments of communal celebration, of merriment and excess, and of extraordinary times followed by a return to the ordinary.

A good illustration of this theatrical challenge to order and its return – one familiar in classical comedy and common to every kind of medieval vernacular comedy – appears in the device of the saucy servant upstaging his master. The routine occurs with amazing frequency in the cycle plays, as can readily be seen in mouthy messenger figures like Garcio, Cain's servant in the Wakefield *Killing of Abel*. At the outset of the play this 'mery lad' defies his master and trades him blow for blow before at last being driven away. The truly defiant servant is of course Cain, who attempts verbally to justify the murder of Abel and is himself driven away into exile by the end of the play, when some sort of moral order is reasserted. Likewise, in the non-cycle plays, the interactions of such characters as Colle and Brundiche in the Croxton *Play of the Sacrament*, already noticed above, show the same process at work. Morality plays encode this carnivalesque process of inversion and return to order as a main structuring device: their vice characters by definition refuse to serve the cause of the virtuous, and sometimes they actively revolt against it, like the team of Mischeff, New-Guise, Nowadays and Nought who taunt Mercy and torment the main character in *Mankind*. In each case without fail, the challenges to current social or religious conventions, as well as the reversals of order or hierarchy, are at first excitingly dramatised but in the end soundly defeated.

Beyond imagining and reasserting social and ecclesiastical order in the plays – however useful those functions may be to understanding their power in political terms – there lay a further festive celebration of a different kind of order. Virtually all medieval English plays dramatised and reflected the sacramental order of Christian life, an order grounded in Catholic doctrine itself. Gail McMurray Gibson has termed this quality an 'incarnational aesthetic', suggesting that the devotional aspects of the plays were inextricably bound up with their theatrical success.[33] The tacit underpinnings of sacramental and affective levels in the plays, rooted as they were in doctrine and practice, need to be noticed in our discussion of medieval theatre history. Towards the end of

33 Gibson coins the term in the first chapter of *The Theater of Devotion*.

the life of medieval theatrical traditions, late in the sixteenth century, doctrinal issues that had sparked and fuelled the English Reformation continued to resonate, and it is no coincidence that these medieval traditions perished with the growth of the reformed church in England.

We might recall too that from their earliest appearance, civic- and parish-sponsored plays were commonly referred to as 'Corpus Christi' plays, signalling not only their centuries-old origins in the feast of Corpus Christi, but also their celebration of what was understood to constitute the mystical body of the church. Indeed, Gibson suggests that during the heyday of cycle and non-cycle plays alike, 'there was a growing tendency to see the world saturated with sacramental possibility and meaning and to celebrate it'.[34] In this sacralised, sacramental order of the church, the most prominent sacrament of worship and dispute was that of the eucharist, embodied in Holy Communion. The consecrated bread and wine, thought literally to be Christ's body on earth, signified at the same time the body of the entire communion of saintly worshippers, a spiritual body with Christ at its head. Whenever the body of Christ was staged, then – as a host, a speaking character, a tortured victim in a passion sequence, or even as a babe in a manger – it acted as social metaphor, one that extended the affective power of the play. As Peter Travis notes, speaking of the Chester cycle, the staged body of Christ 'blesses the material. It bonds with the physicality of its torturers; it extends to the city wall and gates. It is a natural symbol that embraces and is part of the living body of the community.'[35]

The staged body of Christ, then, was a common feature of medieval plays in one form or another, and it always implied or suggested some larger frame of meaning within the sacramental religious culture. So when the sacrament of the eucharist sparked fierce doctrinal controversy that proved central to the English Reformation, the matter had serious implications for drama itself. Certainly some of the most hotly argued controversies during the fifteenth and early sixteenth centuries revolved around the doctrine of transubstantiation, that is, of the sacred presence of the sanctified body of Christ on earth, alive in the host – or, as Jew Jonathas in the Croxton *Play of the Sacrament* puts it, 'Yowr God, that ys full mytheti, in a cake' (line 285). Not only because of its doctrinal significance, but also because of the symbolic resonance of the body of Christ, the issue was far from trivial. As we have seen, upon this very doctrine hinged a key understanding of Roman Catholic identity. The scope of church power

---

34 Ibid., 6.
35 Travis, 'The social body of the dramatic Christ in medieval England', in Tricomi (ed.), *Early Drama to 1600*, 33.

and its authority figured large in the matter, and the acceptance or rejection of this doctrine had far-reaching social ramifications. The issue informs the main action in the Croxton *Play of the Sacrament*. The victim of torture is the consecrated host, but beyond that host lay Christ's body – and by extension the church temporal – and beyond that lay the real target in history, the doctrine of transubstantiation itself. Hence the importance in the play attached to the elaborate mock consecration by the Jews, to their defeat, and to the spectacular proof of the real presence. Hence the utterly triumphant tone accompanying their conversion at the end of the play.

The doctrinal dispute surrounding the sacrament of the eucharist, which figures so prominently here and in other late medieval plays, offers us a taste of the large cultural shift taking place in the background, where Christian history was rewriting itself. During the sixteenth century, religious and cultural transformations occurred at breakneck speed as the Reformation swept across England. In Wittenberg in 1517 Martin Luther had already pioneered a general course of Protestant action in response to the widespread worldliness and corruption in the Roman church. Less than two decades later in England, the accumulated wealth and weakened ideals of that church created ready targets for Henry VIII's greatest desires: to replenish his treasury and to remarry. By 1534 Henry officially and completely made the break with Rome by the Act of Supremacy, the legal act that declared him Supreme Head of the Church in England. To be sure, this act and the others that followed on its heels in subsequent years had political goals, but their main effect was to redefine English religious culture, and that in turn affected the drama. In 1536 the Act of Dissolution of Smaller Monasteries was passed, followed in 1539 by the Act of Dissolution of the Greater Monasteries. The appropriation by the crown of ecclesiastical holdings was ruthless and efficient, and by 1540 the years of inventory came to an end and the plunder began. The monasteries surrendered everything to the crown: their vast estates and income-producing properties, their richly endowed chantries and schools, their immense stores of plate and jewels. During this astonishingly brief time, then – the last twelve years of Henry's reign and the five or six of Edward VI's – an entirely restructured church and government, based upon reformed policies and reformed sensibilities, had become firmly established.

The Protestant reformers specifically eschewed ecclesiastical display of all kinds, and as their influence spread across England so did the conscious narrowing of church ceremony. Painted or sculpted images, decorated ornamentation, elaborate vestments, even ritual customs and practices associated with Roman Catholic routines, were discouraged and abandoned. Both the composition and performance of religious drama – which had been underwritten for centuries in one form or another by the medieval church, came under scrutiny. Ultimately, the sanctions imposed on monastic communities took their toll at the local level, in towns and parishes, and it seems clear now that, as a more or less unintended consequence of closing down the monasteries and of cleansing the church of ceremonial display, medieval theatrical enterprises too came to an untimely end. In any case, the clerical authors of medieval plays, educated in monasteries or monastic schools, were made homeless by 1540, with no possibility of replacement – a fact with real import to the towns and villages where their plays had made welcome entertainment.

At the same time in many towns, a reform-minded oligarchy was on the rise. The new political leaders worked diligently to bring about the demise of those now outmoded festive occasions associated with the Roman church. Some practices they considered intemperate, like parish-sponsored drinkings (or 'ales'); others, like the civic-sponsored plays, which since time out of mind had been performed as proof of piety and displays of power, they disagreed with openly and put down. As the effects of the Reformation took hold in England, then, the tradition of local drama that had been fostered in towns and parishes became ideologically suspect. Some towns, like Chester and Norwich, tried hard to maintain their theatrical traditions by revising their playtexts, and Chester even shifted the date of its play performances from the old Corpus Christi Day to Whitsuntide. But such attempts were doomed from the start, for embedded in the fabric of the plays was the sacramental and incarnational identity of Christ with his church, that old Catholic doctrine of the eucharistic body, temporal and eternal, woven into the texts of even the most familiar Bible stories. The festive celebration of Christ's body had to go, and it did. Within two generations of the dissolution of the monasteries the late medieval flowering of drama had become no more than a curious memory.

In the late fifteenth and early sixteenth centuries, however, a parallel theatrical tradition sprang up, rooted in the rising tide of humanism. Plays springing from this tradition ultimately provided a professional alternative to popular communal and festive plays. Humanism itself had been building as a powerful social and intellectual force since its beginnings in the Italian *quattrocentro*, and on the continent its intellectual ferment surged after the invention of movable type in the 1450s. By 1475 William Caxton had set up a press in Westminster, the first in England, and he began to produce a stream of printed works that fuelled the humanistic enterprise. With the rapid proliferation of books and literacy – now more easily acquired than ever before – learning gained new favour and greater social status. Education, in the broadest sense of the word, was recognised as a politically potent tool for social engineering. When Henry VII ascended the throne in 1485, he relied upon humanists early on to help devise and maintain a system of government that would survive the predictable baronial pillaging that attended the end of the Wars of the Roses. And over the course of his reign (1485–1509), Henry did more: he welcomed internationally celebrated humanists like Erasmus (1466–1536) into the country, and at home actively supported the careers of English humanists like John Colet (1466/67–1519), the founder of St Paul's School.

Given the central role that texts played in humanistic affairs, and given the emphasis on learning as a social tool, it seems natural – perhaps even inevitable – that humanism should turn to drama as a form of expression. Key to this development was the importance of education as an ideal – not only for scholars but also for a ruler and his subjects, for the court and the kingdom. So the king, his children and the court surrounding them were all to be schooled in ancient and modern writings that might help them perform their social roles better. By the end of the reign of Henry VII, there was an established legacy of humanistic learning in the court. King, court and country all participated in an educational project that made England one of the major European centres of Renaissance learning and brilliance. The process was a symbiotic one in courtly circles: humanistic education offered new (though often classically based) intellectual ideals and prospects of moral betterment to courtly audiences, and courtly patronage of humanism in turn offered fresh opportunities for learned, literary and artistic enterprises.

Thus the stage was set for a further development of theatre, and in the 1490s, for the first time ever, new plays associated with humanistic sensibilities were composed and performed specifically for courtly audiences. These plays are the early Tudor interludes. They projected on stage some of the immediate interests and concerns of their audiences, treating subjects of manners and morals and, like the courtesy books to which they are distantly related, they circulated models of proper behaviour for those who were connected – and those hoping to be connected – with the court. The interludes, betraying their humanist roots, drew both on classical sources and on well-known theatrical conventions like those found in the morality tradition. Often set in classical times and portraying classical characters, the plots and actions were unmediated by the familiar biblical stories or religious doctrines that lay at the heart of so many medieval plays. The interludes experimented with dramatic forms of romantic comedies, of classically inspired farces, and even of moral allegories. Whatever shape they took, it is fair to say that with these interludes English drama had turned an important corner, from scholastic learning to classical learning. The path begun here led through the Reformation into the future.

The earliest Tudor interlude that has survived is Henry Medwall's *Fulgens and Lucres*, which was performed at the court of Cardinal Morton (where Medwall acted as chaplain) some time in the 1490s. Set in classical times, the plot dramatises a wooing contest in which Lucres, the beautiful daughter of the Roman senator Fulgens, must choose between two suitors, one of whom is more nobly qualified than the other. The suspense is heightened and the action mediated by two characters, A and B, who act as servants in the world of the play and also watch the proceedings onstage, commenting directly to the audience. After much debate and a good deal of lively dialogue, Lucres decides upon the lower-born suitor. Notable here are two unusual features: an almost Chaucerian concern with the definition of *gentilesse*, or nobility – highly appropriate for a courtly audience – and the placing of responsibility for the marriage choice in the hands of the female character. Notable too is what the play leaves out: any religious, moral, biblical or doctrinal matter altogether. Meanwhile, the witty wordplay foreshadows one main feature of later interludes.

The connections between the early humanist writers of interludes are of more than passing interest. It is no coincidence that the household of Cardinal Morton is where Thomas More grew up, nor that, when *Fulgens and Lucres* was printed in 1500, the job was done by John Rastell. Rastell was to become More's brother-in-law, marrying More's sister Elizabeth; he wrote the interludes *The Nature of the Four Elements* (1518), *Calisto and Melabea* (1527) and *Of Gentleness and Nobility* (1527–30). Another humanist playwright, John Heywood, author of *The Four PP* (1520–2) and *The Play of the Weather* (1525 33), married the daughter of John Rastell and Elizabeth More. These family connections point towards the intimacy of the court itself and its shared humanist concerns with classical texts and education. They highlight too the very real possibility that a small group like the More circle could wield an influence far beyond what its numbers might suggest. The list of humanist playwrights can be expanded to include a number of relatively familiar names like John Redford, author of *Wit and Science* (*c.* 1540), John Skelton, who wrote *Magnificence* (1515–18), and Nicholas Udall, whose *Roister Doister* has long been considered the first 'Tudor comedy'. These writers drew on classical conventions of dramatic structure and character still recognisable in the theatre a hundred years later. The characteristics of that theatrical tradition lie beyond the scope of this essay and properly belong to the discussion of Elizabethan drama that follows. These plays, clearly, mark the future course of British theatre.

But medieval dramaturgy left its mark on the mainline traditions of English theatrical practice too, and if we look forward briefly we can see how influential it proved to be. By the 1590s the native tradition of guild sponsorship of performance was viewed as totally outmoded – not simply old-fashioned and passé, but completely obsolete in doctrine, dogma and ritual echo, open to satiric exploitation. The 'rude mechanicals' of Shakespeare's *A Midsummer Night's Dream* – such clear parodies of guildsmen brimming with theatrical innocence, are now cast in the harsher light and expectations of professional productions in London – and they appear on the public stage without a trace of nostalgia. The break might seem complete, the modes of theatrical experience that cycle and non-cycle plays represented for all practical purposes dead until Brecht's and Pirandello's experiments in the twentieth century. But in fact these medieval theatrical traditions provided bridges from early English stages to Elizabethan and Jacobean theatres and beyond.

As the careers of these plays came to a close – and they had, after all, flourished for a very long time – their dramatic energy was subsumed into some forms and appropriated by others, fragmented into locally sponsored disguisings, for example, or, at the court, into masques. Their stagecraft continued to inform royal entries and civic processions. Their outward interest in historical and biblical matter fed into the more specific history plays and chronicle plays. Their broad strokes depicting internal conflicts and tensions, along with the allegorical map of spiritual and psychological struggle, the *psychomachia*, found representation in more realistically oriented figures, characters who in later guise would display conflicted selves in political, social or polemically charged arenas, and in high-Renaissance tragedies. As the morality plays shaded into sixteenth-century interludes, they also provided characters and character types, thematic resonance, and an emphasis on internal moral struggles, all of which will show up in the next generation of Elizabethan theatre. We might compare, for example, the indulgent and dismissive treatment of Bottom and his 'rude mechanicals' in *A Midsummer Night's Dream* with the roles that the Good and Bad Angels are allowed to play in *Dr Faustus*. Taken directly out of the morality-play tradition, Marlowe's figures are regarded as serious agents and integrated into his play without losing a shred of their original power.

In the later Elizabethan and Jacobean ages, the theatrical emphasis on conversions and inner struggles, so artfully set out in the non-cycle plays, joined with the dramaturgical expertise that had developed over the course of repeated productions. All became fodder for the verbally textured and visually focused professionals who were to follow. Other medieval streams of theatrical tradition joined the long river of theatre history – folk plays, classical plays, learned neo-Latin plays from the universities, Italian *commedia dell'arte* and *commedia erudita* characters and routines. Each brought unique opportunities for creative expansion from a different quarter; each added further important dimensions to the increasingly rich and professional theatrical world. All descended from the long line of medieval theatre that had arisen out of Roman practices, had been reinvented as part of Christian ritual ceremony in monasteries and churches, had been sponsored by towns and guilds and parishes across the land, had arisen in humanist venues, and had at last landed in the lap of London, where court and country would converge at last.

Faith, pastime, performance and drama in Scotland to 1603

JOHN J. McGAVIN

Faded, often damaged and disrupted by prejudice, war and the accidents of time, manuscript witnesses to early Scottish play are only too eloquent about the transience of the pleasures they record.[1] The mainly fifteenth- and sixteenth-century historians, scribes and notaries whose hands left traces of recreation rarely, if ever, did so for the reasons which prompt the modern scholar to read them. Consequently, their silences cannot be easily interpreted either. Although conscious of history, they were not writing for the distant future, and would have been dismayed that education had so declined from its proper subjects and language that scholars would find value in an account of a fool's fee written in Latin or pageant expenses written in Scots. Nevertheless, they have left evidence of variety and continuity in play. From the priest of Inverkeithing who, in 1282, led the young women of the parish in a semi-mimetic phallic dance (with stage prop) to the French tightrope walker whom James VI (1566–1625) astutely employed to divert his court, Scotland enjoyed a heterogeneous and habitual life of play, often showing features which we associate with theatre, but best understood in its hybridity rather than under any strict consideration of genre. Poem, debate and dialogue merged with image, pageant and ritual; procession blended into masque, and all with the frequent inflection of song, music and dance.

Celebration of royal events such as births, baptisms, marriages and visits to important towns constitutes a significant strand in that varied tradition, from rejoicing for the birth of Alexander II (1198–1244) to celebration of the king's nights (5 August and 5 November) when James VI escaped first from the Gowry conspiracy (1600) and then from the Gunpowder plot (1605). How far such activities veered from lay jollity and ecclesiastical ceremony towards

---

1 The records of early Scottish drama, ceremonial and secular music are currently being edited as *Records of Early Drama: Scotland*, under the auspices of the REED project. Unless otherwise noted the records referred to here can be found in Mill, *Medieval Plays in Scotland*.

theatre is sometimes unclear, but the play which linked monarchs with their subjects was not always innocently transparent. The first recorded charivari in Britain, mingled ambiguously with a harvest procession, and further iro-nised in courtly conversation, was offered in admonitory spirit to Robert III (c. 1337–1406) at his coronation in 1390.[2] That event was provincial, rural and largely focused on local and personal issues. However, a national version of such serious play occurred on 2 September 1561 when Mary Queen of Scots (1542–87), newly returned from France, enjoyed a ceremonial entry to Edinburgh. Recre-ation, from its financing to its reception, was often articulated with issues of power and politics: its semiotics frequently subtle and, like language, com-municated in moods other than the indicative. Mary's entry had some of the theatrical motifs and all of the complexity characteristic of royal entries inter-nationally. The circuit which took Mary from her royal quarters to her castle, then to her chief burgh, and finally back to the privy chamber accompanied by the retinue of the burgh inscribed political meaning on the institutional geography of the area: palace, castle and city were linked, but the last of them, which completed the circle, was linked conditionally upon her accepting the textual, choral and spectacular meanings which the burgh had presented in a series of pageants. In a densely iconographic experience she was warned off idolatry; she was flattered as a potentate by the (fairly conventional) masquing motif of exotic 'moors' who accompanied her, but also reminded that her closest aides were the wealthy seigneurs of the town in their velvet gowns and bonnets who carried a canopy over her head. She was given the keys to the town by a descending angel, but with other gifts which enjoined on her responsibility for the reformed religion, and silently qualified her freedom; she saw also how her future fortune rested upon the virtues of Love, Justice and Policy.[3] She was edified by material glory but also by the psalms. Diverted by colour and music, she must have shared nevertheless the irritation of her Catholic friends as they watched the rituals of their faith implicitly criticised on stage. She was praised, exhorted and also warned; treated to the gift of an ornate cupboard, she received a political agenda as well.

Records of elaborate royal entries exist mainly for the principal burghs in the sixteenth century; they reveal cultural emulation, varying degrees of po-litical negotiation, and both competition and cooperation between the towns in managing them. As in other countries, their texts could be provided by

2 McGavin, 'Robert III's "rough music"', *Scottish Historical Review* 74:2 (1995), 144–58.
3 *A Diurnal of Remarkable Occurrents that have passed within the country of Scotland since the death of King James the Fourth till the year MDLXXV*, and Mill, *Medieval Plays in Scotland*, 188–91.

authors of real stature, such as Sir David Lindsay, who wrote for a triumph at St Andrews. They occur on occasions such as the 1503 marriage of James IV (1473–1513) and Margaret Tudor (1489–1541); the arrival in Scotland of Queen Mary, second wife to James V, in 1538; the return of Mary Queen of Scots; the partial majority (thirteen years) of James VI in 1579, and the reception for him and his queen in 1589. They intensively combined allegory (which could be classical in reference), biblical and chivalric allusion, heraldic iconography, tableaux on eclectic subjects, orations, symbolic architecture, such as the artifical gates through which monarchs could 'enter', general civic decoration and (sometimes reusable) stage machinery, often with military and civic procession, and firing of gunpowder.[4] Although to the watching populace the royal party moving before them must have constituted one of the main attractions of the performance, to the party itself, proceeding quest-like through an urban forest of theatrical adventures, the experience was designed to turn spectacle into *speculum*, gaze into political insight. And yet, while such culturally loaded episodes demand historical reading and constitute vital evidence for the forces operating in society, one must remember that they were 'event' as well as 'text'. Although one can read the challenges which her entry would have posed to Mary, one cannot know how her 'moors' felt about it. Perhaps the bejewelled young Edinburgh men who blacked up their legs and arms felt the pull of ceremonial prestige, theatrical commitment and personal display more strongly than any reformist message.

Masquing activities within the court circle had a long tradition in Scotland. Writing in the 1440s, Walter Bower reported the following event at the wedding of Alexander III (1241–86) in 1285:

> a kind of show was put on in the form of a procession amongst the company who were reclining at table. At the head of this procession were skilled musicians with many sorts of pipe music including the wailing music of the bagpipes, and behind them others splendidly performing a war-dance with intricate weaving in and out. Bringing up the rear was a figure regarding whom it was difficult to decide whether it was a man or an apparition. It seemed to glide like a ghost rather than walk on feet. When it looked as if it was disappearing from everyone's sight, the whole frenzied procession halted, the song died away, the music faded, and the dancing contingent froze suddenly and unexpectedly.[5]

---

4 See Kipling, *Enter the King*; Johnston and Hüsken (eds.), *Civic Ritual and Drama*; Gray, 'The royal entry in sixteenth-century Scotland', in Mapstone and Wood (eds.), *The Rose and the Thistle*, 10–37.

5 Bower, *Scotichronicon*, ed. Watt, v. x. 40; 418–19.

There is no independent evidence to confirm Bower's account: Alexander's accidental death some months later may have encouraged a link with a supernatural story. But equally, it reads like a court masque, though not necessarily one of the late thirteenth century. The main problem with such chronicle reports, however, is that they gather contemporary meanings as they roll along. By the time of John Bellenden's translation of Hector Boece's *Historia* (published 1527), the figure whose imminent disappearance brought an end to the dance had become identified with Death, and in William Stewart's translation of Boece (1531–5) it was a phantom with rattling bones, which vanished when the dancers gazed on it. Even if Bower himself imagined it as a Dance of Death, his account hardly justifies this: it is the departure of the mysterious figure, not its arrival, which signals an end to frenzied festivity, the exact significance of which is also difficult to establish. If this was indeed a court masque, it was to have many illustrious and equally striking successors, such as the elaborate, costumed tournaments of the 'Wild Knight' and the 'Black Lady' for James IV in 1507–8; the frequent masques of Mary Queen of Scots, which could involve cross-dressing by men or women; the baptismal triumphs for James VI in 1566, recently described as 'the first truly Renaissance festival' in Great Britain, and then for his son, Prince Henry, in 1594.[6] These were costly, flamboyant and participative 'guising' (festive disguising) activities for the royal family and their aristocratic companions. Their audiences, generic aspirations and political significance were often international; their integration of the poetic and the pictorial involved writers and stage designers of commensurate reputation, and they could be multi-lingual in performance. The cloud which descended to catch up the Black Lady at the end of the eponymous masque was devised by Andrew Forman, Bishop of Moray, whom Pitscottie describes as an 'igromanciar' [conjurer] who 'seruit the king at sic tymes for his pastyme and pleasour'.[7] This device was to be reproduced throughout the century at civic triumphs. During the reign of Mary Queen of Scots, George Buchanan wrote (in Latin) for Twelfth Night celebrations, royal and courtly weddings, and baptismal triumphs.[8] Andrew Melville later wrote for James VI. All this was a far cry from the poor serving girls who scandalised the kirk by dancing in their brothers' hats or jackets, or the apprentices who caused laughter by guising in women's clothes, or the burghers' sons who rode through their towns in green

---

6 For tournament pageantry see Fradenburg, *City, Marriage, Tournament*, 225–64. For the events of 1566 see Lynch, 'Queen Mary's Triumph', *Scottish Historical Review* 69:1 (1990), 1–21.
7 Lindesay of Pitscottie, *The Historie and Cronicles of Scotland*, ed. Mackay, I, 244.
8 See McFarlane, *Buchanan*, 232–4.

jackets as Robin Hood and his men. But all these activities, so separated from each other by power, class, education and money, were satisfying the same desire to display oneself metamorphosed and beyond normal social bounds while still within the permissions of custom.

Scottish civic play on serious religious subjects is unsupported by the weight of record and text which has given such prominence to the English biblical and morality plays. Nevertheless, it is clear that, at least from the fifteenth century, the major Scottish towns enjoyed a rich diet of both processional and static events involving theatrical elements in tableau or scripted form (or perhaps both) at Corpus Christi, Candlemas and other liturgical dates. Aberdeen, for example, had a play of the Holy Blood recorded from 1440 and a play of Belial from 1471. The properties for at least sixty-five participants in Dundee's fifteenth-century Corpus Christi procession suggest that the event would have appeared as an animated version of a book of hours in its selection of biblical and hagiographic scenes. Lanark and Perth were similarly eclectic, combining in Perth's case Adam and Eve, the devil's chapman and St Erasmus, whose intestines, represented by a cord, were drawn out. Lanark, like the others, combined artificial pageant devices such as a dragon, a chapel and Christ's body, with real people. Whether its procession was scripted, involved commentary, or was merely advertised is hard to determine from the record of a quire of paper bought 'to bill the pla', but it is important not to simplify such civic activity generically on the model of either English play cycles or untexted procession. It is quite possible from the extant early sixteenth-century evidence, that Haddington had a Corpus Christi procession and also that the guilds played their pageants in the modern sense, perhaps in the common playfield on the Sands nearby. Similarly, one cannot know whether the John Walcar, alias Hatmaker, to whom Perth regularly turned in the 1540s for 'gemmys, ferchis [farces] and clerk playis making and plaing' contributed script to their Corpus Christi procession.

Scottish towns, like those of England and the continent, found that such communal activities were actually foci for dissent. In the case of Haddington, it is craft rivalry and reluctance to organise that brings their Corpus Christi celebrations into the records.[9] In cases of disputed priority in craft processions, recourse was had by more than one burgh to the precedent of Edinburgh, thus revealing a failure of local tradition to manage what was supposedly

---

9 McGavin, 'Drama in sixteenth-century Haddington', in Higgins (ed.), *European Medieval Drama*, I, 147–59.

communal. Points of breakdown in what were claimed to be shared purposes, and the enforcement of activity purported to be organic to the society can all be identified long before reformation pressures bore upon traditional Catholic practice. The recurring tensions between crafts may have been symptomatic of general financial difficulty and those wider civic antagonisms which show up in burghal and parliamentary resistance to the development of craft working practices. One identifiable rift separates those who wished civic traditions of play to be maintained and those who actually bore the burden of playing. In Haddington craft dilatoriness in the face of pressure from town authorities probably had financial causes, but in Aberdeen absenteeism from the crafts' Candlemas Offering hid deeper resentment. In 1524, most of the craftsmen were missing from this procession, in which they traditionally carried the insignia of their trades. The outrage of the authorities focused on a tailor, John Pill, because he had also insulted the baillies by calling them merchants and inviting them to process with salt pork and herbs in their hands. There seems little doubt that the craftsmen no longer agreed with the authorities that the Offering was an 'auld honorable and lovabill consuetude of the burghe', which is how the official records describe it. Rather it seemed an entertainment for their financial superiors in which craft insignia were visible not to express communal civic pride but as tokens of their subordination. This view is supported by Pill's punishment: since the tailor had not taken part in the public theatre of social control, the provost and baillies required a private humiliation of the same kind: he had to beg their pardon on his knees with a pair of shears round his neck.

In its various manifestations, from the boy bishop watched by Edward I (1239–1307) in the chapel at Dunfermline in 1303–4 through King of the Bean festivities at St Andrews University to civic Abbots of No-rent or Robin Hoods, misrule seems until the later sixteenth century to have been associated more with privileged groups in society. In Aberdeen, the misrule procession was socially restricted in practice because participants had to be on horseback and, latterly, able to provide costumes of green and yellow with bows and arrows. The records suggest that, while the Candlemas Offering was carried out by craftsmen, a preponderance of burgesses, merchants and burgess sons was expected in the Robin Hood riding. Privilege also showed itself in the freedom of the burgess community to change the name, and possibly the form, of its misrule. While adherence to old customs was insisted on for the craftsmen, the council of Aberdeen invoked continuity to cover a change in the figures of misrule whom the burgesses would enjoy. In 1508 they were to ride 'with

Robert huyd and litil Iohne quhilk was callit in yeris bipast Abbot and priour of Bonacord'. Though there may have been a real change to a misrule figure understood against lay rather than ecclesiastical norms, subsequent records are inconsistent in designation, and this is typical of all the terminology of play, whether in Latin or Scots, throughout the period. The expenses of those who figureheaded misrule were usually met from the fees of those seeking the freedom of the burgh; attendance at events could be similarly enforced by loss of this freedom, and taking on the financial and managerial responsibilities of such a post could bring a burgessship and probably hinted at future advancement.[10] Their duties accordingly reflected broader burghal needs, from the manufacture of archery butts to the organisation of a religious play or royal celebration or the provision of music, dancing and general 'jocositeis'. At times of play the burgh could well be on show to visitors – visiting French military watched the Robin Hood plays in Ayr, for example – and the post of Robin Hood or Abbot, though symbolic of disorder (and occasionally the inspiration for genuine disorder), must have required considerable civic skills and commitment.

There was evidently a great deal more play in Scotland than there are texts to show for it. From this period, there are only six extant, complete and original plays in Scots. Only one of these, Sir David Lindsay of the Mount's *Ane Satyre of the Thrie Estaitis* (composed by 1552), is known to have been performed; another, the anonymous Terentian play *Philotus* (published in 1603, but composition variously dated within the latter half of the sixteenth century), has been successfully staged and seems intended for play despite the undramatic appearance of its printed text. The remaining four, Sir William Alexander's Senecan *Monarchicke Tragedies* (composed at the end of the period and published in 1607), fall outside the scope of this study since they are evidently closet drama, though Haddington records suggest that the closet in which they were read might be a shoemaker's as much as those of the more learned.[11] There is also a complete Scots play, John Burel's *Pamphilus* (published 1594 or 1595), translating the Latin *Pamphilus de amore*, though there is no evidence that it was ever played or intended for play. From the hand of George Buchanan are a further two original plays in Latin, *Jephthes* and *Baptistes*, and two translations from Euripides into Latin, *Medea* and *Alcestis*. These works, composed in France in 1542–3, were evidently performed there (with Buchanan's student

---

10 Eila Williamson discusses the career of one such 'Abbot' in 'Drama and entertainment in Peebles', *Medieval English Theatre* 22 (2000), 127–44.

11 *Haddington Burgh Registers: Court Book 1615–23*, 9 December 1617, National Archives of Scotland, B30/10/10, fo. 81[v], Edinburgh.

Montaigne as one of the actors).[12] This list suggests a Latinate and humanistic emphasis in the published canon, but dramatic quality is revealed mainly in Lindsay and Buchanan, with *Philotus* as runner-up.

There are also a palimpsest of a folk play, and a few fragments of plays (mainly masques), all in Scots. From the early sixteenth century there is 'The Pleugh Sang', a musically sophisticated, generically uncertain, and possibly courtly, part-song which probably alludes to and incorporates elements of a folk Plough Play.[13] Opinions have differed about whether it preserves a folk ceremony of renewal or suggests a hiring fair for ploughmen, with accompanying social comment, but it is not *in this form* an authentic folk drama.[14] From *c.* 1509 to *c.* 1515 comes the anonymous 'The Manere of the Crying of ane Play', a stanzaic introduction to a Robin Hood procession of the merchants of Edinburgh.[15] Although the event itself may not have been scripted, and may have involved more spectacle than drama, this comically sexual text constitutes bravura play in its own right. Its speaker directly addresses the mercantile interests of his hearers; exploits visual comedy; imports popular cultural references into the event being announced, and his Rabelaisian claims form part of the misrule which is being celebrated through the city's burghers dressing up as outlaws. This poem belongs to a genre of speeches in which the 'arrival' of the speaker heralds play. Its extravagance has stylistic analogues in the speeches of Fansy and Foly in Skelton's *Magnyfycence*, though the complex relationship of its playfulness to the world of civic order draws it closer to Lindsay's *Satyre*. As poetically detachable elements of theatre, such fragments have lasted more readily than the events which they announced. Alexander Montgomerie's substantial *oeuvre* contains two such speeches, 'The Navigation' and 'A Cartell of the Thre Ventrous Knichts', from the reign of James VI, who was a renowned patron of poetry and music (though, like most Scottish kings, he probably preferred hunting).[16] Narrative in style, the poems praise king, court and country while introducing exotic travellers, such

---

12 Lindsay, *Ane Satyre of the Thrie Estaitis*, ed. Lyall, *Philotus* in *The Mercat Anthology of Early Scottish Literature 1375 1707*, ed. Jack and Rozendaal, 390 432; *The Poetical Works of Sir William Alexander*, ed. Kastner and Charlton; *Pamphilus*: BL MS C 21.b.39; STC 4105. All four of Buchanan's plays are edited, and his own compositions also translated, in Sharratt and Walsh (eds.), *George Buchanan Tragedies*.
13 Text in Elliott and Shire (eds.), *Music of Scotland 1500–1700*, 141–7.
14 Carpenter, 'Early Scottish drama', in Jack (ed.), *The History of Scottish Literature*, I, 200; Ross, *Musick Fyne*, 119–21.
15 The text is included in Mackenzie (ed.), *The Poems of William Dunbar*, 170–4, though there is no strong evidence for the attribution.
16 *The Poems of Alexander Montgomerie*, ed. Cranstoun, 204–14. See also Shire, *Song, Dance and Poetry of the Court of Scotland under King James VI*.

as Turks, Egyptians or knights errant, whose costumes will form part of the delights of the masque, and whose actions will drive the ensuing recreation. Fragments of a masque (1588) by James VI include such a speech, though the significance of the work lies more in its varied classical, theatrical, moral and satirical *dramatis personae*, for whom James attempted some characterisation by style and subject, with comic intention.[17]

As a major figure in the Scottish Renaissance and a tutor of the future James VI, but also as a dramatist of real critical and emotional insight, Buchanan (1506–82) repays study. His version of the story of Jephtha, in particular, takes us into the area of sexual identity, gender politics and the selfishness of rectitude. It reveals (though it does not explicitly decry) the moral escape routes of a patriarchal culture bound to the exigencies of the word and at once seduced by and fearful of a more loving, less rigorous attitude to life. Although male heroic values are reinstated through Jephtha's daughter, who willingly embraces death to fulfil her father's unthinking vow, Buchanan shows that this does not preserve the masculinity of the father, and it does not obscure the rights, values and sufferings of the mother, who is allowed to speak last. Buchanan shares with other humanist educationalists an interest in arguing on both sides of a question, and this extends even to making his two original plays appear like a diptych, for in *Baptistes* (on the execution of John the Baptist) a woman again takes over a man's oath. This time, in the world of *realpolitik*, a craven Herod is protected from the criticism of the public by his queen. Buchanan seems more interested in the psychology of the weak and evil than in the rigour of the good, the play being explicit about dark motivations and wilfulness in dishonest critics. Strategies of self-preservation, the different motives which can be imputed to the same act, how leadership can be variously defined, and the values and dangers of social repression and tolerance all contribute to this sophisticated problem play, which not only shows Buchanan as a powerful dramatist working in a different theatrical mode from his Scottish contemporary Sir David Lindsay (with whom he nevertheless shares some themes), but which is also eerily prophetic of the emotional and moral problems evident in the Scottish Reformation.

We no longer have the text of the interlude version of Lindsay's *Ane Satyre of the Thrie Estaitis*, which was presented indoors before James V (1512–42) at Linlithgow Palace in 1540. We do have a partial manuscript and full printed edition of the two-part, enlarged and revised version which received outdoor

---

17 James VI, 'An Epithalamion upon the Marques of Huntlies Mariage', in *New Poems by James I of England*, ed. Westcott, 47–52.

performance at Cupar in 1552 and Edinburgh in 1554, where the queen regent, Mary of Guise (1515–60), watched it. It has been persuasively argued that this later play, composed after the death of James V, sees a diffusion of power, a loss of royal focus, with accompanying ambivalence about kingship, a failure to present reformation as fully successful, and a promotion of control and punishment in society without an accompanying sense of social improvement.[18] However, as a corollary to this, and with rather different implications, the play can be positioned at the centre of an intense cultural self-referentiality noticeable in sixteenth-century Scotland.

Particularly in the poetry of Dunbar (*c.* 1460–*c.* 1513), but also in the 'Christis Kirk' genre (to which Lindsay contributed), and Gavin Douglas's *The Palice of Honour* (1501), we find direct references to play events and descriptions of them, together with allusions, echoes, satires, imitations and evocations of the world of play.[19] A visual imagination which draws poetic and theatrical traditions together shows up in the penchant for set-piece scenes of observed and interpreted spectacle in non-dramatic Scots writing of the fifteenth and sixteenth centuries. But even if one discounts this as a literary confluence with many possible origins, one still finds mock and real tournaments, fools, minstrels, dances, ceremonial entries, the Black Lady of James IV's tournament, Yule-tide fun, bull-baiting, flytings, court and country entertainments and carnival in the poetry, and it is Dunbar who reminds us that writers, like everyone else, 'Playis heir ther padyanis, syne gois to graif' (play their pageants here; then go to the grave). Even poems which do not explicitly refer to theatre may be predicated on the reader's knowledge of it, as when Dunbar berates the merchants of Edinburgh for the state of their town by taking them through a parody of a royal entry, stopping at key sites of pageantry on the way: 'May nane pas throw your principall gaittis, / For stink of haddockis and of scattis'. At the Cross and the Tron, one meets curds, milk and puddings rather than gold and silk; the town minstrels are good for nothing but singing popular songs, and 'Through streittis nane may mak progres, / For cry of cruikit, blind and lame'.[20] Even the lofty rhetoric of Gavin Douglas's *Palice* is built at one point on action recognisable to the ordinary citizen of any Scottish burgh. In a dream vision he marvels at Venus's court as it processes by him. This extravagant, musically sophisticated pageantry is greater than any real burgh or court

18 For the relationship between the interlude and outdoor versions see Walker, *The Politics of Performance in Early Renaissance Drama*, 134–62.

19 Dunbar, *Selected Poems*, ed. Bawcutt; MacLaine (ed.), *The Christis Kirk Tradition*; Douglas, *The Shorter Poems*, ed. Bawcutt.

20 Dunbar, *Selected Poems*, no. 42, 'Quhy will ye, merchantis of renoun'.

could have managed, but is in the same idiom, and it prompts the unhappy Douglas to interrupt proceedings with a loud and assertive song of inconstant love. 'Tho saw I Venus on hir lip did bite, / And all the Court in haist thair horsis renyeit' (lines 639–40). This is a higher version of the 'hawy strublens [serious disturbance] and vyill myspersoning' which Alexander Kayn's wife offered to the Aberdeen Lords of Bonacord as they passed her in 1542. In equally effective rhetorical vein she called them common beggars and spongers with little to eat for all their 'cuttit hose'. Douglas expects his poetic interruption to be recognisable as an offence against public play

This cross-fertilisation of poetry and play goes some way to compensate for the country's lack of playtexts, but it also creates an impression of Scottish cultural homogeneity centred on pastime, performance and drama. Lindsay's *Satyre* reinforces this. In moving from the relatively secure genre of a hall-based interlude to the multiple staging, extravagant theatricality and generic instability of the play as we have it, Lindsay also developed a strongly metatheatrical strain. Time and again, the *Satyre* addresses 'pastyme with plesance' in its moral and social dimensions. Many popular recreations of Scotland are mentioned, including the dramatic experience which the audience is enjoying. They constitute both common attractions and dangers. Within the *Satyre*, the vices devise their own 'guising' in order for Lindsay to show that the real clergy whom they impersonate are themselves spiritual impostors; clerical accoutrements become stage props to be revealed as artifice in real life. Despite its allegorical characters and action, its explicit didacticism, and its dramatic self-consciousness, the *Satyre* creates an intensely realistic impression, and justifies its claim to be criticising the nation at large by making public theatre out of those events which themselves constituted the theatre of public life: royal display, parliament, civic processions (in this case inverted to a kind of charivari), executions, punishment in the stocks, etc. It insists, especially in the First Part, on the moral responsibility of the spectator to observe and interpret images which are offered both for recreation and illumination. Fifty years before Hamlet set out to catch the conscience of King Claudius by a play within a play, Lady Verity tells those spectators in authority, 'The pepill wil tak mair tent to your deids / Then to your words', as a tableau of the king lolling among the ladies of the court is displayed behind her. Sometimes Lindsay's diplomatic training shows when he moderates criticism by saying that all should be taken 'in play', but this is only one aspect of his polyvalent treatment of the subject. Play is equated with order when it is disrupted by a fight between a pardoner and a pauper, who comes from Lothian, a region whose play traditions had been disrupted by English invasion as recently as the late 1540s. But in the less guarded Second Part, play becomes the medium for a drama of forensic rhetoric, and preaching. Now one character can be told to state his creed fully – 'this is na game' – and the social threat of falsehood means that whoever wrote the stage directions felt the need to adjust theatrical semiotics, shifting from the regenerative folk adumbration of punishment when characters are hanged in effigy to presenting the real thing: 'Heir sall he [Falset] be heisit up, and not his figure'. The climax of Lindsay's metatheatre comes with the closing sections on Foly in which he draws together play and teaching, while also permitting them to keep their own integrity. The outrageous, risible stage business of Foly is prosodically separated from the wisdom of Foly's sermon which succeeds it. Taken together they justify the genre as a medium for recreation and truth, but as discrete elements more powerfully assert the independent necessity of both. The reformed kirk, which was to be founded only six years after the Edinburgh performance of the *Satyre*, continued to wrestle in real life with the problem of play which Lindsay's metatheatricality had exposed and exploited.

An uneasy compromise in this area is reached in the published edition of *Philotus*. Described internally as a 'ferse' and on the title page as a 'Treatise', this play is built upon set-piece speeches between 'interloquitors' in 'rime couée', but contains within a comic structure more than enough disguise, misapprehension of gender, mistaken identity and satire to work well on stage. A tale of young lovers united, and freed from the unnatural restrictions imposed by aged passion and bourgeois money-mindedness, it is spiced with homoeroticism, and an offstage beating for Philotus, who has transgressed against sexual norms. It only veers away belatedly from the kind of sexual revenge that we find in Chaucer's *Reeve's Tale*. Its ribaldry is clarified, and thereby revealed as unattractive, by a commentator who hardly constitutes a vice figure though he operates in a similar environment between action and audience. He is called the 'Plesant', and thus (along with pipers, fiddlers, songsters, fake fools and sturdy beggars) belongs in the category of idle persons without lawful calling which the General Assembly of the kirk explicitly named as contributing to the common corruption of the realm.[21] The play hauls itself back into exemplary mode at the end, making its peace with reformist values when God's grace is invoked, his punishment declared merciful, and older people are advised to master their affections and behave with propriety. A further verse addition from the publisher reinforces this sobriety by dwelling on

21 *Booke of the Universall Kirk of Scotland*, ed. Peterkin, 435. This complaint was made at the Assembly held 26 May (or March) 1596.

the insignificance of human pleasures, before appealing to just those pleasures by listing among his other publications 'The Three Priests of Peebles with merie Tailes' and 'The Freiris of Berwick'.

From its founding in 1560 until the start of the seventeenth century, when James VI forced through episcopal government, the Presbyterian kirk, despite having the support of parliamentary acts, was intermittently engaged in local skirmishes designed not so much to bring an end to play as to establish itself through controlling and changing the *occasions* of play. It aimed to remove recreation (and work) from the Sabbath, and to ensure continued work without recreation at the festivals which had been observed under the Catholic dispensation. In the former case, the kirk's regulations varied between the broadly, but unspecifically, sabbatarian; explicit prohibitions on play during sermons, and prohibition at any time on the Sunday. Consequently, individual cases brought debate from those arraigned as to whether they were actually in contravention of church discipline. As to the calendrical festivals, though there were many celebratory traditions of a local type, in general, it was the Yule period (Christmas to mid January) and May which had to be preserved from the ludic habits of generations and of institutions with varying degrees of independent identity, power and financial resource, such as courts, aristocratic houses, burghs and schools or universities. The 'landwart' (country) population probably felt more loyalty to their local laird, who might be Catholic, and they had to be policed at a time when church-going in such parishes was neither popular nor physically easy.

Furthermore, the reformers themselves, like their counterparts in England and Geneva, were neither blind to the uses of play, free from its traditions, nor immune to its charms. On Easter Day 1535 in Stirling a Friar Killour presented a reforming 'Historye of Christis Passioun' before King James V. This really deserves to be considered the *locus classicus* for such drama, as it used traditional Catholic forms, subject matter and a liturgical occasion in order drastically to revise traditional dramatic meaning: the Catholic authorities were identified with the persecuting Jews, and Christ with those Christians who professed the Gospel. The merchant James Wedderburn also 'nipped the Papists' with plays on John the Baptist and Dionysius the Tyrant on the public playfield of Dundee. He also apparently made dramatic fun out of a friar's conjuring of a ghost, and this linking of Catholicism with spiritualist superstition may have become a popular comic motif for it reappears through a fake exorcism in *Philotus*. Scottish reformist dramatists had the theatrical advantage of counterfeiting what their audiences already believed to be counterfeit. John Knox himself seems to have disliked particular genres rather than the medium. He caustically (and quite erroneously) judged the 'maskings' of the 1561 royal entry of Mary Queen of Scots to be an attempt to imitate France, and earlier that year had helped to cause an apprentices' riot in Edinburgh by joining the provost and baillies in refusing mercy to a man sentenced to hang for playing Robin Hood. The resulting violence, which ended in a victory for the apprentices and the freeing of the man, showed that the authorities had rather overplayed their hand.[22] But Knox was nevertheless present in 1571 in St Andrews University at a play which, in keeping with his views, showed Edinburgh Castle, at that time held for Mary against the regent, being captured and its captain, Sir William Kirkaldy, hanged in effigy.[23] The author of this play, and of another politically dangerous dialogue 'set furth' by several colleagues, was John Davidson, subsequently minister at Prestonpans near Haddington, where another notable reforming minister had also organised a play in 1574. The greater the scholar the more informed the opinion of drama might be: James Melville gave this account of studying with his uncle, the Presbyterian scholar and divine, Andrew Melville: 'He read a Comedie of Tyrence with me, schawing me that ther was bathe fyne Latin langage and wit to be lernit: That of langage I thought weill, bot for wit I merveled, and haid nocht knawin befor.'[24]

When it came to the nexus of faith, pastime and performance, it was the subtleties of context which determined the liberties of the participants. A comedy of Terence read behind closed doors between consenting, and learned, Presbyterians posed little threat. In direct contrast was the comedy of Terence played in Elgin by the schoolmaster and boys in 1600. In this case academic licence was undermined by the season of the performance (May), the place (a kirkyard), and the social consequences, for the schoolmaster's example and his literate assistance enabled craftsmen to seek permission for their own traditional May celebrations, implying civic misrule. Refusal had led to the display of ensigns on the church steeple and other threats to order. The play may also

---

22 *A Diurnal of Remarkable Occurrents*, 63–6. It is put in a more detailed political context in Lynch, *Edinburgh and the Reformation*, 90–6. John Knox (d. 1572) had returned to Scotland in 1559 to become minister of St Giles in Edinburgh, the founding father of the Scottish Presbyterian kirk, and chief irritant to Mary Queen of Scots, after an eventful life which saw him first in priestly orders and then in the French galleys as a slave, following his friendship with the reformer George Wishart and close association with those who had murdered Cardinal Beaton in retaliation for Wishart's martyrdom. Knox had periods of exile in England and Geneva, and a short pastorate in Frankfurt, before his return. He was the most prominent of a group of reformist intellectuals and divines who were either native to the Lothian region outside Edinburgh or worked in it. He wrote a substantial history of the Scottish Reformation.

23 *The Diary of Mr James Melvill 1566–1601*, 22.

24 Ibid., 36.

have blended into dancing (with bells) and piping. The place of the performance and the possibility that the boys collected money at the time rather suggest that Terence had been made accessible to the townsfolk through translation. Nationally, the kirk felt itself under threat from continuing Catholicism, widespread observance of superstitious practices, the need for tougher quality-control measures on its own ministers and the king's episcopalian sympathies: the local session must have felt that Terence's style and wit were inadequate compensation.

Though many original documents are lost, the General Assembly of the kirk would seem to have first specifically addressed the issue of texted plays in 1575, and then from a concern for the transmission of scriptural knowledge. It is no accident that when the Assembly demanded that ministers should be able to understand learned Latin commentaries on scripture it also prohibited 'clerk' plays, comedies or tragedies on the canonical scriptures: the channel by which the truth was disseminated from scholarship through the ministry to the congregation needed to be cleared by both statutes.[25] When John Brown, schoolmaster at the kirk of Strageath, was being harried in 1583 by the presbytery for a 'clerk' play performed by his students, he was told to justify such performances in Latin, which the ministers then examined.[26] The contents of the play and the intellectual proficiency of the teacher had been linked issues from the time of Lindsay's *Satyre*. As for 'prophane' plays, that is texted plays which did not represent authentic scripture (such as *Philotus* and the Elgin play), the General Assembly simply required that their texts be examined before public performance which should not take place on the sabbath. Despite this prohibition, the authorities of Dunfermline requested permission to play on the sabbath the very next year.[27] More irritatingly, kirk officers themselves were not averse to attending even the superstitious May games which had always been an object of the kirk's attack, and which, with Robin Hoods, Abbots of Unreason, May Queens and so on, had actually been banned by Parliament before the reformed kirk was formally instituted.[28] In 1579 the Assembly had to consider what to do with such 'persones that after admonitione will pass to May playes, and speciallie elders and deacones and uthers wha beirs office in the Kirk'.[29]

25 *Booke of the Universall Kirk of Scotland*, 146. Session 7 of Assembly begun 7 March 1575.
26 Kirk (ed.), *Stirling Presbytery Records 1581–1587*, 130.
27 *Booke of the Universall Kirk of Scotland*, 159.
28 Thomson and Innes (eds.), *Acts of the Parliament of Scotland AD 1124 (–1707)*, II, 500: 20 June 1555, no. 40. Quoted in Mill, *Medieval Plays in Scotland*, 30.
29 *Booke of the Universall Kirk of Scotland*, 192.

Although there were long-standing injunctions against certain types of itinerant player and medieval statutes against the misuse of church land for plays
and other irreligious activities, and against such church-based misrule as the
Feast of Fools,[30] it is important to recognise that the Reformation church in
Scotland during the second half of the sixteenth century was *developing* practice,
not simply executing it, and was doing so in conditions which were nationally unpredictable and often locally unfavourable. Its complaints about plays
of misrule sometimes overlapped with the secular authorities' fears about
disorder but equally they sometimes foundered on the inertia (at best) of
landowners; sometimes action against a group of participants was possible,
but on other occasions the strength of local involvement safeguarded all but
ringleaders; sometimes the kirk felt it could be severe, sometimes mercy was
politically expedient. The actions which the kirk took against playing, however immediately or locally successful, and they were not always that, failed
to end some of the most loathed practices of superstition during the period
under review. In 1603, the year that James VI succeeded to the English throne,
the presbytery of Haddington near Edinburgh was still trying to stamp out a
May play (with text) which it had known about for many years. It was also
dealing with suspected celebration of Yule, the striking of a drum through
the streets of Tranent on May Day, and the complaint of a minister that he
could get no congregation because his parishioners 'ga far of and neirhand
to playis and pastymes'. These need not have been theatrical plays, of course:
football, drinking, skittles and playing catch on the church wall on Sunday
afternoon also caused offence.[31] But we know that people congregated from
miles round to enjoy the 'Trik' (play) of Samuelston. Individuals could be just
as determined: in January 1604 one Tiberius Winchester appeared before a kirk
session for guising with a pillow case over his head, almost ten years to the day
after his first offence. In 1599, an embattled kirk failed, in a major dispute with
James VI, to prevent the English players Laurence Fletcher and Martin Slater
from performing 'comedies' in Edinburgh, where the baillies permitted them
to fit out a theatre in Blackfriars' Wynd, in Dundee, where they played in the
Tolbooth and received the substantial sum of £33 6s 8d, and in Aberdeen, where
Fletcher, described in the records as 'sserviture to his maiestie', was made a

---

30 Patrick (ed.), *Statutes of the Scottish Church 1225–1559*, 40, 42, 77, 138–9. Thirteenth-century
   statutes against the Feast of Fools were borrowed from those of Lincoln. Scottish parliamentary statutes against itinerant bards date from 1449.
31 *Haddington Presbytery Records: Minutes 1596–1608*, 29 December 1602, 5 January 1603, 19
   May 1603, 9 May 1604, National Archives of Scotland, CH2 / 185 / 2, Edinburgh.

freeman. In this case, theatre was really the focus for a power play which had had international implications when it was thought that the comedians were going to make fun of the Scots.[32] Fletcher himself subsequently benefited from this royal patronage, his name being added (before Shakespeare's) to the profit sharers of the King's Men when they received their patent from the new king of Great Britain.[33]

In 1603 Scotland was still far from a commodified, textually predictable, indoor theatre led by identifiable professionals whose work was replicable at any licit time and in any part of the country. Behind it, however, lay a tradition of play, in the broad sense of that word usefully forced on us by contemporary terminology, whose records extended to at least the thirteenth century. The departure of the court to England may have removed an immediate source of patronage, but it did not affect those traditions of play which had always been independent of it. Dancers, comedians, May pastimes, devisers and manufacturers of royal entries, plays and a 'summer house' can still be found long after James went south. One presbytery, for example, was still exercised about the superstitious observing of Yule, almost certainly by guising, in 1642, the year the theatres in England were closed.[34]

32 Nicolson to Lord Burghley, 15 April 1598, MS State Papers (Scotland), Elizabeth, 62.19, Public Record Office, Kew.
33 Gurr, *The Shakespearian Playing Companies*, 113.
34 *Haddington Presbytery Records: Register 1639–48*, folios 12[v], 66[r], National Archives of Scotland, CH2 / 185 / 5, Edinburgh.

The Bible as play in Reformation England

PAUL WHITFIELD WHITE

One might suppose that the rise in Bible reading and the literacy it engendered during the English Reformation rendered obsolete the demand for popularly produced biblical plays. For centuries such plays had been among the few means by which the general populace learned about the Bible and its stories, the Catholic church having restricted reading it to those who knew Latin. Indeed, it is widely believed that biblical drama – most notably the 'mystery cycles' and other parish- and civic sponsored scriptural plays – fell rapidly into decline largely because of Protestantism's reverence for the *written* Word of God and its growing hostility towards image-centred representations of sacred history. These factors, in conjunction with state censorship of religious issues in plays, the theory goes, hastened the drama's development towards secularisation which reached its height of achievement in the urban theatre of Shakespeare and his contemporaries.[1]

Without questioning Protestantism's significant role in the eventual cessation of religious drama as a popular pastime in England in the second half of the sixteenth century, we need to reconsider some of our assumptions about both Protestantism itself and religious – and here specifically biblical drama. Protestantism was not a fixed, unchanging cultural entity, it produced a range of religious sensibilities and cultural attitudes, some characterised by excessive zeal and iconoclastic tendencies; others more conservative and accommodating of traditional beliefs and practices. This is especially important to keep in mind in the first phase of the Reformation's cultural formation, a period I would extend from about 1530 to 1580, when the relationship between medieval religious and early modern reformed values, beliefs and modes of worship was *not* everywhere characterised by conflict and opposition.[2]

---

1 I discuss and document this at length in 'Reforming mysteries' end', *Journal of Medieval and Early Modern Studies* 29 (1999), 121–48.
2 For the contingent nature and changing circumstances of religious reform in England, see Haigh, *English Reformations.*

The drama is no less subject to misconceptions. There was not, for example, a steadily evolving progress from the sacred to the secular in sixteenth-century English theatre. Secular drama in the form of Robin Hood plays surged in growth before the century began and as quickly declined just around the time the commercial playhouses were opening in London. Parish- and civic-sponsored religious plays, on the other hand, *increased*, rather than declined, in popularity in many communities in Reformation England.[3] The Chester cycle, for example, which may not have developed into a major, three-day production until 1507, thrived through the second and well into the third quarter of the century. Critics might argue that this was due to the continuing vitality and resiliency of medieval Catholicism, and they are right to a certain extent. But as we shall see below, many communities, including Chester, produced biblical theatre which at least accomplished some measure of religious reform, whereas others were fully brought into line with Reformation teaching and practice. Indeed, I would argue that, in early Reformation England, Bible reading did not curtail but rather generated new interest in the production of biblical drama.

In tracing the history of biblical drama in Reformation England to about 1580, my discussion begins by looking at the attitudes and policies of early Tudor Protestant authorities on drama, which favoured the treatment of biblical subjects. We will then consider the scriptural drama of the early Reformation, centring on the plays of its most original and influential figure, John Bale. The discussion which follows focuses on representative biblical plays of different auspices: *Mary Magdalene* as a typical professional-troupe interlude; *Jacob and Esau* as exemplary of school drama; *Ezechias* as illustrating both court and university drama. Finally, I reconsider the complex role of the Reformation in the final days of the civic-sponsored biblical drama in the provinces, often known as the mystery cycles.

Promoting the Bible on stage

Most of the early reformers approved of staging the stories and teachings of the Bible, and even in the Geneva of John Calvin plays depicting the Acts of the Apostles and other books of the Bible were witnessed by large audiences. In England, where a rich tradition of religious theatre already existed, the patron-

88

age and production of Protestant biblical drama in the 1530s coincided with the central government's campaign to popularise reading the Bible nationwide. The royal Injunctions of 1536, and again those of 1538, ordered that a Bible be placed in every parish church; the following year the 'Great Bible' was published as the official version and made available for purchase.[4] We need to keep in mind that to Protestants the Bible is the infallible Word of God, with exclusive authority (when correctly interpreted of course) on all matters pertaining to doctrine, worship, daily living and political governance. No longer are priestly intermediaries necessary for salvation, since God speaks directly and personally to each individual through his Word in the scriptures. No longer should the humanly devised decrees and directives of the Roman papacy be followed, since universal principles of church order and political rule are plainly evident in the scriptures. These were powerful concepts; they were also controversial – the king himself feared popular access to the Bible might incite religious and political dissent. However, his chief minister, Thomas Cromwell, and Archbishop of Canterbury, Thomas Cranmer, pushed forward their campaign for a vernacular, widely available, translation of the scriptures.[5] As we shall see shortly, Cromwell's suitor, John Bale, wrote biblical plays promoting the new Bible policy, and another reformer with high connections, Ralph Radcliffe, wrote scriptural drama for his Hitchin grammar-school students who performed them before the townspeople in a locally designed theatre. Among the plays he produced were *The Disobedience of Jonah*, *The Afflictions of Job* and *The Deliverance of Susanna*.[6] Bible plays did not challenge but complemented the reformers' efforts to popularise the scriptures.

It would not be until Edward VI's reign that a systematic account of how to write, stage and regulate biblical plays was formulated by the foreign reformer Martin Bucer while serving as Regius Professor of Divinity at Cambridge. In *De Regno Christi*, a political treatise presented to King Edward VI as a new year's gift in 1551, Bucer devotes an entire chapter to plays ('De Honestis Ludis'), proposing that the Christian state should promote religious drama

---

4 See Haigh, *English Reformations*, 130–4.
5 Henry VIII's patronage of the Great Bible is featured on its title page, where the king is shown flanked by Cromwell and Cranmer (see figure 12). The publication and popular purchase of the scriptures began with William Tyndale's *New Testament*, 50,000 copies of which were published (illegally!) by the time of the reformer's death in 1536. The profound importance of the Bible for the development of literacy, not to mention the success of Protestantism itself, is indicated by the eight translations into English of some 200 editions of the Bible between 1520 and 1600. See Haigh, *English Reformations*, 132–5, 193–5; Greenblatt, *Renaissance Self-Fashioning*, 74–114.
6 White, *Theatre and Reformation*, 103–4; Roston, *Biblical Drama in England from the Middle Ages to the Present Day*, 57–8.

as a means 'to strengthen faith in god, to arouse love and desire of God and to create and increase not only admiration of piety and justice, but also the horror of impiety and of the sowing and fostering of every kind of evil'.[7] An appointed team of specialists should be in charge of writing and regulating the plays, 'preventing the performance of any comedy or tragedy which they have not seen beforehand and decided should be acted', and ensuring that characters 'be acted in such a way as to arouse in the audience both a longing to imitate them [i.e. godly figures] and a hatred of bad ways and deeds'. Bucer places particular stress on biblical topics and stories; *they* should be the focus rather than the 'profane plays and stories of the pagans!'. Writing to the boy king, Bucer dwells on the performance of biblical plays by schoolchildren, both for educational purposes and 'to provide their public with wholesome entertainment which is not without value in increasing piety'.

John Bale and early Reformation biblical drama

From the career of the early Protestant reformer John Bale we learn a great deal about the Henrician government's use of drama as a vehicle for promoting its Reformation agenda. Bale was a Carmelite friar who converted to Protestantism in the early 1530s. He tells us he was patronised by the Protestant Earl of Oxford, for whom he wrote some fourteen plays, before his recruitment in 1536 by Thomas Cromwell, the political mastermind of the Reformation in the 1530s. From that point through to the end of the decade Bale was kept busy writing, producing and acting in plays – he records the titles of twenty-four in all – for his own troupe of actors under Cromwell's patronage who appeared at court and toured the country through the remainder of the 1530s. Bale's career extended into Elizabeth's reign when he continued to be involved with the production of controversial religious drama until he died at Canterbury in 1563.[8]

All five of Bale's surviving plays, which date from the mid-to-late 1530s, clearly support the reform measures his patron Cromwell implemented from 1536 to 1540. The plays themselves are saturated with biblical references and illustrate Bale's belief that, just as the Old Testament foreshadows the New, the events of both find their sequel in national history.[9] Thus the prototypes

---

7 Quotations from *De Regno Christi* are taken from Wickham, *Early English Stages*, II (part 1), 329–31.
8 The best study of Bale's drama remains Blatt, *The Plays of John Bale*. See also Happé, *John Bale*.
9 See Blatt, *The Plays of John Bale*, 24.

for the king – and his Reformation successor Henry VIII – in his chronicle play *King Johan* are Moses, Josiah and David, as the audience is told directly at the conclusion of the first act. The iconography of the Great Bible of 1539 makes this identical link of the Old Testament patriarchs, Moses and David, with King Henry VIII[10] (see figure 12).

Although it is allegorical in method and dresses its characters in contemporary garb (most of the Vice figures are Catholic priests), Bale's *Three Laws* is a biblical play, for it both dramatises and chronicles the ages of the three types of divine law set down in the scriptures: the Law of Nature, extending from the time of Adam to the time of Moses; the Law of Moses ruling from that time through to the advent of Christ; and the Law of Christ which dominates from Christ's birth to the end of time. As in *King Johan*, the play attacks the contemporary Catholic church's utter corruption and suppression of God's word and envisages an English nation knowledgeable in the scriptures. A notable moment occurs when the chief Vice, Infidelity, and the Catholic bishop, Ambition, resolve to suppress 'the Byble readers' who threaten the pope's authority in England. In the course of showing how this should be accomplished, Infidelity points to Ambition's mitre, the tall, divided headpiece worn by Roman prelates in liturgical services, and then prompts the prelate to bend forward so that its pointed horns give the appearance of a wolf's gaping mouth.[11] This stunning visual pun must have amused even Bale's Catholic spectators. But its purpose is to satirise the tropological significance which Catholics ascribe to visual images, in this case clerical dress. And by applying an entirely different 'trope' to Ambition's elaborate headwear, one that identifies the bishop with the ravenous wolves of Matthew 7:15 and John 10:12 who deceive and devour the innocent sheep (i.e. 'the Byble readers' of the Reformation), Bale attacks the cruelty of Catholic authorities in persecuting scripture reading Protestants.

Eleven of Bale's twenty-four plays are biblical plays, following in many respects the traditional form of the medieval mystery cycles in featuring scriptural episodes in simple, vernacular verse. They were no doubt intended as a more scripturally accurate and gospel-centred alternative to the Catholic cycles and were designed to complement Cromwell's programme of popularising the scriptures. Included is a linked series of eight plays on 'The Passion of Christ', extending from Christ in the temple through to his resurrection.[12] None of these survives, yet we can get some sense of what such plays were

10 On the iconography of Holbein's title page of the Great Bible, see King, *Tudor Royal Iconography*, 70–5.
11 *Three Laws*, in Bale, *Complete Plays*, ed. Happé, II, 99 (lines 1181–85).
12 Chambers, *The Medieval Stage*, II, 224; Blatt, *The Plays of John Bale*, 24.

Figure 12 Henry VIII and the Reformation Bible: the title-page woodcut of the Great Bible of 1539 by Hans Holbein

like from looking at Bale's *extant* biblical plays, *God's Promises, John Baptist's Preaching* and *The Temptation of Our Lord*, which constitute a separate mini-cycle. These plays lack the ribald and virulent anti-Catholicism of *Three Laws* and *King Johan*, although in *The Temptation* Satan does appear in the 'devout and sad' dress of a Catholic hermit. *God's Promises* is a prophet play which, like earlier and contemporary cycle plays in the *processus prophetarum* tradition, uses liturgical texts and music in its presentation of a series of biblical patriarchs (Adam, Noah, Abraham, Moses, Isaiah, David, John the Baptist), each of whom appears in his own scene conversing with God in a foreshadowing of the advent of Christ. The traditional advent theme, however, has been adapted to convey the covenant theology of early Protestantism. We tend to think of Bale as a radical reformer – and indeed he was in many respects – but *God's Promises* must have appeared to the next generation of Prayerbook Protestants as half Catholic, half Protestant, for it combines Protestant theology with the Latin liturgy familiar to pre-Reformation breviaries, permitting the antiphons prescribed with organ accompaniment at the end of each scene to be sung in Latin (with English as an option), a practice that was heavily frowned upon during Edward VI's reign, and forbidden, for example, in the Lincoln Cathedral injunctions of 1547–48. *John Baptist's Preaching* and *The Temptation of Our Lord* are no less conservative in design and presentation, with the former evidently following medieval precedent in administering the rite of baptism as part of the play performance.[13]

    God's Promises, John Baptist's Preaching and *The Temptation* exhibit the simple language, liturgical character and devotional function of the medieval mystery plays and therefore were probably intended for performance by small parish and civic groups.[14] Since the plays demand little in terms of staging and costuming, however, it is possible that they were in the repertory of Lord Cromwell's Men under Bale's leadership when the professional troupe toured between

13 White, *Theatre and Reformation*, 158–60. Since we know that Bale's acting troupe performed in churches, the question arises whether a baptism instituted according to the official rite in a play would make use of the baptismal font, which in St Stephen's Church, Canterbury, where the troupe performed in 1538, still survives.

14 The only known performance of the three extant biblical interludes was by a local group of players, perhaps his cathedral choristers, in Kilkenny, Ireland, when Bale served as Bishop of Ossory in 1553. There, the 'yonge men' staged the plays, along with *Three Laws*, on the day proclaiming Mary Tudor as new Queen of England, which in Catholic Ireland was celebrated with great festivity. In a move that not even Ian Paisley would attempt, Bale walked in procession to the market cross in Kilkenny, having set aside his bishop's cape, mitre and crozier in favour of carrying a Bible; however, the local Catholic leadership, determined to follow the liturgy, arranged for two priests to carry the mitre and crozier before him. Despite the resulting confusion and protests, Bale got his way, and, with organ-playing and singing, the actors proceeded to perform the plays.

1538 and 1540. *Three Laws*, along with *King Johan*, was certainly designed for touring. Like all of Bale's plays, *Three Laws* works best with five actors, and this is the cast prescribed at the conclusion of the surviving text: 'into fyve personages maye the partes of thys Comedy be devyded'. Bale's directions for 'The aparellynge of the six vyces, or frutes of Infydelyte' are both colourful and controversial: 'Lete Idolatry be decked lyke an olde wytche, Sodomy lyke a monke of all sectes, Ambycyon lyke a byshop, Covetousnesse lyke a Pharyse or spyrituall lawer, False Doctryne lyke a popysh doctour, and Hypocresy lyke a graye fryre. The rest of the partes are easye ynough to conjecture.'[15] Bale also supplies a doubling scheme in which the division of parts among the five actors requires that Bale himself double the play's prologue figure ('Baleus Prolocutor') with the chief Vice Infidelity, the play's dominant and most theatrically taxing role. Described elsewhere as a very tall and imposing man, Bale must have cut an impressive figure on stage, especially in the role of leading Vice.[16] Infidelity requires a physically dexterous actor who is sufficiently skilled at mimicry to assume several identities, including those of a Franciscan friar and the ribald comic of English folk drama, Robin Goodfellow, whom Infidelity unmistakably mimics when he makes his initial, outrageous entrance, equipped with Goodfellow's trademark props, a candle and a broom[17] (see figure 13).

There is little doubt that Bale took his iconoclastic biblical drama to the royal court during the Cromwellian era of the 1530s, but it was before King Edward VI that anti-papal stage propaganda seems to have received its most appreciative royal audience, with an apparently spectacular 1550 Christmas show called *The Tower of Babylon*. Non-extant, this piece may or may not be 'De meretrice Babylonica' ('The Whore of Babylon') authored by the young king himself, who was an enthusiastic supporter of such stage polemic.[18] However, in conflating the tower city of Genesis 11 afflicted with the confusion of tongues (Babel) with the apocalyptic city of destruction in Revelation 18 (Babylon), the title points to a familiar Reformation theme. To the reformers, Babylon

---

15 Bale, *Complete Plays*, II, 121.

16 The reformer's height is revealed in a quarrelsome exchange between Bale's son and a Canterbury youth named John Okeden in 1560, who reportedly exclaimed, 'By God's soul every man saith thy father is an heretic and an Anabaptist, and thou art not his son. Mr. Bale is a tall man, and thou art but a little light knave. Some friar leapt in when he was away and begat thee.'

17 As first noted by Richard Axton, 'Folk play in Tudor interludes', in Axton and Williams (eds.), *English Drama: Forms and Development*, 22.

18 Bale assigns this play to King Edward in *Scriptorum Illustrium maioris Britanniae*. The attribution is plausible. Edward was writing a *Discourse on the Reform of Abuses in Church and State* prior to 1551.

Figure 13 'Robin Goodfellow': a sixteenth-century woodcut

signified Rome, and the infamous Tower of Babel–Babylon, which presumptuously rose to the heavens and housed pagan images and ceremonial objects
for worship, was a powerful prophetic image of the Roman Catholic church
in full decadence and likewise destined for destruction.[19] The tower, specially
commissioned for the occasion, was designed by architectural artist Robert
Trunkey, under the direction of Nicholas of Modena, the celebrated international architect. Built at the Revels Office at Blackfriars, the tower was shipped
upstream to Hampton Court for the performance, and if contemporary illustrations are any indication (see figure 14), its appearance and collapse on stage
must have resulted in a memorable piece of iconoclastic theatre. Unfortunately, we know next to nothing about the *dramatis personae* of the costuming
of *The Tower of Babylon*, only that the king's interluders, along with the players of the Royal Chapel, received their annual reward around the time it was
performed.

19 Luther popularised the theme in his *Babylonish Captivity of the Church* (1520). Edwardian
court spectacle depicted cardinals, popes, bishops, etc. to make this point about the outward glory and inward spiritual corruption of Catholicism. See King, *English Reformation
Literature*, 371f; Aston, *The King's Bedpost*, 71–7.

Figure 14 The Fall of the Tower of Babylon : an etching by Cornelis Anthonisz (1547)

Lewis Wager's *Mary Magdalene* and biblical drama
on tour

Bale's career during the 1530s suggests that he was encouraged, if not commissioned, by Thomas Cromwell, Henry VIII's chief architect of religious reform, to bring the nation's religious drama into line with the Reformation by devising new models for parish- and civic-sponsored biblical drama and for plays performed by professional troupes on tour. As we shall see, this ambitious undertaking was extended by reform-oriented playwrights and play producers through at least the first decade of Elizabeth's reign. Cromwell's policy of using the professional touring troupe as a vehicle of Protestant propaganda was continued by the later Tudor Protestant regimes. Those professional playing companies advancing religious reform were mostly sponsored by the nobility, who, as rich beneficiaries of church property seized by Henry VIII's government, had a major stake in the new religion's success. We know of several biblical (including apocryphal) plays staged by these 'professional' troupes, including *Zacheus*, *Samson* and *King Darius*. Whether the commercial interests of a troupe on tour compromised in any way the religious message of such plays is a valid question to ask and one we will address below.[20]

Perhaps the finest example of a Protestant biblical drama designed for professional touring is Lewis Wager's 'saint play', *The Life and Repentaunce of Mary Magdalene*. *Mary Magdalene* was not printed until 1566 but the statement in the prologue that it teaches 'true obedience to the kyng' (rather than the queen),[21] as well as the play's extensive indebtedness to Calvin's *Institutes* which was widely circulating among university students towards the end of Edward VI's reign, points to an Edwardian date. Its author Lewis Wager, like Bale, was a former-friar-turned-Protestant preacher.[22] On the title page of *Mary Magdalene* Wager is described as 'a learned clarke', and, given the topical satire of young ladies of wealth and noble descent in the earlier scenes, he may have served in a major household as an almoner, chaplain, or tutor, like other playwrighting scholars of the Reformation (e.g. Thomas Becon, Ralph Radcliffe, John Foxe and Stephen Gosson). Historians have noted that the relations between the aristocracy and the monastic orders had always been close and that the more privileged and talented among the ex-religious were well cared for following the dissolution.[23]

Mary Magdalene was written for a nobleman's troupe of 'four men and a boy', the adults doubling thirteen parts among them, and the child actor portraying Mary, as the casting chart on the printed title page indicates. As with Bale's troupe, the players appear to have been experienced singers, with treble, base, and 'meane' parts assigned for the song which concludes the first phase of the action. In offering a moral lesson to youth of aristocratic descent, a performance of the play would have been appropriate for the great hall of a noble household (a reference to 'without the door' suggests an indoor setting), perhaps one where wards and other privileged adolescents were educated, but the play's homely language and lively dialogue and action, as well as its more

---

20 These companies were 'professional' in the sense that they performed in exchange for payment, but as household servants of a great lord they toured usually only one or two seasons of the year.

21 Wager, *The Life and Repentaunce of Mary Magdalene*, in White (ed.), *Reformation Biblical Drama in England*, 2 (line 34). All subsequent references to the play are to this edition.

22 A Franciscan of the Oxford convent, Wager was ordained subdeacon by the Bishop of Sarum on 21 September 1521, and studied at Oxford some time prior to 1540. The next we hear of him is in April 1560 when he became rector of St James, Garlickhithe, London; he was buried in his own parish two years later in July 1562, the administration granted to his widow Elinore. He is probably the father of William Wager, an early Elizabethan clerical playwright known for plays with such Calvinist-sounding titles as *The Longer Thou Livest the More Fool Thou Art* and *The Cruel Debtor*.

23 See Knowles, *Bare Ruined Choirs*, chapter 25.

general evangelical theme of justification by faith through imputed grace, made it also suitable to the diverse audiences on tour. That it was taken on tour is evident from the Prologue, who tells us that he and his colleagues 'haue ridden and gone many sundry waies;/ Yea, we haue vsed this feate at the vniversitie'.[24] It also reveals how a professional troupe earned its keep on the road: spectators are invited to give money for the performance: 'Truely, I say, whether you geue halfpence or pence, / Your gayne shalbe double, before you depart hence.'[25] Perhaps a hat or plate was passed around, as was evidently the case in performances of the medieval *Mankind*.

A particularly interesting feature of *Mary Magdalene* is that it is a rare surviving example of a type of play evidently very popular in fifteenth- and early sixteenth-century England, the saint play. Perhaps more accurately, it is a Protestant adaptation of a saint play. Wager's choice of subject matter is readily understandable when we consider that the Franciscans and other monastic organisations were believed responsible for the many dramatised saints' lives which were presumed destroyed along with the great monastic libraries. Whether Wager was familiar with the many Magdalene saint plays on record for the period,[26] including the surviving East Anglian Digby *Mary Magdalene*, is unknown, but his play does share some features in common with the latter play. Following the Digby author, Wager identifies the profligate woman who washes Christ's feet in Luke 7 with the Mary Magdalene in Luke 8 out of whom Jesus expelled seven demons (and in both plays the exorcism is highly theatricalised), he makes references to Mary's upbringing in the castle of Magdalene, and he depicts at some length the dinner at Simon's house where Mary washes Christ's feet and listens to the parable of the two debtors. In terms of dramaturgy, both plays mingle biblical figures with characters signifying moral abstractions. Nevertheless, the similarities basically end here. As a troupe dramatist, Wager could not remotely accommodate the elaborate staging and casting requirements of the Digby spectacle. As a Protestant, he had no place for the post-biblical miracles and other legendary aspects of the saint so dear to the medieval cult of Mary Magdalene, such as her conversion of the king and queen of Marcylle, her being fed by the angels from heaven and so on. Moreover, while he is no less committed to combining edification

---

24 *Mary Magdalene*, lines 25–6. The 'ridden' here provides further evidence that the strolling players travelled with a horse and perhaps a small wagon.
25 *Mary Magdalene*, lines 43–4.
26 Although their playbooks do not survive, we know of a Mary Magdalene play performed in the parish church at Taunton in 1504, an outdoor production at Chelmsford in 1561 (this may have been the Digby version), and quite possibly another at Magdalene College, Oxford, in 1506–7 (Lancashire, *Dramatic Texts and Records of Britain*, 272, 107, 244).

with entertainment in treating the saint, his play is infused with an entirely different religious outlook, one which is positively hostile to the medieval cult of saints and other Catholic dogma and iconography that underpin the Digby *Magdalene*.

In morality-play fashion, Wager's Calvinist view of religious conversion is made transparent through Mary's interaction with a series of Vices, who tempt her into sin and prolong her unregeneracy, and Virtues (including Christ as Protestant preacher) who bring her to repentance and salvation. The biblical episode of Mary washing Christ's feet in the home of Simon the Pharisee shows her heart-felt love in contrast to the malice and outward sanctity of the accusing Pharisee. Of particular interest is the degeneracy phase of the action which is depicted in lively, comic realism, overlaying the familiar pattern of vice intrigue and spiritual corruption with a topical satire on the youth of the privileged classes. To enhance the play's appeal to youth, particularly to those of noble birth for whom it may have been originally written, Mary is presented as a beautiful, but no less spoiled and coquettish, gentlewoman who has just come into the inheritance of a wealthy estate. Her recently deceased parents, she tells us, brought her up 'In vertuous qualities, and godly literature', and 'nourtred [her] in noble ornature', but they also gave her much liberty and granted her every request.[27] When she first appears before the audience, she is berating her tailors for failing to keep her fitted out in the latest fashions and chiding her maids for insubordination. Expressing her need for assistance to help her run her estate and keep her in good cheer, Infidelity promptly offers his services, along with those of 'persons of great honor and nobilitie, / Felowes that loue neither to dally nor scoffe, / But at once will tell you the veritie.'[28] The Vices now take on a more human (and topical) dimension with Infidelity as Mary's chamberlain and the others as her newly appointed attendants. The action which ensues gives us an engaging glimpse into sixteenth-century women's fashions and beauty-care, recalling the Lisle letters describing the dressing of Lady Lisle's daughters at the royal court.[29] The Vices proceed to instruct the fashion conscious young profligate to dress provocatively in the latest style, dye her hair blonde with the help of a goldsmith and curl it with a hot needle, wearing some of it piled on her forehead, and heighten her looks with cosmetics, all in the interest of alluring rich young suitors. The scene is spiced up with mimicking of courtly manners, a 'song of. iv. parts', much

27 *Mary Magdalene*, lines 249–55.
28 *Mary Magdalene*, lines 294–6.
29 *The Lisle Letters*, ed. Byrne, IV, 166.

sensuous kissing and embracing, and sexually explicit punning. Consider the
following exchange between Infidelity and Mary:

> INFIDELITIE: Mistresse Mary can you not play on the virginals?
> MARY: Yes swete heart that I can, and also on the regals,
>   There is no instrument but that handle I can,
>   I thynke as well as any gentlewoman.
> INFIDELITIE: If that you can play vpon the recorder,
>   I haue as fayre a one as any is in this border,
>   Truely you haue not sene a more goodlie pipe,
>   It is so bigge that your hand can it not gripe.[30]

As Patricia Badir has recently shown, the play's highly charged eroticism extends far beyond this moment,[31] which prompts the question of how a contemporary audience, either noble or popular, responded to this scene and how the
eroticised interaction between Mary and the Vices could be reconciled with
Wager's homiletic intentions. There is little doubt that the burlesquing of
contemporary gentlewomen's fashions and coquettish behaviour would have
delighted Tudor audiences, particularly aristocratic youth who could most
identify with the situation. Scholars have argued, however, that the audience's
warm, sympathetic response to Vice comedy and the pleasurable desires it
evokes are a means of implicating and involving spectators in the very experience of temptation and corruption the protagonist undergoes, and that
this will later lead to the feelings of guilt and conviction of sin necessary for
repentance.[32] As convincing as this argument is in terms of the playwright's
homiletic *intention*, in actual performance it is highly questionable whether
audiences responded so predictably. Indeed, the highly defensive Prologue to
Mary Magdalene, which lashes out at 'Hypocrites that . . . slaunder our facultie'
and question the moral value of their performances, suggests that at least some
members of the troupe's audiences on tour did not find the play so edifying.[33]
The one specific charge against the players, according to the Prologue, is that
they exploit their audiences financially, but the play's opening speech hints
that the now-familiar charge of sexual immorality levelled against the players
by later Elizabethan anti-theatricalists may also have been raised as early as
Edward VI's reign, or at least in the opening years of Elizabeth when *Mary
Magdalene* was published (1564).

---

30 *Mary Magdalene*, lines 837–44.
31 Badir, '"To allure vnto their loue"', *Theatre Journal* 51 (1999), 1–20.
32 The definitive article on this is Jones, 'Dangerous sport', *Renaissance Drama* 6 (1973),
   45–64.
33 *Mary Magdalene*, lines 38–44.

Mary was performed by a male actor, almost certainly a boy, and it is worth distinguishing the use of cross-dressing here from its practice in Bale's *Three Laws*. There, the cross-dressed male is exploited for a specific homiletic purpose: to denounce sexual relations between men associated with that very transvestism; Bale supervised his own productions, so he could ensure that his message got across in performance.[34] On the other hand, the transvestism of the boy actor playing Mary Magdalene had no such polemical purpose, and that cross-gendered impersonation, not to mention the sensuous fondling and kissing clearly called for by the script, might have been made all the more sensational by professional actors more interested in the door-take than in the Protestant evangelism of the play's author. *Mary Magdalene* illustrates the potential disjuncture between the theory and the practice of religious propaganda on the stage, a disjuncture in which the intended 'message' may have been subverted by elements within the text itself and by the interpretation that text was given in performance.

Jacob and Esau and the Reformation youth play

As a Protestant biblical play, *The History of Jacob and Esau* offers an interesting contrast in dramatic style, stage presentation and treatment of biblical subject matter to *Mary Magdalene*. Indeed, the main differences are really those between a popular troupe play following medieval English dramaturgy and an academic interlude in imitation of Roman comedy, a humanist-inspired approach to play composition known as 'the Christian Terence'. In Wager's play, a few well-known biblical scenes are interwoven into a *psychomachia* plot, with Mary's 'character' moving freely among the worlds of biblical story, spiritual allegory and contemporary topical satire; she and her companions, moreover, are self-presentational in that they explain their significance to the audience in direct-address speeches. In *Jacob and Esau*, on the other hand, the action focuses on biblical events throughout (although it gives fictional names to the Hebrew servants: Mido, Ragau, Abra), and the author takes further measures

---

34 In *Three Laws* the transvestism of the male actor playing the old witch Idolatry is explicitly drawn to the audience's attention: at line 425, in act 2, Infidelity says to the old sorceress: 'What, sumtimye thou wert an he!', to which Idolatry replies: 'Yea, but now ych am a she, / And a good mydwyfe per De.' In performance, the focus on gender is accentuated by the fact that the audience has seen the male actor playing Idolatry earlier in the action in the role of Christ's Law. The significance of all this, however, is not made clear to a reading audience until some fifty lines later when Sodomy physically fondles Idolatry. Bale's virulent attacks on sodomy were part of a propagandist offensive against the monastic religious houses.

to give the work a sense of historical reality.[35] According to the title page, the players are 'to be consydered to be Hebrews, and so should be apparailed with attire', which indicates the first known attempt in an English play at 'period costume'.[36] The characters are as naturalistically portrayed as any in the drama of the time, with no breaking out of their roles to summarise the action or comment upon its significance, as one finds commonly in the troupe plays, and they are unaccompanied by personified abstractions. And in contrast to the multiple settings of Wager's play, all the action in *Jacob and Esau* takes place in a single locale, the Hebrew settlement in front of Isaac's tent. Moreover, the school play holds up to the description in the title as a 'mery and wittie Comedie', consistently comic throughout (apart from Esau's angry outburst in act 5), and is generally free of the earthy sexuality, on the one hand, and the long serious sermon-like speeches, on the other, that characterise the dialogue of Vices and Virtues in Wager's biblical interlude. The play's five-act structure is the most salient feature derived from classical comedy.

Jacob and Esau was evidently written by a schoolmaster, perhaps the educator William Hunnis, during Edward VI's reign when two of the play's thematic concerns, the raising of youth and predestinarian theology, were popular subjects for preachers and playwrights alike.[37] Evidence suggests that it was acted by the Children of the Chapel Royal at court (as the concluding prayer suggests) under Edward VI and possibly revived under Mary and Elizabeth. The play's music, especially the hymns, is not unlike that performed at the Chapel Royal, with the solo singing assigned to little Abra clearly written for a specially gifted boy chorister. The parts of both Abra and Mido require skilful coordination of speech, song and movement, as when, for example, Abra sweeps the floor as she sings the play's second song or when Mido mimics the gesturing and speech of his elders. A high calibre of acting was demanded at the Chapel Royal where the master was given free licence by the crown to choose his choristers from any of the choir schools throughout the realm. The play's ten listed acting parts (excluding 'the Poet') seem suitable for the eight children residing at the Chapel in 1553, assuming that Isaac's neighbours Hanan

---

35 The importance of the word 'history' is indicated by its appearance in title, head title and running title.

36 *The History of Jacob and Esau*, in White (ed.), *Reformation Biblical Drama in England*. All subsequent references to the play are to this edition.

37 Serving as boy chorister and gentleman of the Chapel Royal under Edward and Mary, Hunnis was appointed its choirmaster by Queen Elizabeth in 1568, the same year as *Jacob and Esau*'s second printing. In 1557, the year the interlude was registered with the Stationers' Company, Hunnis was imprisoned in the Tower for a plot to dethrone Queen Mary.

and Zethar (who briefly appear in the second scene never to return) involved doubling.

Jacob and Esau's main concern is with the theological problem of predestination versus free will. This issue is explicitly addressed at the outset by 'the Prologue, a Poet', with considerable care taken to ground the notion of predestination in biblical verses from the books of Malachi and Romans, as well as Genesis.[38] The dramatic action that follows illustrates the validity of predestination chiefly through the contrasting characters of the elect Jacob and his reprobate brother Esau. In the twin brothers we encounter two different and irreconcilable types of mankind: the one, God's elect who is destined to inherit worldly prosperity as well as salvation in the next life; the other, an unregenerate without conscience who is deterministically bent on a course leading to eternal damnation. Jacob, as one would expect, is a faithful, obedient son, his mother's favourite, and beloved by all in the community for his piety and quiet disposition. His motives to acquire Esau's birthright and blessing are not selfish or in the interests of self-advancement, but based on his conviction that he is acting in accordance with God's will. Esau, on the other hand, is as wicked as Jacob is unswervingly righteous, a profligate youth so preoccupied with his favourite pursuit, hunting, that he can devote no time or attention to his parents or his responsibilities as the heir apparent.

Like other Protestant youth plays of its time – *Nice Wanton*, *The Disobedient Child*, *The Longer Thou Livest the More Fool Thou Art*, *The Glass of Government*, as well as *Mary Magdalene* – *Jacob and Esau* attempts to reconcile abstract theological doctrine with practical matters of upbringing and education. In juxtaposing older and younger brothers, the play explores the question of how it is that youths, given identical Christian upbringing and education, can turn out so differently. Even more emphatically, the school play illustrates the notion that since all persons are deserving of damnation by reason of original sin and deliberate disobedience, God is not bound to save any child, even if he is born into a righteous family. Esau has been nurtured in the ideal family environment, yet he still grows up to be an inveterate sinner.

What is extraordinary about *Jacob and Esau*, however, is its departure from the orthodox Christian view that the deceptive plotting of Jacob and Rebecca to procure Esau's inheritance was both immoral and totally unnecessary. Instead of showing that they were self-seeking and presumptuously intervening in the divine plan (the standard view of Tudor biblical commentaries), the author attempts to demonstrate that the seizure of the birthright was in fact sanctioned

---

38 *Jacob and Esau*, lines 11–14.

by God as the means of unseating corrupt authority and fulfilling his promise to Jacob. This has led several scholars to recognise a political dimension to *Jacob and Esau*. As David Bevington concludes: '*Jacob and Esau*'s chief ideological purpose is to justify seizure of power, and to insist that the seizure is reluctantly undertaken', and adds that the dramatist's 'theory dangerously sanctions any rebellion when divine command may be taken to oversway established order'.[39] *Jacob and Esau*, in fact, appears to anticipate the political views of such Marian exiles as Bishop John Ponet, the former high-ranking official of the Edwardian church, who settled for a time in Strasbourg, and John Knox and Christopher Goodman, who came under Calvin's influence in Geneva. After witnessing and hearing reports of the Protestant executions under Queen Mary, these exiles abandoned the early Protestant doctrine of non-resistance, hitherto unchallenged in England since Tyndale enunciated it in *The Obedience of a Christian Man*, and adopted the view that the usurpation of corrupt authority is justified on scriptural grounds. While *Jacob and Esau* lacks the strident tone and the anti-Catholic virulence of Bale's plays, the dramatist obviously sees in the analogy of the Old Testament story a two-edged sword against contemporary Catholicism. He uses the analogy of Jacob's supremacy over the elder Esau, first of all, to demonstrate the validity of the doctrine of predestination as opposed to the Roman doctrine of free will and justification by works. And secondly, Esau may be seen as the older generation of English Catholics who have no place in England's future; Jacob, on the other hand, stands for the Protestant elect who are predestined to live in prosperity as the new Israel: 'The one shal be a mightier people elect: / And the elder to the yonger shall be subiect.'[40]

Royal advice and royal rebuke: Nicholas Udall's *Ezechias*

Jacob and Esau's typological application of biblical personages to contemporary political affairs may be traced back to Bale, most notably to *King Johan* where the hero and his present-day pope-defying successor, Henry VIII, are compared to the Old Testament patriarchs, Moses, Josiah and David. Another biblical figure to whom Henry VIII and his Protestant heirs were repeatedly compared was King Hezekiah of II Kings. To Protestants, Hezekiah exemplified the godly monarch who restored his nation to true religion by destroying the

---

39 Bevington, *Tudor Drama & Politics*, 112.
40 *Jacob and Esau*, lines 245–46.

Figure 15 Hezekiah and the Smashing of the Brazen Serpent: an etching by Matthaus Merian (1630)

superstitious idols worshipped by his people, the most notorious being the serpent of brass twisted around a pole, which in the earlier age of Moses possessed the magical property of curing, on sight, those Israelites poisoned by deadly snake-bites. Whereas Catholics favoured the Moses story of the hanging brazen serpent recounted in Numbers, chapter 11, as a directive to worship the cross of Christ (John 3: 14–15 later compares the brazen serpent to Christ), Protestants more frequently cited – and illustrated (see figure 15) – Hezekiah to show that worshipping the cross or the crucifix was a horrible superstition and that such idols needed to be destroyed.[41]

Nicholas Udall, the playwright and schoolmaster, was among the first to make the comparison of the Old Testament king to Henry VIII in the introduction to his 1549 translation of Erasmus's *Paraphrase of St Luke's Gospel*, yet he may have made it as much as a decade or more earlier in *Ezechias*, his dramatisation of the Old Testament king. Was this the play performed before Henry VIII when Udall arranged for a production by his Eton students

41 I am indebted here to Aston, *King's Bedpost*, 113–27.

at court in 1537 which Cromwell sponsored? The play's one recorded performance, however, took place several years after Udall's death, in 1564, when
a large cast of Cambridge students staged it before Queen Elizabeth during
her royal visit to the university that year. The decision to revive this old play
before the young monarch is not so surprising when we consider the repeated
parallels in contemporary writings of Elizabeth to Hezekiah, not the least
of which being that both were twenty-five when they succeeded a wicked
predecessor to the throne.[42] Perhaps due to her gender, perhaps due to her
presumed political naiveté, Elizabeth during her first decade on the throne
was frequently given pointed – and often unwelcome – advice from both the
stage and pulpit.[43] *Ezechias* provides an interesting example. As Margaret Aston
has shown, the message to Elizabeth was double-edged: on the one hand, she
was being commended, as she had been in numerous contemporary writings,
as the present-day Hezekiah who crushed the superstitious religion of her
predecessor on the throne; on the other hand, in the play's highlighting of
the destruction of the hanging brazen serpent, she was being reminded of
'the Queen's own idol', the crucifix she stubbornly maintained on the altar
of the Royal Chapel.[44]

Although the text of Udall's biblical interlude does not survive, Abraham
Hartwell's eyewitness account in verse of the performance in King's College Chapel makes it possible to envisage the action in general terms and
to draw further conclusions about its staging.[45] Following II Kings 18–19, the
play opened in iconoclastic fashion with King Hezekiah's destruction of the
idolatrous brazen serpent, along with the pagan altars and other superstitious
images worshipped by the Israelites. Hezekiah's restoration of true religion,
however, proved short-lived, for, in the action which followed, priests, elderly
men and women, and others among the ignorant populace, were depicted defying the true forms of worship and returning to their superstitious ways. This
provoked the appearance of the Prophet (Isaiah), who warns of impending
retribution, which subsequently manifested itself on the stage in the form of
the heavily armoured Assyrian invaders, many of coal-black complexion and
led by Rabsaccus. In response to Rabsaccus's threatening speech demanding

---

42 Ibid., 113.
43 *Gorboduc* and the no-longer-extant *Juno and Diana* are plays which address questions
   of royal marriage and succession; both were sponsored by Robert Dudley. During a
   performance of the latter play, the queen reportedly turned to the Spanish ambassador
   and said, 'This is all against me.' See Wilson, *Sweet Robin*, 155.
44 Aston, *King's Bedpost*, devotes a chapter to the crucifix controversy.
45 Hartwell's account and other reports of the play are reproduced and discussed by Boas,
   University Drama in the Tudor Age, 89–98.

surrender in the name of pagan religion, King Hezekiah goes to the altar and prays for God to intercede on Israel's behalf. The play concludes with the invaders mysteriously dying in their sleep the night before battle, although it is unclear whether this is shown on stage or merely reported by a chorus or messenger.

The great oak-wood stage, raised five feet and extending across the eastern half of the nave in King's College Chapel, would have easily accommodated what appears to have been a sizeable cast of characters (not unusual for university productions). In addition to the historical figures of King Hezekiah, the Prophet Isaiah and Rabsaccus, they included various social types among the Israelites – priests, old women, old men and 'the rustic crowd' (the latter quite possibly a single character like Bale's Common Crowd in *John Baptist's Preaching*), and a host of soldiers among the Assyrians. The actor playing the Assyrian leader must have towered over the other performers, for Rabsaccus is described by Hartwell as 'Huge in armament and of a huge body'.[46] Hartwell's description suggests that a large image of a serpent was shown on stage, along with pagan altars, incense boxes, 'incense-burning gifts' and other objects of superstitious worship. These images must have received special significance within the church setting. The overthrowing of the pagan altars and the breaking up of the brazen serpent performed right in the chapel would have evoked fresh memories in many of the spectators of the iconoclastic campaigns of Elizabeth's father and younger brother which officially sanctioned the smashing of statues, paintings and stained-glass windows in parish churches and cathedrals throughout the realm. The destruction of images in *Ezechias* suggests that, in addition to lecturing the queen on her private habits of worship, the play was intended in part to justify, and celebrate, the iconoclastic policy of the Protestant Tudor administrations, as the *Tower of Babylon* (discussed earlier) had done under Edward VI.

Ezechias was by no means the first controversial biblical play staged at Cambridge. Two years earlier, John Foxe's *Christus Triumphans* was performed at Trinity College with the purpose 'to transfer as far as possible from the sacred writings into the theatre those things which pertain primarily to ecclesiastical affairs'.[47] Foxe inherits Bale's apocalyptic vision of history, in which the one true biblical chronicle envisaged by St John in Revelation is repeated in almost endless variation up to the present when the heroic proponents of the true

---

46 Noted by Boas, ibid., 96; for this translation of Hartwell's text see Nelson (ed.), *REED: Cambridge*, II, 1141.
47 John Foxe, *Christus Triumphans*, ed. and trans. Smith, *Two Latin Comedies by John Foxe the Martyrologist*, 209.

A lively Picture, describing the weight and substance of Gods
most blessed Word, against the doctrines and vanities
of mens traditions.

Figure 16 The Word of God versus Popish Superstition: a woodcut from John Foxe, *Acts and Monuments* (1560)

gospel defeat the villainous emissaries of the popish Anti-Christ (see figure 16). Performed in Latin, which was the norm rather than the exception for drama at the universities, Foxe's Cambridge-sponsored play of Christ markedly contrasts with the relatively non-controversial drama of Bale's friend Nicholas Grimald, whose resurrection play, *Christus Redivivus*, and dramatised life of John the Baptist, *Archipropheta*, were performed in the more conservative environs of Oxford in 1541 and 1548 respectively.

Protestant intervention in provincial biblical drama

Since the days of E. K. Chambers, scholars have widely recognised the use of court-sponsored interludes, professional troupe plays and school and university drama to propagate, explicate and celebrate reformed religion. Many of these, as we have seen, centre on biblical stories and were deemed suitable because their allegorical and homiletic structures could be easily adapted to convey the new reformed ideology and because they were produced under the auspices of institutions – the royal court, noble households, academic centres – at the forefront of religious change. On the other hand, the theory persists that provincial parish and civic-sponsored religious – and specifically biblical – drama was the object of systematic government suppression due to its image-centred dramaturgy and celebration of banned Catholic holidays like the feast of Corpus Christi. It is true, of course, that in many parts of the realm, especially in the northern towns where Catholicism remained vital and popular, Roman teaching and habits of worship continued to be represented in their cycle plays – York, for example – but in such towns as Chester the biblical drama appears to have been an uneasy mix of traditional and reformed elements, and there is no evidence that the provincial biblical drama was the victim of a nationwide campaign of suppression. We need to recognise that the plays themselves were routinely subject to revision; consequently, some adapted to the changing circumstances of the Reformation and indeed participated in the Tudor Protestant regimes' promotion of the Bible.

Let us begin with the Shropshire town of Shrewsbury. After the Reformation, and indeed during the first decade of Elizabeth's reign, the town bailiffs and guild members joined up with the local grammar school to stage a series of pageant plays centring around 'The Passion of Christ' over a three-day period at Whitsuntide before reported audiences of between 10,000 and 20,000. The performances took place within a theatre located in a quarry just outside of town. The generous town subsidy and large contributions levied from the local occupations indicate that 'the greate playe', as it was called, was lavishly produced. The author of 'The Passion of Christ', or perhaps its reviser – since Whitsuntide pageants in the quarry were traditional at Shrewsbury – was Thomas Ashton, the headmaster of the grammar school known for his 'godly preaching'.[48] Like Lewis Wager, Ashton was a devout Calvinist; he introduced puritan-like reforms to the school's regulations and curriculum, including the use of Calvin's *Catechism*.[49] He was also an energetic advocate of acting and theatre: every Thursday, beginning in 1564, a comedy was to be rehearsed by the students, who included Philip Sidney and Fulke Greville. Despite objections from some Protestants to representing the deity on stage (the best known of these are the ecclesiastical commissioners at York who tried to censor the Wakefield cycle on this basis in 1576), Ashton and the civic

48 See Somerset (ed.), *REED: Shropshire*; and Somerset, 'Local drama and playing places at Shrewsbury', *Medieval and Renaissance Drama in England* 2 (1985), 1–32.
49 See *REED: Shropshire*. Ashton appears to have been close to the strongly Protestant Sidneys; he travelled with Sir Philip on at least one journey while at Shrewsbury.

leadership at Shrewsbury followed John Bale in depicting the crucifixion and other events in the life of Christ. The arrangement for the Mercers' and other guilds to buy for the production vestments and 'certayne coppes' suggests an anti-Catholic dimension to the performance.

The Protestant passion play of Ashton is lost. This is also true of Bale's *The Passion of Christ*, which, as noted earlier, formed part of a cycle of eight plays extending from Christ in the temple through to his resurrection. These must have resembled in many ways Bale's extant biblical plays, yet taken together the latter are not designed for elaborate staging over several days. Such *is* the case, however, of an anonymous biblical play entitled *The Resurrection of Our Lord*, surviving in fragmented form and written and printed sometime between 1526 and 1570.[50] *The Resurrection*, like civic biblical drama staged in a number of communities across Britain through the third quarter of the six-teenth century, is designed for performance over two, perhaps three, days; and it presents the usual biblical characters found in the cycle resurrection plays: Christ, the Marys, several disciples, the Jewish priests Caiaphas and Annas, Pilate and various soldiers. The play's continuity with medieval Catholic tra-dition is evident in its establishing Peter's preeminence among the disciples, a major claim supporting the office of the papacy; 'as for thee Peter', Christ says at one point, 'amoungst my Disciples all/I choise thee heade, and governer principall.'[51] Yet in other important respects the play betrays an allegiance to reform. Pilate, for example, resembles the Protestant magistrate or monarch in his scepticism about priestly power and the dangers of sedition. More signif-icantly, the theology of this play is explicitly Protestant, as demonstrated by the expository speeches of 'Appendix', who appears at intervals throughout the action to direct the audience's attention to its significance. Appendix's harsh criticism of those authorities ('Hereticks' he calls them) who oppose Bible reading, the play's faith in individual interpretation of scripture, not to men-tion its reliance on Tyndale's New Testament, suggest that it, or at least this version, dates from around the time of Cromwell's 1536 and 1538 Injunctions, when the order for a Bible to be placed in every parish church throughout the realm provoked vehement protest from Catholic conservatives.[52] The play is so concerned about preserving the sanctity of Holy Writ (and perhaps coun-tering charges of fictionalising scripture raised in *A Tretise of Miraclis Pleyinge*

---

50 *The Resurrection of Our Lord*, ed. Wilson and Dobell. All subsequent references are to this edition.
51 Ibid., lines 548–9.
52 Tyndale is the source for the New Testament, while the Vulgate remains the source for Old Testament references.

and elsewhere) that at one point Appendix delivers a long speech justifying the insertion of dialogue between Christ and Peter only hinted at in the gospels.[53]

Especially interesting, however, is Appendix's identification of the Jewish priests or bishops with modern-day opponents of scripturalism, an unmistakable reference to the Roman Catholic clergy. The author may have been familiar with Tyndale's other works as well, where the reformer identifies the opinions, demeanour and outward appearance of the Pharisees with 'popish prelates'. This equating of the Pharisees with Catholic prelates, of Old Testament legalism and 'traditions' with Catholicism, is a recurring feature of early Reformation polemic, and is especially evident in Bale's writing and drama. Indeed, as we have seen, Bale exploited the visual resources of the theatre to make the point devastatingly effective by costuming his fictional advocates of the old law in the vestments of the Catholic clergy. It is difficult to underestimate the impact on popular audiences of this visual conflation of the villains of medieval biblical drama with Roman priests and bishops. Notably, the old clerical attire was readily available from 1536 onward, when all over England vestments in churches and seized monastic institutions were sold off in large numbers, many for dramatic productions. The selling of old copes, surplices, stoles, mitres, etc. became a significant source of revenue for some cash-deficient parishes.[54] In *The Resurrection of Our Lord*, Caiaphas and Annas are repeatedly referred to as 'Bishops', to a far greater extent, for example, than we find in the cycle resurrection plays, and my guess, based on the Protestant bias of the dialogue and the example offered by Bale's dramaturgy, is that they would have appeared in the vestments of Roman Catholic prelates. In the N-Town cycle and other pre-Reformation drama, the contrast in attire points to the corruption and decadence of a worldly and materialistic religious establishment (that of the Jews) intolerant of Christ's spirituality, but in Protestant England that convention was, as noted, used as a polemical weapon by identifying those lavishly dressed Pharisees as Roman Catholic priests. In effect, very little revision is needed to bring these plays into line with Protestant interests: a few polemically oriented costume changes and new Protestant-oriented commentary.

The surviving playbook of *The Digby Conversion of St Paul* seems to have undergone precisely this kind of textual revision, as Heather Hill-Vasquez has recently argued. The playbook has been traced to Chelmsford, Essex, in the 1560s when detailed local records show the revival and flourishing of the

---

53 The *Resurrection* of our Lord, lines 590–618.
54 Most of the REED volumes document the sale or rental of vestments during the Reformation era, many for acting purposes.

civic-sponsored religious drama there.[55] Expense accounts and costume listings indicate that the banned Catholic vestments of Mary's reign were used in the Whitsuntide performances, a point made in John C. Coldewey's article arguing for Chelmsford as the Elizabethan setting for *The Conversion of St Paul* and other Digby plays.[56] Hill-Vasquez argues that the play's interpolated devil scene, added at the time of the Reformation (*c.* 1530), imposes a new interpretation upon the St Paul conversion narrative, one that sees it as prefiguring the plight of the reformers faced with Roman Catholic opposition, represented by the vestment-clad Annas and Caiaphas, and perhaps the devils Belial and Mercury as well. What is interesting about the Essex towns of Chelmsford, Braintree and Maldon is that the religious drama evidently stopped completely under Queen Mary only to be immediately revived after Elizabeth's accession. Chelmsford, in particular, was a Protestant stronghold from the days of Henry VIII. Following the 1538 Injunctions for Bibles to be placed in every parish church, one William Maldon relates how several poor men in Chelmsford bought a New Testament and 'on syndays dyd set redinge in [the] lower ende of the churche, and many wolde flocke about them to heare theyr redinge'.[57] I would suggest that the marked rise in popular scripture reading in Essex towns and elsewhere after the Reformation did not impede but rather generated interest in the production of biblical drama, and may help to explain the increase of such plays in the region between 1530 and 1570.

The situation at Chelmsford in the early 1560s might cast light on the civic drama at Chester, where the post-Reformation Banns make the claim that the cycle was Protestant from the beginning when its alleged fourteenth-century monastic author, Ranulph Higden, risked Catholic persecution, even death ('borninge, hangeinge, or cuttinge of heade') for writing such a work of faith. The claim, of course, is a pretty fantastic one, but most of the extant cycle plays (exceptions are noted below) exhibit little that would have proved deeply offensive to moderate Protestants. Indeed, local traditionalists might have been offended by some of the Protestant revisions. Lacking the pronounced sacramentalism of the York cycle, the Chester plays make repeated references to biblical authority and, to guard against too much immediacy and openness of meaning, expository passages foregrounding the spiritual and theological significance of the action are not uncommon. Nevertheless, the defensive posture of these Banns suggests that they were responsive to critics in Chester

---

55 Hill-Vasquez, 'The possibilities of performance', *REED Newsletter* 22 (1997), 2–20.
56 Coldewey, 'The Digby plays and the Chelmsford records', *Research Opportunities in Renaissance Drama* 10 (1967), 103–21.
57 Nichols (ed.), *Narratives of the Days of the Reformation*, 348–50.

who did not see the plays quite the same way, and certainly by 1570, when Queen Elizabeth was excommunicated by the pope, the more radical Protestants in the city, apparently led by the returning Marian exile, Christopher Goodman, solicited the intervention of Archbishop Grindal and the Earl of Huntingdon, the newly appointed Lord President of the North, to put a stop to the plays.[58] It is this anti-theatrical perspective of the cycle as 'ye popish plaies of Chester' which becomes the solely represented Protestant position in the records of later generations, beginning with David Rogers's *Breviary* (1609) and some parts of 'the Mayors Lists'. The Chester cycle was, at best, an unevenly reformed cycle, with some guilds less cooperative than others in Protestantising their plays.

Finally, in the city of Coventry there are compelling indications that efforts were made to revise the civic religious cycle along Protestant lines. Shortly after Queen Mary's restoration of Catholicism in 1553, we are told by John Foxe in his *Acts and Monuments*, a weaver named John Careless was imprisoned for religious dissent but temporarily released by his gaoler to perform in the local pageant play. However, by the time Careless shows up in the records, Coventry had a long-established reputation for religious fervour and dissent, and no doubt its early reception of Protestantism was partly due to the strong Lollard following in the city dating back to the mid fifteenth century. Protestant control of the city council can be dated at least from Edward VI's reign, and it continued well into the reign of Mary when the mayor and council were sufficiently defiant of Catholicism to warn religious radicals to flee the town when ordered by the Bishop of Lichfield to apprehend them for questioning. Not surprisingly, the Privy Council intervened to force a Catholic mayor into office in early 1556, yet by this point the city already had 'great numbers zealous for evangelical truth', as one contemporary reported.[59] Given the extent to which Protestantism was received within the civic leadership and among large segments of the citizenry, and given the control exercised by the city council over the town's annual religious pageants, can one seriously doubt that those pageants were enthusiastically supported by Chester Protestants? I believe this to have been the case.

Although we cannot rule out Old Testament plays entirely, the cycle of ten plays staged at Coventry appears to have centred on the life of Christ (like Bale's lost 'mystery cycle' of eight plays noted earlier). According to Pamela

---

58 Goodman's role in the controversy was recently discovered by David Mills. For the various measures Grindal and state authorities took against the cycle and the Chester mayors in the 1570s, see Clopper (ed.), *REED: Chester*, 97–117.

59 The words of the Marian exile, Thomas Lever. See Robinson (ed.), *The Zurich Letters*, 86–7.

King, reformist elements are discernible at Coventry as early as 1534/35 when the pageants staged by the Shearmen and Taylors and by the Weavers (the same guild to which John Careless belonged) were 'newly translate[d]' by the local playwright Robert Croo. King believes that the expository passages by the Prophets, which Croo evidently wrote to link episodes in the two plays and to provide an interpretive frame for the action, 'suggest a preoccupation with Lutheran or Zwinglian ideas, far from the confident sacramentalism which pervades the plays in the York Register'.[60] Nevertheless, if Croo was an early advocate of religious reform, he left both extant Coventry plays remarkably free of controversy on matters of worship and doctrine, which may have been intentional; striving after consensus among religious conservatives and advocates of reform may help to explain the Coventry cycle's longevity well into Elizabeth's reign.

During the period of 1530 to 1575, Coventry's play-producing guilds continuously revised and rewrote their pageants. In 1561, for example, the Drapers' play added two new characters named 'wormes of Conscyence'; they also paid eight pence for 'playing of the protestacyon', which appears to have been a piece attacking the old religion. It seems to me highly likely that the four pageants the queen witnessed during her visit to Coventry in 1567 would have supported the Elizabethan Settlement of religion. By the mid 1570s, the letter commonly ascribed to Robert Laneham seeking royal patronage for the *Hock Tuesday Play* indicates that certain Coventry preachers were hostile to the drama, and by this point no doubt the town experienced the same sorts of conflict over traditional recreations evident elsewhere in the realm, but it does not mean, as is routinely assumed, that such voices were representative of *all* serious reformed opinion about the propriety of stage playing. The civic biblical drama continued virtually uninterrupted through to 1579, and, despite the city's reputation for advanced Protestantism, there is no surviving evidence of opposition to it. What is more, for the last production of the cycle, as well as for the historio-religious drama of 1584, *The Destruction of Jerusalem*, the guilds contributed unprecedented sums for their pageants.[61] It would appear, however, that during the 1580s changing religious attitudes, combined with less willingness on the part of the guilds involved to finance the civic religious drama, led to its cessation in Coventry.

The Coventry cycle was the last of the great 'mystery plays' to end (in 1579), and although scriptural drama found a place on the professional stage in early

60 King, 'The York and Coventry mystery cycles', *REED Newsletter* 22 (1997), 20–6.
61 See Ingram, '1579 and the decline of civic religious drama in Coventry', in Hibbard (ed.), *Elizabethan Theatre*, VIII, 120–1.

modern London – a dozen or so plays can be identified as such – their decrease and eventual disappearance from England's popular theatrical culture was due largely to an increasing Protestant reverence for the Bible as the literal word of God, with its concern that nothing be added or omitted in modern expositions or renditions of original biblical texts. This in turn conflicted with the trend on the London stage towards greater complexity in plot design. Yet, as we have seen, biblical drama fulfilled a vital role in Reformation England. It continued its traditional function of celebrating the story of redemption through Christ and explaining Christian theological and moral doctrine in concrete dramatic terms. It helped propagate the Tudor Protestant policy of popularising Bible reading among the laity, and in turn this reading of the scriptures may have rejuvenated interest in biblical drama. Where biblical drama most markedly departed from the past was in its appropriation for polemical purposes, to justify Reformation iconoclasm with its denigration of perceived Catholic superstition and corruption, and to advocate, in at least one case (*Jacob and Esau*) the radical doctrine of resistance against unjust rulers.

4

Drama in 1553: continuity and change

PETER HAPPÉ

This choice of a single year in British theatrical history is rather like a geological transect which makes an arbitrary cut through different strata. In doing so, it leaves some doubt about exactly how far the evidence which emerges is a true reflection since the theatrical process under examination, rather like a geological one, is subject to continuities and changes which cannot be wholly understood by reference to the sample alone. There is also the problem of near misses, since we find that although some theatrical events certainly did occur precisely in the calendar year 1553 (new style), what happened in adjacent years ought to be taken into account if it colours what we know about the year in question.

The attraction of this particular year is partly that it marks a period of great political turmoil as Queen Mary came to the throne. Daughter of Catherine of Aragon, she had remained a Catholic, and her assumption of power meant a reversing of the increasingly Protestant tendencies of the brief reign of her brother, Edward VI (1547–53). She was proclaimed on 19 July, her brother having died thirteen days earlier, and the intervening period being marked by the attempt of the Duke of Northumberland to preserve the Protestant monarchy, and his own ascendancy, by proclaiming as queen his daughter-in-law, Lady Jane Grey. Alongside these momentous political events there are several theatrical items which can be definitely attributed to this particular year making it unusually rich in such occasions. Besides the entertainment at court, some of which is closely related to the political and public circumstances, there is a now-discernible range of dramatic and paradramatic events which increasingly challenges our concepts of drama, as well as indicating that many people in this particular year must have devoted resources of intellect and material means to participate in theatrical events of many kinds. As there were performers and technicians, who may have been earning the whole or a part of their living by their activities, spreading over much of England and Scotland, so there must have been a heterogeneous variety of participating audiences in cities, towns and villages, comprising many social levels, and coming to dramatic events for all sorts of different reasons.

What emerges from this transect is that the drama was entertaining and lively – a fact which we can still perceive today when modern companies restore it to life on our stages – and that the entertainment was richly diverse. Besides this, the surviving material, chiefly in the form of playtexts and records about dramatic performance (usually concerned with expenditure, but very revealing all the same), shows an interweaving of medieval and Renaissance concepts and practices. It allows us to consider the challenges which authors, actors, directors, technicians and musicians addressed, revealing the sophistication which these artists had achieved. It also presents some important information about the patronage of drama and the means by which cultural pretensions (not solely artistic ones) were reflected in the use of resources. This last is also an ideological process which came into visible prominence in this chosen year. It is apparent that the great change in the political climate was reflected in the drama, especially as things acceptable under Edward now became unwelcome, and vice versa. This particularly affected the mystery cycles and religious drama in general.

For convenience I will divide consideration of samples of this material into four categories:

local drama and paradramatic activities;
drama with a distinctly academic or educational context;
drama of a primarily religious nature, the cycle plays in particular;
drama whose context is primarily the court with implications of the power
    struggle.

In setting up these convenient headings, however, we should bear in mind that they are too categorical for many examples which could undoubtedly feature under more than one of them. Moreover, the mystery of time itself means that many of them were going on simultaneously, so that, to the vision of an all-seeing theatrically sensitive eye transcending the boundaries of time and space, the kingdom would seem a seething mass of dramatic activities, complete with preparation and aftermath, interwoven in the fabric of the religious and secular life of the year. We can point to one further significant distinction between types of drama, one which reflects upon the limits of the transect mentioned above. On the one hand there were items like the ephemeral court masques developed in the first part of the year for the ailing king, with a projected life of only one performance; and in contrast there were the mystery cycles, some of which had a history of performance going back, in some form or other, more than a century and a half before 1553.

Local drama and paradramatic activities

In many local communities there were traditional ceremonies and festivals which occurred every year. Unfortunately the records, copious in some places, are disobligingly incomplete, and their failure to survive does not necessarily mean that nothing was going on. Certainly there were places where ceremonies based upon Robin Hood, in association with Maid Marion and the other conventional characters, Little John, Friar Tuck and Much, the miller's son, were annual events. In Scotland by mid century the ceremony had become more popular than the festivities associated with the Abbot of Bon Accord which was medieval in origin, and was still observed in some places, as in Aberdeen in 1552/3.[1] Most of the English observations of Robin Hood were south of Nottingham, the traditional locus of the story, and information has survived from the valleys of the Thames and the Severn and the west country, particularly Devon. Of specific places for 1553, we know of Robin Hood at Shrewsbury, Yeovil, Ashburton and at Chagford (in 1554). In general the events were associated with Whitsun, and they tended to be on a parochial basis. At Yeovil in the early 1550s there were payments to different men to play the part of Robin Hood; and it seems that in the Thames valley some of these individuals were of reputable status, even to the point of being likely to uphold the social order rather than to subvert it.[2] At Ayr in 1553/4 gunpowder was provided for the Robin Hood plays.[3] But the activities of Robin Hood were not simply matters of rural entertainment. He appeared with Little John at Exeter in 1553–4,[4] and he had reached the court in Edinburgh in 1550. By the end of the decade in London there was a morris dance which was followed in procession by Robin Hood, Friar Tuck and Maid Marion (see figure 17).

There were other central characters for annual festivities, among which Lords of Misrule were common. In London on 8 March 1553 the sheriff apparently became Lord of Misrule in a procession, with other traditional characters including the devil, giants and a doctor.[5] Sometimes this character was associated with Christmas festivities up to Twelfth Night, and there was often a

---

1 Mill, *Medieval Plays in Scotland*, 30. In the same year at Haddington it became clear that the abbot was being discouraged and this was promulgated by the statute of 1555.
2 Johnston and Hüsken (eds.), *English Parish Drama*, 96–7.
3 Mill, *Medieval Plays in Scotland*, 167.
4 Wasson (ed.), *REED: Devon*, 145.
5 Lancashire, *Dramatic Texts and Records*, no. 1080.

Figure 17 Title page of *A Mery geste of Robyn Hoode and of his lyfe* (*c.* 1560) showing Robin and Littlejohn

link with fools and jesters at this time. The Lord of Misrule's function was largely secular, and he appeared at court as well as in small local communities. He continued to be popular for many years until he attracted Puritan condemnation, as at Shrewsbury in 1618–19 and Gloucester in 1623.[6] Henry VIII's assault upon many church practices had swept away in the late 1530s the popular boy-bishop ceremonies at Christmas (recorded at Wells cathedral up to 1537, and at Hereford until 1543). These had provided, in ecclesiastical settings, the inversion of the normal values which the Lord of Misrule was now perpetrating in the 1550s. One could say that his work was shared by other figures such as the Summer Lord at Thame in the early 1550s where he was attended by Vices who played the fools, and the Christmas Lord in 1554 at Swaffham and Trinity College, Cambridge. The Abbot of Marham appeared at Shrewsbury in 1551–2, his name connoting disruption.[7]

Details of what actually occurred on these occasions are sparse, but it is clear that there was impersonation (sometimes the leading characters were elected), a probably unwritten plan which involved processions and dancing as well as the presence of fools. For processions there may well have been a traditional order for the participants, as at Wells where, by the 1550s, there was a King's Watch at Midsummer in which companies of craft guilds paraded in a prescribed order.[8] On the other hand it seems likely that there were many impromptu items and the occasions presumably inspired improvisation. No doubt a festive atmosphere obtained because these shows took place upon the official holidays, especially at Whitsun and Christmas, though there were manifestly many local variations. Similar events, presumably secular rather than ecclesiastical in origin, took place at Midsummer, as for example the Midsummer Watch, which is traceable in 1554 at Totnes and at Chester, where there were payments for the carriage of pageants and to painters in 1553.[9] The word 'pageant' here and elsewhere is difficult to interpret. It may well have been an image rather than a play or a wagon for a performance. At Bristol there were many payments year by year, at this period, for carrying the 'pageants' belonging to craft guilds, and here most likely these were images not plays, for they could be carried by one man, who had to be strengthened

---

6 Somerset (ed.), *REED: Shropshire*, 310; Douglas and Greenfield (eds.), *REED: Cumberland, Westmorland, Gloucestershire*, 346.

7 Wiles, *The Early Plays of Robin Hood*, 5; Galloway and Wasson (eds.), *Records of Plays and Players in Norfolk and Suffolk, 1330–1642*, 101; Nelson (ed.), *REED: Cambridge*, 1, 186; Somerset (ed.), *REED: Shropshire*, 203. See also MacLean, 'Reassessment of a popular pre-Reformation festival', in Twycross (ed.), *Festive Drama*, 233–41.

8 Stokes (ed.), *REED: Somerset*, 11, 480.

9 Wasson (ed.), *REED: Devon*, 279; Clopper (ed.), *REED: Chester*, 55.

by liquid rations. There are records that in 1553 and 1554 the Bakers' pageant was carried.[10] Where the festivities were essentially local, the relationship between the audience and the performers must have been a very special one since each would know the other personally, and this would allow interaction between them which could be rich in comic effect. However, the assumption of a persona by the participants was no doubt a liberating procedure which enabled things to take place outside normal decorum. It is this challenge to what was permitted and acceptable which may account for the continuing popularity of these paradramatic events.

It is not clear whether church ales, which were fund-raising events, also involved impersonation. Many of the surviving records were made to note the extent of the income to church funds. At South Littleton in Worcestershire, for example, a receipt (for 3s 7d) is recorded for the church ale in May 1553, and there is a note of 'what the maydons dyd gethur thys yere' for May–June 1554. For such events there was an outlay for 'strykes' (bushels) of barley or malt.[11] In Somerset the practice of 'hoggling', an unspecifiable entertainment accompanied by collection for church funds, occurred in a number of parishes including Banwell in 1553–4.[12] A regular event which took place annually at Coventry until its suppression in 1561 was the Hock Tuesday Play.[13] Occurring on the Tuesday after Easter Sunday, this was a game between the sexes in which men were held to ransom by women, and vice versa. This would seem another example of inverting normal social structures. It allegedly was a memorial of heroic work by women against the Danes in the eleventh century, and apparently raised considerable sums.

The records of expenditure by civic and local authorities, and also those by some independent households, show that music formed a great part in entertainment, and often these costs can be associated with the festivities we have been discussing. Thus in 1553 at Newcastle payments were made for minstrels on St John's Eve (23 June) and St Peter's Eve (28 June) at/by Trinity House; and at Chester waits were rewarded on St Martin's Eve (10 November). Norwich made regular payments to the city waits each quarter in 1552–3 and 1553–4. Barnstaple had minstrels in church in 1552–3, and in the following

---

10 The accounts were rendered in November 1553 and December 1554 and presumably relate to events in the previous summers, such as Corpus Christi, Midsummer or St Peter's day: Pilkinton (ed.), *REED: Bristol*, xxviii, and 60–1.

11 Klausner (ed.), *REED: Herefordshire, Worcestershire*, 391, 357.

12 Stokes (ed.), *REED: Somerset*, Appendix 2, 11, 641–3, 655.

13 Ingram (ed.), *REED: Coventry*, xx and lxiii (note 15). The play was apparently revived for Elizabeth I's visit to Kenilworth in 1575.

year 'my Lord of Bathes minstrelles' were rewarded there.[14] In Kent the Lord
Warden's minstrels were paid at Canterbury, Dover, Faversham, Lydd and New
Romney in 1553. For some of these places the position is more elaborate in that
the minstrels of other patrons are recorded in this year, and the queen's jester
was also paid for a visit at Lydd in 1553 and at Canterbury in 1554.[15]

These itinerant entertainers are often difficult to disentangle from companies of actors which were also on the road. If someone 'played' it may well
be ambiguous. They usually had aristocratic patronage, though this became
more necessary as legislation against vagabonds was tightened later in the century. Even in 1552–3 companies belonging to the Duke of Suffolk and the king
were paid at Dover.[16] The membership of such companies may have been very
unstable and the members themselves may well have been able to combine
acting with music. At the time with which we are concerned Lord Russell's
minstrels and / or players were rewarded at Canterbury in 1553, Barnstaple and
Shrewsbury in 1552–3, and Norwich in 1553–4. However, after the accession
of Mary there was trouble at Norwich where William Mason was put in the
pillory for singing 'unfitting' songs, and the unfortunate Robert Gold also had
his ear nailed for the same offence. On 10 May 1554 James Wharton, one of
Lord Russell's minstrels, was interrogated about unfitting songs touching the
honour and dignity of the queen's highness which were found on him. He
sought to shift the blame onto an unnamed minstrel of Wymondham.[17] The
records show that there were several other active groups or indeed individuals
such as the queen's trumpeter who turns up at Winchester and Trinity College, Cambridge, in 1553. Some recent work on the movements of such groups
of entertainers has suggested that they followed well-established routes which
took in urban centres, ecclesiastical establishments and the houses of national
or local grandees.[18]

Alongside these professional or semi-professional companies – the distinction is hard to make when membership was variable – there was interchange
between towns and villages of what were probably amateurs, actors and performers for a day. For example, at Shrewsbury in 1551–2 'Histrionibus' and
waits from Bridgnorth were paid for.[19]

---

14 Anderson (ed.), *REED: Newcastle-upon-Tyne*, xv; Clopper (ed.), *REED: Chester*, 52; Galloway (ed.), *REED: Norwich 1540–1642*, 32, 33; Wasson (ed.), *REED: Devon*, 41.
15 Dawson (ed.), *Records of Plays and Players in Kent, 1450–1642*, 12, 42, 58, 106, 136.
16 Ibid., 42.
17 Galloway (ed.), *REED: Norwich 1540–1642*, 33–5.
18 For reconstruction of routes of travelling players in the 1530s see Westfall, *Patrons and
   Performance*, 146–7, and White, *Theatre and Reformation*, 22–7.
19 Somerset (ed.), *REED: Shropshire*, 203.

Academic and educational drama

Schools and universities were very active in 1553 in promoting dramatic activities. Drama offered training in a number of ways. It helped with public speaking and the art of rhetoric, which was fundamental to Tudor education. It brought students into contact with classical models and practices. It developed an appreciation of the use of language in both classical languages and the vernacular. However, the subject matter and perhaps the scope of drama in education was by no means entirely drawn from literary origins. For example at least two Cambridge colleges, Christ's and Trinity, had a Christmas Lord in 1553.

The interest in drama in schools is evidenced by the statutes of Aberdeen grammar school which prescribed the study of Terence in 1553.[20] The school at St Paul's became very active in the performing of plays, sometimes at court, especially under the mastership of Sebastian Westcott who is thought to have been appointed from February 1553. He worked in collaboration with John Heywood at that time for the presentation of a play by the boys for the Princess Elizabeth at Hatfield. Boys from the same group also performed at a wedding in the household of Sir William Petre, either in London or at Ingatestone.[21]

There is plenty of information suggesting that Cambridge colleges were active in the drama in 1553. William Stevenson, a don at Christ's, was concerned with presenting, and possibly writing, plays for a number of years, and there is reference in the college records to meeting his expenses, and those of others who laid out money in 1552–3. In the following year he was again reimbursed for expenses on waits, coals and horse hire for fetching apparel. He was still being paid in 1559–60.[22] This brings us to *Gammer Gurton's Needle* which was printed in London in 1575, but has the following attribution on the title page:

> Played on Stage, not longe ago in Christes Colledge in Cambridge.
> Made by Mr. S. Master of Art.

From this there is no doubt that the context was Christ's College, and Stevenson's authorship seems probable (see figure 18).

---

20 Lancashire, *Dramatic Texts and Records*, no. 1633.
21 Ibid., nos. 754, 789. There is a tradition that in 1553 Thomas Ashton, who became headmaster of Shrewsbury School, produced his first play, followed by others in the 1560s. Somerset (ed.), *REED: Shropshire*, 204 and 266 (note 204).
22 Nelson (ed.), *REED: Cambridge*, I, 177–8, 184–5, 207. Whitworth points out that, as Stevenson disappears from the list of Fellows between 1553 and 1559, he may have been a Protestant sympathiser excluded under Mary, *Three Sixteenth-Century Comedies*, xxiv–xxv.

Figure 18 Title page from William Stevenson's *Gammer Gurton's Needle*, quarto edition 1575

That this play is the product of an educational preoccupation is evidenced by its close adherence to Terentian structure, but this is masked or even transformed into something much more mischievous in that it avoids that other Tudor preoccupation, the moral instruction of its audience. It is this which makes it seem more likely that the play was aimed at some kind of topsy-turvy festival entertainment within the college community. The action comprises a complex but nonsensical search for a lost needle and the effects on a village community until it finally turns up in a pair of breeches. The rural setting invites comment, however, because it can be related to just that kind of village life to which the entertainments discussed earlier belonged. Some of the speeches are deliberately 'mummerset', and the character of Diccon, for example, is apparently a 'Bedlam' (a village idiot), and yet he is a comic master of those around him. The classical influence is also apparent in the brilliant exploitation of the language, as in Hodge's soliloquy (4.2.5–28) in which every line ends with 'see now', and which is really a reported narrative of offstage events in the approved classical manner.

The staging of the play raises a significant aspect of educational drama in that it is elaborate enough to require an acting space outside the view of the audience, an upper layer, and a hole for Dr Rat to crawl into.[23] The point at issue here is that there would have to be considerable preparation and expenditure in arranging this set, a fact which may account for the payments noted above. Elaborate settings certainly were a feature in Cambridge colleges at this time, as the activities at Queens' make clear. This college had a vigorous dramatic tradition and a good deal is known about productions there through the sixteenth century. In 1546–7, the consolidation of the college statutes prescribed the penalty of expulsion for students below the status of MA refusing to take part or be present at performances of a comedy or tragedy.[24] The statute notes that these plays would be paid for from the common treasury of the college. It was reinforced in 1558–9:

> And lest our youth, trained perhaps in other respects, remain crude in pronunciation and gesture and unpolished, we wish the professor of the Greek language . . . to be responsible for putting on two comedies and tragedies every year between the twentieth day of December and the beginning of Lent.[25]

In 1552–3 at Queens', Nicholas Robinson's comedy and Richard Thorpe's tragedy were performed at the Christmas period. In January Dowse was paid for taking down the theatre and Thorpe's and Robinson's expenses were met. John May's costs for a dialogue were paid in January, and he received garments kept in the college tower for a play about Theano (Thraso?). A stage and altar were put up by Dowse in February or March, and the comedy Stichus (Plautus) was put on. Beaumont borrowed more garments a little later, including a coat for Thraso (the braggart in Terence's Eunuchus)[26] (see figure 19). These items suggest a strong emphasis upon classical models, but they also show that the stage could be put up and taken down when required, and that the college was alive to performance.[27] Though the records at Queens' are exceptionally

---

23 Ibid., xlix, for speculation on how this might have been arranged at Christ's.
24 Nelson (ed.), REED: Cambridge, II, 1117–18.
25 Ibid., II, 1130.   26 Ibid., I, 181–6.
27 See Nelson, Early Cambridge Theatres, 16–37, especially 34–5, for the years 1550–4.

Figure 19 Terentian actors gesturing, from *Andria*

detailed, such theatrical activities can be paralleled in several Cambridge colleges, as well as at Oxford where a tragedy was performed at New College *c.* 1553–6, and the dean and chapter of Christ Church allowed funds for two comedies and two tragedies in Latin and Greek at Christmas 1554.[28]

Religious drama

During the reign of King Edward there are signs that the performances of the mystery cycles had been affected by the shift towards Protestantism. At York in 1548 the plays on the Death, Assumption and Coronation of the Virgin were omitted, and at Wakefield there are marginalia reflecting anti-Catholic sentiment.[29] Nevertheless the impulse to perform them was still apparently strong. Year after year, in the spring, the minutes of the York city council show the order going out for the arrangements for performance to begin. These were brought to a successful conclusion in 1548, 1549, 1553 and 1554. The play was

28 Lancashire, *Dramatic Texts and Records*, nos. 1287, 1288.
29 Stevens and Cawley (eds.), *The Towneley Plays*, I, xxiv.

also performed in 1551, but fear of large gatherings in a time of plague caused the number of stopping places to be reduced to ten. The play was suspended completely in 1550 because of the plague, and in 1552 the original instruction had subsequently to be reversed for the same reason. Some of this enthusiasm and persistence may well be attributed to the civic and political situations in individual cities where the cycles had become part of the social context. There was also a religious concern in as much as the cycles gradually became a site for contention between differing views. Naturally they were originally associated with Catholicism, but the Protestant response might have been either to abolish them or to adapt them to a style more in accordance with Protestant views. The latter, however, were not necessarily of one piece as we can see from the struggles among Protestants later in the sixteenth century at Chester.[30]

We have significant detail, in varying amounts, about mystery-play performances in 1552–3 and 1553–4 at York, Chester, Coventry and Newcastle. The texts we have present us with some problems for these performances. At York the only text was written out in 1461–73 and annotated in various ways for nearly a century afterwards,[31] and at Chester all the complete surviving texts were copied after the plays had ceased to be performed in 1575. From Coventry and Newcastle only fragments survive, some of them in copies of much later date. Elsewhere there may have been performances of cycles of plays in these years at the following places:

- Wakefield,[32] where there is an extant cycle (i.e. *The Towneley Plays*) which may never have been performed in the form in which it is found in the sixteenth-century manuscript, but for which there is evidence of performance of some kind in the 1550s;
- Norwich, where one play survives;
- Kendal, where there is no text but a late reference mentions a Corpus Christi play in former times;
- Lincoln, where there was an indoor performance of a Corpus Christi pageant not now known in 1554;
- Exeter, where there was a play as far back as 1414, but later records are wanting;

---

30 Mills, *Re-Cycling the Cycle*, 146–52.
31 See Beadle (ed.), *The Cambridge Companion to Medieval English Theatre*, 91–2, and Meredith, 'John Clerke's hand in the York Register', *Leeds Studies in English* 12 (1981), 245–71.
32 I retain, for convenience of reference, the traditional ascription of these pageants to Wakefield, about which there is some doubt.

– Beverley, where the thirty-six pageants of 1520 are lost;
– New Romney, where parts for a Passion Play were written in 1554 for a performance in 1555.[33]

The case of Hereford poses a number of typical problems in relation to Corpus Christi ceremonies. There is a list from 1503 of some 27 pageants, from Adam and Eve to the Knights at the Tomb 'for the procession of Corpus Christi', but there is nothing to back this up later, and no way of deciding whether these were tableaux or full plays within the procession.[34]

A different set of circumstances is presented by the surviving corpus of Cornish drama. The cyclic *Ordinalia*, with sections on the Origin of the World, the Passion and the Resurrection, exists in a manuscript in a fifteenth-century hand (MS Bodley 791). Some stage directions were added later in the same century and these have been interpreted as indications that it definitely was produced. The language is thought to be Middle Cornish of the late fourteenth century, and the play was probably written at or near Penryn. The seventeenth-century manuscript of *The Creacion of the World* (*Gwreans an Bys*) is partly adapted from the *Ordinalia*, but it is an original work in its own right which may have been staged in the middle of the sixteenth century. The saint play on Meriasek (*Beunans Meriasek*) survives in a manuscript dated 1504. These three large dramatic works argue a vigorous dramatic life in Cornwall throughout the sixteenth century. They are supported by local records which show unspecified plays at St Ives in 1573, and at Camborne (of which Meriasek was the patron saint) where 'a piper at the play' was paid in 1550. As to other dramatic forms in Cornwall, Robin Hood is known at Stratton (1536), at St Breock (1588) and St Columb Major (1589, 1595), some of these being associated with morris dancing.

The implication of this information is that in 1553 there must have been a vigorous interest in drama in Cornish towns and villages, and that the drama would most likely be similar in many respects to the English-language religious drama as well as to local festivals. Richard Carew's generalised account of performances at playing places, the *plen-an-gwaries*, suggests that people walked miles to be present.[35]

Two things emerge about mystery cycles from this data. One is that this form of play, though possessed of a national reputation, was comparatively rare

33 Johnston and Hüsken, *English Parish Drama*, 138–9.
34 Klausner (ed.), *REED: Herefordshire, Worcestershire*, 115–16.
35 *The Survey of Cornwall* (London, 1602), quoted by Bakere, *The Cornish Ordinalia*, 12–13: the information used here is drawn from her account, 1–44.

in England.[36] The majority of dramatic activity was plainly of a different nature. The second point is that the plays were not identical, and though in four of the texts mentioned above (York, Chester, Wakefield and Beverley) we do know that the cycle consisted of a narrative sequence from Creation to Doomsday, we may not conclude that all the other cycles followed this pattern. Indeed, cycles elsewhere in Europe rarely did. References to a Corpus Christi play refer more certainly to the time of the year when it was performed than to a uniformity of content or manner of performance. At York, Chester, Coventry, Newcastle, Norwich and possibly Wakefield the performance involved craft guilds taking over individual episodes, but this again cannot be applied automatically to other places. The evidence from the first three, where pageant carts processed through the streets along a traditional route, suggests that this arrangement was highly organised and involved very large casts, as well as making the whole city a theatre for the performance. At York for the 1554 performance there were sixteen stopping places along the route where each episode was performed, and as there may have been nearly fifty items, the day must have been a very long one and the traffic problems created by so many pageant carts gigantic.

By this time the York play customarily took place on Corpus Christi, the Thursday after Trinity Sunday. On the following day the civic procession normally went through the streets, and there were other significant festivities for St George. In 1554 his procession went on 23 April and was repeated on Whit Tuesday. It is apparent that at York there were also alternatives to the cycles in the Creed Play and the Pater Noster Play (both now lost). These were less frequent than the cycles, but their importance lies in the increase in awareness and activity of this culture of street performance in the city. There was a similar richness at Chester, where the cycle was performed in 1553, though it was not done annually. From 1521 it had been moved to Whitsun week, where it later acquired a three-day configuration. It was rivalled by the Midsummer show which is thought to go back to the fifteenth century, and, being less theologically sensitive, was probably more frequent than the plays. It is recorded in 1554 and descriptions from slightly later refer to a variety of exotic wild animals, giants, naked boys and at times characters in costume from the Whitsun plays.[37] At Coventry there was a continuous run of cycle performances from 1548 through to 1554. For each of these years there are records of expenditure

36 By comparison, some 181 *mystères* survive from France; Runnalls, *Les Mystères français imprimés*, 14.
37 'Also this yeare the Playes were playde', Clopper (ed.), *REED: Chester*, 54; Mills, 'Chester's Midsummer Show', in Twycross (ed.), *Festive Drama*, 132–44.

on preparations of stage equipment, on rehearsals and on payments to actors whose parts are named. For most of these years these guilds and some others also spent money on the Midsummer watch, and in 1553 the Mercers paid for six suits of armour for the procession on Fair Friday.[38] We have already noted that the Hock Tuesday play was an annual event.

Though it is difficult to sum up the qualities of the mystery plays in a short space, we may begin from the sense of community implicit in the previous account. Often the actors were drawn from the guilds, though payments were in some cases large enough to suggest actors from elsewhere. For the music, which forms a large part of the performance, it has recently been suggested that the musicality demanded of those playing the shepherds might well have been of professional standard.[39] Many of the acting parts were also very demanding, and in different ways. Some scenes, like the Trial before Herod, required very close interaction between the performers, especially those playing the contrasting villains Annas and Caiaphas. The roles of the Devils and other evil characters like Herod required bravura acting, especially Herod's rage (in pictorial representations he was often shown with his legs crossed in violent frustration). Though it is difficult to establish authorship for each cycle, two things are evident. They were written by people fully aware of biblical, theological and exegetical traditions, suggesting that the authors were clerics; and they were written in local dialect or regional speech. The latter is an integral part of the poetic effects of these works. The versification, which is usually stanzaic, and follows schemes and conventions which are still not properly understood, is varied and sophisticated, depending upon alliteration as well as rhyme. Modern reconstructions have shown that it is most effective in open-air performance. But even so, as the life of the York cycle was about 200 years of performance, it is difficult to believe that the text as we have it is the work of one writer, even though there are many structural aspects which help to unify it. Perhaps the text itself is partly the result of modification in performance: after all, these texts were developed only with that in mind. Unlike France,[40] there is no hint that in England anyone except John Bale (see below) ever thought it worth printing the cycles, and the texts remain records of what is inherently an aural and visual experience. Perhaps, too, the traditional nature of the guilds and the circumstances of performance meant that practices in acting and singing could be handed down within individual guilds and possibly families. Once again the presence of local people using

---

38 Ingram (ed.), *REED: Coventry*, 196.
39 Rastall, *The Heaven Singing*, I, 356–8, 364.
40 Runnalls, *Les Mystères français imprimés*, passim.

local speech must have enhanced the relationship between performers and audience.

Compared with other dramatic forms in 1553, the cycles had a special function in religious experience. It has been noted that the *mystères* did not function as a means of instructing the people so much as appealing to a faith already well established.[41] Though there are moral elements which are used to interpret scriptural history in terms of divine intervention, the main thrust of the cycles is a celebration of celestial justice. The presence of local actors, local speech and contemporary costume would bring these cosmic issues into an everyday context, and one which the local authorities would seek to encourage as it reflected their own political status.

One performance of part of a cycle in 1553 is especially worth mentioning because it reflects the use that could be made of scriptural history. In the 1530s John Bale, probably under the stimulus of the Protestant requirements of Thomas Cromwell, had reconceived ten episodes from the mystery cycles to make a continuous sequence acceptable to the newly evolving religious views. His rewriting involved putting greater emphasis upon scripture and the role of preachers interpreting it, and reducing the element of the miraculous found in the traditional cycles. In 1552 his appointment by King Edward to the bishopric of Ossory in southern Ireland projected him into a hostile environment where his lack of tact probably made him many enemies among the local Catholics. In *The Vocacyon of Johan Bale*, an account of his adventures in the years 1552 and 1553 probably drawn from a journal, he describes how he protested on 20 August 1553, the day Queen Mary was proclaimed at Kilkenny. He records that three of his plays (printed at Wesel in 1547–8) were acted by the young men: *God's Promises* in the morning, with songs and organ music, and *John Baptist's Preaching* and *The Temptation of Our Lord* in the afternoon. If he meant to provoke a reaction, he was successful, for he barely escaped from Ireland with his life.[42]

Apart from the cycles, there are other plays, usually known as interludes, which deal with religious themes at this period, mostly by means of a moral allegory. For most of them the dating is imprecise and we cannot be sure that they occurred strictly in 1553. The exception is *Respublica* whose manuscript is specific about date, but which we will deal with in the setting of the court drama below. Most of these interludes survive in printed form, and their survival is probably an indication that they were acceptable to the Protestant authorities,

---

41 '[Le jeu] n'enseigne pas la foi, il la suppose'; Bordier, *Le Jeu de la Passion*, 754.
42 Happé and King (eds.), *The Vocacyon of Johan Bale*, 59.

and for some, publication was delayed until after the accession of Elizabeth I in 1558. The following plays are representative of this genre, with approximate dates of composition:

1547–53	*Nice Wanton*
1547–66	*The Life and Repentance of Mary Magdalene* by Lewis Wager[43]
1550?	*The Disobedient Child* by Thomas Ingelond
1550–3	*Lusty Juventus* by Richard Wever
1554–5	*Wealth and Health*
1553–8	*Impatient Poverty*

Most of these have a distinct political or religious flavour, and, with the exception of *Impatient Poverty*, they have a Protestant orientation. In recent years it has become more and more apparent that the interlude was widely accepted as a means of making clear an ideological position.[44] The customary dependence upon abstract characterisation and the freedom to develop plots in accordance with such a preoccupation were probably the most attractive aspects of these plays to authors and polemicists. There is a good deal in them which could support lively theatrical presentation through singing and dancing, grotesque characterisation of the devil, and some associated vices, and disguise. Performance of these plays was usually either by boys' companies, or by small groups of adult players who did the play in a number of places, and kept down the costs by the extensive use of doubling. The importance of these plays for this account is that although they cannot necessarily be claimed for 1553, their survival indicates that there was an appropriate means of writing and performing such political entertainment at this time.

Drama at court

Thanks largely to the Loseley Manuscripts which recorded many of the dramatic entertainments at court throughout 1553, we can consider a number of theatrical events in relation to political events.[45] The young King Edward, though ailing, was provided with a variety of shows. At Christmas 1552 Ferrers

---

43 The emphatically Protestant style in language and characteristion of this play owes much to John Bale's plays, especially *Three Laws* which he attempted to revive in Hampshire in 1551: see Happé, 'The Protestant adaptation of the saint play', in Davidson (ed.), *The Saint Play in Medieval Europe*, 205–40.

44 White, *Theatre and Reformation*, 13–15, and Walker, *The Politics of Performance in Early Renaissance Drama*, 66–75.

45 Feuillerat (ed.), *Documents Relating to the Revels at Court in the Time of King Edward VI and Queen Mary*, 116–50; Streitberger, *Court Revels 1485–1559*, 292–4.

was appointed Lord of Misrule, and there was a joust with hobby-horses at Greenwich on 1 January, followed by his entry into London a few days later (four fools were noted). On 6 January George Howard's 'triumph' of *Venus, Cupid and Mars* was presented at court. Further entertainments were planned in February for Candlemas and Shrovetide, but the king's illness caused a postponement until Easter (2 April) when the Revels Office set up five 'masks'. This word seems to have meant almost any kind of quasi-dramatic show, and on this occasion there were apes who played bagpipes; cats; medioxes (probably half men and half figures of Death); Greek worthies; and tumblers who walked on their hands. The mixture of these topics suggests a desire for exotic and surprising shows, but perhaps the medioxes were an attempt – we do not know how tactful – to comment upon Edward's illness. The Revels documents show that considerable skill was expected from the makers of costumes and effects, and several different crafts, including skinners and goldsmiths, were employed. At the same time William Baldwin's lost play, *The State of Ireland*, was performed, and John Heywood prepared a play for twelve boys. This latter item was repeated on 1 May with some others.

By now, as Edward's health deteriorated, Northumberland was jockeying to maintain his position. For 25 May he ordered for Durham House two masks from the Revels for a triple wedding, including that of his son with Lady Jane Grey. On her accession Queen Mary reacted sharply against activities which concerned doctrine. Her edict of 18 August imposed restraint on preaching and the printing of any inappropriate books, and it specifically ordered that no one was 'to playe any interlude, except thay have her graces speciall licence in wrytynge the same'.[46]

The coronation procession on 30 September, which was designed by Florentine merchants, followed the traditional route for royal entries: northwards across London Bridge, through Fenchurch Street where there were giants; along Gracechurch Street, past an angel and a fountain; at Cornhill she met Virtues; and passing along Cheapside she reached St Paul's churchyard where John Heywood, the playwright and a long-standing and probably favoured supporter, gave an address to the queen in English and Latin.[47] His speech is lost, but the themes of the entry, an intricately planned affair following upon and deliberately varying from an ancient tradition, brought out, through classical iconography, her unique and almost unprecedented role as queen regnant. Links were established with the wisdom of Athena, and Marian

---

46 Dutton, *Mastering the Revels*, 19–20.
47 Lancashire, *Dramatic Texts and Records*, no. 1083; Anglo, *Spectacle, Pageantry, and Early Tudor Policy*, 319–22.

'bunting' (lines 768–9). Besides the name and disguise games which he plays, giving aliases to his associates Oppression, Adulation and Insolence, his part is full of word-play, and it is pithy with ambiguities. He misleads Respublica and is finally exposed by Nemesis and sentenced, allegorically, to being squeezed like a sponge. In the cast list he is called 'the vice of the plaie', and this term, 'the Vice', was at this time becoming the name for the leading part in many interludes: it was perhaps a development of characters invented by Heywood and Bale, and it remained popular for a generation of playwrights. There is also the possibility that Avarice, in this instance, was played by an adult, a schoolmaster, perhaps, among his pupils.

It has long been appreciated that there is a strong political intention in this play. Most likely, as Walker has recently emphasised,[55] the intention was to expose the corruption of the Protestant courtiers who, under Edward, had indulged in profiteering against the church. Several of these men still retained office under Mary, but although the author revives the traditional Catholic dialogue between the Four Daughters of God as part of the process of amelioration, he is careful to concentrate his condemnation (and his fun) upon these secular matters rather than aspects of Protestant doctrine. It must be admitted, however, that the precise flavour of this political commentary is quite difficult to pin down. No doubt in this first year of Mary's reign there were many uncertainties, the policies which led to the later executions not yet manifest, though perhaps feared. One of the functions of court drama, as John Skelton and John Heywood had discovered years before, was to try to persuade and to bring about shifts in policy through entertainment, and this author is no doubt following suit. Heywood, it will be remembered, was still at court.

The dramatic activities considered here may illustrate the variety of modes which were active in the kingdom in 1553. Many of them, religious or secular, were traditional in concept, but in the interludes at least there was scope for innovation. The fascination inherent in this material lies in the ways dramatic form may be made entertaining, and also how, by means of such key devices as impersonation, disguise, plot and theatrical language, a dramatic event may present as well as comment upon the opinions and aspirations of people in a social context.

55 *Politics of Performance*, 174–8.

PART II

*

ELIZABETHAN THEATRE

5

The development of a professional theatre, 1540–1660

JANE MILLING

The writing of a theatre history reveals almost as much about contemporary tastes and values as it does about the cultural world of the past. Historians tend to organise their material into familiar explanatory or narrative structures, most often, the rise, the fall and the rise and fall. If we consider the dramatic literature produced during the period 1540–1660, historians from the mid eighteenth century onwards have preferred a story of rise and fall. In their narratives dramatic literature charted an upward trajectory from the primitive dramatic texts of mummings, mysteries and moralities, blossomed into theatre proper embodied by the sophisticated genius of Shakespeare, before collapsing, exhausted, into Cavalier and Caroline degeneracy. An outspoken example of this kind of narrative from the eighteenth century is Chetwood's *A Short View of the Rise and Progress of the English Stage* (1752). Chetwood cannot mourn the paucity of pre-Shakespearian theatrical literature:

> A more particular knowledge of these Things, any further than as it serves to show ... the progressive Refinement of our Language, was so little worth preserving, that the Loss of it is scarce to be regretted ... Though Tragedy and Comedy began to lift up their Heads, yet they could do no more for some time than bluster and quibble ...[1]

Chetwood had little time for drama before or after Shakespeare and Jonson. While we might smile at his offhand dismissal of swathes of dramatic endeavour, his assessment of dramatic quality employed a model that remained a powerful truism in the literary study of early modern drama. The story of the flowering of theatrical literature in Elizabethan and Jacobean England has been central to the establishment of a national English literature and cultural identity. The publishing history of dramatic texts and literary criticism from the period continues to display a similar formulation.

---

1 Chetwood, *A General History of the English Stage*, v–viii. Although Chetwood is able to take some satisfaction in that 'Imperfect as they were, we had made a far better Progress at this time than our Neighbours, the French.'

Histories of theatre and performance, as opposed to dramatic literature, have followed a slightly different narrative, but one also inflected with a romantic nostalgia for the glory days of Shakespeare. Since the Restoration the history of theatres and theatre workers has been constructed primarily in economic terms, with success measured by the generation of an expanding market-place, the professionalisation of playing and the multiplying of adult theatre companies. These theatrical histories tell of the rise and rise of the theatre, before the brutal interruption of the Interregnum. In James Wright's *Historia Histrionica* (1699), an early dialogue history, the character Truman usefully lists the troupes functioning before the Interregnum:

> All these Companies got Money, and Liv'd in Reputation, especially those of the Blackfriars, who were men of grave and sober Behaviour.
> *Lovewit*: Which I admire at; That the Town much less than at present, could then maintain Five companies, and yet now Two can hardly subsist.[2]

We remain fascinated by the theatrical market-place and the theatre industry of early modern Britain. Of course, actors and theatre workers would not have thought of themselves as part of an industry, although many thought of themselves as industrious. The language of industry, although anachronistic, usefully emphasises that there were commercial imperatives which helped to condition the development and mode of operation of theatres. The focus on economic history does not preclude moral commentary, and the anti-theatrical battle was played out within discussion of commercial success in early theatre histories. For theatrical supporters, the story of the rise of the actor in cultural status was in direct proportion to the financial potential of stage playing. Yet, for John Stowe, in his *Survey of London*, the professionalisation of acting was not a positive move. Playing 'which was once a Recreation, and used therefore now and then occasionally, afterwards by Abuse became a Trade and Calling . . . in Process of time it became an Occupation' to the detriment of church going and social decency.[3] For Stowe the appearance of the professional actor was a fall in every sense.

The nationwide phenomenon of theatre was highly disparate but this chapter seeks to trace one of the leading features of the emergent professional theatre: the theatre company. The professionalisation of the theatre was to a large degree produced by the development of theatre companies. A focus on company histories would seem to chime with the current fascination for the economics of theatre, and the company certainly functioned as a complex

---

2 Wright, *Historia Histrionica*, 5.
3 Chetwood, *A General History of the English Stage*, x.

economic unit. But in the 1540s it was not an economic given that actors would form themselves into stable groupings or fraternities as companies, nor that those companies would be successful. Recent studies arising from the Records of Early English Drama (REED) project have reconstructed from fragmented household records, parish, civic and court documents the complex patterns of touring and company economics. This work has generated many curiously revealing micro-histories. A study of Kent, for example, suggests a burgeoning of touring theatre companies during the sixteenth century, in keeping with national trends. As the seventeenth century rolled on, many Kentish towns experienced a gradual decline in official sanction and a reduction in the number and frequency of troupes that visited, coupled with a reduction in local civic and community theatricality.[4] Meanwhile, in London those same theatre companies maintained an optimistic expansion of repertoire, playing spaces and courtly interaction throughout the early Stuart period.

The chapter will attempt to chart some of the complexity surrounding the development of the professional theatre company, 1540–1660, in particular by looking at its relationship to systems of patronage, to actors, entrepreneurs, playwrights and audiences. Andrew Gurr's study of the Shakespearian-era companies collates a wide range of material to offer an overview of the mechanisms of company operation. Scott McMillin and Sally-Beth MacLean and Roslyn Knutson have examined the distinct flavours and repertoires of leading companies. These studies also place the companies in their specific political and social context and it is undoubtedly true that the appearance of the professional theatre company was as much a result of political forces as it was of economic ones.

The story of the rise of the professional theatre company might seem to imply a concomitant fall in patronage relationships. However, the commercial imperatives always operated beside and beyond modes of patronage. William Ingram argues that the development in economic status of the London-based playing company in the mid Tudor period and the concomitant growth of the Elizabethan theatre were conditioned by political enthusiasm for the potential of theatre. As Paul White illustrates in his chapter in this volume, the stage's potential for propagating Protestant polemic was grasped by Henry VIII, and more particularly by Thomas Cromwell. Protestantism itself was by no means inimical to the theatrical; indeed one of the earliest treatises on dramatic theory, *De Honestis Ludis*, which was presented to Edward VI in 1551, was written by Martin Bucer, Professor of Divinity at Cambridge. He urged, after a study of

4 Gibson, 'Stuart players in Kent: fact or fiction?', *REED Newsletter* 20:2 (1995), 1–13.

classical material, that 'acting comedies and tragedies provide their public with wholesome entertainment which is not without value in increasing piety'.[5] Edward VI was to encourage a brief resurgence of enthusiasm for radical political and religious polemic within interludes and courtly entertainment.[6] The telling point here is not that the monarch or court influenced the texts and thematic content of plays, although this seems certainly to have been the case in the work of individuals like John Bale. Theatre can never be simply propaganda and it is extremely difficult at this distance to assert that the interpretative work of an audience would be completely circumscribed by the apparent message of a text. In fact, by the 1540s the court was growing uncomfortable with the licence to discuss religious and political matters that interlude writers and players were taking and attempts were made to limit their excesses. Much more significant than the content of dramatic texts was that the government's enthusiasm for the potential of performance had encouraged the development of the theatre companies themselves. This development was one increasingly sponsored by leading nobles as a useful form for the dissemination of their policies and influence.[7]

The structure of patronage relationships and the notion of household membership was a powerful conditioner of the form, stability and even the touring mechanisms of the early professional theatre companies, although they were not strictly household employees. Indeed, James Burbage had to request explicit confirmation from his patron, the Earl of Leicester, in 1572, that his company were 'your houshold Servaunts and daylie wayters' in order to travel freely under the Elizabethan proclamation against vagabonds.[8] Early in Elizabeth's reign the interrelation between the royal court and theatre companies was minimal; rather, the theatre industry thrived because of the culturally significant use patrons were able to make of their companies' offerings. Patrons of playing troupes which appeared at court in the early part of Elizabeth's reign include Robert Dudley, Earl of Leicester, and his brother Ambrose, Earl of Warwick. Significant post-holders were expected to maintain a theatre company. When Thomas Radcliffe, Earl of Sussex, became lord chamberlain in 1572 he patronised a company. His successor, Henry Carey, Lord Hunsdon, the queen's cousin, took on the role of chamberlain in 1585 and with it responsibility as patron of the theatre company. The Lord Admiral's Men, who were led by Edward Alleyn until the end of the century, were patronised by post-holders

5 Wickham, *Early English Stages*, III, 206.
6 Edwards et al., *The Revels History of Drama in English*, IV, 20.
7 Ingram, *The Business of Playing*, 90.
8 Chambers, *The Elizabethan Stage*, II, 86.

Edward Clinton, Earl of Lincoln, and, after 1572, Charles Howard, Baron of Effingham.[9] The demonstration of significance and power that a successful theatre company could muster reached its apogee with the formation of the Queen's Men in 1583. McMillin and MacLean read this move as a politically inflected act, created to further the Protestant polemic that Leicester's own company had been propagating. Under Walsingham and Leicester's direction, the Queen's Men were 'a company designed to increase the prestige of their patron throughout the land, to harness the theatre in the service of a moderate Protestant ideology, and to add a vivid group of travellers who might serve the [Privy] council's needs for secret information about recusants or foreign visitors'.[10]

Although the impact of a patron on the content, genre or style of plays was limited, a patron was able to bask in reflected glory as the companies became more commercially successful, some of them establishing extended playing runs in London playhouses before the end of the century. And a company's commercial success might occasionally be influenced by the powerful support of their patron. For example, Gurr reads the Privy Council ruling of 1597, which ordered the Curtain, Theatre and all playhouses to be 'plucked downe', as part of Henslowe's attempt to dominate theatres on the South Bank. Francis Langley had just wooed Pembroke's Men to his Swan theatre in direct competition to Henslowe. The response of Charles Howard, lord admiral and privy councillor, was, Gurr argues, 'either a ham-fisted response to [Henslowe's] appeals for help, or else an exceptionally ingenious manoeuvre which [Henslowe] knew about in advance'.[11] When the system of patronage altered under James I, and all theatre companies had to shelter under patronage from members of the royal household, ironically the significance of the patron to a company was reduced. What might occur on occasions though, as Richard Dutton's chapter on *A Game at Chess* ponders here, was that the playing companies might find themselves voicing the interests of a particular faction at court. By the succession of Charles I, who permitted two companies to operate without a patron, at the Red Bull and, later, in Salisbury Court, royal patronage had become practically irrelevant. Instead, there was a system of renewable licences run from the Revels office. This more tenuous system of patronage indicates not only the extent to which the professional playing companies had become something other than household players, but also perhaps that the overridingly commercial concerns of the professional troupes had rendered them far less dangerous in the court's eyes.

9 Astington, *English Court Theatre, 1558–1642*, 167.
10 McMillin and MacLean, *The Queen's Men*, 24.
11 Gurr, *The Shakespearian Playing Companies*, 107.

The court had never been a monolith, of course, and a good illustration of this is in the complexity of court patronage of theatre companies by the queens' households of the seventeenth century. Queen Anne was a keen masquer herself and supporter of the theatre. In 1603, when James came to the throne, she took over Worcester's Men as an adult company, as well as Blackfriars Boys as Children of the Queen's Revels, the latter, most interestingly, with a separate Master of the Revels and censor from her household, Samuel Daniel. Leeds Barroll offers an intriguing view of the political significance of Anne's court as a potential centre of oppositional feeling to the new regime, into which the early work from the boy company quickly fed with *Eastward Ho!*, *The Isle of Gulls*, Daniel's own *Philotas* and other scurrilous works. Anne attended 'these representations in order to enjoy the laugh against her husband' according to the French ambassador.[12] The explicit experiment of a separate household censor, and a self-regulating company, was speedily brought to an end. Charles I's queen, Henrietta Maria, was not only a keen masquer, but took the unprecedented step of performing spoken drama at court, as well as attending the public theatre; four visits to Blackfriars are recorded, including trips to see Lodowick Carlell's *Arviragus and Philicia* (1636) and William Davenant's *The Unfortunate Lovers* (1638), although it is possible that these were specially commissioned evening performances.[13] Her influence extended far beyond the tenor of court entertainment, where her encouragement for versions of platonic and pastoral tropes was read in a highly politicised way. Public theatre writing from those of her circle occasionally infiltrated the repertoire of the King's Men at Blackfriars or the theatre at Salisbury Court in which Edward Sackville, Earl of Dorset, one of her circle, had a considerable interest. Her pro-French enthusiasm, expressed in her taste for the French *précieuses* and their salon, romance tradition, was a useful emblem for the broadly Protestant opposition voices at court for a considerable period of Charles's reign, as Janette Dillon discusses here.[14]

Companies and actors

It is difficult to identify when acting companies in England first became professional troupes, and when actors earned a living primarily from their playing. There was a well-established tradition of individual touring entertainers or small groups, such as minstrels, through the medieval period. However, early

12 Chambers, *The Elizabethan Stage*, I, 325.
13 Bentley, *The Jacobean and Caroline Stage*, VI, 34–6.
14 See also Butler's *Theatre and Crisis*.

Tudor household players often held other posts in the household, even though they might spend a considerable time on tour. Many of the early players also list themselves as trade freemen; for example, George Mayler, a merchant tailor or glazier, whom we know to be one of Henry VIII's actors from law-suits concerning costume hire, and his apprentice actor, Thomas Arthur.[15] Elizabethan stage players are often known in official documentation by their membership of livery companies, as much as for their status as players. Later performers were also often guild freemen: Martin Slater was an ironmonger, John Heminges a grocer, John Shanks a weaver, and Robert Armin and Andrew Cane goldsmiths. So when, in *Histriomastix* (1600), Marston draws a satirical picture of Sir Oliver Owlet's Men as a scratch company including Gulch, Clout, Belch the beard-maker, Gut the fiddle-string maker and Incle the pedlar, he is taking a dig at the rather more reified status of the adult companies as freemen of a variety of trade guilds.

It is true that, by 1581, some players considered themselves as in effect professionals, and were recognised as such by the Privy Council who, in a minute from 3 December, allowed them licence to play in London after the plague closure:

> in respecte of their pore estates, having noe other meanes to sustayne them, their wyves and children but their exercise of playing, and were only brought up from their youthe in the practise and profession of musicke and playeng...[16]

Financial stability within the profession seems to have depended on whether a player was a shareholder or not, with a capital investment in the performing company. Shareholder Edward Alleyn was to become a highly respectable and wealthy London citizen after his retirement. Those performers who were hired men fared less well on a small, sometime irregular salary, although some, like Christopher Beeston, were to go on to economic success as company managers and shareholders. However, financial achievement was not the same as social standing, as the university wits and satirists were only too fond of reminding those 'copper-lace gentlemen'.[17] It is impossible to generalise about the status of players over the period, as that depended largely on the company they belonged to, their perceived talent and the point of view of the commentator. As we have seen, actors in those theatre companies that were central to courtly entertainment and display gained some distinction from their appearance

---

15 Chambers, *The Elizabethan Stage*, II, 81.
16 Gurr, *The Shakespearian Playing Companies*, 280.
17 Chambers, *The Elizabethan Stage*, IV, 247.

before the monarch. Will Kemp, Robert Wilson and Robert Browne were valued sufficiently by the Earl of Leicester to be included in his flashy entourage on his 1585 expedition to Flushing to command the English troops in the Low Countries. A telling illustration of the potential improvement in the status of the player by the Caroline era was Joseph Taylor, who appeared at court, not as a performer, but as an acting coach. John Pory observed the preparations made by Queen Henrietta Maria, who was to perform with her ladies in Walter Montague's *Shepherd's Paradise*, and noted that 'Taylour the prime actor at the Globe goes every day to teache them action.' Taylor was to have 'the making of a knight given him' for his trouble.[18]

In the early Tudor period actors were not always thought of, nor considered themselves, as allied to companies and it was not a given that the theatre company would become the primary structure of professional theatricality. In 1550 the Court of Aldermen in London bound eighteen common players, as individuals, not to play in the city without licence. At this point, although the eighteen men may well have been working together in groups, they were not identified by company. Under the later Tudors the days of the common player or masterless man were numbered.[19] Legislation certainly helped condition the development of the companies under Elizabeth. All Tudor monarchs had paid some attention to controlling wandering players in rulings which were implemented with varying degrees of enthusiasm and effectiveness. It would be misleading to think of the development of legislation as a gradual, planned and coherent programme of repression or control. Statutes and rulings, precedents and licences were *ad hoc*, often temporary and usually reactive, but they did, cumulatively, help to produce the theatre industry as we recognise it. One of the first significant moments was the 1572 statute, *An Acte for the punishement of Vagabonds*, which gave towns and boroughs, including London, powers to arrest anyone travelling who was 'not belonging to any Baron of this Realme or towardes any other honorable Personage of greater Degree'.[20] Would companies have sought noble patronage, simply in the tradition of household playing, without this ruling?

Undoubtedly the legal establishment of theatre companies had seemed to offer the Elizabethan authorities a solution to the difficulty of common, masterless players wandering around unchecked. However, the thirst for theatrical entertainment throughout the country produced a proliferation of patronised companies. In the summer of 1575 alone, Londoners were able to appreciate

18 Edwards et al., *Revels History of Drama in English*, IV, 13.
19 Ingram, *The Business of Playing*, 84.
20 Chambers, *The Elizabethan Stage*, IV, 270.

the talents of players patronised by the Earls of Leicester, Warwick, Sussex, Oxford, Lincoln, Pembroke and Essex, as well as troupes belonging to Lord Howard, Lord Rich, Lord Abergavenny and Sir Robert Lane, and these are only the companies that appeared in official documentation or letters. By the end of the 1590s 'unregulated patronage itself came to be seen as a problem'.[21] The system of royal patronage under James I was a response to this, but was never to be wholly watertight and was allowed to lapse under Charles I. Companies received a roughly annual licence to play from the Master of the Revels, which gives some indication of the relaxed sense of stability the playing companies were felt to have, although, ironically, the Caroline companies were much less stable groupings of individuals, and their relationship to playing places in London was similarly unsettled. The independent touring professional company remained the most usual supplier of theatrical entertainment, even past the point where the theatre venues of London were closed to them and gathering for a performance was legislated against in 1642.

Once companies were established, part of their enduring success was that they offered a level of financial security not available to looser groups of performers. Both sharers and acting hired men tended to remain with a company unless the company itself split or folded with the death of their patron or financial difficulties, usually because of plague.[22] For example, it took the intervention of Sir Francis Walsingham and the Earl of Leicester to produce the Queen's Men in 1583, when the premier performers from the troupes of the Earls of Leicester and Sussex and possibly the Earl of Oxford as well were head-hunted for the queen's troupe.[23] It is rarer to find references to players moving or leaving of their own volition. Was it Alleyn's move from the Admiral's Men in 1591 that prompted its split into a provincial and an international touring group or was he biding his time during the company's low period before eventually becoming the lynch-pin of a new Admiral's company in May 1594? After all, as Gurr ponders, Alleyn continued to maintain the lord admiral's livery in 1591 while he was performing with Strange's Men. Will Kemp is perhaps a clearer example of this rare phenomenon, the independent actor, since he sold his share and left the Chamberlain's Men in 1599, apparently to pursue a solo career of dancing feats, before joining Worcester's Men in 1600. Kemp is truly anomalous in fact, because we have so very few records of solo performances, although this may be because they did not enter legal or civic documents in

21 Ingram, *The Business of Playing*, 85.
22 Streitberger, 'Personnel and professionalization', in Cox and Kastan (eds.), *A New History of Early English Drama*, 347.
23 McMillin and MacLean, *The Queen's Men and their Plays*, 12.

the same way as companies. There is one tantalisingly elusive reference to a solo female performer from Richard Madox. On 22 February 1583, he 'went to the theater to see a scurvie play set out al by one virgin, which there proved a fyemarten without voice, so that we stayed not the matter'.[24] This unfortunate young woman may have been a singer offering something akin to Moll Frith's entertainment at the Fortune in 1611.

Clearly shareholding actors had a capital investment in the company they joined, but for the average player and performing hired man it was also in their interest to maintain relations with one employer, who provided regular playing. Ingram's warning about interpreting financial information in relation to players is timely here. He offers a detailed study of fragments of the life of John Garland, one of the Queen's Men. Ingram challenges the reader to interpret Garland's decision to stay with the company in 1595 when plague meant that other players were relocating, and in which year he received a daily stipend of 2 shillings for life from the queen. Was this 'a reward for Garland's freely declared allegiance, or was it the price he exacted for his continued membership'?[25] We shall probably never be able to determine in what proportion the relative stability of actors within companies grew from friendly solidarity, loyalty to a patron, company status or economic wisdom.

There is little indication of the way in which companies recruited performers, or how they assessed their skills. Some useful hints about where players came from lurk in the negative criticism of Stephen Gosson, in his *Plays Confuted in Five Actions* (1582). He attacks the idle players as 'either men of occupations, which they have forsaken to live by playing, or common minstrels, or trained up from their childhood to this abominable exercise and have now no other way to get their living'.[26] Training young men within a company seems to have been a significant feature of the profession after the 1560s, when boy players became useful additions to adult companies. The apprentice was most usually contracted to an individual player within a company and was maintained by him. Henslowe himself seems to have considered a boy player a useful capital investment: 'Bowght my boye Jeames brystow of william agusten player the 18 of desember 1597 for viij li'.[27] By 1600 Henslowe was charging companies 3 shillings a week for the use of his boy.

What the actual 'training' of these apprentices comprised, other than the experience of performing and the discipline of learning parts and observing

---

24 Chambers, *The Elizabethan Stage*, I, 371n.
25 Ingram, *The Business of Playing*, 52.
26 Chambers, *The Elizabethan Stage*, IV, 218.
27 Rutter, *Documents of the Rose Playhouse*, 127.

their elders, is not clear. By 1629 Richard Gunnell and William Blagrave were licensed to form a separate company to train boys as players to supply the professional companies. Later companies, like Lady Elizabeth's company and Beeston's Boys, may also have been primarily training ventures.[28] The child actors were not only valuable members of the troupe, but also versatile publicists for the company. In a lawsuit over *Keep the Widow Waking*, Benjamin Garfield, whose family was pruriently depicted in the play, protested that boy actors from the Red Bull pointed up at Anne Elsden's window, and said 'there dwelte the widdowe waking'.[29] The training for full involvement in the company meant that the boy apprentices might go on to become performing hired men, sharers, theatre managers like Christopher Beeston or playwrights like Richard Brome. Adult players who joined the companies may have come from household or regional troupes, the many hidden companies that only surface in documents as borrowers of costumes or disturbers of the peace. We have no record of how these players were assessed or auditioned before they joined. At our most cynical we might suspect that some performers bought their way in, as seems to be the case with William Bankes and Prince Charles's company in 1635. Bankes introduced himself to the company and 'did agree to pay the said company one hundred pounds and to become an actor'. The company might have rued the day, since they had occasion to criticise his 'disorderly behaviour' and to defend themselves against him in a lawsuit in the late 1630s.[30] Shareholders tended to get the larger, meatier roles in each company, although shareholding itself was not necessarily an indication of acting ability, rather of financial significance.

What was the experience of acting for the performers? Certainly there are hints about nerves before going on stage, particularly for the prologue speaker. Dekker's *Gull's Hornbook* paints a picture of 'the quaking Prologue [who] hath by rubbing got colour into his cheeks and is ready to give the trumpets their cue that he's upon point to enter'.[31] Heywood's three prologuers in the induction to *Four Prentices* describe the 'signes of a Prologue': 'Do I not looke pale, as fearing to be out in my speech?'.[32] Whatever the nature of their action and skill, the players appear to have generated that curious attractiveness that we still attribute to those who perform. In 1592, a group of English travelling players was a great hit in the Netherlands where, despite the language barrier, 'many

28 Streitberger, 'Personnel and professionalization', 350.
29 Bentley, *The Jacobean and Caroline Stage*, III, 255.
30 Bentley, *The Profession of Player*, 44.
31 Pendry, *Thomas Dekker*, 100.
32 Cited in Greenfield, *The Induction in Elizabethan Drama*, 74.

young virgines fell in love with some of the players, and followed them from citty to citty'.[33] An anonymous 1587 letter to Walsingham complains that 'two hundred proude players jett in their silkes' in London.[34] In their satire *The Return from Parnassus* (Christmas 1601), even the university wits conceded that players were glamorous:

> England affordes those glorious vagabonds,
> That carried erst their fardels on their backes,
> Coursers to ride on through the gazing streetes,
> Sooping it in their glaring satten sutes . . .   (V i)

There seem to have been plenty of players on hand to supply the companies when they divided for touring, and perhaps the profession had become rather attractive. There are nearly a thousand players we know of by name during the period, and there were probably many more.[35]

We might also be curious as to whether actors were political creatures, with an investment in the attitude of the play they were performing, as we assume playwrights were, or were the players merely 'Puppets, that speake out of their mouthes'?[36] We know that Robert Shaa, along with fellow actor Ben Jonson, was imprisoned when the Privy Council took action against Pembroke's Men for presenting at the Swan in 1597 a satirical play called *The Isle of Dogs*. The text has not survived, but it contained, in the Council's view, 'very seditious and slanderous matter'. Shaa and Jonson were surely articulating something of their own point of view in the text and performance they helped to generate. Much later, Andrew Cane seems to have developed his own satiric streak. He is cited by the Privy Council for satirising monopolies and ecclesiastical officials in the lost play, *The Whore New Vamped*, produced by the Prince's Men at the Red Bull 'for many days together' in September 1639. Cane is specifically mentioned for a patch of comic dialogue criticising the monopoly on wine and its patentee, London alderman William Abell.[37] The king-in-council ordered the attorney-general to call to account the actor Cane, the poet and, intriguingly, the licenser himself. Unfortunately it is not clear what the outcome was, but Cane had certainly garnered a reputation as a politicised performer, and in 1641 he appears as a character in the pamphlet *The Stage Players Complaint: In a Pleasant Dialogue Between Cane of the Fortune and Reed of the Friers*, which touched on theatrical and political matters. His effectiveness

33 Chambers, *The Elizabethan Stage*, I, 343.
34 Ibid., IV, 304.
35 Nungezer, *A Dictionary of Actors*.
36 Rutter, *Documents of the Rose Playhouse*, 216.
37 Butler, *Theatre and Crisis*, 235.

as a writer and performer of jigs also allowed him space to express his own satiric point of view. Somewhat surprisingly, he was for the king during the Civil Wars, and is found coining for the royalists in 1644 and was possibly imprisoned in the late 1640s for his support.

Of course, because we have so very little information even about which performer played which range of parts it can be dangerous to speculate about political or religious persuasion, let alone casting and typecasting within a company, or to distinguish between the acting styles of different companies. The reader may sympathise with Lovewit of *Historia Histrionica* who wails:

> I wish they had Printed in the last Age ... the Actors Names over against the Parts they Acted, as they have done since the Restauration. And thus one might have guest at the Action of the Men, by the parts which we now Read in the Old Plays.[38]

It is unlikely that there was a uniformity of performance skills; some actors were clearly considered more impressive, in contemporary terms, than others and it was not only the quality of the plays that marked out the leading companies. If actors were working for rival troupes at houses across London, or off on tour, were they able to see each other perform? This must have been true to a certain extent as companies amalgamated or shared a bill at court. A young player must surely have been curious to see Kemp, Armin, Burbage or Alleyn at work and to learn from their success. When Paul's Boys satirise the adult players in the induction to *Antonio and Mellida* (1599), and 'Feliche' mocks the braggart 'Matzagente' for his 'Rampam scrampum, mount tufty Tamburlaine!', he is mocking the performance register of a Tamburlaine, modelled on Alleyn's towering rendition of the role. What must have been true of all performers was their versatility in singing, stagefighting, doubling, memorising an inordinate number of parts, performing in many genres, pitching their work for many spaces in London and on tour, playing male and female roles, kings and petty officials and extemporising where necessary. As the theatre industry developed and theatre companies grew in size, doubling and all the dextrous use of quick change, vocal and physical distinction that that required, became less necessary. Perhaps the need to extemporise also declined. An important part of much early Tudor work, extemporisation was probably less free improvisation as we now understand it, and more *commedia* style, solo semi-prepared diatribes or flexible riffs and gags with a partner, as in the early *All for Money*:

38 Bentley, *The Jacobean and Caroline Stage*, II, 692.

Here the Vice [Sin] shall turn the proclamation to some contrary sense every time All-For-Money hath read it, and here followeth the proclamation.[39]

As late as 1611 Greene's *Tu Quoque* offers the stage direction 'here they two talk and rail what they list'.[40] By the time Brome is writing for Caroline audiences, that kind of improvisation has become a nostalgic motif of an earlier, fictional theatre. As an exchange in *The Antipodes* teases:

> LETOY: But you, sir, are incorrigible, and
> Take licence to your self to add unto
> Your parts your own free fancy . . .
> BY-PLAY: That is a way, my lord, has been allowed
> On elder stages, to move mirth and laughter.
> LETOY: Yes, in the days of Tarleton and Kemp,
> Before the stage was purged from barbarism . . .
>
> (2.2.41–3, 48–51)

How much Tarlton and Kemp or any actor did improvise within performance is lost to us now. By the late 1630s extempore playing had come to be regarded as the somewhat dated province of the popular play and playhouses, as interest in acting technique had turned elsewhere.

Companies and entrepreneurs

We have only fragmentary traces of the operation of some theatre companies during the period of this study. These traces almost certainly do not offer us the whole story. During the Elizabethan period company size grew from four to six to much larger troupes with twelve or more shareholders and many hired men. The hired men were mostly musicians, tiremen, gatherers, stagekeepers and bookkeepers rather than performers, although they might have been called on to make up numbers in a scene, as marginal notes in playbooks suggest. Some of them were asked to post a bond to indicate their willingness to stay with a company. A draft contract for a typical hired man at the Rose in 1599 indicated 'viiii s a wecke as longe as they playe & after they lye stylle one fortnyght then to geue hime hallfe wages'.[41] There was also differentiation between London and touring salaries. In 1597 Henslowe hired William Kendall at 10 shillings a week for playing in London and 5 shillings

39 Schell and Shuchter (eds.), *English Morality Plays and Moral Interludes*, 454.
40 Rasmussen, 'Setting down what the clown spoke', 134.
41 Rutter, *Documents*, 161.

for the country.[42] By the late Elizabethan period companies were in the main organised with player-shareholders providing capital which went towards the purchase of plays and costumes, renting of space and the equipping of the troupe. In London shareholders took a cut of the profits on the door, whilst playhouse owners like Henslowe took a cut of the income from the galleries.

The financial transactions that held a company together had always been complicated. Henry Crosse levelled the charge of money-lending against the companies in his tract, *Vertues Common-wealth* (1603); 'not fewe of them usurers and extortioners', he darkly intoned.[43] Indeed it does seem that the entrepreneurs James Burbage and John Brayne, his brother-in-law, were doing a little moneylending on the side in the late 1560s, while developing the Red Lion playhouse.[44] Henslowe's papers have opened him to considerable aspersion on this score from modern commentators, although Carson thinks that they 'do not look like the accounts of a professional money-lender; they have more the appearance of the rather casual efforts of a man to keep track of his personal loans'.[45] Either way it is clear that the company functioned as a complex economic unit. By the Jacobean period the King's Men were employing twenty-one hired men in December 1624. The value of a share during the Jacobean period increased; in 1612 Queen Anne's Men reckoned on £80 a share, and the less significant Prince Charles's Men estimated a share was worth £70 in 1615. By the Caroline period company organisation was a little different and shareholders were not always players, with the healthy mix of financial and artistic stability that that system had provided.

The likely internal regulation and responsibilities of a company were illustrated as early as May 1574, in a patent for Leicester's Men which allowed them to perform music and plays which had been seen and allowed by the Master of the Revels, both in London and elsewhere. Rather than a document of control, this patent might be read as liberating, offering the company extensive opportunity for commercial expansion, in the teeth of disapproval from the authorities in the towns they visited. Rulings from the court and regulatory attempts on the content of plays by the Revels office were only one aspect of pressure on the company. The regulation of playing places, seasons and times generated a continual battle with the aldermen of the City of London, and increasingly through the century with the civic bodies of towns visited on touring routes. This mattered because provincial touring remained

---

42 Ibid., 127.
43 Chambers, *The Elizabethan Stage*, IV, 247.
44 Ingram, *The Business of Playing*, 40.
45 Carson, *A Companion to Henslowe's Diary*, 10.

a significant element of most companies' activities. Companies might double their profits by dividing and running a London and a provincial troupe under one licence; the doubled licence was called an exemplification. Sometimes companies toured illegally under feigned patents, as Lord Chandos's Men did in 1592, when the Norwich authorities were disturbed to discover that, having paid out 10 shillings to one company, 'a nother Company of his men that cam with lycens presently after saying yat thos that Cam before were counterfetes & not the Lord Shandos men', and had to pay out 20 shillings to the real troupe.[46]

Martin Slater was an acting-entrepreneur who made something of a success out of touring companies under exemplifications. In 1607 he was taken to the Court of Common Pleas by Thomas Greene, manager of Queen Anne's Men, with whom Slater was also a sworn member. Slater had been touring with a group and posting bills under the name of Her Majesty's Servants, and he received £12 on the understanding that he would discontinue the practice unless he had at least five members of the troupe in his group.[47] It was not only the companies themselves that tried to regulate the abuse of this erstwhile useful practice of exemplifications. Slater is one of those named in the 1617 ruling by the Earl of Pembroke, sent to the Norwich authorities, condemning the use of duplicate patents, wherein Slater is cited as one of 'the Queens Mats company of Playors haveing separated themselves from their said Company'.[48] By 1617, then, the number of roving companies had grown far beyond the original number envisaged under the royal patents, but the effectiveness of Pembroke's action may be deduced from the fact that Slater continued to tour widely and successfully with his own company, under the guise of a Queen's Man, until his death in 1625.

There was also a complicated relationship between the player-shareholders of a company and those entrepreneurs who saw the theatre and its institutional needs primarily as a source of income. Apart from the Globe and Blackfriars, all theatres in London were solely or jointly owned by entrepreneurs. It is interesting to ponder why it was not considered a wise investment to develop theatre-specific buildings and a resident company in other important centres outside the capital. It may be that there was not a sufficient population to guarantee a regular audience, or that the city authorities in other major towns were less tolerant of activities in their penumbra. A Bristol inn was briefly converted into a playing place in 1604; York and a village in Lancashire

---

46 Gurr, *The Shakespearian Playing Companies*, 315.
47 Bentley, *The Profession of Player*, 148.
48 Bentley, *The Jacobean and Caroline Stage*, II, 574.

had also tried this earlier.[49] Most intriguingly, there was a scheme mooted in York in 1608–9 to establish a theatre with its own company as 'a means to restrayne the frequent comminge of other stage players'. This curious piece of double-think seems not to have been followed through.[50] Whilst playgoing and the theatre industry were burgeoning in London in the Jacobean period, elsewhere the records of local authorities show a marked increase in the number of playing troupes turned away with a payment for *not* playing, as well as a decrease in participatory dramatic events at the level of the city and community. Peter Greenfield discusses the reasons and significance of these records of provincial playing in this volume. During the late Elizabethan and Jacobean period the significance of playing at court and the cultural resonance of playing in London as a trial for a potential royal audience had greatly increased. Once James had reorganised the licensed playing companies under royal patronage, entertaining at court was no longer about the status of the company's patron, but about the status of the company and players themselves. And playing in York hardly facilitated an invitation to the Christmas revels with the monarch.

Companies and playwrights

Some see the Elizabethan and Jacobean period as the 'golden age' of English dramatic writing. The Renaissance fascination with classical drama, readily attainable in recent translation, and its impact on the kind of education offered in the grammar schools, coupled with a burgeoning popular and civic theatricality, was fruitful ground for the development of the theatre industry. However, the crop of playwrights who flourished and the quality of the plays that they produced cannot be considered in isolation from their central relationship to the theatre companies for whom they wrote. The number of plays from many 'great' playwrights, and the survival of this outpouring in print, in itself attests to the commercialisation of theatre companies, notably the attractions of longer stays in London, and to the success of printed playtexts in the developing publishing industry.

Surveys of the printed playtexts show that authors were rarely credited on the title pages of plays in the Elizabethan years, where 'less than twenty percent of the extant published plays featured the name of the author' and common-born authors were even less often recognised on the cover.[51] It was

---

49 Gurr, *The Shakespearian Playing Companies*, 105.
50 Chambers, *The Elizabethan Stage*, I, 336.
51 Brooks, *From Playhouse to Printing House*, 10; McMillin, 'Professional playwrighting', in Kastan (ed.), *A Companion to Shakespeare*, 225–38.

much more usual to find an acknowledgement of the company which owned and performed the play. Recent studies from Brooks, Dutton and Masten have revealed that some playwrights were themselves investigating the nature of dramatic 'authorship' in prefaces, dedications and their printed works. The developing literary aspirations of dramatists, and the improving status of the dramatic poet, perhaps find their most extreme expression in the rash of courtly or amateur writers for the stage during the Caroline period, who are cruelly mocked by the professional Brome. He styles himself simply:

> Our Playmaker (for yet he won't be call'd
> Author, or Poet) nor beg to be install'd
> Sir Lawreat)
> (*The Damoiselle* Prologue, lines 1–3)

The telling possessiveness of that 'our' in the mouth of the player runs through many of the prologues and inductions of the century written, of course, by the playmakers themselves. Even Jonson, the most aspirational of poets, at the very moment he draws up a contract with the audience as the 'author' of *Bartholomew Fair*, also figures himself as in the theatre with Lady Elizabeth's Men, the listening poet 'behind the arras',[52] just as he had offered his putative, sweating presence in the tiring house in the induction to *Cynthia's Revels* (1600). A residual anti-theatrical prejudice has too often encouraged us to think of a dramatic author as a literary specialist who diversified from poetry, translation or the more down-market pamphlet writing, into dramatic form. What benefits or insights might we gain by thinking of the professional playwright as a company employee or factotum? In the light of the evidence left us in company documents, manuscript playtexts and printed plays from the period, how are we to interpret the relationships between playwright and theatre company?

Playwriting could be a lucrative activity. As McMillin estimates, leading companies were paying £5 to £6 for a play in 1598, as much as 'a run-of-the-mill writer of "fine" literature might earn' in a year.[53] In 1614 Henslowe's papers indicate that he had negotiated, on behalf of Lady Elizabeth's Men, to pay Robert Daborne £20 for his play, although this sum may have included the price of making up a 'fayr written' playbook and production costs.[54] By the 1630s it seems that Richard Brome was regularly earning £20 a play. Lack of company documentation makes it difficult to assess whether these later prices were paid to playwrights across the board. It seems unlikely that inflation

---

52 Ben Jonson, *Bartholomew Fair*, Induction l.8
53 McMillin, 'Professional playwrighting', 227.
54 Carson, *A Companion to Henslowe's Diary*, 55.

would account for the four-fold increase, so does the higher cost indicate an increase in the value of a playtext to a company? This at a time when the market for new plays was reduced as companies found revivals of stock favourites an effective financial alternative. Whatever the significance of this improved sum, in 1635 Brome thought it worth his while to forgo one-off payments for a regular salary and a benefit day. It is true that, although the price per play or contribution to writing was always healthy, the vagaries of playing, plague and prohibition meant that few dramatists managed to live within their means, or to subsist entirely on income from playwriting. The more economically successful playwrights tended to be linked to companies for stretches of time although these were rarely monogamous relationships (see Roslyn Knutson in this volume). Shakespeare is unusual in writing almost all plays after 1594 for one company, the Chamberlain's / King's Men. His position as a company shareholder made this a more effective economic proposition, as it did for Thomas Heywood.

The language we use about playwrights from the period tends to imply that they fell into two groups, the contracted and the freelance. It is difficult to assess whether this is true and to weigh up the significance of those categories if it is. Although Henslowe's papers are peppered with contracts with players, there are none with playwrights. The two agreements with Porter and Chettle are not contracts, but bonds against their debts with the Admiral's Men. In terms of documented evidence for contracts, there appear to be only two. One dates from the early stages of the profession, in 1572, when Lawrence and John Dutton, freemen weavers, and Thomas Gough, barber surgeon, all players with Sir Robert Lane's company, and later with the Earl of Lincoln, entered into contract requiring Rowland Broughton of London to supply them with some eighteen plays over the course of the next thirty months for a company of boy players to be set up. Although it is not clear whether Broughton was contracted to write them or simply to supply them, the matter was serious enough to take to law when difficulties arose.[55] Interestingly this illustrates that the market for playtexts was exploding even prior to the settled emergence of multiple London playhouses and longer spells in one place. It was the formation of a new company that produced an increased need for repertoire.

The other playwright's contract is at the other end of our period, and is of quite a different nature. Depositions about Richard Brome's contracts of 1635 and 1638 illustrate two radical innovations. Firstly, Brome seems to have been directly contracted to the impresario Richard Heton rather than to a

55 Benbow, 'Dutton and Goffe versus Broughton', *REED Newsletter* (1981), 1–9.

company of sharers. This chimes with the breakdown of traditional company organisation and licensing under Charles I that we have noted above. Secondly, Brome was paid a weekly salary, rather than price per play. This was a departure from the usual method of working, and, judging from the lawsuit, one which didn't take. Despite the salary, Brome sold a play to Beeston for a fee in the old way and eventually rejected his contractual obligation, moving to Beeston at the Cockpit.[56] Broadly speaking almost all playwrights were free agents, employed on a job-by-job basis. This was a cheaper way of operating for companies and allowed them to draw on the talents of a wide range of writers. Playwrights were not sharers in a company unless they were also performers as even Shakespeare, however unimpressively, was.

Thomas Heywood offers a good example of the complex connection that might exist between playwright and company. His first theatrical connection seems to have been with the Admiral's Men as a playwright, when they borrowed 30 shillings in 1596 to purchase 'hawodes bocke'. Two years later they hired him as a player and 'covenante searvante for ii yeares'.[57] By 1602 Heywood had transferred allegiance to Worcester's Men, where he was registered as a shareholder. He wrote for them and played for them too. We have some record of his dealings with the company through their stay at the Rose where Henslowe was landlord. In February 1602/3 Heywood was writing a new play, *A Woman Killed with Kindness*. Before the final instalment was delivered Henslowe records:

> pd unto Thomas hewode the 5 of febreary 1602 for A womones gowne of black velluett for the playe of A womon kylld with kyndnes some of vi li 13 s.[58]

Perhaps Heywood's position as sharer might explain in part his sense of responsibility towards the production, but was it also as playwright that he became a procurer of costumes?

Heywood's case also illustrates the extent to which a playwright was not owner of his own labour. In the preface to *The English Traveller* (1633) he explains the absence of a collected works since 'many of them by shifting and change of Companies, have been negligently lost, Others of them are still retained in the hands of some Actors, who thinke it against their peculiar profit to have them come in Print, and a third, That it never was any great ambition in me to bee in this kind Voluminously read'.[59] Even as a sharer in Worcester's / Queen

---

56 Haaker, 'The plague, the theater, and the poet', *Renaissance Drama*, n.s. 1 (1968), 283–306.
57 McLuskie, *Dekker and Heywood*, 2.
58 Rutter, *Documents of the Rose Playhouse*, 209.
59 Brooks, *From Playhouse to Printing House*, 194.

Anne's Men, he was not able to ensure possession of his own plays. The curious notion of individual player-sharers holding on to plays from the companies' repertoire is also illustrated by Henslowe's accounts. The Admiral's Men had to rescue five playbooks from Martin Slater after his retirement in July 1597, and in January 1599 *Vayvode* was bought back from the retired Edward Alleyn for 40 shillings, when Chettle probably revised it for performance.

There has been much debate about the apparent conflict between performers and playwrights at the turn of the seventeenth century, cultivated largely by the university wits, who were moaning about their lack of recompense, and by those pitted against the stage for religious or political reasons, like Henry Crosse, who wished that the 'admired wittes of this age, Tragaedians, and Comaedians, that garnish Theaters with their inuentions, would spend their wittes in more profitable studies, and leave off to maintain those Anticks, and Puppets, that speake out of their mouthes'.[60] Of course, theatre writing might be a profitable study. By James's reign the professional and commercial imperative of playmaking was ironically glossed by Dekker, who commented on the industry in *The Gull's Hornbook* (1609):

> The theatre is your poets Royal Exchange upon which their Muses – that are now turned to merchants – meeting barter away that light commodity of words for a lighter ware than words – plaudits . . . Players are their factors who put away the stuff and make the best of it they possibly can.[61]

Dekker continued to insinuate an economic conflict between players and playwrights in his pamphlet work, as in the address to the reader of *The Wonderful Year*, where he presents the players as 'ingratiating hacks, careless of the value of the work they perform'.[62] This demonstrates that he was able to pitch the tone of a best-selling pamphlet as cannily as his best-selling plays. Bemoaning the players' economic success at the expense of the impoverished playwright became an almost conventional trope and appears again, most ironically in Heywood's *Divers Crab-tree Lectures* as late as 1639, where a wife goads her poet husband:

> The first step to beggary, is to write for the stage. The players . . . have the wit to keep you poor that they themselves may prank it in plush.[63]

Brome inverts the conventional position in the epilogue to *Court Beggar*, where he has Swaynwit, a blunt country gentleman whose juicy insults have enlivened

60 Rutter, *Documents of the Rose Playhouse*, 216.
61 Pendry, *Thomas Dekker*, 98.
62 McLuskie, *Dekker and Heywood*, 3.
63 Edwards et al., *The Revels History of Drama in English*, iv, 36.

the play, complain about begging on behalf of a playwright whom the players have already paid. Overall it seems extremely unlikely that the playwrights' venom was truly aimed at the companies and players who paid for their wares.

So to what extent were the playwrights independent creative thinkers, generating material as the mood took them? There is certainly evidence that playwrights pitched ideas to companies, as in Jonson's bid to the Admiral's Men in the fall of 1597, following his release from prison after the *Isle of Dogs* affair, to write 'a boocke which he showed the plotte unto the company'.[64] However, the popularity, and high frequency, of sequels gives some indication of the extent to which the market the companies perceived for themselves and their texts conditioned what they requested from playwrights. Not only did linked plays seem a canny commercial move – Heywood's *Age* plays are an extreme example – where runs of connected titles followed a successful offering, but they sometimes revived an old play with an up-to-date follow-on, as Fletcher did with his sequel to *The Taming of the Shrew* in the 1620s.[65] There is evidence that plays originally planned as solo pieces were adapted to allow for a sequel. Albert Tricomi argues that this happened to *Bussy d'Ambois*, and Edward Rasmussen argues that *Troilus and Cressida* was revised to keep Troilus alive for the sequel.[66]

Companies and playtexts

The significance of the playtext to a company changed over time. In the Elizabethan and Jacobean period there is no support for the idea that companies routinely pirated each others' plays, or that printing a text contributed to this. As Richard Dutton suggests, licence to perform a play rested with a specific company.[67] Prior to publication playwrights themselves might try to sell, and occasionally succeed in selling, the same play to different companies but this might well result in legal action. The regularity with which companies revisited similar source material or topics, which were then crafted by playwrights to suit their particular style or audience, also throws into question the notion of piracy from printed texts – why run the risk of invoking the Master of the Revels' wrath for unlicensed performance, if you could ask for your own

64 Rutter, *Documents of the Rose Playhouse*, 126.
65 Gurr, *The Shakespearian Playing Companies*, 86.
66 Tricomi, 'The revised *Bussy D'Ambois* and *The Revenge of Bussy D'Ambois*', *English Language Notes* 9 (1972), 233–45; Rasmussen, 'The revision of scripts', in Cox and Kastan (eds.), *A New History of English Drama*, 460.
67 Dutton, 'The birth of the author', in Brown and Marotti (eds.), *Texts and Cultural Change in Early Modern England*, 155.

play on a popular topic?[68] A rare exception becomes a moment of theatrical irony in the induction to *The Malcontent*, where Condell and Burbage, playing themselves at the Globe, explain how they acquired a play from the Blackfriars' Boys:

> CONDELL: Faith, sir, the book was lost, and because 'twas pity so good a play
>   should be lost, we found it and play it.
> SLY: I wonder you would play it, another company having an interest in it.
> CONDELL: Why not Malevole in folio with us, as Jeronimo in decimo-sexto
>   with them? They taught us a name for our play: we call it *One for Another*.
>
> (Induction lines 89–97)

If plays were the valued property of theatre companies rather than authors, what are the implications of this for the way we view the playtext? The playtext as a printed object, complete, stable and authorised, was a chimera. The texts of plays were working documents and company stock and were primarily experienced in pieces, or as a collection of 'writings', including, perhaps, compositional sections from collaborative hands (such as Dekker's 'two sheetes of paper conteyning the first Act of a Play' which was to become *Keep the Widow Waking*, submitted in September 1624), the playbook with cuts, additions and revisions, actors' parts, the tiring-house plot, and property writings, like letters.[69] The printed playtext captured one version of a text that took a multiplicity of forms over time, and editors of early modern drama have battled with the complexities ever since.

In the composition and the revision of texts, collaboration was the norm rather than the exception. We know that even Shakespeare collaborated (with Fletcher, Middleton and the largely forgotten George Wilkins). Much of our understanding of how collaboration between playwrights worked comes from studying Henslowe's *Diary* and papers, and is discussed by Knutson in this volume. A playwright's input to a collaborative writing task might range from a plot or scenario to the writing of multiple acts, involve as little as a speech, prologue or epilogue or as much as the co-ordination and binding together of elements into a full version. Even when writing solo works, the playwright is not often figured as a solitary literary creature 'close in his studie writing hard' as John Day ironically paints himself.[70] The dramatist's study was rarely the closeted space of meditation and solitude. Kyd shared a room with Marlowe, as his anxious deposition about 'wrytinge in one chamber twoe yeares since'

---

68 Knutson, *The Repertory of Shakespeare's Company*, 168–77.
69 Bentley, *The Jacobean and Caroline Stage*, III, 255.
70 John Day, *Isle of Gulls*, induction, line 22.

records. This sharing of space with another writer or performer had become romantic orthodoxy in the minds of Restoration commentators, in Aubrey's account of Beaumont and Fletcher who 'lived together on the Bank side', and Kirkman's admiration for the hard-working Heywood who 'not only Acted almost every day, but also obliged himself to write a sheet everyday ... but many of his Playes being composed and written loosely in Taverns occasions them to be so mean'.[71]

If we are to think of the professional playwright as closely linked to the company he is writing for, we might not only wonder about collaboration with other writers, but also wonder about collaboration with actors in the creation of performance. Firstly, we could note that many individuals who considered themselves primarily as actors also wrote for their companions, in particular those who gained a reputation for themselves as clowns. Henslowe's papers also show 'players' collaborating with 'playwrights'. For example, the debacle of *The Isle of Dogs*, despite the frustrating loss of the text, indicates an intimate interaction between company and playwright. Nashe defends himself by protesting: 'I having begun the induction and first act of it, the other foure acts ... by the players were supplied.'[72] The suppliers were probably Jonson, Gabriel Spencer and Robert Shaa, and the Privy Council imprisoned one of the actors of the piece because he was 'not only an actor but a maker of parte of the same plaie'.[73] Secondly, when plays were revived or had been in production for some time, was it only playwrights who offered revisions? Masten has suggested that actors revised scripts in ways that may not have eventually registered in the text we have.[74] For example, both McMillin and Rasmussen make a strong case for reading the interpolations from 'Hand B' in the manuscript version of *The Book of Sir Thomas More* as those that a scribe jotted down from memory of the Clown's improvisations, when the play was revived several years later and the Elizabethan vogue for improvisatory clowns was on the wane.[75] Finally, in attempting to understand the text as material generated quickly and rehearsed immediately and briefly, there is also an inevitable question of improvisation. Rasmussen argues that the clown figure in *Sir Thomas More*, without 'Hand B', would be silent in the text, indicating room for improvisation. As we have seen there are also occasional stage directions for plays as late as 1611, which leave room for extemporisation.

71 Cited in Masten, 'Playwrighting: authorship and collaboration', in Cox and Kastan (eds.), *A New History of English Drama*, 360, 365; Brooks, 194.
72 Nashe, *Works*, ed. McKerrow, III, 154.
73 Ibid., v, 311n.
74 Masten, 'Beaumont and/or Fletcher', *English Literary History*, 59 (1992), 344, 350.
75 Rasmussen, 'Setting down what the clown spoke', 130, 135.

So the audiences may have heard more or different text in performance from that which we have preserved on the page, sometimes to the horror of the dramatists on site. A hint that this might be the case comes from Edward Pudsey's commonplace book, where he records lines substantially different from those in the printed texts of the plays we have today. Was this a case of Pudsey's poor memory, or preference for his own coinage, or a suggestion that what was printed and what was spoken might differ?[76]

After their costumes, the playbook was the most valuable capital asset a company had, and possession of the book seems in the early years to have been mainly with company shareholders. The ambiguous wording of Henslowe's *Diary* seems to imply that Henslowe as manager 'was in possession of a set of playbooks which he loaned along with his playhouse to the visiting companies. Unfortunately . . . there is nothing to say if he rented such playbooks out or whether they were freely available with the playhouse.'[77] This would explain why some plays, notably *The Jew of Malta*, seem to have travelled from company to company. McMillin argues that the book was rather the property of Henslowe's son-in-law, Alleyn, and travelled with him.[78] If Henslowe did own the books, and it seems uncharacteristically unprofitable that he did not take the opportunity to rent them separately and more widely if he did, it would be an early example of what would later be a feature of the impresario management style of entrepreneurs like Christopher Beeston and Richard Heton during the Caroline era.

The financial significance of the playbook was not diminished over time. In 1615 actors from Lady Elizabeth's company drew up a long complaint against Henslowe, their administrator, accusing him among other things of keeping the manuscripts for which they had paid £200, as well as their costumes. The Shrove Tuesday riot of 1617 in the newly completed Phoenix damaged not only the building belonging to Queen Anne's company, but more seriously the apprentices cut 'the players apparell all in pieces, and all other theyre furniture and burnt theyre play bookes'.[79] Likewise, Palsgrave's Men suffered a considerable setback after fire destroyed the Fortune (1621) and 'all their apparell and play-bookes lost, wherby those poore companions are quite undon'.[80] These glimpses suggest that playbooks were stored in the theatre when a company was in London, and travelled with the company on tour, in part because the

76 Bodleian MS Eng. Poet.D.3.
77 Gurr, *The Shakespearian Playing Companies*, 95.
78 McMillin, 'Sussex's Men in 1594', *Theatre Survey*, 32 (1991), 214–23.
79 Edwards et al., *The Revels History of Drama in English*, IV, 87, 90.
80 Gurr, *The Shakespearian Playing Companies*, 249.

Master of the Revels' signature in the book was a guarantee of the play's, and players', legitimacy. It seems very unlikely that an established company would tour with all its books, but only those they were keeping in the repertoire. The rather high number of books (fourteen) the Salisbury Court company toured with in 1634, Gurr considers, was an indication of their disquiet about the security of their London playhouse.[81] Once a play had dropped out of the repertoire the book became less significant and printers who later required the texts to publish ran into difficulties. Humphrey Moseley reports his trials in tracking down Beaumont and Fletcher's *Wild Goose Chase* for the folio of 1647, since 'a Person of Quality borrowed it from the Actors' and never returned it. The actors obliged by recording what they actually played, perhaps an indication that a real old favourite needed no book, since its performance was almost second nature to a stable troupe.[82] This might challenge the notion that the loss of the book, say in a fire as the Palsgrave's Men experienced in July 1623, necessarily meant the loss of repertoire. Although the troupe commissioned thirteen new plays in the following eighteen months, of which shareholder Gunnell and actor Rowley provided five, this was not necessarily the sum total of their repertoire, since the company was able to tour during this period with something.

The only extant actor's part from the professional theatre is Edward Alleyn's role for Orlando in Greene's *Orlando Furioso*, preserved in Dulwich College. There is evidence that professional players' practice was echoed in the amateur sphere by players at university.[83] The play was probably read through to the company, but after that the 'parts' system offered no further sense of overview of the play to the actors. There is even the hint in Henslowe's papers that the actors were given their roles and presumably began learning them before hearing the whole play, or before the play was finished. Robert Daborne's heartfelt note to Henslowe in the summer of 1613 records 'I have took extraordynary payns with the end and altered one other sean in the third act which they have now in parts.'[84] To what extent this hampered the players is not clear. For example, Carnegie's study of play parts for university production finds there is enough material in the part of 'Poore' to reconstruct a fairly detailed plot summary for the lost play. One distinction that Carnegie notes between amateur and professional parts, is that the university actor had longer cue phrases

81 Ibid., 429.
82 Dutton, 'The birth of the author', 169.
83 Carnegie, 'Actors' parts and the "Play of Poore"', *Harvard Library Bulletin*, 30:1 (1982), 5–24.
84 Greg (ed.), *Henslowe Papers*, 73.

than Alleyn's roll with its two-word introductions. Carnegie argues that this might have offered the university actor time for a 'more consistent characterization or a more coherent reaction to plot action than minimal parts and negligible rehearsal time would have allowed his professional counterpart'.[85] This intriguing suggestion seems to imply, somewhat contentiously, that the university thus produced better-based acting than the professional theatre. The induction to *Antonio and Mellida*, when the boys enter in a liminal state, dressed as their characters but 'with parts in their hands', hints at ways in which the professional stage might have fleshed out the single role through discussion and complex conventional understandings. The profession had effective short-hand mechanisms which must have been part of the working life of the company, like the 'plot'. There are several extant plots, which Bradley has analysed, but which might have come into existence in the most casual way, as suggested by a 'doodle' of a plot preserved in the Alleyn collection, which was made by Robert Shaa in November 1599 while listening to the reading of a play about the flight and capture of the Duke of Buckingham and the landing of Henry Richmond.[86]

Although in the Elizabethan playhouse not many plays stayed in the repertoire more than a year, as the companies continued to play there were many revivals and old favourites recurred.[87] By the 1630s the King's Men were not buying more than three or four new plays a year, compared with the twenty or more of the 1590s, since they had almost all of Shakespeare's work, nearly all of Beaumont and Fletcher, and much of Massinger, Middleton and Jonson.[88] Playwrights often revamped their own work; for example Heywood worked up or rather cut down his *Age* Red Bull plays for Beeston's Cockpit in the 1620s. Although we have very few manuscript playbooks in which the evidence of cutting, additions and revisions remain, Ingram offers a timely reminder of the economic imperative behind paper-saving devices of cutting, pasting and writing in the margins of these books, since 'the paper alone in the *Sir Thomas More* manuscript thus represents an investment, in modern terms, of almost £20'.[89] Paul Werstine and William Long have done much to aid modern interpretation of the manuscript playbooks and the playhouse practices of revision and addition that they reveal, which offers fresh challenge to the modern editorial presentation of Renaissance playtexts.

---

85 Carnegie, 'Actor's parts and the "Play of Poore" ', 13.
86 Foakes and Rickert (eds.), *Henslowe's Diary*, 287–8.
87 Knutson, *The Repertory of the Shakespeare's Company*, 33.
88 Bentley, *The Jacobean and Caroline Stage*, I, 108–34.
89 Ingram, *The Business of Playing*, 37.

Companies and the audience: in touch with the audience

For all the importance of the company, patron and playwright, one of the most significant factors in shaping a piece of theatre, both in the writing and performing, was the audience. The development of professional theatre in England over the period to 1660 charts an ironic trajectory from household performance, either courtly or noble, through the entrepreneurial development of commercial touring routes and function-specific buildings, to surreptitious household performance once more during the Interregnum. As the plays themselves indicate, and playgoing records suggest, audiences differed considerably in these various contexts, in size, composition and the kind of relationships a group of performers might be able to forge and maintain with their spectators.

Although a little earlier than the period we are looking at here, we have two plays from Henry Medwall, writer and notary in the household of Archbishop Morton, which vividly demonstrate the sophisticated actor–audience relationships available in household performance. Possibly written for the Christmas entertainment honouring the Flemish and Spanish ambassadors in 1491, *Fulgens and Lucrece* was designed to set off a day of eating and to celebrate a specific event for a specific audience. The performers were probably chapel choristers from the archbishop's household, professionals in their way, highly skilled in singing and with the full resources of the household at their disposal. In the banqueting hall, with the full range of household members and dignitaries gathered under the eye of their patron and employer, the performers were able to game with the audience very freely. Two actors, A and B, begin as audience members, eager for the players to arrive, but gradually take on tasks within the fiction. Part II, after the banquet, starts with a long prologue by actor A who grows increasingly uncomfortable when left on his own to entertain the hall audience. At last, with relief, he cries:

> A: Ah! There cometh one, I hear him knock
> He knocketh as he were wood.
> One of you go look who it is.
>
> *Enter B*
> B: Nay, nay, all the meinie of them I wis
> Cannot so much good:
> A man may rap till his nails ache
> Or any of them will the labour take
> To give him an answer.

> A: I have great marvel on thee
> That ever thou wilt take upon thee
> To chide any man here.
> No man is so much to blame as thou
> For long tarrying.
>
> (Part II, lines 73–85)

This instruction to answer the door, addressed to an unsuspecting audience member, punctures any notion of a distinction between the 'stage world' and the audience-crammed banqueting hall. The gag is beautifully written, so that, whether the unfortunate audience member starts across to the door or not, B's entry in gloomy bad temper still works. Later, as A and B move from their roles as actors and prologuers to figures within the fiction of the text as retained servants, they maintain this possibility of direct interaction with the audience. A offers an even more physically compelling threat to the audience, when he loses a love letter from his master that he was supposed to deliver to Lucrece:

> And here he sendeth you a letter –
> God's mercy I had it right now.
> Sirs, is there none there among you
> That took up such a writing?
> I pray you, sirs, let me have it again.
>
> (Part II, lines 324–328)

Thinking he has lost it on his way into the hall, he goes back to interrogate the audience members he brushed past on his entry. The physical proximity of the audience, on the same level as the performers and packed into the hall on all sides, offers a thrilling theatrical moment in performance.

Medwall takes the idea even further in *Nature*, probably written and performed around 1495–1500. Once again in Morton's banqueting hall, Worldly Affection, left on his own while Pride takes Man to try on new clothes, decides to warm his hands by the hall's fire and, in the absence of stage furniture and stage servants, orders an audience member:

> Get me a stole Here may ye not se
> Or ellys a chayr Wyll yt not be
> thou pyld knave! I speke to the
> How long shall I stande?

If the performers were indeed members of the chapel, presumably the man playing Worldly Affection would be able to make even more of this joke in his choice of the particular spectator who becomes the 'pyld knave'. Both these plays, and others designed primarily for household performance, are bold in their direct address and the physical integration of the spectators. John Heywood's *The Play of the Weather* (*c.* 1528), with an evening performance by boys, possibly for Henry VIII, has actors push past into the performing space, as Merry Report insists 'let me go by ye, Thynke ye I may stand thrustyng amonge you there?', and elsewhere the Vice instructs a servant standing nearby 'Brother, hold up your torch a little higher!' so that he is better lit. More than merely an acknowledgement of the theatrical event, these plays demand physical intervention from the audience, and presuppose a well-behaved gathering, who would not take this licence to intrude upon the playing space and fiction too far. If banter or talking back was expected by the performers it does not find its way into the text, either in instruction to the performers or in the provision of jokes or action to recover the initiative for the stage players. Pieces written specifically for household and courtly performance throughout the period allow physical interaction between audience and performers; at its most tame, the invitation to dance at the end of the masque, more boldly, Nashe's entertainment for Archbishop Whitgift in 1592 displays many of these games with the audience through the figure of Will Summers.

To what extent there was cross-over in personnel between household players and the professional troupes that were retained by nobles is difficult to assess. However, many noble households of the Tudor period expected to be entertained by professional players, either those they maintained themselves or those who visited them. It is difficult to trace the texts used by specific early troupes, but the plays undoubtedly drew on the conventions of household playing as well as the popular tropes of mystery plays, carnival, contest plays and mummings. The Tudor playtexts we have, which were 'offered for acting' probably by these professional troupes, employ a presentational style of performance and plenty of direct address to the audience. In the Edwardian interlude *Lusty Juventus*, the eponymous anti-hero enters singing to the audience and in lieu of his friends, or players, asks the spectators:

> Is there any man here that wil go to game.
> At what soever he wyl play
> To make one, I am ready to the same . . .
> Who knoweth where there is ere a mynstrell,
> By the masse I would fayne go daunce a fitte.
> (lines 58–60, 64–5)

It is not only the hero or the Vice who addresses the audience; Good Councell introduces Knowledge to Juventus, but Knowledge turns to address the 'good christian audience' and introduces himself to them a second time. In *Wealth and Health*, probably written for Queen Mary's interluders early in her reign, the cheerful Wealth and Health roll in singing a ballad to introduce themselves, after which Wealth upbraids the docile audience:

> Why is there no curtesy, now I am come
> I trowe that all the people be dume
> Or els so go helpe me and halydum
> They were almost a sleepe.
> No wordes I harde, nor yet no talking
> No instruments went nor ballattes synging
> What ailes you all thus to syt dreaming
> Of whom take ye care?
> Of my coming ye may be glad.   (lines 1–9)

This bold opening of a potential dialogue with the audience suggests skilled performers, ready to extemporise, and a relatively containable audience. The troupes on their travels might indeed have played in households or guild halls, where the presence of grandees and the context of a small audience of guests, or communities of known individuals, might account for the surprising need for the actors to wake up their audience. If the performers also offered these texts in inn-rooms or on trestle stages in the yards, what kind of audience could have resisted the opportunity to respond?

Once the troupes were travelling more widely and developing commercial audiences in London the function of the spectators and the kind of audience itself changed. Like the outdoor playing spaces in inns, the new playhouses in London all utilised a raised stage and offered a range of seating, altering the physical possibilities of the actor–audience relationship. The last bastion of household-style playing, the boys at St Paul's, introduced a raised stage in their tiny auditorium when it was revamped and reopened in the late 1590s. Even in the intimacy of the indoor playhouses physical interaction with a privileged audience was no longer invited, as *The Knight of the Burning Pestle* illustrates in vibrant satiric form. Once the stage was established, entering the same playing space as the actors was considered riotous disorder, 'the spectators frequently mounting the stage, and making a more bloody Catastrophe amongst themselves then the players did'.[90] Although Gayton suggests that such 'mutinus attemptes' occurred every holiday, records imply that they were more probably very occasional events, usually as part of the upending behaviour of Shrove Tuesday riots.[91]

---

90 Gayton, *Pleasant Notes upon Don Quixote*, p. 271.
91 Cook, 'Audiences', in Cox and Kastan (eds.), *A New History of English Drama*, 313.

The only permitted sharing of the playing space was the commercially successful habit of allowing selected individuals to have a stool on stage. These audience members were not invited by the performers to participate in the fictional or theatrical world; indeed they were vilified for any attempt to engage with the action. Stage-sitters were most often pictured on the private theatre stage as the 'twelve penny stool Gentlemen',[92] and are explicitly referred to in inductions to *Cynthia's Revels* (1600–1), to Marston's *What You Will* (1601), or John Day's *Isle of Gulls* (1606). However, Dekker's satiric advice in *The Gull's Hornbook* also hints that the public stages employed the practice. The young gull is to pay 'the gatherers of the public or private playhouse' and 'advance himself up to the throne of the stage'. It is difficult to assess which 'public' houses used the practice, since it seems that the Globe did not encourage the custom, as Webster's additional induction to *The Malcontent* (1604) implies. Although this induction at the Globe opened with the tireman following an errant audience member onto the stage with a stool as if to seat him, the tireman warns him that the 'gentlemen will be angry if you sit here'. The audience member, played by Will Sly, wonders why since 'We may sit upon the stage at the private house.' Later in the same speech, Sly indicates why it might have been less common practice in the public arena: 'Dost think I fear hissing?'. The mechanisms of household control did not apply in this commercial setting, where the stage audience were rather too keen to perform themselves, distract attention from the play or, worse, to leave. As Dekker implies, it must often have been the 'scarecrows in the yard' who controlled the stage gallants, by hissing or catcalling if they proved too distracting.

Although the *gentleman* stool-sitter is most often pictured, there are also suggestions, admittedly in satiric portraits, that the Jacobean stage stools were not necessarily monopolised in terms of class or gender, theatres 'allowing a stool as well to the farmer's son as to your Templar'.[93] It was the citizen's wife who sat on stage with her husband in *The Knight of the Burning Pestle*, and in Jonson's late play *The Staple of News* (1625), four gossips come to take up their places and comment on the action. The inconvenience of seats on stage did not quell the practice, although playwrights complain about the absence of 'elbow-room'.[94] Jonson's prologue to *The Devil is an Ass* in 1616, is still moaning:

92 *Roaring Girl*, 2.1.151.
93 Pendry, *Thomas Dekker*, 98.
94 Ibid., 101.

Yet, grandees, would you were not come to grace
Our matter, with allowing us no place . . .
Do not on these presumptions force us act,
In compass of a cheese-trencher . . .
. . . When you will thrust and spurn,
And knock us o' the elbows, and bid turn;
As if, when we had spoke, we must be gone . . .

(lines 3–4, 7–8, 11–13)

In John Jones's *Adrasta*, as late as 1635, the Prologue enters and promptly falls over a gentleman seated on stage. The professional playing troupe clearly found sharing a stage space in the playhouses with self-aggrandising gallants or self-righteous citizens less of a delight. One wonders how these induction sequences and pointed remarks might have been taken by those audience members already settled on their stools on stage.

Regulating the house

Questions about the social make-up of the London playhouse audiences during the period have been fought to an impasse by Cook, Gurr and Butler, who all agree that, whatever the relative significance of elite, citizen or 'mechanick' attenders, most audiences were heterogeneous. No longer were these playgoers, particularly in the outdoor houses, self-regulated by hierarchical structures of household obligation or the presence of civic and guild dignitaries, patrons or employers. This, coupled with the increased capacity and, we must assume, the size of the audience a group might play to in the new purpose-built playing spaces, argues strongly for the necessity of a different actor–audience interaction, out of sheer self-preservation. Westfall suggests that in the portrayal of actor–audience interaction in *Hamlet*, *The Taming of the Shrew* and *A Midsummer Night's Dream*, Shakespeare:

> may betray the irritation of a dramatist writing in a time when the aesthetics of response were beginning to change, when players were beginning to resent audience invasion of the stage space, when dramatists were attempting to close the stage, to encourage suspension of disbelief rather than the reverent and absolute identification of the liturgical form.[95]

In work written for the commercial houses, direct address by *players* to audiences is more often contained by induction sections, prologues, epilogues and

95 Westfall, *Patrons and Performance*, 133.

occasional choral commentaries. However, this might well have been driven less by resentment and a tendency towards the illusory than by the pragmatics of a changed audience and setting. Moreover, 'characters' continue to be written with address to the audience through soliloquy, asides and rhetorical tropes. The development of acting styles and the potential of actor–character relationships on the Tudor and Jacobean stages have been discussed by Lesley Soule, who argues that for audiences the person of the actor was never fully subsumed by the persona or character. Thomson in this volume touches on these ideas in the figure of the clown and fool. Not yet accustomed to illusionistic playing, the audience was always aware of both the performer and the part. Satirists note the tendency of the player to share with the audience; even 'when he doth hold conference upon the stage; and should looke directly in his fellows face; hee turnes about his voice into the assembly for applause-sake'.[96] In *A Mad World My Masters*, Sir Bounteous finds this kind of overt playing to the audience ridiculous, when the real Constable unwittingly arrives on stage in the middle of a play and tries to address him:

> To me? Puh, turn to th'justice, you whoreson hobby horse! This is some new player now; they put all their fools to the constable's part still.   (5.2.82–4)

Most performers, whatever the pejorative language of the satiric prologues and epilogues, must have relished the power of contact with the audience in performance.

In playing to the commercial, masterless audience, one method of monitoring and containing potential audience responses was fully to acknowledge and discuss them. What could be more satisfying for the audience at the Fortune than to be inspected by the actor/characters on stage in *The Roaring Girl*. The character of Sir Anthony shows off his 'galleries – How bravely they are trimmed up' and 'below, / The very floor, as 'twere, waves to and fro, / And like a floating island, seems to move / Upon a sea bound in with shores above' (1.2.14–15, 29–32), before arranging the characters on stage and settling down to tell his story to both on- and offstage audiences. The prologues, induction sequences and epilogues are full of commentary about spectators, assuring them that they have been noticed by the performers, although not always in complimentary terms. Sly, playing an audience member in the induction to *The Malcontent*, ponders with the actors John Lowin and Henry Condell:

---

96 Cited in Gurr, *Playgoing in Shakespeare's London*, 237.

SLY: I do use to meditate much when I come to plays, too. What do you think
    might come into a man's head now, seeing all this company?
CONDELL: I know not, sir.
SLY: I have an excellent thought: if some fifty of the Grecians that were
    crammed in the horse-belly had eaten garlic, do you not think the Trojans
    might have smelt out their knavery?   (lines 134–41)

In these metatheatrical moments, players and playwrights celebrate the audience's complicity in the theatrical exercise, that 'each one comes / And brings
a play in's head with him; up he sums / What he would of a roaring girl have
writ.'[97]

The writing of these introductory sections frequently attempted to manipulate audience expectations of the generic and theatrical content of the
afternoon: 'expect no noyse of Guns, Trumpets nor Drum, / No Sword and
Targuet; but to heare Sense and Words, / Fitting the Matter that the Scene
affords.'[98] The diverse tastes of the spectators were acknowledged either satir-
ically, 'Neither quick mirth, invective, nor high state, / Can content all: such
is the boundless hate / Of a confused Audience',[99] or apologetically, as the
players and playwrights attempted to reconcile them:

> The rest we crave, whom we unlettered call,
> Rather to attend then judge; for more than sight,
> We seek to please, the understanding eare
> Which we have hitherto most gracious found.[100]

That audience members, as well as performers, understood the potential of
these modes of direct address as controlling mechanisms is indicated in comments from theatregoers. For example, in one of Edmund Gayton's anecdotes,
he demonstrates just how anarchic a riotous theatre audience was when it
could not be quelled by the usual means:

> It was not then the most mimicall nor fighting man, *Fowler*, nor *Andrew Cane*
> could pacifie; Prologues nor Epilogues would prevaile; the Devill and the fool
> were quite out of favour.[101]

All of these elements imply direct address from a player. The reason that
the conventions of direct performer and character address persisted, particularly in introductory material, was surely that it offered the players space

97 *Roaring Girl*, prologue, lines 3–5.
98 *Two Merry Milkmaids* (1619), prologue, lines 2–4.
99 John Day, *Isle of Gulls*, induction, lines 140–3.
100 *The Brazen Age*, prologue.
101 Bentley, *The Jacobean and Caroline Stage*, II, 691.

to acknowledge and prepare audience expectations, to establish auditorium conventions and generate illustrations of optimal spectators or mockery of inappropriate audience behaviour as a way of building an orderly, attentive and responsive community of viewers and listeners.

However, the performers' attempts to control the auditorium were often severely stretched by their concomitant desire to provide a whole afternoon of entertainment. At the end of the play the theatre might suddenly fill even more, as the 'great multitude' show up for the 'lewde Jigges songes and daunces', which some managed to get in to see for free. The Middlesex General Session ruling of 1 October 1612 singled out the Fortune for its unhealthy attraction to the mass of 'ill disposed persons', but further attempted to ban all endpiece 'jigs, Rymes and dances' in all theatres.[102] The jig might follow any kind of play, comic or tragic. Thomas Platter's account spends longer describing the slipper jig he saw at an unnamed theatre than *Julius Caesar* at the Globe, surely not an indication that the jig was more theatrically stimulating? These were indeed, as Jonson had complained in his dedication of *Catiline* (1611), 'Jig-given times'.[103] A jig might well have contained bawdy references or political relevance, and was very likely to have involved moments of extempore performance and direct interaction with the audience. Certainly in the Elizabethan theatre there was often a jig, dance or rhymed 'song extempore' at the end, as the satirical figure of Posthaste promises, who finishes the piecemeal offering of Sir Oliver Owlet's men with a 'theame'.[104] Rasmussen takes a hint from Nashe's *Pierce Peniless* about 'the queint Comaedians of our time, / That when their Play is doone, do fal to ryme' and suggests that: 'Tarlton and Wilson won reputations for "themes" which seem to have been verse improvisations based upon topics suggested by the audience, performed at the conclusion of Elizabethan plays.'[105]

Calling for the jig, or the convention of audience interaction at the end of the play, continued well into the Jacobean and Caroline era, as Shirley's *The Changes* (1631) implies:

> Many gentlemen
> Are not, as in the days of understanding,
> Now satisfied without a Jig, which since
> They cannot with their honour, call for after
> The play, they look to be serv'd up in the middle.
>
> (4.2)

102 Edwards et al., *The Revels History of Drama in English*, IV, 82.
103 Brooks, *From Playhouse to Printing House*, 51.
104 *Histriomastix*, 2, 295–311.
105 Rasmussen, 'Setting down what the clown spoke', 128.

Jigs were often more politically daring and topical than the plays they followed; a phenomenon guaranteed to generate interest among audiences, drawing directly on the political and cultural world beyond the theatre experience.

Within the plays themselves spectatorship and playgoing are referred to regularly in metaphors and as indication of character. Sometimes theatregoing is a sign of good taste, as More's welcome to the touring players indicates in *Sir Thomas More*, or of sophistication in comparison with a country fellow who does not understand theatre conventions, as in Sly's confusion in *The Taming of the Shrew*. Just occasionally, attending performance is a symbol of ignorance, usually in choosing to watch the denigrated forms of jig or puppetry (as in Hamlet's rebuke to Polonius or Cokes's 'interrupting vapours' at *Bartholomew Fair*'s puppet show). There are frequent presentations of spectatorship by characters within the plays and this self-referential theatricality not only reflected on playmaking and performing, but also offered the audience satirical, entertaining or instructive pictures of themselves. The figure of the understanding audience member is presented on stage in ways as diverse as Jonson's chorus in *Every Man out of His Humour* (1599) and Brome's therapeutically driven theatregoers in *The Antipodes* (1638). These stage audiences occasionally comment on the interpretative work of spectatorship, with varying degrees of perspicuity. Sir Bounteous and Harebrain watch Follywit desperately improvising:

> HAREBRAIN: How moodily he walks! What plays he, troth?
> SIR BOUNTEOUS: A justice, upon my credit; I know by the chain there.
> FOLLYWIT: *Unfortunate justice!*
> SIR BOUNTEOUS: Ah-a-a-.[106]

Intriguingly, and no doubt to some extent due to staging pragmatics, almost all of the pictures of stage spectatorship are of orderly, yet commentating, small-scale audiences, often within noble or courtly communities, self-regulated by strict codes of hierarchy.

In London the practice of playgoing for noble and common audience members changed over the century. No longer an occasional event, theatregoing could now be an almost daily affair, and the diet of new plays of all kinds was seemingly unending. For the first time the commercial theatre offered opportunities for a theatre aficionado to emerge. Edward Pudsey's commonplace book notes lines from a range of Blackfriars plays of the turn of the century.[107] Most of the prologues and inductions, as well as the plays themselves, assume

---

106 *A Mad World My Masters*, 5.2.55–8.
107 Bodleian MS Eng. Poet.D.3.

a theatre-familiar audience, and cross-refer to characters and scenarios, actors and theatres. When characters within plays discuss going to the theatre, their observations tend to be written to draw knowing laughter from the audience. Inductions which celebrated the hidden realm of theatre backstage or in rehearsal, or generic debates, attest to the powerful attraction the idea of drama and theatricality itself had for an audience. The role of playgoing within culture was evolving. Theatregoing in London was more often about an individual's opportunity to exert economic power in leisure, to appreciate and be seen to appreciate significant cultural events or to indulge a fascination with the transformational narratives of the performers. It was much less a community event, or an activity designed to demonstrate respect for the nobleman whose company was visiting, or civic status through attendance at the mayor's show in the guildhall. Clearly established theatre conventions prevailed in the London playhouses, which set out to manage this audience of individuals carefully.

When the theatres closed in 1642 and it became clear that they were to remain closed for some time, household-style performance may have reappeared, with audience members rubbing shoulders more closely with performers in tavern rooms and private houses, as Cosmo Manuche's *Loyal Lovers* (1652) implies. James Wright recalls surreptitious private performance just outside London 'where the Nobility and Gentry who met (but in no great Numbers) used to make up a sum for [the actors]'.[108] The companies relied on word of mouth and often used their apprentices, like Alexander Goffe, as a 'Jackal' to gather and inform nobles of surreptitious performances. These can only have been very select gatherings, as the performances which may well have flourished in private country houses, as at the Earl of Northampton's seat at Castle Ashby, must have been. Rather more public affairs did still survive, with Beeston setting up a training school for boys in the old Cockpit, returning to the conceit that if boys were performing it was educational exercise rather than public theatre.[109] There is evidence of a broader, more boisterous audience which gathered at occasional performances that were allowed in one or two of the old playhouses, notably the Red Bull at fair time, and at unauthorised playings at other times.[110] Davenant managed to generate some income from several playhouses in the 1650s and his staging of 'operas' at Rutland House, in 1656 and after, might also count as private performance, although

108 Bentley, *The Jacobean and Caroline Stage*, ii, 695.
109 Hotson, *The Commonwealth and Restoration Stage*, 94–8.
110 Bentley, *The Jacobean and Caroline Stage*, ii, 695.

customers paid. Overall, these small and select audiences were probably more exclusive than those who had frequented the public playhouses in the pre-Interregnum years. Certainly the generic choices and content of the plays and the performers' relationship to this audience were modelled more consciously on courtly entertainments, for political as well as pragmatic reasons, as Janet Clare discloses in this volume.

6

Drama outside London after 1540

PETER H. GREENFIELD

Local dramatic activity

The dominant trend outside London from 1540 to 1642 was the disappearance of late medieval traditions of dramatic activity without the creation of new forms to replace them, so that by the time parliament prohibited public performing in 1642, very little remained. Economic distress in both provincial towns and rural areas contributed to the decline in dramatic activity outside the capital, but the Reformation had the greatest impact. In fact, to plot in space and time the suppression or abandoning of forms of entertainment ranging from biblical cycles and parish plays to king ales, maypoles and morris dancing is effectively to map the progress of the Reformation across the English landscape. That progress was gradual, at first affecting only those elements of the traditions that too obviously reflected Roman Catholic theology and practice. The feast of Corpus Christi was suppressed in 1548, forcing the biblical cycles to shift to Whitsun or some other convenient date, and some plays were dropped from the cycles around this time. The reign of the Catholic Mary Tudor briefly reversed the process in the mid 1550s, but when the Protestants returned to power with Elizabeth, they intensified their efforts to eradicate anything associated with the Roman church, eliminating the major cycle plays in the 1560s and 1570s. Other town- and parish-sponsored drama lasted as long, and often longer, especially in places remote from London. Eventually, however, the traditionalists gave way before the increasing numbers and power of those whom they called 'puritans', those who valued the sober industriousness of

---

* Much of the material used in this chapter has been drawn from the published and as yet unpublished findings of the Records of Early English Drama (REED) project, based at Victoria College, University of Toronto (where some of the unpublished documents are available for consultation). Published volumes are listed in the Works Cited section of the present volume. Unless there are special reasons to cite published volumes, only unpublished collections are listed in these notes. I am grateful to the editors of these collections for allowing me to see and refer to their findings.

the individual and the preaching of God's word over the festive communal rituals provided by the old dramatic traditions.

We know more about these traditions in their last decades than over the rest of their existence. Documents like churchwardens' accounts survive in much greater numbers from the second half of the sixteenth century than from before 1550. Such documents tell us something about dramatic activity when it was a regular, often annual feature of life, though they provide less detail than we would wish, since what is usual is unremarkable. Ironically, however, the attempts to suppress dramatic activity generated court cases and other documentary material that tell us a great deal about what people did and why they did it.

At York, the Reformation's first major impact on the drama came when religious guilds were dissolved in 1547, forcing the city to take over responsibility for the Creed Play, previously produced by the Corpus Christi Guild, and the Pater Noster play, originally performed by St Anthony's Guild.[1] The cycle continued to be performed, but some efforts were made to bring the plays in line with Protestant theology: in 1548 three plays on the Death, Assumption and Coronation of the Virgin were excised as too popish. At the accession of the Catholic Queen Mary they were restored to the cycle, and then suppressed for good in 1561. In 1568 the council decided the Creed Play should be performed, rather than the cycle, and asked Matthew Hutton, Dean of York, to make any emendations necessary to make the text acceptable. Hutton instead advised that it should not be played, for he found 'manie thinges, that I can not allowe, because they be Disagreinge from the senceritie of the gospell'. The cycle was performed for the last time in the following year.

The Chester cycle was altered somewhat during Edward's reign, including the suppression of the Baker's play of the Last Supper. Under Elizabeth the text of the entire cycle was extensively revised in the hope of satisfying Protestant authorities, and it is that text which has survived. In 1572 the city council ordered the performance of the plays, but they were almost prevented by the Archbishop of York, whose prohibition arrived too late. In 1575 the city again decided to produce the plays, but moved the performance to Midsummer, and limited the performance to a single day and location. This time the archbishop had the mayor, John Arnewaye, summoned to the Privy Council to answer for the city's actions, and the cycle was never performed again.

What the reformers most objected to in the mystery cycles can best be seen in the ecclesiastical commissioners' letter to the bailiff and burgesses of

1 Johnston and Rogerson (eds.), *REED: York*, i, xv–xvi.

Wakefield in 1576. It directed 'that in the said playe no Pageant be vsed or set furthe wherein the Maiestye of god the father god the sonne or god the holie ghoste or the administration of either the Sacramentes of Baptisme or of the lordes Supper be counterfeyted or represented/or any thinge plaied which tende to the maintenaunce of superstition and idolatrie or which be contrarie to the lawes of god or of the Realme'.[2] It is easy to see that if all the pageants in which one of the persons of God is represented were eliminated, there would be almost nothing left in any of the surviving cycles.

Coventry's cycle saw its final performance in 1579, and only in the far north-west did the tradition survive. Preston had something called a 'Corpus Christi play' in 1595, nearly a half century after the feast was suppressed, and Kendal's lasted until 1605. These plays probably were not full biblical cycles, but the Kendal play at least involved several pageants organised by the craft guilds.

The great biblical cycles of York, Chester and Coventry were relatively unusual; in the south the parish, not the city, was the more common sponsor for plays. These plays were much more modest in scope, put on to raise money for the parish. Some plays felt the effects of the Reformation almost immediately. Bishop's Stortford in Hertfordshire had a play involving a dragon, presumably a St George play, that was performed regularly until the 1530s. The 'dragon made of hoopis couered with canvas' appears in an inventory of church goods taken in 1543, but not the one taken in 1548, and the profits from the play found in earlier churchwardens' accounts no longer appear in the 1540s.[3]

Other parishes, especially ones in rural areas far from London, preserved their performing traditions much longer. New Romney, in Kent, had a passion play, or rather four plays, that began with Christ's baptism and ministry and concluded with the Ascension. This passion play had existed since at least the early fifteenth century, and received its last performances in 1560 and 1562.[4] Several Essex towns performed plays with biblical subjects in the 1560s, Maldon stopping by 1564, but Chelmsford continuing to 1574 and Braintree to 1579.[5] In Lincolnshire, Donnington had a play about Nebuchadnezzar and his attempt to burn the three boys as late as 1563. Spalding had a play of the battle between St Michael and the Devil that included fireworks and machines. People from

---

2 Cawley (ed.), *The Wakefield Pageants in the Towneley Cycle*, 125.
3 Hertfordshire Record Office: D/P 21 5/1, *passim*.
4 Gibson, ' "Interludum Passionis Domini" ', in Johnston and Hüsken (eds.), *English Parish Drama*, 137–45.
5 Coldewey, 'The last rise and final demise of Essex town drama', *Modern Language Quarterly* 36:3 (1975), 257.

Stamford, Peterborough and other towns in the region attended, and the play may also have travelled to those towns into the 1570s.[6]

Tewkesbury, in northern Gloucestershire, also rented out its 'players' geare', which was clearly intended for plays on New Testament subjects, as it included garments for Christ made of sheep-skins, a mask for the devil, and wigs and beards for the apostles. Payments for rental on these costumes continued until 1585, and as late as 1600 the parish put on three 'stage plays' at Whitsun, in order to finance a new battlement on the tower. The churchwardens paid to hire costumes and musicians, and to construct a 'a place to playe in'.

While all these examples probably represent survivals or adaptations of me-dieval dramatic traditions, the case of Sherborne, Dorset, cautions us against assuming that is always so. Sherborne was dominated by its Benedictine abbey during the Middle Ages, but in 1540 the lay parish of Sherborne took over the former abbey as its parish church. Rosalind Hays has argued that the parish 'seems to have celebrated its triumph over the abbey with the substitution of a play for the old Corpus Christi procession'.[7] Records from the 1540s mention both playing garments and a playbook, but by the 1550s the book had disap-peared from the churchwardens' inventories, and the garments were rented out to other parishes, and finally sold in 1562 to the parish of Yeovil.[8] Then, in the early 1570s, the parish once again put on a play at Corpus Christi, and the wardens had to pay for costumes for Lot's wife and the inhabitants of Sodom, and they even spent 6d 'for a peacke of Wheatten meal for to macke louttes Wyfe', presumably when she had been turned into a pillar of salt.[9] The story of Sodom and Gomorrah and Lot's wife must have seemed more appropriate for a Protestant parish, but as at Chester, where the ancient texts were revised in the 1570s to eliminate the most egregious elements of papistry, in the end the plays must still have smacked too much of the popish past, and Sherborne's Corpus Christi plays, like Chester's, received their last performance in 1575.

In addition to the fact that they did not attempt to dramatise all of Christian history from creation to Doomsday, most parish and town plays also differed from the cycles of York, Chester and Coventry in that the latter involved a great deal of expenditure on the part of the cities and their guilds. The smaller-scale parish plays, especially in southern England, were put on with the specific purpose of raising money, usually for poor relief and the upkeep of the church fabric.

---

6 James Stokes (ed.), 'REED: Lincolnshire', unpublished transcriptions.
7 Hayes, 'Lot's wife or the burning of Sodom', *Research Opportunities in Renaissance Drama* 33 (1994), 105.
8 Ibid., 105–6.   9 Ibid., 99.

At both Tewkesbury and Sherborne, the parishes were under special pressure to raise funds, as at the Dissolution both had purchased large monastic churches from the crown to be the parish church, resulting in significant debts, along with the heavy maintenance costs on the large buildings. The method they chose to deal with their heavy expenditures was one parishes had been using for at least the two previous centuries. The religious plays were offered in conjunction with, and perhaps as a legitimation of, an ale: grain, purchased from or donated by parishioners, was brewed into ale, and the ale sold at a feast accompanied by a play. The wardens also made collections, to which the parishioners contributed, perhaps more generously than they would have without the lubricating effects of the ale on their purses. The plays and ale of 1600 made Tewkesbury's churchwardens some £45 toward the £66 they had spent constructing a battlement on the church tower to replace a fallen spire.

While Tewkesbury's plays were biblical, the charitable purpose of these ales, and the collecting – perhaps coercing – of money from those attending made it entirely appropriate that in many parishes Robin Hood and not religion was the focus of the plays. In the majority of the cases it might be better to call these events not plays but games having mimetic elements.

Perhaps the best attested is the Robin Hood game which accompanied the Whitsun ale at Yeovil, where it was the principal parish fund-raiser until at least 1577. Robin Hood, Little John and a sheriff, accompanied by musicians, walked the streets of the town, carrying people on a cowlstaff, and demanding money of onlookers to avoid the same fate. The degree of mimesis involved is partly indicated by mentions in the churchwardens' accounts of costumes and props for this game, including a sword for the sheriff and arrows for Robin Hood. Yeovil's Robin Hood was not really an outlaw figure, as he was always played by one of the respected former wardens of the parish. Other Robin Hoods might have been less respectable, like the ones who prompted William Dyke, a preacher of St Michael's parish in St Albans, to complain of the Whitsun ale at Redbourn, where they had 'Maid Marion comyng into the Churche in the time of prayer and preachinge to move laughter with kissinge in the church'.[10]

Records of Robin Hood plays are most plentiful from the counties west of London – from the Thames valley down through Somerset and into Devon. And again, they lasted longer the further one went from London. In Lancashire the authorities tried to suppress Robin Hood and May games at Burnley in 1579, and in Shropshire, Bridgnorth had a Robin Hood play as late as 1588. A Star Chamber case of 1607 tells of the great Wells Show of that year, which was

10 British Library MS Lansdowne 61, no. 25, fo. 74.

a kind of compendium of provincial traditions of entertainment, including Robin Hood, morris dancing, a maypole, and shows and pageants by the city's six craft guilds. Evidence of these activities in Wells in the late sixteenth century has not survived, but we can reasonably assume that the Wells Show was an elaborate version of living traditions of popular entertainment, or a revival of traditions only recently abandoned or suppressed.

Robin Hood is frequently associated with May games and summer games, and the distinctions between Robin Hood and king games and summer lords are often blurred. King games and summer games usually accompanied Whitsun ales, and centred on the choosing of a mock king or lord – and sometimes a queen or lady, as well, much as Perdita is chosen queen of the sheepshearing in *The Winter's Tale*. A fifteenth-century court case from Wistow, in the West Riding of Yorkshire, describes the parish summer game, in which a king and queen were chosen by lot, and led in procession by a minstrel and the youth of the parish to a barn, designated the 'Somerhouse'. There the king and queen held court on thrones, while others took the roles of knights and a steward, as the assembled parishioners engaged in plays or games for the rest of the day.[11]

Hampshire is rich in records of such games, usually called 'king ales' in that county. Some may not have survived the Reformation, though Bramley, which had an elaborate king ale in the 1530s, may simply have hidden the continuation of that tradition in the churchwardens' terse later recording of their 'clear gains at Whitsuntide', a formula which appears in the accounts well into the seventeenth century.[12]

Other Hampshire parishes continued their king ales well beyond 1540. Crondall and Weyhill still held theirs in the 1570s, Stoke Charity theirs in the early 1580s. At Newton Valence in 1580, John Smith may have been swept away by the part he was playing, since a consistory court case charged that he had proposed marriage to Clarice Baker, when he 'was somer lord & the said Clarice was somer lady of newton'.[13] At St John's, Winchester, the wardens paid for 'payntynge of the clothe vpponn the somerloge' in the mid 1550s, and the king ale held in that lodge lasted until 1597.[14]

11 Palmer, ' "Anye disguised persons" ', in Johnston and Hüsken (eds.), *English Parish Drama*, 82–3; Billington, *Mock Kings in Medieval Society and Renaissance Drama*, 58–9.

12 Hampshire Record Office: M63M70/PW1, *passim*. Transcriptions from these records will appear in the Records of Early English Drama collection for Hampshire, being edited by Peter H. Greenfield and Jane Cowling.

13 Deposition Book of the Consistory Court of Winchester Diocese, Hampshire Record Office: 21M65/C3/8, p. 128.

14 Churchwarden's accounts for 1554–1557, Hampshire Record Office: 88M81W/PW1, fo. 14r, and *passim*.

Latest of all in Hampshire was the parish of Wootton St Lawrence, where the wardens recorded king ales covering several days in 1600, 1601, 1603, 1605 and 1612. In addition to large sums spent on food and drink, the wardens also paid for liveries for the summer lords and ladies, and hired minstrels. Immediately following the payment for the lords' and ladies' liveries in the accounts for 1600 is an intriguing entry: 2 shillings paid 'to Whitburne for his play'. It seems most likely that 'for his play' meant that Whitburne was the leading performer in that year's king game, but the phrase does raise the question of whether these games included anything that might be called a play, in the sense of written dialogue. One doubts that there were written texts, though there may have been traditional dialogue, preserved through oral transmission, and certainly the games had mimetic elements that allow us to see them as manifestations of a popular dramatic impulse.

These late Hampshire examples show that people clung to their traditions despite the opposition of the reformed church. A 1585 diocesan letter of Thomas Cooper, Bishop of Winchester, expresses a view typical of ecclesiastical authorities:

> Wheras a heathenish vngodly custome hath bene vsed before time in many partes of this land aboute this season of the yeare to have Church Ales, maygames, morish daunces, and other vaine pastimes vpon the Sabath Dayes, and other dayes appointed for common prayer, which they have pretended to be for the relief of their Churches, but indeede hath bene only a meanes to feed the mindes of the people and specially of the youth with vaine sightes, alluring them from Divine service, and hearing of the woord of God, and inducing them to the prophaning of the Sabath, to the provoking of Gods heavy wrath and Indignation against vs ... [It] is a straunge perswasion among Christians, that they can not by any other meane of contribution repaire their Churches, and set forth the service of God, but that they must first do sacrifice to the Devill, with Dronkennes and dauncing, and other vngodly wantonnes. These are therfore to charge all Ministers Churchwardens, and other like Officers, together with the discreetest of the parishes, that as they tender the true Seruice of God, and will avoide such penalties as may comme vnto them by lawe, that they suffer not any such Church Ales, morish daunces, or Riflinges [gambling], within their parishes ... And hereof faile you not as you will aunswere to the contrary att your perilles.[15]

In Wootton St Lawrence at least, the churchwardens continued to 'suffer' and themselves organise king ales for another three decades. As Cooper suggests,

---

15 Surrey Record Office, Guildford Muniment Room: Loseley MS Cor 3/377, mb. 1d.

they may have believed that they had no other way of maintaining the parish economy. Certainly the churchwardens' accounts of many parishes reveal that ales, with or without plays, provided most of the parishes' income, and that the seat money or rates that replaced the ales often made considerably less. Another motive for continuing such festivity was expressed by the people of Rangeworthy, Gloucestershire, who explained to the court of Star Chamber that their traditional Whitsun revel had not only been used 'for the refreshinge of the mindes & spirittes of the Countrye people', but also 'for preservacion of mutuall amytie acquaintance and love and decidinge and allayinge of strifes and discordes and debates between neighbour & neighbour'.[16]

Such motives could not hold out against the reforming fervour of those the traditionalists called 'puritans' and 'precisians', and who were often found among the local constabulary. The early seventeenth-century records of Star Chamber are full of disputes like the one from Rangeworthy, where the constable tried to stop the revel in 1613 on the grounds that it was in fact 'a most disorderly Riotous and vnlawful assembly'. At Alton, Hampshire, in the same year, a like-minded constable tried to prevent a group of parishioners from dancing in the 'somer howse' to the music of an itinerant minstrel, only to be beaten for his trouble.[17] The Alton dancers may have won a kind of victory, but only a temporary one. The court records of this period – of Star Chamber, county quarter sessions and ecclesiastical courts – may tell us more about seasonal festivity than we can learn from any earlier records, but they also record the steady decline of such festivity from a customary feature of the life of every parish, to infrequent and unusual events found only in places far from London where Catholic recusancy remained strong.

Lancashire was certainly one of those places, yet even there the growing sabbatarianism of the civil and ecclesiastical authorities threatened to eliminate all the popular pastimes of people in agricultural communities, who had no time to participate in games and sports during the work-week. In 1617 petitioners from Lancashire complained to King James, who issued *The Book of Sports* to declare the right of all his subjects to engage in lawful recreations after divine service. James's declaration permitted dancing, May games, Whitsun ales and maypoles, as well as athletic contests, though not interludes, bull- or bear-baiting, or bowling.

Despite the king's support, seasonal festivities and other pastimes with dramatic elements dwindled to a small fraction of their pre-Reformation numbers.

16 Public Record Office: STAC 8/239/3.
17 Public Record Office: STAC 8/262/11.

One activity permitted by *The Book of Sports* that did remain popular in some northern parishes well into the seventeenth century was the rushbearing, a ceremonial procession bringing bundles of fresh rushes to strew the floor of the church. In this basic form, the rushbearing has nothing dramatic about it, but often music and dancing was involved, and the most elaborate rushbearings included representational elements. At Cawthorne, Yorkshire, in 1596, the people 'did arme & disguyse themselves some of them putting on womens apparell, other some of them puttinge on longe haire & visardes, & others arminge them with the furnyture of Souldiers, & beinge there thus armed, & disguised, did that day goe from the Churche, & so wente vp & downe the towne showinge themselves.'[18] A late example of 1633 from Hornby, Lancashire, found the bearing of the rushes accompanied by morris dancers, a lord of misrule, clowns and giants, and again men dressed as soldiers.[19]

As soon as it was issued, *The Book of Sports* became a focal point of contention between moderate and more radical Protestants, and between the crown and parliament as well. By 1625 parliamentary resistance to the declaration succeeded in forcing the king to assent to an act outlawing Sunday sports. Charles I reissued *The Book of Sports* in 1633, an act that many at the time thought contributed significantly to bringing the nation to the point of civil war. Archbishop Laud aggressively promoted Sunday sports as a means of combatting puritanism, but even his support, and the threat that clergy might lose their livings if they did not comply, did little to reverse the disappearance of traditions of local dramatic activity outside London.[20]

Travelling performers

In addition to locally produced dramatic activity, the provinces also enjoyed the visits of travelling players, some of them based in London, others with entirely provincial itineraries. A popular misconception has it that players toured the provinces only when they could not perform in London, either because they had no theatre of their own or because the authorities had temporarily closed all the theatres, usually because of the threat of plague. In fact, touring the provinces was the rule rather than the exception for companies of actors in this period. A troupe as prominent as the Earl of Leicester's Men regularly took to

---

18 Palmer, ' "Anye disguised persons" ', 86.
19 Baldwin, 'Rushbearings and maygames in the diocese of Chester before 1642', in Johnston and Hüsken (eds.), *English Parish Drama*, 34–5.
20 Hutton, *The Rise and Fall of Merry England*, 189–99.

the road, though they often appeared at court and after 1576 had the Theatre as their London base. In 1572 they asked their patron for a licence 'to certifye that we are your housould Servaunts when we shall have occasion to travayle amongst our frendes as we do usuallye once a yere'.[21] This pattern of annual tours continued even after the company constructed their own purpose-built theatre in the capital.

Troupes like Leicester's Men followed touring routes long used by itinerant minstrels; payments to visiting performers appear in the earliest accounting records of most provincial towns, as early as the late thirteenth century in the case of Canterbury.[22] These traditional routes tended to take the form of loops leading out from London and returning, at least for those companies lucky enough to perform regularly in London and at court. One such loop went north-east through East Anglia to Norwich, the second-most populous city in the nation at the time, and might include stops at Cambridge, Ipswich and other towns, as well as a number of aristocratic residences. Another went south-east through Canterbury to Dover and the other Kentish ports, following the coast as far south as Rye before bending back toward London. A south-western loop led to Southampton, and then west along the Dorset coast, or inland to Salisbury, eventually reaching Exeter or even Plymouth before turning north for Bristol and Bath. The actors might then return east to London, or pursue a more ambitious tour further north, travelling up the Severn valley through Gloucester to Worcester and Shrewsbury, or turning up the Avon toward Coventry, perhaps visiting Stratford on their way. An especially long tour might combine several of these loops, and reach as far north as York, Newcastle, Kendal or Carlisle. Many got no further than Coventry or Leicester, returning to London by the Great North Road, or down the Thames valley through Oxford and Abingdon (see figure 20).

Roads and topography partly determined these routes. Players encumbered by a cart loaded with costumes and props would take the best roads they could, which probably explains the number of companies that visited Southampton, but bypassed Winchester, though it appears to have been on their way. The main road used to move goods from Southampton's port to London passed a few miles east of Winchester, and the connecting road was hilly and poorly maintained. Water courses offered relatively easy travel, so that players visiting Gloucester followed the Severn south to Bristol or north to Worcester. To go

---

21 Chambers, *The Elizabethan Stage*, II, 86.
22 James Gibson (ed.), 'REED: Kent, diocese of Canterbury', unpublished transcriptions.

Figure 20 Map of touring theatre company routes after 1540

east to Oxford, roughly the same distance away, would have meant struggling to move their gear up the steep Cotswold Edge. Similar concerns may have kept companies from visiting Guildford and Farnham, despite their proximity to London, due to the ruggedness of the North Downs. On the other hand, quite small places might see travelling players frequently because of their location, as did Ashburton in Devon, roughly halfway between Exeter and Plymouth.

Though topography partly guided the routes the players took, so did their basic motives for taking to the road: profit and serving their patrons. Profit, or at least financial survival, must have been possible outside London, since the major companies regularly went on tour, and lesser ones functioned for years in the provinces without ever having a London base. Unfortunately, the archival research that has revealed a good deal about where the players went, has discovered considerably less about how much they made. The best-known description of a provincial performance, from R. Willis's *Mount Tabor*, reports that

> In the City of Gloucester the manner is (as I think it is in other like corporations) that when the Players of Enterludes come to towne, they first attend the Mayor to enforme him what noble-mans servants they are, and so to get license for their publike playing; and if the Mayor like the Actors, or would shew respect to their Lord and Master, he appoints them to play their first play before himselfe and the Aldermen and common Counsell of the City; and that is called the Mayors play, where every one that will comes in without money, the Mayor giving the players a reward as he thinks fit to shew respect unto them.

The records tell us the amounts of such rewards from the civic purse, or from the head of the household when they gave a private performance. What the records cannot tell us is how much income the players derived from other sources. In some towns the recorded rewards were supplemented by collections from the audience or an admission fee: unlike Gloucester, where no one was charged to attend the 'Mayor's play', at Leicester the chamberlains regularly indicated that the amount they paid the players was in addition to whatever 'was gathered'.[23] Moreover, the performances we know about from the accounts represent only a fraction – perhaps a small one – of the total number of performances a company gave on tour. The Gloucester 'Mayor's play' was only the first play a visiting troupe performed in the city, perhaps the first of several. In 1580 Gloucester sought to restrict the number of performances in the city by passing an ordinance that limited the queen's players to three plays within three days, and players of patrons holding the rank of baron or greater to two plays in two days. Norwich gave rewards to few companies, but licensed many others to play for periods ranging from a day to a week or more. At some performances the players charged an admission fee, as the Queen's Men did in 1583, when they played at the Red Lion inn in Norwich, and a fight broke out when 'one wynsdon would have intred in at the gate but

---

23 Alice Hamilton (ed.), 'REED: Leicester', unpublished transcriptions.

woold not haue payed vntyll he had been within'. In other places the players may have had to rely on taking a collection among the audience, as the players of *Mankind* did, when they interrupted the performance to require payment before the great devil, Titivillus, would appear. No doubt the players' skill at working an audience, an audience softened up by ale when the performance occurred at an inn, meant that passing the hat could be quite lucrative.

Certainly the players would have needed the income from admission fees and collections, because even the companies with the best actors and the most important patrons could not have survived on the payments that appear in the records. A recent estimate of the cost of touring in the late sixteenth century suggests that it would have cost at least a shilling per day per member of the company – 6 pence for the evening meal and 6 pence for a bed for the night – and twice that if they hired horses.[24] A small company, say the 'four men and a boy' of the play within a play of *Sir Thomas More*, would have had to take in at least 5 shillings a day, 35 shillings a week just to break even. A more prominent company with ten to fifteen actors might well spend a pound a day on the road, and, if they had only the officially recorded payments to defray those expenses, they might well have suffered a fate similar to that of Pembroke's Men in 1593, when they went on tour to escape the plague raging in London, but soon found themselves in such dire straits that they had to return to London, dissolve the company and sell their wardrobe to pay their debts.[25]

The spotty survival of relevant records makes it impossible to reconstruct the finances of an entire tour, but occasionally we get enough information to give us a reasonable glimpse at what happened over a brief period. For one four-day period in 1594, the Queen's Men made 52 shillings in recorded rewards: 12 shillings from Lord Berkeley at Caludon Castle near Coventry on 1 July, and 40 shillings from the city of Coventry on 4 July.[26] Since it is likely that the company numbered fourteen at that time, even the minimum expenditure of a shilling a day per man would add up to 14 shillings a day or at least 56 shillings for the four days.[27] Most likely, however, the Queen's Men showed a substantial profit for those four days, rather than a deficit of a shilling or more

24 Ingram, 'The cost of touring', *Medieval and Renaissance Drama in England* 6 (1993), 58–9.
25 Foakes and Rickert (eds.), *Henslowe's Diary*, 280.
26 Greenfield, 'Entertainments of Lord Berkeley', *REED Newsletter* 8 (1983), 16.
27 Several plays associated with the Queen's Men were published or entered in the Stationer's Register in 1594, and an analysis of the casting requirements for those plays puts the size of the company at that time at fourteen players (McMillin and MacLean, *The Queen's Men*, 108). A shilling per day per man is probably too low a figure for expenses for the monarch's company, which we would expect to be well equipped.

a day. The players quite likely performed on the 2 and 3 July as well, and the gate from those performances, and perhaps from the Coventry performance on 4 July as well, must have added substantially to the 52 shillings in recorded rewards.

Perhaps even more important is the fact that their expenses would have been considerably reduced, even eliminated, while they were visiting Lord Berkeley. We know from pantry accounts of the third Duke of Buckingham at Thornbury and Francis Clifford at Londesborough that the players were guests in these households, receiving meals and presumably beds.[28] Often they received only a single reward, but were housed and fed for two or more days. In fact, as a travelling singer testifed in court, performers might live entirely by going 'from gentilmans house to gentilmans house vpon their benevolence'.[29] An especially welcoming household would be well worth a journey off the direct route between towns; many troupes may have planned their itineraries around such households, seeing the towns as mere stepping stones between more comfortable and lucrative visits to aristocratic residences.

If aristocrats were important to travelling players in the role of host, they were vital in the role of patron. Being a patron to a company of players was a different matter from being a poet's patron, because patrons gave their players little direct financial support. Lord Berkeley, for example, gave his servants an annual gift at New Year, and his musicians received such a gift in each of the seven years for which household accounts survive, as well as rewards at other times of the year, suggesting that they spent much of their time with the household. Berkeley's players, however, received a New Year's gift only once during those seven years, though they were active elsewhere in the country.[30]

The most valuable thing a patron gave his players was his (or occasionally, her) name. Legally, that name, appearing at the bottom of a piece of paper, was the players' licence to tour. The 1572 *Acte for the Punishemente of Vacabondes* required players to have a licence from someone of at least the rank of baron in order to move around the country; if they did not, they faced the same imprisonment as rogues, vagabonds and sturdy beggars. And the name that kept them out of prison also helped the players earn their living. As Willis tells us, the first thing a company did on arriving in a town was to see the mayor 'to enforme him what noble-mans servants they are', because a 1559 royal proclamation gave mayors the power to license performances, and the

---

28 Douglas and Greenfield (eds.), *REED: Cumberland, Westmorland, Gloucestershire*, 356–8; Wasson, 'REED: Clifford family', unpublished transcriptions.
29 Somerset (ed.), *REED: Shropshire*, 280.
30 Greenfield, 'Entertainments of Lord Berkeley', 12–24.

patron's name was the key to getting the mayor's permission. Willis also tells us that the mayor would request a 'Mayor's play' and reward the players 'if the Mayor like the Actors, or would shew respect to their Lord and Master'.

Showing respect to the patron certainly seems to have determined the size of the rewards towns gave players. The monarch's players universally received the largest rewards; other companies got less, on a scale having much more to do with the patron's rank and local influence than with the size or skill of the company. The Queen's Men made 30 shillings from Gloucester's mayor in 1582–3, while the Earl of Oxford's players made 16 shillings and 8 pence, and Lord Stafford's only 10 shillings. In the same year the city gave 20 shillings to the players of Lord Chandos, who lived at nearby Sudeley Castle and represented the county in Parliament, his local influence meaning even more than the Earl of Oxford's rank. Lord Berkeley had extensive holdings in Gloucestershire but resided further away and was less in favour at court than Chandos, so his players received the lower reward of 13 shillings.

It made sense, then, for a company to tour where its patron held land, titles or other forms of influence. Thirty-five of the fifty-six known provincial visits of Lord Berkeley's players occurred near his lands and residences, including visits to Gloucester, Bristol, Bath, Bridgwater, Abingdon, Coventry and Caludon Castle. Moreover, all the visits to Gloucester, Bristol and Bath took place when Lord Berkeley's principal residence was at Yate Court in southern Gloucestershire. Most of the visits to Coventry came after 1590, when he moved his principal residence to Caludon, just outside that city. Other companies had similarly limited itineraries: the players of the Lord Warden of the Cinque Ports, and those of the Lord President of the Council in the Marches of Wales appeared almost exclusively within their patrons' spheres of influence. The monarch's players predictably covered the entire country, their range approached only by the companies whose patrons combined power with considerable ambition, like the Earl of Leicester.

Itineraries reflected the extent of the patron's influence because that made financial sense for the players, but also in order to serve the patron. Just as the patron's name was more important to the players than the limited financial support the patron provided, so the spreading of the patron's name on tour was the main way the players served their patron, more important than providing pleasure with the occasional performance in his presence. For the monarch, the travels of the royal players functioned much like a royal progress to remind people throughout the country of the power of the sovereign. Such reminders were particularly important in the sixteenth and early seventeenth centuries, when dynastic and religious upheaval threatened to pull the country apart. The formation of the Queen's Men in 1583 was probably associated with Walsingham's development of a nationwide intelligence system of surveillance against Catholics who continued to resist Queen Elizabeth and the dominance of English Protestantism. The queen's players did not actually have to spy for their visits to spread the image of a monarch whose vigilance extended throughout the provinces.[31]

At the same time, a tour visit to a town also resembled a royal entry in allowing the town a symbolic assertion of its own sovereignty. Royal entries enacted the town's acceptance of royal authority, but usually began with the civic officials meeting the royal party at the outer gate or boundary to welcome the ruler into the town. By requiring the players to obtain a licence to perform, civic officials asserted their own limited local authority, at the same time as they recognised the patrons' influence by granting the licence and paying the players a reward. The situation was much the same, if less formal, when the players offered to perform in a private household. Each touring performance thus involved the negotiation of a reciprocal relationship between the players' patron and whoever authorised the performance. In the seventeenth century, when relations became strained between the crown and aristocracy on the one hand and urban elites on the other, it became much harder for players to make a living on the road.

In the second half of the sixteenth century, however, most towns remained receptive to the visits of itinerant players, despite suffering from economic decline made worse by substantial population growth. The resulting poverty led to social tension, while most of the public ceremonies that had provided ritual reaffirmation of the community's social structure in the late Middle Ages had disappeared. The suppression of Corpus Christi not only affected the plays performed on that feast, but also eliminated the annual procession in which the civic officials and guilds marched, advertising the structure of the local hierarchy through their ceremonial garb and the order of the procession.[32] Urban elites had to turn to other symbolic measures to engender 'the civic deference necessary for effective government', including enlarging the ceremonial mace, giving the mayor a chair of office, and building or renovating the town hall.[33] To license travelling players to perform, and to locate the performance in a space that represented civic authority, was to transfer some of the symbolic

---

31 McMillin and MacLean, *The Queen's Men*, 23–8.
32 Davis, 'The sacred and the body social in sixteenth-century Lyon', *Past and Present* 90 (1981), 40–70; James, 'Ritual, drama, and social body in the late medieval English town', *Past and Present* 98 (1983), 3–29; Phythian-Adams, 'Ceremony and the citizen', in Clark and Slack (eds.), *Crisis and Order in English Towns*, 57–85.
33 Tittler, *Architecture and Power*, 98–128.

impact of a touring performance as an advertisement of power and influence from the patron's purposes to that of the local elite.

Town halls are the most frequently mentioned playing places in the accounting records that give us much of our knowledge of touring companies. Performances in inns, churches and private houses may have occurred just as often, and perhaps even more frequently, but have gone unrecorded unless connected with legal action. At Gloucester, the mayor's play seen by R. Willis was staged in the town hall or Bothall, and performances before the mayor and council also took place in town halls like the Leicester Guildhall, the Norwich Common Hall and the hall over the Bargate in Southampton, all three of which survive[34] (see figure 21). At Norwich, the players also performed at the Red Lion Inn, as we know from the story of the 'affray' in which the Queen's Men became involved in 1583.[35] At Southampton in 1620 an ordinance prohibiting further performances in the town hall blamed stage players for the miserable state of the hall, from broken benches to 'fleas and other beastlie thinges', and ordered 'That hereafter yf anie suche staige or poppett plaiers must be admitted in this towne That they provide their places for their representacions in their Innes', the last pronoun suggesting that inns were familiar playing spaces to the players and to Southampton's council.[36] Outdoor performances are rarely attested; a single mention of the Queen's Men playing in the cathedral churchyard at Gloucester in 1590 contrasts the several references to the town hall there. Church houses were used in some rural parishes, as at Sherborne, Dorset, and in others the church itself, as was the practice at Doncaster.[37] Only Bristol could offer touring companies purpose-built theatres like the Wine Street playhouse and Redcliffe Hall, which operated in the the first two decades of the seventeenth century.[38]

We know very little about what plays touring players performed in these spaces. Civic accountants faithfully recorded the amounts paid and usually the patron's name, but showed lamentably little interest in play titles. Even the depositions concerning the 'affray' at Norwich in 1583 never mention the name of the play given at the Red Lion, though the many folios of witnesses' testimony do mention the names of several of the queen's players, and that

---

34 McMillin and MacLean, *The Queen's Men*, 67–83; Somerset, ' "How chances it they travel?" ', *Shakespeare Survey* 47 (1994), 54–60.
35 Galloway (ed.), *REED: Norwich*, 72–3.
36 Southampton Court Leet Book, SRO: SC6/1/37, fo. 16v.
37 Hayes, 'Dorset church houses and the drama', *Research Opportunities in Renaissance Drama* 31 (1992), 12–23; Wasson, 'The English church as theatrical space', in Cox and Kastan (eds.), *A New History of Early English Drama*, 36.
38 Pilkinton (ed.), *REED: Bristol*, xxxvii–xl.

Figure 21 Interior of Leicester Guildhall

they left the stage with rapiers in their hands, because those details were germane to the case. Bristol records from the 1570s do mention a few titles or descriptions for what sound like moral interludes: 'what mischief worketh in the mynd of man' and 'the Court of Comfort'. Willis described a similar play at Gloucester in the same decade:

The play was called (the Cradle of security,) wherin was personated a King or some great Prince with his Courtiers of severall kinds, amongst which three Ladies were in speciall grace with him; and they keeping him in delights and pleasures, drew him from his graver Counsellors, hearing of Sermons, and listning to good counsell, and admonitions, that in the end they got him to lye downe in a cradle upon the stage, where these three Ladies joyning in a sweet song rocked him asleepe, that he snorted againe, and in the meane time closely conveyed under the cloaths were withall he was covered, a vizard like swines snout upon his face, with three wire chaines fastned thereunto, the other end whereof being holden severally by those three Ladies, who fall to singing againe, and then discovered his face, that the spectators might see how they had transformed him, going on with their singing, whilst all this acting, there came forth of another doore at the farthest end of the stage, two old men, the one in blew with a Serjeant at Armes, his mace on his shoulder, the other in red with a drawn sword in his hand, and leaning with the other hand upon the others shoulder, and so they two went along in a soft pace round about by the skirt of the Stage, till at last they came to the Cradle, whereat all the Courtiers with the three Ladies and the vizard all vanished; and the desolate Prince starting up bare faced, and finding himself thus sent for to judgement, made a lamentable complaint of his miserable case, and so was carried away by wicked spirits. This Prince did personate in the morall, the wicked of the world; the three Ladies, Pride, Covetousnesse, and Luxury, the two old men, the end of the world, and the last judgement.

Small provincial companies may have continued to offer plays of this kind into the seventeenth century, but the major London companies would surely have brought on tour what was most successful in the capital. In 1593, Edward Alleyn and Lord Strange's Men performed 'hary of cornwall' at Bristol, a play they had performed several times at the Rose.[39] *Henry of Cornwall* does not survive, but the plays of Marlowe, Shakespeare and Jonson must have found similar paths into the provinces. Touring companies could have cut their repertories to a few tried-and-true favourites, since they gave only a few performances in any one town or household before moving on. Doing so would allow them to reduce the number of costumes and props they had to transport, and would avoid the effort and risk involved in putting on a new play. In fact, relying on a few plays familiar to the actors and proven before audiences may have been one of the few compensations for the rigour of life on the road.[40]

To do their London repertory essentially intact, the London-based companies would have had to take most of their number on provincial tours, and household accounts of the Cliffords record troupes as large as fifteen. When the Earl of Derby's players visited Francis Clifford at Londesborough in 1598, he provided meals for twelve of them. Many companies the Cliffords received had only six or seven actors, however, and six may have been a common size for a minor itinerant company. *The Cradle of Security* requires a cast of six,

---

39 Foakes and Rickert (eds.), *Henslowe's Diary*, 16–18.
40 Somerset, ' "How chances it they travel?" ', 60.

and – according to his will – Simon Jewell had put up 'the sixth parte' of a company's investment in apparel, horses and a wagon for a proposed tour.[41] Though extensive doubling would have made plays with many characters possible, these smaller companies must have continued to perform older interludes throughout the period or heavily adapted the newer plays written for the London theatres.

Touring outside London waned in the seventeenth century; it had all but disappeared by the time public performing was banned by Parliament in 1642. At Coventry, where the city leaders paid travelling players more often than at any other provincial town, rewards to visiting troupes averaged six a year in the 1590s and eight a year in the first decade of the seventeenth century. Between 1610 and 1619 that average decreased to four, and shrank to only two in the 1620s and 1630s. Other towns saw similar reductions in the frequency of rewards to players, and in many places such payments became sporadic or ceased altogether. Aristocratic households continued to welcome players, especially those in places distant from London. Still, fewer companies were on the road, and those that remained found touring a struggle, even under royal patronage.

The same cultural changes that led to the decline of local dramatic activity contributed to the decline of provincial touring, particularly the growth of puritanism among urban elites. Increasing tension between those elites and the crown meant that mayors might no longer wish to 'shew respect to [the players'] Lord and Master'. Not only did rewards from towns decline through the first four decades of the seventeenth century, but more and more often the players were paid 'not to play', or more brutally, 'to rid the town of them'. Many towns passed ordinances designed to regulate or even eliminate public performance. Canterbury was one of the earliest: in 1595 the court of Burgmote prohibited playing on the sabbath, and restricted any visiting company to performing for no more than two days out of any thirty. Moreover, those performances had to end before nine o'clock at night. These restrictions appear to have discouraged most companies from even trying Canterbury. A popular stop for travelling performers for several centuries, from 1603 to 1642 Canterbury made only twenty payments to players, and fifteen of those were to leave town without performing.[42]

As long as such restrictions were relatively rare, players could still survive on the road, performing where they could, and making brief forays into less

41 Edmond, 'Pembroke's Men', *Review of English Studies*, n.s. 25 (1974), 129–36.
42 Gibson, 'Stuart players in Kent: fact or fiction?', *REED Newsletter* 20:2 (1995), 7–8.

7

'An example of courtesy and liberality': great households and performance

SUZANNE WESTFALL

A prince ought also to show himself a patron of ability, and to honour the proficient in every art . . . Further, he ought to entertain the people with festivals and spectacles at convenient seasons of the year; . . . and show himself an example of courtesy and liberality. . . .

Niccolo Machiavelli, *The Prince*

Twenty years ago, a volume on early modern theatre would not have contained an essay or chapter about household performances; very likely the term 'household' would not even appear in the index. But ironically, an awareness of household theatre and noble patronage has always silently haunted practically every volume about Renaissance drama. Whenever a performance at court is described, whenever a travelling troupe of players is mentioned, whenever minstrels are noted, whenever an interlude is analysed, whenever the antics of a fool are admired, household performance haunts the writing. So, it turns out we have been covertly discussing this topic for some time; all it takes is a slight shift of the lens, a change from background to foreground to produce this essay and other studies of patronage.

In our own time, the students and scholars of early modern theatre have focused primarily on the plays of the public stages, but long before the existence of the Blackfriars, the Rose, or the great Globe itself, private household auspices had offered cultural experiences that differed significantly from their vastly more famous progeny. Records of Early English Drama (REED) publications are verifying that during the peak years of the London stage, performances sponsored by noble patrons in the provinces, at households and towns, were increasing, which challenges the popular notion that the public stage replaced the private. So theatre historians, perhaps under the influence of New Historicism, have turned their attention to matters contextual to printed plays, and consequently such venues as the great households of England have become a focus of study rather than an incidental footnote. Ecclesiastical households and university auspices, both of which share some of the qualities of the aristocratic households, also demand more consideration, since their not-for-profit performances were as thematically potent and structurally sophisticated as many of the revels at the royal court.[1]

There are several reasons for this shift in the paradigm. The continuing work of the REED project in cataloguing references to performance has unearthed hundreds of references to households and their entertainments, references which have led to many new publications.[2] Recent transitions in criticism from textual analysis of playscripts to theatrical analysis of performances have also reoriented our attention to the contexts as well as the texts of theatrical entertainments. Theatre historians interested in social history, specifically in the fundamental importance of patronage to the structure of early modern culture, have discovered that household auspices were much more significant in the history of drama than we had heretofore assumed them to be. In fact, patronage studies have led to re-evaluations of the function of women as 'producers' of these entertainments, and to speculations about the role of this 'private' theatre in the formation and development of the 'public' stage.[3] Looking at early modern theatre from the perspective of patronage and households allows us to re-evaluate the meaning and purpose of theatre, to understand better the power structures and hierarchies of Elizabethan England, and to reassess noblemen's and noblewomen's roles in creating Renaissance theatre.

There are also many explanations for the fact that household revels have been neglected or have been relegated to biography, antiquarian studies and social history. Entertainments in great households were almost always occasional, ephemeral and frequently non-textual due to their multi-mediality. Consequently, they are extremely difficult to recover without documentation such as visual representation, musical score, or some description of movement and dance. In addition, great-household production values are difficult to reconcile with our highly rhetorical concept of drama. Tournaments, masques

1 I mean to concentrate here on the baronial households, since space precludes the discussion that the university auspices deserve. Alan Nelson has already produced a thorough study, *Early Cambridge Theatres*.

2 See, for example two works that exploit REED discoveries: McMillin and Maclean, *The Queen's Men*, and Gurr, *The Shakespearian Playing Companies*. Sally-Beth MacLean and Alan Somerset have also constructed a marvellous website that makes patronage data easily available at www.utoronto.ca/patrons. (David Kathman's biographical index to Elizabethan theatre is also invaluable: http://www.clark.net/pub/tross/ws/bd/kathman.htm.)

3 Dutton, *Mastering the Revels*; White and Westfall (eds.), *Shakespeare and Theatrical Patronage*.

and jests, though meaningful politically to sixteenth-century participants, may be incomprehensible to us, and therefore seem trivial in comparison to extant playscripts. But any discussion of household theatre automatically engenders a profusion of other issues, from the influence of patronage (ideology, religion, touring), to the aesthetics of non-verbal performance (jousts, disguisings, masques, cookery, heraldry, ceremony), to architectonics (great halls, chapels, outdoor, domestic versus public space).

Obviously a short essay such as this cannot hope to cover all these issues. Here I will concentrate on refocusing our lens by considering some of the most important issues involved in the study of patronage and household theatre: 1. the structure of the household, both human in the form of retained personnel and physical in regard to potential stage spaces; 2. the collaboration of the retained artists and the aesthetic this synergy suggests, an effect that frequently distinguishes household theatre from public theatre; 3. patrons and players, the topic that has heretofore formed the nucleus of Tudor theatre history; 4. an occasional performance, a great household wedding, as an example of how such performances were framed; 5. some of the texts that might have been enacted in the households; and 6. the roles that women played, both on stage and off, in their revels.

Since until recently scholarship has focused on writers and texts, let me begin with scripts, and with exploring some analogues. In the often-omitted induction scene of *The Taming of the Shrew*, Christopher Sly, convinced that he is the patron of an aristocratic household, prepares to watch an entertainment constructed for his pleasure. During the wedding scene in *A Midsummer Night's Dream*, Duke Theseus chooses from a number of proffered entertainments, sorting out what manner of performance is 'suitable' for his marriage banquet; Beatrice–Joanna's wedding in *The Changeling* will last for three days and include a dance by the mad folk of the local asylum. Hamlet's party view a play adapted and directed specifically to reflect household events, while Prospero treats his guests to a thematically appropriate masque in a style worthy of Inigo Jones and Ben Jonson, whose own *Volpone* maintains a fool, a dwarf and a castrato. All of these scenes remind us that theatre happened not just on the public stages in London, but also at aristocratic courts, in the halls and chapels, in the castles, manors, parks and gardens of British nobility all over England.[4] Household theatre is not important because these men are writing about it, they are writing about it *because* it is important.

---

4 I have discussed literary analogues at length elsewhere; see ' "The actors are come hither" ', *Theatre Survey*, May 1989, 56–68.

Household structures and stages

We know from various primary sources – chronicles, letters of ambassadors, household account books, books of ordinances, university accounts, civic records and aristocratic correspondence – that these households were indeed powerful cultural centres (sometimes at odds with or in competition with the royal court) that produced multi-media entertainments specific to occasions, to domestic politics, and to local interests. Such household theatre frequently comprised marginalised forms – tournaments, jests, ceremonies, interludes, disguisings and masques – that have not survived in published form; indeed, scripts may never have existed. But household books of ordinances do give us some idea of the structures of occasional theatre and the retainers who were expected to provide it. Edward IV's *Black Book*, for instance, is a particularly valuable record of household management for resident and non-resident performers. Henry Algernon Percy, fifth Earl of Northumberland, kept a volume now entitled *The Second Northumberland Household Book*, which gives detailed instructions about every aspect of family ceremonial occasions. An earlier household book (1311–12) survives for Queen Isabella. So, although we may not have dialogue, we do have stage managers' 'bibles' to guide us.[5] These 'bibles' also confirm that household theatre was meticulously planned and precisely stage-managed, in marked contrast to the improvisation and haphazardness of the film and pop-culture versions of 'medieval' feasts and Renaissance 'fairres'.

A great household, whether ecclesiastical or aristocratic, was not a specific architectural structure, not a 'place' *per se*. Rather, these 'sites' of culture were collections of people assembled to serve an aristocrat in the maintenance of person and property. So the Tudor noblemen and noblewomen (for many women kept their own courts within the household auspices of husbands, brothers and fathers) formed an epicentre for a semi-itinerant company of family, bureaucrats, officers and servants. Thus, a household is itself a paradoxical establishment – it is both static and active, both private and public, both domestic and commercial. Moving from property to property, from manor to castle to London townhouse, a superstructure of servitors and household

---

5 Grose (comp.), 'Northumberland's Household Book'. *The Second Northumberland Household Book* is preserved in Bodleian MS Eng. hist. B. 208. For Edward IV's household see Myers, *The Household Book of Edward IV*. See also Blackley and Hermansen (eds.), *The Household Book of Queen Isabella of England for the Fifth Regnal Year of Edward II*. Household account books, preserving payments but not procedures, are also invaluable. Chamberlain's accounts survive for Robert Dudley, Earl of Leicester (Leicestershire Record Office BRIII / 2 / 52, mb2.; his household book is in the archives of Christ Church, Oxford, Evelyn MS 258b), and for the Middleton household (Nottingham University Library MS MiA62, fol. 14) .

'stuff' (known as the 'riding' household) would progress periodically throughout an aristocrat's far-flung holdings.

Family 'seats' were rather public private homes to the resident household – a nobleman, his extended family, his staff and their families, as well as all of their servants. The numbers in a household could range from the small group of servitors for a country knight to 250 or more for Edward Stafford, third Duke of Buckingham, eighty-six of whom formed the household of his duchess, Eleanor Percy. These servants expected to be fed, clothed, sheltered, entertained and sometimes protected at the expense of the patron. Small wonder that provincial families panicked when the royal household was headed their way, expecting the hosts to foot the bill for food, lodging and entertainment for two entire households – their own and the travelling monarch's.

For a household was also an economic unit, a corporation of managers and workers who happened to live (occasionally) under the same roof. Consequently, entertainments in the noble households tended to represent a curious mixture of the sacred and the secular, the public and the private, an opportunity for the formal performance of largesse as well as the casual celebration of personal leisure. Entertainments, as a result, became rather complex affairs with complex motives, for they were designed both to reflect and to reinforce the patron's political power, to secure the loyalty of his domestic 'army', to spread his influence to other areas when his retainers toured the provinces (sometimes acting as spies and messengers[6]) and to communicate his ideology to other households and populations, a function that became crucial after the Reformation. In addition, the forms and structures of these frequently extravagant and expensive entertainments assisted in the social construction of a desired reality, reflecting the audience and projecting the philosophies of the producers.

While the geographical space of the household is changeable, the duties and privileges of the personnel are remarkably specific. Besides salary and gratuities from the patron and his friends, lodging (and perhaps jobs and lodging for family members), diet, candles and fuel, a retained performer expected a suit of livery once a year; one actor even expected burial costs from the Countess of Pembroke.[7] Often resident entertainers served in more than one occupational capacity. For example, in 1311 Richard Pilke and his wife Elena were retained by the royal court as both minstrels and pastry chefs; much later Anthony Hall, of the Duke of Rutland's household, was provided with board

---

6 McMillin and MacLean, *The Queen's Men*, 22–4.
7 Ibid., 29. Streitberger, *Court Revels*.

for four weeks because he was 'lernyng a play to pley in Christemes' and 'scowrying away the yerthe and stones in the tennys playe'. Many have noted Richard Gibson's dual functions of player and yeoman of the wardrobe, or John English as Henry VII's interluder and tailor.

We have a job description for Edward IV's heraldic trumpeters. In return for their perquisites, they are to provide:

> blowinges and pipinges, to such offices as must be warned to prepare for the king and his houshold at metes and soupers, to be the more redy in all seruyces, and all thies sitting in the hall togyder, whereof sume vse trumpettes, sume shalmuse and small pipes.

The king also warned his minstrels not to 'be too presumptuouse nor to familer to aske any rewardes of the lordes of his lond'; further orders are given that some minstrels 'com to court' only at the 'v festes of the yere', to take 'iiijd ob. a day', and to 'auoyude the next day after the festes be don', showing that the household was not inclined to support all its entertainers on a full-time basis.[8] So here we have an institutional reason for all those touring minstrel troupes we find in civic and other household record books.

Occasions for performance were also frequently specified. Northumberland's Chapel, for example, was directed to perform the Nativity play on Christmas morning, the Resurrection play on Easter morning, and an unspecified play in the great hall on Shrove Tuesday. What exactly these entertainers performed is unrecorded, but it is tempting to envision great-household performers enacting something akin to the appropriate episodes of the cycle plays, especially since Northumberland's chaplain assisted in the writing of the Beverley plays.[9] *The Second Shepherd's Play*, with its complex musical requirements, specific seasonal allusions, and explicit references to chapel functions, seems a particularly good candidate for household production, as I have argued elsewhere.[10] Northumberland's *Household Book* also requires the services of actors, singers, dancing henchmen and musicians in the ordinances for Twelfth Night and for family weddings.[11]

As physical stages, the properties of the noble patrons provided various venues. In actuality any space, from bedchamber to tents at the Field of the Cloth of Gold in France, could and did become stages, a fact that challenges

---

8 Myers, *The Household Book of Edward IV*, 131–2.
9 Grose, 'Northumberland's Household Book', 61, 92, 97, 199.
10 Westfall, *Patrons and Performance*, 49–52.
11 Grose, 'Northumberland's Household Book', 256–8. Lancashire, 'Orders for Twelfth Day and Night', *English Literary Renaissance* 10 (Winter 1980), 7–45.

twentieth-century assumptions about 'appropriate' theatre space, and suggests that early modern aristocrats conducted their lives with a complex understanding of 'public privacy'. Household revels blur the distinction between
communal and personal space, public and private experience, liturgical and
secular activities. Participants, both performers and spectators, mingled in the
most popular household entertainment, the disguising or masque. Henry VIII,
in particular, was fond of dancing in disguise, and once performed dressed as
Robin Hood with a woman as Maid Marion for the Spanish ambassadors
in Queen Catherine's bedchamber. On another occasion, Hall records the
amazement that ensued when the king broke 'fourth wall' conventions
and chose dancing partners from amongst the spectators, a convention that
quickly became popular.[12]

Performances could and did take place in chapels, taking advantage of lofts
and surrounding rooms, and of course in great halls where the banquets took
place (thus prompting some scholars to interpret the Latin term *interlude* as
entertainments *between* courses). Richard Southern began looking at great
halls as performing spaces, though his conclusion that the hall screens were
customarily used as backdrops and the minstrel's gallery as playing space has
been challenged repeatedly by more recent studies. John Astington shows that
performances did not invariably use the expanse of the hall or the screens, and
that the platform stages constructed for specific events were elaborate, often
painted three-dimensionally, and equipped with ingenious mechanical devices.
Nelson has demonstrated the complexity and sophistication of reusable stages
at Cambridge, and MacLean and McMillin have beautifully photographed a variety of spaces that indicate the diversity and adaptability of household space.[13]
At family occasions such as christenings and weddings, the entire property
could become theatre space, as ceremonial processions progressed throughout the space from chapel, to antechamber, to great hall to bedchamber, and
outdoors for hunting and dancing.

Allegorical tournaments and jousts, athletic events that incorporated all the
conventional elements of drama – dialogue, conflict, plot, costume, character
and set – were framed by banquets, music, emblematic 'devices' and disguisings. These were usually staged by the royal household (which could afford
the economic and political expense of mock battle), and would naturally occur
outdoors, often with elaborately constructed 'sets'. There are, however, some

12 Hall, *The Vnion of the Two Noble and Illustre Famelies of Lancastre and Yorke*, 516; Streitberger,
   Court Revels, 255.
13 Astington, *English Court Theatre*; McMillin and MacLean, *The Queen's Men*, 68–81: Nelson,
   Early Cambridge Theatres; Southern, *The Staging of Plays Before Shakespeare*.

notable exceptions to the royal venue for jousts among the upper, most trusted nobility. Henry Herbert, second Earl of Pembroke, and Sir Philip Sidney produced tilts at Wilton; Pembroke's son William celebrated his wedding to Mary Talbot, daughter of the privy councillor Earl of Shrewsbury, with emblematic tournaments. A patron might also erect temporary structures or banqueting houses, an action so popular that the royal household eventually resorted to creating offices of Tents and Works as subdivisions of the office of the Revels to take care of the constructions at Hampton, Richmond, Greenwich and St James.[14] City walls, streets and squares were constantly used by civic producers welcoming visiting dignitaries, and noble patrons could make use of such 'environmental theatres' when the monarch went on progress.

Collaboration and multi-mediality

One major difference between these private 'sites of culture' and the public venues was the multi-medial nature of the entertainments produced in the great households. Since most households retained resident performers of different sorts, including musicians, actors, jesters, animal trainers, acrobats and choristers (both adult and child) for their chapels, they could expect their entertainers to combine forces for performances. In addition, resident actors and chaplains could be commissioned to write interludes for the household. Indeed, virtually every known playwright (and probably most of those 'anons') occupied some position in one or more of the patronage networks, so that to some extent we might say that the great household patrons were fundamental to Renaissance public theatre.

The most ubiquitous troupes in the great households were the musicians without whom, it appears from period household accounts, no 'respectable' household could function. Certainly throughout the so-called high Middle Ages, heraldic minstrels were indispensable for martial and ceremonial occasions, and the nobility almost always travelled with a small contingent of trumpets and drums. In addition, soloists on harp, psaltery, lute, organ and virginals, and 'mixed consorts', usually comprising rebec, lute, tabor, viols and fiddles are found in the accounts of most families above the degree of knight. These musicians were responsible not only for playing, but also for preserving family history, carrying messages, repairing instruments and teaching music to family members, who frequently purchased songbooks of their own to exercise their musical abilities in private amusement.

14 Streitberger, *Court Revels*, 12–13 ff.

Music was also frequently provided by resident chapel clergy and Children of the Chapel (so despised by Hamlet in his 'What, are they children?' tirade of 2.2.337–44), who numbered from six to twelve, depending on the size of the household. These were literate musicians, preachers and singers who were responsible primarily for religious service, but also performed as a theatrical company. For example, Edward IV employed thirty-seven in his chapel, eight of whom were children; the fifth Earl of Northumberland retained six children in his chapel of twenty-eight. Households which did not retain chapel personnel often employed boy companies, as when Edward Seymour, lord protector, hired Paul's Boys for New Year's Day; Sir William Petre did the same for his daughter's wedding in 1560.[15] These non-touring entertainers were required to be 'in descant clene voysed, well relysed [blended] and pronouncyng, and eloquent in reding both English and Latin'. Most households owned numbers of antiphons and prick-song books, indicating that these boys could also read music.[16] Chaplains, almoners and chapel gentlemen were among known playwrights, including John Redford, John Heywood, Nicholas Udall and William Hunnis.

Chapels commanded specific play spaces in the chapels, nether chapels and lofts, as well as the great hall for more secular entertainments. They had access to the household wardrobes and vestments for costumes, and chapel plate for set decoration. At Northumberland's household in the early 1500s, besides the plays I have mentioned above, the chapel was specifically directed to perform concerts at Christmas, All Soul's Day, New Year's Day and Easter.

As we know from financial accounts and Hamlet's complaint, boy choristers were popular actors on the public and private stages of England. Chapel boys were also frequent performers in plays and disguisings at the royal courts, and no doubt at the courts of other aristocrats. In fact, many interludes from the mid fifteenth century to the mid sixteenth seem to require chapel involvement, including *Wisdom, Youth, Fulgens and Lucrece, Godly Queen Hester, Wit and Science, Roister Doister, Respublica* and *Jacob & Esau.* All of these plays require large casts that cannot be doubled, music and dance, ingredients specific to chapel productions, as I have explored at length elsewhere.[17] It is interesting that most of these plays are polemical – arguing specific political or religious agenda – another luxury of great household performance.

A full example of such topical and multi-medial entertainments occurred at Henry VIII's court on 6 May 1527, to celebrate Princess Mary's betrothal to

---

15 Westfall, *Patrons and Performance*, 15–16.
16 Myers, *The Household Book of Edward IV*, 135–7.
17 Westfall, 'The Chapel', *English Literary Renaissance* 18.2 (1988), 171–93.

Francis I's son, with the accompanying Anglo-French treaty. After elaborate allegorical jousts, the company retired to a 30 metre by 90 metre temporary banqueting house (which, according to Richard Gibson's accounts, took five months to build and decorate), gilded with gold and blue in compliment to France, hung with tapestries, with windows cut into the walls. There, two chambers were connected by a gallery via an arch with a minstrels' gallery above, whose cost alone for construction and decoration mounted to a little over £574. The king's jewel-encrusted gold and silver plate was on display everywhere in the dining hall, which was lit by elaborate candelabra and a 'pagiant of Lightes' – twenty figures holding candles.

Here, after an elaborate banquet, the company viewed a disguising, which began with a Latin oration praising the kings of France and England as well as the ubiquitous Cardinal Wolsey. The *debat*, entitled *Love and Riches* and featuring chapel gentlemen and children, reiterated the chivalric themes of the morning jousts. Most notably, the performers asked Henry VIII himself to judge the debates, once again blurring the line between spectator and performer. The transparent fourth wall disappeared totally when Princess Mary then entered in a rich disguising with eight gentlemen and ladies, followed by eight more maskers including the king and the French ambassador.[18]

This extravagant revel, united by theme and including several different types of entertainment, was typical of Henry VIII's household revels. Lesser nobility, to be sure, could not afford (either politically or economically) to imitate the complexity of these revels, but we have some evidence that they did mark religious feasts and family occasions with expensive celebrations. For example, the third Earl of Northumberland celebrated Christmas with a tri-partite entertainment. After a torchlight procession into the hall, carefully and hierarchically orchestrated (the earl and duchess entering last and proceeding to the dais), the Twelfth Night revels began with an elaborate banquet accompanied by the chapel choir and minstrels performing carols. A play followed, produced probably by the earl's own troupe, who were ordered to attend him at Christmas. Then minstrels escorted gentlemen and gentlewomen into the hall to perform a disguising, which was interrupted by the entrance of a pageant vehicle out of which burst forth noble henchmen performing a morris dance, almost in the style of an antimasque. At the close of the morris, the disguisers resumed their dances to end their portion of the evening's entertainment. The morris dance, or fool's wooing, actually seems strangely appropriate to

---

18 Streitberger, *Court Revels*, 124–8, supplies records and a detailed description of the extravagant decoration for 'the hovs kalled the long hovs'.

the celebrations for a marriage, which perhaps accounts for Middleton's and Rowley's choice of a dance of madmen and fools for the wedding in *The Changeling*. After the henchmen and disguisers had departed, general dancing and gaming followed.[19]

Players and patrons

While chronicles, financial accounts and household books allow us to recover some aspects of such non-verbal entertainments, we have long been more comfortable tracing the actions of professional player troupes, who performed at royal and baronial courts all over England, subsidised by aristocratic patronage. In fact, McMillin and MacLean assert that by 1583 the Earls of Leicester, Sussex, Oxford and Derby had retained all the most prominent actors in England.[20] This has been a matter of record and a focus for early modern theatre studies for the past century, so I will not labour the issues here, except to point out that in hundreds of thousands of civic and aristocratic account books, records indicate the presence of actors not by their origins, or their names, or their texts, but by the names of their patrons.

Some scholars have assumed that such patrons acted in name only, but more recent study makes clear that the patron–retainer relationship was far more complex. Andrew Gurr reconstructs the company histories of almost twenty companies patronised by the nobility, noting their composition, repertoires and touring details, which allows us to form a much sharper picture of the interactions we have long simply surmised.[21] Certainly the central government assumed that the nobility had some control over their entertainers. As Richard Dutton has observed, potentially seditious materials were sometimes permitted to be performed in household auspices. As early as 1285 the Statute of Winchester addressed the problem of masterless vagabonds, and the statute was reactivated by royal proclamation in 1527 with a reminder in 1531. Years later Elizabeth once again renewed the Act against Retainers and the Act for the Punishment of Vagabonds. The crown also began issuing patents to

---

19 Grose, 'Northumberland's Household Book', 254–7; Lancashire, 'Orders for Twelfth Day and Night', 7–45. Having directed a reconstruction of the earl's Twelfth Night at the Great Hall in University College, University of Toronto, in 1978 (starring the late Robertson Davies as the Earl and Dr Alexandra Johnston, executive editor of the Records of Early English Drama project, as the Duchess of REED), I can bear witness to the complex organisation, opportunity for specific topical allusion and the aesthetic sophistication of the *mise-en-scène*.

20 McMillin and MacLean, *The Queen's Men*, 1.

21 Gurr, *The Shakespearian Playing Companies*, 161–437.

control the patronised troupes, and regulations to control seditious content in plays.[22]

Besides wielding the law, Elizabeth also practised more covert methods to control the use and arguments of her theatre. In a ground-breaking and thorough study that makes splendid use of the REED records, MacLean and McMillin have focused on the Earl of Leicester and his part in helping to create and maintain the Queen's Men. Their work affirms my argument that patrons, even in the heyday of the public theatre, still took active roles in the administration and in the repertoires of their troupes. MacLean and McMillin conclude, for example, that part of the reason that Leicester and other noblemen were willing to contribute their best players to an amalgamated troupe under the queen's titular patronage was that such a 'monopoly' (later to be replaced by the 'duopoly' of the Lord Chamberlain's Men and the Lord Admiral's Men) increased Privy Council control over public playing, thereby ensuring that the interests of the patrons in political and religious issues were properly represented.

Most interestingly, MacLean and McMillin go on to suggest that this bold move, while reducing the likelihood of recusant themes, also protected the players against the slings and arrows of the radical Protestants, intent on attacking the public stage. In support of the politics of the creation of the Queen's Men, we do indeed find that the troupe toured very actively, so that it could properly serve the function for which it was born. These discoveries once again affirm the importance of household theatre, even after the public theatres of London were in their full strength; touring players were far more effective as spies, emissaries and messengers, stopping at towns and other noble households, than were the stay-at-home London actors.[23]

Noble patronage might also inspire higher wages and rewards on tours, Mary Blackstone has convincingly argued. For example, in 1540/1 the city of Dover rewarded their local patron the Duke of Suffolk's players 6 shillings and 8 pence, whereas more far-flung communities gave them only the typical 12 pence. The Earl of Northumberland's household book institutionalises this practice, specifying that performers retained by a 'speciall Lorde Frende or Kynsman' receive higher rewards than others.[24]

Household accounts also note the popularity of novelty entertainers such as court fools (both natural and artificial), and bearwards (who travelled with

---

22 Dutton, *Mastering the Revels*, 41–5.
23 McMillin and MacLean, *The Queen's Men*, 18–30.
24 Blackstone, 'Patrons and Elizabethan dramatic companies', in McGee (ed.), *Elizabethan Theatre X*, 112–32; Dawson (ed.), *Records of Plays and Players in Kent*, 39, 69; Grose, 'Northumberland's Household Book', 253.

trained animals). Edward I was entertained by his fool Bernard and fifty-four of his 'companions' dancing naked before the king. Odd references to such antics as 'minstrelsy with snakes' and to the multi-talented Roland le Fartere, who was rewarded for 'making a leap, a whistle, and a fart', enliven the account books. Henry VII rewarded two Flemish women that 'did pipe, dance, and play' an exorbitant £8.[25] The royal court paid the Earl of Oxford's bearward, players 'with mamettes' for a puppet show at the May game, for a 'disare [storyteller] that played the Sheppert before the Quene' and for 'setyng vppe of the may pole at Westmynster', just to show that not all court revels were 'highbrow' like Wolsey's entertainment of a banquet, a disguising featuring the king, a classical pageant of Venus and Senex, and Plautus's *Menaechmi* in Latin at York Place in 1527. A payment to William Cornish for 'paving gutters of lead for urinals' for a 1516 Greenwich joust both brings us down to earth and demonstrates the foresight of those charged with producing household performances.[26] These sorts of entertainment occur in household account books incidentally, with no discernible pattern in date or reward, leading to our impression that courts were always open to originality and that enterprising performers might expect generous rewards for feeding the appetite for novelty.

Occasional celebrations

Unlike the public stages, private households employed all those resident artists who could collaborate to create a theatrical 'event', a phenomenon with which we are extremely familiar from accounts of the masques of Jonson and Jones at the court of King James. These sorts of entertainment, however, had been staged at least since the accession of Henry VII in the houses of rich noblemen. Sidney Anglo has written in detail about the court entertainments of Henry VII, including the elaborate wedding revels for Prince Arthur and Princess Catherine of Aragon, for which minstrels, actors, painters, confectioners and a variety of other artists and labourers were put to work.[27] When a great household celebrated a major religious feast or secular festival, it strove to amalgamate, to produce a multi-dimensional entertainment by enlisting the co-operation of many people, from cooks to composers, from priests to players.

These household performances are unique in form, content and motivation. Because entertainments tended to be occasional – specific to social, liturgical

25 Westfall, *Patrons and Performance*, 91.
26 Streitberger, *Court Revels*, 244–5, 249, 252, 263, 272 and *passim*.
27 Anglo, *Spectacle, Pageantry, and Early Tudor Policy*.

and political events – they would also be geared to a specific audience, and intended to define, to self-fashion as it were, the aristocratic patron. Fixed or temporary stages and household possessions provided sophisticated set and costume opportunities, the variety of entertainers encouraged collaboration in design and performance, while the non-profit (at least in real money) nature left the designers considerably freer to experiment and over-produce, since the patron absorbed the cost, at least until frugal Elizabeth found a way to make other patrons pay.

These factors clearly distinguish private household drama from that of the public stage. Aristocratic, educational and ecclesiastical households had the money, the space and the personnel to produce such entertainments. The closest comparison might be to the civic organisations, which also produced ephemeral and occasional pageants with similar production values to welcome visiting dignitaries or to celebrate civic occasions like royal weddings, Lord Mayor's shows, coronations, or progresses. These occasions were also elaborate, expensive and non-profit, except for the political benefit that a city might expect from an honouree.

These household aesthetics were put into action on a specific occasion, the revels surrounding the marriages of the fifth Earl of Northumberland's sister and/or his daughter, between 1511 and 1515. This Order demonstrates that art often reflects life; through a co-operative effort of household servants, the wedding revels illustrate the ideology and aesthetics of noble marriage. The revels are theatre, with specific sets, hierarchical characters, indexual costumes, precise blocking and linear structure, prescriptions that destroy any remaining notion that household entertainments were casual, unconstructed and potentially wild events. Rather, these revels were carefully directed and stage-managed, commingling public and private space, public and private experience, as the participants progress through the geographical space of the household.

At first glance, a family wedding may seem a private and secular event, and, in comparison to the great religious feasts, it certainly is. In fact, in pre-Reformation England a religious service was not required, only a civil contract and 'betrothal'. Nevertheless, when two aristocratic families merged, the marriage became a public and liturgical event, requiring the participation of the clergy, in this case specifically Percy's chapel. In addition, a Tudor marriage was likely to be a political and economic event, attended by many guests who brought with them their own entertainers, and who bore public witness not only to the alliance, but also to the political, economic and social power of the families involved.[28] Consequently, the family produced a public show of their 'private' life, displaying family treasures of plate and arras, providing lavish banquets[29] with every variety of food the earl's far-flung properties could provide or exotic delicacies his unstinting purse could purchase. In addition to these displays, entertainments by the earl's retained artists demonstrated the sophistication of his private life, and ensured that wedding guests left in suitable awe of their host.

The twelfth order of the *Second Northumberland Household Book* shows that the earl took the opportunity to display his wealth, almost as set decoration for the theatre that was to come. Thus the earl 'produces' a social space, marking his territory by transmogrifying the church (which many might consider an egalitarian and public space where all the assembled company could be equal in the sight of God) into a chamber within his home, foregrounding his possessions. The first four of the six articles within the order stipulate that the high altar, the choir, the body of the chapel and the two altars at the chapel door were to be covered with 'the best stuf that they have', hung with 'arras

28 The political effect of wedding celebrations may be observed in the royal weddings celebrated during the reign of Henry VII. When Henry married Elizabeth of York, daughter of Edward IV, the wedding revels must have been subdued, for they pass almost without comment. Hall notes only that: 'lyke a good prynce accordyng to his othe and promes, he did both solempnise and consummate [the marriage] in brief tyme after, that is to say on the xviij daye of Ianuary' (*Vnion*, 424–5). Henry was adamant that his subjects recognise that the throne was his through his own noble lineage, conquest and divine right rather than through his marriage to the heiress of the previous monarch. In marked contrast, when Henry married his heir Prince Arthur to Princess Catherine of Aragon, the king required that the world bear witness to the alliance, for the marriage symbolised international recognition of the Tudor dynasty. Consequently, this marriage was marked by perhaps the most elaborate revels of his reign, including a tournament, four elaborate banquets and disguisings. Similarly, when Princess Margaret was married by proxy to James IV of Scotland in 1502, Henry once again seized the opportunity to broadcast the alliance by staging a tournament and disguising. Although this second wedding was celebrated more simply than the previous year's (perhaps due to the recent deaths of the queen and prince), it certainly outshone the king's own wedding in 1486.
29 Although the menu is, of course, non-extant, Percy's household accounts provide some indication of the foods that may have been served. Over the twelve days of Christmas, the revellers consumed venison, swans, cranes, herons, pheasants, peacocks and other birds (Grose, 'Northumberland's Household Book', 103, 167). In 1552, when Sir William Petre celebrated his daughter's wedding, he hired a master cook and four apprentices, and entertained 400 guests for two days (Emmison, *Tudor Food and Pastimes*, 32). Percy's wedding festivities may well have been on the same scale, if his banquet and entertainment of Princess Margaret in 1502 are any indication. Each item of the dinner is served separately, by a gentleman usher, household officer or yeoman usher bearing a towel over his arm, like a contemporary maître d' hôtel. Each servitor makes his obeisance, serves the bride, then departs. Only after the bride has been served are her attendants served. Thus, a gentleman usher and yeoman usher bring the basin and towel for her to wash. They retreat, the chaplain says grace, and then the carver and server process to the bride with the first course. They in turn are succeeded by the cupbearer (Bodleian MS Eng. hist. B. 208. fols. 27v–29).

or counterfeat arras'; Percy's silver and gilt church plate was displayed on the high and doorway altars.[30] In the midst of this 'set' Percy's chapel singers performed the polyphonic music for which they were distinguished.

Other orders dictate precedence, the province of the earl's chamberlain who was responsible for ensuring that each link in the chain of social order was properly placed. Concerned primarily with matters of hierarchy and protocol, the orders ensure that each person is properly placed according to rank, facilitate the precise timing of the procession, and prescribe the attendance and dress of the bride, depending upon her marital history – whether she were a maiden, a widow or previously betrothed. While these ceremonial matters have long been considered the province of social and legal history, they have become intriguing to theatre historians as well, for ceremonials are clearly theatrical – they employ set, costume and choreography and suggest themes and plots in their constructions and executions.

The sixth article also stipulates that the earl himself was waiting in the choir to give the bride away 'yf their be not A better to yef her that Day'.[31] This last comment is particularly interesting, for it indicates that rank was more significant than kinship, that the family patriarch customarily relinquished his paternal right if a guest of higher rank were in attendance, clear evidence that the private, domestic aspect of marriage was, in aristocratic nuptials, turned inside out, with the private publicly reconstructed and displayed, and the small play of social hierarchy acted out. Even the blocking of the wedding ceremony would be emblematic: the daughter of an earl or baron was to be married at the choir doors, that of a knight at the chapel door, and women below that status outside the church door entirely.[32]

Subsequent orders describe in detail the wedding ceremony, the wedding supper and festivities, including an afternoon of dancing, accompanied by the earl's retained minstrels and minstrels that noble guests had brought along. It is possible that visiting entertainers – local jugglers, acrobats or players (reminiscent of the 'hard-handed men that work in Athens' at Theseus's wedding in *A Midsummer Night's Dream*) – might conveniently fit into the revels here without disturbing the preordained design. In the evening, during a 'bankett', the guests viewed an entertainment performed by disguisers and players, followed by the rather public 'bedding procedures' so necessary to the aristocratic cult of virginity and legitimacy.

After the great effort and expense of the preparations for the wedding, after many guests had travelled various distances to participate, it is unlikely that

---

30 Bodleian MS Eng. hist. B. 208. fol. 23.
31 Ibid., fol. 24.   32 Ibid., fols. 25–31v.

Percy's wedding revels ended after one short day. Beatrice–Joanna's continued for three days in *The Changeling*; the 1563 Talbot–Herbert union was celebrated for four days; royal marriages such as Prince Arthur's and Princess Margaret's went on far longer. The wedding orders in the *Second Northumberland Household Book* describe only the activities of the marriage day, but feasting, dancing, hunting and theatrical performances may well have continued afterwards.

Such combinations of music, dance, banquet, play and disguising appear to be a popular structure for most great household revels. At about the time of the marriage of the earl's female kin, Henry VII marked the wedding celebration of his daughter Margaret to James of Scotland in similar fashion. Although no plays are specifically mentioned (we know, however, that the king's players, led by John English, performed a 'moralitee' at the wedding), the revels did include a disguising with pageant device and a banquet.

Several facets of performance unique to the disguising made it extremely popular as a courtly entertainment. Like a play, a disguising could be commissioned to celebrate a specific occasion by referring to particular events and people and by employing allegory complimentary to the interests of the household. A play performed by a small troupe of interluders could never hope to be as extravagant a theatrical display as could a disguising that involved a greater number and variety of performers. Chapel gentlemen and children, singing and perhaps speaking, joined with minstrels and dancing gentlemen and gentlewomen to create a visual and aural extravaganza that interluders could not match, as Sydney Anglo, W. R. Streitberger, and Steven Orgel and John Astington have all amply demonstrated in their work on the masque and disguising.

Other qualities of the disguising made it an ideal entertainment for a patron who wished to impress his guests with his wealth and artistic sophistication. A disguising was expensive, including costs for costumes and scenic devices, and was never intended to be recreated; since it could never return a profit or even meet expenses, the household absorbed the entire expense. In addition, the disguising involved the guests in a fashion that a play could not. Some may have participated themselves as disguisers, others recognised friends among the dancers. Never intended for general-admission audiences, the disguising not only entertained the elite but flattered them as well, complimenting their intellect with its often classical themes, and reflecting their own courtly lifestyle, while at the same time impressing on the surrounding servitors of all classes that they were in the familial embrace of powerful and sophisticated people, the equivalent of the twenty-first century's 'beautiful people'. The sole profit to the patron, the grandeur of the impression, made it a splendidly wasteful display.

Percy would have been even more inclined to include a play in his wedding revels because he would be hesitant to produce the entertainment that figured most prominently in the royal weddings: the allegorical tournament. Both Prince Arthur's and Princess Margaret's weddings were marked by chivalric jousts, the former lasting an entire week. The nobleman who felt secure enough to stage his own tournament under Henry VIII's rule was rare, for obvious reasons; no monarch would smile at a martial display from a powerful vassal, and few aristocrats could afford either the financial expense or the risk of treason that the tournament could imply. This situation had changed by Elizabeth's time, as evinced by the jousts organised for weddings by Pembroke and Sidney, mentioned above.

In these noble weddings, the private lives and spaces of the aristocratic family were intentionally turned inside out, made public for the occasion. Masculine and feminine worlds, choreographed like a pavane, meet, retreat and mingle once again in great chamber and bedchamber. The hospitality of the home is enlarged and orchestrated into a corporate event employing hundreds of family retainers. Rather than the domestic intervening in the outside world of politics and economics, the domestic becomes a cauldron for these forces.

Texts

In this context, household theatre comprises many forms and intricate socio-political patterns. Playtexts produced within the households serve these characteristics, since both their forms and their contents differ considerably from the public theatre, whether the cycle plays, miracle plays and saint plays under civic and ecclesiastical patronage, or the plays of the London theatres under public patronage.

What sorts of plays might we expect to find in the households? Certainly from 1580 onwards we find many of the same plays that we find on the London public stages, for, after all, the premier household in England is the queen's, and her revels demand that the best troupes in the city perform before her. I would never suggest that all plays were written for households of course, but playwrights would clearly see the financial advantages of offering their work to both a generous patron and/or the Revels office at the same time as they sold it to the public stages. But before the 1570s, many of the plays that we call interludes or moral plays do indeed seem to have been commissioned by aristocratic patrons, performed within their households, and, if the production values of the text were appropriate, toured by their players. It should surprise no one that these plays often reflected the politics, religions and aspirations of their patrons.

Before the Tudor era *Wisdom Who is Christ, or Mind Will and Understanding* (*c.* 1460–74) is very much the sort of play we should expect to be staged in a great household. Rather than being an anomaly, as some would have it, the play encompasses precisely household aesthetics. To begin with, the subject and form indicate a fairly learned audience, since it contains more than a smattering of Latin in its complex philosophical arguments about maintenance and authority, themes very near to the aristocratic heart and oft-repeated in the interludes of the period. In addition, Wisdom is a king and the sins mentioned (simony, 'worldly worschyppe', promiscuity, etc.) are not generally the trespasses of a rural or working-class audience. The play also requires a large cast (five speaking roles and five who double as wits, demons, whores and other extras – notably courtiers of both genders), which indicates to me the co-operation of a troupe of resident actors and chapel children. Some have suggested an ecclesiastical household as auspices, but the intensely secular humour, including a mime of prostitutes, seems to discourage that theory. *Wisdom* also demands very high production values and the budget necessary to provide them.

In style, many have found the piece stagey, rather more like the later masque than a lively play, which is precisely the way I would describe great-household performances, without, of course, the condescending implication that masques are not 'lively'. Elaborately costumed henchmen (another household fixture) follow Mind, Will and Understanding in a complex dance, which certainly provides the spectacle and 'liveliness' the audience would crave. This effect also discourages touring, which again reinforces the conclusion that this play is intended to be ephemeral and occasional, to be a not-for-profit offering in a household that could afford the financial and artistic commitment.

Even though the play, through the Macro Manuscript in which it has been preserved, has often been associated with Bury St Edmond's, Alexandra Johnston makes a persuasive case that *Wisdom* was commissioned by local nobility, perhaps by the Duke of Norfolk or Suffolk, both of whom lived nearby. Johnston points out that REED volumes contain no evidence for drama originating within the priories, though there is ample evidence of performance in ecclesiastical establishments by touring troupes under the patronage of the nobility.[33] This seems to decide the argument for auspices in favour of a lay

---

33 For a thorough discussion of staging, see Riggio, *The 'Wisdom' Symposium*.

rather than an ecclesiastical household. The central point is, of course, that either way *Wisdom* is a household play.

During the past twenty-five years, many scholars have been working to attribute anonymous early Tudor playtexts to patrons and great household auspices. Early on, Sydney Anglo's *Spectacle, Pageantry, and Early Tudor Policy* and David Bevington's *Tudor Drama and Politics* proved, as if we had any doubt, that theatre was central to court life as early as the turn of the fifteenth century. Henry VII's taste for continental style in extravagant revels developed during his exile in the Burgundian court, as well as his commitment to establishing, in both reality and fantasy, the rightness of his violent deposition of the Plantagenets, produced entertainments that exploited specific allegories designed to reinforce and compliment the new Tudor dynasty. Bevington's argument, that drama was naturally polemical and that patrons either chose or commissioned works that would communicate their own ideologies, has become an assumption for scholars studying patronage and player repertories.

More recently, McMillin and MacLean, in their detailed discussion of the repertoire of one particular company, the Queen's Men, connect players and specific texts, an achievement that years ago we could but wish for. Their research once again confirms Bevington's prediction, that the ideologies of the patrons affected, if not dictated, the texts of their players. The Queen's Men (with the support of Protestants like Walsingham and Leicester) were engaged in promulgating ideological state apparatuses, in discouraging recusancy and more radical puritanism simultaneously, which also happened to be the ideological concerns of their patrons.[34]

This conclusion is not new. Paul Whitfield White explores in detail the relationship among plays, patrons and religious polemics. We have known for years that 'bilious Bale' and his 'felowes' worked for Thomas Cromwell during the 1530s, with his virulently anti-Catholic *Kynge Johan*, performed at Canterbury in the household of Archbishop Cranmer, forming almost a model of the political use of the stage. Bale's other extant plays, *Three Laws, God's Promises, Johan Baptystes Preachyng* and *The Temptation of Our Lord*, clearly toe the royal and Cromwellian party-line, while the titles of the lost plays (*Concerning the Deceptions of the Papists, On the Papist Sects, The Knaveries of Thomas Becket,* for example) leave little to the imagination about Bale's religious opinions.[35]

Of course the religious card could be played both ways. John Lyly, who counted the Catholic Earl of Oxford among his patrons, seems to try to

---

34 McMillin and MacLean, *The Queen's Men*, 86ff.
35 White, *Theatre and Reformation*, 12–27.

temper the queen's attitudes by recommending tolerance toward Catholics in *Endymion* and *Midas*. Sir Richard Cholemeley's players, who performed *King Lear* and *Pericles* for the household of Sir John Yorke (*c*.1609–10), got into serious trouble with the Star Chamber for their recusant interpretations of plays, suggesting that Shakespeare's plays might be interpreted in ways sympathetic to the sufferings of the northern Catholics. Just two years later, the same Sir John was once again in hot water for harbouring priests and sponsoring a seditious interlude as well as a saint play in his household; these revels seem to create public space for recusant festivity, including fireworks, lightning, thunder and the expulsion of known anti-Catholics who later testified that the Church of England had been ridiculed. Even Shakespeare has been claimed as a playwright at least sympathetic to the recusancy, with patronage ties to the Houghton family.[36]

Women and households

Household theatre, besides revealing the contours of the religious landscape, also complicates our views of gender roles in Tudor and Stuart performance, for household theatre gives women a role they were denied on the public stage, in spite of the irony that two women sat on the throne. Feminist criticism has inspired some of the most refreshing discoveries in household patronage, showing that women took a vital role in artistic production in early modern England. We have known for ages that women were proscribed from the stage except at the two social extremes – as vaudeville-type travelling entertainers and court fools or as noble dancers in masques and disguisings – all of these exclusively household entertainments. Here, women found freedom to produce and perform in disguisings and masques beginning during the reign of Henry VII and culminating in the Stuart court masque that Jones and Jonson helped Queen Anne to produce. A woman might also have some aesthetic control over her revels, as when the queen, desiring some exotic (and erotic?) fantasy, requested Ben Jonson to compose a masque in which she and her ladies could appear 'all paynted like Blackamores face and neck bare', inspired perhaps by the spectacle of Africans dancing 'naked in the snow in front of the royal carriage' at her own wedding.

We know that several women, including seven queens (Catherine of Aragon, Anne Boleyn, Jane Seymour, Mary I, Elizabeth, Anne and later Henrietta

---

36 Honigmann, *Shakespeare: the 'Lost Years'*; Sams, *The Real Shakespeare*; Honan, *Shakespeare: a Life*.

Maria), served as patrons to artists and playwrights who created household entertainments. Noble women such as Susan Vere, Countess of Montgomery, Lady Anne Herbert and Lady Mary Wroth performed. Even after the government closed the theatres in 1642, the women of the Cavendish household produced their domestic theatrical *The Concealed Fancies*. David Bergeron has identified, through dedications of dramatic texts, at least fourteen women who served as patrons.[37] Through patronage and purse strings, a few women did indeed have a say in the theatrical art of their era. And in more indirect fashion, women in the audiences, both public and private/household, served as patrons, a situation satirised in quite controversial style in *The Knight of the Burning Pestle*.

Women could participate in private household entertainments in a variety of ways. Many, like Margaret Beaufort, mother of King Henry VII and patron of the poet/playwright John Skelton, headed their own households and therefore acted as patrons to poets and performers within them. Lady Honor Lisle went shopping in 1538 and purchased the text of an interlude called *Rex Diabole*, then presumably produced it for her household. Denied roles in the civic and public theatre, women sang, played musical instruments, spoke text and danced in disguisings and masques. Matilda Makejoy, one of the very few female minstrels on record, entertained the royal court with dances and acrobatics in the early fourteenth century. Aemilia Lanyer, feminist poet and (at least to A. L. Rowse) Shakespeare's 'dark lady', was a member of the recorder-playing Bassano family who served Henry VIII, receiving in the process a monopoly on Gascon wine and the confiscated London monastery of Charterhouse.[38]

And, of course, women often provided the theme and point of entertainments, as countless prologues and epilogues demonstrate. It would be impossible for me to list the innumerable compliments to Elizabeth that trod the boards during her reign, but I will indulge in a couple of the more extreme examples. John Lyly, who held a post in the household of Queen Elizabeth's lord high treasurer, William Cecil, Lord Burleigh, was also under the patronage of Edward de Vere, Earl of Oxford; his *Endymion*, drawing freely from Eliza's identifications with Diana and the moon, has always been considered a thinly veiled compliment to the chastity of Queen Elizabeth and the devotion of her courtiers, as have many of his other classically influenced plays. The extremely artificial end to George Peele's *The Araygnement of Paris*, in which

---

37 Bergeron, 'Women as patrons of English Renaissance drama', in Lytle and Orgel (eds.), *Patronage in the Renaissance*, 274–90.
38 Lasocki, 'Professional recorder playing in England, 1500–1740', *Early Music* 10.1 (1982), 23–8.

the prize golden apple rolls to the queen's feet, demonstrates just how blatant appeals to feminine influence might be.

Conclusion

Throughout this essay I have referred to patronage and patronage networks, socio-political structures that inform not only theatre but also Tudor culture. Household revels and patronage are inextricably wound together, as the former is an expression of the latter. Consequently, investigating household theatre leads to speculation about its function within the political system, and ultimately its value to the people who paid the pipers. Clifford Geertz, writing from the anthropological wing, puts it best:

> At the political center of any complexly organised society . . . there is both a governing elite and a set of symbolic forms expressing the fact that it is in truth governing. No matter how democratically the members of the elite are chosen (usually not very) or how deeply divided among themselves they may be (usually much more than outsiders imagine), they justify their existence and order their actions in terms of a collection of stories, ceremonies, insignia, formalities and appurtenances that they have either inherited or, in more revolutionary situations, invented. It is these – crowns and coronations, limousines and conferences – that mark the center and give what goes on there its aura of being not merely important but in some odd fashion connected with the way the world is built. The gravity of high politics and the solemnity of high worship spring from liker impulses than might first appear.[39]

Clearly great household performances are exactly the 'set of symbolic forms' that express the political power of the patron. As REED editors discover new records, as scholars stitch those records into coherent narratives, we are finding that what we had once assumed to be a rather monovalent monarchy, a so-called 'great chain' is showing its stress lines. Rather than one unified ideological state apparatus, we find many – sometimes competing and conflicting. In spite of repeated attempts at control by the city and crown, we find that art will discover a way to express the hearts and minds of its authors and audiences, as we find at Sir John Yorke's celebration of Catholicism. Instead of the Revels office as censor, we find an office dedicated to balancing patronage and patrons to produce the most profit from theatrical pleasure.

Studies of household theatre and patronage also balance our view of the public stage in London as the centre and epitome of performance in the

---

39 Geertz, *Local Knowledge*, 124.

Elizabethan era. Years ago we abandoned the 'big bang' theory that secular drama was expelled from nave to market-place because of its comic coarseness; perhaps it is also time to acknowledge that Shakespeare did not spring, fully grown with quill in hand, from the trap of the Globe, and that London public theatre was not the only high-quality performance in the land. Provincial theatre flourished then, just as it does now.

I do not mean to suggest that theatre happens only from the top classes down. Throughout these times we also see an intertwining line of popular theatre, as Michael Bristol has pointed out so clearly, [40] a line that frequently intersects patron theatre in such activities as the Feast of Fools, folk festivals (or their imitations in court disguisings) and the various 'vaudeville' entertainers at any aristocratic fête. By the end of the sixteenth century, obviously, these lines had intertwined so that companies like the Queen's Men, the Lord Chamberlain's Men and the Lord Admiral's Men clearly had two patrons – the monarch *and* the paying public. In some cases these two patrons worked at cross purposes, but in most cases they appeared to be quite comfortable as bedfellows, implying that aristocratic patronage offered perquisites that the public could not, and that the public offered economic rewards that the patrons were (if we can believe, for example, in Queen Elizabeth's frugal habit of getting others to pay for her entertainment) reluctant to distribute.

Household revels, then, provide us with a unique cross-section of early modern theatre. In multi-medial, occasion-specific events the patrons, in the dual roles of producers and spectators, exercised and manifested their power, both aesthetically and politically. Employing their retained artists – performers, painters, writers, cooks and carpenters – as collaborators in a non-profit entertainment, household patrons had long served as suppliers of theatre. Perhaps the increasing competition among patrons and the replacement of the feudal system with incipient capitalism, based heavily on patronage politics, finally encouraged some actors to market their commodities in more lucrative and rewarding ways. But for the Catholics in the provinces, the women in country households, the aristocrats with political or religious convictions and the liveried players touring through the land, these auspices offered opportunities not only to connect with the way the world is built but also to contribute to the construction of their culture.

40 Bristol, *Carnival and Theater.*

8

The birth of an industry

DOUGLAS BRUSTER

The period of literary history we call the English Renaissance has at its core the new commercial theatre of the sixteenth and seventeenth centuries. While the term 'Renaissance' may initially call to mind courtly writings, such as *The Faerie Queene* and *Astrophel and Stella*, it is the surviving texts of the commercial playhouses that have most strongly shaped our fascination with this period. So frequently are these plays edited, read, taught and performed, in fact, that they can seem freestanding monuments, dramatic stories left to history by the grace of a culture replete with literary talent. Yet in their own time, the dramas of such playwrights as Shakespeare, Marlowe, Jonson, Middleton and Webster were commodities, and perishable ones at that. Far from the glorified, handsomely adorned things that we encounter in classrooms, and on stage and screen, they were instead part of a bustling new theatrical business that may with justification be called an 'entertainment industry'.[1]

At first blush, the term 'industry' may seem too formal for use in this regard. Given its sometimes rag-tag players, secondhand costumes, impoverished playwrights, noisome playhouses and uncertain conditions of employment, the business of theatre at this time seems to have been so unpredictable, and generally so financially unrewarding, that to call it an industry risks implying a stability it did not possess. When seen from historical distance, and from the perspectives of those who worked within it, however, the business of theatre in the sixteenth and seventeenth centuries was indeed an industry; on the whole it offered the commercial production and sale of theatrical spectacle in a regularised, highly competitive environment. Playing companies retailed these spectacles in playhouses built expressly for this purpose, as well as in many other venues.

Accordingly, this essay explores the industry which playing constituted in England during the sixteenth and seventeenth centuries, paying attention to

---

1 For this phrase, see McLuskie, 'The patriarchal bard: feminist criticism and Shakespeare', in Dollimore and Sinfield (eds.), *Political Shakespeare*, 92.

the economic aspects of the playhouses, playing, writing plays, playgoing and the publication of playbooks. These economic aspects are described here broadly, in the hope that together they may supply a meaningful context for understanding how and why the plays we have come to admire were originally written and performed. The essay closes by discussing what we have to gain, as well as what we risk, by sustaining an economic focus on the theatre of this time.

The playhouses

We could begin examining the business of playing in sixteenth- and seventeenth-century England by taking note of the structures built for that purpose. During the formative years of the 1560s and 1570s, four playhouses were constructed near London for professional playing. The Red Lion, built about a mile to the east of London, began the trend in 1567. It was followed, in 1576, by three other playhouses: the Theatre and the Curtain, both built that year in Shoreditch, to the north-east of London; a mile below the city, in another county, a playhouse was built at Newington Butts. Before this time, and even after it, actors had of necessity adapted themselves to the spaces they found: the hall of a great house; an innyard; a city street; a large chamber at court. These places and more were used for the presentation of plays, and continued to be used when the companies left their base in London's playhouses. This was especially the case when productions at the new playhouses were made difficult by weather or epidemic (the latter of which led to prohibitions on playing when deaths in London from the plague reached a certain number). With the rise of the purpose-built playhouses actors had, for the first time in English history, places dedicated primarily to the business of playing, regular sites of theatrical commerce. That the theatre could be good business is apparent from the playhouses built in the decades which followed, among which were the Rose in 1587, the Swan in 1595–6, the Globe and the Boar's Head in 1599, the Fortune in 1600, the Red Bull in 1605, and the Hope in 1613.[2]

The centralisation of playing in these newly constructed and adapted buildings formed part of a larger cultural movement; the same impetus that led to the development of these structures led as well to the construction of financial institutions like Gresham's Exchange (1566–7) and the New Exchange (1609).

2 Two of these playhouses – the Boar's Head and the Red Bull – appear to have been converted from inns, rather than constructed from the ground up.

Clearly, individuals sought the regularising influence of physical structures to help them manage the growing complexities of business. Just as apparent is that theatre and finance were profitable enough to have structures dedicated to their operations. The parallel chronology of these institutions and buildings asks us to think across English culture, and to expand the kinds of question that we ask about the business of playing. How did the construction of the Globe playhouse in 1599, for instance, relate to a social fact like Elizabeth's signing of documents the following year, legitimating the transactions of the East India Company? To what degree were the plays which we understand as art understood by those within the theatrical industry of their time as commodities? To ask such questions is to begin to acknowledge a larger historical narrative involving the consolidation of cultural activities in new forms, practices and structures.

Many of these playhouses were situated in the outskirts of London, in the areas generally known as London's 'liberties'. Because the liberties were outside the easy reach of the authorities, and often associated with lawlessness, it is sometimes held that the playhouses must have been somehow lawless themselves, presenting activities and ideas that challenged the status quo. As Steven Mullaney argues in *The Place of the Stage*, the liminal position of these theatres was paralleled by transgressive material in the plays offered there. This argument is not without supporting evidence: those who criticised the playhouses during the sixteenth and seventeenth centuries often described them in language which stressed licentiousness, transgression and even subversion. But the argument from location fails to acknowledge that not all playhouses were in the outskirts of London, or that location need not imply a political source or orientation. We might sense a greater truth about the status of the playhouses during this period, in fact, by noting that when the Blackfriars theatre was challenged by its neighbours, it was censured not because of its ideological implications, but in relation to the noise and traffic it would bring to the area – complaints not unfamiliar in urban settings today when new enterprises are proposed.

Theatre buildings were most often situated in the liberties, perhaps, not because actors and playwrights had discernible political agendas, but because (at least in relation to the exterior liberties) rents were cheaper there than in areas closer in, and because in the liberties theatrical companies could elude much of the interference of city neighbours and regulations, the latter of which tended to impede business operations. Such is the conclusion of Melissa Aaron, whose reading of Shakespeare's *Henry V* as a business document refers to the liberties as 'enterprise zones', places 'attractive to theatrical companies seeking economic freedom'.[3] In his study *The Business of Playing*, William Ingram also supports this interpretation, when he submits that the Act of Common Council of 6 December 1574 can be read as enabling, rather than suppressing, theatrical business in London. That is, the bureaucratic fees and fines imposed in the Act may have been a bid by the city officials to benefit financially from the presentation of plays and interludes in the many inns of London, by taxing the places of playing. If Ingram's theory is correct, by situating their playhouses further out, the playhouse entrepreneurs (actors and investors alike) were evading the authorities' desire for profit while advancing their own.

However much these interpretations counterbalance readings which exaggerate the ideological potential of this era's dramas, it may be misleading here to sustain an opposition of economics and politics. For what separates the two, perhaps, is more the gulf between current critical assumptions and emphases – between, on the one hand, those critics who see the playhouses as primarily challenging the orthodoxies of their day, and, on the other, those who see them as primarily diverting and entertaining audiences for money – than any real disjunction between commerce and ideology. Although Paul Yachnin is surely right to argue that the sixteenth- and seventeenth-century theatres were politically 'powerless', it might have been the case that some of those writing for and acting in them, as well as those attending the performances, believed otherwise; and such a belief in itself could have had consequences.[4]

It is relevant here to note that the most popular production of the entire era – 'popular' here taken to mean the ability to hold the stage – was Middleton's *A Game at Chess*, which played at the Globe for nine consecutive days (excluding Sundays) in August of 1624. Here any opposition between 'entertainment' and 'politics' necessarily dissolves, for this anti-Spanish satire succeeded in doing political work only by being thoroughly entertaining, and entertained its audiences only by offering focused political satire. Politics and entertainment, in this play, went hand in glove.

On the whole, however, plays of this era seem to have succeeded by being enjoyable pastimes. As Richard Perkins asked, rhetorically, in a poem prefacing Thomas Heywood's *Apology for Actors* in 1612, 'Thou that do'st rail at me for seeing a play, / How wouldst thou have me spend my idle hours?' Those in attendance were delighted both visually and aurally, for theatres offered a

---

3 Aaron, 'The Globe and *Henry V* as business document', *Studies in English Literature 1500–1900* 40:2 (2000), 277–92. I am grateful to Aaron for sharing this and other of her work with me prior to its publication. See also Rappaport, *Worlds within Worlds*, 35.

4 Yachnin, 'The powerless theater', *English Literary Renaissance* 21 (1991), 49–74, later included in his *Stage-Wrights*.

rich montage of attractions. We can see this in a contemporary document advertising a production of *England's Joy* at the Swan playhouse on 6 November 1602. In a printed playbill, Richard Vennar gives a synopsis of the drama in nine heads, each episode of which involves impressive characters, costumes and action. The concluding ninth episode is especially rich in detail:

> Lastly, the Nine Worthyes, with seuerall Coronets, present themselues before the Throne, which are put backe by certaine in the habit of Angels, who set vpon the Ladies head, which represents her Maiestie, an Emperiall Crowne, garnished with the *Sunne, Moone* and *Starres*; and so with Musicke both with voyce and Instruments shee is taken vp into Heauen, when presently appeares, a Throne of blessed Soules, and beneath vnder the Stage set forth with strange fireworkes, diuers blacke and damned Soules, wonderfully discribed in their seuerall torments.

Unfortunately, Vennar's play existed only in his head; it was a hoax production which, in not transpiring, led to the vandalising of the Swan by playgoers unhappy to be defrauded in this way. Nevertheless, even as all successful advertisement speaks to the content of existing fantasies, Vennar's tantalising 'plot' of *England's Joy* tells us something about what people went to the playhouses for: spectacle, sumptuous costumes, fascinating props, ceremony, instrumental and vocal music, even fireworks.

One might analogise what happened in a theatre to the way an empty fairground or market-place becomes gradually full of people during the day – offering many goods, events, sights, sounds and smells – before emptying again as the day ends. In a similar way, the playhouses drew large numbers: Andrew Gurr estimates that, in the sixteenth and early seventeenth centuries, 'well over fifty million visits were made to the playhouses' in London.[5] Apart from any food and drink purchased in the playhouses, what people went home with were primarily memories of productions: recollections of stories, actors, characters, costumes, music, sword fights, speeches and striking phrases. The playhouses took money and in return gave audiences what Samuel Daniel would call 'Punctillos of Dreams and shows'.

Whether we choose to analogise the playhouses to well-stocked shops, to ships laden with goods or plunder, to museums, or even to 'the great globe itself', it is clear that during a typical production they gathered, before displaying and dispersing, a dense variety of events, experiences, ideas, words, languages and costumes. We might gain some sense of how thoroughly the playhouses absorbed the larger culture of which they were a part by noting

---

5 Gurr, *Playgoing in Shakespeare's London*, 4.

references to various forms of entertainment and activity in *The Taming of the Shrew*. This play not only multiply defines the possibilities of its own genre or mode as a 'pastime passing excellent', a 'Christmas gambold [or] tumbling trick', a 'kind of history', and a beguiling of the 'old folks' by the 'young folks [who] lay their heads together', but invokes various other practices and genres. These include cony-catching, the *commedia dell'arte*, puppetry, wooing dances, rope tricks, pornography, revenge tragedy plots, chronicles, hangings, dreams, school and education, musical performance, animal racing, animal training, hunting and feasting. These, again, are only a few of the many modes of action and representation that the play calls upon, sometimes only rhetorically, in developing its plot. In this way, *Shrew* typifies the playhouses' centripetal relation to English culture.

This voracious appetite for things, practices, ideas and words gave the playhouses an odd status in their day. As Howard Norland points out, a signal transition had occurred in English drama with the Reformation. Whereas in 1485 'drama extended to all corners of the commonwealth and to every level of society', by 1600 its scope had been narrowed to considerably fewer venues.[6] An unintended consequence of the Reformation, the commercial playhouses capitalised on the decline of public drama – drama understood, that is, as a social given. Although forms like the masque and allegorical shows survived, and although humanism was responsible for the recovery of traditions long unavailable to playwrights and readers, the Reformation was bad for English drama, broadly conceived. With the widespread consolidation of Protestant authority which accompanied this religious and social revolution, the *places* where dramatic activity might occur dwindled. The commercial playhouses thus enjoyed a niche of freedom in relation to the sometimes anti-theatrical orthodoxy of Elizabethan authority. They exercised this freedom by absorbing and refashioning various dramatic forms and genres. One might say that the potent heterogeneity of the 'Shakespearian' moment and after depended on the collocation of diverse genres, plots and topoi; the multiplicity of this theatre stands in part as a survival of earlier dramatic practice. what was sold in these plays – drama that seemed to contain the whole world – once permeated English society.

Players and playwrights

Actors in the sixteenth and seventeenth centuries probably had more in common with thespians from every period than they did with contemporary

6 Norland, *Drama in Early Tudor Britain, 1485–1558*, xvii.

workers in other occupations. The reason for this seems close at hand: throughout the centuries, the theatre has drawn individuals for whom other forms, and other places, of work are less capable of giving the satisfaction that results from a successful performance before an appreciative audience.[7] Hence a strongly economic explanation of the motivation for playing – one which ignored the eternal lure of theatricality – would be inadequate at best. To be sure, there circulated in England at this time fantasies of striking it rich from theatre, some of which we hear in the plays themselves. One might think of Bottom and the mechanicals' dreams of what will come from pleasing Theseus's court with their production of *Pyramus and Thisbe*, or the countrymen's cry, 'A mad woman? We are made, boys!', upon finding the Jailer's Daughter in *The Two Noble Kinsmen*, or the greedy thoughts of Alibius, the asylum-master in *The Changeling*, who speaks of the 'reward' and 'bounty' which will follow the parade of madmen he devises for an impending nuptial celebration. Significantly, the plays from which these fantasies are drawn frame such utterances as the naive hopes of rank amateurs. For although some individuals earned wealth, status and celebrity from the business of playing, most actors travelled more than they acted, and even then had to endure long periods between tours.

However much the foregoing describes actors of every era, the players of this time shared the following with their contemporaries: like much of the population in practice, and all of it in theory, they were servants to their social betters. The prominent companies we know – for example, the Chamberlain's Men and the Admiral's Men – were descendants of earlier groups which lacked the strong base near London that Shakespeare and others would possess, and which had relied more heavily upon aristocratic patronage. Earlier dramatic productions had been intensively local in nature; following the Reformation, however, the religious theatre of the Middle Ages went into a steep decline. Stepping into this void were companies of players who enjoyed the political sponsorship of aristocrats (hence the names of celebrated companies later on: Lord Strange's Men, the Lord Chamberlain's Men, the Queen's Men). Such companies could travel from a great house in the countryside to London, performing before the court, as well as to other venues in England. Bestowing upon these actors their patronage, powerful aristocrats offered them livelihood, a place to act and political protection. The last of these benefits became increasingly desirable during the sixteenth century, as the links between actors and communities became ever more attenuated, even hostile. An Act of 1572, for instance, criminalised 'rogues, vagabonds and sturdy beggars', including

---

7 For commonalities in the psychology of playing over the centuries (with special reference to Elizabethan theatre), see Skura, *Shakespeare the Actor and the Purposes of Playing*, 9–28.

in this category all 'common players of interludes and minstrels' unless they could prove they had aristocratic patronage.

If the players benefited from such patronage, so did the patrons. Such plays as *The Changeling* and *A Midsummer Night's Dream* show us that actors were depended upon as a chief source of entertainment for aristocratic weddings and feasts. As Greg Walker argues, however, earlier in the sixteenth century such companies, and the plays they enacted, gave their patrons more than entertainment; they often staged political messages so pointed that they can fairly be described as having lobbied for their noble (sometimes royal) sponsors.[8] We may recognise the specially commissioned play-within-the-play in *Hamlet* (Hamlet gives its title as *The Murder of Gonzago*) as a historical 'memory' of such political theatre: its point is to do political work to Hamlet's benefit. By the time *Hamlet* was performed, however, this kind of argumentative repertory had given way to a vital commercial theatre responsive more to the ebb and flow of popular taste (for instance, the broad appeal of *A Game at Chess*'s anti-Spanish sentiment) than to the winds of aristocratic intrigue. Roslyn Knutson's research into the repertory system at this time shows that theatrical companies quite frequently produced new plays in genres whose popularity had been demonstrated by other companies.[9] *As You Like It*, for example, needs to be read not only as a pastoral comedy of late Elizabethan England, but also as a 'Robin Hood' play related to instances of this genre performed by rival companies in the 1590s. Other examples abound: theatre at this time was a business which attended closely to what its audiences wanted, a tendency famously spelled out in such titles as *What You Will* and *As You Like It*.

Like most businesses, and in spite of the relevant term 'sharer', acting companies were at least partly hierarchical in nature. Although it is dangerous to generalise from the information we possess about some of the more prestigious groups of this day, many acting companies in London seem to have been divided in similar ways. We can draw three major distinctions. The first involves the difference between permanent members and part-time actors, or 'hired men', who would complete the company's personnel by taking minor roles, especially in plays with expansive casts of characters. Hired men earned less than the sharers of the company; they appear to have been paid approximately 5 to 10 shillings a week.[10] As the term implies, 'sharers' in acting companies theoretically shared the labour, the property (including the company's 'stock', which comprised playscripts, costumes and props) and the

8 Walker, *Plays of Persuasion*, 7–8.
9 Knutson, *The Repertory of Shakespeare's Company*.
10 See Bentley, *The Profession of Player in Shakespeare's Time*, 106–12.

profits from its productions. Shares were investments in the company, and entitled the sharers (primarily, but not always, actors in the company) to benefit from its success. Shares were purchased by actors who bought their way into companies in this manner, and either sold them upon leaving the company or passed them along as part of an inheritance.

Besides the division between sharers and hired men, there came a second qualification when certain actors became part-landlords of the theatres themselves. These were called 'householders', and by virtue of their more substantial investment and risk relating to the physical structure and property lease, householders were entitled to a share not only of the company's profits, but of the initial takings at the door. Finally, there obtained a third division, between the sharers and the boys who were employed to play women and children. As Andrew Gurr relates, these boys 'seem always to have been contracted to specific players, in bonds involving some form of contract rather like that of a trade apprenticeship'.[11] Within any acting company, then, one might expect to find a variety of employees, many of whom had radically different talents and responsibilities, who related to the company in disparate ways, and who would accordingly be compensated for their labour at varying levels.

One might encounter still another kind of work being performed by a member of an acting company, as a few actors were also playwrights. Among these were Shakespeare, Jonson, Thomas Heywood, Nathan Field and William Rowley. To be such a *factotum* was the exception rather than the rule, for the great majority of playwrights at this time did not act, however closely they accompanied the players. Nor did they tend to act alone when they wrote: most plays were the products of multiple hands; collaboration was the primary form of dramatic composition throughout the era. Further, we might see the work of writing plays as a thoroughly materialistic endeavour. Most playwrights were the sons of mechanical men, of bricklayers, glovers, dyers, scriveners, drapers: people who worked with their hands. Writing plays was perhaps not so different a labour, as dramatists often pieced together their plots from popular books, shaping their plays to fit not only what the public and the acting company demanded, but also the particular contours of the company's personnel. One company's famous clown, for instance, might require an extended moment of low comedy; another's celebrated tragedian, a series of eloquent soliloquies. In this way, writing plays was much like another business to which it was sometimes compared: that of the tailor.

11 Gurr, *The Shakespearian Playing Companies*, 100. In this regard Gurr cites Bentley, *Profession of Player*, 113–26.

The playhouses themselves had a strong dependence on clothing, in the form of costumes worn there. The scripts of new plays cost the companies less to purchase, in fact, than some of the elaborate costumes in their 'stock'. These costumes were necessary in the continual quest to delight the eyes of Londoners at this time. While the 'book' of a play was an important template for any production, it was only part of a larger montage of attractions that made up a performance. Perhaps because of escalating competition with other playing companies, playwrights were increasingly aware of the importance of an audience's good will toward such attractions. The induction to Jonson's *Bartholomew Fair* facetiously alludes to the variety of ways a play could appeal to its audience even as it introduces the production at hand with mock 'Articles of Agreement' between the audience and author:

> IMPRIMIS, It is couenanted and agreed, by and betweene the parties abouesaid, and the said *Spectators*, and *Hearers*, aswell the curious and enuious, as the fauouring and iudicious, as also the grounded Iudgements and vnderstandings, doe for themselues seuerally Couenant, and agree to remaine in the places, their money or friends haue put them in, with patience, for the space of two houres and an halfe, and somewhat more. In which time the *Author* promiseth to present them by vs, with a new sufficient Play called BARTHOLOMEW FAYRE, merry, and as full of noise, as sport: made to delight all, and to offend none. Prouided they have either, the wit, or the honesty to thinke well of themselues.

Jonson goes on to offer a strict economy of contribution (that is, the price one has paid to be admitted) and criticism (what, and how much, a person may judge): 'It shall bee lawfull for any man to iudge his six pen'orth, his twelue pen'orth, so to his eighteene pence, 2. Shillings, halfe a crowne, to the value of his place: Prouided alwaies his place get not aboue his wit.'[12]

This last ratio appears to have been the model for a more familiar version of the correspondence between cost and content, price and judgement. This is, of course, the opening address to what the First Folio of Shakespeare calls 'the great variety of readers'. There Shakespeare's colleagues, John Heminges and Henry Condell, mime Jonson's contract, though with a difference:

> From the most able, to him that can but spell: There you are number'd. We had rather you were weighd. Especially, when the fate of all Bookes depends vpon your capacities: and not of your heads alone, but of your purses. Well! It is now publique, & you will stand for your priuiledges wee know: to read,

12 Lines 73–91 of the induction to *Bartholomew Fair*, in Herford and Simpson (eds.), *Ben Jonson*, VI.

and censure. Do so, but buy it first. That doth best commend a Booke, the Stationer saies. Then, how odde soeuer your braines be, or your wisdomes, make your licence the same, and spare not. Iudge your sixe-pen'orth, your shillings worth, your fiue shillings worth at a time, or higher, so you rise to the just rates, and welcome. But, what euer you do, Buy.

The tone here is, like Jonson's, humorous and ingratiating, but without Jonson's veiled resentment. The difference may rest, in part, with the various personalities involved, Jonson being (in print, at least) notoriously irascible. But the decade between the two documents might also have helped transform Jonson's mock contract into a more serious one. That is, the differences might signal a growing accommodation, on the part of those involved in the business of playing, to an ever-competitive market for dramatic entertainment.

Playbooks

This market extended to the reading public, for in addition to attending dramatic productions, playgoers could obtain a printed copy of the plays they saw. The 1590s and early 1600s, in fact, witnessed a comparative 'boom' in the printing of playbooks. Printed versions of many scripts, often with what appear to be only modest alterations from the versions provided to the companies themselves, flooded numerous booksellers' stalls in the busy yard of St Paul's cathedral, and elsewhere. Compared to the sumptuous folio collections of the plays of Shakespeare, Jonson and Beaumont and Fletcher, these printed playbooks were smaller and relatively inexpensive, giving rise to Thomas Bodley's notorious characterisation of them as 'baggage books'. They were nonetheless an important part of London's book trade at the time.

Significantly, some of the 'best sellers' of this genre were plays that have subsequently found an almost permanent place in the canon of English literature; these include such dramatic texts as *The Spanish Tragedy*, *Doctor Faustus*, *1 Henry IV* and *Richard III*. Yet other play texts that sold editions in significant numbers did not make this same impression on later generations of readers. Plays that, from the evidence of numbers of editions, appear to have been much more popular in their own day than in ours include, among others, the anonymous *Mucedorus* and *Wily Beguiled*, Dekker's *The Shoemakers' Holiday*, Heywood's (?) *How a Man May Choose a Good Wife from a Bad*, Heywood's *1 If You Know Not Me You Know Nobody* and *1 & 2 Edward IV*, Beaumont and Fletcher's *A King and No King*, *The Scornful Lady* and *The Maid's Tragedy*, and Greene and Lodge's *A Looking Glass for London and England*.

By far the most detailed discussion of the printed playbook occurs in Peter W. M. Blayney's essay, 'The publication of playbooks'.[13] In this essay Blayney strenuously seeks to disabuse literary critics of certain beliefs concerning the value of these published playbooks. We can call this pattern of beliefs the 'golden playbook' myth. Because Blayney's essay offers a trove of information about published playbooks, and because it will be looked to as an authoritative account, we may benefit here from scrutinising some of his assumptions and claims. In the end, Blayney may be said to provide an over-correction of past theories about these playbooks. That is, where earlier scholars may well have overestimated the cultural and commodity status of published playtexts, Blayney systematically underestimates their significance.

As rehearsed broadly in the essay's conclusion, the golden playbook myth runs as follows:

> Greedy publishers (usually mistaken for printers), impatient to make a quick fortune from the insatiable demands of hordes of eager play collectors, therefore spend much of their time conspiring with disaffected bit-part players. Having procured an illicit text they carefully conceal their involvement from the private ledgers of the Stationers' Company – while nevertheless proclaiming it on the printed title page.[14]

What keeps this myth alive, Blayney holds, is the anachronistic projection of our values: 'Literary scholars are predisposed to assume that their own attitudes toward highly valued texts were shared by the public for whom those texts were first printed'.[15] In seeking to puncture the myth of the golden playbook, Blayney establishes in detail what we know about the publication and purchasing of playbooks during this era. He closes by carefully estimating the costs and expected profits involved with the publication of a hypothetical text from the commercial theatre. Examining these figures, Blayney concludes that publishing playbooks was rarely lucrative, and that the supply of playbooks far outstripped the demand for them.

Blayney argues against the notion – key to the golden playbook myth – that 'the sale of printed texts might itself reduce the demand for performance'.[16] In contrast, he advances 'a perfectly plausible reason why … players … flood[ed] the market with scripts. The strategy is known today as "publicity", or "advertising"'.[17] This is an intriguing theory, for the large-scale release of playbooks might indeed have been used as a spur to playgoing following the

13 Blayney, 'The publication of playbooks', in Cox and Kastan (eds.), *A New History of Early English Drama*, 383–422.
14 Ibid., 415.   15 Ibid., 384.   16 Ibid., 386.   17 Ibid., 386.

'down time' of the plague. To it, though, we need to add Andrew Gurr's argument (made later in the present volume) that this release of playbooks had another kind of economic spur: the need of various acting companies to raise capital for the construction of new playhouses. Gurr, too, holds that advertisement might have been a motivation. These two suggested motivations – advertisement and the need for capital – appear quite similar, in that they share a common source: a desire for money. Actually, however, they offer radically different evaluations of the playbooks themselves. That is, while the 'advertising' theory privileges productions as the source of value (playbooks being valuable as enticements to play*going*), the 'capitalisation' theory privileges the playbooks themselves as the primary locus of worth (playgoing having led to a demand for play*books*).

This potential contradiction is important to understanding Blayney's essay, for crucial to the golden playbook myth is the belief that repertories held playbooks too valuable to publish without overwhelming warrant. Blayney argues against this belief for two reasons: one involving the absence of evidence that 'any player ever feared that those who bought and read plays would consequently lose interest in seeing them performed';[18] the other that 'the London [acting] companies seem for the most part to have respected each other's repertories, printed plays included'.[19]

To make these points, Blayney has to argue against three often-cited passages typically read as testifying to the attractiveness of unpublished playbooks. These are Webster's (?) induction to *The Malcontent*, which refers to intercompany play appropriation; the epistle prefixed to the second state of *Troilus and Cressida*, which speaks of certain stingy 'grand possessors', perhaps of playbooks; and Thomas Heywood's epistle before *The English Traveler*, which refers to 'some Actors, who thinke it against their peculiar profit to have them [i.e. certain of Heywood's plays] come in Print'. Blayney's argument comes up short when considered in light of these passages, for they reveal that it was quite possible to believe that playbooks were valuable, however much that belief runs contrary to a logic we embrace.

The 'market' should not be thought of as a list of prices and rules, in abstraction from the people who both worked within it and helped to give it its specific shape. For example, Blayney holds that 'Andrew Wise . . . struck gold three times in a row in 1597–8 by picking what would become the three best-selling Shakespeare quartos as the first three plays of his brief career'.[20] We might ask whether the description here is supple enough to account for

---

18 Ibid., 386.   19 Ibid., 386.   20 Ibid., 389.

Wise's freedom beyond the initial selection. For that matter, even the selection of these three plays could have involved a more-than-fortunate acumen regarding what would sell. Perhaps such an acumen was the result of Wise's theatregoing. Might there also have been something outside the qualities of the plays themselves that accounted for their rapid reprinting? That is, could Wise not have had special skill as a promoter of his wares? Special contacts? Could his sales of these texts have been influenced by his sentiments as to their salability? That is, could a belief in the essential marketability of these plays have been a factor in Wise's promotion of them; and could such promotion in turn have influenced their distribution, and reprinting as best-sellers? Because much of Blayney's account unfolds as the story of individuals tossed about by forces over which they have little control, Wise's success sounds more happenstance than needs be. Comprehending the market means understanding that individuals often had more agency than can be explained by broad and otherwise impersonal pictures of an era.

One of the most demonstrative aspects of Blayney's essay is its statistical contextualisation of published playbooks. In two tables, he shows that published playbooks were outsold by various other texts. Religious 'best-sellers', in particular, far exceeded published playbooks in terms of editions. Even among what we would define as literary texts, Blayney argues, playbooks fell behind such texts as 'Daniel's verse'.[21] Blayney concludes that 'no more than one play in five would have returned the publisher's initial investment inside five years. Not one in twenty would have paid for itself during its first year – so publishing plays would not usually have been seen as a shortcut to wealth'.[22] This is an unobjectionable conclusion, yet we should ask whether the principle it is based on – a quarter-century view of the economics of publishing – is adequate to the questions we need to ask of the period. That is, what Blayney knows about publishing in this era could have been *known*, in the strong sense of that word, by no publisher of the time. The 'truth' of the risky playbook may appear undeniable to us from the vantage-point of the *Short-Title Catalogue*, but it would not have been so apparent, if apparent at all, in 1593, or to Andrew Wise and his competitors in 1600.

21 Blayney justifiably conflates the two texts of *Doctor Faustus* in his tabulation, though it is open to question whether to count, as one text, the various editions of Daniel's verse (in Greg's order: STC 6243.4, 6243.5, 6243.6; STC 6261; STC 6236; STC 6239; STC 6240, 6242; STC 6238). I would also like to suggest here two emendations to his first table on p. 388. According to my count, there were six (rather than five) editions of Heywood's *1 If You Know Not Me You Know Nobody* from 1605–23 (STC 13328, 13329, 13330, 13331, 13332, 13333); and likewise there were six (rather than five) editions of *Richard III* from late 1597 through late 1622 (STC 22314, 22315, 22316, 22317, 22318, 22319).
22 'The publication of playbooks', 389.

The truth of '1600–20' may not be true before or after that period, or even during individual years of that period. Likewise if we move our window of tabulation to (for instance) 1623 (which would include the First Folio), or 1642, the number of play editions looks more significant. This also suggests that we need to adjust our figures in relation to the total number of titles published per year, as a playbook published in the context of 600 other titles should not be considered in the same light as a playbook published in the context of 200 other titles. There is a certain flattening out of the difference of times and numbers in Blayney's essay, something unavoidable given its own constraints of space, but something we need to be aware of when employing its findings.

Published playbooks *were* consequential, both in terms of the economics of the publishing industry and in terms of the cultural scene of England at this time. According to my own research, during the 1590s and early 1600s the percentage of literary texts grew in relation to the numbers of titles published, and playbooks made up a significant part of those numbers.[23] In 1602, for instance, 278 book-length imprints were brought out. Of these titles, 56 – or 20.14 per cent – were what we would define as 'literary' texts. Among these were 15 plays, which accounted for a full 5.39 per cent of that year's imprints, and 26.78 per cent of the imprints of a literary nature. Thus, more than one out of every four 'literary' titles published that year was a playbook. To be sure, Blayney relates that in the long run new play titles accounted for only 1 to 2 per cent of all titles. But to someone alive in 1602 such was not yet a truth. What *was* apparent at that time was that over the past two decades the publication of plays written in English, for presentation in commercial venues, had overtaken the domestic publication of plays by Plautus, Terence and Seneca. What this meant in England at that time is perhaps most apparent in such documents as Francis Meres's *Palladis Tamia*, which finds reason to announce a level of literary attainment that later generations would call a Renaissance.

Economy and interpretation

The story of commerce told in this essay holds that the plays of Shakespeare and his contemporaries were commodities within a vital theatrical industry. As such, they indicate the aptness of the phrase 'early modern', in addition to 'Renaissance', as a way of describing this era. With 'early modern' comes, among other things, an indication of the growing market economy which,

---

23 The following figures are drawn from my own research in progress, a year-by-year subject analysis of the imprints in the *Short-title Catalogue*.

to many, has been the motor of history as experienced since the seventeenth century.

Placing these dramatic texts within such a narrative has a number of consequences for literary criticism, among which is the risk that this narrative will overwhelm – at the very least, diminish – other approaches to the texts at hand. That is, the more we focus on the business side of the theatre, the less sensitive we may be to its aesthetic, social and historical aspects. Perhaps like a business person worried about the 'bottom line', we will be less attentive to the variety of the product itself – in this case, to the content and contours of the lines written for actors to speak. Although the protocols of historicism ask that we try to inhabit imaginatively the positions of those who have gone before, we need to remember that those positions were complex in nature: thus, a concern for profit might well have stood alongside an interest in aesthetic affect, in addressing and solving formal problems, in social themes, in issues of particular political significance, in placating or irritating various members of a company – the list could be extended. An economic approach to these plays, and to the business of playing, must not be seen as a master logic or explanation. Instead, such an approach should complement – sometimes extending, sometimes qualifying in other ways – existing ones.

If we need to resist becoming overwhelmed by questions of commerce as they relate to these plays, we also should resist seeing the rise of the commercial playhouses as an entirely beneficent thing. It has been observed that, following upon the Reformation, these playhouses capitalised on the decline of a pervasive social theatricality in England: what had earlier existed as quasi-public celebration and carnival became available only to those with money to spend. In an essay on questions of patronage and economics of the theatre at this time, Kathleen McLuskie and Felicity Dunsworth also caution against fitting the business of playing into too neat a box:

> Every historian knows that any route taken through the forest of documentation involves exclusions that arise from a thesis, if not a larger view of the world. We should, however, become especially suspicious both when the path taken follows the tracks of contemporaries too firmly and when it speeds down the superhighway of a modern historiographical teleology. The view that the economics of theater moved from a system of patronage to one of commerce follows both of those roads. For the early modern antitheatricalist, it fed nostalgia for an ordered, coherent community; for the modern historian, it fits the grand narratives of modernization and commercialization.[24]

24 McLuskie and Dunsworth, 'Patronage and the economics of theater', in Cox and Kastan (eds.), *A New History of Early English Drama*, 438.

To the extent that it warns against a facile account of the theatrical industry, this paragraph is worth heeding. Yet this warning is founded on a strange premise. McLuskie and Dunsworth are uncomfortable with the 'view that the economics of theater moved from a system of patronage to one of commerce', though their reason for this discomfort – that it too closely fits beliefs about the theatre both in the sixteenth and seventeenth centuries, and in contemporary historiography – is difficult to understand. Although both shoes 'fit', McLuskie and Dunsworth are reluctant to try either on.

I offer that what we see in the paragraph quoted above is a reluctance conceived in anxiety. The anxiety may have at least two sources. First is the fear that a simple-sounding story could be true: that society, for instance, has become more secular, or more commercial, or more (or less) democratic in nature. As such, the anxiety is understandable; academics thrive on complexity rather than simplicity, and fail to benefit from easily grasped narratives. Accordingly, we tend to overvalue exceptions to general rules, and make a fetish of departures from the norm. A second possible source for the odd reluctance shown in the paragraph quoted above is the fear that the present may be profoundly similar in some ways to the past. That is, if we grant the existence of a theatrical industry in the sixteenth and seventeenth centuries, it opens the floor to questions about this industry's similarity to practices of acting and playwriting in our own day. Like the problems posed by simple narratives, our potential commonalities with those of the past are sometimes unwelcome in academic enquiry today.

The predicament is perhaps familiar to critics and scholars interested in economic issues relating to the early modern theatre. With the construction of the third Globe playhouse in London, tensions between British and American, art and commerce, and past and present have come to the fore. Supporters of contemporary productions of sixteenth- and seventeenth-century plays, at the Globe and elsewhere, are simultaneously open to charges of both mawkish nostalgia and venal consumerism when it comes to the business of such theatre in the twenty-first century. If there is anything that studying the production and reception of sixteenth- and seventeenth-century plays tells us, however, it is that an enormous variety of motivations and orientations was involved in the business of theatre at that time, none of which seems likely to have been extinguished in the intervening centuries.

What we get when we follow the money in regard to the commercial playhouses of sixteenth- and seventeenth-century London is a rich language – one of many such languages – with which to address questions of agency. That is, when we study plays of the early modern era, we most often try to explain how they got to be the way they are, asking questions which we may render in sum as 'Who or what gave this object this particular shape, how, why, and with what effect?'. Realising that these plays were commodities, that they were fashioned, bought and sold in a theatrical industry, by workers highly conscious of and responsive to the business of theatre, provides us with a richer set of terms and ideas with which to address such questions. It reminds us of the 'general equivalent' – that is, the money – which changed hands within London's theatrical industry as individuals pursued various desires. Following the money helps us understand that pursuit. We need to remember, of course, that no equivalent, and no single logic or story, can account for every desire, action and belief held by any person of any era. The rise of the market in the sixteenth and seventeenth centuries thus helps explain the institutional form of London's theatres to us, and illuminates certain forms of business activity within them, but we cannot think that it may fully explain what happened in the theatres themselves, or the texts that have survived as witnesses to the business of playing.

9

Theatre and controversy, 1572–1603

DIANA E. HENDERSON

The sixteenth century was a time of great change. Inflation, expansion and new forms of mobility were challenging and displacing centuries-old patterns of social order, religious belief, political structure and economic value. The population of England and Wales grew by more than 45 per cent to over four million people in 1600. Land was enclosed, workers displaced and real wages for the poor declined; at the same time, more men had access to education, the state took control of religion without causing a full-scale civil war, and luxury goods poured in from newly accessible foreign lands. Interpreting the place of theatre within this flurry of activity is a complex task. To invoke an analogy popular among cultural critics, looking at sixteenth-century theatre is like looking at an anamorphic perspective painting such as Holbein's *The Ambassadors*: the first impression is one of profit and delight, but another image gradually emerges to complicate the picture. Viewed the more direct and obvious way, the last three decades of Elizabeth's reign inaugurated the great era of English drama. Professional theatre companies flourished and a remarkable variety of performance genres and styles came into being, producing great and memorable playscripts that have come to dominate the classical repertory of English-language theatre. But buried within this picture of artistic energy, productivity and innovation lies the skull, the reminder of what was dying and the sign of future problems that the rich surface could not entirely obscure. With the death of old ways came fears of the new and the foreign: fears of this theatrical world and fears expressed by its participants. They worried about the public theatre's social functions but also about the socio-political and economic changes shaping it and the society it was helping to transform. Thus the professional theatre emerged in a context of controversy and debate.

Not surprisingly, attacks on theatre's very existence were particularly intense and vitriolic during its first years as part of the professional London entertainment industry. While small bands of professional players had toured the country for years and would continue to do so throughout Elizabeth's reign, the construction of purpose-built theatres in the London area signalled a new stage of commercialisation and centralisation. It also meant that playing now took place alongside bearbaiting, cockfighting, and other less edifying forms of amusement in the 'liberties' outside the city limits. Although free from the Common Council of London's strict regulation, theatre was not thereby exempted from the criticism that it corrupted its audiences. Thomas White's *Sermon preached at Pawles Cross* (1577) signals how quickly these London theatres became a popular success but also how extreme was the opposition:

> Looke but uppon the common playes in London, and see the multitude that flocketh to them and followeth them: beholde the sumptuous Theatre houses, a continuall monument of Londons prodigalitie and folly. But I understande they are nowe forbidden bycause of the plague. I like the pollicye well if it holde still, for a disease is but bodged or patched up that is not cured in the cause, and the cause of plagues is sinne, if you looke to it well: and the cause of sinne are playes: therefore the cause of plagues are playes.[1]

Outbreaks of plague repeatedly closed (or provided an excuse for closing) the theatres, most notably during 1592–4. But the industry, if not particular companies, survived – much to the dismay of the radical Protestant preachers.

Professional competition clearly aggravated their moral indignation. As John Stockwood lamented in a 1578 sermon, 'Wyll not a fylthye playe, wyth the blast of a Trumpette, sooner call thyther a thousande, than an houres tolling of a Bell, bring to the Sermon a hundred?'.[2] John Northbrooke concurred that plays have 'stricken such a blinde zeale into the heartes of the people, that they shame not to say, and affirme openly, that playes are as good as sermons, and that they learne as much or more at a playe, than they do at god's worde preached'.[3] Not entirely averse to scholastic drama, this preacher focused his anger on the public theatres, women's attendance and corruption thereby, and playing upon the sabbath – the 'abuse which is generalie found fault withal', according to another pamphleteer.[4] Indeed, when stands at the Paris Garden collapsed on Sunday 13 January 1583, killing seven and injuring scores of spectators at the bearbaiting, John Field took it as an omen to those 'frequenting the *Theater*, the *Curtin* and such like, that one day those places will likewise be cast downe by God himselfe'.[5]

And yet, *not* playing on the sabbath meant playing on a work-day, and hence led to another form of attack. Phillip Stubbes argued that theatres 'maintaine a great sort of ydle Persons, doing nothing but playing and loytring, having their

---

1 Chambers, *The Elizabethan Stage*, IV, 187.
2 Ibid., IV, 199.   3 Ibid., IV, 198.   4 Ibid., IV, 210.   5 Ibid., IV, 211.

lyvings of the sweat of other Mens browes, much like unto dronets devouring the sweet honie of the poore labouring bees' (*The Anatomie of Abuses*, 1583).[6] Apprentices, whose youth and numbers led them to be perceived as a threat to public order (sometimes with reason), were particularly avid theatregoers. Not only did theatre draw young workers into idleness and unruliness, the critics argued, but it took away their money – and gave it to those other unruly idlers, the players. Such attacks came from the divines but also from 'reformed' playwrights, including Stephen Gosson and Anthony Munday, the presumed author of *A second and third blast of retrait from plaies and Theaters* (1580). The latter asks rhetorically of players, 'Are they not notoriouslie knowen to be those men in their life abroad, as they are on the stage, roisters, brallers, il-dealers, bosters, lovers, loiterers, ruffins? . . . the principal end of all their interludes is to feede the world with sights, & fond pastimes; to juggle in good earnest the monie out of other mens purses into their own hands.'[7] Theatre was tainted both by being a business and drawing others from theirs, both by being a commodity and leaving the buyer with nothing (or worse, a corrupting model of bad behaviour). Not that it didn't remain powerful: according to Gosson (1582), his fellow reformer Munday has returned to the theatre, 'like ye dog to his vomite, to plays againe'.[8]

What lured him back? Was it lewdness, drunkenness, idleness, or pride – all common charges against players, their audiences, and the very stories they represented onstage? Perhaps the answer lies in his own words: ' Such like men, under the title of their maisters or as reteiners, are priviledged to roave abroad, and permitted to publish their mametree in everie Temple of God, and that through England.' As retainers of the nobility or her Majesty, the players had unusual freedoms of mobility in what was still officially a stiflingly hierarchical society. Gosson admits they could traipse about onstage 'under gentlemens noses in sutes of silke'.[9] This wearing of hand-me-downs from aristocrats challenged the whole code of sumptuary laws, which were meant to establish one's social position by restricting what one could wear. The symbolic power of playing was great indeed, allowing men of the 'middling sort' or lower to play the king. And even if playwrights often failed to gain financially in selling their scripts to acting companies (as Gosson and later Robert Greene lamented), they might hope to attract aristocratic patronage, while actors might strive to become sharers (part-owners) in their company. Most would fail, but in the fast-growing city filling with more and more over-educated, under-employed young men, the chance and comparative freedom

6 Ibid., IV, 222.   7 Ibid., IV, 212.   8 Ibid., IV, 218.   9 Ibid., IV, 204.

must have been attractive. Some players seem to have been serving the crown and particular court factions covertly as well as overtly, acting as spies and messengers when on tour while also presenting entertainments congenial to their patrons' political interests.[10] The most controversial of playwrights, Christopher Marlowe, was not the only spy in town.

Munday may have been led back to his craft by the power of representation itself, a power acknowledged by both theatre's critics and defenders. As the temporarily reformed playwright remarked, 'Are not our hartes through the pleasure of the flesh; the delight of the eie; and the fond motions of the mind, withdrawen from the service of the Lord, & meditation of his goodnes?'.[11] Within the decade, Marlowe would create a great play illustrating this very truth. But by allowing his audience to empathise with as well as to judge Doctor Faustus, and perhaps to question God's 'goodnes' as much as his tragic hero's, he leaves one to meditate upon, rather than simply accept, the analogy between corrupting spectacle and his own dramaturgy. Underlying much theatrical debate is the larger social controversy which historians such as Patrick Collinson dub 'iconophobia', the Reformation fear of the power of images.[12] Some scholars now argue that theatrical practitioners themselves acknowledged and incorporated their sense of the danger of images within their plays, creating in essence a 'reformed' theatre. Others counter that, as in Marlowe's case, self-consciousness may as likely have led to challenges and mockery, if not the 'atheism' of which that playwright was accused. In any event, the very medium of theatre, involving words and images, and often the imitation of immoral behaviour by actors, became an occasion for debate: did one learn from representations of 'evil' or not? Could images function (as Sir Philip Sidney argued in his *Defense of Poetry*) as positive exempla, moving men to do good? Did the fiction and performance so blur that both became corrupting, or did the audience's awareness of that distinction allow them to become more discerning? Did the fantasy itself fulfil a purpose, as carnivalesque activities have been argued to do? That is, did it work as an 'escape valve' for the pressure of a society in which subservience was a given for most people (the play thus ultimately serving the dominant social order)? Or was it a form of subversion subtle enough to elude direct censorship and punishment (making the play a mechanism for long-term societal change)? The critical debates now, as then, rage on.

As well as confronting practical concerns about pickpockets, the spread of disease, violence, cross-dressing, illicit assignations, heterogeneous audiences

---

10 McMillin and MacLean, *Queen's Men*, 22–9.
11 Chambers, *The Elizabethan Stage*, IV, 210.
12 Collinson, *From Iconoclasm to Iconophobia*.

confusing and challenging social order – in other words, the ongoing conditions of the professional London theatres – players and playwrights also became directly involved and implicated in more specific political and religious controversies. These cases worried many who seemed indifferent to the preachers' polemics or the city magistrates' managerial dilemmas. The incendiary potential of theatre to communicate seditious opinions to a large crowd obviously concerned the crown, Privy Council, and their primary overseer of entertainments, the Master of the Revels. In 1581, the current master, Edmund Tilney, received a special commission:

> to warne commaunde and appointe in all places within this our Realme of England, aswell within francheses and liberties as without, all and every plaier or plaiers with their playmakers . . . to appeare before him with all suche plaies, Tragedies, Comedies or showes as they shall have in readines or meane to sett forth, and them to presente and recite before our said Servant or his sufficient deputie, whom wee ordeyne appointe and aucthorise . . . to order and reforme, auctorise and put downe, as shalbe thought meete or unmeete unto himself . . .[13]

While motivated by the desire to find the best and cheapest entertainment for Queen Elizabeth, this commission enlarged Tilney's responsibility and control over playing to a national scale. He used that authority sometimes to protect players from more rigorous local magistrates, as in London, but also as a form of censorship. Tellingly, the only manuscript to survive with Tilney's marginalia as well as 'editing' reveals his concern with sedition and public disorder: in the margins of *Sir Thomas More* (c. 1594), Tilney instructed the players to 'Leave out the insurrection wholy & the Cause ther off & begin with Sr. Tho: Moore att the mayors sessions with a reportt afterwardes off his good service don being Shrive off London uppon a mutiny Agaynst the Lumbardes only by A shortt reporte & nott otherwise att your own perrilles. E. Tyllney.'[14] Again, it is *representation* that constitutes a particular threat: a 'shortt reporte' of 'mutiny' had less incendiary potential than an enacted encounter, even if, as in this case, the point of the scene was to laud More's success in suppressing, not encouraging, rebellion. Nevertheless, even verbal mention of the mutineers' particular cause is forbidden, and with some reason: they had been participating in anti-foreigner riots. Tilney was writing when once again English xenophobia, compounded by poor grain prices, inflation and uncertainty about the royal succession, had led to anti-foreigner demonstrations.

---

13 Chambers, *The Elizabethan Stage*, IV, 286.
14 Ibid., IV, 32.

Having had a cousin executed for his involvement in the Catholic Babington plot to assassinate Queen Elizabeth (1586), Tilney might also have been more than usually sensitive to the material here. Nor was Tilney the only control upon the players and their plays.[15] In 1572, a royal decree declared actors without the specific support of court aristocrats to be vagabonds, subject to arrest. From the beginning of Elizabeth's reign, local authorities could prohibit plays 'wherein either matters of religion or of the governaunce of the estate of the commonweale shall be handled, or treated' (1559). Similarly, the crown tried to root out all remnants of Catholic drama. Although the feast of Corpus Christi, which had been the occasion for Christian mystery cycles, was suppressed by decree in 1548, mysteries continued to be performed (especially in the north) and more decrees followed: the 1581 prohibition of mystery cycles themselves, and later of any scriptural or biblical drama. Actual control remained harder to enforce than to legislate.

Tilney's markings in the *More* manuscript illustrate the tight connections throughout the period between religion, politics and control of the theatre. The links appear even more directly in the 'Martin Marprelate' pamphlet war (1588–90), which was also an occasion for extensive theatrical participation in a raging controversy. The vitriolic (and often amusing) exchange began with an attack on episcopal corruption within the Church of England by 'Martin', most likely the pseudonym for a number of puritan sympathisers. Earlier attempts to destroy theatre having failed, these puritans appear to have enjoyed some of the Queen's Men's performances and decided to use the players' satiric techniques. Rather than let be, Richard Bancroft, Canon of Westminster, (no doubt backed by Archbishop Whitgift) encouraged counter-attacks on the Martinist pamphlets. The theatre took up the gauntlet. Both in print and on stage, players and playwrights got involved: John Lyly and Thomas Nashe wrote pamphlets mocking 'Martin'. The writers seemed eager to prove themselves allies of the powers-that-be, and with good reason; the radical Protestant attack had after all found inspiration in earlier stage satires. Although the great comic actor Richard Tarlton had died in September 1588, he was cited positively by a Martinist writer for his role in Robert Wilson's *The Three Ladies of London*, in which he exposed simony as 'the bishops lacky' (playing Simplicity, however, Tarlton could not defeat Lady Lucre's knaves, who also included Usury, Fraud and Dissimulation). By the summer of 1589, the continuing insults spurred

15 The crown may have consciously attempted to limit their numbers and touring in order to control them more effectively, argue McMillin and MacLean, *Queen's Men*, 12–36. On Tilney and regulation, see Dutton, 'Censorship', in Cox and Kastan (eds.), *A New History of Early English Drama*, 287–304.

Francis Bacon to write an *Advertisement Touching the Controversies* in which he lamented the church's involvement in 'this immodest and deformed manner of writing lately entertained, whereby matters of religion are handled in the style of the stage'.[16] Not just in the style, too: Martin was made into a stage character and satirised mercilessly. An anti-Martinist pamphlet vaunts that:

> These Jigges and Rimes, have nipt the father [Martin] in the head & kild him cleane, seeing that hee is overtaken in his owne *foolerie*. And this hath made the yong youthes his sonnes, to chafe and fret above measure, especiallie with the Plaiers, (their betters in all respects, both in wit, and honestie) whom saving their *liveries* (for indeede they are hir Majesties men, and these not so much as hir good subjects) they call *Rogues*, for playing their enterludes, and Asses for travelling *all daie for a Pennie*.[17]

Again reminding us (and his audience) that theatre is now a business, the pamphleteer has his mock-Martin conclude that the actor who will 'play the foole but two houres together, hath somewhat for his labour', whereas Martin gets nothing for his folly.

Signalling official desire to quiet the fractious religious controversy it had helped protract, by October 1589 Lyly was lamenting that the players were not allowed to perform all their anti-Martinist comedies (for then 'I am sure he would be decyphered, and so perhaps discouraged').[18] The pamphlets soon devolved into personal attacks. Highlighting the power of the theatre upon public opinion, Gabriel Harvey attacked Lyly as:

> a professed jester, a Hickscorner, a scoff-maister, a playmunger, an Interluder... All you that tender the preservation of your good name, were best to please Pap-hatchet [Lyly]... for feare lesse he be mooved, or some One of his Apes hired, to make a Playe of you; and then is your credit quite un-done for ever, and ever: Such is the publique reputation of their Playes. He must needes be *discouraged*, whome they *decipher*. Better, anger an hundred other, then two such; that have the Stage at commandement, and can furnish-out Vices, and Divels at their pleasure.[19]

Harvey proved correct in this at least: the players fairly destroyed his reputation – with a bit of help from himself.[20] Yet it is also true that the Queen's

---

16 Chambers, *The Elizabethan Stage*, IV, 229.
17 *Martins Months Minde*, cited in ibid., IV, 230.
18 Chambers, *The Elizabethan Stage*, IV, 232.
19 *An Advertisement for Papp-Hatchett* [Nov. 1589], cited in ibid., IV, 232–3.
20 Peele mocked Harvey as Huanebango in *The Old Wives' Tale* and Shakespeare sent him up as Holofernes in *Love's Labour's Lost*.

Men took to the touring road again and gave fewer court performances after their involvement in this controversy, and Lyly and his boys' troupe were fairly silenced – albeit whether for his role as an anti-Martinist, we cannot now be sure.

The children's acting companies did not regain their popularity until the end of the 1590s, when they became embroiled in another controversy more squarely focused on the shape of their professional field itself, hence known as the 'war of the theatres'. From John Marston's *Histriomastix* (1599) through Ben Jonson's *Cynthia's Revels* and *Poetaster* to Thomas Dekker's *Satiromastix* (1601), the playwrights combined personal invective and satires on one another's writing styles with acrimony concerning the re-emergence of boys' companies as rivals to the men's troupes. Shakespeare too contributed his brief aside from the adult players' perspective, in Hamlet and Rosencrantz's discussion of the 'little eyases' drawing crowds away from the players who are therefore touring to Elsinore. (Shakespeare's company, the Lord Chamberlain's Men, had been financially affected by the boys performing in Burbage's second Blackfriars theatre, after the local population prevented the men from moving into their renovated hall in 1597.) While the professional rivalry between playwrights and companies was undoubtedly real, this 'war', like the Marprelate controversy, arguably served the theatre business as a whole: it attracted patrons eager to be *au courant* and enjoy another form of topical humour in the wake of the 1599 bishops' ban on printed satire.

Other controversial involvements did not so benefit the players: most notably, those spurred by *The Isle of Dogs* (1597) and the playing of *Richard II* (presumably Shakespeare's) on the eve of the Earl of Essex's rebellion (1601). In the former case, Thomas Nashe was again involved, as the play he co-authored with Ben Jonson caused an outcry. The exact source of consternation remains unknown, for the play itself does not survive. Circumstantial evidence points towards an insult to the Polish ambassador. But whatever the reason for anger, the consequences were severe. Along with some of the other actors, Jonson was put in jail; Nashe took off. Whether two official actions followed from *The Isle of Dogs* scandal or merely coincided with it remains a source of debate, but on 28 July 1597 the City petitioned for the suppression of the playhouses and the Privy Council ordered them destroyed. Although this draconian policy was not enacted, the following February the Privy Council did restrict playing to only two troupes, the Lord Chamberlain's and Lord Admiral's Men, under direct authority of the Master of the Revels (a reduction of the competition which the lord chamberlain had been pushing for since 1594). This strict level of control did not last long, but it did institute new and stronger assumptions about centralised regulation of the London theatre business, and had immediate fall-out. Pembroke's Men, the company that had performed *The Isle of Dogs*, was put out of business, while the owner of the new Swan theatre where it played lost hundreds of pounds and sued his actors for breach of contract.

In 1601, the Lord Chamberlain's Men got off more lightly – though Essex himself did not. By late 1599 when the earl returned prematurely from his unsuccessful campaign in Ireland (where he had knighted dozens of his followers without permission, yet failed to put down the Tyrone rebellion), Elizabeth felt the behaviour of her dashing favourite had gone too far. For several years Essex had been a magnet for aspiring young men. Poets vied for his patronage and praised his military feats, most notably the destruction of the Spanish fleet at Cadiz in 1596. Moreover, writers had drawn surprisingly direct parallels between Essex and Bolingbroke, the duke who two hundred years earlier had deposed Richard II to become Henry IV. Essex's end would in fact more closely resemble that of another of Richard's relatives, the uncle who was made into a plain-speaking hero of the English people in the early 1590s play *Woodstock*. Thomas Woodstock was put to death by Richard's orders, as Essex would be by Elizabeth's. For Essex miscalculated badly, discounting the commoners' personal loyalty to the queen and revulsion at rebellion (reinforced if not instilled by the church's *Homily Against Rebellion*). When he decided to rise against the queen (or, more specifically, her counsellors) in September 1601, his conspirators paid the Lord Chamberlain's Men to perform their play 'of King Henry the Fourth, and of the killing of Richard the second' the night before, a play the earl had frequently attended. Clearly the rebels hoped to abet their insurrection by providing an historical precedent. Just as clearly, Elizabeth perceived the threat in such analogies, reportedly fuming soon after Essex's death, 'I am Richard II, know ye not that?'. When the coup failed to gain the support of London, Essex was tried for treason and eventually beheaded, and the Lord Chamberlain's Men were interrogated. Augustine Phillips, the players' representative, stressed that the conspirators had paid the company an extra £2 to perform a play the professionals asserted (perhaps disingenuously) was 'so old and so long out of use'.[21] Phillips's wise choice of a financial rather than political excuse worked, and the players were cleared. Nevertheless, the deposition scene of *Richard II* was not published until the fourth quarto (1608), well after Elizabeth's death. Moreover, the incident remains indicative of how English chronicle histories were being used throughout the 1580s and 1590s

21 See Andrew Gurr's introduction to *Richard II* (1984), 6–7.

to create topical drama – drama that sometimes became more dangerously topical than its authors might have wished or intended.

The Essex rebellion itself was symptomatic of the elite culture's restiveness under a female monarch. As the century waned, worries about who would rule after childless Elizabeth were growing more acute by the year. From the start of her reign, the succession question had been a source of controversy. Few had confidence that a woman could rule alone, and all believed that a direct male heir was crucial for future stability. Elizabeth's counsellors pushed her to marry (though they were never able to agree on whom), and used performances among the elite to reinforce that message: Thomas Sackville and Thomas Norton's Inns of Court play *Gorboduc* (1561–2) and the Earl of Leicester's 'princely entertainments' at Kenilworth Castle (1575) are two famous instances of dramatic lobbying. Elizabeth, however, developed other strategies for keeping power. Having herself been endangered during her elder sister's reign by rebellion on her behalf, Elizabeth refused to name any successor who might in turn become the focus for those discontented with her rule. She played powerful European realms against one another in hopes of forestalling a united Catholic attack; for years she held out the prospect of marriage to royal foreigners, including her sister's widower Philip II of Spain and the French duc d'Alençon. She appeared seriously to consider marriage to Robert Dudley early in her reign and to Alençon around 1580, in each case sparking furious protests and scurrilous attacks in print. The suits came to nothing, and Elizabeth then stressed her singular devotion to her nation, as prince and 'mother' to her people. But the threats to her policy were many. When her Catholic cousin and potential challenger Mary Stuart fled a hostile Scotland in 1568, Elizabeth kept her under guard but avoided finding Mary guilty in the murder of her second husband, Lord Darnley. Despite repeated plots on Mary's behalf and pressure from extreme Protestant counsellors, Elizabeth resisted executing her for almost two decades. But Mary Queen of Scots was always a dashing figure shadowing Elizabeth, and the pressure to account for her marks even the most laudatory court plays (such as Lyly's *Endymion*) and poetry (Spenser's *Faerie Queene*). Spenser makes her the duplicitous double of his heroines Una and Britomart, and Lyly presents her as a seductress tempting chaste Cynthia's worshipper. When Mary's involvement in the Babington plot and an imminent Spanish invasion made this Catholic rival too dangerous, Elizabeth reluctantly consented to her beheading (1587), still worried about the precedent of executing a fellow royal and descendant of Henry Tudor. And although the fortuitous defeat of the Spanish Armada in 1588 was hailed at the time and can be seen retrospectively as a watershed moment in England's emergence as a powerful nation-state, it ended neither the prospect of foreign invasion nor plotting against the queen. Thus, while it became generally assumed that Mary's (Protestant-reared) son James Stuart would reign after Elizabeth, she refused to make an official pronouncement. Indeed, she put a leading Member of Parliament, Peter Wentworth, in the Tower of London for arguing in print that James had the best claim. But as evidenced by the 1590s interest in plays focused on England's 'weak kings' (*Edward II*, *Richard II*) and civil wars and rebellions (the several *Henry IV* and *Henry VI* plays, *Edward IV*), her policy also sparked worry and discontent.

The succession controversy was but one of the many confusions spurred by England's having a female ruler. Within a society founded on social hierarchies, male supremacy being among the most basic, the exception of honouring a woman at the top of the political order confounded many. The work of justification included political propaganda accentuating England's uniqueness and mystifying Elizabeth as a divine anomaly. In court plays of the 1580s, she was represented as a uniquely inaccessible goddess (*Endymion*) or, more intriguingly, as the first among many lauded goddesses (George Peele's *Arraignment of Paris*). But by the 1590s, the gap between reality and representation caused obvious discontent, traces of which surface even in a court play (Marlowe and Nashe's *Dido Queen of Carthage*), as well as in Shakespeare's mockery of an ass-loving fairy queen in *A Midsummer Night's Dream*. Some popular playwrights presented Elizabeth as embodying a distinctive English goodness (see Thomas Dekker's *Old Fortunatus*); but most of the public stage's iconography of Good Queen Bess would come after her death. Then the difficulties caused by her bodily presence were safely distanced, and she could more easily be incorporated into nostalgia for a mythic English past.

The exceptional queen was, in fact, the proverbial tip of the iceberg in terms of sixteenth-century gaps between social theory and practice: 'women on top' were perceived as but one aspect – and sometimes the cause – of widespread topsy-turvyness. European fears of change and social instability often led to vilification of those who were supposed to be of lower status yet seemed (or were imagined) to possess power: village 'wise women' became 'witches', women who talked were dubbed 'scolds' or 'shrews', servants were suspected of tricking their masters, the rural poor regarded as filthy vagabonds and the urban poor as thieves. In many cases, these putative 'upstarts' were punished, tortured and even killed through the use of pillories, ducking stools, cartings, bridles, brandings, whippings, the gallows, dismemberment and burning. On the stage, social fears were conveyed through both comedies and tragedies in which subservient 'familiars' became dangerous.[22] In *Arden of Faversham* (c. 1587–92), the corruption invades a man's very home: his wife and his tenant conspire to kill the master. What is covered over in this stage version of an actual crime is the complicated instability of the master's own status. Whereas the historical Thomas Arde(r)n was a 'new man' made wealthy by the sixteenth-century court patronage system rather than by birth, the play represents his murder as a conspiracy of the uppity and unruly against the stable old order.[23] Life resisted traditional theories and explanation more thoroughly than did stage fictions.

In an attempt to create stability, English gentlemen concocted false pedigrees, as did the monarchy – tracing its roots back to a mythic grandson of Aeneas, Brute. Elizabeth could thereby symbolise the inexorable movement of empire westward, the *translatio imperii*: from ancient Troy, to Rome, to Britain. Discounting ruptures in the royal line caused by successive invasions and untimely ends was again but the tip of the iceberg: more fundamental and wide-ranging was the attempt to create 'pure' Englishness out of an impure history. An obvious sticking point for this project was the presence and persistence of Celtic Britons, undeniably indigenous but often hostile and seemingly 'other' in language and culture. At the same time, it has been estimated that a hundred years before, half the inhabitants of the British Isles were still Celtic speakers of some variety.[24] The fact that the queen's own family bore the Welsh name of Tudor was a reminder of the ethnic and cultural mixing that had gone on for centuries, defying any clear ethnic or geographical boundaries of 'Englishness'.

Take Wales: along with Cornwall, it was the most successfully colonised of the Celtic 'fringe' areas. Yet despite Acts of Union under Henry VIII, the status of Wales was not resolved. The official language and the common law might now be English, but Welsh circuit courts had some autonomy and most of the population continued to speak Welsh. Despite many gentry families' loyalty to the Tudors and hence to the English crown, signs of Wales's foreignness persisted in English culture, exemplified on stage by Lady Mortimer's Welsh speech and song in Shakespeare's *Henry IV, Part I*. A Privy Council letter of

---

22 On forms of legal punishment, see Dolan, *Dangerous Familiars, passim*; Underdown, 'The taming of the scold', in Fletcher and Stevenson (eds.), *Order and Disorder in Early Modern England*, 116–36; Ingram, *Church Courts, Sex and Marriage, 1570–1640*; and Boose, 'Scolding bridles and bridling scolds'.

23 On this play's relation to domestic culture, see Orlin, *Private Matters and Public Culture in Post-Reformation England*; and Henderson, 'The theater and domestic culture', in Cox and Kasten (eds.), *A New History of Early English Drama*, 173–94.

24 Maley, ' "This sceptred isle" ', in Joughin (ed.), *Shakespeare and National Culture*, 96.

January 1584 reflects continued worry that the Welsh coast might provide an inroad for foreign troops: it instructs the county muster-masters of Anglesey, Merioneth and Caernarvon to assemble trained men in readiness to fight during 'these dangerous times'.[25] One trusts that they were more serious in the endeavour than was Shakespeare's Falstaff.

Ireland remained the most unruly area of Celtic resistance. Essex stood at the end of a long line of English noblemen who failed to quell Irish rebellion against colonisation and cultural suppression. Those 'beyond the Pale' of English settlement fought back, prompting justifications for iron-fisted rule such as Spenser's *A View of the Present State of Ireland*. But despite the massacres and confiscation of property he defended, Spenser himself was forced to return to England in 1598 after his Irish estate was sacked. From Henry Sidney through Lord Grey of Wilton to Essex, patrons of the arts also carried scars from their Irish encounters. Not until Lord Mountjoy's brutal campaign at the start of the seventeenth century did the English have any lasting control over the Irish population. Its enforcement would create a legacy of hate and violence still unresolved.

With a few notable exceptions, the stage trivialised and mocked characters from these untamed parts of the British Isles. Humour diffused anxiety over the seriousness of threats to the emergent nation, as in the famed flare-up between Captains Fluellen of Wales and Macmorris of Ireland in act 3 of *Henry V*. Insatiate Welsh widows-on-the-make and pontificating Welshmen appear in comedies such as *The Merry Wives of Windsor* (1597), *Patient Grissil* (1600) and on into the Jacobean works of Thomas Middleton. If Celtic culture could not be killed by force, the theatre did its part to 'domesticate' it through laughter.

Efforts at colonisation across the Atlantic were even less successful. Sir Frances Drake circumnavigated the globe and optimistically claimed California en route (1579), but settling proved harder than voyaging or claiming. Sir Walter Ralegh was granted a patent to establish a colony in 'Virginia', that all-encompassing name for the eastern seaboard of North America meant to honour Elizabeth. Ralegh organised an expedition which in 1585 established the Roanoke settlement in what is now North Carolina. This outpost soon earned its place in history as the 'lost colony', its inhabitants disappearing and suspected to have been kidnapped or killed by native Americans. From 1589 through 1602, Ralegh supported five voyages to locate and relieve the colony, further motivated by the fact that he would lose his patent (and monopoly) if

---

25 Jones, *A New History of Wales*, 55–6.

there were no permanent settlement. Hostilities with Spain made the attempt even more difficult, and Ralegh failed. As a result, the first successful Virginia colony would be named for the king who reigned when it was established in 1607: Jamestown. Nevertheless, the 'new world' voyages and failures provided fascinating news for Elizabethans. They melded with older (largely fictional) accounts such as the best-selling *Voyages and Travels of Sir John Mandeville* to create visions of the exotic and perilous, of potential wealth and adventure despite disease, want, 'savages' and 'cannibals'. These images begin to appear in stage speeches and occasionally even representation, mixing with and informing the reception of less fanciful cultural 'others'. Thus, a conquered Amazonian queen appears and an Indian boy plays a crucial but unseen role in *A Midsummer Night's Dream*; and the Moor Othello speaks of encounters with 'the Cannibals that each other eat, / The Anthropophagi, and men whose heads / Do grow beneath their shoulders' (1.3.145–7).

Many representations of racially, geographically or religiously different characters were more overtly hostile. Despite (and because of) ample evidence of change and the gap between social theory and practice at home, the English often turned on those deemed foreign, who could more complacently be made into the villains threatening an emergent national identity. Specific political plots and controversies sometimes coincided with a spate of such representations. Yet stage plays also call attention to contradictions within the categories themselves, refusing easy oppositions and blurring the lines between domestic and foreign, holy and barbaric, civilised and savage.

Black characters such as Muly Mohamet in George Peele's *The Battle of Alcazar* (1589), Aaron the Moor in *Titus Andronicus* (c. 1591) and the Prince of Morocco in *The Merchant of Venice* (c. 1596) are mocked and/or feared. All three are designated as Moors from North Africa but seem to have been represented as if they were sub-Saharan Africans, implying a hazy understanding of, or at least interest in, ethnic differences. More recently, such representations have been the source of scholarly debate, as we try to differentiate racial, religious and geographical categories and compare their importance in early modern minds. While it would be anachronistic to project pseudo-scientific models of nineteenth-century racism back in time, anxiety about the presence of 'negroes' in Elizabethan England cannot be ignored. In 1596 and 1601, the queen issued warrants for the expulsion of 'blackamoors'. In the first case, eighty-nine black servants were to be exchanged for an equal number of English prisoners who had been held by the Spanish; the licence adds that 'those kind of people [blackamoors] may be well spared in this realm, [it] being so populous and numbers of able persons . . . perish for want of service'. She assumes masters will provide their servants voluntarily, 'considering her majesty's good pleasure to have those kind of people sent out of the land'.[26] Such trading in human flesh also reminds us that the privateer John Hawkins, active in breaking Portuguese control of the seas along the African coast, was already initiating English involvement with the African slave trade.

Yet the queen at least said she found the slave trade repugnant, and kept two black attendants herself. Such 'exotics' were also used in entertainments and pageants as signs of new English wealth and grandeur. More important politically, England was making alliances across racial and religious lines, with the Moroccans and the Turks. The Moorish ambassador of the Islamic King of Barbary came to England for half a year in 1600, during which the Lord Chamberlain's Men performed at court. Years before this visit and Shakespeare's tragedy of the converted Moor of Venice, moreover, Peele's *Battle of Alcazar* presented a good Moor to balance its bad one. Peele's honourable Moor was even Islamic and allied with the Turks, whereas the bad Moor worked with the English (Catholic-affiliated) character Thomas Stukeley and the Christian king of Portugal, Sebastian. The historical battle from which the play derives (4 August 1578) was a disaster for Portugal if not 'Christendom'; Sebastian's death there ended Portugal's royal line as well as his dream of a Christian crusade against Islam. It soon led to Portugal's annexation by Spain (1580–3; a subsumption Kyd's *The Spanish Tragedy* represented in fictional form). Given England's attempts at colonial expansion through shipping and its antagonism with Spain, the decline of Portugal was in fact a more pressing issue for England than whether Catholics or Muslims won North African battles. This dramatisation captures the complexities of its contemporary scene, with religious, ethnic and national positions defying simple oppositions. Here too the recent historical past and present collided, as English alliances shifted dramatically in the face of more immediate European threats. Although the great sea battle of Lepanto (1571) effectively ended Ottoman encroachment into western Europe, and despite an Anglo-Turkish treaty, mythic memories of past fears and losses to the Turks remained haunting: traces appear in *Tamburlaine, Selimus* and even *Othello*.

Similar oddities appear in the representation of Jewish characters. All Jews had officially been expelled in 1290, but a few Jews and Jewish converts to Christianity did live in Elizabethan London, including the queen's own physician, Roderigo Lopez. Between the time when Marlowe's satire *The Jew of Malta* was performed (c. 1592) and the time of Shakespeare's subtler portrait of

---

26 Cited in McDonald, *The Bedford Companion to Shakespeare*, 296.

Shylock in 1596–7, Doctor Lopez was accused and found guilty of plotting to poison the queen. In 1594 he was condemned to a traitor's death, still affirming (according to William Camden) 'that he loved the Queen as well as he loved Jesus Christ; which coming from a man of the Jewish profession moved no small laughter in the standers-by'. The collision of pathos and mockery here, as at moments in the stage representations, indicates the cultural contradictions regarding Judaism. Jews were blamed for being usurers yet needed by Christian merchants to help finance their early capitalist ventures; blamed for being Christ's killers yet recognised as upholding the culture of the biblical patriarchs; forbidden to practise their religion yet mistrusted as converts. On-stage, Jewish characters (like Moors and Turks) could also serve to unmask Christian hypocrisy, especially when representatives of these cultures were brashly juxtaposed, as in the plays of Marlowe.

Tellingly, *The Jew of Malta* and *Othello* are located within the Mediterranean basin, within the 'known' world but on islands at the margins of European control. They were islands for which Turks and Christians battled during the sixteenth century. The loss of Rhodes and Cyprus to the Turks and the unsuccessful siege of Malta by forces of Suleiman the Magnificent (1565) were still fresh memories. But these locations also foreground the linkage between foreign threats and mercantile expansion, pragmatic interests in shipping lanes and trade motivating new awareness of and attitudes toward 'others'. When the first European 'new world' voyagers set out, they were after all seeking wealth and trade with the East, not the unknown Americas. Increased desire for luxury goods whetted English interest in trade with (and soon, attempted domination of) Asian nations. Hakluyt added new material about Asia to his final edition of *Principall Navigations* (1598–1600) and prompted the first Englishman's account of travel in India. Trading via the Ottoman Empire had been proceeding apace; in 1588, the ship *Hercules* returned from Syria with 'silk from Persia, indigo and cotton from India, cinnamon from Ceylon, pepper from Sumatra and nutmegs, cloves, and mace from the Moluccas'.[27] In 1600, English merchants formed the East India Company, and soon began to see remarkable returns on their investment in Asian trade. We do not see representations of first encounters in foreign lands on the Elizabethan stage, however; instead, we begin to see evidence of the battling among Mediterranean powers that would shape the colonial era to come.[28]

27 Hakluyt 1904: III, 328; cited by Loomba, 'Shakespeare and cultural difference', in Hawkes (ed.), *Alternative Shakespeares*, II, 183.
28 See Raman, *Framing 'India'*, passim.

For economic as well as religious reasons, then, most threats to English-ness on stage were represented as coming from the European continent, and especially from the Catholic regions of Spain and Italy. The Italian threat was represented as cultural, though along with immorality and decadence came an emphasis on mercenary motivations. The political theorist Machiavelli, badly understood through intermediary texts such as the *Contre-Machiavel*, became the prototype for scheming villains – appearing directly in the prologue to *The Jew of Malta*. Italy was also the land of the pope, now dubbed the Anti-Christ by fervid Protestants and English nationalists. The mockery of the pope in *Doctor Faustus* is a particularly brash (and complicated) example of the re-sulting treatment of Catholic churchmen onstage. The practice roots back to mid-century Protestant moralities such as John Bale's *King Johan*, in which the pope 'doubles' as Usurped Power. But recent events increased English anger at the specific popes in power. In 1570, Pope Pius V had excommunicated and officially 'deposed' the English queen as a heretic; ten years later, Pope Gregory XIII proclaimed that assassination of Elizabeth was not a mortal sin, thereby licensing murder of the English sovereign. As tensions increased, some Catholic English exiles, trained by the Jesuits on the continent, returned to their homeland. In 1581, Elizabeth countered with a gruesome demonstration of sovereign power: she had the Oxford-educated priest Edmund Campion and two other Jesuits executed for treason – including the punishment of being drawn and quartered, a horror often commuted in the case of gentlemen. Finally in 1587, in alliance with the Spanish, the pope announced a religious crusade against England. The following year saw the attempted invasion of England by the Spanish Armada.

The Spanish had the military strength to put the pope's words into action. Anglo-Spanish relations had deteriorated mightily since mid century, when Elizabeth's sister Mary Tudor had married Philip II. After several years of unsuccessful wooing, Philip realised that Elizabeth had no intention of fol-lowing in her sister's footsteps. He was, moreover, a dedicated Catholic who believed in the necessity of returning a renegade nation to the fold. He also had economic and political incentives for curbing England. In 1576, the Spanish sacked Antwerp, attempting to control that crucial trading port and solidify their claims in the Netherlands. The move instead led to political resistance under their Protestant leader William of Orange and unification of the Dutch provinces against Spanish rule. In the meantime, however, the loss of Antwerp hurt the English wool trade badly, and wool was the premier English ex-port. Thus, when William of Orange was assassinated in 1584, Elizabeth could no longer sustain her 25-year-old policy of avoiding foreign entanglements (military as well as marital). The following year, she sent an army headed by the Earl of Leicester to help the Dutch states. With brief remissions, England was essentially at war with Spain for the rest of Elizabeth's reign.

The Armada's 1588 defeat was a remarkable victory of English small ships over huge galleys, greatly abetted by Spanish delays, the unruly English Channel and stormy weather. It became immediately symbolic of the little island nation's emergence on the European historical stage, a Protestant David having destroyed the Spanish Goliath. It also coincided with a trend towards history plays: if not itself the spark, the victory certainly provided impetus for interest in England's historical past and present. Sometimes histories were distinguished from romance and plots derived from humanist study of the classics, but at other times the interests merged (as in Robert Greene's *Friar Bacon and Friar Bungay* and *James IV*). What might later sound like empty jingoism found an eager audience in that perilous moment: *The Famous Victories of Henry V* (perhaps the first English history play) revels in French defeat, and particularly the moment when the dauphin is forced to kneel before the English king. Robert Wilson's *The Three Lords and Ladies of London* directly celebrates the victory over the Armada, and in *The Troublesome Reign of King John*, the barons unite, proclaiming, 'If England's Peers and people join in one, / Nor Pope, nor France, nor Spain can do them wrong' (lines 1195–6). Obviously Protestantism and the imagined nation were integrally connected by this point.[29] As the reality of the Armada defeat sank in, it was also treated with a lighter touch: in *Love's Labour's Lost*, Shakespeare creates a 'fantastical Spaniard' with the resonant name Don Adriano de Armado, who is easily outwitted by that pint-sized 'juvenal', Moth.

Shakespeare's comedy takes place in a romanticised Navarre, with the proposed marriage of its king and the princess of France at its centre: the happy ending, however, is delayed. The play thereby emblematises the uncertainty of France's own attempted happy ending at this political moment. Given its religious civil wars throughout the latter half of the century, this other great continental power presented a more difficult case for English representation. France was sometimes an ally and sometimes a Catholic threat. 1572 was a benchmark year: on St Bartholomew's day (24 August), the extreme Catholic faction of the French court, headed by Catherine de Medici and the duc de Guise, persuaded Charles IX to eliminate the Protestant (Huguenot) problem by a mass killing. The streets of Paris ran with blood, quite literally, in a shocking slaughter witnessed by young Philip Sidney and later memorialised

---

29 See McMillin and MacLean, *Queen's Men*, esp. 18–36.

in Marlowe's *The Massacre at Paris*. The event aggravated religious fears in Protestant England. Although the duc d'Alençon (later, Anjou) was viewed by Elizabeth and her chief counsellor Lord Burghley as a force of toleration opposed to the radical Catholics, his being the French king's brother made his wooing of the queen anathema to many Englishmen. They saw their opposition as loyalty to both Protestantism and Elizabeth, even if she thought otherwise. When the author of a virulently anti-Alençon pamphlet, John Stubbes, had his right hand chopped off as punishment, he used his other hand to raise his hat and proclaim 'God save the Queen'. After the death of Alençon in 1584 and the murder of Charles IX's successor Henri III in 1589, England openly supported the Huguenot leader Henri de Navarre (whose Paris wedding with Princess Marguerite of France had provided the occasion for the 1572 massacre). Navarre's victory brought joy, but swiftly on its heels followed the great capitulation: deciding he could only rule effectively as a Catholic and that Paris was 'worth a mass', he converted. Nevertheless, in 1596 a wounded England signed a treaty of alliance with France against Spain, and the death of Philip II soon after (1598) marked the end of Spain as a major threat. That same year, the Treaty of Nantes allowed Huguenots freedom of worship and equal French citizenship. If not in Shakespeare's comedy, in the political world Navarre had indeed 'married' France, becoming the venerated Henri IV.

The French wars brought an influx of Protestant refugees from the continent, with the Huguenots soon joined by Flemish merchants and craftsmen after the sacking of Antwerp. Many resident aliens found themselves the object of English anger rather than sympathy: they were regarded as taking skilled jobs away from 'true' Englishmen, especially in years of greater unemployment, inflation and famine. 1572 marks the beginning of state-wide legislation attempting to address these economic problems, beginning with classifications and prohibitions on 'vagabonds' and the establishment of a uniform 'poor rate', and culminating in the harsh Poor Laws of 1597–8 and 1601. These laws, in effect until the nineteenth century, vainly tried to stop the poor from moving among parishes and included severe punishment for begging. When soldiers returned from the continent (especially around 1597), the labour market became even more strained. The theatre presented returning soldiers with both sympathy and scepticism – the most outright rogue being *Henry V*'s Pistol, who plans a post-war career in England as a thieving beggar pretending to have got his scars 'in the Gallia wars'.

Expansion of trade, new capitalist ventures and greater reliance on foreign markets were in great part accountable for the new patterns of fluctuating employment, but symptoms were easier to discern than causes. There were

thirty-five riots in London between 1581 and 1602, with a record twelve occurring in June 1595. The complaints ranged from anger at the lord mayor to
the need to release prisoners, from patent abuse to hunger to hatred of the
alien residents. Apprentices took the lead, but successive bad harvests during
the mid 1590s also stirred the working poor and villagers who could not afford to buy grain. Discontent spread beyond the usual suspects and the nearly
ritualistic Shrove Tuesday apprentice riots. In the countryside, the policy of
enclosure increased the anger: wealthy landowners fenced in fields that had
long been commonly farmed by villagers, so that the pastures now fed animals
instead of people. Anti-enclosure riots doubled in frequency after 1590. In 1596
in Oxfordshire, the peasants rebelled, threatening to kill the gentry and march
on London. The gap between rich and poor was growing, and new goods and
signs of wealth – especially evident in London – aggravated the situation.

Understandably, signs of fear at this social unrest appeared onstage, as in
Shakespeare's portrayal of Jack Cade's rebellion in 2 Henry VI (and, later, the
food rioters in Coriolanus). Others treated the plight of the working poor
and less privileged sympathetically. In Dekker's The Shoemakers' Holiday, the
journeyman shoemaker Ralph sadly goes to war – unlike the 'nobleman' Lacy
who evades service – and returns lamed. This story nevertheless reaches a
happy conclusion due to the goodness of his beloved Jane and his master Simon
Eyre, in a fantasy world where Shrove Tuesday brings not rioting but Henry V,
who comes to dine with benevolent craftsmen and apprentices. The play also
treats interactions with a Dutch skipper comically. An Englishman for My Money
(1598), among the first 'city comedies', likewise makes light of the difficulty
of telling the foreign from the domestic, the orderly from the unruly in a
new world of markets and exchange. Finally, some used these social upheavals
to create new types of heroes: not only the infamous shepherd-turned-ruler
Tamburlaine and other Marlovian aspirers, but more familiar members of the
'middling sort' in London, such as Simon Eyre and Heywood's Four Prentices
of London – who rove all the way to Jerusalem.

These heroes were indeed a sign of things to come: of new perspectives on
class, value and the power of the individual citizen to 'fashion' a distinctive self.
And in initiating that modern project, the work of one playwright continues to
stand out and surprise. It is no coincidence that the name of Christopher Marlowe has arisen repeatedly in these pages: one cannot find a more controversial
figure in the theatre than this great stylistic innovator and social subversive.
To see the strains between the energetic new and the haunting old in late
sixteenth-century society, we need only turn to his plays: to the retelling of
an episode from classical epic that seems to challenge if not undo the courtly

logic of Elizabeth's 'cult' (*Dido Queen of Carthage*); to the Scythian slaughterer who defies God, humanity, morality and social hierarchy (*Tamburlaine*); to the upwardly mobile Wittenberg scholar who seeks knowledge and power, taunts popes, devils and commoners, but is finally damned to hell (*Doctor Faustus*); to the money-grubbing, nun-poisoning Barabas who turns out to be no more (nor less) 'politic' than Christians, Turks and Moors (*The Jew of Malta*); to the scathing portraits of power politics that give the lie to religious and moral righteousness at the French court (*The Massacre at Paris*) and in English history (*Edward II*). Who knows what other idols he might have smashed, what beliefs he might have satirised had he not himself been so controversial? For the space of theatre remained embedded in that hierarchical society, despite its challenges and liminality; players might vaunt, but when the man who wrote their parts did, the guardians of order (or at least power) intervened.

The details of Marlowe's end in a bar-room brawl remain a matter of speculation, as do the true motivations behind his being charged with heresy a month prior. But one episode during the month he was murdered provides documentary evidence of the close involvement of Marlowe's role in the theatre and the social controversies swirling in London. In early May 1593, a doggerel poem known as the 'Dutch Church libel' harangued the resident aliens whom the apprentices had already been threatening with violence. It was signed 'Tamburlaine'. Marlowe was out of town and certainly not the libel's author, but any connection at all would not have helped Marlowe's case with those trying to maintain social control. Hearkening back to 1572 and Marlowe's recent representation of the St Bartholomew's day massacre, the libel threatens the Dutch immigrants: 'We'll cut your throats, in your temples praying, / Not Paris massacre so much blood did spill.' The debates, controversies and confusions of sixteenth-century culture shaped Christopher Marlowe, who in turn reshaped them for the stage in a radical new style. But the London audience also did their own controversial reshaping.

When Marlowe was charged, the testimony of paid informants (Richard Baines) and tortured ex-roommates (the playwright Thomas Kyd) was duly produced, and perhaps had a modicum of accuracy. After all, the expression of unconventional desires (for tobacco and boys) and humorous defiance (of religion, propriety and social controls) is of a piece with Marlowe's stage representations. Whether his mouth or his behaviour, his subservience to Walsingham's spy service or his rebellion against church doctrine, led Marlowe into trouble, what remains fascinating about the case is the difficulty of distinguishing forces of order from those of disorder at that particular moment in 1593. Like the texts he left behind, Marlowe's life leaves scholars debating, interpreting in nearly antithetical ways. How appropriate, then, that Marlowe himself can now stand as a final image of Elizabethan theatre and controversy. He was no icon standing *for* a definable position, but an Englishman who epitomised the upheavals in material conditions and *mentalité* that defied simple understanding. Out of those conditions, and like the theatre for which he wrote, he produced great fear – and great wonder.

10

The condition of theatre in England in 1599

ANDREW GURR

England in 1599

It was not a good year for facing the future with confidence. Seven successive bad harvests with their effect on prices and human well-being, a long war against Spain fought across the North Sea in the Netherlands, threatening more Armadas and draining the government's treasury, the major distraction of a new and costly rebellion in Ireland, a virgin queen now long past the hope of bearing any heir and so prompting fears of a disputed succession, all these troubles, along with the recurrent epidemics of bubonic plague, made the Bible's four horsemen of the apocalypse into an ominous symbol of life's realities as the new century loomed. Famine, war, pestilence and death were on show throughout the country.

Probably the largest fear was over the succession. With Catholics oppressed more and more by the church establishment, and getting active support from the Spanish enemy, the danger that civil war would return whenever the sixty-three-year-old Elizabeth died was a constant concern. The Catholics had a case, and a candidate. Elizabeth's elder half-sister Mary, whom she succeeded, had married Philip of Spain. Mary died without bearing any heirs, but her marriage gave her husband an interest in the English throne that he tried to enforce in 1588 with his Armada. English Catholics who kept the old faith had reason to assert Elizabeth's bastardy and her dubious claim to the throne. The pope had given them even more dangerous arguments. The Papal Bull that excommunicated Elizabeth in 1570 encouraged the most militant Catholics to believe that it could be right to assassinate a heretical prince. By 1599 the network of spies and informers set up by Francis Walsingham for the Privy Council in the 1580s was more active in ferreting out the subversive activities of recusants than ever. Bright young men like Anthony Munday and Christopher Marlowe were paid to pretend to have been converted to Catholicism and go to France to learn the enemy's techniques and plans. The hot war with the might of Spain across the North Sea in the Netherlands had in no way been checked by Henri IV's suspension of the religious wars in France in 1596, and threats of new Armadas kept recurring. In 1599 England was fiercely at war, both outside and in.

War

William Camden's *Annales*, telling the story of the last fourteen years under Elizabeth, comprehended the 'Two and Fortieth Yeere of her Reigne', 1599, with an account almost exclusively given over to the Earl of Essex's activities. First he describes him arguing for the lord deputyship in Ireland, then from March conducting and misconducting his campaign, and in September returning in disgrace and high dudgeon to his detention in the hands of the lord keeper. Camden's account ends, before two last short pages about the deaths of famous men such as Hooker, 'And now let us leave the Earle of *Essex* under custody.'[1] Essex and the Irish fiasco did dominate the thinking of the English court that year. But underneath its ludicrous extravagance and the many deaths that accompanied it, there was always the war with Spain.

The defeat of the first Armada was already ten years old, and England had been sending its troops and its navy to fight in the Netherlands for thirteen years by 1599. The threat of another attempt at invasion by the Spaniards was ever-present. In March stories started circulating about a Spanish fleet being gathered to take advantage of the fact that the English forces were on their way to Ireland as well as busy in the Netherlands. Twelve large warships were said to be gathered at Ferrol. In April twelve more were seen in the Bay of Biscay. The number of ships rumoured to be gathering escalated week by week through the summer, and by 1 August a massive Spanish fleet was said to be heading for England. That day John Chamberlain, writing from London to his patron in Ostend, reported that troops were mustering throughout the south in consequence of a report that 'the Adelantado hath an Armada redy at the Groine of 30 gallies and 70 ships (though some say more)'.[2] Nine days later he wrote, 'Upon Monday toward evening came newes (yet false) that the Spaniards were landed in the yle of Wight, which bred such a feare and consternation in this towne as I wold litle have lookd for, with such a crie of women, chaining of streets and shutting of gates as though the ennemie had ben at Blackewall.'[3] In all, the rumour called thirty thousand men to

---

1 Quoted from the English translation by Thomas Browne (1625), 251.
2 *The Letters of John Chamberlain*, ed. McClure, 1, 78.
3 Ibid., 1, 81.

arms in the south and in London. Chamberlain further reported on the fresh speculation that this muster of so many soldiers prompted: 'The vulgar sort cannot be perswaded but that there was some great misterie in the assembling of these forces, and because they cannot finde the reason of yt, make many wilde conjectures, and cast beyond the moone, as sometimes that the Quene was daungerously sicke...'[4]

With Jesuit pamphlets about the succession printed abroad and widely distributed in England, with ordinary Catholics increasingly oppressed by the new church establishment, and getting active support from the Spanish enemy and their Jesuit missionaries and propagandists, the fear that civil war would start when the increasingly fragile Elizabeth died was never far from anyone's mind. Questions about dynastic and inheritance rights lurked under the taciturn surface. One in particular related to Salic law, a recurrent issue about the legitimisation of dynasties. And by the end of the 1590s, for all the continuing bellicosity of the hundreds of sermons and printed pamphlets still flowing from the presses, some hints of war-weariness were beginning to appear.

Famine

The long run of bad harvests created massive price inflation which the government could do nothing to control, and serious famines developed, especially in the north, where heavy eruptions of the plague kept recurring in more isolated pockets. In 1598 Kendal in the Lake District lost 2,500 adults, most of its inhabitants, to the plague. Penrith lost nearly as many, and famine continued to take a toll through the next year because farmers were reluctant to bring their goods to such dangerous markets.[5] In Yorkshire and all the northern counties families starved.

Like the rest of the country, London was suffering from the successive bad harvests, with their heavy effect on prices and the social unrest they generated. Robin the ostler in 1 *Henry IV* had reason to lament as early as 1596 the scale of the losses in Eastcheap 'since the price of oats rose' (2.1.13–14). London also had by far the largest of the country's contingent of sick and discharged soldiers and seamen, who by 1599 were a fast-growing addition to the already heavy civic burden of parish poor. London had enjoyed its special identity as the country's leading city for centuries already. The shift under the Tudors when

---

4 Ibid., 1, 83.
5 Mullett, *The Bubonic Plague and England*, 94.

central government began its slow leaching of power from the great lords into more local hands, accelerating when the Reformation took power and lands away from the church, meant that London's citizens grew stronger and proud of their strength and their civic responsibilities. Every town of any substance built its guildhall as a locus for the administration of justice and control of prices. In London especially, pride in its traditions grew. The playing company at the Rose celebrated its London affinities, only established formally five years before, with *The Shoemakers' Holiday*, a celebration of citizen pride in its ruling livery companies and citizen generosity in the story of Simon Eyre, like Dick Whittington one of London's legendary lords mayor. The staging of Dekker's play in 1599 coincided with the publication of that other great celebration of London and its traditions, the loyal citizen and former whiffler John Stow's great *Survey* of London's history and geography.[6]

Pestilence

By no means one of the worst years for epidemics of the plague, the summer of 1599 still saw sixteen Londoners die from it. After the massive death-toll from the epidemic of 1593–4, the four years from 1597 to 1600 were thought to be relatively free from plague. Only 48 people died from it in London in 1597, 18 in 1598, 16 in 1599 and 4 in 1600. Those numbers were never sufficient to impel the Privy Council to renew its periodic bans on public gatherings and attendance at plays, although the wealthier citizens and the gentry of the royal court and the courts of law still made sure they took their summer vacations, when the plague was at its worst, well out of the city. The next major epidemic affecting London did not come until 1603, when Elizabeth died. Nonetheless, onsets of plague were still terrible throughout the north and through Wales, from 1597 and through 1599. It was not socially selective, either. The Bishop of Carlisle died of it at his episcopal palace in 1597.[7] The apocalypse might not be in evidence yet, but at least two of its horsemen, Famine and Pestilence, gave ample cause to fear them right across the country.

Death

At such a time death was never far from anyone's thoughts, and fears about the human soul's tragic place in the divine comedy were a constant theme in

---

6 'Whifflers' cleared the way for the official figures parading on foot or on horse in London's annual processions.

7 Shrewsbury, *A History of Bubonic Plague in the British Isles*, 254.

the churches, where the anti-recusancy laws required everyone to attend. The first months of 1599 saw Shakespeare laying down cash to help build the Globe, finishing *Henry V*, a non-tragic story of war, and writing *Julius Caesar*, about a tragedy that started a war. Was war fever abating? The ending of *Henry V*, especially the long speech by the Duke of Burgundy about war's devastation of France's richly fertile garden, does celebrate a peaceful conclusion to the ride of the horseman of war through France. In reality, for the English in 1599 the fighting in the Netherlands was as intense and as costly as ever. What was worse, Ireland was again in revolt, and the Earl of Essex's campaign had drawn many of the nation's hotheads into it. The question of the succession to the crown was more intense than ever, while open discussion of it was firmly suppressed. References to what was uppermost in people's minds had, when made public, to be covert and indirect. That may have influenced some of the changes that Shakespeare's company, now readying itself to move to the Bankside, made in performance to *Henry V*. The Chorus insists on the rightness of Henry's cause, and the valour in all English hearts. Death is threatened at Agincourt, but hardly touches the English. In time of war, heroic success was of higher value than tragedy and death. Death was treated very carefully in these times. It belonged with the question of lawful rule and succession, but chiefly it was seen as the punishment for ill-doing. Shakespeare, about to embark on his first tragedies since *Titus Andronicus* and *Romeo and Juliet*, knew that as well as anyone.

In keeping with the mood of the time, *Julius Caesar*, for all its political assassination and at the end the tragic death of 'the noblest Roman of them all', was written much more as political analysis than personal tragedy. As a new play about Rome at the moment of its transition (conceivably a backward step) from the republican government which had made it great to its older form, monarchy, the Globe's resident writer was launching a fresh series of plays based on known history. Perhaps mercifully, more likely deliberately, the new series was released from the old question of correct title to rule and succession through legal inheritance that *Richard II* had broached and that *Henry V* contemplates. *Richard II* was already being used as an analogy to the relations of the queen with Essex, as the historian John Hayward learned to his cost in February 1599, when his history of Richard's deposition was published, with a dedication to Essex that was immediately removed from the printed text. Instead *Julius Caesar* studies raw power and scheming for personal advantage. Antony is shown swaying the Roman mob against his assassins with promises from Caesar's will which he soon discards. The noblest Roman, Brutus, is shown to be honest but incompetent. *Julius Caesar* appears to have built into it several of the current concerns of 1599, such as the much-debated anomalies of the Julian calendar, now eleven days out of season, and the damage it was doing to the dating of England's religious calendar. Its central subject, though, personal ambition in government, where questions of right to rule and individual freedom, the 'liberties of the weal', get lost under the forces of might, reflects a possibly cynical and yet quite fresh approach to England's immediate political problems.

While *Julius Caesar* was being written, the Earl of Essex increasingly clearly was posing the threat that might subvert such right as Elizabeth herself had to the throne. He had already asserted his own ancestry as traceable back to the sons of Richard II. Early in 1601 his followers were to employ Shakespeare's players to identify him as the new Bolingbroke who would replace Elizabeth's Richard. In believing that, the Essex group showed they were not uncareful readers of Shakespeare's earlier histories. His reinscription of the story of English kings from Richard, rightful heir to the royal title but wrongful user of it, through the rightful use by the wrongful usurper Bolingbroke as Henry IV, in effect nullified the significance of title to rule while asserting, with Henry V, the need of the dubiously titled ruler to act rightly, and acknowledge the public interest in order to hold public support. If Elizabeth was losing public support, Essex had a chance to make himself as rightful a ruler as Henry IV or his son.

There is good evidence that this was a deeply difficult political matter in 1599. It has been claimed quite plausibly that the notorious bishops' ban of June 1599 which ordered the burning of nine recent books of satirical verse, was prompted by Archbishop Whitgift's anxiety over Essex, whose feats in Ireland were then the subject of massive speculation. It was in effect an attempt to suppress publications containing critical verses that might be thought to refer to him.[8] Certainly a book by John Marston's cousin Everard Guilpin, *Skialetheia or a Shadowe of Truth*, which has at least one verse that could have been applied to Essex, was included in the ban, along with two of Marston's own. *Skialetheia* comments on 'great *Foelix*', behaving exactly like the Bolingbroke of Shakespeare's *Richard II*, who 'vayleth his cap to each one he doth meet', even a humble 'broome-man', in order 'T'entrench himselfe in popularitie, / And for a writhen face, and bodies move, / Be Barricadode in the peoples love'. In 1598 that was a comment on what many Londoners could see of Essex, while he waited impatiently for his commission to quell the rising in Ireland. He left for Ireland towards the end of March. By the summer his return was expected

8 Clegg, *Press Censorship in Elizabethan England*, chapter 9, esp. 211, 216.

as the 'conquering Caesar...bringing rebellion broachèd on his sword' that Shakespeare's fifth Chorus for *Henry V* anticipates. Nerves were stretched, and the succession question loomed over Essex more than anywhere.

It is probably true that such nerves as Archbishop Whitgift showed with his ban were a reflection of the Elizabethan authorities' capacity for cock-up rather than conspiracy.[9] The burning of the books did, nonetheless, show how careful every writer had to be. The Archbishop's Order to the Stationers' Company to suppress the nine books included an instruction that no books of history should be printed without prior allowance from the Privy Council, nor any plays that had not been officially authorised for publication. The inclusion of books about history was a twitch from the problems that arose earlier in the year over Hayward's *History of the Reign of Henry IV*. Shakespeare, never concerned about the appearance of his plays in print, may still have felt it wise to switch his attention from the history of England to that of Rome, and to replace the local Caesar with the real one.

He saw all too clearly the way things were going in English politics. He may even have had a vision of a future based rather more firmly on titles to rule than Essex's evidently simple and self-interested reading of King Richard's story and his idea that the might of Bolingbroke could be utilised in the present time to replace Richard's right.[10] There are two particularly local concerns set out in *Henry V*. One is the question of the place of Salic law, denying succession through the female, in dynastic issues, the other attitudes to the enemy in the north. The single most extraordinary and anomalous feature of *Henry V* is the figure of Scottish Jamy amongst the four captains in Henry's army.[11] At the time of Agincourt almost all the Scots fighting in France were fighting for the French, and the danger of the Scots invading England while the English

---

9 Clegg writes 'The cultural practice of literary censorship seen through the fixed window of 1599 looks less like an efficient government system, stringently enforced and compliantly followed, than an improvisational play of competing personal interests acted out on a stage of perceived national emergency' (ibid., 217).

10 The judges at Essex's trial in 1600 over his conduct of the Irish campaign accepted evidence that casually muddled history with theatre in their view of what Essex had done. Thomas Wright, a Jesuit who testified against Essex at the trial, mixed the fact of the publication of Hayward's ill-timed history of the deposition of Richard, a book prefaced by an Epistle dedicated to Essex and censored in March 1599, with Essex's enthusiasm for the story as depicted in Shakespeare's play. His accusations against Essex included 'his underhand permitting of that most treasonous booke of Henry the fourth to be printed and published being plainly deciphered not only by the matter, and by the Epistle itself, for what ende, and for whose behalf it was made, but also the Erle himself being so often present at the playing thereof, and with great applause giving countenance and lyking to the same' (quoted in ibid., 203).

11 See Gurr, 'Why Captain Jamy in *Henry V*?', *Archiv* 226 (1989), 365–73.

army fought in France is dealt with thoroughly in the play's second scene. To add a comic Welshman and even an Irishman to the English troops in France was understandable, but a Scot in the English army was quite exceptional. Holinshed mentions only one Scot in Henry's entourage, the young King James I, a long-term captive of the English since the age of eight, when he was shipwrecked off the Yorkshire coast.[12] For Shakespeare to add a Scottish James as an ally of the English in 1599 was a remarkable and in the event a uniquely prophetic choice. In 1599, unlike most of the Welsh and many of the Irish, Scotland was no friend of England, and certainly not a military ally. Jamy, not presented with as comic an accent as Llewellyn (Fluellen) or Macmorris, but with his distinctive form of English written in as carefully as those of his fellow captains, has a name and role that resonate intriguingly in the play. Shakespeare was anticipating the union of the kingdoms that the succession of King James VI to the English throne was to bring about in 1603, joining the four realms into one for the first time since the united Britain of ancient mythology.

Elizabeth had forbidden any discussion of her likely successor from early in her reign, and grew more insistent as age began to weigh on her. She put the MP Peter Wentworth in the Tower in 1594 for proposing King James of Scotland as her legitimate successor. Nobody dared say anything about the succession in public, although the long-running correspondence between the Cecils in London and King James in Edinburgh shows what was really expected and hoped for by all non-Catholic citizens. Putting Scottish Jamy into Agincourt in 1599 suggests that a place in the national brotherhood was recognised for Scotland, in a united Britain that Shakespeare was only able to celebrate more explicitly, in *King Lear* and *Cymbeline*, after 1603 when King James came to unite his two thrones and revive the ancient kingdom of Britain. The addition of Jamy to the other captains may have been an afterthought (his lines can be taken out with little adjustment to the sense of that scene),[13] but it was certainly made in 1599 as a remarkable act of prophecy. Ironically, his one scene could not have survived after 1603, when the influx of hungry Scotsmen to London had made the accent far less of an innocent gesture to political union than it was in 1599. Certainly by 1605, when the royal James was audience to a performance of the play at court, the inclusion of a Captain Jamy would have made a sharp test for the players' awareness of court sensitivities.

---

12 King James, by then aged twenty-four, joined Henry in France in 1420, to help him counter the threat from an army of 7,000 Scots who had been sent to join the dauphin's forces at Chatillon.

13 See Brown, 'Historical context and *Henry V*', *Cahiers Elizabethaines* 29 (1986), 77–81.

The other issue was an English nuance of Salic law, which in its French use is rehearsed so specifically and disingenuously by the Archbishop of Canterbury. Its denial of the right to inheritance through the female line underlaid the present dynastic issue in England. Salic law was not peculiar to France. One particular aspect was at issue in these years in England: the right of noble titles to pass through the female line by marriage. That not only challenged the right of any husband of Mary or Elizabeth inheriting the crown, like Philip of Spain, but was directly an issue in the Yorkist claim to the English crown, since their title came from the Earl of Cambridge's marriage to a royal daughter who was senior to any male in the line of descent from Edward III. Their child could inherit, but it was a matter of current dispute in English law whether a husband could assume his wife's title. Sir John Oldcastle, of whom there is more to be said later, was known as Lord Cobham in the right of his wife's title. It was a tender legal issue, and the 1599 play about him calls him 'Lord Cobham' in the text, but gives him his own name in the title. Shakespeare knew the law from his own family's attempt to register his mother's right to her Arden titles. Patriarchal law applied, but such sore points as the primacy of primogeniture as against bequest by paternal testament, including Henry VIII's will which laid down his choice for the succession and in the process called King James of Scotland's title to the English crown into question, raised enough doubts, at a time when the succession to Elizabeth was in everyone's mind, to make Salic law a far more intriguing issue than we find it now.[14]

Theatre in 1599

For all the apocalyptic perils of the time evident in the plays, in the theatre plainly commercial pressures had their say. It was a year for major changes in playgoing. Each of the two companies given an exclusive licence to perform in London provided three plays at court over Christmas as usual. But that settled system was now at risk. In 1599–1600 they did follow almost exactly the same pattern at court as in 1598–9: the Chamberlain's Men performed on Boxing Day (St Stephen's Night), and the Admiral's the following night. In February 1599, as the forty-day fast of Lent loomed, the Admiral's closed the festivities with a play on the 18th and the Chamberlain's on the 20th. In the 1599–1600 season they played at court on the same days, but with one

---

14 For a note about its implications, see *Henry V*, ed. Gurr, 17–23.

ominous change. In February 1600, instead of the Admiral's, it was Derby's Men who gave a performance. This was the first time in six years that a company other than the two duopolists was admitted to play at court. Competition was growing. Through the previous ten years plays had begun to establish themselves as a massively successful feature of London's leisure, and a highly profitable activity for those putting them on. As a result, new companies were beginning to press on the London duopoly. Equally ominously, new companies of boy players now joined the array of entertainers.

Both of the monopoly companies had their own troubles. The Admiral's Men in fact suffered chiefly from the method the other chose to get out of its own problems. Having lost both of their playhouses at the beginning of 1597,[15] Lord Hunsdon's Men, renting the old Curtain to play in, were struggling to raise the money for a new one. In late December 1598 and through the first months of 1599 they retrieved (or, as the owner of the land claimed, stole) the framing timbers from their old playhouse, the Theatre, and used them for the skeleton of the Globe on Bankside. To fund it they set up a collaborative deal where some of the players, one of them Shakespeare, became co-owners of the new building. It was a time of high investment and high risk. And in the middle of it all, they lost their chief clown. Will Kemp at first gave his share of the money for the Globe, but then withdrew it and himself in order to do his famous feat of morris-dancing all the way from London to Norwich through that winter's wet weather.

At the Globe Kemp was famous for his jigs and his imitation of Richard Tarlton's country-clown extempore acts. It is not clear exactly when Robert Armin took his place as comedian in the playing company – he may have been on hand already – but Shakespeare's 1599 comedy contained a comment on Kemp's departure. *As You Like It*, the first play to celebrate the Globe's completion, with Jaques's 'All the world's a stage' speech echoing the new playhouse's motto, featured an inversion: not Kemp's country clown making his way to the court but a court jester who makes his way into the country. Touchstone, the mark by which other characters see themselves, is not the 'natural' fool which Kemp played, but a jester, an 'artifical' fool. In his *Foole uppon Fooles, or Six Sortes of Sottes*, printed in 1600 once he was firmly established with the London company, Armin wrote an account of six 'natural' fools he had known. On Jack Oates, and his 'new Motley Coate', he wrote:

15 For a short account of the Blackfriars, built and banned at the end of 1596, and the Theatre, closed down in April 1597, see Gurr, 'Money or audiences', *Theatre Notebook* 42 (1988), 3–14.

> Naturall fooles are prone to selfe conceit,
> Fooles artificiall, with their wits lay waite
> To make themselves fooles, likeing the disguises
> To feed their owne mindes, and the gazers eyes.
>
> (B2)

Armin's prefatory note to his printer suggests that he must be an 'Atlas' to carry such a load, which may refer to the new Globe's emblem, and the weight of the costs they were carrying with their new theatre.

A new era in playwriting was beginning, but it did not fall into place all at once. Both the leading companies of players were under stress. Both companies started selling their most popular playbooks to the press to help raise funds for their new playhouses, and, as the schedule for court performances over Christmas 1599 showed, both were being threatened by other companies moving into the London scene. The fact that the one company built their new Globe barely fifty yards from their main rivals' Rose playhouse was to them a minor factor in these troubles. But it bothered Philip Henslowe, the Rose's owner, and his son-in-law and partner as leader of the Rose's players, Edward Alleyn, and it certainly reduced their takings at the Rose severely.

The Rose prospered wonderfully until the spring of 1599. But when it re-opened after the customary closure for Lent its takings began to shrink drastically. Almost certainly the drastic fall in its income reflected the presence of the Globe rising only fifty yards away, and opening for its first performances in the early summer.[16] The other company's move from the northern suburb of Shoreditch to join them on Bankside was a major challenge to the Admiral's Men. Through the autumn and winter the Rose's takings dropped still further, so its owners decided they would have to move in the opposite direction. Accordingly, in December Edward Alleyn took out a lease on a site in Golden Lane just outside Cripplegate, not far from the modern Barbican, in the northern suburbs that stretched into Middlesex. It was conveniently close to the office of the Revels in Clerkenwell, where the companies took their plays for rehearsal and approval before the annual performances at court. A contract to build the Fortune on the new site was drawn up on 8 January 1600 with the master carpenter who had recently completed the Globe.

The beginning of autumn was a time for new policies. By late September, just before the hopes of the militant Essex party at court were dashed by his

---

16 Building the Globe started in early January. Accounts of the time its construction took vary, but, with its builders working from an existing prefabricated framework, it was not likely to have taken more than four or five months.

return in disgrace from Ireland, the Globe was staging *Julius Caesar*, and the company at the Rose was facing up to the consequences of its main competitor now being only fifty yards away. Henslowe commissioned a new play, *Sir John Oldcastle*, to call attention to its neighbour's former trouble with Falstaff. The original name given to Falstaff, his most famous character, had been Sir John Oldcastle. Oldcastle was a Protestant martyr, and his descendant became the new lord chamberlain soon after *1 Henry IV* appeared. Late in 1596 the name was changed to Falstaff. Henslowe paid over the odds for his new play that rubbed in the Chamberlain's Men's error, and added another ten pounds 'as a gefte' when it was staged.[17] How much he thought of that bonus as the price of his revenge for being dispossessed from his home territory on Bankside we cannot tell.

The new play put a lot of emphasis on the rival company's portrayal of the original Oldcastle as a fat and sinful coward. Its prologue asserted that:

> *It is no pampered glutton we present,*
> *Nor aged Councellor to youthful sinne,*
> *But one, whose vertue shone above the rest,*
> *A valiant martyr.*

Such a claim depended on the listeners knowing that Shakespeare's Falstaff had originally been named Oldcastle, and that the company was forced to change it because the new lord chamberlain objected to his wife's ancestor being misrepresented in such a scandalous fashion. But the prologue's last line was really disapproving. It condemned the *'forg'd invention former time defac'd'* with the moral superiority of the historically correct. The oppressed Rose writers were fighting for their livelihoods, and pulled no punches.

And yet they also made thorough use of their rival's successes, in ways which show graphically what was popular on stage then. They started with the story of Oldcastle as a Protestant martyr, told at length in Foxe's hugely popular *Acts and Monuments*, better known as the *'Book of Martyrs'*, which gave Henslowe's four writers their main story, and at least one of the four took care to show several other historical misrepresentations in the Shakespeare version. The silence in *Henry V* about the conspirator Cambridge's claim to the English throne, for instance, is emphasised in scene 7 of *1 Sir John Oldcastle*, where the three conspirators of Shakespeare's scene argue the justice of their resistance to Henry with a French agent. Cambridge rehearses his wife's lineage as traceable back to Edward III's grandson Clarence, an older son of the Black Prince than

---

17 See Rutter, *Documents of the Rose Playhouse*, 169.

Henry's grandfather John of Gaunt. Cambridge himself, Richard Plantagenet, son of the Duke of York, therefore claims that his wife (no mention is made of Salic law) has a better title than Henry to the English crown. This was, indeed, the basis for the Yorkist claim against Henry's Lancastrian title that eventually launched the Wars of the Roses. The play underlines the political errors in the Shakespeare version, while offering its own far more respectful reading of the life of one of England's early Protestant martyrs.

At the same time, the play, dealing with only the first half of Oldcastle's long-running opposition to the Catholic church under Henry, is filled with devices from the Shakespeare plays that evidently proved popular with the audiences of the 1590s. Falstaff's role was transferred to a false priest, Sir John of Wrotham, whose woman is called Doll and who robs the disguised King Henry, both of them complaining about having been robbed themselves by Falstaff, Peto and Poins. Sir John later loses his winnings by gambling with the still-disguised king and his nobles. His language follows Ancient Pistol more closely than Falstaff, an unpriestly habit that a noble reproves him for in scene 2: 'it ill becomes / One of your coate, to rappe out bloudy oathes'. He later describes himself as a wolf in sheep's clothing, 'A priest in shew, but in plaine termes, a theefe' (line 308). His punishment is to be tricked by Henry into revealing himself as a thief, through a device rather like that of Williams and the glove in *Henry V*, and being threatened with hanging until Henry reprieves him. The play also has a comic Irish thief, who is not reprieved from execution.

Competition between the two companies that formed the now long-standing duopoly was bound to sharpen as the financiers of the Admiral's Men laid their plans to build the Fortune. Part of this plan included putting a third company in at the ageing Rose, to intensify the competition. It became a turning-point in London's theatre history, a year that saw the two companies of 1594 rise to five. It also saw the beginning of a new flow of plays into print. The first flood had come in 1594, when the major playing companies were losing their patrons, and most groups were breaking and re-forming. That was a time of major changes in the system, as the controllers on the Privy Council gave exclusive rights to their two new companies and excluded all the others from London. Now the same two companies had to reorganise themselves and raise funds for their new playhouses, the Globe and the Fortune, and at the same time advertise their most popular wares against their new competitors.

In 1599 eight plays appeared in print for the first time, and another eight were reprinted. The new plays included some from the established London companies, *An Humorous Day's Mirth* from the Admiral's and *A Warning for Fair*

Women from the Chamberlain's. Others came from their fading competitors, *Edward IV* and its sequel from Derby's, and *George a Greene* from Sussex's. The reprints included the Admiral's *Spanish Tragedy* and the Chamberlain's *Romeo and Juliet* and *1 Henry IV*. Some plays from a decade or more earlier also now came into print, like the Queen's Men's *Clyomon and Clamydes*, Peele's *David and Bethsabe* and Greene's *Alphonsus of Aragon*. The new habit of reading playbooks was turning into a respectable custom with the gentry. Sir John Harington, courtier and wit, augmented his library with copies of all the plays published in 1599.

Playing was now clearly established as massively profitable, and the commissioning of new plays went ahead at an unprecedented rate. While the Globe played *Henry V*, *As You Like It* and *Julius Caesar* as their newest offerings, no doubt along with other plays now lost, the players at the Rose ran an even busier programme, buying plays both by single authors and by groups, most of which have survived only as titles. Besides Dekker's *Shoemakers' Holiday*, Chapman produced *All Fools*, Heywood *Joan as Good as my Lady* and *War without Blows*, Henry Porter a sequel to *The Two Angry Women of Abingdon*, Chettle *Troy's Revenge* and with Porter *The Spencers*, Chettle and Dekker *Agamemnon*, which may have become the Rose's *Troilus and Cressida*, and *The Stepmother's Tragedy*, possibly also known as *The Orphan's Tragedy*, William Haughton *The Poor Man's Paradise* and with Chettle *The Arcadian Virgin*. A consortium of four wrote *Sir John Oldcastle*, Robert Wilson wrote *2 Henry Richmond*, a play which seems from the brief plot summary that survives to have been a version of the last two acts of Shakespeare's *Richard III*, Ben Jonson and 'other Jentellman' put together *The Scots Tragedy*, also called *Robert II, King of Scots*, Haughton and Day wrote *John Cox*, and Haughton, Dekker and Chettle *Patient Grissell*. The busy Dekker also wrote *Bear a Brain* and at the end of the year *Old Fortunatus*. At least two other plays were paid for in part, but never finished. In all, besides the plays already in the repertoire, the Rose players bought more than twenty new plays that year from the various groupings of more than ten different writers.

Old Fortunatus was a special case. Produced, or possibly revived, for the value of its name as a reference to the new playhouse, Dekker revised it for a performance at court that Christmas. Alleyn leased the site for the new Fortune on 24 December, and three days later they proclaimed the proposed new playhouse's name in the title of the play at court. Shakespeare had already celebrated his own new playhouse's motto with Jaques's extremely quotable speech about all the Globe being a stage in *As You Like It*. If it is true that the Globe's motto was '*Totus mundus agit histrionem*', and its flag did show

'Hercules and his load too', as it was put in *Hamlet*,[18] we might expect the summer's best comedy to celebrate the new playhouse. Alleyn followed the same game for his new playhouse's name with *Old Fortunatus*, and later with *Fortune's Tennis*.

As You Like It was remarkable in 1599 not just for its celebration of its company's new home and motto, but for launching a new concept of comedy. Its successor, *Twelfth Night*, acquired a similar title, 'What you will', the name that John Marston gave to one of his comedies for the boy players at St Paul's. Its oddity has provoked a lot of discussion, mostly inconclusive. It certainly had the title from the outset, since the name was used for a 'staying entry' when the play was first taken to the Stationers' Company to license it for printing, in the year following its initial success.[19] There it was noted in the Register along with three other plays of the Lord Chamberlain's Men, including its predecessor, *Much Ado About Nothing*, on 4 August 1600 under the name '*as yow like yt*'. In the event it did not appear in print until the Folio of 1623. The name is almost off-hand, an acknowledgement that the players were willing to indulge the known tastes of the audiences coming to the new playhouse.

More competition was developing in 1599 than just from the companies of adult players like the Earl of Derby's Men, some of whom were later to play at the Rose. John Chamberlain told his correspondent in Ostend that the sixth earl, William Stanley, was busy 'penning plays for the players'. They were presumably intended for his own company. Stanley, however, was moving down more than one path, as another letter-writer, Rowland Whyte, affirmed. His pen and his money were also making work for the newly revived playing company of boy choristers at St Paul's.

Two hungry boy companies were unleashed on the London stages in 1599 and 1600.[20] One was a resurrection, the singing boys of St Paul's, with their tiny playhouse in a corner of the cathedral, protected from city hostility by its location inside the cathedral precinct, where the dean and chapter ruled, not the City. The other was a new group, using the Burbages' vacant playhouse, built in 1596 in the same Blackfriars complex where Richard Farrant had run a playhouse for boys between 1576 and 1582. In 1599 and for a few years after, there was a higher social cachet in performances by boy players than in those

---

18 See Dutton, '*Hamlet, An Apology for Actors*, and the sign of the Globe', *Shakespeare Survey* 41 (1989), 35–43.

19 For a note about the much-debated 'staying entry', see *Henry V*, ed. Gurr, 217–20.

20 There is no precise indication about just when they restarted, after the government in 1590 suppressed the one company run by John Lyly that played at the Paul's playhouse, but one of the new boy companies was certainly performing by 1599, and possibly both.

of the adults. The boy company impresarios claimed to offer 'private' shows, in contrast to the 'public' showings by the adult companies, which were controlled by the Master of the Revels. For the next eight or nine years the boy companies offered plays free from direct official censorship. The sponsors of the little eyases made use of the Burbages' Blackfriars, and the tiny playhouse abutting the cathedral ran a more frankly commercial operation than the earlier boy companies, which maintained the pretence that they were educating the boys who performed their plays. For a while they made deep incursions into the territory of the adult players.

Edward Pearce, appointed from the Chapel Royal to replace the dying Thomas Giles as choirmaster in the middle of 1599, quickly recognised that his stipend could not do much for the boys under his charge. He needed extra income, and commercial performances by the boys at the empty playhouse still nestling under the cathedral's walls were the means to it. So it was that in November or December 1599 John Marston gave the Paul's Boys their first success with *Antonio and Mellida*.

Aged twenty-three, and already noted by Henslowe as a likely writer in his collaborative teams, Marston, a student at the Middle Temple, was the first of a new group of younger writers who chose to write for the boy companies, the most prolific of whom was to be Thomas Middleton. Like most of these writers, Marston lived and wrote for the immediate present of the theatre world in London. Playgoing was still a fresh feature of London's social life, and the one thing new writers were sure of was that their audiences were frequent playgoers who knew their favourite repertoire. *Antonio and Mellida*, carefully designed as an introductory play for the new Paul's Boys, was written in a deliberate mélange of current styles. Packed with allusions to the plays of the adult players' duopoly, it was an Italianate romantic drama with overt affinities to *Romeo and Juliet*, except that it closes on a happy note with the re-establishment of 'our houses unitie' (line 1959),[21] and an assertion that 'here ends the comick crosses of true love' (line 1978).

In many ways the play demonstrates how small and intimate the theatre world of London was. The so-called 'war of the theatres', in which Marston figured along with Ben Jonson and other writers for the new boy companies, was yet to serve its purpose as publicity for the new boys and their unlicensed plays, but self-consciousness about the innovation runs through all Marston's early plays.[22] *Antonio and Mellida* starts with an induction bringing the chief

---

21 Quotations are from the Malone Society Reprint, 1921, ed. W. W. Greg.
22 Reavley Gair's introduction to his Revels edition of *Antonio and Mellida* gives an extensive account of the circumstances.

boy players on stage in cloaks and with their parts in their hands, to discuss their characters and how they will act them. One boy even declares he cannot possibly act a woman's part, a neatly self-conscious reference to the roles of the boys in the adult companies. Mazzagente roars some lines of Marlovian verse, and the reaction by another boy is 'Rampum scrampum, mount tuftie *Tamburlaine*. What rattling thunderclappe breakes from his lips?' (lines 96–7). That allusion to the Rose repertory is matched by Balurdo the clown, who identifies the Globe repertory by saying his role is 'The part of all the world' (line 34), or to be exact 'the foole' (line 36). Marston delighted in the riches the twenty-year-old novelty of London commercial theatre gave him – for the first time ever, poets had captive audiences in their hundreds listening to their verse – and he filled his lines with neologisms ('unpropitiously', lines 585–6, is one ironic instance) that soon brought Jonson's scorn down on him in *Poetaster*, written for the other boy company.

Even though the cost of keeping a boy company of twenty or so young singers was much smaller than a company of adult players, the small roofed playhouses the boys used, with their capacity at less than a fifth of the open amphitheatres, could not possibly survive by charging similar prices. To get a comparable income, they had to charge more. This meant that they had to aim at customers with a markedly higher income-level than the citizens, artisans and apprentices who formed the bulk of the amphitheatre audiences. So from the start the boys aimed at the gentry and nobility, the more educated and fashion-conscious end of the wide range the adults in the amphitheatres catered for. Marston acknowledged this by his parodies of the adult plays, by his appeal to those who knew Latin, and by his explicit expectation that his audience would behave more gently than those in the open-air playhouses. The whole ambience was different from that of the 'public' playhouses. Boys could not imitate the realism of men or the grandeur of Edward Alleyn as Tamburlaine. They could, however, memorise long parts written in prose rather than verse, they were well-trained singers, and they had good musicians to amplify their performances. The small auditorium at Paul's and the Blackfriars required them to use woodwinds rather than the brass of the amphitheatre trumpets, but that was no loss. *Antonio and Mellida* has a sennet played on recorders or 'still Flutes' at line 1883, and specifies the use of cornets rather than trumpets at 219, 1766 and 1842, and it featured eight songs and five part-songs in the performance. The composer Thomas Ravenscroft was an eight-year-old chorister in 1599, and may have played in Marston's play. He was later to praise his choirmaster and play producer, Edward Pearce, as the most admirable of mentors.

At the end of *Antonio and Mellida* the epilogue asks, in typical Marstonian polysyllables, for *'applausive incouragements'*. It was a new venture, and it needed cheering on its way. But it got its encouragement, and through the next eight years first Paul's and then more and more distinctly the Blackfriars boys were to become the main talking-point of the town. Never financially secure, and never given official approval, the 'private' performances did encourage the bolder spirits to voice their views about their time. In June 1599 Marston's early satirical and erotic verses had been burned on the official bonfire. The plays of the boy companies offered him and his fellow wits a new and more profitable venue free from episcopal control. 1599 may not have been a year full of cheering prospects, but it initiated radical changes for poets and for playgoers in London. For Shakespeare and others at their new playhouses, 1599 preluded a decade of unmatched growth and prosperity.

Ben Jonson's *Every Man in His Humour*:
a case study

RICHARD ALLEN CAVE

The use of the term, *case study*, in the sciences yields some interesting ambivalences. In the physical sciences it tends to be applied to a study which determines the *representative* qualities of a system, process or type; and similarly in the natural sciences the intention is generally to define through a close observation of the individual example the nature of the species or *genus* (genre) to which the sample belongs. The impetus here is to generalise from the particular. In the psychological sciences and psychoanalysis, a different intention is usually to be observed in operation: the case history investigates that which subtly distinguishes the particular individual undergoing study from the norm, defines his/her exceptional or unique qualities of being that determine selfhood. What is presented to our understanding is a *specific* psyche and sensibility; and the focus of study is directed towards those qualities that make for originality.[1]

But why begin this essay by determining different applications of the term, case study? Jonson's *Every Man in His Humour* is unusual amongst extant texts of Renaissance plays in that it exists in two distinct versions. So, of course, do *Hamlet* and *King Lear* and several other major works of the period; but the revised texts in these instances were effected relatively close in time to the original compositions, even if one of the versions chanced not to be printed until some two decades later.[2] *Every Man in His Humour* was first printed as a quarto in 1601, three years after it was successfully staged by the Lord Chamberlain's Men. Though the folio edition of Jonson's *Works* did not appear till 1616, it is

---

1 Jonson and many of his contemporaries have suffered for too long from a critical bias that has set them up as the 'dark', 'othered' side of an oppositional binary in which their artistry is measured in terms of deviations from the grand Renaissance norm which is Shakespeare. For a full discussion of this issue, see Cave, Schafer and Woolland, *Ben Jonson and Theatre*.

2 The publishing history of *Hamlet*, for example, involves two quarto texts (1603 and 1604) and the folio version (1623), but the compositional history covers a shorter time-span.

known that the dramatist began to prepare his plays for this publication some four years before its release. As *Every Man in His Humour* is the first play in the volume, it has generally been assumed by editors and critics since Herford and Simpson that revisions to this particular work date from 1612 (internal evidence and references in the text would support this dating). We have then a quarto text that is Elizabethan and a folio text that is Jacobean. The first dates from the early years of Jonson's career as playwright; the revision, if the 1612 dating is accepted, would have occurred at some point between the completion of *The Alchemist*, staged in 1610, and *Bartholomew Fair* in 1614, while Jonson's invention as a writer of comedies was at its zenith. The quarto marks Jonson's shedding of apprentice status and discovery of an individual *voice*; the folio text was effected when that voice had come to its full maturity of range and resonance. In respect of the two definitions of the term 'case study', the 1598/1601 version of *Every Man in His Humour* has to be seen within the context of Elizabethan drama for its unique qualities, as the assertion of a wholly new style of comedy. However, the Jacobean version is best studied for its representative nature, as Jonson brings the play into line with a genre and a tradition that by 1612–16 he has securely established, largely but not entirely at the expense of older styles of comic playwriting. As a case study, the play claims our attention, by virtue of its compositional history, in two distinct ways.

In the 1598–9 season in which the first performances of *Every Man in His Humour* were given, the Lord Chamberlain's Men also staged Shakespeare's *Much Ado About Nothing*. Setting aside the obvious fact of the more polished work of the more experienced dramatist, it is instructive to compare the two comedies, since Shakespeare's at this date is clearly, and in the best sense of the word, traditional. It has all the characteristics of what till this moment in time had constituted *Elizabethan* comedy. *Much Ado* has an Italianate setting; its main plot line (the intemperate and wrongful repulsing of a young woman, Hero, by her intended husband, Claudio, who has been tricked into supposing her unfaithful) draws heavily on popular literary sources deriving from the Italian stories of Bandello and Ariosto; its most prominent characters, Beatrice and Benedick, are largely tangential to the plotting and are engaged on wittily deciding whether or not to fall in love with each other; the play ends with the two couples marrying and the sense that this is what a stable society requires of its young inhabitants. Most stage time in performance is given over to Beatrice and Benedick and their searching for sensible social and emotional grounds for trusting each other to a degree that would enable them confidently to enter into wedlock. Where Hero and Claudio fall instantly in love with scant knowledge of each other beyond the attraction of appearances, Beatrice and Benedick for all their playful banter are seeking to come to a serious understanding of each other's sensibility, values and intellect.[3]

Behind *Much Ado About Nothing* one could trace a tradition going back to the Greek New Comedy of Menander with its focus on the means by which lovers are reconciled and brought into a fruitful union. But more strongly behind Shakespeare's play lies the influence of an Elizabethan writer who took the constituent elements of New Comedy and in rearranging them brought more strongly to the foreground of interest the issue of a proper decorum (of words, sentiments, gestures, conduct) in courtship. John Lyly had initially achieved literary fame with *Euphues or The Anatomy of Wit* (1578), which set a standard for elegance of expression (though it quickly came to be lampooned for its rhetorical excesses). His plays, written exclusively for performance by the companies of boy actors, adapted that practice of wit to elevate prose, the preferred medium for comedy, to a tone suited to the anatomy of intense feeling. 'Elevated' is perhaps the best epithet to describe the impact of his plays: they are generally set in mythical or legendary worlds, and take for their themes enduring, courtly or platonic love (as in *Endimion* of 1591, which examines the love of a mortal for the moon goddess in a manner that makes it clear it is an allegory about a courtier's ideal relation to Queen Elizabeth, who was herself continually represented in contemporary propaganda as an earthly incarnation of the classical goddess, Diana) or heroic magnanimity (as in *Alexander and Campaspe* of 1584, where the Greek conqueror relinquishes his claim to Campaspe once he appreciates the depth of her love for the artist, Apelles, whom he has commissioned to paint her portrait). Always the dramatic interest lies in the correct use of language and an ability on the part of the characters to frame words to define the heart's truth for those listeners sensitive enough to perceive the emotional and moral scruple that ideally determines the speaker's choice of diction. This would doubtless seem very precious, were these grandiloquent characters not offset by others who laughably fail to meet the required standards of expression, because motivated by passion, lust or folly rather than high-mindedness and integrity. These are literally prosaic characters, usually male, whose rhetorical inflations produce only bathos to the amusement of their accompanying pageboys, who take great delight in ridiculing the pretensions of their masters. If Lyly's comedies extend to satire, the focus is still on powerful emotion and the follies that

---

3 We are here entering characteristically Shakespearian thematic territory in investigating the complex interrelationships between perception, appearance and dissembling, all within the context of choosing a marital partner.

it reduces undisciplined individuals to manifest. The plays sustain a careful thematic unity.

While Lyly's younger contemporaries borrowed heavily from his technique, they attempted to include in their comedies a greater diversity of material. Robert Greene, for example, in *Friar Bacon and Friar Bungay* (acted in 1594) seized for his main plot the popular ballad story of the young prince Edward (later Edward I) and his rivalry with Lord Lacey for the love of a country girl, Margaret, which ends with Edward surrendering her to Lacey as magnanimously as Lyly's Alexander surrendered Campaspe. Lyly is a clear influence on Greene's conception. Elsewhere the comedy takes for subject the magical exploits of Bacon and Bungay, where the more satirical side of Lyly's drama has been transformed into an engagement with the fantastical. This allows for moments of spectacle, which Lyly firmly resisted. By pitching the tone of the magic scenes between the awe-inspiring and the absurd, Greene keeps his audience in a state of moral detachment from such a dangerous subject as the black arts. While Greene achieves considerable diversity in his comedy, his polarising of the amatory and the satirical is at the expense of thematic unity. Both plot lines are, however, concerned with the extra-ordinary, whether the subject be courtesy in love or superhuman power and knowledge through magic.

Shakespeare achieved diversity, but by a wholly different means: he brought an acute psychological verisimilitude to bear on the subject of courtship, exploring a range of potential for emotional fulfilment but within more credible human relationships than either Lyly or Greene explore. Magnanimity gives place to generosity; and what satirical impulse is present is less barbed, since the interest is now in discriminating different modes of engaging in the pursuit of love and marriage and the different manners that are consequently displayed by the lovers in question. Beatrice and Benedick are carefully distinguished from Hero and Claudio in *Much Ado*, while in *As You Like It* (*c.* 1600) the four couples who present themselves before Hymen in the final scene are precisely individualised (and Jaques with shrewd insight foretells what the very different marital futures of those couples are likely to prove to be). Courtship in these comedies has been anatomised in relation to temperament, psychology and sensibility, and the potential for future fidelity assessed. While Shakespeare humanises Lyly's subject matter, he respects Lyly's preoccupation with decorum, but rather in terms of showing how in courtship each couple must create their own particular and shared understanding of what constitutes decorum in relationship for the two of them. Decorum here is not, as with Lyly, some grandly Platonic ideal, but a more relative, privately defined basis of trust.

Together Lyly, Shakespeare and the likes of Greene created and sustained a tradition of comedy that may be defined as the Elizabethan norm. To turn from any of the plays just discussed to *Every Man in His Humour* is to confront a wholly different kind of comedy: the tone is quite new; there is little in the way of what conventionally passed for plot; and courtship is marginalised almost to the point of exclusion. Though one can trace a lineage behind the play, Jonson treats the elements of that style of comedy as freely (one is tempted to write as arbitrarily) as he subordinates the features of romantic comedy. Roman comedy in the hands of Plautus and Terence, while it clearly derived from Greek New Comedy, was generally much harsher in its tone and approach. The bringing of a young couple into relationship still provided the framework for the action, but far more stage time was devoted to the range of elderly or bizarre suitors for the heroine's affections and their eventual discomfiting, which was usually effected through the cunning schemes of a wily slave intent on furthering the hero's interests in the hope of his own eventual profit. Jonson received a goodly diet of Roman drama while at Westminster School, and Plautus so profoundly influenced the writing of Jonson's first extant comedy, *The Case Is Altered* (usually dated earlier in 1598), that one is inclined to see the play as little more than clever adaptation.[4] If the dating of the play to the same year as the composition of *Every Man in His Humour* is accurate, then it is astonishing how rapidly Jonson as apprentice-playwright outgrew his Latin models. There are vestiges of the Plautine types behind the characterisation of Musco (Brainworm) as wily servant, Matheo (Matthew) as daft suitor, Bobadilla (Bobadill) as braggart soldier, Giuliano (Downright) as angry man and Lorenzo Senior (Kno'well) as anxiously protective father; but even to intimate this is to see at once how differently they are treated. And, too, there is a host of characters for which there are no Plautine blueprints. Plautus will remain a shadowy presence behind many future Jonsonian comedies, especially where master–servant relations are being explored (Volpone and Mosca, Jeremy and Lovewit in *The Alchemist*, Fitzdottrel and Pug in *The Devil Is an Ass*, the Host and Fly and to some degree Frances and Pru in *The New Inn*); but invariably that Roman ghost is evoked to point up Jonson's originality of invention.

It is worth pausing a moment to consider one significant change between the quarto and folio texts of *Every Man in His Humour*: the translating of the characters' names from Italian to English. It suggests that for Elizabethan audiences

---

4 What is distinctive about *The Case Is Altered* is Jonson's decision to elide two of Plautus's plays, *The Pot of Gold* (*Aulularia*) and *The Prisoners* (*Captivi*), in creating his own; the result is a virtuosic exercise in plotting but at the expense of creative originality.

the dangerous art of comedy had to be rendered 'safe' by being situated in far-fetched, Arcadian, foreign or historical settings (it was not until *Epicoene* in 1609 that Jonson was finally to set a comedy in London). The Italianate dimension permits a further comparison with Italian comedy: writers such as Machiavelli, who developed Plautine material beyond mere imitation, did so into the territory of sex comedy, exploring adulterous liaisons (the unsuitable rival to the hero, Callimaco, for the affections and bed of Lucrezia, the heroine in *Mandragola*, is none other than Lucrezia's husband, Messer Nicia) or exploiting conventional devices of comedy such as disguise to permit all manner of bawdy innuendo and allow libido unrestrained expression. Jonson does not eschew adultery as a subject, but he does not realise it as a situation within his comedy. Instead the *fear* of adultery and of his becoming a cuckold plagues the imagination of one of his characters, Thorello (Kitely); the dramatic focus is on how that private fear distorts his perceptions and renders his public actions absurd to the bewilderment of his wife and relations. His fear makes him vulnerable to characters who, perceiving his condition, choose for their own ends to manipulate and trick him. When he, his wife and Lorenzo Senior converge independently on Cob's house hoping to find evidence of adultery or illicit sex, the audience knows that all three of them have been duped into going there by either Prospero (Wellbred) or Musco and so the focus of the laughter is on their utter gullibility. The humour in Jonson's play is altogether more innocent and benign than in Machiavelli's; and this is chiefly because his thematic interest is no more in analysing lust than it was in investigating courtship.

Every Man in His Humour is remarkable precisely because it makes a bid to open up *any* experience to comic scrutiny; but in doing this Jonson perceives that he has to create an innovatory dramatic structure through which to express his new subject. Though the play when staged proved a success (as is implied by the reference on the 1601 title page to its being acted 'sundry times'), the actors in the Lord Chamberlain's company were apparently wary at first of tackling the piece (or so legend has it). This is hardly surprising, if true, since the comedy requires a different mode of ensemble acting from what the actors were accustomed to. Contemporary comic dramatists offered Elizabethan actors a purchase on a play by containing their individual roles within the strong framework provided by the storyline, which – from what we know of rehearsal and performance conditions of the time – must have functioned in a manner like one of the established scenarios for a *commedia dell'arte* troupe. It was a known shape within which they could place their learned parts and quickly recover their position if something chanced to go wrong. Jonson's play offers no such traditional support; there is no overarching plot line (such plotting as occurs tends to extend over no more than two or three scenes); what we are invited to contemplate at length is people's social behaviour, how this relates to their private conceptions of themselves and how such potential disjunctions within individuals can lead to disturbing the sense of community amongst a social group. Comings and goings to and from the stage are not motivated by the need to advance a story: Matheo and Bobadilla leave because they want breakfast, while Cob exits earlier to go to work; Lorenzo Junior decides to visit a friend in town; and Thorello has a thriving business to attend to which requires his going off stage to meet with a lawyer, a magistrate or a customer; Musco is perhaps an exception here and his functions in the play will be discussed later, but he cannot be described, like Mosca in *Volpone*, as the engine who sets the play continually in motion. The characters, as Jonson represents them here, *exist*: for our amused contemplation at first, and then for our hilarity and delight when they come into unexpected but invariably troublesome confrontations, which further amplifies our insight and understanding. What gives the play its unity is its precise thematic focus, and actors must be alert to this fact in working together as an ensemble. That theme is never precisely stated; an audience has to infer it; and the actors must help to guide them to that particular way of reading the performance. Jonson's comedy presupposes an intelligent (not necessarily an intellectual) audience and actors of some scruple and sensitivity.

The theme is first sounded by Stephano, when he asks to his uncle's astonishment whether he might borrow a book from him about 'the sciences of hawking and hunting', since he has 'bought me a hawk, and bells and all' and so lacks 'nothing but a book to keep it by'. Confronted by Lorenzo Senior's ridicule, Stephano attempts to justify himself: 'Why, you know, an' a man have not skill in hawking and hunting nowadays, I'll not give a rush for him. He is for no gentleman's company...'[5] Lorenzo's irony about Stephano wasting his little means by casting away money on a buzzard is replaced by a sternly admonishing tone:

> I would not have you to intrude yourself
> In every gentleman's society,
> Till their affections or your own desert
> Do worthily invite you to the place;
> For he that's so respectless in his course

5 Most editions of the play print the 1616 text. All citations in this essay are to Lever (ed.), *Every Man in His Humour: A Parallel-Text Edition of the 1601 Quarto and the 1616 Folio*. The quotations here are on pp. 12 and 14 (1.1.29–40).

> Oft sells his reputation vile and cheap . . .
> Cousin, lay by such superficial forms,
> And entertain a perfect real substance.
> Stand not so much on your gentility . . .
>
> (p. 16: 1.1. 62–7, 74–6)

He speaks to deaf ears, for he has scarcely finished when a stranger enters, a serving-man, who is promptly treated to an account of Stephano's superior gentrified position, his precise income and his financial expectations, and all from Stephano himself. When the servant defers politely to him, Stephano promptly decides the man is being insubordinate, tries to pick a quarrel and generally throws his weight around till his uncle dismisses him as a 'peremptory ass' from the scene.

In one short episode we have learned a great deal about Stephano: he has, more by luck than direct inheritance, come into a reasonable income and small property; and he stands, were his cousin Lorenzo Junior to die before him, to inherit his uncle's far larger estate (£1000 a year). There is a marked contrast in this scene between uncle and nephew respecting how their position as gentry affects their dealings with and manner of address to servants. Where Lorenzo is unfailingly direct and polite, Stephano is downright rude, because a patent snob. He has aspirations to be thought genteel but has no sense of what that entails and so he needs books to give him guidance over how to manage not only a hawk but also himself. Stephano's loud assertiveness is actually proof of a deep insecurity. It is noticeable later in the play (2.2), when Lorenzo Junior takes him to meet a group of his peers, that he is utterly silent with embarrassment till Prospero (Wellbred) effects his introduction to everyone else on stage. This done, Stephano again lapses into silence, studying the other men closely and imitating their gestures, postures and modes of swearing. It is a characteristic Jonsonian technique that a silent character (whom it is easy to forget in reading the text of a play) is not necessarily one to be ignored in a staging or reduced to being merely a player who makes up the overall scenic picture. The situation gives the actor playing Stephano considerable leeway to invent a wealth of comic business in his attempts to cultivate gentlemanly airs and graces: business which, far from being a distraction, is meticulously harnessed to the thematic drive of the whole play. That opening scene has directed us to look closely at the ways in which men present themselves socially as an expression of their particular status; or to put it another way, *Every Man in His Humour* is quickly established as a play preoccupied with what precisely constitutes a gentleman. With the introduction of the jealous

Thorello (Kitely) that theme expands steadily till the play begins to investigate where lies true manliness. Earlier Elizabethan comedies took definitions of gender on trust; in choosing to interrogate concepts of masculinity, Jonson is staking out a whole new territory for comedy; also original is his decision to base comedy on social insecurities (anxieties about 'fitting in', particularly if one has designs on improving one's status).

Throughout his adult life Jonson admired Sir Philip Sidney and took him as a kind of *exemplum* of the best that a man might shape himself to be as courtier, soldier, scholar, poet. Sidney seemed to be an embodiment of all the qualities praised in what had become internationally a cult book of the Renaissance period defining proper manly conduct, *Il Cortegiano* by Baldassare Castiglione (1528), which had been magnificently translated into English by Sir Thomas Hoby in 1561. Castiglione devises a series of evening conversations between a group of Italian aristocrats from which emerges an image of an ideal man in his social and private capacities as courtier and as lover; but the secret of perfect gentility and manliness is defined as *sprezzatura*, the ability to demonstrate so absolute a mastery of a range of accomplishments (physical, emotional, intellectual, imaginative) that one can carry them off with an easy grace as if they are natural and innate, not learned through study and careful practice. The merest hint of anxiety or effort would undermine one's stance as gentleman: self-possession is essential. Countless conduct books were published in the wake of Hoby's translation, increasingly towards the end of Elizabeth's reign as a growing mercantile class based on the City of London began to press for increased power and to effect a degree of social mobility, which was rapidly to develop over the reign of James I. The very nature of a book about proper conduct is disturbingly ambivalent: it implies that the attributes of a class can be learned; and that then such knowledge might be exploited like a disguise, a mask to hide one's true origins and social status. This would create anxieties at both ends of the social spectrum: for the *parvenu*, the would-be gentleman, there would be the fear that the assumption of the disguise might not be complete and tell-tale vestiges of lowliness mar the impersonation; for the born gentleman there would be an increasing worry about how to detect the real thing from its imitation (to what extent could one trust that one's seeming peers were in fact one's genuine social equals). It is this uneasiness which Jonson makes the site of his comedy.

Lorenzo Junior and Prospero have brought together three upstarts for their private amusement. Stephano with his preoccupations with wealth, hunting and flaunting his position is overawed by the sight of the other two. Matheo (Matthew), a fishmonger's son, has designs to improve his position by paying court to a merchant's sister, and spends his scant income on buying books of poetry (Marlowe and Daniel) which he plagiarises to make up poems to address to his beloved; being a melancholic writer, he believes, is the best way to demonstrate one's credentials as a courtly lover. Bobadilla (Captain Bobadill) smokes, swears and expatiates about his superior skills as a fencer and soldier under the impression that such *machismo* is proof of true manliness. Where Matheo borrows the poetic terms which in his hands become jargon, Bobadilla has full command of the language of fighting, the stance and flourishes of the fencer; it is actual experience and aptitude with the sword or the foils that he lacks. Having given the three of them the stage, Jonson invites the audience to relish their absurdity as two of them go through their motions and the third tries to ape from them everything the audience finds preposterous. Stephano is quite taken in by Matheo and Bobadilla; his close watching of Matheo and Bobadilla increasingly renders what they do a performance, an assumption of roles that they cannot fully embody.[6]

This display of gulls takes place in Thorello's house, which serves to aggravate his rather different anxieties. He is a successful merchant who has married a squire's sister (Jonson is meticulously precise about his characters' social origins) and he is desperately afraid of being made a cuckold. The implication is that this social distinction between husband and wife provokes in Thorello a fear of sexual inadequacy, which undermines his trust in Biancha (Dame Kitely). That this is a complete fantasy on his part is evident, both from her cheerful self-possession in her position as wife (she is no sex-starved matron the like of Lady Would-Be in *Volpone*), and from the absurdity of Thorello's assumption that men as totally self-obsessed as Matheo or Bobadilla could be infatuated with his wife. Also stalking the house is Thorello's brother-in-law, Giuliano (Downright), whose contempt for the three gulls finds expression in a self-righteous rage so undisciplined that he is moved eventually to give Bobadilla a hearty drubbing. Giuliano's inclusion in the play is interesting: he is the least developed of the fool-figures and, though his anger serves to create the mayhem that brings Thorello racing back to his house suspecting that a lewd orgy has broken out as numerous suitors vie for his wife's favours, he has no overt function to fulfil within the drama, except in overreacting to the likes of Bobadilla. Scruple, the matching of response to experience, is a necessary gentlemanly virtue; and Giuliano lacks this in being morally outraged

---

6 This kind of metatheatrical strategy, in which characters on stage become like an audience and observe the actions of others, thereby making the actual spectators in the theatre self-conscious about their own function in relation to the performance, was a device that Jonson was to deploy over his career with ever-increasing subtlety.

by individuals who merit only laughter. Taking them seriously is to view fools on their own terms. Deflating their pretensions by seeing them as objects of amusement, as Lorenzo and Prospero do, is the fittest response to the three gulls morally and socially. Jonson, while not precisely directing the audience's judgement, is offering through Giuliano and Prospero contrasting modes of response and inviting spectators to discriminate. He is characteristically showing how viewing comedy can be an educative process.

Giuliano's anger is worth further exploration. Rage reduces his stature to the same comic level as the fools he attempts to chastise. It would have been easy for Jonson in conceiving this roll-call of gulls to have adopted a superior attitude and judged them harshly, made them simply caricatures and, as such, butts of ridicule in the manner of the Roman comedy. The satire in *Every Man in His Humour* is matched, however, by creative insight and sensitivity, which is what has made the central roles consistently attractive to actors with a developed comic technique.[7] Thorello, for example, may be fixated in his jealous temper, but, far from being blind to his condition which would render the role a caricature, in Jonson's account he is fully cognisant of the extent to which he is in the grip of an obsession. Sadly, no amount of self-awareness can loosen its hold over his mind's activity. No one can diagnose his 'disease' better than Thorello himself:

> First, it begins
> Solely to work upon the fantasy,
> Filling her seat with such pestiferous air
> As soon corrupts the judgement; and from thence
> Sends like contagion to the memory,
> Still each of other catching the infection,
> Which as a searching vapor spreads itself
> Confusedly through every senseive part,
> Till not a thought or motion in the mind
> Be free from the black poison of suspect.
> (p. 80: 1.4.203–12)

Wearily he ends this soliloquy with what he already knows is a vain hope: 'Well, I will once more strive...myself to be' (p. 80: 1.4.215–16). This is a complex moment, too replete with pathos to elicit dismissive laughter.

---

7 David Garrick excelled in the role of Kitely. Henry Woodward, equally notable in that period as Bobadill, initially played opposite Garrick. Charles Dickens had great fun with Bobadill in 1845; so too at Stratford did Frank Benson in 1903, Donald Wolfit in 1937 and Pete Postlethwaitc in 1986. The Kitely in that RSC revival was a moving as well as hilarious creation by Henry Goodman.

While Bobadilla clearly derives from the type of *miles gloriosus* of Roman comedy, he too exceeds the conventional limitations of the type. Though he is never less than bizarre, one is captivated by the imaginative grandeur of his fantasies (such as eliminating an enemy army by single combat over a matter of months with a party of twenty picked swordsmen, trained in his own secret techniques) and his sensual depiction of the joys to be offered the smoker by differing kinds of tobacco. He has an undeniably poetic way with words that outdoes all Matheo's versified effusions. Above all else it is the tone Jonson invents for Bobadilla's speech which shows a masterly command of how to relate local effect to larger thematic issues. Bobadilla affects a hilarious devil may-care insouciance; his every speech has a laid-back tenor as if nothing shakes his self-control or awareness of his own brilliance: recalling some six men who simultaneously attacked him, he concludes: 'By my soul, I could have slain them all, but I delight not in murder' (p. 202: 4.2.42–3). This is an exquisite travesty of what Castiglione meant by *sprezzatura*, a carefree nonchalance; and one might be tempted to take it for the real thing, except that no gentleman by Castiglione's definition would so advertise either his proficiency in arms or his generosity of impulse. What in performance takes one completely by surprise is Bobadilla's response to being given a beating by Giuliano. Matheo races from the stage abandoning his companion to his assailant's wrath; Bobadilla, though armed, takes his drubbing passively, claiming he has had a 'warrant of the peace' served on him (though the law would allow him to fight in self-defence). The portrayal of Bobadilla might end here with the fantasist confronted by a painful reality, but Jonson unexpectedly extends the comedy further. Matheo returns to the wounded hero and shamefacedly asks the inevitable question:

MATHEO: I wonder, Signior, what they will say of my going away, ha?
BOBADILLA: Why, what should they say, but as of a discreet gentleman, quick, wary, respectful of nature's fair lineaments? And that's all.
MATHEO: Why, so; but what can they say of your beating?
BOBADILLA: A rude part, a touch with soft wood, a kind of gross battery used, laid on strongly, borne most patiently; and that's all.

(pp. 222 4: 4.4.1–7)

The nonchalant manner remains despite what has happened and, in so far as it now embraces magnanimity towards Matheo and stoic acceptance regarding himself, Bobadilla achieves a modest dignity in the face of trying reversals. Something of Castiglione's required ideal illuminates Bobadilla's behaviour briefly before Matheo gets his prompt agreement to the suggestion that they seek revenge on Giuliano by invoking the law to get him arrested. The grand moment dissipates into bathos when the ever-impecunious pair next discover that, if they are to afford the cost of a warrant, then they have to pawn the last insignia they possess that support their claims to gentlemanly status (Matheo's earring and Bobadilla's silk stockings). The rapidly shifting tones in the sequence require a highly flexible mode of response from the audience (now sympathetic, now critical); but always the invention illuminates the overriding preoccupation with the nature of manliness.

There are, of course, degrees of sophistication in the ways that the various characters are represented. Cob for instance is not so subtle a creation as Thorello, yet even the apparent predictability of his boorishness and his lame joking is undermined by the sudden violence he metes out to Tib when he suspects her of adultery. Cob's whole life is focused inward on himself: his jokes play on the potential for puns in his name (cob = broiled salt herring) through which he endeavours to create a bizarre history for himself – 'I do fetch my pedigree and name from the first red herring that was eaten in Adam and Eve's kitchen'[8] (p. 42: 1.3.12–14) – and such cobs are the constant subject of his meditations. Tib is his property by marital right and he takes care that she stays within the confines of his house. When that house (wrongfully) is cited as a brothel and Tib as its presiding bawd, his authority as married man is doubly challenged and violence is his only felt means of reclaiming it. The portrayal is a cunning indictment of the patriarchal mind-set (obsessed with lineage and ownership) as yet another questionable manifestation of manliness meriting Jonson's interrogation; it is the funnier and the more shocking for being developed as the pretensions of the lowliest character in the play. Cob also affords a valuable contrast with Thorello who, when he similarly believes himself to be unmanned, turns violent but directs that violence inward, compelling himself to suffer within a tortuous labyrinth of despair. Fear of cuckoldom as provoking loss of a secure identity is viewed contrastingly from both social and private perspectives. Jonson's control over the thematic architecture and patterning of the play is masterly.

It has been necessary to investigate the representation of character in terms of degrees of complexity to avoid a rather limiting critical approach to Jonsonian comedy, which, taking the word 'humour' in the title as justification,

---

8 In the revised folio text, the point is emphasised by a reordering of the phrasing and the addition of a further detail: 'The first red herring that was broil'd in Adam and Eve's kitchen do I fetch my pedigree from, by the harrots' [heralds'] books.' The resulting joke is characteristically ambivalent: it establishes the absurdity of Cob's fixation but it also looks teasingly at the equally absurd details of a family's former history on which aristocratic heraldry often draws for its emblems.

has tried to impose an overly cerebral agenda on the play as a kind of dramatised treatise along with its successor (*Every Man out of His Humour* of 1599)
on the Elizabethan theory of humours. Scientific doctrine in the period promoted the view that health in an individual was profoundly affected by the
balance or otherwise of the elements of water, air and heat within the particular physiology, which in turn controlled the production of blood, phlegm and
the varieties of bile related to the promoting of choler or melancholy. Mental
stability was directly related to a balanced bodily system. To categorise the
characters of the play in terms of the mental and emotional disorders which
were said to derive from particular forms of imbalance within the disposition
of humours is to risk reducing them to precise and predictable types. This
is virtually to accuse Jonson of robbing his characters of theatrical vitality in
favour of presenting them as intellectualised constructs. While Jonson may
initially encourage an audience to feel they can *place* figures like Bobadilla,
Thorello or Cob, it is the better to serve his purpose, which is to deploy such
figures to illuminate his theme precisely when they take on unexpected dimensions. He allows his creations stage-time to *grow* in spectators' understanding.
Far from working reductively from the particular to the generalised (making
characters conform to the theory of humours), Jonson is more accurately seen
as working expansively from the general to the particular. This alone would
explain the attraction of the play to the likes of Burbage and Garrick: it is in the
particularising that Jonson allows full scope to the actor's powers of invention.
The actor playing Bobadilla must find the means to be bragging *and* nonchalant, socially down-at-heel yet a rich fantasist, at once pathetic and comic. To
play the character as simply exemplifying the choleric type in the role of *miles
gloriosus* is to miss the theatrical potential of Jonson's creation and so lose most
of the fun. If characters merely perform what is expected of them, there is no
room for an audience's insight to be challenged, discomfited or developed.

To take another example: if Matheo were just a bad poet and plagiarist,
the comedy would quickly run dry. But Matheo is much more than a silly
ass: he is seeking through poetry to court a superior woman as his means
of expressing the current vogue amongst the Elizabethan upper classes for
melancholia; and behind that affectation lies the desire of a shopkeeper's son
for the genteel leisure enjoyed by his social superiors.[9] If Matheo makes a pal of

---

9 In the earlier version of the play Matheo's pretensions to be a poet are offset by Lorenzo
  Junior's far more serious claims to the status. His delight in composing poetry is what
  in this version most excites his father's anxiety (even though Lorenzo Senior admits
  to versifying at his son's age). Late in the play Lorenzo Junior is given an impassioned
  defence of the art of poetry when his father accuses him before Doctor Clement. This

Bobadilla, it is because the latter can give voice to fantasies of dashing brilliance that feed his own weak imaginings and take him out of a world of depressing contingencies. To see Matheo in these terms is to perceive the extent to which he is a forerunner of the many gulls in *The Alchemist* who come to Subtle and Face in the hope of bettering their social position by acquiring wealth or luck. Face and Subtle feed their gulls' upwardly mobile ambitions. *Every Man in His Humour* is Jonson's first attempt at what he would develop into his own style of city comedy where the prevailing subjects are class, status, sexual mores, manners and money. To suggest this is both to realise the extent to which Jacobean comedy distanced itself from the prevailing tenor of Elizabethan comedy established by Lyly and to appreciate Jonson's crucial role in effecting that transformation. To claim this is also to intimate the presence in the early comedy of many features, devices, strategies and techniques which Jonson would develop into his mature artistry. Three such 'presences' are Lorenzo Junior, Prospero and Musco (Brainworm).

Lorenzo and Prospero have none of the diversity of the characters explored so far; they serve functions chiefly, being the means by which the principal fools are initially brought together, and by which Thorello confronts the absurdity of his suppositions at Cob's house. They are vastly entertained by the folly of others but we are offered no motivation for this: it seems just youthful high spirits. There is none of the complex moral duplicity which underlies Mosca's and Volpone's attracting of corrupt fools into their presence, or Face, Subtle and Doll's luring of gulls to Lovewit's house in his absence, where in both cases Jonson examines the questionable excitements of gulling as much as the qualities which expose an individual to being gulled. By comparison with the two Jacobean comedies, *Every Man in His Humour* presents gulling as an altogether innocent diversion. To write of Musco as the prototype of Face or Mosca is again to discriminate a greater geniality in Jonson's first essay. All three are evolved from the wily slave of Roman comedy, but Musco lacks the malevolent cunning and cynical amorality of Mosca or Face's outright materialism. What they all share is a delight in disguise and acting. Musco is a trickster, a merry devil, whose manipulation of other characters has no dark ulterior motive: he does it all for the sheer hell of it, and is ultimately praised for his superior *wit* in devising his schemes and in carrying them off

theme is somewhat played down in the revision and, though Old Kno'well refers to his son's taste for poetry in the final act, it is now Justice Clement who speaks rapturously of the art. This is one revision for which there seems no clear justification; and, though the RSC in its 1986 revival played the folio text, the director chose (justifiably) to insert Lorenzo's defence of poetry from the quarto.

with such expert bravado. He plays with *character* by continually dressing up and assuming identities as *roles* – four in all in the course of the action – and we are invited, through the responses of Lorenzo Junior and later Doctor Clement, to admire his vivacity and daring: with each impersonation he gets costume, voice, diction, temperament and mind-set right, to the point where no one recognises him as Musco till he chooses to reveal himself.[10] To create Mosca Jonson had to elide the functions of Prospero and Musco, but before he attempted that his creative vision had confronted the lethally evil games with role play that beset Tiberius's Rome in *Sejanus* (1603). Impersonations thereafter could no longer be a source of easy laughter.

What impresses in the Folio revision of the play is Jonson's refusal to attempt a complete rewriting that would bring the early work into line with his more experienced artistry and more intricate moral scruples. Beyond the obvious changing of the location from Florence to London, most of the revision is devoted to sharpening the effects and strategies he originally devised. Overall there is a better sense of how to pace episodes: where to expand, where to compress to achieve a tighter action and greater clarity. By 1612, city comedy was the staple comic format of the Jacobean theatre, and Jonson along with Middleton had created its most enduring examples: the exception had become the rule. But if in his city comedies Jonson was to develop his preoccupation in the early play with duplicity and the exposure of follies, class unrest and the problems and dangers of social mobility, several works (*Epicoene, The Devil Is an Ass, The New Inn*) turn back to another theme that in *Every Man in His Humour* exercised his discrimination: masculinity in its social, emotional, gendered and political manifestations. In all these plays, though there is no loss of social and political concern, the thematic focus is centred on the patterns of behaviour by which a man defines his masculinity, especially in relation to how he conducts himself with women; and this creates a style which anticipates the comedy of manners of the Restoration era. *Every Man in His Humour* was ground-breaking in 1598; the revision of 1612 confirms its status as initiating two new forms of comedy. On both counts it merits exploration as a case study.

---

10 Jonson adds to the folio text at the point where Musco reveals his identity to his master the following line for Old Kno'well: 'Is it possible! Or that thou shouldst disguise thy language so, as I should not know thee?' (p. 263: 5.1.144–5).

12

London professional playhouses and performances

MARTIN WHITE

On 21 January 1560, Queen Elizabeth's treasurer of the chamber recorded a payment to

> The Lord Robert Dudley's players and to Sebastian Westcott, Master of the Children of Paul's... in way of the Queen's Majesty's reward for playing of Interludes before her highness at Christmas – to either [each] of them vj^{li} xiij^s iiij^d.[1]

There were at this time no permanent playhouses in London. The Children referred to – scholars and choristers – performed only occasionally and in private. The small groups of adult actors – around six men in each company – were attached to the households of some nobles but were, for most of the year, itinerant performers, performing where they could find a venue and, in London especially, constantly oppressed by civic authorities.

The first step in the adults' attempts to secure a foothold in London came in 1567, when John Brayne, a grocer from Bucklersbury, paid for a permanent playhouse to be erected in the suburbs of London – the Red Lion. Our knowledge of this project is derived entirely from the records of a dispute between Brayne and his carpenters.[2] According to the details of the ensuing court case, the Red Lion was a 'messuage or farme house', and not, as was previously thought, an inn used, like other inns, as an occasional venue for plays. There, in the adjoining garden, Brayne erected what is so far as we know the first purpose-built playhouse in England, essentially combining a platform stage

---

1 £6 13s 4d was the standard fee for a performance at court, though it rose to £10 (equivalent to a good day's box-office take) later in the period.
2 Brayne hired one carpenter, William Sylvester, to build the scaffold seating and another, John Reynolds, to construct the stage. For relevant documentation and commentary, see Wickham, Berry and Ingram (eds.), *English Professional Theatre*, 290–4. See also Loengard, 'An Elizabethan lawsuit', *Shakespeare Quarterly* 34 (1983), 298–310.

of the kind erected by travelling players with galleries for spectators such as those found in bearbaiting arenas and innyards.[3]

Once Sylvester had completed the 'galloryes', John Reynolds was instructed to erect a stage 40 feet (12.20 metres) wide, 30 feet (9.15 metres) deep and 5 feet (1.52 metres) high (the only contemporary reference to stage height) and to leave a 'certain space' unboarded for the trap to be inserted. On this stage, Reynolds was to 'set upp . . . one convenyent turrett of Tymber' 30 feet (9.15 metres) in height from the ground, with a floor 7 feet (2.13 metres) from the top. This 'turrett' is something of a puzzle since, with only one floor specified, and that 18 feet (5.5 metres) above stage level with no obvious form of access, it seems unusable. Presumably, however, with the addition of other floors and some form of stairs, it was intended to provide raised performance and viewing areas such as one finds in later playhouses. No mention is made anywhere of a roof, tiring house, or walls.

It is misleading to think of Elizabethan open-air playhouses, constructed over a period of more than fifty years, as identical structures. In fact, they varied considerably in shape, size, architectural features and level of finish, were owned and managed under different systems, and staged distinct repertoires to different kinds of audiences. Nevertheless, the Red Lion appears to have included many of the features that are repeated, and varied, by subsequent builders of open-air playhouses. Brayne's brother in law was James Burbage, formerly a joiner but by 1567 a leading actor with Leicester's Men. Burbage is not actually mentioned anywhere in connection with the Red Lion, but given his knowledge of carpentry and acting it seems unlikely he would not have been involved in some way. If he were, it raises the likelihood that the Red Lion project influenced not only the design of Burbage's own playhouse, the Theatre (1576), but also the design of the first Globe (1599), given the evident similarities between those two playhouses.[4]

In general terms, outdoor playhouses were polygonal structures, with three tiers of covered galleries with bench-seats at different prices offering spectators a choice of view and comfort, but where they might also stand. These galleries surrounded a yard, open to the weather, for standing spectators, in which stood a large stage which sometimes contained a trap door. At the rear of

---

3 See Brownstein, 'A record of London inn playhouses from *c.* 1565–1590', *Shakespeare Quarterly* 22 (1971), 17–24, and 'Why didn't Burbage lease the Beargarden?', in Berry (ed.), *The First Public Playhouse*, 81–96.

4 In 1635, Cuthbert Burbage, James's son, described his father as 'the first builder of playhouses' which may suggest his involvement with the Red Lion venture.

the stage was a tiring house where the actors could conceal and prepare themselves, and which had a gallery above the stage for use by actors, musicians and spectators.[5] Although not mentioned in the Red Lion documents, other outdoor playhouses appear to have had a roof of some kind over the stage, usually supported by two pillars, and with a trap through which things could be lowered to, and raised from, the stage.[6]

There is no record of the Red Lion's artistic achievements, but the venture does not seem to have been a commercial success. Perhaps the playhouse's location in Mile End, some way to the east of the city, was too remote to sustain an audience in these early days of playgoing, or perhaps there was as yet simply an insufficient mass of potential audience members to support any public playhouse.

With limited opportunities to play in London, companies continued to tour, although it was a practice increasingly fraught with difficulty. In 1572, Queen Elizabeth issued a decree limiting the right of her subjects to retain 'unordinary servants', which prompted Leicester's company to petition their patron 'to certify that we are your household servants when we have occasion to travel'. Two years later, the benefits of having a powerful patron were strikingly demonstrated when, on 7 May 1574, the Privy Council issued a royal patent authorising Leicester's Men, alone among companies, to 'use, exercise, and occupie the arte and facultye of playenge . . . as well within oure Citie of London and liberties of the same, as also within the liberties and fredomes of anye [of] our Cities, townes, Bouroughes &c . . . thoroughte our Realme of Englande'. This not only eased the dangers of touring for this particular company, but presumably encouraged James Burbage to make a second attempt at establishing a permanent playhouse in London.[7]

In 1576, Burbage leased land on the site of the former Holywell Priory in the north-east suburb of Shoreditch, outside the jurisdiction of the city authorities where, with financial help from grocer Brayne, he erected a playhouse. Having planned to spend about £200, they had in the end to find the considerable sum of £700, much of which they had to borrow. They named it the Theatre – the Roman name (*theatrum* in Latin means 'seeing place') intended, no doubt,

---

5 Later playhouses appear to have had a designated 'Music Room'; Gurr, *The Shakespearean Stage*, 147–9.
6 No roof is recorded in any document referring to the Theatre or the Curtain, and it may be that the Swan was the first playhouse to have its stage covered.
7 For relevant documentation see Chambers, *The Elizabethan Stage*, IV, 269–72. See also Ingram, 'The economics of playing', in Kastan (ed.), *A Companion to Shakespeare*, 313–27, for a discussion of links between the upsurge of playhouse building in the late 1570s and the 1571 statute against usury.

to signal the magnificence of the new structure as a magnet to attract the audiences vital to the project's success. A sermon preached at Paul's Cross in August 1578 referred to the Theatre as the 'gorgeous playing place',[8] and the sumptuousness (or the illusion of such) of the playhouses was to be one of the charges most frequently levelled against them. Burbage installed his own company, Leicester's Men, in his new property, taking the entire gallery receipts as rent.

Visitors refer to the Theatre as an amphitheatre with three galleries, but the only contemporary illustration – an engraved 'View of the Cittye of London from the North towards the South', made around 1597–9 – is too unclear to provide any detail of its structure. It has been suggested that – especially if it had no cover – the Theatre's stage might have been portable, to allow the yard to be cleared for 'feats of great activity'[9] (it *was* used on occasions for sword-fighting competitions) or perhaps even animal baiting. If Brayne and, possibly, Burbage had got their fingers burned with the Red Lion venture, such caution would be understandable.

Within a year, another playhouse – the Curtain, a name derived from curtain, or defensive, walling in the vicinity – opened not far from the Theatre, a clear sign of the growing demand for dramatic entertainment. Even less is known about this playhouse, though it, too, was a polygonal structure, a 'wooden O'. Indeed, it was possibly at the Curtain in 1599, while they were waiting for the Globe to be completed, that the Lord Chamberlain's Men performed Shakespeare's *Henry V*. In the event, this playhouse lasted in use longer than any other – from 1577 to 1625 – and was standing until at least 1698. Another playhouse had also been, or was soon to be, erected, some way further south of the city, in Newington Butts. However, like the Red Lion, it was perhaps in too suburban a location to survive, demanding a whole day's outing rather than just an afternoon stolen off work. A Privy Council warrant, dated probably in mid 1592, states that 'by reason of the tediousnes of the waie ... plaies have not there been used on working days'. When it closed is not known for certain. It is possible that by 1599 the playhouse had been replaced by domestic dwellings, but a disparaging reference to the crude verse popular there – a 'Newington conceit' – in a play dated around 1609 might suggest it was at least fresh in the audience's memory as a venue.[10]

8 Chambers, *The Elizabethan Stage*, IV, 199–200.
9 The phrase is George Puttenham's, and is used in his description of Roman theatres in *The Arte of English Poesie*. Puttenham's description, like De Witt's later comments on the Swan, suggests similarities between Roman and Elizabethan amphitheatres.
10 Ingram, *The Business of Playing*, 150–81. The play is Nathan Field's *A Woman Is a Weathercock*, 3.3.

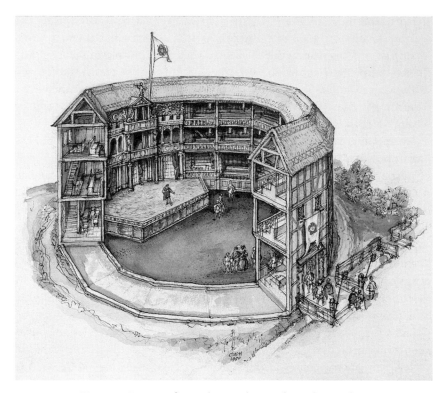

Figure 22 Interior of Rose theatre, drawing by Walter Hodges

But it was the area south of the Thames that was in the long term to prove the most profitable location for playhouses. In 1585, Philip Henslowe, originally a dyer, but by the mid 1580s a successful financier, acquired the lease to a property in Southwark known as Little Rose, a stone's throw from what is now the southern end of Southwark Bridge. There, in 1587, he paid a carpenter, John Griggs, to build him a playhouse. It cost £360, about half as much as Burbage's Theatre, and was named the Rose.

In 1989, excavations for a new office block revealed the foundations of the Rose (see figure 22). The discovery forced theatre historians to rethink many opinions on the nature of Elizabethan playhouses. The excavations, of about two-thirds of the site, revealed a polygonal building, confirming previous assumptions, but one with fourteen sides and an external diameter of about 22 metres. These dimensions indicated a structure much smaller than had been previously assumed to be the norm for all amphitheatres, but were in line with Thomas Dekker's description of the Rose in his play *Old Fortunatus* (1599) as 'this small circumference'. Indeed, the marginal note in the 1592 quarto of *The Spanish Tragedy* (3.2.25) that a letter should be written in 'Red incke' confirms the impression that many in the audience would be able to pick up the smallest detail.

The remains of the internal foundations indicated that the timber galleries, rising about 10 metres to the roof ridge, were about 3 metres deep and 4.5 metres across, while an erosion trench circling the perimeter of the yard, caused by water dripping from the roof, showed it was a thatched building – gutters cannot be fitted to thatched roofs. The yard was about 15 metres from east to west and 9.5 metres north to south. It had been generally assumed that playhouse yards were flat, but the Rose's (when first built) appeared to have been level in the rear half, and then to have sloped downwards at an angle of 14 degrees towards the stage. This arrangement would have aided drainage of the yard (via a barrel-head sump connected to a pipe to carry the water to the Thames) and improved the sight-lines for those standing at the back. The floor of the yard was mortar, over which was laid a mix of ash, clinker and hazelnut shells, a by-product of local soap factories used for road surfacing and used here, presumably, to improve drainage.

There were further surprises. The Rose stage faced south-south-east, into the afternoon sun, counter to the evidence of the Boar's Head, and of Hollar's *Long View of London* (1647) which shows the stages at the Second Globe and Hope facing north.[11] Nor was the stage rectangular, as seems to have been the norm elsewhere. Like the stage shown in the illustrated title pages of William Alabaster's *Roxana* and of Nathaniel Richards's *Messalina* (see figure 23), the Rose stage tapered from about 11 metres at its widest point to about 8 metres at the front. It was about 4.75 metres in depth, giving a total area of only 46 square metres compared to the colossal 114 square metres specified at the Red Lion. No evidence of a stage-trap emerged during the excavations, and there is no compelling textual evidence for such a feature in plays known at this time to have been staged at the Rose.[12] The excavations did not clarify the nature of openings in the *frons*, but evidence from plays performed at the Rose suggests there was a central opening, possibly curtained, which could be used for ceremonial entrances and 'discoveries', with a balcony 'above' which could also be used by the actors. The excavations did not indicate whether the front wall (the *frons scaenae*) of the Rose tiring house was angled or straight.

11 Berry, *The Boar's Head Playhouse*; Foakes, *Illustrations*, 36–8.
12 Wickham, 'Notes on the staging of Marlowe's plays', in *Shakespeare's Dramatic Heritage*, 121–31.

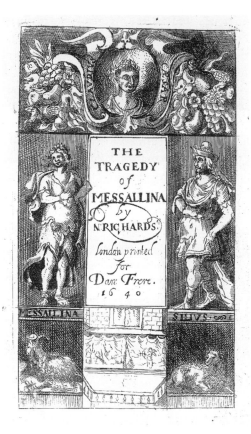

Figure 23 The title page to Nathanael Richards's *Messalina* (1640)

If angled it would have increased the stage depth while severely limiting the available space in the tiring house, but would have improved sight-lines to both the balcony and upper level.

In either configuration of *frons* – straight or angled – the Rose stage is shallower than at other outdoor playhouses. A surviving drawing of *Titus Andronicus*, which conflates two separate scenes (1.1 and 5.1), is possibly dated around 1594, the year Shakespeare's play was performed by Sussex's Men, probably at the Rose, on 23 and 28 January and again on 6 February, with Edward Alleyn in the title role (see figure 24). Whether the artist, Henry Peacham, who was eighteen or nineteen years old at that time, was recollecting an actual performance is open to conjecture. But if he were, the linear position of the actors might reflect the nature of blocking required at the Rose as opposed to

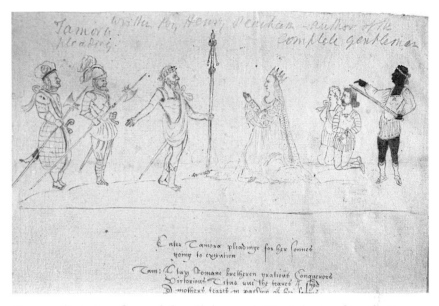

Figure 24 Illustration of a speech from Shakespeare's *Titus Andronicus*, drawn by Henry Peachum (*c.* 1594)

the sharper diagonals possible on deeper stages, such as are illustrated in the frontispiece to Francis Kirkman's *The Wits* (1673) (see figure 25).

Henslowe had made a shrewd investment. The Rose's location in the liberty of the Clink, amidst the pleasure grounds of the south bank with its animal-baiting houses, public gardens, inns and brothels, and close to the Thames, was ideal. The proximity of the river – the main thoroughfare of the city – does much to explain the subsequent growth in the popularity of Southwark as a venue for playhouses; Henslowe paid 8 shillings for 'wharfyng' and mooring rights in 1592–3, and the following year bought his own barge. Business evidently flourished, since, from February to April 1592, Henslowe spent well over £100 to expand and improve the Rose. The northern end of the playhouse was moved back, extending the gallery and increasing the size of the yard by more than a third. The yard was made more level. The stage was moved back nearly seven feet, but it kept the same alignment and – perhaps strangely, given its apparently small size – was enlarged by no more than one foot in depth. Nor was the tiring-house made bigger – increased box-office income was Henslowe's priority, not the actors' comfort.

As the actors' landlord, it was Henslowe's initial practice to take 50 per cent of the total gallery receipts as rent from whichever company was using

Figure 25 Title page to Francis Kirkman's *The Wits* (1673)

his playhouse. In 1592, for example, when *Henry VI* was performed at the Rose by Lord Strange's Men, Henslowe's cut amounted to £3 16s 8d, which has been calculated to reflect a gallery audience numbering between 1,400 and 1,600. Adding the 'groundlings' in the yard, calculated to number around 500 when full, suggests a capacity of around 2,000 in 1587, rising to around 2,400 after the 1592 works. Henslowe's own financial records indicate that his average audience was more like 600. It has been estimated that Henslowe's average annual income from his playhouse was about £250, rising to £400 for a particularly good year – a very satisfactory return on his initial investment.[13]

It is not absolutely clear whether the Rose was originally provided with a cover over the stage, though plays known to have been staged there after the 1592 works clearly indicate that stage posts were used in the action. If the 1587 Rose stage *was* unroofed, it may suggest Henslowe (possibly like Burbage at the Theatre) was hedging his bets, keeping his costs down and investing in a building that could, with its stage removed, house other entertainments (though its raked yard might argue the opposite). By 1592, if this supposition of earlier portability is correct, Henslowe's confidence in playgoing as a reliable commercial concern was presumably strong enough to justify his alterations.

Case study 1: *The Spanish Tragedy* at the Rose playhouse, 1592

On 14 March 1592 Henslowe recorded a performance of 'Jeronymo' by a company made up of Lord Strange's and the Lord Admiral's Men. This was undoubtedly Thomas Kyd's play, called by the name of its central character, and the title by which it is frequently referred to throughout the period. The play made only modest production demands on the company. There are never more than thirteen characters on stage at any time (in 1.4, including a musician) and a doubling chart reveals that any number of possible combinations would permit a performance with twelve actors, two of whom needed to be specialist female impersonators.

Weaponry (swords, dagger, pistol) is standard, while furniture is confined to thrones, stools and a table. As in many Elizabethan plays the props list is not extensive, with only the scutcheons (shields painted with heraldic emblems) perhaps having to be specially made:

---

13 By comparison, the wage of a skilled tradesman, such as a dyer, was fixed at £5 per year.

a chain of office
various papers and documents
a crown
a scarf
3 decorated shields (scutcheons)
3 crowns
items for a banquet
gold coins/purse
blood-stained handkerchief
various letters
box
rope
two books
pen-knife
pen

The text of the 1592 quarto specifies the use of an upper level and at least two entry doors on to the stage. The stage direction at 3.11.8 reads 'He goeth in at one door and comes out at another.' While the indefinite article may hint at a third entrance there is no specific reference to, or need for, a central opening, though if there were one, it is possible to see how it might be useful. The stage direction indicating 'They bind [Alexandro] to the stake' (3.1.48) might suggest the use of a stage pillar, though the moment would be simple enough to stage without such a permanent feature.

The prologue. Elaborate costume and stage effects were important elements in the entertainment offered by the Elizabethan theatre. If there *was* a trap in the stage floor it is possible that Andrea's Ghost (dressed in silver or white and with the actor's face made pale with make-up) and Revenge (dressed in black, possibly carrying a flaming torch) entered through it at the opening of the play, perhaps accompanied by smoke and fireworks.[14] More probably, they entered through one of the rear doors.

At l.90 Revenge announces 'Here sit we down to see the mystery'. But where do they sit? The question is of more than just practical interest, since throughout the play the Ghost and Andrea act as chorus and audience, observing events and interjecting after each act to help shape the audience's perception of the action. Placed – metaphorically if not literally – between the

14 Thomas Dekker, in his prose satire *The Seven Deadly Sins of London*, refers to a character wishing he might rise up '(like the Ghost in Jeronimo) crying "Revenge" ', though that might refer to a later performance at the Fortune and there is no specific evidence that the Rose possessed a trap.

audience and the stage they are essential to the metatheatrical structure of Kyd's play. Building on the Renaissance image of 'the world as a stage', the real and fictive audiences are confronted with the terrifying blurring of the boundaries between life and art. So did the Ghost and Revenge sit in one of the downstage corners of the stage, mirroring, perhaps, the position of the later onstage audience in act 4? Or, as some editors suggest (or assume), were they located on the balcony at the rear of the stage? If so, when did they make their way there? There is no obvious moment in the dialogue when they could make the ascent to the balcony from the main stage. So did the Ghost and Revenge perhaps make their first entry on the upper level? The balcony is frequently used in contemporary plays as a position from which characters observe and comment on the action below (see case study 4 below), and Andrea's and Revenge's use of it would therefore be appropriate. Nevertheless, even allowing for the small scale of the Rose and the possible angling of the tiring-house wall, it may seem strange to play the whole of the prologue, which contains key narrative and character information, from such a position. Indeed, if it were played from the balcony, it would appear to be the longest upper-level scene in any extant play of the period. The upper level is also designated as a place for other characters to occupy at points in the play. In 2.2, the quarto text specifically places Balthazar 'aboue', in the 'secret' place from which he and Lorenzo spy on Horatio and Bel Imperia on the main stage, a simultaneous use of the physical levels of the staging that strikingly reflects the two levels of dialogue. In 3.9 it represented the window from which Bel Imperia speaks. At such moments, presumably, if Andrea and Revenge remained 'above' throughout, they would simply draw back while other actors used the space.

Following the prologue the word 'Enter' is not used to precede the lines spoken by the Ghost and Revenge in 1.5 and 2.6. In 3.15 and 4.5, however, their interjections are preceded in the 1592 quarto by the direction 'Enter', directions which are invariably omitted by editors on the grounds that they are redundant. But their inclusion in the quarto raises the possibility that – at the end of the play at least – the Ghost and Revenge might leave the balcony to reappear on the main stage, returning to the opening image and appropriately framing the intervening action.

I have dwelt on this issue at some length in this first case study to underline how speculative our attempts to reconstruct staging must be, even when, as in this case, we have a reasonably reliable text to apply to a playhouse about which we have real concrete evidence.

Act 1 scene 4. At line 115 there is the stage direction 'Enter the Banquet, Trumpets...' Banquets are common in Elizabethan and Jacobean plays. They are often conceived of as fairly casual affairs, but the direction 'sit to the banquet' (line 127) suggests something more formal here. A stage direction from a later indoor play, Thomas Drue's *The Bloody Banquet* (3.3), gives an insight into how – with the addition of stools – such a moment might be staged using four stagehands / servants:

> Soft music, a table with lights set out. Arras spread . . . Loud music. Enter 2 with a Banquet; other 2 with lights; they set 'em down and depart . . . Loud music, Enter Roxano, Mazeres and the 4 Servants, with dishes of sweet meats, Roxano places them: each having delivered his dish makes low obeisance [and exits].

Unlike the practice at indoor playhouses (see below), amphitheatre productions ran uninterrupted, which partly helps account for the running time of two to three hours to which contemporaries frequently refer and which differs from much of our own experience of watching Elizabethan plays. It is perhaps significant, therefore, that the scene following the banquet, 1.5, is a short, nine-line exchange between Andrea and the Ghost, which may (if played from the balcony) be designed to provide a shift in the audience's focus while the stage is cleared.

Act 2 scene 4. Horatio and Bel Imperia meet in a secluded arbour. Unknown to them, Pedringano betrays them to Lorenzo who, with Balthazar and others, takes the lovers by surprise. Having seized Horatio, 'they hang him in the arbour' before stabbing him. It is not clear from the text how the scene was staged, but it is possible that a structure representing an arbour – perhaps similar to that shown in the frontispiece of the 1615 edition (see figure 26) – was brought onto the stage. The structure is the focus of the next scene, 2.5, but since the Rose stage was surely too small to permit the structure to remain on stage, another short scene between Andrea and the Ghost (2.6) could again be used to cover its removal. Of course, 2.4 could have been staged differently, possibly using one of the pillars in some way or, if there were a central opening in the rear wall, employing that. There is a further hanging in the play, when Pedringano is tricked by Lorenzo (3.6). If there were an arbour it is possible that this (turned round, perhaps) was used for this scene, too. It was certainly used again in 4.2, where a stage direction refers to the arbour being 'cut down' by the grief-racked Isabella. Such structures were evidently not uncommon. Henslowe's own 1598 property list includes items that sound as if they might have been substantial, such as a 'wheel and frame in the Siege of London' and a 'hell mouth'.[15]

---

15 Henslowe's inventory of his costumes and properties is reproduced in Rutter, *Documents of the Rose Playhouse*, 133–7.

The Spanish Tragedie:

OR,

Hieronimo is mad againe.

Containing the lamentable end of *Don Horatio*, and
Belimperia; with the pittifull death of *Hieronimo*.

Newly corrected, amended, and enlarged with new
Additions of the *Painters* part, and others, as
it hath of late been diuers times acted.

LONDON,

Printed by W. White, for I. White and T. Langley,
and are to be sold at their Shop ouer againſt the
Sarazens head without New-gate. 1615.

Figure 26 Frontispiece to Kyd's *The Spanish Tragedy* (1615 edition)

Since the 1560s, many groups of professional actors had formed themselves into companies, merged with each other, dissolved and reformed under a variety of patrons. By the end of the 1580s, for example, the earls of Berkeley, Essex, Lincoln, Sussex, Warwick, Worcester, as well as Leicester and Queen Elizabeth, were among those who had had companies in their names. During the repeated plague years of the early 1590s, however – with playhouses closed for months on end – survival became particularly difficult, and many companies failed, or 'broke', to use Henslowe's evocative term.[16] The evident precariousness of the companies and the implication for theatrical entertainment in London to meet the demands of the monarch were undoubtedly major factors in the decision taken in 1594 by Henry Carey, the lord chamberlain, to regulate the companies. With the support in the Privy Council of Henry Howard, the lord admiral, Carey gained agreement that two companies only – the Lord Chamberlain's Men, consolidated with members of various other companies, and the Admiral's Men – should be authorised to play in the capital. At the same time, to mollify the city authorities, the Privy Council finally forbade playing at any inn within the city. The two companies appeared together at the Rose for a brief period in 1594, before the Lord Chamberlain's Men moved permanently to the Theatre. The Lord Admiral's Men stayed on at the Rose where they remained until the end of the decade. The Admiral's first season was long – it ran from mid June 1594 to Lent 1595 – and successful. During the 1595 Lent break Henslowe hired a painter to freshen up the Rose and in June paid a carpenter £7 2s 0d for work that included 'mackinge the throne in the heuenes' – the use of the word 'making' suggesting, perhaps, the installation of new technology in the form of flying gear, rather than a repair.

From this date these two companies dominate the London theatre until the closure of the playhouses in 1642. While all Elizabethan acting companies operated to some extent as co-operatives, the Admiral's and Lord Chamberlain's Men were also in part family businesses. Henslowe was the father-in-law and business partner of Edward Alleyn, the company's leading actor, while the Burbage family remained at the core of the Lord Chamberlain's / King's Men until their own deaths. In addition to the 'sharers' (shareholders), who included the leading actors, 'hired men', paid by the week, took the supporting roles, while the boys who played the female roles were apprentices, and lived, like their counterparts in other trades, with their masters. From the turn of

---

16 In 1625 the plague was so severe that all companies except the King's Men were bankrupted.

the century the average size of a London company, including all actors and musicians, was between twenty and thirty.[17]

While Henslowe was, in effect, the financier of the Admiral's Men, charging for production costs and taking a cut of the box office in rent for the playhouse, the Chamberlain's Men developed a unique management system. By 1597 the core of the company were the six sharers, who financed productions, paid the theatre owner (James Burbage) and the hired men, before taking their share of the profits. Around 1611, one of the sharers, John Heminges, appears to have ceased acting in order to concentrate on managing the company's business affairs.

The increased security of the Chamberlain's Men (during Christmas 1596 they provided all the command performances at court) combined with the restriction on the use of inns and James Burbage's awareness that his lease on the Theatre was soon to run out, may have prompted him to purchase the lease on a property in Blackfriars, intending to 'convert and turne the same into a comon playhouse'.[18] Unfortunately, opposition from neighbours (who included the Dean of St Paul's and, ironically, the company's own patron) put a stop to the plans. The building remained empty until after James's death (in 1597) when his sons leased it to the Children of the Chapel. It was over twelve years before the Chamberlain's Men could finally move in and achieve their aim of possessing a summer and winter venue.

Others, too, were seeking to build playhouses, though without Burbage's vision of a commercial indoor venue for adults. In 1595, the monopoly of the Rose and Theatre and their resident companies was challenged when Francis Langley, a money broker and speculator, opened the Swan, near to Henslowe's playhouse. It was a serious rival. As Johannes de Witt, a Dutch visitor to London in 1596, observed, while all were of 'notable beauty', the playhouses in Southwark were even finer than those in the northern suburbs, with the Swan – a large timber-framed building with the interstices being not the usual wattle and daub but 'an accumulation of flint stones' and 'borne up on wooden columns so painted over in marble-seeming colour as to deceive even the most probing observers'[19] – being 'the largest and most distinguished' of all.

17 In 1624, the King's Men's personnel were listed in a document exempting them from arrest during the period of revels at court. In addition to the twelve sharers, there were twenty-one apprentices and hired men, of whom seven have been identified as musicians.
18 In 1635, Cuthbert Burbage recalled that his father 'purchased [the Blackfriars] at extreme rates and made it into a playhouse with great charge and trouble'.
19 De Witt's description, and other documents related to the Swan, are given in Wickham, Berry and Ingram (eds.), *English Professional Theatre*, 437–51.

In the event, Langley's playhouse has achieved greater distinction in our time than it seems to have done in its own, mainly because of the drawing de Witt made of its interior, which he included in a letter to a friend, Arend van Buchell. In fact, the 'de Witt Drawing', as it is known, is a copy of the original made by van Buchell, and it is this copy, the only known illustration of the interior of a contemporary public playhouse, which, until the discovery of the Rose, provided the key evidence for the outdoor playhouses. It remains of considerable value, but must be treated with caution.

From a point apparently high up facing the stage de Witt drew a circular-looking building with the conventional features of an outdoor playhouse at this date. It reminded De Witt of a Roman theatre and accordingly he labelled its features in Latin: *tectum* (roof); *porticus* (walkway: was De Witt suggesting audiences might stand here rather than sit?); *sedilia* (seats); *orchestra* (very good seats); *proscenium* (stage); *mimorum aedes* (tiring house). The small staircases labelled *ingressus* (entrance) seem to indicate that an audience member could move from the yard to the galleries, which matches the arrangement described by Thomas Platter, a Swiss visitor to the Curtain in the late 1590s:

> anyone who remains on the level standing pays only one English penny, but if he wishes to sit he is let in at a further door, and there he gives another penny, while if he desires to sit on a cushion in the most comfortable place of all, where he not only sees everything well, but can also be seen, then he gives yet another English penny at another door.

Such a system of entry would not require staircases to be built on the exterior of the playhouse, and, on the face of it, the earlier playhouses – Theatre, Curtain, Rose and Swan – had none, their introduction coming with the Globe in 1599. But, seemingly in contradiction of Platter and other evidence, there are indications that the Swan definitely, and the Theatre and Rose possibly, possessed at least one external staircase.[20] Furthermore, de Witt's drawing, though it includes a stage roof, does not show an alignment between the line of galleries and tiring house, perhaps suggesting that its tiring house, like that at the Red Lion and possibly at the Theatre, but unlike the Rose, was a separate structure, not part of the frame of galleries. Such problems of interpretation remind us how speculative our conjecture must be in the light of frequently contradictory evidence.

The drawing shows figures watching the play from the rear balcony. No other audience is illustrated, which may suggest that de Witt was keen to

---

20 Gurr, 'The bare island', *Shakespeare Survey* 47 (1994), 29–43.

emphasise this particular viewing position. These, it is generally agreed, were the Lords' Rooms, the most prestigious place from which to view, reminding us that the Elizabethan playhouse was essentially a theatre-in-the-round, if an unevenly distributed one.[21]

1597 was an eventful year for London's theatre workers: in February, both James Burbage – 'the first builder of playhouses' – and his lease on the Theatre expired, and in July the scandal caused by a play presented by Pembroke's Men at the Swan threatened the very survival of London's professional theatres. Following a performance of *The Isle of Dogs*, by Thomas Nashe and Ben Jonson (and, possibly, others too), a complaint was made to the Privy Council by the lord mayor and aldermen, as a result of which the Privy Council wrote to the justices of Middlesex and Surrey with instructions that 'those playhouses that are erected and built only for such purposes shall be plucked down'. In the event, although the playhouses were shut for a while, the demolition order was not carried out. Nor does it appear that the Privy Council ever expected it would be. Indeed, the whole business might have had as its specific aim the destruction only of Langley's venture – which challenged the well-being of Alleyn's company at the nearby Rose in particular – rather than the end of all playing. Whatever the truth, Henslowe and the Burbages were busy planning further expansion of their activities well before the deadline set by the Privy Council for the playhouses to be destroyed. Neither the Swan nor its owner ever fully recovered from the scandal, however. After the summer of 1598 regular playing at the Swan ceased for the next twelve years, though precisely why is not known. It was used sporadically between 1610 and 1614 and again in 1620–1, and then stopped altogether: the Swan had operated, in total, for a mere nine years. In 1632, Nicholas Goodman wrote of 'three famous amphitheatres', the Globe, the Hope and one which, 'being in times past as famous as any of the other – was now fallen to decay and, like a dying Swan hanging down her head, seemed to sing her own dirge'.[22]

Following James Burbage's death, his son Cuthbert, who acted as a kind of manager for the Chamberlain's Men, took over discussions on renewing the lease on the Theatre, but was unable to agree new terms, and negotiations

---

21 The advantages of the Lords' Rooms as a point from which to see, sometimes disputed by theatre historians, has been proved to my mind at the Globe reconstruction, where their comfort, the opportunity for privacy or display, and an uninterrupted view seem precisely the benefits that a patron would expect.
22 See Wickham, *Early English Stages*, II, part 2, chapter 10, for a full discussion and analysis of the *Isle of Dogs* affair, and Chambers, *The Elizabethan Theatre*, IV, 321–3 for relevant documents.

broke down completely in the autumn of 1598. The original lease had given Burbage the right to remove the actual playhouse structure, and despite opposition from the landowner, Giles Allen (who claimed that as the lease had expired the clause was invalid), on 28 December 1598, they, their carpenter, Peter Street, with ten or twelve helpers, dismantled the Theatre and transported at least the main timbers across the Thames to Southwark. There, close to the Rose and Swan, on land of which they owned the lease, they erected the playhouse which, primarily because of its association with William Shakespeare, has become the most celebrated of all Elizabethan playhouses – the Globe.

The Globe was a polygonal (evidently twenty-sided), timber-framed playhouse with three galleries and a thatched roof, over which flew the flag bearing the company's emblem – possibly Atlas supporting the Globe on his shoulder[23] – and its motto, *Totus mundus agit histrionem* ('the whole world moves the actor'). A roof covered the stage, and Hamlet's reference to 'heaven fretted with golden fire' undoubtedly refers to the decoration of the underside through which it was possible to raise and lower a throne. There was a large trap in the centre of the stage floor; the two doors which flanked almost certainly a larger central opening (probably curtained) had grilles in them to aid audibility backstage and to prevent collisions between actors entering and leaving the stage; there was an upper level that could be used for spectators and, centrally, a balcony for musicians and actors.

Archaeological evidence for the first Globe is minimal. The majority of the site lies beneath a terrace of listed buildings, and at the time of writing there is no sign of English Heritage giving permission for the scale of excavation that would be required. In 1998, a radar scan revealed what appears to be part of a stair tower, part of the outer and inner gallery walls and evidence of hazelnuts in the flooring, as found at the Rose. Calculations based on analyses of the second Globe shown in Wenceslaus Hollar's *Long View of London* (1647) and on the very limited excavation that has to date been possible on the site of the second Globe have advanced a figure of 30.5 metres for the external diameter. A 1634 report indicating that the second Globe, opened exactly a year after the fire in June 1613 that destroyed its predecessor, was built 'upon an old foundation', has been used as evidence for the first Globe also having a similar diameter, though some scholars think this is too large.[24] But Henslowe increased the size of his Rose playhouse only five years after it opened, and it would seem equally possible that the King's Men would make the most of the destruction of their

---

23 It seems likely that the same 'impresa' appeared on the Globe stage's *frons scenae*.
24 The Globe reconstruction in London is built with a diameter of 30 metres.

playhouse, and take the opportunity to expand and improve it. Comments by contemporaries (such as John Chamberlain who remarked, 'I hear much speech of this new playhouse, which is said to be the fairest that ever was in England', or the description in Stowe's *Annales* of the playhouse being 'new builded in far fairer manner than before'), though to a degree conventional and not related specifically to the building's size, would seem to confirm its difference from, rather than similarity to, its predecessor. Perhaps the phrase 'an old foundation' means no more than 'on the same site'. Certainly, when the owners of the Fortune came to rebuild their playhouse after a fire in 1621, also on the same site as its predecessor, they evidently took the even more radical decision to replace their former square building with the more usual amphitheatre.

What was more innovatory than the Globe's architecture, however, was the system of ownership and management. With much of their capital tied up in the Blackfriars project, and despite recycling the fabric of the Theatre, the Burbage brothers were in severe financial difficulties. Consequently, while they contributed what could be salvaged from the Theatre, the remainder was put up by five of their seven fellow sharers who each contributed £100, the Burbages each owning 25 per cent of the enterprise, the five sharers the remaining 50 per cent. And so, for the first time, actors became joint owners of the playhouse in which they worked, and the Globe became the first playhouse designed for a specific company. From the opening of the first Globe in May 1599 to the closure of the second in September 1642 the playhouse was used solely by the Chamberlain's/King's Men.

Case study 2: The King's Men at the Globe, *Henry VIII*, 1613

Henry VIII (or *All Is True* to give the play its Jacobean title) is Shakespeare's last play, written probably in collaboration with John Fletcher, and first staged at the Globe in June 1613. The Folio (and only) text of the play indicates the use of two stage doors (1.1, 2.1, 4.1), the upper level ('a window above' in 5.2.18), and the central opening (2.2.60) where Henry is revealed reading, but from which he emerges promptly onto the main stage where he is fully visible. Music – played from the Globe's Music Room, installed after the King's Men regained use of the indoor Blackfriars – is required throughout to announce entries, for dances and to underscore action.

It is a notable feature of Elizabethan and Jacobean plays that they invariably make few production demands, relying instead on a contract of imagination between stage and audience. At times, however, the companies produced scenes of considerable spectacle, and *Henry VIII* is notable for its elaborately staged and costumed scenes, often involving very large numbers of actors. It is not known if the King's Men ever performed *Henry VIII* at the Blackfriars, but many scenes seem to be designed more for the bigger Globe stage. Sir Henry Wotton described the play being performed there 'with many extraordinary circumstances of pomp and majesty, even to the matting of the stage; the Knights of the Order, with their Georges and garters, the Guards with their embroidered coats, and the like'.[25]

At the opening of 2.4, for example (the trial of Queen Katherine) a fanfare played on trumpets and cornets announces the arrival of no fewer than twenty-two characters, many carrying emblems of state, church and justice – Cardinal Wolsey's eminence being underlined by the 'two great silver pillars', symbols of dignity and high office, that are carried before him. The King takes his place on the throne, under the 'cloth of state'. The Folio gives some detail on where the actors place themselves, but merely instructs the 'rest of the attendants [to] stand in convenient order about the stage', suggesting, perhaps, some conventional practices in staging such scenes.

The scenes of spectacle allow striking contrasts to be drawn – visually and thematically – which dramatise the sharp distinction between the show and substance of government. In the following scene (3.1), Katherine sits, in private, with her women, sewing, the trumpets and cornets of the preceding scene replaced by a single voice, singing to a lute. In 3.2, Wolsey's isolation is starkly underlined as he stands, unaware that he is being observed by Henry and a group of nobles, before the King exits 'frowning upon the Cardinal, the Nobles throng after him smiling and whispering' (3.2.203). Scenes such as these indicate that the authors – who knew the playhouse intimately – considered the stage well-suited to intimate, more conversational scenes. As Mark Rylance has observed, though many people expected the Globe reconstruction in London to demand large-scale, bravura acting, experience has shown that it is equally responsive to 'naturalness' in performance style.[26]

Act 4 consists of two pageants, their juxtaposition embodying the themes of worldly and heavenly glory. The opening scene brings onto the stage (or perhaps the upper level, a common observation point) two Gentlemen who have come to take their 'stand' (or 'viewing place') from which to observe Queen Anne's coronation. Heralded by 'A lively flourish of trumpets' and

25 Pearsall Smith (ed.), *The Life and Letters of Sir Henry Wotton*, II, 32–3.
26 Rylance, 'Playing the Globe', in Mulryne and Shewring (eds.), *Shakespeare's Globe Rebuilt*, 169–76.

accompanied by choral singing and music, a glittering procession (described in great detail) enters, 'first passing over the stage in order and state' before exiting. This common stage direction probably means that, entering by one door, the actors took a route around the perimeter of the stage, described by the two Gentlemen (acting like television commentators), before leaving through the other door.[27]

Scene 2, which follows, is initially in strong contrast, bringing on stage the abandoned Queen Katherine, sick, supported by her usher and her woman, the emblematically named Patience. At line 78 Katherine bids her musicians (offstage in the Music Room) to play, and the stage direction notes that 'Sad and solemn music' is heard, possibly played by viols and recorders.[28] The Queen sleeps, and we witness the act's second pageant – the vision she sees in her sleep, a blend of a masque-like dance and dumbshow. Figures emblematically dressed in white and carrying bay and palms, symbols of triumph and immortality, dance a formal measure, their dance a challenge to the transient values of this world. Suddenly the Queen, in her sleep and 'as it were by inspiration', makes 'signs of rejoicing, and holdeth up her hands to heaven', the dancers 'vanish' and the Queen wakes. The music, however (which has prompted the dream), continues, underscoring the ensuing dialogue and helping shape the onstage mood.

The text also illustrates how, on the Elizabethan stage, the location of scenes is indicated by the use of significant items of furniture. In 1.2, for example, the text specifies a throne of state, which was probably either carried on through the central opening by the stagehands in their distinctive blue coats or flown in.[29] It comprised one or, in the light of the direction at l.8, ('King...placeth her [the Queen] by him'), perhaps two, thrones, raised on a dais with perhaps four steps, allowing the Cardinal to place himself 'under the King's feet'. Above the throne was a canopy. This use of simple signifiers allowed flexible and fluid use of the stage space. In 5.2, for example, the action is located outside the council chamber but at l.34 shifts, without a scene break, into the interior of the chamber – the change of location being established by 'A council-table . . . with chairs and stools' brought on stage and 'placed under [i.e. in a subordinate position to] the state'.

27 See Dessen and Thomson, *A Dictionary of Stage Directions*.
28 For this suggestion, and others, of performance practice, see the excellent introduction to the New Cambridge Shakespeare edition of the play, ed. Margeson (1990).
29 In the prologue to *Everyman in His Humour* (1598), Ben Jonson lists the moment when 'the creaking throne comes down' (line 16) as one of the crowd-pleasing effects to be seen at the playhouse.

But what of the remainder of the playhouse as a performance site? There is no evidence that the actors used the yard at the Globe or elsewhere, though the physical presence of the audience is directly invoked in a number of plays. In 5.3 of *Henry VIII*, for example, the Porter's and the Man's lines, suffused with playhouse references, seem designed to identify the fictional crowd gathered for the christening of the infant Princess Elizabeth with the actual playhouse audience who will witness its enactment, so binding actors and spectators in a shared experience that reflects the unity promised by the new princess. Certainly, experiments at the new Globe in London have demonstrated the ease with which actors can move from the yard to the stage, and how effective placing actors within the standing crowd can be.[30]

Henry VIII has many qualities that seem likely to have appealed to a contemporary audience. Stephen Gosson once loftily observed, in a sermon preached at St Paul's Cross in 1598, that 'in public theatres, when any notable show passeth over the stage, the people arise in their seats and stand upright with delight and eagerness to view it well'.[31] For the spectators at the Globe on the afternoon of 29 June 1613 there was spectacle enough to bring them to their feet when 'the [play]house was fired with shooting off a chamber which was stopped with towe [wadding] which was blown up into the thatch of the house and so burned down to the ground'. No one was hurt, though the reports interestingly refer to a child being in the audience. A year later, almost to the day, the Second Globe opened.

Prompted, possibly, by the arrival of their grand new neighbour, Henslowe and Alleyn decided to move their operations away from the south bank and into the north of the city. They faced the customary opposition from the city authorities but must have been encouraged by a petition in their support, signed by twenty-seven local residents. Between Golden (or Golding) Lane and Whitecross Street in Cripplegate, in the liberty of Finsbury, an up-and-coming area, they erected a new playhouse, the Fortune, which, similar to

---

30 The production of *Julius Caesar* in the summer of 1999, almost exactly 400 years after its original Globe premier, was a case in point. The mechanicals in the first scene were placed among the crowd in the yard, establishing a vigorous relationship between stage and audience. The Soothsayer, too, was placed there ('in the press', l.15) in 1.2, and was lifted to the stage on Caesar's line 'Come from the throng' (l.21). In 3.2, Brutus played his oration to the crowd from the remote upper level, close to the 'aristocracy' in the highest-priced seats, whereas Mark Antony sat right at the edge of the stage, close to 'the people', declining, as indeed the text may suggest, to take the 'public chair' (3.2.65). The effect on this scene of the playhouse architecture, the characters' language and their actions reinforcing each other was particularly striking.
31 Quoted in Gurr, *The Shakespearean Stage*, 226.

the inn conversions but unlike any other known purpose-built playhouse, was square rather than polygonal in plan. It was the second playhouse built for a specific company. The builder's contract survives in Alleyn's papers at Dulwich College, and is informative and frustrating in almost equal measure. The contract gives specific dimensions for the overall structure. The timber frame was to be built on an 80 feet (24.40 metre) square plan, probably with twenty bays like the Globe. The galleries were to be 12 feet and 6 inches (3.8 metres) deep, with the lowest 12 feet (3.6 metres) high, the middle 11 feet (3.35 metres) and the top 9 feet (2.75 metres), measured floor to floor. The top two galleries were to 'juttey forwards' by an extra 10 inches (25 centimetres). The yard was 55 feet (16.8 metres) square and the stage, laid with deal boards, was to be 43 feet (13 metres) by 27 feet 6 inches (8.38 metres) and have a 'shadow or cover' over it. The chosen builder was Peter Street who had only recently finished dismantling the Theatre and, we presume, setting up the Globe. His acquaintance with the Globe allowed his new employers to refer to it as a measuring stick for their own building, requiring him, without going into detail, simply to do certain things in 'the manner and fashion of the saide howse called the Globe', a phrase which continues to tantalise theatre historians.[32] In *The Roaring Girl*, performed at the Fortune around 1611, the authors, Middleton and Dekker, give a description of the packed playhouse viewed from the stage. First the crowded seats:

> Stories of men and women, mixed together
> Fair ones with foul, like sunshine in wet weather;
> Within one square a thousand heads are laid
> So close that all of heads the room seems made . . .

And then, the crowd in the yard:

> Then sir, below,
> The very floor, as 'twere, waves to and fro,
> And like a floating island seems to move,
> Upon a sea bound in with shores above.
>
> (1.2.17–20, 29 32)

32 The plan that would have accompanied the contract is lost, but the contract itself informs us of the playhouse's basic dimensions, that there were to be four 'convenient divisions' of the galleries to provide 'gentlemen's rooms' and other divisions to make 'two-penny rooms'. The lowest gallery was to be paled in with oak boards and 'fenced with iron pikes', presumably to prevent those in the yard clambering into seats. There were to be two main changes from the Globe – the main posts were to be square (rather than round) and the 'lesser beams' were to be more substantial. In Orrell's view, the Fortune was 'nothing but the Globe squared', 'Designing the Globe', in Mulryne and Shewring, *Shakespeare's Globe Rebuilt*, 64.

On 22 June 1600 the Privy Council issued an order again limiting the number of 'allowed...howses' and companies to two, and restricting the occasions on which they could play. The Lord Chamberlain's Men were to be given the choice of 'one...and no more' of the bankside playhouses (they chose the Globe) while Edward Alleyn's company would occupy the newly built Fortune.[33] The order makes no reference either to the Rose or the Boar's Head, but less than two years later the Privy Council gave permission for a company made from an amalgamation of Oxford's and Worcester's Men to use the Boar's Head in Whitechapel (recently converted from an inn) as its permanent home, bringing the number of regular venues and allowed companies to three. More significantly still for the security of the leading companies, in May 1603 the Lord Chamberlain's Men were taken directly under the patronage of the king and became the King's Men with, soon after, the Admiral's becoming Prince Henry's Men and Worcester's the Queen's Men.

The Fortune was the last purpose-built amphitheatre devoted solely to presenting plays.

In 1604, Aaron Holland began to construct the Red Bull in and around the yard of a former inn, and it appears to have started operating in 1607. Its features were apparently similar to those at other outdoor playhouses. Some evidence, however, suggests that spectators not only stood as well as sat in the galleries (as suggested, perhaps, in De Witt's term 'porticus') but may have also sat on the stage, as was the custom indoors. The Red Bull's reputation was as a more downmarket venue (John Webster blamed the lack of a 'full and understanding auditory' for the failure of *The White Devil* there in 1612) and by the end of the period it was frequently mocked for its repertoire and standards of playing. It was regularly used for illegal performances after the closure in 1642 and again, briefly, when playing resumed in 1660. It seems to have been abandoned as a playhouse by 1663.

In 1614, Henslowe and Alleyn returned to the south bank, where, in partnership with Jacob Meade, a waterman, they had a new amphitheatre – the Hope – built near to, or on, the site of a former baiting house. We may speculate that some earlier structures retained the possibility of dual use, but the Hope was specifically designed to accommodate playing *and* baiting and the surviving contract specifies how this was to be achieved. The building was to be based on the conventional polygonal design and to be of 'suche large compasse, fforme, widenes, and height' as the nearby Swan, with many of

---

33 Permission for the Fortune was given on the understanding that the Curtain was to be demolished or 'put to some other good use', though this was not implemented.

the same features, including a tiled roof and external staircases. There were, however, to be two major differences. The Hope's stage, supported on strong trestles, was to be made so it could be 'carryed or taken awaie', and, as a result, the Heavens, covering the whole stage, was 'to be borne or carryed without any postes or supporters to be fixed or sett upon the saide stage'.[34]

Performance spaces – indoors

The company that shared provision of the royal entertainment during Christmas 1560–1 with Leicester's Men was drawn from the choristers at St Paul's Cathedral. In both choir and grammar schools dramatic exercises were used to develop the children's oratorical and rhetorical skills, and they gave a number of occasional, amateur performances. Boys had also been providing entertainment at court for years, and between 1564 and 1576 appeared there at least twice as often as the adult performers. The commercial potential of the children's performances was soon apparent, however, and companies of boys presenting theatrical entertainment to a paying audience emerged in London in the mid 1570s.

In 1575, Sebastian Westcott (the Master of St Paul's choir school, mentioned in the account entry quoted above) opened his own playhouse, the second regular theatre in London following the Red Lion in 1567. Little is known of the Paul's playhouse, though it seems to have been situated in a 'private house' in the liberty of the cathedral (and so outside the jurisdiction of the city). The playhouse was evidently small, with an audience capacity of perhaps only fifty to a hundred.[35] The stage was tiny, backed by a wall with three entrances – the middle of which formed a discovery space – and with a curtained alcove above. The following year, around the time James Burbage was opening the Theatre in Shoreditch, Richard Farrant, a musician, master of the Children (the boy choristers) at Windsor Castle and deputy to the master of the Children of the Chapel Royal, opened a playhouse situated in the former Dominican Priory in Blackfriars, a district at that time still free of the city's control. Farrant's playhouse (usually known as the First Blackfriars) occupied a room in the upper storey of the Old Buttery, a hall 26 feet (8 metres) wide and 95 feet (29 metres) long, though the precise dimensions of the playhouse itself, or any other details, are not known.

---

34 For the Hope, see Wickham, Berry and Ingram (eds.), *English Professional Theatre*, 595–606.
35 See ibid., 306 for further thoughts on the playhouse's location and size.

Farrant died in 1580, Westcott two years later. In 1583, the Paul's company was amalgamated with the Chapel Children, a merger soon terminated when, in 1584, the boys lost the use of their Blackfriars playhouse. The Chapel Children disbanded, but Paul's boys continued under a new manager, Thomas Gyles, and with John Lyly as a kind of resident playwright. Lyly's elaborate language (often termed 'copious', or 'euphuistic') was well matched by the boys' oratorical and rhetorical skills, and they thrived, appearing at court on a number of occasions. However, it may have been Lyly's satirical interventions in the 'Martin Marprelate' religious controversy that got the company into sufficiently hot water for it to be dissolved in 1590/1.[36] For the next ten years there were no public or court performances by children, allowing the adult companies to secure their hold on the theatre in London.

In the winter of 1577, with his new outdoor playhouse open, James Burbage had sought the lord chamberlain's support in persuading the lord mayor of London to permit his company to use an inn for playing. Permission was refused, and it was nearly twenty years before Burbage once again sought to run both an outdoor and indoor venue. On 4 February 1596, Burbage purchased property in the same complex in Blackfriars that had housed the playhouse used by the Chapel Children since 1576. He acquired a hall – the Upper Frater – 110 feet (33.5 metres) long and 46 feet (14 metres) wide, which was divided by a number of partition walls, most of which Burbage removed, leaving an open space 20 metres in length. He built a stage across the space, backed by a tiring house, which on the textual evidence of plays performed there contained three entrances at stage level – two doors at each side and a larger, curtained central entryway – with a balcony above. The ceiling above the stage contained suspension gear, and there was a stage trap though, unlike the outdoor playhouses, no onstage pillars were needed to support the roof over the stage. The audience – probably numbering around 800, though estimates vary – was all seated, on benches facing the stage or in curved galleries (possibly as many as three) that ran right round the playhouse from the front edge of the stage. The stage was flanked by boxes and some audience members could sit on stools on the stage itself.[37] It is possible, too, that gallery seating was available at the rear of the stage as it seems to have been at the later Phoenix in Drury Lane (see below). The side boxes at stage level, each perhaps 10 feet (3 metres) deep, plus the space taken by the stage sitters, reduced the usable

36 See Gair, *Children of Paul's*, 110–12, for a brief discussion of the controversy and the writings of 'Martin Marprelate'.
37 A document of 1603 refers to 30 shillings a week being collected from stage-sitters, a significant sum.

width of the platform to perhaps as little as 14 feet (4.3 metres) or so – certainly Ben Jonson claimed it left the actors no more space than the 'compass of a cheese trencher'.[38]

Unfortunately for Burbage, powerful Blackfriars residents successfully petitioned the Privy Council to prevent the company moving in. On Burbage's death in 1597 the property passed to his son, Richard, who in 1600 leased the playhouse to the Children of the Chapel. The year before, a children's company under Edward Pearce reopened at St Paul's, probably using the same playhouse as their predecessors. Child drama was again available to London audiences, but after a decade of inactivity both companies found the theatrical environment much changed. It was more than a year before the Chapel Children appeared again at court, and the Children of Paul's did not receive the royal summons until 1603, when they provided Queen Elizabeth with one of the last entertainments before her death.

Around the turn of the century the term 'private' emerges to distinguish the children's playhouses from the 'public' ones occupied by the adults. They were in practice, however, open to anyone who could afford the price of admission, though the basic indoor ticket price of sixpence for the upper gallery – as opposed to one penny for the yard outdoors – inevitably narrowed the social range of the audience. The indoor playhouses provided warmer, drier, all-year venues, with the entire audience seated. One shilling and sixpence paid for a bench in the pit, two shillings and sixpence for the most expensive boxes, while two shillings (though not at Paul's where it was not permitted) bought a stool on the stage itself.[39] The stage and auditorium were candle-lit, and there was extensive use of music and song – before, during and after performances. In some ways indoor venues were like private clubs, their audiences known to each other, sophisticated playgoers alert to all trends in theatrical taste and fashion, attracted too by the often-provocative work of young dramatists such as Middleton and Marston. Unlike their adult counterparts, the boys performed less regularly – twice rather than six times a week – and at a slightly later time of day, beginning around four o'clock at Paul's, for instance, rather than at two o'clock. Thomas Middleton, in 'Father Hubburd's Tales', described the child actors at Blackfriars as a 'nest of boys able to ravish a man', his phrases stressing both their youth (Shakespeare used similar language when he called them 'little eyases') and their allure.

38 Jonson, *The Devil Is an Ass*, the prologue (line 8). Jonson also writes that the audience will, once the stage becomes crowded, wish the actors were transparent, made of 'muscovy glass' (line 17), an indication of a level of concern over sight-lines.

39 Dekker includes a satirical description of the – often disruptive – behaviour of stage-sitters in *The Gull's Horn Book*.

The Paul's company developed a varied repertoire, but the Children of the Chapel (known as the Children of the Queen's Revels after Queen Anne became their patron in 1604) rapidly became identified with sharply topical, often scurrilous plays. Unlike the adults, whose plays had to be licensed by the Master of the Revels, the patent awarded to the Children of the Queen's Revels in 1604 entrusted this responsibility to the poet and playwright, Samuel Daniel, who was in the queen's service as a groom of the chamber. In effect, this meant no control at all, since Daniel showed little inclination to restrain the company in any way, and during the 1605–6 season they presented a sequence of plays that brought the company into eventually disastrous collision with the authorities. Daniel's own play *Philotas* (1604) was perceived to refer too closely to the Essex rebellion and he was sacked. Apparently undaunted, the company courted further trouble with productions of *Eastward Ho!* and *The Isle of Gulls*, both of which gleefully satirised James I and the Scots. As a result, they lost the queen's patronage and the leading boy actors were imprisoned. In March 1608, they performed a lost play which again mocked James's Scottish friends, and when the French ambassador complained to the king about another production (probably one of Chapman's *Biron* plays) the company lost its playhouse and was dissolved, the lease being surrendered to the Burbage brothers.

Case study 3: *The Wonder of Women, or, Sophonisba*, by John Marston, at the Blackfriars, 1606

Sophonisba was entered in the Stationer's Register on 17 March 1606, and published in quarto later that year. John Marston himself had begun his career, and made his reputation, writing satirical comedies for the emerging children's companies. But the Preface 'To the general reader' of *Sophonisba* suggests that he saw this play, which drew directly on Roman history, as an attempt to produce a more serious piece of work, far removed from the scandalmongering repertoire that was proving the undoing of the company.

In the preface to another of his plays (*The Fawn*, performed at both Paul's and Blackfriars) Marston had drawn a clear distinction between a text printed to be read and a play in performance. 'Comedies are writ to be spoken, not read', he wrote, since 'the life of these things consists in Action'. The quarto text of *Sophonisba* is rich in implicit and explicit guides to its likely staging at the Blackfriars. Indeed, after the epilogue, Marston entreats his reader 'Not to taxe me, for the fashion of the Entrances and Musique of this Tragidy, for know it is printed onely as it was presented by youths, & after the fashion of the private stage'.

In addition to the differences in their aims and capabilities as performers, compared with the adults, the children offered a distinct theatrical experience to their audiences. Two of the ingredients central to this were the opportunities offered by candle-lit performances (see case study 4) and the use of music. Music was not unknown in the open-air playhouses, of course, but it was employed far less extensively than indoors, where the boys made the most of their chorister origins, and where the orchestra – especially at Blackfriars where it was installed in its own music room above the stage – was an attraction in its own right. The text also reveals a complex and sophisticated stagecraft that makes extensive use of symbolic and emblematic action and which shows Marston embodying the themes of his play in the staging.

Act 1 scene 2. In this scene Marston presents a version of the bedding ceremony used for Jacobean newlyweds, here given classical and ritualistic overtones. It opens with the entrance of 'Arcathia, Nycea with Tapers, Sophonisba in her night attire followed by Zanthia', the tapers and night-dress signifying this as a 'dark' scene (perhaps with some accompanying dimming of the permanent illumination; see case study 4). Music begins to play off-stage and at line 33 the stage direction indicates that 'The Ladies lay the Princes in a faire bed and close the curtaines.' No direction is given for the bed to be brought on stage, so it is possible that it is 'discovered' within the central space and that the curtains referred to are those used to close that entrance. However, the bed is a significant and emblematic item in this and other scenes, and it seems more likely that a bed, with its own curtains, would have been 'thrust out' onto the stage as other directions in other indoor (and outdoor) plays suggest was common practice.[40] The bridegroom, Massinissa, enters, also in a nightgown, accompanied by his friends and 'four boys, antiquely attired, with bows and quivers, dancing to the cornets a fantastic measure', who then draw the curtains to reveal Sophonisba. To a chorus of voices – possibly the other onstage actors – accompanied by the organ and cornets, Massinissa 'draws a white ribbon forth of the bed as from the waist of Sophonisba', a symbol of her chastity. As Massinissa prepares to enter the bed, the mood is shifted and the emblematic image extended by the appearance of Carthalo, 'his shield stuck full of darts', a striking intrusion that symbolises the public demands of warfare that challenge those private ones of marriage, a central concern of the play.

40 Dessen and Thomson identify 'roughly 150 examples' many of which refer to beds being 'thrust/drawn/in/out/forth', *Dictionary of Stage Directions*, 24.

This scene concludes Act 1 and, as usual in the indoor playhouses, the act change is covered by music, which in this case accompanies a dumbshow, perhaps while the bed is cleared from the stage. At the end of the dumbshow Gelosso, 'as much offended, impatiently starts up and speaks'. If the music concluded as abruptly as the actor moves, it would have provided an arresting opening to the scene.

Music in the Jacobean theatre – often specially composed but also apparently improvised, as instructions for 'loud', 'soft' or 'dreadful' music seem to indicate – made use of specific associations with particular instrumentation.[41] In *Sophonisba*, for example, cornets are used throughout to signify a martial mood, while organ and recorders are used to introduce other textures and tones. Perhaps the most complex integration of staging, music and theme comes in the single scene that comprises act 4, and in the opening scene of act 5.

As the cornets that signal the end of act 3 are replaced by the sound of 'organs, viols and voices' to start act 4, it is possible that some adjustment is made to the stage lighting, perhaps by raising the candelabra above the stage into a position higher than normal, as a result of which the introduction and then the setting aside of hand-held lights will also be more effective.[42] At 4.1.90, Syphax, determined to have sexual intercourse with Sophonisba, summons help from the witch Erictho. While 'Infernal music plays softly' to accompany Syphax's invocation, the spirit enters (perhaps through the stage trap, perhaps with smoke) and pledges to help him. A bed is presumably pushed on stage, though there is no printed direction. The infernal music continues to play (perhaps from under the stage)[43] while the erotic strains of a 'treble viol, and a bass lute, play softly within the canopy', meaning, possibly, within the hangings of the bed itself. Then, immediately before 'Sophonisba' appears, we hear a 'short song to soft music above'. In this heady, sensual mix of sound, Erictho enters, 'in the shape of Sophonisba, her face veiled' (perhaps the same actor, or maybe another in an identical costume) and 'hasteth in the bed of Syphax'. Syphax hurries into the bed too, and 'a base lute and a treble viol play for the act' which presumably signifies the sexual activity. Act 5 opens as Syphax, drawing the curtain, discovers Erictho, restored to her normal shape, and, as horrified as she is amused, he calls for lights as the music halts.

41 Edwards, 'Consort music', in Sadie (ed.), *The New Grove Dictionary of Music*, IV, 672–5.
42 Experiments on the reconstructed Inigo Jones stage at Bristol have demonstrated the ease and effectiveness of this manoeuvre. On artificial lighting in indoor (and outdoor) playhouses generally, see Graves, *Lighting the Shakespearean Stage*.
43 Such a direction is found in the Folio text of Shakespeare's *Antony and Cleopatra*, 'Musicke of the Hoboyes [oboes] is under the Stage', sig. 2y4 (4.3.12).

In August 1608, the Burbage brothers eventually regained the lease on the Blackfriars. They divided the title between seven men, keeping a share each and selling the remaining five. One went to a financier called Thomas Evans. The remaining four went to fellow sharers – Heminges and Shakespeare (the surviving original housekeepers from the Globe), Condell and Sly, who died before negotiations were complete, leaving six sharers, of whom four were actors. Plague kept the playhouses closed until December 1609, when the King's Men opened for business at the Blackfriars. The neighbours protested again, but it is a clear sign of the company's increased status that neither these objections, nor any of those lodged at later times, got anywhere. From that point the company used the Globe as a summer house, playing there from May to September and moving to the Blackfriars for the winter. At first they presented much the same repertoire in both playhouses, but as with other outdoor and indoor venues the gap in audiences and programme gradually widened. The Blackfriars was not used for illegal performances after the closure of 1642, and was finally sold by William Burbage, Richard's son, in 1651 for the sum of £700. It was pulled down four years later and replaced with tenements.

Surprisingly, perhaps, the disgraced Chapel Children were allowed to continue under new management, moving briefly to the Whitefriars playhouse, of which little is known. More remarkably, perhaps, they continued to appear at court, though more rarely than in the past. In 1610 the company reformed once again as the Children of the Queen's Revels, though many were by now well over twenty years of age. In 1613 they amalgamated with the Lady Elizabeth's Men (an adult company) with whom they may have performed Middleton's *A Chaste Maid in Cheapside* at the Swan, the presence of the youths perhaps accounting for the unusually large number of female roles in that play. Paul's boys also seem to have stopped regular playing around 1606, and to have ceased operations entirely one or two years later. The Whitefriars playhouse closed in 1615.

The King's Men remained the only adult company with an indoor playhouse until, around 1616, Christopher Beeston, a veteran actor with the Queen's Men but with aspirations to be an impresario, moved his company from the Red Bull in Clerkenwell to the more upmarket location of Drury Lane, close to fashionable residential districts and the Inns of Court. There he opened, and managed, an indoor playhouse, initially called the Cockpit as it was built on the foundations of one. Unlike the King's Men, however, Beeston had no intention of retaining an outdoor playhouse as an alternative venue, and on 4 March 1617, Shrove Tuesday, a crowd of Clerkenwell apprentices, angered at the loss of their local entertainment, attacked the new playhouse. The

Case study 4: *Love's Sacrifice*, by John Ford, at the
Phoenix, Drury Lane, *c.* 1631

'Action gives many poems [plays] right to live' wrote Ford in his commendatory verses to Philip Massinger's *The Great Duke of Florence*, and Ford's own plays demonstrate the extent to which he was alert to the full range of staging opportunities available to him and the care and detail with which he constructed stage action and images. In *Love's Sacrifice* he skilfully utilises the full scope of the physical characteristics of the Phoenix, but I want to focus on his use of candlelight. Act 2, scene 3 opens with the following, typically detailed, stage direction:[46]

> Enter Colona with lights [candles or tapers], Bianca, Fiormonda, Julia, Fernando, and D'Avolos; Colona placeth the lights on a table and sets down a chess-board.

In this, as in his other work, Ford clearly expected his audience to recognise his 'quotations' from other plays, in this case, Act 2, Scene 2 of *Women Beware Women*. Though not so developed as in Middleton, the game allows for a range of suggestive language as Bianca and her would-be lover, Fernando, play, observed and commented on by the scheming Fiormonda and D'Avolos. At line 27, pleading illness, Fiormonda makes an excuse to depart, and she and all except Bianca and Fernando exit, taking 'lights' with them. This leaves the two characters alone, with the emblem of a game (in which the aim is to 'mate' the highest ranking piece) on a stage darkened to enhance the erotic potential of the moment. Almost immediately the game is forgotten as Fernando, who according to the stage direction 'often looks about' (presumably to check they are not watched), suddenly kneels and confesses his love for the Duchess. Unseen by either, however, D'Avolos has entered 'behind' – possibly on the balcony,[47] but more likely through the curtains of the rear entrance, employing the traditional concealment role of the arras. Strangely, although close enough to observe them, he totally mishears their dialogue (one of many instances in the play where characters misinterpret what they see and hear). The Duchess, having rebuked Fernando for his 'baseness' and received an apology, calls for lights, their reintroduction bringing this intense section to an end.

---

46 All directions are as given in the 1633 quarto, with modernised spelling. See also the edition in the Revels series, edited by A. T. Moore, Manchester University Press, 2002, which is very alert to the play in performance.

47 As in my own production of the play on a full-scale, candle-lit reconstruction based on the Inigo Jones drawings. For further details on this reconstruction see my *Renaissance Drama in Action*, 156–76.

The following scene is a night scene, too. The removal of the hand-held lights at the end of the previous scene will aid the sense of increased darkness and the mood of sexual activity and desire, further emphasised by Bianca's state of undress and loosened hair:

> Enter Bianca, her hair about her ears, in her night-mantle. She draws a curtain, where Fernando is discovered in bed, sleeping; she sets down the candle before the bed, and goes to the bedside.

In performance, given the strength of her words to Fernando at the close of the previous scene, this opening will come as no little surprise to the audience. As in the scenes in *Sophonisba*, the question is raised of where the bed is situated. Does the curtain refer to the hangings of the bed or to the curtain across the rear entrance? Again, it seems likely (assuming for the purposes of this discussion that the Inigo Jones drawings represent the Phoenix) that it is the former, given the width of the opening. The dialogue indicates that Ferdinand remains in the bed, or on it, until at least line 30, surely too long to play within the recess, and it seems to me likely that the whole scene is played on or around the bed. If so, the opening direction probably indicates that she draws the curtain at the rear of the stage and that the bed, with Fernando on it, is pushed out to a more central position:[48] as we have seen, the stage direction 'discover' implies a process, not necessarily a static moment.

The scene concludes the act. If, as I suggest, the illumination has been dimmed, this interval, presumably with appropriate music, and used to trim the candles, could be used to readjust the playhouse lighting. The process in these scenes is a common one in indoor plays. Lights are brought onto the stage, then removed, making the stage seem darker than it was. 'Dark' scenes tend to be grouped together, since any change in the lighting state, though effective, obviously took time to achieve.

Another sequence that calls for reasonably complex and elaborate staging – the entertainment that masks the murder of the licentious Ferentes – is also placed directly before an act break. It is signalled with a very formal dumbshow, accompanied by music and singing, in the closing moments of 3.3:

> Loud Music. Enter 3 or 4 [servants] with torches; after, the Duke, Fernando, Bianca, Fiormonda, Petruchio, Nibrassa at one door. Enter at another door two Friars, Abbot and Attendants. The Duke and Abbot meet and salute; Bianca and the rest salute, and are saluted; they rank themselves, and go out, the Choir singing. D'Avolos only stays.

48 We found it perfectly possible to move a bed on and off stage through the central doors of the reconstruction.

The appearance of Petruchio and Nibrassa at the start of 3.4, 'with napkins, as from supper', heralds the return of 'the Duke, Abbot, Bianca, Fiormonda, Fernando, and D'Avolos' preceded by 'some [attendants] with lights'. The Duke bids them be seated and the entertainment begins. The stage direction is detailed and explicit, with the action mirroring the pattern of a masque and reflecting the actions and attitudes of the characters:

> Enter in an antic [comic grotesque] fashion, Ferentes, Roseilli and Mauruccio at several [different] doors; they dance a little. Suddenly to them enter Colona, Julia, Morona in odd shapes, and dance: the men gaze at them, are at a stand, and are invited by the women to dance. They dance together sundry changes; at last they [the women] close Ferentes in, Mauruccio and Roseilli being shook off, and standing at several ends of the stage gazing. The women hold hands and dance about Ferentes in divers complimental offers of courtship; at length they suddenly fall upon him and stab him; he falls down, and they run out at several doors. Cease music.

The women return almost immediately 'unmasked, every one having a child in their arms'. They attack Ferentes verbally and, in Julia's case, once more with a knife. Ferentes's dying speech (which begins 'Pox upon all codpiece extravagancy') intrudes a brief vein of comedy into the violence, the mixture of tones that is typical of Jacobean drama, and which surfaces throughout *Love's Sacrifice*. The act break that follows allows the stage management team an opportunity to reset the stage.

An example of a static discovery within the central opening is provided by 5.1. The scene opens with Fiormonda entering 'above' while, below, 'A curtain [is] drawn' to reveal 'Bianca in her night attire, leaning on a cushion at a table, holding Fernando by the hand'. They kiss, while Fiormonda comments on their behaviour. A cry from 'within' (i.e., offstage) coincides with the entry on the main stage of the Duke 'with his sword drawn, D'Avolos in like manner, Petruchio, Nibrassa and a guard'. D'Avolos comments on the tableau of the lovers, who continue seemingly oblivious to the intrusion before Colona's second shout from within jolts Ferdinand into an awareness of the Duke's presence. Ferdinand is manhandled from the stage, before the Duke orders all to leave, the doors to be 'shut up' and his wife to 'stand forth', presumably meaning she moves forward to join him more centre stage. It may seem strange to set key action in the discovery space, where it cannot be viewed by those in the expensive seats on the balcony. Interestingly, Fiormonda is placed in a similar position to the audience adjacent to her, her responses, like theirs, dependent on what is heard, rather than seen, recalling John Webster's definition of a theatre audience as a circumference of ears.[49]

If 3.4 challenged the resources of the stage and company – with six characters dancing and eight watching, seated among their real-life counterparts, the stage-sitters – the final scene of the play is even more demanding, and more difficult to imagine in terms of the original staging. It is set out in the quarto in considerable detail:

> A sad sound of soft music. The Tomb is discovered. Enter four [attendants] with torches, after them two Friars; after the Duke in mourning manner [dress and behaviour]; after him the Abbot, Fiormonda, Colona, Julia, Roseilli, Petruchio, Nibrassa and a Guard. D'Avolos following behind. Coming near the tomb they all kneel, making show of ceremony. The Duke goes to the tomb, lays his hand on it. Music cease.

With the rest of the characters kneeling (perhaps to aid sight-lines), the Duke finishes his oration to his dead wife (whom he killed in 5.1) and instructs the Guard to 'set ope the tomb, that I may take / My last farewell, and bury griefs with her'. At that moment, however, as the tomb is opened, 'out . . . rises Fernando in his winding sheet, only his face discovered; as [the Duke] is going in he puts him back'. But where – and what – is the tomb? The idea of the Duke trying to enter the tomb (assuming there is no trap door) may suggest the use of the central rear entrance. But the fact that the Duke can lay his hand on it, and that Fernando can *rise* out of it, may suggest a tomb brought onto the stage, like the bed earlier. Indeed, the sudden appearance of Fernando in a winding sheet may productively recall the previous image – and repeat the surprise – of his discovery in bed wrapped in a sheet in 3.4. Equally, following the suicide of both men, if the tomb were on stage, it would result in a typically resonant stage image to conclude the play.

The last commercial indoor playhouse to be built before the 1642 closure – Salisbury Court – opened in November 1630, and was situated on the eastern side of Water Lane (now Whitefriars Street), inside the city, but outside the walls. It was built in a barn, converted at a cost of around £1,000, and was originally home to a new company, the King's Revels, ostensibly a company of children, but actually one made up of adults. It appears to have been small, but to have had seats, boxes and what a contemporary document describes as 'viewing rooms' (possibly the balcony at the rear). In 1639, the king issued an order forbidding audiences to sit on the stage and reimbursing the actors for

---

49 Webster, 'An excellent actor', in *Works*, ed. Lucas, IV, 42–3.

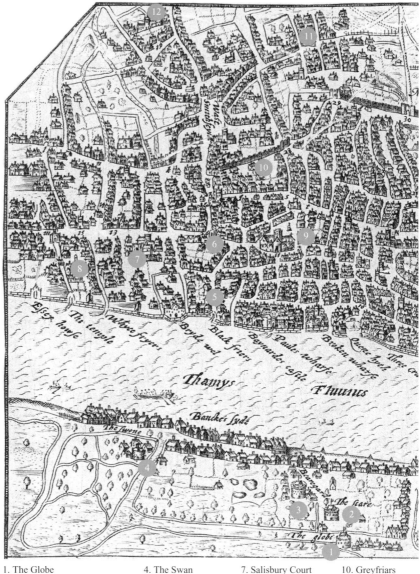

1. The Globe	4. The Swan	7. Salisbury Court	10. Greyfriars
2. The Rose	5. Blackfriars	8. Whitefriars	11. The Fortune
3. The Beargarden/The Hope	6. Bel Savage Inn	9. St Paul's	12. To the Red Bull

Figure 28 Map of London theatres, from John Norden's *Civitas Londini* (1660)

13. The Theatre   15. Bull Inn   17. Bell Inn   19. Boar's Head
14. The Curtain   16. Cross Keys Inn   18. Saracen's Head   20. Red Lion

Figure 28 (*Continued*)

the lost revenue. The playhouse was destroyed in the Great Fire of London in 1666.

In the sixty years between the opening of the Red Lion and Salisbury Court, if one includes conversions (including inns) and total rebuilds, twenty-three commercial playhouses were opened in London. It was a scale of theatre building probably unmatched in any other city at any other time in history, and a tangible measure of the outburst of dramatic activity that characterised the English Renaissance.

PART III

*

JACOBEAN AND CAROLINE THEATRE

13

Working playwrights, 1580–1642

ROSLYN L. KNUTSON

If a complete list of playwrights for the commercial stage from 1580 to 1642 were to be discovered in a London archive, few students of early English drama would recognise many of the names. Until the mid 1580s, most commercial drama was written by players for their companies; while there are some lists of players in this period, there are no lists of those players who were also dramatists. After 1585 players continued to supply companies with plays: for example, Richard Tarlton, Robert Wilson, Robert Armin, Samuel Rowley, Charles Massey and Nathan Field. A few players became known chiefly as playwrights: William Shakespeare, Benjamin Jonson and Thomas Heywood. By the late 1580s there were also authors who devoted a significant part of their time to playwriting. Many came to London from the provinces (Robert Greene, John Day, John Fletcher); some were Londoners born (Thomas Dekker, James Shirley). Many had fathers in trade (Thomas Kyd, scrivener; Anthony Munday, draper), some were themselves members of guilds (Henry Chettle, stationer), and some were of gentle birth (Francis Beaumont). Many acquired a university education (George Peele, Oxford; Christopher Marlowe, Cambridge); some continued to an Inn of Court (John Marston and John Ford, Middle Temple). In *Palladis Tamia*, or *Wits Treasury* (1598), praising those authors best in tragedy and comedy, Francis Meres cuts across lines of class, education, commercial venue and professional commitment to include the player Wilson, the provincial Greene, the Londoner Dekker, the tradesman's son Kyd and the university graduate Marlowe, along with men with modest vitas such as Richard Hathaway and Henry Porter.

The conditions of playwriting as evident in the work habits of the commercial playwrights are likewise various, yet there are common denominators. Most men worked both in collaboration and independently. Most wrote with a particular playing company in mind, though that choice of company might change over time. Most did other kinds of writing, whether for reasons of economics, aesthetics or prestige. Most, as dramatists, had no commercial relationships with stationers, but some had such relationships in their roles as poets. Most stayed in the life until they died. The individual careers of Shakespeare, Dekker and Shirley illustrate different combinations of the factors that define the work of playwriting during the years 1580–1640.

Collaboration

Receaved by vs Richard hathway & Willm Rankins in
part of payment for the play of Hanniball & Scipio
the summe of forty shillynges we say receaved the
3 day of Januarye 1600   xxxx[s]
By vs   Wi: Rankins   Ri: Hathwaye.[1]

Until Edmund Malone published extracts from the diary of Philip Henslowe in *The Plays and Poems of William Shakespeare* (1790), historians of the theatre had not given much thought to the habits of playwrights in regard to their working in collaboration or independently. Shakespeare was the ideal model of solo composition, for he was believed to have written most of his plays, and all of the best ones, by himself. Yet there was the model of Beaumont and Fletcher, whose collaboration produced many excellent and excellently regarded plays. Confronted with the payments in the *Diary*, nineteenth-century scholars saw that playwrights who sold plays to companies at Henslowe's Rose collaborated frequently and promiscuously. Predisposed to prefer Shakespeare's plays and therefore his putative habit of working alone, Shakespearians came to regard the dramatists who supplied other companies as hacks and collaboration as an inferior method of composition that necessarily produced inferior playtexts. There was even the suspicion of fraud: collaborators, because they accepted partial payment for piece-work, needed to produce more plays, or to appear to, to stay out of debtors' prison. Currently scholars have a very different view. Extending G. E. Bentley's perspective in *The Profession of Dramatist in Shakespeare's Time* that collaboration was a sign of professionalism, Jeffrey Masten in *Textual Intercourse* emphasises the collaborative nature of the theatrical enterprise itself, artistically and economically. In a description of the work habits of early modern English dramatists, Neil Carson explains in *A Companion to Henslowe's Diary* that collaboration was good for dramatists and companies.

---

1 Foakes and Rickert (eds.), *Henslowe's Diary*, 65. Subsequent references to the *Diary* appear in the text as *HD*.

In October of 1597, after having provided lists in his business diary of performances by various companies at the Rose since February 1592, Philip Henslowe, the owner of the playhouse, began to enter payments for playbooks and apparel for the Admiral's Men, who had been in residence since June 1594. These payments indicate that at least 50 per cent of the company's new plays each season were written in collaboration. According to Neil Carson, dramatists occasionally belonged to an exclusive partnership or syndicate, but these alliances were brief. In the fall and winter of 1599–1600, for example, 'Drayton and Munday collaborated with Hathaway and Wilson; Chettle and Dekker worked with Day and Haughton'.[2] By May 1603, however, Dekker had also worked with Munday, Hathaway, Drayton, Middleton and Webster; Day had also worked with Smith, Hathaway and a poet unnamed. In 1602–3 Chettle was no longer working with Dekker or Haughton but he was with Day.

In mid 1600 the Admiral's Men moved to their new playhouse, the Fortune. Henslowe, who continued to keep their books, began also to record payments for Worcester's Men, who leased the Rose in August 1602. This period, July 1602 to May 1603, shows how collaboration worked for both dramatists and companies. On behalf of the Admiral's Men, Henslowe made payments for eighteen new theatrical pieces from July 1602 to March 1603. Five were written in collaboration. Henry Chettle worked on two pieces: with a man named Robinson on 'Felmelanco', and with Thomas Heywood on part one of 'The London Florentine'.[3] John Day and Richard Hathaway worked together with Wentworth Smith on 'As Merry as May Be' and with one or more others on 'The Boss of Billingsgate'. Dekker and Middleton collaborated on *The Honest Whore*. On behalf of Worcester's Men, Henslowe made payments for seventeen new theatrical projects from August 1602 to May 1603. Eight were written in collaboration. Henry Chettle contributed to four of these: the unnamed play with Heywood; on 'Christmas Comes but Once a Year' with Heywood, Dekker and Webster; on 'Lady Jane' with Webster and Smith; and on 'Shore's Wife' with Day. The same team of dramatists – Day, Hathaway, Smith and the 'other poete' – worked on the two parts of 'Black Dog of Newgate'. These four plus Heywood wrote 'The Unfortunate General'.

Chettle, perhaps more casual than his fellow collaborators in the choice and timing of partners, worked with eleven playwrights at one time or another, according to records in Henslowe's *Diary*: Day, Dekker, Drayton, Haughton, Heywood, Jonson, an 'other gentleman' (perhaps Marston), Munday, Porter,

---

2 Carson, *A Companion to Henslowe's Diary*, 59.
3 The titles of plays for which texts survive are in italics; the titles of lost plays are in quotation marks.

Robinson and Wilson. Typical of playwrights who collaborated routinely, Chettle worked not only with one partner but also in consortia of three (*Patient Grissel*) and four (the 'Cardinal Wolsey' plays). Also typically, he worked as quickly with a collaborator as alone. The payments to him and Robinson for 'Felmelanco', and to him and Heywood for the first part of 'The London Florentine' span two to three weeks, the average of the span of payments to him for solo scripts (i.e., 'Brute', eight weeks of payments in 1598; 'All is not Gold That Glisters', one week of payments in 1601). Chettle also worked alone while he worked in collaboration. In 1602–3 he worked alone on *Hoffman* and part two of 'The London Florentine'.

Henslowe's records for 1602–3 show that playwrights could work in more than one partnership and for more than one company at a time. Dekker, who collaborated with Day in a project for the Admiral's Men, collaborated with Smith, Chettle, Webster and Heywood in two projects for Worcester's Men. Apparently, too, Dekker sold a play, 'Medicine for a Curst Wife', to Worcester's Men in September 1602 for 130 shillings even though he had already been given 80 shillings for the project by the Admiral's Men. Heywood, who had been writing for the Admiral's Men for several years, worked on 'The London Florentine' for them while he worked on six projects for Worcester's Men. Henry Chettle also worked for both companies, and the sequence of his projects illustrates the busy yet normal activity of a commercial playwright: with Robinson, Chettle supplied the Admiral's Men with 'Felmelanco' in September, during which time he was also getting payments on a tragedy from Worcester's Men; in October, he and two others supplied Worcester's Men with 'Lady Jane'; in November, he and three others supplied Worcester's Men with 'Christmas Comes but Once a Year'; in December, he sold *Hoffman* to the Admiral's Men (perhaps the tragedy for which Worcester's had been paying him); in January he and Heywood supplied the Admiral's Men with 'The London Florentine' and Worcester's Men with a play described as his and Heywood's; in March, he started the second part of 'The London Florentine' for the Admiral's Men, while working with Day on 'Shore's Wife' for Worcester's Men.

In addition to joint efforts in the production of a script, playwrights revised and amended playtexts, sometimes not their own, an activity that Jeffrey Masten calls 'a diachronic form of collaboration'.[4] The best-known examples occur in connection with the revival of old plays. The Admiral's Men paid Ben Jonson in September 1601 and June 1602 for additions to *The Spanish Tragedy*,

---

4 Masten, *Textual Intercourse*, 14.

which Thomas Kyd had written c. 1587. The Admiral's Men paid William Bird and Samuel Rowley £4 in November 1602 for additions to *Doctor Faustus*, which Christopher Marlowe had written by the end of May 1593. Sometimes, however, dramatists mended, or altered, new plays, as indicated by payments to Chettle for work on part 1 of 'Cardinal Wolsey' while it was being written in June 1601 and on part 2 when it went into production in May 1602. Also, a dramatist might be commissioned to write new parts when a play was to be put on at court; Middleton was paid to write a prologue and an epilogue for 'the play of bacon for the corte'. In some instances a play acquired revisions or additions when it changed companies. Worcester's Men paid Dekker for additions to one or both parts of *Sir John Oldcastle* in September 1602 when they acquired the play from the Admiral's Men. John Marston wrote new parts to his own *The Malcontent* when the King's Men acquired it from the boys' company at Blackfriars, but John Webster also contributed additions.

No doubt the most famous partnership of dramatists in Shakespeare's time was that of Francis Beaumont and John Fletcher. Both men wrote plays independently for a year or two, but by 1609 they had teamed up in the composition of *Philaster*, and together they wrote more than a dozen plays before Beaumont retired in 1613. Considerable scholarly energy in recent years has been devoted to the identification of Beaumont's parts as discrete from Fletcher's parts, but as Jeffrey Masten points out, 'the collaborative project in the theatre was predicated on *erasing* the perception of any differences that might have existed, for whatever reason, between collaborated parts'.[5] Fletcher, who also wrote a play or two with William Shakespeare, teamed up with Philip Massinger after Beaumont retired; he and Massinger were occasionally joined by Nathan Field or William Rowley.

It would be easier to identify individual hands in collaborative projects if the playwrights had assigned pieces of the plays by established patterns. However, the evidence in Henslowe's *Diary* and his correspondence with playwrights suggests a variety of collaborative assignments: sometimes one dramatist oversaw the entire project (as Robert Daborne did on 'The Arraignment of London'), sometimes the playwrights divvied up the work by scenes (as Jonson, Chapman and Marston did on *Eastward Ho!*), and sometimes a collaborator contributed his own part as well as a speech in someone else's part (as Dekker did on 'Keep the Widow Waking'). The best test of collaborative practices is the plays themselves, and these suggest remarkably seamless compositions. If there were not proof to the contrary, who could tell by reading the text or seeing a production

5 Ibid., 17.

that two dramatists worked on *A King and No King*, three on *Patient Grissell* and four on *1 Sir John Oldcastle*?

For one play, *Sir Thomas More*, there is evidence of multiple authorship in the manuscript, which preserves the hands of the collaborators (and that of the censor, Edmund Tilney). Because this play was revised, the handwriting provides clues to issues of collaboration not only in the identification of a writers' syndicate and the assignment of parts but also in the mending of someone else's composition. The manuscript of *Sir Thomas More* is written in six hands by men who worked on either the original or revised version of the play. Scholars generally agree that Hand A is Henry Chettle, Hand E is Thomas Dekker, and Hand S is Anthony Munday. Hand B is possibly Thomas Heywood and Hand C possibly a playhouse scribe. Hand D has been controversially identified as William Shakespeare. In *The Elizabethan Theatre and 'Sir Thomas More'*, Scott McMillin is primarily interested in the integrity of the *More* manuscript for use in the playhouse, but he also sorts out the 'original writers' from the revisers, giving the job of alterations to Hands B, C and E.[6] He notes that Hand B, having substituted a clown for a mute in the original, added new dialogue for the clown in scenes not otherwise revised. Hand D appears to have composed a single scene.

If Hand D is William Shakespeare, the identification confirms the ubiquity of collaboration, even among dramatists who usually worked alone. But scholars have been hesitant to accept the implication of the identification because it suggests that Shakespeare, having collaborated once in the manner of the playwrights in Henslowe's records, might have done so often. Also excepted from the category of routine collaborators are Marlowe (despite his partnership with Nashe on *Dido Queene of Carthage*), Peele, Greene, Kyd, Chapman, Marston, Webster, Ford, Brome and Shirley.

Ben Jonson would have put himself in such a category, for he seems to have thought that his reputation would be enhanced if he were judged only by his solo work. Jonson collaborated on projects early in his career, but when he published a collection of his poems and plays in *Works* (1616), he omitted his theatrical collaborations. These included 'The Isle of Dogs', on which he had worked in 1597 for Pembroke's Men. Another collaborator on 'The Isle of Dogs' project was Thomas Nashe, who later claimed in a marginal note in *Nashes Lenten Stuffe* (1599) that he had written the introduction and first act and that the players had written the rest (presumably Jonson and the players Gabriel Spencer and Robert Shaa, with whom Jonson was imprisoned due to

6 McMillin, *The Elizabethan Theatre and 'Sir Thomas More'*, 145.

official objections to the play). Jonson also excluded three collaborations for the Admiral's Men: 'Hot Anger Soon Cold' (with Porter and Chettle), 'Page of Plymouth' (with Dekker), and 'Robert King of Scots' (with Dekker, Chettle, and an 'other Jentellman'). And he excluded *Eastward Ho!*, on which he had worked with Chapman and Marston for the Children of the Queen's Revels at Blackfriars in 1605. No doubt Jonson had other criteria for the selection of plays included in *Works*, for he excluded both *The Case Is Altered*, which he wrote apparently independently for Pembroke's Men in 1597, and 'Richard Crookback', which he wrote solo for the Admiral's Men in September 1602. But it is fair to assume that the suppression of his collaborations was one motive for his choice.

Relationships with companies

Lent vnto harey porter at the Requeste
of the company in earneste of his boocke
called ij mery wemen of abenton the some of fortyshellengs
& for the Resayte of that money he gaue me
his faythfulle promysse that I shold haue alle
the boockes wch he writte ether him sellfe or wth
any other wch some was dd [vpon] the 28 of febreary
1598 I saye thomas downton Robart shawe (*IID* 105)

On 28 February 1599 Henry Porter bound himself to write exclusively for the Admiral's Men; on 25 March 1602 Henry Chettle signed a similar bond with the company. Such entries imply that dramatists worked on contract with playing companies, and that might have been the case, especially in the 1600s when most dramatists appear to have affiliated themselves primarily with one company at a time. Probably, though, such arrangements began more informally. In the late 1580s and 1590s, there was such a demand for scripts that a writer could successfully work free-lance.

According to Henslowe's *Diary*, playwrights such as Chettle, Dekker, Hathaway, Heywood, Middleton and Smith, who had been writing for the Admiral's Men, wrote for Worcester's Men in 1602–3 also. Dekker, who usually wrote for the Admiral's Men (or, in 1602–3, for Worcester's Men), sold *Satiromastix* to the Chamberlain's Men in 1601. William Hathaway and William Rankins, who were writing together for the Admiral's Men in the spring of 1601, bought back the part of 'John of Gaunt' in April that they had sold to the Admiral's Men; unless they meant to scrap the project, they were probably planning to sell it to another company. The letters of Robert Daborne speak to the issue of sales outside a current affiliation. Daborne began writing for the boys' company at Whitefriars in 1610 or thereabouts, and he continued with them when the company merged with Lady Elizabeth's Men in 1613. By way of Nathan Field (a player–dramatist with the company), Daborne negotiated payments for plays and advances against the completion of those plays in correspondence with Philip Henslowe in 1613. By November of that year he had supplied the company with 'Machiavel and the Devil' and was at work on 'The Bellman of London'. Needing yet another 10 shillings advance, Daborne tried to prompt Henslowe's generosity by hinting that the King's Men wanted to buy his play and would pay Henslowe an extra 30 shillings into the bargain ('the kings men hav bin very earnest w^{th}me to pay y^u in y^r mony ... whearin y^u shall have 30^s proffit').[7] Henslowe, too experienced a businessman to be much moved by the attempt at extortion, sent Daborne 5 shillings instead of the requested 10 shillings, and acquired the finished script a month later.

The careers of John Marston and Thomas Middleton illustrate serial company affiliations. Marston, after a flirtation with the Admiral's Men in September 1599, sold his work to the Children of Paul's at their newly reopened playhouse. In 1603 he began to trade with the boys' company at Blackfriars. In an instance of outside sales, he resold *The Malcontent* to the King's Men in 1604, revising the text to accommodate their players. Middleton went from writing for the Admiral's Men and Worcester's Men in 1602 to supplying scripts such as *Blurt Master Constable* for the Children of Paul's. When that company folded, he transferred affiliation to the remaining boys' company, and he went with them in the merger with Lady Elizabeth's Men. Eventually, he appears to have written largely for the King's Men. Between affiliations with Lady Elizabeth's Men and the King's Men, he wrote plays for the Prince's Men: *The Roaring Girl* with Dekker and *A Fair Quarrel* with William Rowley.

Free-lance sales are sometimes impossible to differentiate from a temporary affiliation with a company. Ben Jonson was writing for Pembroke's Men in 1597 but transferred to the Admiral's Men when playhouse closings and the uproar over 'The Isle of Dogs' caused Pembroke's Men to break with Francis Langley, owner and mismanager of the Swan playhouse. The Admiral's Men paid him in earnest in early December 1597 for a play due by Christmas. Apparently he did not finish that work, but he was back in August 1598 in a consortium with Porter and Chettle to supply 'Hot Anger Soon Cold'. In August and September

---

7 Greg (ed.), *Henslowe Papers*, 88.

of 1599 he worked with Dekker, then Dekker, Chettle and a third poet, on two projects, 'Page of Plymouth' and 'Robert King of Scots'. Meanwhile, however, he had been supplying texts written solo to the Chamberlain's Men: *Every Man in His Humour*, on stage by September 1598; and *Every Man out of His Humour*, on stage by September 1599. It may be that Jonson was seeking an affiliation with the Chamberlain's Men that did not materialise. An affiliation did materialise briefly with the Children of the Queen's Revels, who opened at Blackfriars in 1600, for whom Jonson wrote his next two plays, *Cynthia's Revels* and *Poetaster*. However, this alliance was not exclusive; in fact, Jonson supplied more plays to the Chamberlain's / King's Men in the next few years (*Sejanus*, 1603; *Volpone*, 1605) than to the Children of the Queen's Revels (*Eastward Ho!* 1605).

The brief affiliations of Jonson with different companies stand in contrast to the relations of Thomas Heywood with Worcester's / Queen Anne's Men and John Fletcher with the King's Men (also Shakespeare with the Chamberlain's / King's, see below). Heywood, who contracted in March 1598 to play exclusively with the Admiral's Men, wrote for the company also into 1603; he wrote for Derby's Men also in 1599–1600 (if the two-part *Edward the Fourth* is his); but his allegiance in playing and writing came to be Worcester's / Queen Anne's Men. With Beaumont, Fletcher sold plays to the boys' company of the Queen's Revels, but in 1609 or 1610 the pair apparently arranged to supply the King's Men exclusively. After Beaumont's retirement, Fletcher and his new collaborator, Philip Massinger, continued that alliance. A suit brought by the manager of the Salisbury Court theatre against Richard Brome suggests that agreements between playwrights and companies in the 1630s and 1640s had become more common, but they had not changed since the contract Henry Porter signed in 1599 except perhaps to specify the number of plays to be supplied.

There were obvious advantages for the playwright who wrote with a specific company in mind. Scott McMillin, in suggesting Strange's Men as the likely company and the early 1590s as the date of the original version of *Sir Thomas More*, bases his thesis on evidence that the playwrights knew the size of the company and the stamina of its leading player, Edward Alleyn. They could therefore introduce a crowd scene early, and feature the star character himself in a part longer than eight hundred lines. Nonetheless, the fact that playwrights did occasionally sell scripts outside their current alliance suggests that Elizabethan stages and habits of casting were sufficiently similar for a dramatist to write a play that was marketable to more than one company.

Finances

Mr Hinchloe I haue harde fyue shetes of a playe of the
Conqueste of the Indes & I dow not doute but It wyll
be a verye good playe tharefore I praye ye delyuer them
fortye shyllynges In earneste of yt & take the papers
Into yor one hands & on easter eue thaye promyse to make
an ende of all the Reste

Lent the 4 of ap^{r}ell	Samuell	
1601 – xxxx s.	Rowlye	(HD 294)

In order to get money for his work, a dramatist might present the plot of his new drama to the players and receive their approval, as Ben Jonson did in December 1597. Or he might read the script to the company, as Drayton, Dekker or Chettle did with the book of 'The Famous Wars of Henry the First' at the Sun tavern in New Fish Street in March 1598. The company, as a rule, paid 20 shillings in earnest, which is the sum Jonson received for his plot. It paid, as a rule, £6 to £10 for a finished script; the team writing 'The Famous Wars' received £6 5s. It paid £2 for an old play such as 'The Conquest of Brute', which John Day sold to the Admiral's Men on 30 July 1598. The cost of scripts to the company gradually rose; in 1613 Robert Daborne contracted for a payment of £20. Basing his figures on payments in Henslowe's *Diary*, G. E. Bentley estimates that the income of William Haughton was £47 for a 23-month stretch from August 1599 to November 1601; that George Chapman earned £28 10s in fourteen months from May 1598 to July 1599; and that Henry Chettle averaged 'about £25 a year'.[8] In 'The Economics of Playing', William Ingram calculates an income of £10 a year as a 'benchmark annual wage' for working men such as journeymen in guilds, hired servants, and even players.[9] By this measure playwrights did very well.

Earnings, however, are not the full economic picture. Henslowe left records of loans to playwrights, and these suggest more about cash flow across periods of employment and disruptions of work. Yet they too do not fully reveal a dramatist's economic situation, as the loans and payments to Henry Porter illustrate. Porter borrowed £5 from Henslowe on 14 December 1596 and another £4 the following March. On 30 May 1598 Porter received £4 for the script of 'Love Prevented' (some loans and payments might not have been recorded). Between June 1598 and March 1599, he received an additional £22 in payments for various projects. His loans from January through May 1599

---

8 Bentley, *The Profession of Dramatist in Shakespeare's Time*, 100.
9 Ingram, 'The economics of playing', in Kastan (ed.), *A Companion to Shakespeare*, 315.

total £1 19s 3d. His account should therefore have been in the black. However, on 16 May 1599, Porter borrowed 12d, and Henslowe specified that he had to pay back not only the 12d but also the £10 he already owed or else forfeit the £11 'wch deate wase vnto me xxv^s wch he hath not payd acordinge to his bond & so hathe forfetted vnto me'. Apparently, Porter was still in debt. Yet Henslowe loaned him another 14s 10d after the forfeiture. Porter was killed by John Day in a quarrel on 6 June 1599, less than two weeks after he had accumulated this additional debt. It is obvious, then, that the £27 in payments for plays and the £1 19s 3d in loans show only a portion of Porter's net income during the last year of his life.

A few wills of dramatists survive, and these offer an additional perspective on the economics of playwriting. Samuel Rowley, player and playwright (best known for the collaboration with William Bird on additions in 1602 to *Doctor Faustus*), made out his will on 23 July 1624. For a man of modest background, Rowley left a respectable estate, including books, several properties in Middlesex, and sufficient cash to bestow legacies including 40 shillings to the poor of his parish. However, it is impossible to determine the portion of this estate that might have been acquired from playing, not playwriting. Edward Sharpham and John Marston had shorter theatrical careers than Rowley, and while they were writing plays they had no other apparent sources of income. Sharpham's will, dated 22 April 1608, itemises only bequests of apparel, goods and chattels such as a damson-coloured cloak with a black velvet lining and a 'Rapyer beinge hatched with syluer, and a girdle and hangers trymed with syluer belonginge to the same' to his brother.[10] Marston's will, dated 17 June 1634, itemises a number of monetary bequests ranging from £28 to 40 shillings. Unlike Sharpham, who died in the midst of his playwriting career, Marston had been retired from the theatre for twenty-five years when he died, making it impossible to determine the portion of his estate acquired from plays.

Marston might have had family money to supplement his income from writing; other playwrights had to seek support from patronage and publication. Ben Jonson received commissions and gratuities including an annual pension of £66 from King James in 1616. Jonson also wrote masques and entertainments, as did Beaumont, Chapman, Daniel, Dekker, Middleton, Munday and Shirley. In 1611 Jonson was paid £40 each for *Oberon the Fairy Prince* and *Love Freed from Ignorance and Folly*; presumably other writers of masques were similarly well paid. Playwrights also wrote Lord Mayor's shows, which were funded by the guild of the newly elected lord mayor and performed on 29 October.

---

10 Honigmann and Brock (eds.), *Playhouse Wills, 1558–1642*, 78.

Anthony Munday wrote nine Lord Mayor's shows between 1605 and 1623; Thomas Heywood wrote seven between 1631 and 1639. Other playwrights who derived income from Lord Mayor's pageants were Peele, Dekker, Middleton and Webster.

Playwrights also wrote non-dramatic literature. Daniel, Drayton, Lodge and Shakespeare wrote sonnet sequences; Marlowe, Lodge, Marston and Shakespeare wrote epyllia; Jonson and Marston wrote satires; Jonson wrote epigrams. Drayton, in *Poly-Olbion*, and Daniel, in *The Civil Wars*, wrote historical, nationalist epics. Some dramatists were also translators: Marlowe for Ovid; Chapman for Homer. Some wrote prose. John Lyly made his name with the prose narrative *Euphues: the Anatomy of Wit* (1578), then turned in the 1580s to writing plays for the boys' company at Paul's. Robert Greene, who first wrote the prose fictions *Pandosto* (1588) and *Menaphon* (1589), took up writing plays and remorseful pamphlets such as *Greene's Farewell to Folly* (1591) and *A Groatsworth of Wit* (1592) at about the same time. Munday, Chettle, Dekker, Heywood and George Wilkins wrote prose tracts. Thomas Nashe, who collaborated with Marlowe on *Dido Queene of Carthage* but wrote *Summer's Last Will and Testament* (1592) by himself, was more pamphleteer than dramatist. His bread and butter was picaresque fiction such as *The Unfortunate Traveler* (1594) and prose tracts such as *Pierce Penniless's Supplication to the Devil* (1592) and *Nashes Lenten Stuff* (1599). It was in the last of these that he commented on 'The Isle of Dogs' affair, thus inviting conjecture that he might have done work on other plays for London companies in the mid 1590s.

Although dramatists received income from the publication of their non-dramatic works, they did not from their playscripts. These had already been sold to the playing company. The company might sell the script to a stationer, but, because there was no system of royalties such as exists now, any money made in that sale went to the company. Thus, several instances of publication that interest scholars now were of no immediate financial interest to dramatists at the time. For example, dramatists for the Queen's Men made no money from Thomas Creede's publication of plays from the company's stock, 1594–9; nor did dramatists for the Chamberlain's Men profit from that company's trade with James Roberts, who registered such plays as *A Larum for London*, *The Merchant of Venice*, *Hamlet* and *Troilus and Cressida* at Stationers' Hall and subsequently printed some of these for various publishers.

One wonders, in fact, how dramatists might have reacted to the appearance of their scripts in print. In his 1997 essay, 'The publication of playbooks',[11] Peter

---

11 In Cox and Kastan (eds.), *A New Companion to Early Modern Drama*, 383–422.

Blayney points out two bursts of publication, one from December 1593 to May 1595 and a second from May 1600 to October 1601. Even if they did not receive payment, dramatists might have gained publicity if their authorship had been advertised on the title page of the quarto, but few were so identified. In the second period, for example, most of the title-page advertisements include the name of the company owner but only half advertise the dramatist. All seven plays belonging to the Admiral's Men that were registered and/or printed between February and December 1600 carried title-page advertisements of the company (and therefore, significantly, their patron), but not one named Munday, Drayton, Wilson, Hathaway, Dekker or Chettle, who had sole or partial responsibility for one or more of the plays. Munday, Drayton, Hathaway and Chettle were never to be named as authors on the title pages of plays. If publicity did have a commercial value, two playwrights for the Chamberlain's Men fared somewhat better than did the playwrights of the Admiral's Men. Seven plays from the repertory of the Chamberlain's Men were printed between May and October 1600. One advertised Ben Jonson (*Every Man in His Humour*); four advertised William Shakespeare (*2 Henry IV*, *Much Ado About Nothing*, *A Midsummer Night's Dream* and *The Merchant of Venice*). However, the quartos of *Henry V* and *A Larum for London* carried no authorial advertisements.

When dramatists made arrangements on their own with stationers, as Samuel Daniel did with Simon Waterson, they did receive appropriate payment. Waterson published Daniel's first play, *Cleopatra*, and advertised Daniel on the title page (1594). Subsequently Waterson published not only Daniel's other plays, *Philotas* (1605) and *The Queen's Arcadia* (1606), but also his sonnet sequence (*Delia*, 1595), poetical essays (1599), poems (1605) and *Whole Works* (1623). Thomas Thorpe apparently had professional relationships with Marston, Chapman and Jonson, the trio of dramatists who wrote *Eastward Ho!*, because he published the play with William Aspley in 1605 and advertised the authors on the title page (however, he might have had the relationship instead with the company owners). Thorpe and Aspley had already registered and published *The Malcontent*, and Marston's name was advertised on the title page of subsequent printings. Thorpe himself registered *What You Will* in 1607, and he named Marston on the title page as the dramatist. Thorpe also published some of Chapman's plays with advertisements of authorship: *All Fools* (1605), *The Gentleman Usher* (1606) and the two parts of *Bussy D'Ambois* (1608). He published Jonson's *Sejanus* (1605), *Hymenaei* (1606), *Volpone* (1607) and *The Masques of Blackness and Beauty* (1608) with title-page advertisements of authorship. Jonson had previously had an arrangement with Richard Read and/or Walter Burre, printer and publisher of *Cynthia's Revels*, for two presentation copies for potential patrons, and he worked closely with William Stansby on the printing of *Works* (1616). In establishing relationships with stationers, Jonson anticipated the actions of subsequent dramatists, such as James Shirley, who supervised the publication of their non-dramatic and much of their dramatic work.

Most playwrights remained in the profession until their deaths, but a few retired to other pursuits. John Marston left the theatrical world in 1608 for the ministry. He had written plays for nine years; he was to preach sermons for twenty-five. Francis Beaumont, who is named as author with John Fletcher on the title pages of the great anthologies in 1647 and 1679, in fact worked on only five of the fifty plays there printed (*The Coxcomb*, *The Captain*, *The Honest Man's Fortune*, *Bonduca* and *Valentinian*), for, after six years of writing plays, he married an heiress and retired to the country where he died within two years. Cyril Tourneur also left playwriting; after a brief theatrical career, he returned to government service in the Low Countries and elsewhere. By contrast, Thomas Heywood, who was already writing for the stage in 1596, stayed in the profession until his death in 1641. He may have written more pamphlets and Lord Mayor's shows in the 1630s than plays, but his claim in the epistle to *The English Traveller* (1633) that he had had a hand in 220 plays during his career speaks with sufficient eloquence to the daily labour of commercial playwriting.

Shakespeare, Dekker and Shirley at work

> Nay . . . into so lowe a miserie . . . is the sacred Arte of Poesie falne, that tho a wryter . . . wast his braines, to earne applause from the more worthie Spirits, yet when he has done his best, hee workes but like *Ocnus*, that makes ropes in hell; for as hee twists, an Asse stands by and bites them in sunder, and that Asse is no other than the Audience with hard hands.[12]

In *Shakespeare at the Globe* (1962) Bernard Beckerman dispelled the misconception that Shakespeare's company was significantly different in its repertorial and marketing practices from companies at the Rose and other playhouses. It remains for scholars to dispel the misconception that Shakespeare was significantly different in work habits and commercial incentive. The belief in Shakespeare's and his company's difference has been based largely on a bias toward solo composition, loyalty to a company, writing for art's sake, the attraction of genteel audiences and personal financial success. To scholars with

---

12 Dekker, *A Knight's Conjuring* (1607), ed. Robbins, 157.

these prejudices, Thomas Dekker represented a class of inferior playwrights because he was a frequent and indiscriminate collaborator, with debts and without an exclusive company affiliation. James Shirley, though similar to Dekker in serial company affiliations, was nonetheless a cut above because he successfully acquired patrons and succeeded to Shakespeare's place as chief poet with the King's Men. In fact, as theatre historians now agree, the differences among these playwrights have less to do with their work habits than with their financial choices and the vicissitudes of the climate for theatre in their time.

Scholars of the old view seem to have been right about one thing: Shakespeare worked alone most of the time. It appears that, if he is Hand D, he collaborated early in his career on *Sir Thomas More* with the consortium of Chettle (Hand A), Munday (Hand S) and the man known only as Hand C (possibly a scribe). He might also have contributed scenes to *Edward III*. Scott McMillin persuasively assigns Hand D's work on the original version of *Sir Thomas More* to the company of Strange's Men some time between the summers of 1592 and 1593; and this period, or the summer of 1594, is a reasonable time also for *Edward III* to have been written. The date of summer 1594 is significant because the Chamberlain's Men were formed by early June, and Shakespeare joined the company at that time. His stint as a free-lance dramatist, in which he sold *Henry VI* to Strange's Men early in 1592, the rest of the tetralogy to Pembroke's Men in 1592–3 and *Titus Andronicus* to Sussex's Men early in 1594, was over; his lifetime affiliation with the Chamberlain's/King's Men had begun. He was to have another period of collaboration at the end of his career, when he worked (apparently) with George Wilkins on *Pericles*, and with John Fletcher on 'Cardenio', *Two Noble Kinsmen* and *Henry VIII*.

Shakespeare's primary contribution to the repertory of the Chamberlain's/King's Men was to provide new plays, but he probably did more piece work for the company than can be proved by surviving evidence. In *Shakespeare's Professional Career*, Peter Thomson uses the contract signed by Richard Brome with the King's Revels company at Salisbury Court in 1635 to suggest what Shakespeare's 'smaller jobs' might have been: writing prologues, inductions, epilogues and songs; and revising old plays.[13] This work is lost except for some kinds of revision (Masten's diachronic collaboration). One kind – the rewriting of other dramatists' plays, for example, turning *The Taming of a Shrew* into *The Taming of the Shrew* – might have been a facet of his apprenticeship. However, Shakespeare used old play materials throughout his career, turning *The Famous*

13 Thomson, *Shakespeare's Professional Career*, 117.

Victories of Henry V into the Henriad, *The Troublesome Reign of King John* into *King John*, the 'Hamlet' in Henslowe's June 1594 playlist into *Hamlet* and *King Leir* into *King Lear*. The possibility that he did another kind of revision – the rewriting of his own plays – has some support among textual scholars. No one disputes his hand in minor alterations such as changing the name 'Oldcastle' to 'Falstaff' in *1 Henry IV*, but scholars are still arguing whether Shakespeare himself made the more substantial revisions represented by the differences between quarto and folio texts such as those of *Hamlet* and *King Lear*.

Because he was regularly available to the Chamberlain's / King's Men, Shakespeare might also have provided them with plays for a special occasion. There is an old story, popularised by Nicholas Rowe in a biography accompanying his edition of Shakespeare's plays in 1709, that Queen Elizabeth, having been charmed by the character of Falstaff, asked for a play of him in love; and Shakespeare obliged with *The Merry Wives of Windsor*. Scholars who have found such tales the stuff of legend, not history, have nonetheless been willing to grant that an occasion such as a wedding, royal ceremony or performance for a royal visitor might have prompted Shakespeare to write (for example) *A Midsummer Night's Dream*, *Twelfth Night* or *Macbeth*. The evidence for such occasional writing is tenuous, but it is certainly true that Shakespeare, like his fellow playwrights, expected his plays to be performed at court; at some level, therefore, he anticipated audiences of royals and nobles as well as citizens of London and the provinces. Recently, in the search for cultural messages in a supposedly subversive Elizabethan theatre, scholars have given much attention to the political climate of Shakespeare's plays. However, the only documented instance of a performance for a political reason is the revival of *Richard II* at the Globe in February 1601, a performance commissioned by supporters of the Earl of Essex. The players, called before the lord chief justice to answer for their role in the subsequent Essex rebellion, minimised the politics of the situation and emphasised the commerce. Augustine Phillips, their spokesman, claimed that the players agreed to perform *Richard II*, which they thought too old to attract a good audience, only because the earl's supporters promised them a 40-shilling bonus on top of their receipts.

Politics and the court notwithstanding, Shakespeare kept an eye on the theatrical market in subject matter and genre. The history play was still a hot ticket in 1592–3, and four of his early works, the three parts of *Henry VI* and *Richard III*, reflect that demand. These same plays represent another successful commercial strategy: the extension of a narrative into a serial or sequel. There were precedents in the two-part *Tamburlaine* and *The Troublesome Reign of King John*, but Shakespeare may have been the first to construct three- and four-part serials and the first to apply the concept to a romantic comedy, if *Love's Labour's Won* did exist and did complete the wooing of *Love's Labour's Lost* (as its name suggests). In some cases, the appearance of a Shakespeare play when another company was offering a play of the same subject and/or genre cannot always be coincidental. For example, the first part of *Henry IV* was on stage some time in 1596. In writing the play, Shakespeare used material from *The Famous Victories of Henry V*, which belonged to the Queen's Men and might have been played by them at the Swan playhouse at its opening in 1595–6 (*Famous Victories* was printed in 1598 advertising the Queen's Men). The Admiral's Men also had a history play about Henry V; theirs debuted at the Rose in November 1595 and remained in performance through July 1596. Shakespeare spun out his version of the narrative into three plays over three years, offering his company *2 Henry IV* in 1598 and *Henry V* in 1599. In the process, he provided a spin-off, *The Merry Wives of Windsor*, which featured a battery of 'humours' characters along with Falstaff. If its composition was mid 1597, *The Merry Wives of Windsor* was ready for performance soon after the Admiral's Men's *Comedy of Humours* began to draw great crowds to the Rose in May and June 1597.

A similar phenomenon occurred with the revenge play. Whether or not Shakespeare wrote *Hamlet* in 1599–1600 before Marston wrote *Antonio and Mellida* and *Antonio's Revenge* for Paul's Boys, both dramatists were responding to renewed interest in the genre marked by a revival of *The Spanish Tragedy* at the Rose in January 1597. In 1602–3 Chettle contributed *Hoffman*, and *Hamlet* was being performed in London, Oxford and Cambridge (as advertised on the title page of the 1603 quarto). However, by 1603 Shakespeare was already at work on another play of revenge, which he was adapting to the newer fashion of plays about domestic relations. Perhaps initiated by Chettle, Haughton and Dekker's *Patient Grissel* (1599–1600), the formula developed comedic versions such as *How a Man May Choose a Good Wife from a Bad* (1602) and tragic ones such as Heywood's *A Woman Killed with Kindness* (1603). Shakespeare's *Othello*, which debuted in 1604 and was revived (at least) in 1609–10 and 1612–13, opened a strain of domestic violence to which the playwrights of *The Revenger's Tragedy* (1605–6) and *The Second Maiden's Tragedy* (1611–12) responded, as did Webster in *The Duchess of Malfi* (1613–14).

Being a fixture with the Chamberlain's/King's Men, Shakespeare must have had relationships with numerous dramatists, but only two stories suggest what his relationships were. Both involve Ben Jonson. In one, Jonson brought a play to the Chamberlain's Men, and they rejected it; however, Shakespeare saw it, liked it, and praised Jonson publicly as a result. This story is meant to show Shakespeare's professional geniality. In the other, when Jonson attacked commercial theatre in *Poetaster*, Shakespeare joined Dekker in a counter-attack. Dekker's riposte was a trussing in *Satiromastix*; Shakespeare's was a 'purge', perhaps the ridicule of Jonson in a satirical portrait in *Troilus and Cressida*.[14] This story is meant to show Shakespeare's righteous professional outrage. Both stories emphasise a cult of personality popularised by scholars of the old school, and neither gives sufficient credit to Shakespeare the businessman. Working with other playwrights, whether as a collaborator or merely as a fellow contributor to the repertory, was a constant in Shakespeare's theatrical life. In order to add twelve to sixteen new plays to the repertory, the Chamberlain's / King's Men probably traded with six, eight, or more dramatists a year. Shakespeare undoubtedly had friends among these men, though apparently not ones as close as were Beaumont and Fletcher, who reportedly shared not only rooms but a woman. He undoubtedly had enemies, though apparently he avoided the kind of quarrel that led John Day to kill Henry Porter. Given his instincts for business, Shakespeare must have welcomed the return of Jonson's plays to the repertory in 1603, as well as the affiliation of Beaumont and Fletcher in 1610 and their new tragicomedies (a vogue they were themselves promoting). Moreover, even though scholars have dismissed such material as hackwork, Shakespeare must have had commercial respect for plays such as *A Warning for Fair Women*, *The Merry Devil of Edmonton* and *A Larum for London*, and therefore for their authors, because he understood the value of popular stories and formulas in the company's offerings, year after year.

Shakespeare had another reason for welcoming successful plays into the company repertory: he received a cut of the gate receipts in each of his roles as player, sharer and investor in the Globe and Blackfriars playhouses. He had published *Venus and Adonis* in 1593 and *The Rape of Lucrece* in 1594, but the sums he received from his printer, Richard Field, were negligible (Field, however, would have profited from the many subsequent editions). There is no evidence that Shakespeare received a gratuity from Henry Wriothesley, Earl of Southampton, to whom he dedicated both poems. Thomas Thorpe published the sonnets in 1610, but he might not have acquired the manuscript from Shakespeare and the mysterious Mr W. H. might not have returned the courtesy of the dedication with a financial gift.

Shakespeare died in April 1616, and his will is evidence that he had made money from his work and investments. At his death, he left cash, goods and

---

14 Nicholas Rowe's *Life of Shakespeare* tells the story of Shakespeare's endorsement of Jonson: a character in *The Second Part of the Return from Parnassus* alludes to Shakespeare's 'purge' of Jonson but does not link the purge specifically to an episode in a play.

property to his family and friends. His sister Joan received title to her house, his wearing apparel and money. His daughter Susanna received the estate of New Place as well as considerable property in the surrounding county. His daughter Judith received £150 with the promise of £150 more. His wife Anne received (famously) the second-best bed. In comparison with Samuel Rowley, who left 40 shillings to the poor of his parish, Shakespeare left £10. In comparison with Sharpham, who left clothing and silver-appointed weaponry to friends, Shakespeare made provisions for rings to be purchased by friends who included his fellows John Heminges, Richard Burbage and Henry Condell. As indicative of his financial success as any single bequest, Shakespeare identified himself in the will as a gentleman, thus declaring in his last piece of writing that his life's work had enabled him to rise above his birth.

Thomas Dekker once seemed to scholars to be Shakespeare's opposite in significant ways. He did not often work solo, he did not work for one company exclusively, and he spent six years in debtors' prison. True, Dekker often collaborated in the writing of scripts. The records in Henslowe's *Diary*, 1597–1603, indicate that he collaborated with Chettle, Day, Drayton, Haughton, Heywood, Jonson, Middleton, Munday, Smith, Webster and Wilson. After 1603 he continued to collaborate with Day, Middleton and Webster, adding projects over time with Ford, Massinger and Rowley. True, Dekker did not work exclusively for the Admiral's/Prince's Men. He wrote for a while for the Children of Paul's (*Westward Ho!*, *Northward Ho!*), and he sold at least one play to the Chamberlain's Men (*Satiromastix*). True, Dekker was in the King's Bench prison for debt from 1613 to 1619. However, in scholarship today, Dekker and playwrights similarly labelled 'hacks' by old-school scholars are being re-evaluated. Criteria such as solo composition, exclusive company affiliation and personal prosperity are being supplanted by criteria that reflect commercial and cultural issues. Judged by his contributions to the theatrical market-place, Dekker is more similar to Shakespeare as a professional playwright than different.

Dekker did not write exclusively for the Admiral's/Prince's Men throughout his 35-year career, but during the stretches that he did write for them he was an asset to their political and commercial agendas. For example, he was available to prepare plays to be shown at court. In 1599–1600, the Admiral's Men had two court dates, and Dekker had plays ready for these performances: *Old Fortunatus*, which he was just finishing and for which he was paid an additional 40 shillings for a court epilogue; and *The Shoemakers' Holiday*, which, when published, carried a title-page advertisement of a court performance on New Year's night 1600. The next year, when the Admiral's Men again had two court dates, Dekker had ready his old play, 'Phaeton', having been paid

40 shillings for alterations. The revisions to 'Phaeton' and *Old Fortunatus*, as well as alterations to 'Pontius Pilate' and the old 'Tasso's Melancholy' in the winter of 1602, illustrate the small jobs that, as a company-affiliated playwright, Dekker was on hand to perform. He was also available for a very special occasion in the life of the Admiral's Men: their move to the Fortune playhouse in the summer or autumn of 1600. He had already written *Old Fortunatus*, which fortuitously advertised the company's new theatre; and in September he was paid 20 shillings for a project called 'Fortune's Tennis'.

From 1597 to 1603, Dekker worked on projects for the Admiral's Men that suggest his knack for repertorial commerce. For example, he helped the company with new plays on topics long popular: mythology and classical history. A sampling includes 'Phaeton' and 'Hannibal and Hermes' in 1598; 'Troilus and Cressida' and 'Agamemnon' in 1599; and 'Truth's Supplication to Candlelight', 'The Golden Ass, or Cupid and Psyche' and 'Fair Constance of Rome' in 1600. He also contributed to the diversity of the company's offerings in genre. With *Patient Grissel* in the winter of 1599, he may have provided the seminal play in the soon-to-burgeon genre of domestic relations. Subsequent projects illustrate some directions into which the genre developed: 'Page of Plymouth', domestic crime; part one of 'Fair Constance of Rome', Greek romance; and *The Honest Whore*, contemporary realism. With 'The Spanish Moor's Tragedy', he contributed to the strain of revenge play in which the main character, like Barabas the Jew in *The Jew of Malta*, is a villainous alien.

With such plays as the two parts of 'Earl Godwin', and the four parts of 'The Civil Wars of France', Dekker contributed both to the always-popular history play (domestic and foreign) and to audiences' taste for narratives in serial. The four parts of 'The Civil Wars of France' illustrate Dekker's participation in the market strategy of duplication, or cloning, of a company's own or its competitors' offerings. The Admiral's Men had performed Marlowe's *Massacre at Paris* in 1594–5 and they were to revive it in January 1602; between these runs, they had Dekker's collaborative 'Civil Wars' plays, which shared at least the character of the Guise with *The Massacre at Paris*. Meanwhile, the Chamberlain's Men had a four-part history of civil war also, namely, the Wars of the Roses plays known as the three parts of *Henry VI* and *Richard III*. These were surely played at the Theatre in 1594–5 in competition with Marlowe's play at the Rose. Given their reprinting in 1600, the second and third parts of *Henry VI* might have been revived at the Curtain (1598–9) or Globe (1599–1600) in competition with the 'Civil Wars' plays at the Rose, 1598–9. Derby's Men competed as well, offering the two parts of *Edward IV* at the Boar's Head, 1598–9.

And yet Dekker had trouble making ends meet, and he apparently turned to prose writing in 1603 to give himself a broader financial base. His plays had begun to appear in print in 1600, and he began to be credited publicly in the title-page advertisements with *Satiromastix* in 1602. In 1603 he began to publish prose works. Some tracts such as *That Wonderful Year* (1603) and *The Bellman of London* (1608) went through several editions, making money for their stationers but no extra for Dekker. Then, despite this additional industry, some combination of personal financial disaster and harsh creditors finally landed him in the King's Bench from 1613 to 1619. During his imprisonment, Edward Alleyn, star player and businessman for the Admiral's / Prince's Men, provided Dekker with charity, no doubt a sign of his former value to the company. When Dekker got out, he resumed writing and publishing; two of the shows he wrote for the Lord Mayor's pageant were published in the 1620s. He died, in 1632 or soon after, apparently still poor.

A few weeks before Charles I became king on 27 March 1625 and just as the playhouses were to be closed for six months because of plague, James Shirley began writing for the stage after a stint as schoolmaster of St Albans Grammar School. His first play, *The School of Compliment, or Love Tricks*, was performed at the Cockpit playhouse managed by Christopher Beeston. During his career Shirley wrote most of his thirty-eight plays independently, affiliated himself with a company, directed his plays at a specific audience, published the plays with title-page advertisements of his authorship, and courted a variety of patrons. These patterns became the norm in the years leading up to the official closure of the playhouses in 1642. Similar in long affiliations with a single company and an instinct for pleasing audiences, the conditions of Shirley's career were significantly different from Shakespeare's and Dekker's in alliances with stationers and the aggressive pursuit of patrons.

Like Shakespeare, Shirley worked solo, although the heavy influence of Fletcher, Shakespeare and Ford was collaboration of a kind. Presumably he signed a contract with Beeston, perhaps a prototype of the Brome contract in 1635, to supply Lady Elizabeth's Men, later Queen Henrietta's Men, with two plays a year. This affiliation lasted until 1636, when plague again shut down the playhouses. Shirley then moved to Ireland and wrote for the theatre in Dublin. When he returned to London in 1640, he affiliated himself with the King's Men at Blackfriars and the Globe. Both at the Cockpit (later Phoenix) and Blackfriars playhouses, Shirley addressed audiences more routinely upscale and female than Shakespeare and Dekker would have known. The tastes of these audiences are reflected in Shirley's favourite genres: the realistic–instructional–social comedy, tragicomedy and romantic tragedy.

Shirley, more like the poet Samuel Daniel than the prose writer Dekker, published his own work through specific stationers. After the playhouses closed in 1636, Shirley arranged with William Cooke and Andrew Crooke to publish sixteen of his plays including *Hyde Park*, *The Lady of Pleasure*, *The Young Admiral*, *The Gamester*, *The Maid's Revenge* and *Love's Cruelty*. His work had already appeared in print. *The Wedding* (1629) was the first of his plays to be published, and its title page is typical of subsequent Shirley publications in advertising not only him as author but also the company owners and theatrical venue. After the close of the playhouses in 1642, Shirley again turned to publication. With Humphrey Moseley, he published a collection of poems (1646), many of which were prologues and epilogues from his plays; a number of masques; and plays, six of which including *The Doubtful Heir* and *The Cardinal* had belonged to the King's Men and were collected in a volume in 1653.

Shirley allied himself with coteries of politicians at Gray's Inn, English and Irish courtiers, Catholics, and literati who could provide the patronage he sought. Of these patrons, William Cavendish, Earl (later Duke) of Newcastle, not only supported Shirley's playwriting but allegedly collaborated on *Captain Underwit* (1639–41). A list of the dedicatees of Shirley's plays and poems includes such notable men and women as Francis Manners, Earl of Rutland; Thomas Wentworth, later Earl of Strafford; William Tresham; Henry Rich, Earl of Holland; Lady Dorothy Shirley; and the sisters Tufton. King Charles was also Shirley's patron. According to a story told by Henry Herbert, Master of the Revels, the king gave Shirley the story idea for *The Gamester*, which was later performed at court and for which event Shirley presumably received a generous reward. Another event suggests the benefit to Shirley of using plays for patronage. In an ironic dedication of *The Bird in a Cage* to William Prynne, author of *Histriomastix* (1632), Shirley defended the queen against the puritan's rabid attack on her playacting; as a result, he secured the commission to write *The Triumph of Peace* for the Inns of Court.

Shirley died in 1666, having lived through the closing of the theatres in 1642, the restoration of Charles II, the return of the country to orthodox Protestantism and the great plague year of 1665. The great fire of 1666, however, proved one disruption too many; both he and his wife reportedly died due to the shock of having been driven from their home by the fire. Shirley's will is evidence of his financial success as playwright but even more of the insurance provided by patronage in a playhouse world destabilised by plague and civil war. Shirley gave legacies of £200, £180 and £150 to his sons, as well as generous bequests to his daughters, wife and friends. To his children, he also gave jewellery, household valuables and clothing. He made several monetary bequests to friends, and a bequest of £5 for the poor of St Dunstan in the West. He left the remainder of his estate to his wife. Shakespeare, it seems, had acquired a more substantial fortune in real estate, but Shirley did well for himself, considering that his profession was officially outlawed for eighteen years.

Commercial playwrights in the generation after Shirley followed his example in making patronage a key to their economic security. Shakespeare, because of his investment in the Chamberlain's / King's Men and their playhouses, was able to amass a comfortable estate; Dekker, with only the products of his pen, lived always on the edge. All three men wrote industriously and co-operatively, alert to the rhythm of audience taste and cultural discourse; they therefore deserved to prosper in their profession. But certain fluctuations in the theatrical market-place were beyond their control. Plague would come, the risk of offending a powerful nobleman was ever-present and a once-generous patron might become fickle. Increasingly, as the theatre lost its popular base and depended more on the support of the elite, playwriting became more a political game than a commercial one.

14

Theatre and controversy, 1603–1642

JANETTE DILLON

Two kinds of theatre were in a state of abeyance during the first year of King James's reign. The first was commercial performance in London, the playhouses having been closed when Elizabeth was dying in 1603, and remaining closed on account of increased plague deaths following James's accession. The second was ceremonial theatre, in that James's coronation pageant had to be postponed until the following year. This too was due to the plague, though it later became clear that James was also personally somewhat unwilling to take part in this public show. The reasons for this absence of theatre in 1603–4 tell us something about how theatre was perceived at the time. Closure on a monarch's death was a measure of the authorities' fearfulness of theatre as a potential instigator of disorder. Not only were plays liable to contain 'dangerous matter' (Henry Herbert's phrase; see again below) that might put ideas into people's heads; they also, regardless of their content, presented the occasion for very large assemblies of people to gather, including those at the lower end of the social scale. Any large gathering might be regarded in times of stress as a riot waiting to happen, and it was not uncommon for theatres to be closed at other times of unrest, as, for example, during the anti-alien riots of summer 1592. When James Burbage first tried to open the Blackfriars for public performance in 1596, residents voiced the same fear as the London authorities, and successfully petitioned against it on the grounds that it would lead to 'the great resort and gathering together of all manner of vagrant and lewd persons that, under colour of resorting to the plays, will come thither and work all manner of mischief'.[1] It was also the fact of the sheer volume of people assembled in one place for public performances that led to the closure of playhouses in times of plague.

This anxiety about theatre as a potential public menace is also evident in the legislation that had accumulated before and during the reign of Elizabeth.

---

1 Gildersleeve, *Government Regulation of the Elizabethan Drama*, 185.

Both the state and the city of London sought to limit theatre's potential to incite disorder in various ways: by forbidding Sunday and Lent playing; by restricting the hours of performance; by attempting to ban performance in particular places; and by setting up systems for the licensing of both plays and players. The details of such legislation make clear that the two most prominent areas of danger, in the eyes of the authorities, were the subject matter of the plays and the nature and size of the audience, and that the two were inextricably tied together. What was considered dangerous subject matter played in English on a public stage might well pass without exception if played in Latin before a university audience. Both the legislation and the circumstances of the new reign foreground perhaps the single most important point about theatre and controversy: the importance of time and place in determining both what could be staged and the meaning of what was staged.

Meanings were being made even during and by the absence of public performance in 1603. One of the king's first acts on coming to England was to adopt the Lord Chamberlain's Men as his own company, the King's Men, and to rename Worcester's Men and the Admiral's Men as Queen Anne's and Prince Henry's Men respectively, thus effectively bringing all the major companies under royal patronage. This could be interpreted both as a stamp of approval and as a way of taking control. (Richard Dutton has argued that it was merely the logical development of a process that built gradually under Elizabeth;[2] but this does not, I think, change the basic point about control, however it came about.) Though the players' status rose as a result of becoming servants of the court, they might also think carefully before biting the hand that fed them. The withholding of the coronation procession was readable, especially after the event, as indicating a certain aloofness in the new monarch. The coronation itself went ahead as planned, on 25 July 1603, but without the ceremonial entry, which finally took place in March 1604. But the royal entry of 1604 was not only detached from the actual coronation, but also cut short at various points so that 'His Majesty should not be wearied with tedious speeches'.[3] According to the seventeenth-century historian, Arthur Wilson, the king made his displeasure in the proceedings evident. At that point, then, it became possible to read events of the preceding year as symptomatic of the new relations between monarch and subjects pertaining from James's accession.

The conditions of the new reign differed in several ways from conditions during Elizabeth's reign. First, the new monarch was a man, following almost

---

2 Dutton, 'Censorship', in Cox and Kastan (eds.), *A New History of Early English Drama*, 297.
3 Thomas Dekker, in *Jacobean Civic Pageants*, ed. Dutton, 115.

fifty years of female reign. This created the space for a completely different kind of mythology and image-making around the royal presence. Where the mythologising of Elizabeth had centred on virgin-goddesses, like Cynthia and Diana, or on the biblical judge, Deborah, James turned to ancient Rome, and in particular to Caesar Augustus, for the images of imperial absolutism that became characteristic of his style. He also saw himself primarily as a peacemaker, and both his domestic and his foreign policies laid great emphasis on harmonising differences. The Hampton Court conference, with its attempt to find a middle way between Catholic and puritan hard-liners, and the Treaty of London, bringing the war with Spain to an end, spoke clearly to the nation on two fronts in 1604. To many of James's English subjects the irony of moving from the potentially emasculating position of being led in war by a mere woman to that of being forced into peace by a man was cruelly disappointing, and the Treaty of London was received with widespread hostility. Adding insult to injury, James also addressed his first parliament in 1604 on the subject of union with Scotland, a project dear to his heart, which again met with a cold reception amongst his English subjects. Disregarding this response, James nevertheless had himself proclaimed king of 'Great Britain' in October of the same year, and the issue continued to dominate subsequent parliamentary sessions for some years.

Another significant difference between James and the Virgin Queen was that James had a wife and three children, including two sons, when he came to the English throne. On the one hand, this meant that the worry about the succession, which had become increasingly insistent in Elizabeth's lifetime, disappeared; but on the other, new causes for concern arose as a result. The court expanded to become virtually three courts (as the titles of the new playing companies indicate), and the costs of supporting the monarch and his family escalated. This king, furthermore, was a foreigner, and not only a Scot, but the son of the Catholic Queen Mary, executed by Elizabeth for plotting against her. This raised worries about the new king's religious and political affiliations, worries which his enthusiasm for union between England and Scotland did nothing to calm. Nor did James's personal style, which combined extravagance with open favouritism and aloofness with imperial aspirations, endear him to his English people.

These concerns can be seen shaping both the subject matter and the reception of the various different kinds of theatre on offer throughout his reign and into the reign of his son, Charles. First impressions of the new reign seem to register surprise at the apparent freedom with which the players commented on politics, religion and the king himself. In June 1604 the French ambassador wrote expressing his own sense of the inappropriateness of such freedom: 'Consider for pity's sake what must be the state and condition of a prince, whom the preachers publicly from the pulpit assail, whom the comedians of the metropolis bring upon the stage, whose wife attends these representations in order to enjoy the laugh against her husband',[4] while Samuel Calvert, in a letter written the following year, was similarly disapproving: 'The play[er]s do not forbear to represent upon their stage the whole course of this present time, not sparing either King, state, or religion, in so great absurdity, and with such liberty, that any would be afraid to hear them.'[5] Yet censorship was unpredictable in these years, and those who gave offence could find that repercussions were much more severe on some occasions than on others (as in the case of *Eastward Ho!*, discussed below).

The King's Men, despite their name and patron, were the first to offend with two plays: *Sejanus* in 1603 and a play about the Gowry conspiracy (an attempt on the king's life in 1600) in 1604. As Jonson told Drummond of Hawthornden, he was called before the Privy Council for his *Sejanus* by his 'mortal enemy', the Earl of Northampton, and 'accused both of popperie and treason by him'.[6] Popery and treason represented the two kinds of subject matter most likely to run into trouble with the authorities: matters of religion and matters of state. From the earliest attempts to legislate for the stage, religion was singled out as a taboo subject, precisely because it was also a matter of state. English monarchs, whether Protestant or Catholic, legislated against public performances touching on the topic of religion. Under Henry VIII the Act for the Advancement of True Religion (1543) allowed the performance of moral plays rebuking vice and promoting virtue provided that they did not 'meddle ... with the interpretacions of Scripture, contrarye to the doctryne set foorth or to be sett foorth by the Kinges Majestie'; under King Edward the Act of Uniformity (1551) outlawed plays attacking the new Book of Common Prayer; under Queen Mary a proclamation of 1553, issued within a month of her accession, fulminated against 'evil disposed persons' who played interludes or wrote books 'concerning doctrine in matters now in question and controversy touching the high points and mysteries of Christian religion' and forbade them to continue; and under Queen Elizabeth, in a proclamation of 1559, a mere

---

4 Chambers, *The Elizabethan Stage*, I, 325.
5 Ibid., I, 325–6.
6 *Conversations with Drummond of Hawthornden*, item 13, in *Ben Jonson*, ed. Herford and Simpson, I, 141.

six months into the reign, matters of 'the governance of the estate of the commonweal' were explicitly paired with matters of religion as 'no meet matters' for plays to deal with.[7]

Sejanus offers an instructively ambivalent lesson on the importance of time and place in shaping the meaning of performance. First, though the play was first performed in 1603–4 (the Folio title page dates the play's first performance to 1603, which in old-style dating means somewhere between 25 March 1603 and 24 March 1604), Jonson may have been writing it over a period of up to two years prior to that. Secondly, it is unclear whether Jonson was indicted in 1603–4, following the play's first performance, or in 1605, following its publication. And thirdly, within the context of these foregoing uncertainties it is impossible to be sure what it was about the play that seemed seditious. One possibility, argued for by Philip Ayres in introducing his edition of the play, is that the primary point of reference was the treason trials of Sir Walter Ralegh and Lord Cobham in late 1603. Since the theatres were closed, however, from March 1603 to April 1604 (as noted above), this argument depends on either the assumption that the play was performed at court or the possibility that the theatres were briefly opened at some point in that year. Others have argued for allusion to the fall of the Earl of Essex, which was certainly the political framework that caused the trouble surrounding Daniel's *Philotas* in 1604. (As Richard Dutton points out, the fall of Essex had continuing resonance at the start of the new reign since it had created the networks of power in force at the Jacobean court.)[8] A final irony, separate from both these arguments, is that the name of Sejanus later came to be understood as a figure for the Duke of Buckingham, and when Buckingham was assassinated in 1628 Jonson was briefly arrested, even though Buckingham could clearly in no way have influenced the writing of the play twenty-five or more years before.[9]

The play, set in classical Rome, which Jonson had used before as a transparent mask for topical allusions, follows the rise and fall of Sejanus at the court of Tiberius and has as its centrepiece a trial scene in which those of whom Sejanus wants to rid himself are set up, accused and condemned in a blatant parody of justice tacitly mocked by Arruntius in a sequence of asides and openly condemned by Silius, one of those on trial:

---

7 Luders et al. (eds.) *Statutes of the Realm*, III, 894; Hughes and Larkin (eds.), *Tudor Royal Proclamations*, II, 5–6, 115.
8 Dutton, *Mastering the Revels*, 170.
9 Patterson, *Censorship and Interpretation*, 56–7.

> This boast of law, and law, is but a form,
> A net of Vulcan's filing, a mere engine,
> To take that life by a pretext of justice
> Which you pursue in malice.
>
> (3.244–7)[10]

The trial scene also contains an attack on censorship itself in Cordus's passionate plea for freedom of speech. His books are burnt regardless of his plea; but the brief exchange that follows makes Jonson's own views clear:

> AFER: It fits not such licentious things should live
> T'upbraid the age.
> ARRUNTIUS: [Aside.] If th'age were good, they might.
>
> (3.467–8)

Yet all these speeches remain in both the quarto (1605) and the folio (1616) editions of the play, and were therefore presumably not thought sufficiently offensive to be eliminated, even though we know the play was cut for printing, since Jonson goes out of his way to make this point in his address to the readers, and thereby to transfer some of the responsibility for offence to an unnamed collaborator: 'I would inform you that this book, in all numbers, is not the same with that which was acted on the public stage, wherein a second pen had good share' (lines 38–40). One of the difficulties of trying to make sense of controversial plays after the event is that the printed text is rarely likely to represent what was performed, and we are not usually in a strong position to second-guess what was cut out and why. Even in the rare cases where a manuscript survives with evidence of the censor's hand, it is not always possible to know which cuts to attribute to censorship and which to other kinds of revision and annotation.[11]

The Gowry play does not survive, which may or may not be accidental. A contemporary letter by John Chamberlain certainly implies censorship.

> the tragedie of Gowrie with all the action and actors hath ben twise represented by the Kings players, with exceeding concourse of all sortes of people, but whether the matter or manner be not well handled, or that yt be thought unfit that princes should be plaide on the stage in theyre life time, I heare that some great counsaillors are much displeased with yt: and so is thought shalbe forbidden.[12]

10 Quotations are from Philip Ayres's edition.
11 See, for example, Anne Lancashire's discussion of the annotations to *The Second Maiden's Tragedy* (1611) in her edition of the play.
12 Gurr, *The Shakespearian Playing Companies*, 290.

Yet both *Sejanus* and the Gowry play must have been licensed for performance in the first place. Active intervention and suppression seem often to have struck in a way unpredictable even to contemporaries; and material extant in printed plays can look either innocent or unaccountably risky to us at this distance. Controversy over whether the differing quarto and folio texts of *King Lear*, for example, represent changes in the performance text, authorial/artistic revision, or evidence of censorship indicate something of the difficulty of really getting at a sense of precisely how time and place situate playtexts.

It was not, however, the King's Men who took the most provocative line in their repertory, but the children's company at the Blackfriars, patronised at the start of the reign by Queen Anne, who granted them a royal patent and appointed Samuel Daniel as their master. The queen, as the French ambassador's comment above suggests, may have had reason to encourage satire against her husband, and it would seem that the issue of a royal patent authorising Daniel to approve the plays performed by the boys successfully bypassed the authority of the Master of the Revels, to which adult companies were routinely subject for the licensing of their plays. The furore caused by *Eastward Ho!* (1605), however, raises some doubt about the legitimacy of their bypassing the Master of the Revels, since Chapman, co-author of the play with Jonson and Marston, apologises in a letter to the lord chamberlain for failure to seek his 'allowance'.[13] One might think, too, that Jonson, having been summoned by the Privy Council with regard to *Sejanus* and previously imprisoned for his share in *The Isle of Dogs* in 1597, was hardly likely to put himself in jeopardy again with another controversial play or to seek to stage provocative matter without a licence, and yet these are precisely the apparent anomalies that confront us. The Blackfriars Children were also willing to go on playing with fire, it seems, in choosing to stage *The Isle of Gulls* the following year. Both the authors and the company paid for their mistakes in 1605–6, however, though this was not always the case. Jonson and Chapman were imprisoned for their part in *Eastward Ho!* (Marston seems to have escaped imprisonment), and the Chapel Children lost the queen's patronage some time in late 1605 or early 1606. The importance of powerful patrons for those engaged in making theatre at this time is demonstrated by the fact that Chapman and Jonson were apparently saved by the intervention of prestigious patrons from the punishment of having their ears and noses cut, and were released from prison.

---

13 Dutton discusses the complex question of authority over the children's companies more fully in *Mastering the Revels*, ch. 7.

What then was the controversial subject matter of *Eastward Ho!* that caused the king to take exception to it? Jonson's *Conversations with Drummond of Hawthornden* briefly allude to 'writting something against the Scots in a play Eastward hoe'; and one of Chapman's letters states that the 'chiefe offences are but two Clawses'.[14] There are indeed two points in the play at which the text seems to have been altered as it was going through the press, pointing respectively to anti-Scottish and anti-court sentiment as the grounds of the offence. The first is the deletion of a reference to:

> a few industrious Scots, perhaps, who, indeed, are dispersed over the face of the whole earth. But, as for them, there are no greater friends to Englishmen and England, when they are out on't, in the world, than they are. And for my part, I would a hundred thousand of 'em were there, for we are all one countrymen now, ye know; and we should find ten times more comfort of them there than we do here.
>
> (3.3.44–52)

The other is the substitution three lines further on of 'any other officer' for 'nobleman' in a passage implying that noblemen have to fawn on their superiors to establish their status.[15]

Yet, as with *Sejanus*, it is a measure of how far our understanding must fall short of adequacy that the offending clauses seem no more offensive than material that stands untampered with in the printed play as we have it. Sir Petronel Flash, for example, embodies an open gibe at the ease with which knighthoods were to be bought under James; and not only does Gertrude's ten-line set-piece on the inadequacies of contemporary knights compared with knights of the past stand uncensored, but so too does even this dialogue between two unnamed gentlemen, the first speaking in a clearly signalled Scottish accent:

> 1 GENTLEMAN: I ken the man weel; he's one of my thirty-pound knights.
> 2 GENTLEMAN: No, no, this is he that stole his knighthood o' the grand day for four pound, giving to a page all the money in's purse, I wot well.
>
> (4.1.197–200)

Equally difficult to come to terms with is the fact that, despite the punitive response to the play in performance, the play was printed three times in 1605. Since the Master of the Revels did not take on responsibility for licensing

---

14 *Conversations*, in *Ben Jonson*, ed. Herford and Simpson, 1, 140; *Eastward Ho!*, ed. Van Fossen, 218. References to the play are to Van Fossen's edition.

15 For possible evidence of further censorship, see Van Fossen's edition of *Eastward Ho!*, 48–9.

plays for print until 1606, the authorities who licensed plays for print and for performance were different, printed books being under clerical control. Even so, it seems unlikely that there would be a vast divergence of views between the two authorities over most issues, and the discrepancy of approach remains puzzling.

Eastward Ho! is an instructive test-case in many ways for the kinds of controversial matter that routinely find their way on to the public stage. Besides dabbling in political waters that on this occasion attracted the attention of the censoring authorities, the play is full of topical satire on everything from affected manners in dress and speech to religious extremism, mercantile thrift and social mobility at every level. It mocks the city as much as the court and makes as much fun of virtue as it does of vice. Touchstone the goldsmith, spouting bourgeois wisdom in tired proverbs and empty phrases, or Golding, his smugly well-behaved apprentice, are as much caricatures as those who glorify themselves above their station, like Touchstone's daughter, Gertrude, and the newly knighted Sir Petronel Flash.

It also engages with theatre itself as a subject of satire and controversy. Quicksilver, the unreliable apprentice, quotes lines from famous plays when he is drunk (2.1), and the play inserts a brief appearance, completely irrelevant to the plot, by a footman called Hamlet, who goes mad (3.2). Its characteristic mode is a flippant and fickle relation between morality and the knowing wink. The play dedicates itself to the city in the prologue and returns to that sober morality in Touchstone's last words to the audience:

> Now, London, look about,
> And in this moral see thy glass run out:
> Behold the careful father, thrifty son,
> The solemn deeds, which each of us have done;
> The usurer punished, and from fall so steep
> The prodigal child reclaimed, and the lost sheep.
>
> (5.5.218–23)

But the epilogue, spoken by Quicksilver, moments after offering himself as a spectacle of the penitent prodigal, happily trashes the moral perspective for a commercial one that compares this show with London's Lord Mayor's show and expresses the hope that the audience will keep coming back for more. It precisely invites them, then, to pursue their pleasures rather than follow the sober example briefly set within the illusion. The fact that the epilogue is apparently spoken with all the characters still on stage highlights the intrusion of one world into another and the impudence with which theatre sometimes chooses in this period to stage its knowingness about its own controversial status.

Four years later, Heywood's *Apology for Actors* tries to reaffirm the argument that plays can be defended as

> either animating men to noble attempts, or attacking the consciences of the spectators, finding themselves toucht in presenting the vices of others. If a morall, it is to perswade men to humanity and good life, to instruct them in civility and good manners, shewing them the fruits of honesty, and the end of villany.[16]

The structure of his treatise, however, targets the children's companies as the fly in the ointment. For Heywood, mounting the moral defence of theatre, the children's companies represent an 'abuse' of theatre's 'quality' which he feels bound to acknowledge and disavow at the close of his treatise:

> The liberty which some arrogate to themselves, committing their bitternesse, and liberall invectives against all estates, to the mouthes of children, supposing their juniority to be a priviledge for any rayling, be it never so violent, I could advise all such to curbe and limit this presumed liberty within the bands of discretion and government. But wise and judiciall censurers, before whom such complaints shall at any time hereafter come, wil not (I hope) impute these abuses to any transgression in us, who have ever been carefull and provident to shun the like.[17]

Heywood's own plays may offer a window onto the kind of coverage of potentially controversial material that was acceptable in his generation. His two-part play on the life of Queen Elizabeth, *If You Know Not Me, You Know Nobody*, for example, produced in 1604–5, was a huge popular success which openly placed itself in both religious and political terrain, but never, so far as extant records show, encountered any hostility from authority. The first part dramatises the life of Princess Elizabeth during the reign of her Catholic sister Mary, and belongs within a genre that derives its authority from Foxe's *Book of Martyrs*, itself both popular and 'safe' during the reign of a Protestant monarch. First published in English in 1563, and dedicated to Queen Elizabeth, Foxe's work came out in a further four editions before 1600 and four more over the next century. Following the second edition of 1570, copies of it were placed alongside the Bible in parish churches and other public places so that all

16 Heywood, *An Apology for Actors from the edition of 1612*, with introduction and notes by J. P. Collier, 53.
17 Ibid., 61.

could have access to it. Plays dramatising its narratives of Protestant martyrdom represented the kind of material likely to have wide popular appeal and unlikely to disturb the authorities except in special circumstances. Heywood is more interested in demonstrating the faith and determination of the princess in her sufferings than in matters of doctrine, and more concerned with the loyalty of most of her English subjects at every social level than with anti-Catholic or anti-foreign polemic. Far from highlighting matters of controversy that might divide English loyalties, the play addresses its audience as though Englishness and Protestantism were virtually indistinguishable and seeks to portray the movement from Mary's reign to Elizabeth's, and from Catholicism to Protestantism, as a miracle worked by God's own hand.

Yet a different historical context and agenda demonstrate how the Foxeian play could stray into unacceptable terrain within the reign of a Protestant monarch. Thomas Drue's *The Duchess of Suffolk* was licensed for performance in 1624. In granting it a licence, Henry Herbert, the Master of the Revels, noted that it, 'being full of dangerous matter was much reformed'.[18] As Jerzy Limon has shown, the theatre season of 1623–4 offered an unprecedented concentration of plays dealing with political matters, primarily foreign policy.[19] (*A Game at Chess*, discussed in chapter 17 below, was one of the plays of this season.) Negotiations between England and Spain regarding a marriage between Prince Charles and the Spanish infanta had been continuing over several years. Many in England were hostile to a Catholic marriage for the prince, and that hostility was exacerbated when, in 1620, James's daughter, Elizabeth, and her husband, Frederick,[20] Elector Palatine and recently elected King of Bohemia, were forced out of Bohemia by the Spanish, within the political context of a conflict that represented the early stages of the Thirty Years' War. As always in this period, religion was inseparable from politics, and James's failure to offer help to his daughter and son-in-law while continuing marriage negotiations with Spain was seen as a betrayal of English Protestantism. Within this context of mounting public hostility the king imposed tougher legislation on freedom of speech and information in an attempt to suppress popular protest.

18 Bawcutt (ed.), *The Control and Censorship of Caroline Drama: the Records of Sir Henry Herbert*, 148.
19 Limon, *Dangerous Matter*.
20 Elizabeth was married to the Protestant Frederick in 1613, as part of a policy on James's part to show even-handedness towards both Catholic and Protestant foreign states. In 1611 James was negotiating this marriage for his daughter alongside a Catholic marriage for his son, Henry, who died in November 1612, shortly before his sister's marriage in February 1613. Elizabeth's Protestant marriage was always more popular in England than the Catholic matches proposed for her brothers.

A proclamation of 24 December 1620 'against excess of Lavish and Licentious Speech of matters of State' had to be reissued seven months later, and a further proclamation 'against the disorderly Printing, uttering, and dispersing of Bookes, Pamphlets, &c' was issued in September 1623, reiterating a Star Chamber decree of 1586.[21] The king also tried to gag the clergy and parliament, ordering clerics not to 'meddle in their sermons with the Spanish match nor any other matter of state' in December 1620 and forbidding parliament to debate foreign policy in 1621, which caused the Commons to petition for renewal of the 'ancient Liberty of Parliament for Freedom of Speech'. Following a further exchange, the Commons' journal recorded their insistence on this as a matter of right. James's response was to tear out the page and dissolve parliament.[22] When Prince Charles and the Duke of Buckingham returned from Spain in October 1623 admitting the failure of the marriage proposal, there was elation in London and a continued keen public interest in political affairs.

The outburst of politically oriented plays in 1623–4 may be seen as both paradoxical and necessary within the context of the regime at its most repressive. The very force with which the king attempted to suppress debate was likely to make the need to speak all the more urgent, though how Thomas Drue originally tried to speak in *The Duchess of Suffolk* cannot be known, since, yet again, the play as we have it is a censored version. Robert Raines has suggested that anti-Catholic, and possibly anti-monarchic, passages have been erased, but Jerzy Limon argues that the censor was more likely to have intervened to tone down the criticism of James's foreign policy, which is left merely implicit in the extant play.[23] The Palatine's (or Palsgrave's) Men, the company who presented it, were appropriately placed to stage a play in support of Frederick and Elizabeth, since Frederick had been their patron since 1612, following the death of Prince Henry. The life of the Duchess of Suffolk, their subject, was taken from Foxe, who included the duchess as an example of a woman active in her support for Protestantism, forced into exile when Queen Mary succeeded her brother Edward in 1553, and unable to return until after Mary's death. Several features of the duchess's life in exile provided parallels with the plight of Frederick's wife, Elizabeth, and various changes made to the facts of her life by the dramatist make his intention to use the material as a veil for dealing

---

21 Larkin and Hughes (eds.), *Stuart Royal Proclamations*, 1, 495–6, 519–21, 583–5.
22 Clare, '*Art Made Tongue-tied by Authority*', 153–4; Patterson, *Censorship and Interpretation*, 76–7.
23 Raines, 'Drue's *The Duchess of Suffolk*', 35–7; Limon, *Dangerous Matter*, 58–9.

with the current situation in Bohemia clear. Like the duchess, Elizabeth had to flee alone, in snow, heavily pregnant, and undergo various sufferings before being offered a home, with her husband and family, by a foreign prince. Jerzy Limon discusses these changes in more detail, arguing that fictional features of Drue's King of Poland (notably his courtship of the duchess and his status as the Protestant ruler of a Protestant country) allow crucial political equations to be made between him and two contemporary figures: Maurice of Nassau, Prince of Orange, who offered shelter to Elizabeth and Frederick, and Frederick himself, an elected king like the Polish king of the play.[24] Within the volatile political climate in which it makes its appearance, the play becomes a propagandist intervention in support of the Protestant cause.

It was not only public theatres and companies like the Palatine's Men, however, that risked staging inflammatory material. The king's own company, whom we already saw in trouble at the beginning of the reign, were responsible for *A Game at Chess* (see chapter 17 below), staged while the king was out of London; and court masques sometimes dared to offer careful critiques to the king himself. We should beware of making simplifying equations between writers, patrons and politics. Just as popular theatre could be conservative and patriotic, so court theatre could be adversarial and push in radical directions. Thomas Scott, author of an anti-Spanish pamphlet, *Vox Populi*, published in 1620, wrote in 1624 that 'Wee see sometimes Kings are content in Playes and Maskes to be admonished of divers things'; but Scott was by that time writing from exile in Utrecht, where he had been forced to flee after overstepping the line in his pamphlet.[25] The new Caroline court staged no court masques for the first five years of the reign (with the possible exception of a birthday masque for the king and/or queen in November 1626), a fact which may have been underpinned by economic considerations, but which, given the context of James's attempt to suppress criticism towards the end of his reign, might also be read as a politic sealing off of the opportunity for expressions of discontent at court. Once masques became more regular again in the early 1630s it is clear that they still had the potential to convey criticism as well as flattery. The figure of Momus in Thomas Carew's *Coelum Britannicum* (1634), for example, offers some pointed allusions to contemporary abuses, and Bulstrode Whitelocke comments of James Shirley's *Triumph of Peace*, performed by the four Inns of Court at the Banqueting House the previous month, that its antimasque 'pleased the Spectators the more, because by it an Information was covertly

24 Limon, *Dangerous Matter*, ch. 2.
25 Butler, 'Reform or reverence?', in Mulryne and Shewring (eds.), *Theatre and Government under the Early Stuarts*, 121.

given to the King, of the unfitness and ridiculousness of these Projects against the Law'.[26]

Under King Charles, most critics agree, it becomes more appropriate to speak of an 'oppositional' drama, and theatre becomes an increasingly important forum for the representation of controversial issues. This is partly demonstrated through the rising number of overtly political plays, but can also be linked to a notable nostalgia for old plays at this time. As Martin Butler has shown, Elizabethan plays could be produced precisely in order to incite scepticism towards current ideology and to invite support for older values seen nostalgically from the political and temporal distance of Caroline England.[27] As in James's reign, the plurality of courts also created the conditions for factionalism. Queen Anne and Prince Henry had on occasion marked their difference from the king through sponsoring masques that gave voice to values that called his own into question;[28] but Charles's queen, Henrietta Maria, seems to have fostered particular interest groups in a much more consistent way. Through much of the 1630s her ties were broadly anti-Spanish and pro-puritan. (As Erica Veevers has shown, this was not a position in conflict either with her Catholicism, which was a moderate form known as Devout Humanism, or with France's political alignment, which was typically with Holland and Sweden rather than Spain.[29]) According to one contemporary, writing in 1630, the court 'was never so full of factions and enmities and emulations as it is now'.[30]

Henrietta Maria's court was strongly female-centred, with that focus primarily fixing on the person of the queen. Like Elizabeth, this queen was happy to surround herself with male courtiers declaring their political allegiance in terms of romantic love and to encourage extravagant expressions of that love. Since Henrietta Maria was also a great lover of theatre and much more active in fostering drama at court than her husband, plays were a favoured medium of expression for the political 'love' her courtiers bore her, and the characteristic dramatic mode was pastoral and platonic. From her arrival in England, Henrietta Maria was actively involved in theatricals, not just as a sponsor, but also as a performer, having been brought up to take part in court theatre in France. It must be remembered, however, that, if theatre itself was a field of

---

26 Orgel and Strong (eds.), *Inigo Jones*, II, 542.
27 Butler, *Theatre and Crisis*, ch. 8.
28 See, for example, Lewalski, *Writing Women in Jacobean England*, 28–43; Butler, 'Courtly negotiations', in Bevington and Holbrook (eds.), *The Politics of the Stuart Court Masque*, 20–40.
29 Veevers, *Images of Love and Religion*, 5–7 and ch. 3.
30 Quoted in Butler, *Theatre and Crisis*, 26.

controversy, women in theatre were especially controversial in England. The position of women, like that of theatre, was already an area of controversy that polarised views in very extreme ways. Public-theatre plays like *The Roaring Girl* (1611), with its redefinition of the cross-dressed heroine, or *The Witch of Edmonton* (1621), with its revisionist attitude towards women and 'witchcraft', are only two among many that stage debate about the place of women. Yet for all the boldness of these two in opposing traditional ideas about silence, chastity and obedience, no English company ever employed female actors, who by definition threatened notions of a woman's place in the home, subject to husband or father. Henrietta Maria and her ladies, however, not only took speaking parts on stage within the first year of Charles's reign, a thing unprecedented in England,[31] but played male roles. The fact that the performance was given before a carefully selected audience did not insulate it from shocked reactions, and several contemporaries commented disapprovingly on seeing women wearing beards and male apparel and hearing the queen herself speak on stage.[32] Yet the gap between the power of queens to remake cultures and the relative impotence of less prestigious agents is made starkly visible by the visit of French actresses to the Blackfriars Theatre three years later. Though spectators flocked to see them, according to William Prynne's report, it was not to applaud them but to barrack them, and they were hissed and pelted from the stage.[33] It was not only in Prynne's eyes that female actors were 'notorious whores' (the phrase is from the index to his *Histriomastix*, discussed below).

The queen's behaviour and Prynne's condemnation of theatre combined to make the issue of women actors a very public controversy that was to cost Prynne his ears. Again, time and place came together in an unforeseeable and highly volatile manner. Though the queen's first performance on stage took place in 1626, her performance in Walter Montague's pastoral, *The Shepherd's Paradise*, in January 1633, happened to coincide closely with the publication of Prynne's *Histriomastix*, a huge volume which Prynne claimed to have begun writing in 1624. This had been licensed for publication in 1630 and gone through most of the printing process before the end of 1632. Bulstrode Whitelocke explains how prelates whom Prynne had angered by his attacks on Arminianism and the powers of bishops went to the king

---

31 Tricomi argues that Queen Anne's household performed imitations of plays they had seen (*Anticourt Drama in England*, 11); but the term 'child plays' in Arabella Stuart's description, as quoted by Tricomi, seems to me more likely to mean children's games than plays. More importantly, they are clearly improvised entertainments, not rehearsed performances.
32 Orgel and Strong, *Inigo Jones*, 1, 384–5.
33 Bentley, *The Jacobean and Caroline Stage*, 1, 25.

the next day after the Queen had acted her Pastoral, shewed Prynne's Book against Plays, to the King, and that place of it, 'Women actors notorious Whores', and they informed the King and Queen, that Prynne had purposely written this Book, against the Queen, and her Pastoral, whereas it was published six weeks before that Pastoral was acted.[34]

At Laud's instigation, according to Whitelocke, Prynne's books were examined and Prynne was prosecuted, charged with 'writting and publishinge a scandalous and a libellous Booke againste the State, the Kinge, and all his people' and encouraging his readers to think 'that ytt is lawfull to laye violent handes uppon Princes that are either actors, favourers, or spectatores of stage playes'.[35]

While he was imprisoned in the Tower, awaiting trial, a play probably also written some years earlier now acquired particular pointedness in this context. James Shirley's *The Bird in a Cage* may have been written in 1629–30, but it was printed early in 1633, and the title page states that it was performed at the Phoenix in Drury Lane (also known as the Cockpit), where Henrietta Maria's Men played. Shirley is described on the title page as 'Servant to Her Majesty', because he was at the time a *valet de chambre* of the queen. The play presents a princess and her ladies agreeing to perform a play and specifically highlights the issue of their sex. Donella, the most forceful of the group, encourages the others to have confidence in their own abilities: 'Doe not distrust your owne performance, I ha knowne men ha bin insufficient, but women can play their parts' (3.3. (p. 42) 1–3),[36] and there are jokes about women wearing beards and playing the parts of kings and gods. The printed edition carries a sarcastic dedication to William Prynne, in his 'happy Retirement' (i.e. imprisonment), in which Shirley delights in warning him how far the printed text must fall short of the pleasures of performance: 'for it comprehending also another *Play* or *Interlude*, personated by Ladies, I must referre to your imagination, *the Musicke, the Songs, the Dancing*, and other varieties, which I know would have pleas'd you infinitely in the Presentment' (lines 9, 18–22).

The wording makes it clear that Prynne was in prison at the time the dedication was written, but he was not sentenced until February 1634. The sentence, when it came, was brutal. The book was condemned to be burned

---

34 Orgel and Strong, *Inigo Jones*, II, 539. Contemporaries differ on the date of Prynne's publication in relation to the performance of *The Shepherd's Paradise*. Sir George Gresley agrees with Whitelocke that *Histriomastix* was printed shortly before the performance, while Justinian Paget says it was published the day after (Bentley, *The Jacobean and Caroline Stage*, IV, 919).

35 Gardiner, *Documents*, I, 2.

36 Quotations from the play are taken from Senescu's edition, which begins each page at line 1.

by the hangman, and Prynne himself was 'to bee degraded of all degrees, eyther att the Universitye or Innes a Courte, to stand on the pillorye att Westminster and Cheape side, to loose an eare att eyther place, to weare papers declareing his offence, and to bee perpetually imprisoned, and paye a fyne of 5000^li [pounds]'. Four years later 'the court examined whether Prin had any eares left', found they were incompletely cropped, ordered the rest to be cut off and reiterated the sentence of lifelong imprisonment.[37] As Annabel Patterson argues, both sides broke the unwritten rules of censorship in this case, Prynne by attacking 'one of his culture's main media of indirection', the drama, and Star Chamber by refusing to accept the usual defence of a gap between intention and interpretation.[38] (Prynne's prosecutors reported that 'Itt is said, hee had noe ill intencion, noe ill harte, but hee maye bee ill interpreted'; but went on to argue that 'That must not bee allowed him in excuse, for he should not have written any thinge that would beare construccion.'[39]) The severity of Prynne's sentence may seem unbelievably harsh at this distance, but is partly explained by the bigger issues underlying the controversy about theatre: issues of class, religion and individual freedom. Prynne was a middle-class puritan, while both Shirley and Henrietta Maria were Catholics, and respectively courtier and queen. Prynne's hostility to theatre not only seemed to fit within a long tradition of Protestant attacks on the theatricality of Catholicism and the depravity of theatre, but, in appearing to target the court as a specific locus of depravity, Prynne also seemed to be mounting an unacceptably impudent attack on his social superiors.

Patterson's point about indirection highlights the fact that, despite the increasingly rigorous legislation inhibiting free speech, theatre was an arena in which the protective armour of fiction and analogy could create a space for the voicing of contentious issues; and because theatre, at least in London, was so widely accessible even to the illiterate, it was perhaps the form that spoke to the largest constituency of the king's subjects. In representing controversial matters as readable from different perspectives it gave audiences ways of thinking about things that might conflict with the conformity that the king attempted to enforce by burning books, instructing preachers what to preach, forbidding discussion of particular topics and punishing those who infringed these edicts. It is worth remembering that, although the theatres did not in fact close until 1642, there were moves from various quarters throughout the period to close them down.

37 Gardiner, *Documents*, 17, 75.
38 Patterson, *Censorship and Interpretation*, 46.
39 Gardiner, *Documents*, 16.

Ironically, *The Bird in a Cage*, though it mocked Prynne, deprived of his liberty, was itself centrally concerned with questions of individual freedom at a time when the increasing absolutism of a monarch determined to rule without parliament was making itself felt. The play's main plot opens with a duke depriving his daughter of her liberty so that she cannot marry without his consent. The scene plays up the princess's sense of outrage at being 'cag'd up' (1.1. (p. 7) 6), and the plot turns to the duke challenging Rolliardo (who is in fact the princess's beloved Philenzo in disguise) to gain access to the imprisoned princess. Again, much is made of Rolliardo's unrestricted movement ('it seemes he makes himselfe free of all places'; 1.1. (p. 11) 32), and images of freedom and imprisonment dominate both the language and the action. Bonamico regains the duke's favour by making him a gift of a huge cage filled with various birds (used to introduce allusions to various contemporary political figures and events); the princess and her ladies take the story of Jupiter and Danae (a princess confined in a seemingly inaccessible tower) as the subject of their interlude; and Rolliardo finally manages to penetrate the princess's captivity by having himself conveyed in Bonamico's birdcage. Rolliardo steps into the princess's view at the moment she opens the cage and declares himself 'the truest Prisoner' (4.2. (p. 57) 34). The comedic ending resolves itself into freedom for both Philenzo/Rolliardo and the princess. If Prynne, in prison, ever saw a text of the play so pointedly dedicated to him, he might have reflected with some bitterness on the relative freedom of princesses, whose loss of liberty in stories is always a prelude to a happy ending, and who, in real life, are freer to break the rules than their social inferiors. Though both sides may have broken the rules, only one party was punished. The other continued to pursue her pleasures at public expense.

Resentment of the king and court and concerns about personal liberty became widespread over the next decade. Increasingly it seemed that the king set himself above the law and that the only way to freedom for ordinary people was in moving out of the established framework of institutions altogether. This is the thrust of Richard Brome's play, *A Jovial Crew*, which, performed in 1641, 'had the luck to tumble last of all in the epidemical ruin of the scene' (Brome's dedication, lines 26–7), meaning that it was performed just before the closing of the theatres.[40] The plot moves around three groupings: Oldrents (whose name denotes his care for his tenants and refusal to move with the times) and his daughters; Justice Clack (who drowns out opposition by incessant monologue) and his son and niece; and the beggars, who find contentment in cutting free

---

40 Quotations from *A Jovial Crew* are taken from Haaker's edition.

of institutionalised social ties, offering duty only where they choose. In the words of Springlove, Oldrents's steward, who rejoins the beggars on the road every summer: 'Where duty is exacted, it is none, / And among beggars, each man is his own' (1.1.258–9).

The politics of the play are overtly hostile to court and city in favour of 'country' values, and the concept of 'nature' is idealised as a criterion for what is right. The court is denounced for its 'tramplings on the country's cost' (2.1.338) at the end of a scene in which Oldrents's daughters denounce the trivialities of elegant social and city life in pursuit of everything the beggars appear to have that they want, namely 'absolute freedom' (2.1.18). On the other hand, the play clearly shows the hardships of the beggars' lives in a state that hounds them as a threat to its own structures. Images of birds, caged and uncaged, recur here, as in Shirley's play, to call attention to the contrast between conditions constructed respectively as imprisonment and freedom; but Brome understands freedom in a much more radical and nuanced way than Shirley, who plays with it as a fictional device without ever putting it to overtly political use. For Brome there seems to be no such thing as the 'absolute freedom' that Oldrents's daughters think they see. Yet it is clear that for him the beggars, despite the fact that they are fugitives from the law, constantly subject to the threat of whipping and dependent for their livelihood on begging from those in positions of power who mostly despise them, are freer subjects than their oppressors.

As in *The Bird in a Cage* too, characters stage a play-within-the-play that represents their own situation as a way of trying to make a point to those characters within the play whose views need changing. But throughout the play, in between the set speeches about behaviour and morality, politics are also coded into lyric form. Spontaneous song and dance characterise the beggars' mode of living and communicate to the audience the sheer pleasures of that existence by contrast with the discontent displayed by the leisured class. The presence of song, dance and theatre within the fiction of the play also highlights Brome's awareness of the parallel to be drawn between beggars and players, constructed as vagabonds by the 1572 statute wherever they could not show a licence or evidence of attachment to a noble patron. The epilogue pointedly draws the analogy between players and beggars, as the actors, no longer 'beggars of the crew' (5.1.503), that is, now standing outside the fictional frame, beg the audience's approval. Controversial theatre here, as so often, is as knowing about itself as it is about the other issues it calls into question.

15

The Stuart masque and its makers

DAVID LINDLEY

There is probably no literary genre more elusive of reconstruction, more fugitive of interpretation, yet more significant as a cultural symptom than the court masque. In its fully developed form it lasted only from 1604 to 1640; the scripts that survive (and by no means all of them do) give a very partial sense of the mix of words, music, scene, dance and audience participation that characterised the entertainments. Dismissed by Francis Bacon (in his essay 'Of masques and triumphs') as 'but toys', and regarded by many outside the court with horror both for their inordinate expense and their supposed encouragement of wantonness, they yet set out to display the magnificence of the court, especially to the foreign ambassadors who competed for invitations, and reported back, with varying degrees of accuracy and enthusiasm, on what they saw. At the same time the techniques of staging and the developments of musical style engendered by these evanescent entertainments were to be of profound significance for theatrical practice in succeeding centuries.

The Stuart masque most often formed a central part of the court's extended Christmas festivities, alongside plays and other entertainments, though they were also performed at other times of the year, and frequently celebrated significant political events – the investiture of Prince Henry as Prince of Wales in 1610, or the marriage of Princess Elizabeth in 1613, for example. The genre was dominated by two figures   Ben Jonson, who provided the words for the majority of Jacobean masques, and Inigo Jones, the designer (appointed Surveyor of the King's Works in 1615). Their combative and frequently acrimonious partnership began in 1605, with *The Masque of Blackness*, and continued until *Chloridia* in 1631. After that date Jones himself took the dominant role in the invention of the devices of the masque, in partnership with a number of different authors. Though these two names most frequently figure in discussion of the genre there were many others, musicians and dancing masters as well as other poets, whose contribution was of central, if often undervalued, importance.

At the heart of every masque was the entry of masked figures who first performed specially designed dances, and then took out members of the audience to dance in 'the revels'. Masquers were generally courtiers, who did not themselves usually speak. Their roles were explained by allegorical figures, often personated by professional actors, and, as the genre developed, their arrival was prefaced by one or more 'antimasques' functioning, as Jonson put it in his preface to *The Masque of Queens* (1609), as 'a foil or false masque', a 'spectacle of strangeness' which set in relief the virtues symbolised by the main masquers.[1] The development and variation of the relationship between antimasque(s) and main masque was to be a central feature of the genre throughout its history; it might be one of dialectical opposition, in which the vices of the antimasque are overturned by the glowing presence of the virtues of the main masquers, or it might involve a more complex narrative of reformation in which excess is redirected. In the later Jonsonian masques antimasques frequently operate as 'realistic' comedic preludes, and in the Caroline masques the sequence of comic or grotesque entries of antimasques was much elaborated.

The Stuart masque did not, however, emerge *ex nihilo*. The main entry of masquers had its roots in 'disguisings' or 'mummings' which can be traced back into the Middle Ages, and were an often anarchic part of Christmas revelry at every level of society. Throughout the Tudor period there are records of revels at court involving variously disguised masquers, both male and female, who might be drawn in upon 'pageants' or wagons, parade through the hall, offer gifts to the monarch, dance and then invite spectators to join them. On occasion the monarch might participate in the masque itself. In 1512 Henry VIII and eleven of his court, according to Edward Hall,

> were disguised, after the maner of Italie, called a maske, a thyng not seen afore in Englande, thei ... came in, with six gentlemen disguised in silke bearyng staffe torches, and desired the ladies to daunce, some were content, and some that knew the fashion of it refused, because it was not a thyng commonly seen. And after thei daunced and commoned together, as the fashion of the Maskes is, thei toke their leave and departed.[2]

Shakespeare's *Love's Labour's Lost* presents us with just such a simple disguising, when, in act 5 scene 2, the King of Navarre and his fellows attempt to prosecute

---

1 Lindley (ed.), *Court Masques*, 35, lines 12, 17. Where possible, references throughout the essay are to this (*CM*), and the other most widely available anthology of masque texts: Spencer and Wells (eds.), *A Book of Masques* (*BM*). Also referred to is Orgel and Strong (eds.), *Inigo Jones* (*IJ*). (Orgel and Strong reproduce all Jones's extant drawings and designs for the masque, and are an essential resource.)

2 Welsford, *The Court Masque*, 130.

their love of the Princess and her ladies by entering disguised as Muscovites, though their efforts at 'commoning together' are comically undercut since the ladies themselves have donned masks. Enid Welsford suggested that it was this element of 'commoning' or conversing that gave novelty to Henry VIII's entry, and love was to remain a constant theme of the masque. Indeed it was precisely the opportunity that the masque's dances seemed to provide for amorous conversation that in part prompted hostility to the genre. The Stuart masque is always aware of its vulnerability to such attacks, and frequently negotiates carefully the moment when masquers take out the members of the audience in the revels. In *Pleasure Reconciled to Virtue* (1618), for example, the masquers are instructed:

> Go, choose among, but with a mind
> As gentle as the stroking wind
>   Runs o'er the gentler flowers;
> And so let all your actions smile,
> As if they meant not to beguile
>   The ladies, but the hours.
> Grace, laughter, and discourse may meet,
>   And yet the beautie not go less;
> For what is noble should be sweet,
>   But not dissolved in wantonness.
>
>   (*CM*, 124)

In the Caroline masque the theme of love was further developed, as the platonic love between Charles and his queen, Henrietta Maria, became a politicised emblem of the harmony of court and nation, and the purification of passion is a central theme in masques such as Townshend's *Tempe Restored* and Carew's *Coelum Britannicum*. The frequency with which masques allegorise the amatory implications of the dance underlines, even as it attempts to control, the awareness that the masque was always at bottom the occasion for a party – a party that could get out of hand, as in the infamous pageant presented to Christian IV of Denmark at Theobalds in 1606, memorably recorded by Harington: 'The entertainment and show went forward, and most of the presenters went backward, or fell down; wine did so occupy their upper chambers.'[3]

But if at one level the masque was a communal celebration, at the same time it drew upon a long tradition whereby court entertainments reflected directly upon the current political situation. In the context of a discussion of 'Devices to be shewed before the quenes Majesty by waye of maskinge, at Nottingham

---

3 McLure (ed.), *The Letters and Epigrams of Sir John Harington*, 119.

castell, after the meteinge of the quene of Scottes' in 1562, W. R. Streitberger observes that 'by long established precedent in the Tudor period revels held to celebrate state occasions of this kind were connected thematically to the substance of the negotiations'. As he explains: 'The political and diplomatic subjects that Elizabeth I and Mary were to negotiate are dealt with principally through a moral allegory complete with personified abstractions, a struggle between virtues and vices, and a poetic debate which is referred to as stylised combat.'[4] In an analogous fashion the Elizabethan entertainments of which the most complete accounts survive, those produced by courtiers to entertain the queen on her progresses during the summer months, coupled extravagant praise of the monarch with advice or instruction offered to her. So, for example, the Earl of Leicester in his entertainments at Kenilworth in 1575, and again at Wanstead in 1578 (in Sidney's *Lady of May*), made coded efforts to bid for the royal hand. Obviously advice had to be offered cautiously – Queen Elizabeth was quite capable of reacting directly and angrily to what she construed as presumptuous address: she stormed out early from Kenilworth, and pointedly honoured the 'wrong' figure at Wanstead. But the delicate balance between praise and advice, the negotiation between the sponsor of the entertainment and the monarch to whom it was offered, so conspicuous in these progress entertainments, remain constant features of the court masque throughout its history.

The allegorical representation of the politics of Elizabethan courtiership, in which the abstractions of medieval courtly romance jostled with classical deities, was continued in the next century. Indeed the allegorical habit of mind was pervasive in tiltings and tournaments, the annual series of Lord Mayor's pageants in the City of London, and masque-like entertainments in other environments – at the Inns of Court, or in the houses of substantial families far away from London. The court masque, in this respect, is but a particular symptom of a general practice, and one not, of course, specific to England. Hall attributed the fashion of Henry's 1512 masquing to Italy, and continental practice exerts a powerful influence throughout the whole period. The international dimension of court culture has been somewhat marginalised in a good deal of recent criticism of the masque, but the effects of Burgundian, French and Italian entertainments on the shape and design of English court revels was substantial. Jones's designs derive from the published descriptions of French and particularly Italian entertainments, and were deeply influenced by his journey to Rome in 1614–16. And even though Jonson was ostensibly

4 Streitberger, 'Devising the revels', *Early Theatre* 1 (1998), 55–74, 62.

contemptuous of things Italian, a number of his masques – from *Hymenaei* in 1605 to *Chloridia* in 1631 – derive details from Italian entertainments.[5] Campion's *Lords' Masque* of 1613 drew upon the Florentine intermedii, and Townshend's 1633 masque, *Tempe Restored*, was a rewriting of perhaps the most famous of French entertainments, the *Ballet Comique de la Reine* (1581). Nicholas Lanier, one of the important composers of music for the masque, also travelled on the continent and his style may have been influenced by his exposure to the Italian avant-garde. Queen Anne and Queen Henrietta Maria, each of great importance to the evolution of the genre, themselves brought their continental experience to bear upon the masques in which they performed. At every level the English court entertainments placed themselves competitively within a European context.

The court masque, then, was deeply embedded in traditions of celebration and habits of representation which had a long history. What perhaps more than anything gave the Stuart masque its particular character, however, was the imperiousness with which Ben Jonson sought to impose upon these disparate elements an intellectual and philosophical rigour. In the preface to *Hymenaei* (1605) he provided the clearest statement of his aims, and familiar though it is, its centrality is such that it is worth quoting in its entirety:

It is a noble and just advantage that the things subjected to understanding have of those which are objected to sense, that the one sort are but momentary and merely taking, the other impressing and lasting. Else the glory of all these solemnities had perished like a blaze and gone out in the beholders' eyes. So short lived are the bodies of all things in comparison of their souls. And though bodies oft-times have the ill luck to be sensually preferred, they find afterwards the good fortune, when souls live, to be utterly forgotten. This it is hath made the most royal princes and greatest persons (who are commonly the personators of these actions) not only studious of riches and magnificence in the outward celebration or show (which rightly becomes them) but curious after the most high and hearty inventions to furnish the inward parts, and those grounded upon antiquity and solid learnings; which, though their voice be taught to sound to present occasions, their sense or doth or should always lay hold on more removed mysteries. And howsoever some may squeamishly cry out that all endeavour of learning, and sharpness in these transitory devices especially, where it steps beyond their little or (let me not wrong 'em) no brain at all, is superfluous, I am contented these fastidious stomachs should leave my full tables and enjoy at home their clean empty trenchers, fittest for such airy tastes; where perhaps a few Italian herbs picked up and made into a salad

5 See Peacock, 'Ben Jonson and the Italian festival books', in Mulryne and Shewring (eds.), *Italian Renaissance Festivals*, 271–88.

may find sweeter acceptance than all the most nourishing and sound meats of the world. For these men's palates let me not answer, O muses. It is not my fault if I fill them out nectar and they run to metheglin. (CM, 10)

Jonson here recognises the primary function of the masque to declare the 'magnificence' of the court in its 'outward show', but his preface is directed principally at countering the transitoriness of the single night's entertainment by claiming that if the device is founded upon some 'removed mystery', an allegorical programme validated by its learning, then it has the capacity to reach beyond its moment, to affect and to educate its performers and beholders. In his claim for the efficacy of such learning Jonson echoes the neo-platonic aspiration of French court entertainments in the latter part of the sixteenth century which sought, through the union of myth, poetry and music, to recover the transformative moral effects imagined as having been possible in the art of Ancient Greece.[6] From such a perspective the outward show of the masque shadows moral truth, and elicits from the spectator a response generated by that higher reality. It is this belief which underlies, for example, Jonson's verses accompanying the dancers in *Pleasure Reconciled to Virtue* (1618):

> For dancing is an exercise
>   Not only shows the mover's wit,
> But maketh the beholder wise,
>   As he hath power to rise to it.
>   (CM, 123)

This moral, educative ambition conditioned all Jonson's masques, and the seriousness with which he viewed their proper foundation in 'solid learning' is evident in the extensive annotation of a number of his published masques. In his dedication of a manuscript of *The Masque of Queens* to Prince Henry, Jonson explained that he had provided the commentary (so elaborate that it threatens to overwhelm his text) at the prince's request, and complimented him as one of those 'who do not only honour [Poetry] with your ear, but are curious to examine her with your eye and enquire into her beauties and strengths' (CM, 226). As in the preface to *Hymenaei*, Jonson is fully aware that not all his audience cared for the 'removed mysteries' he so carefully constructed, and his anxiety is echoed by Campion in *The Lords' Masque* (1613, BM, 107) and by Chapman in his preface to *The Memorable Masque* (1613, CM, 79). The

---

6 For a detailed discussion of the French entertainments see Yates, *The French Academies of the Sixteenth Century*, especially chs. 3 and 11.

surviving reports of responses to entertainments certainly suggest that they were right to suspect that the audience's attention was only too likely to focus upon the richness of costume and display rather than attending to abstruse mythological programmes. But Samuel Daniel objected more profoundly to Jonson's aggressive learning in his preface to *Tethys' Festival* (1610), where he wrote:

> And shall we who are the poor engineers for shadows and frame only images of no result, think to oppress the rough censures of those who, notwithstanding all our labour, will like according to their taste, or seek to avoid them by flying to an army of authors as idle as ourselves? (*CM*, 55)

In the masque itself Daniel articulates his views in one of the songs:

> And can shadows pleasure give?
> Pleasures only shadows be
> Cast by bodies we conceive,
> And are made the things we deem,
> In those figures which they seem.
> But these pleasures vanish fast,
> Which by shadows are expressed.
> Pleasures are not, if they last,
> In their passing is their best.
> Glory is most bright and gay
> In a flash, and so away.
> Feed apace then, greedy eyes,
> On the wonder you behold.
> Take it sudden as it flies,
> Though you take it not to hold.
> When your eyes have done their part,
> Thought must length it in the heart.
> (*CM*, 63)

In this exquisite lyric Daniel subverts, even reverses Jonson's claims; here it is precisely the evanescence of the show and the transitoriness of the pleasure it generates which validate the bravery of the night. (Shakespeare also reflected on this debate in *The Tempest*, where the dissolution of Prospero's act 4 masque for Ferdinand and Miranda provokes his famous speech: 'Our revels now are ended. . .'.) Daniel's contest with Jonson was not merely a conflict of personality; in their opposed views of the nature and function of the masque they reflect debates also prosecuted on the continent about the nature of courtly entertainment.[7] But he was certainly aiming directly at his opponent when he concluded his preface with these words:

> But in these things wherein the only life consists in show, the art and invention of the architect gives the greatest grace, and is of most importance, ours the least part and of least note in the time of the performance thereof; and therefore have I interserted the description of the artificial part, which only speaks Master Inigo Jones. (CM, 55)

In the Jonsonian aesthetic of the masque the 'show' belonged to its 'body', not its 'soul'. In his embittered 'An Expostulation with Inigo Jones', written after the final collapse of their partnership, he ironically exclaimed:

> O shows! Show! Mighty shows!
> The eloquence of masques! What need of prose,
> Or verse, or sense, to express immortal you?[8]

But, as has been recognised more and more in recent years, Jones himself was committed to a view of spectacle informed by exactly the same neo-platonic theories as Jonson brought to bear on the texts of the masque.[9] So, for example, in *Tempe Restored* (1632) the entry of the masquers showed 'the magnificence of the court of England' (CM, 160), but the purpose of the costume of Henrietta Maria, who figured Divine Beauty, was 'that corporeal beauty, consisting in symmetry, colour, and certain unexpressible graces, shining in the Queen's majesty, may draw us to the contemplation of the Beauty of the soul, unto which it hath analogy' (CM, 164) (see figure 29). But more can be claimed for Jones's work than this. As John Peacock puts it:

> Jones's contribution to the masques is doubly didactic: his teaching is aesthetic as well as moral. Not only is he using 'picture', in collaboration with Jonson's poetry, to communicate philosophical, ethical and political ideas; he is inducing his audience to revise radically their ideas about what 'picture' is, to adopt a wholly new concept of visual art.[10]

The stage for the masque had to be erected quickly in the halls employed for the entertainments, and equally quickly dismantled afterwards, yet for thirty-five years Jones continuously developed techniques of staging and display, informed

7 See Peacock, 'Ben Jonson's masques and Italian culture', in Mulryne and Shewring (eds.), *Theatre of the English and Italian Renaissance*, 73–92.
8 *Ben Jonson*, ed. Donaldson, 463, lines 39–41.
9 See Gordon, 'Poet and architect', in Orgel (ed.), *The Renaissance Imagination*, 77–101, and the introduction to *IJ*.
10 Peacock, *The Stage Designs of Inigo Jones*, 6–7.

Figure 29 Henrietta Maria as Divine Beauty from *Tempe Restored* (1632)

by neo-classical theory and continental practice, that were to become part of the standard scenic vocabulary of the theatre for the next 250 years. It was he who introduced the use of perspective scenes, and, as has frequently been pointed out, they were designed to be viewed from the position directly in front of the stage, where the monarch was placed, emphasising the controlling vision of the principal spectator.

The masque was founded upon transformation, and Jones steadily sophisticated the means by which such transformation could be executed. In the early years he relied upon the *machina versatilis*, or 'turning machine'. It was employed, for example, in *The Masque of Queens*, where, as the antimasque of witches gave way to the entry of heroic queens:

> the whole face of the scene altered, scarce suffering the memory of any such thing. But in the place of it appeared a glorious and magnificent building, figuring the House of Fame, in the top of which were discovered the twelve masquers, sitting upon a throne triumphal, erected in form of a pyramid, and circled with all store of light. (CM, 45)

Then, after Heroic Virtue introduces the masquers:

> Here the throne wherein they sat, being *machina versatilis*, suddenly changed, and in the place of it appeared *Fama Bona* as she is described in *Iconologia di Cesare Ripa*, attired in white with white wings, having a collar of gold about her neck and a heart hanging at it; which Orus Apollo in his *Hieroglyphica* interprets the note of a good fame [see figure 30]. (CM, 46)

From 1611 onwards, however, Jones moved increasingly to a more flexible mode of transformation, the *scena ductilis*, or series of painted flats set in grooves on the stage, which could be opened in turn to reveal a sequence of varied scenes (see figure 31). The variety of scene also encompassed the use of upper and lower levels, for, as Orgel and Strong observe, 'cloud machines and flying devices played the crucial role in establishing the reality of the masque's apotheoses' (IJ, 18). From the appearance of the moon goddess in *The Masque of Blackness* in 1605 'in the upper part of the house, triumphant on a silver throne' (CM, 5) to *Salmacida Spolia's* discovery of Henrietta Maria in 'a huge cloud of various colours... descending to the midst of the scene' in 1640 (CM, 210), the exploitation of 'heavenly' discovery played a large part in many of the masques. After 1631, when the stage included a fly gallery for the first time, such aerial scenes became ever more complex. The provision of quasi-magical visual 'wonders' was very much part of the masque designer's purpose, and the descriptions of masques are full of testimony to the excitement of the spectators at such spectacular effects. In Campion's *Lords' Masque*, for example:

> According to the humour of this song, the Stars moved in an exceeding strange and delightful manner, and I suppose few have ever seen more neat artifice than Master Inigo Jones showed in contriving their motion. (BM, 110)

And twenty years later, in *Coelum Britannicum*, Jones produced a hill from under the stage which 'by little and little grew to be a huge mountain' and

Figure 30 The House of Fame from *The Masque of Queens* (1609)

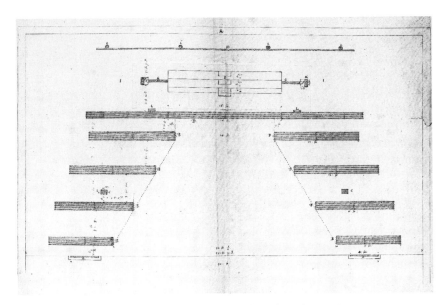

Figure 31 The floor plan to *Salmacida Spolia* (1640)

'gave great cause of admiration, but especially how so huge a machine, and of that great height, should come from under the stage, which was but six foot high' (*CM*, 187, 189).

It is important, however, to remember that such descriptions do not necessarily give the whole truth. In Campion's *Lord Hay's Masque* the masquers, encased in trees, sank, we are told, by means of 'an engine placed under the stage. When the trees had sunk a yard, they cleft in three parts, and the masquers appeared out of the tops of them' (*CM*, 28–9). But in a rare moment of honesty Campion in a side-note recorded:

> Either by the simplicity, negligence, or conspiracy of the painter, the passing away of the trees was somewhat hazarded, the patterns of them the same day having been shown with much admiration, and the nine trees being left unset together even to the same night.   (*CM*, 224)

The picture of noble masquers struggling to get themselves out of the trees is wonderfully deflationary. But the elaborate machinery on which the masque's transformations depended must have been frequently clumsy and noisy. The Florentine ambassador, for example, reported on Campion's *Somerset Masque* that 'the music done, the Florentine engineer [Constantino de Servi] let drop his portcullis and the lords came down without any music, with no other sound but the screeching of the wheels'.[11]

As the ambassador suggests, music could serve the functional purpose of covering the noise of machinery, but as symbol and enactment of cosmic harmony, and as an imagined reflection or representation of the music of the spheres, it underpinned the philosophical designs of Jonson and Jones at a much more profound level. In many masques the musicians appear as priests, or servants of Harmony, and their songs and music do not merely accompany the action, but in important respects seem to initiate it – particularly at the moments of transformation where, as Peter Walls has pointed out, songs 'use imperative verbs – a way of insisting that the songs themselves effect the transformations'.[12] The interaction of words, scene and music is dramatised in Campion's *Lords' Masque*, where Entheus (poetry) and Orpheus (music) are joined by Prometheus, who symbolises the visual display of the masque. Entheus appeals to him:

> Patron of mankind, powerful and bounteous,
> Rich in thy flames, reverend Prometheus,
> In Hymen's place aid us to solemnise
> These royal nuptials; fill the lookers' eyes
> With admiration of thy fire and light.

To which Prometheus replies:

> Entheus and Orpheus, names both dear to me,
> In equal balance I your third will be
> In this night's honour.   (*BM*, 109)

This 'equal balance' is important, for, as Peter Walls suggests, Jones's neo-classical architectural principles of proportion were themselves cognate with, even derived from, musical theory.[13] The symbiotic relationship of music, words and spectacle is enacted in the final moments of *Salmacida Spolia*, where:

the scene was changed into magnificent buildings composed of several selected pieces of architecture. In the furthest part was a bridge over a river, where many people, coaches, horses and such like were seen to pass to and fro. Beyond this on the shore were buildings in prospective, which, shooting far from the eye, showed as the suburbs of a great city.

---

11 Orrell, 'The agent of Savoy at *The Somerset Masque*', *Review of English Studies* 28 (1977), 303.
12 Walls, *Music in the English Courtly Masque*, 47.
13 Ibid., ch. 5, 'Music for the eyes'.

Figure 32 The apotheosis of *Salmacida Spolia* (1640)

From the highest part of the heavens came forth a cloud far in the scene, in which were eight persons richly attired, representing the spheres. This, joining with two other clouds which appeared at that instant full of music, covered all the upper part of the scene; and at that instant, beyond all these, a heaven opened full of deities; which celestial prospect, with the chorus below, filled all the whole scene with apparitions and harmony [see figure 32].

(*CM*, 211–12)

The words of the song which accompanied this transcendent vision of a transformed London turned spectacle into political instruction:

> *To the King and Queen by a chorus of all*
> So musical as to all ears
> Doth seem the music of the spheres,
> Are you unto each other still,
> Tuning your thoughts to either's will.
>
> All that are harsh, all that are rude,
> Are by your harmony subdued;
> Yet so into obedience wrought
> As if not forced to it, but taught.

The translation of music into an emblem of the harmony engendered by the monarch was a familiar trope, but while we have the description of the scene, and an illustration of Jones's design, of the music, composed by Lewis Richard, Master of her Majesty's Music, no trace survives. This is not untypical. Even if music was published, as, for example, were some of Alfonso Ferrabosco's songs for the earlier Jonsonian masques, it was adapted for domestic consumption, and most of the manuscript material that does survive is represented in an outline form (usually tune and bass line) which gives little sense of how it might have sounded. Many further problems attend the attribution of such dance tunes as are still extant to particular masques.[14] Yet the experience of the music made a major contribution to the event at every level. Able to draw on the singers of the Chapel Royal, and the full resources of the royal musical establishments, as well as on musicians from the theatres, composers had at their disposal a range of resources unavailable in any other place. Thomas Campion, himself a musician as well as poet, left the most comprehensive description of the scope and arrangement of these resources in his account of *Lord Hay's Masque*:

> The great hall (wherein the masque was presented) received this division and order: the upper part, where the cloth and chair of State were placed, had scaffolds and seats on either side continued to the screen; right before it was made a partition for the dancing place, on the right hand whereof were consorted ten musicians with bass and mean lutes, a bandora, a double sackbut and an harpsichord, with two treble violins. On the other side, somewhat nearer the screen, were placed nine violins and three lutes; and, to answer both the consorts (as it were in a triangle) six cornetts and six Chapel voices were seated almost right against them, in a place raised higher in respect of the piercing sound of those instruments.   (CM, 20–1)

Together with the singers and instrumentalists who performed in the masque itself, there were, as Campion proudly tells us, a total of forty-two musicians who combined in the masque's climactic praise of King James. Used as we are to symphony orchestras and ear-bursting electronic excess, it is easy to underestimate the visual and aural opulence of this sound to the Stuart audience; but the unparalleled assembly of musicians in the Christmas entertainments contributed as much as the richness of costume and elaboration of the setting to the declaration of the magnificence of the court.

---

14 See ibid., *passim*. The ascription of music to masques in Sabol, *Four Hundred Songs and Dances from the Stuart Masque* – the main modern source for the music – has been much challenged.

Like Jonson and Jones, composers brought a purposeful innovation to their work. Because songs commented on or directly initiated the action of the masque, composers were led towards a style which ensured the audibility of the words. Whether or not the English masque composers were directly influenced by continental developments in declamatory style has been a subject of some contention amongst musicologists, but the presence of many foreign musicians in the royal musical establishment and the continental travels of a number of composers make it likely that, just as Jones was profoundly influenced by the architecture and theatrical designs of Italy, musicians too naturalised a continental musical style – even if Orazio Busino, chaplain to the Venetian embassy, in his report on *Pleasure Reconciled to Virtue*, was rather sniffy, remarking that 'this performance was not much to our taste, accustomed as we are to the elegant and harmonious music of Italy' (*IJ*, 283). In the 1640 Folio of Jonson's works it is claimed that Nicholas Lanier's music for *The Vision of Delight* and *Lovers Made Men* (both 1617) was sung in *stylo recitativo*, and, though the absence of this direction in the 1617 quarto of the latter work has led some to doubt its veracity, it would seem probable that the masque saw the arrival in England of this innovative style, later to be developed in Restoration opera.

The musical world of the main masque, then, had a self-conscious novelty and refinement, often explicitly contrasted with the sounds of the antimasque, where grotesque or comic figures were frequently accompanied with a miscellany of percussion instruments, or with unspecified 'wild music', demarcating the territory of difference.[15] In *Britannia Triumphans*, for example, the first antimasque to emerge from the suburbs of hell was 'of a mock-music of five persons . . . one with a viol, the rest with: tabor and pipe, knackers and bells, tongs and key, gridiron and shoeing horn' (*IJ*, 664), for some of which Jones's drawings survive (see figure 33).

Many of the most important musicians of the period were involved in composing for and performing in the masque, and if even the work that survives of Ferrabosco, Lanier, William and Henry Lawes, for example, is little known today, they deserve to be acknowledged as highly significant 'makers' of the genre. But if these figures are shadowy, those who choreographed the dances for antimasque and masque have almost entirely disappeared from view. Their importance to the event can be measured by the fact that they were frequently paid more for their services even than Jonson or Jones, yet they are only fitfully acknowledged in the published texts, and until very recently have been largely

---

15 See Walls, *Music in the English Courtly Masque*, chs. 2 and 3, and Lindley, 'The politics of music in the masque', in Bevington and Holbrook (eds.), *The Politics of the Stuart Court Masque*, 273–95.

Figure 33 Antimasquer with bells and knackers

ignored by scholars. Yet, as Tom Bishop trenchantly observes, 'dancing was where the real action was', and in the elegant novelty of masque dancing 'the hieroglyphics of invention, the elaborated learning, the machinery of the *impresa* are condensed and absorbed into the body and make their address through it'.[16]

The dances for the masque fall into three distinct categories. First, the antimasque dances, then the choreographed dances of the masquers themselves, and finally the social dancing which occupied the greater part of the

16 Bishop, 'Tradition and novelty in the Jacobean masque', in Bevington and Holbrook (eds.), *The Politics of the Stuart Court Masque*, 96, 98.

evening. Though the texts give little precise sense of the way these dances were performed, antimasques seem to have been marked by exaggerated and 'indecorous' movement, such as that described in Campion's *Lords' Masque*:

> At the sound of a strange music twelve Frantics enter, six men and six women, all presented in sundry habits and humours . . . that made an absolute medley of madness; in midst of whom Entheus (or Poetic Fury) was hurried forth and tossed up and down, till by virtue of a new change in the music the Lunatics fell into a mad measure, fitted to a loud fantastic tune.   (*BM*, 106–7)

In the Caroline masque, under the influence of French fashion, the sequence of antimasque dances was much elaborated – in *Salmacida Spolia* there are no less than twenty 'entries' of various kinds of eccentrics, grotesques and foreigners, 'all which antimasques were well set out and excellently danced, and the tunes fitted to the persons' (*CM*, 207).

The dances of the courtly masquers themselves were designed to contrast with the ebullience of the actors in the antimasques, declaring the dignity of the aristocratic performers and attempting to reflect symbolically the theme of the entertainment. For several weeks before the performance the masquers were occupied in intensive rehearsal – leading on occasion to amabassadorial complaints about the unavailability of important court figures. (Indeed, if Chamberlain is to be believed, it could be a life-threatening business – he attributes the death of Henry Bowyer in 1613 to his over-exertion in rehearsal for the marriage of Frances Howard and Robert Carr.) These dances seem often to have traced geometrical figures – as in *The Masque of Queens* where the dancers spelled out the letters of the name of Prince Charles – but beyond that nothing is known of their detailed choreography. The music for these dances was probably contrived by the dancing masters themselves from their repertoire of conventional musical phrases – most of the dance tunes that survive are musically rather undistinguished. Nonetheless, virtually unknown though they now are, dancing masters such as Jeremy Herne, Thomas Giles, Nicolas Confesse and Jacques Bochan amongst others played a major role in bringing to life the 'curious mazes' of the masquers' dances, and, since many of them were French, imported the fashionable styles of continental dancing to England.

International fashions undoubtedly affected, too, the dances of the revels. It is easy to underplay the importance of these social dances, for though they are represented in the printed texts by a single word or brief sentence, they might last for several hours, and provided significant opportunity for courtiers to make their mark. Some sense of what might be at stake during the revels is indicated by Busino's account of *Pleasure Reconciled*:

> They did all sorts of ballets and dances of every country, such as passemeasures, corantos, canaries, Spanish dances, and a hundred other beautiful turns to delight the fancy. Finally they danced the Spanish dance once more with their ladies, and because they were tired began to lag; and the King, who is by nature choleric, grew impatient and shouted loudly, 'Why don't they dance? What did you make me come here for? Devil take all of you, dance!' At once the Marquis of Buckingham, his majesty's favourite minion, sprang forward, and danced a number of high and very tiny capers with such grace and lightness that he made everyone admire and love him, and also managed to calm the rage of his angry lord. Inspired by this, the other masquers continued to display their powers one after another, with different ladies, concluding with capers, and lifting their goddesses from the ground. We counted 34 capers in succession cut by one knight, but none matched the splendid technique of the Marquis.
> (*IJ*, 283)

It was precisely the possibility of self-advancement through such courtly display which prompted Sir John Holles to instruct his son as he set out for France to 'practice your riding, weapon and dancing seriously and diligently that you may be a proficient and master in each occupation, all which qualities adorn not only, but are so necessary to a young gentleman, as who can not express himself in them as he ought shall be disesteemed'.[17] The *sprezzatura* of Castiglione's ideal courtier, manifested in graceful ease and confident role-playing, was an important means of securing attention and place at the Stuart court.

The court masque, then, was a synthesis of different arts, a fusion of the fashionably up-to-date with longstanding traditional elements, a genre with high aspiration to learning and moral education, and yet at the same time an expensive celebration which acted as an arena for courtly display and individual self-promotion. It was also a profoundly occasional event. As Chapman observed: 'all these courtly and honouring inventions...should expressively arise out of the places and persons for and by whom they are presented' (*CM*, 79), and in recent years the masque's reflection of and intervention in the political culture of the period has been central to critical discussion. In his important and highly influential book, *The Illusion of Power*, Stephen Orgel asserts: 'Masques were essential to the life of the Renaissance court; their allegories gave a higher meaning to the realities of politics and power, their

---

17 Quoted in Ravelhofer, 'Unstable movement codes in the Stuart masque', in Bevington and Holbrook (eds.), *The Politics of the Stuart Court Masque*, 255.

fictions created heroic roles for the leaders of society.'[18] The praise of the monarch was not merely a central element of the text of the masque, but in it 'the ruler gradually redefines himself through the illusionist's art, from a hero, the center of a court and a culture, to the god of power, the center of a universe'.[19] This powerful view of the masque as a coercive idealisation of an increasingly absolutist monarchy has recently been tempered by recognition of more complicated ways in which these works negotiated the realities of the political world. In the first place, it is a simplification to speak of the 'royal court' as a single arena; Queen Anne and later Prince Henry maintained their own courts, and it was, indeed, the queen rather than her husband who initiated the development of the court masque. She commissioned Samuel Daniel to provide the first such entertainment in 1604; in 1605 it was by her request that Jonson's first masque at court presented the queen and her ladies in blackface, and, according to the introduction of *The Masque of Queens*, she suggested to Jonson the devising of the antimasque of witches so significant to the evolution of the form.[20] The masques for Prince Henry's investiture as Prince of Wales, especially Jonson's *Oberon*, struggle to reconcile the political agendas of father and son, and it would appear that some at least of the masques for the marriage of his sister, Princess Elizabeth, negotiated between the pacifism of the king, and the hopes for a more aggressive Protestant union which the prince himself espoused. (Though the prince's early death in 1612 caused the festivities for the marriage to be postponed, it is evident that the masques were already planned and assumed his presence.) Later, Henrietta Maria was not only instrumental in encouraging the importation of French fashion into the Caroline entertainments, but in her own masques was capable of articulating a religious and political position distinctly her own.[21]

Secondly, not all masques were sponsored directly by the royal family. Francis Bacon, for example, invested a substantial sum in presenting *The Masque of Flowers* for the marriage of Frances Howard and Robert Carr with the intention of ingratiating himself with the monarch and his favourite. It was also possible for courtiers to use the occasion to proffer, however carefully, advice

18 Orgel, *The Illusion of Power*, 38.
19 Ibid., 52.
20 For the importance of Queen Anne, see Barroll 'Inventing the Stuart masque', in Bevington and Holbrook (eds.), *The Politics of the Stuart Court Masque*, 121–43; Lewalski, *Writing Women in Jacobean England*. On Prince Henry, see Strong, *Henry, Prince of Wales and England's Lost Renaissance*.
21 On Henrietta Maria, see Veevers, *Images of Love and Religion*.

to the king. Campion's *Lord Hay's Masque*, for example, sponsored by relatives of the bride and groom whose Anglo-Scottish marriage it honoured, is in part a commentary on James's much desired, but highly contentious project of uniting the kingdoms of England and Scotland, and suggested tactfully the need for reformation of the court's intemperance and due respect for English sensibility if the union was to succeed.[22] Masques were also provided by the Inns of Court, and, in both Chapman's *The Memorable Masque* and Shirley's *Triumph of Peace* (1633), registered independence from the political vision of the monarch. In the first, an offering for the celebration of the marriage of Princess Elizabeth, there is an encouragement of colonial ambition in Virginia which seems to chime with the expansionist views of Prince Henry rather than those of his father; in the second, the six antimasques of 'projectors', according to Bulstrode Whitelocke, 'pleased the Spectators the more, because by it an Information was covertly given to the King, of the unfitness and ridiculousness of these Projects against the Law' (*IJ*, 542).[23] Such 'covert information' might be offered in other antimasques where figures of riot or excess could function as reminders to the monarch – and to the courtiers themselves who participated in the celebrations – of potential abuses that needed reformation. Masques, then, 'even if they did not subvert the King's authority ... might function as mechanisms through which the balance between differently empowered groups at court could be opened to reconfiguration'.[24]

The extent to which the masques were able to express or articulate varied, even dissentient, political views should not be overstated. Scenic apotheoses and panegyric verse insisted on the centrality of the monarch, and music could easily be converted into a manifestation of the harmoniousness engendered by James's peace, or by the mutual love of Charles and Henrietta Maria. But even masques which appear unproblematically to replicate a royal agenda might be threatened in other ways, especially by the mismatch between their idealising vision and the actualities of the political world. When Jonson dramatised the justice of the King in *The Golden Age Restored* (1616), for example, his audience would have been only too well aware of the attempt embodied in the masque to put the best possible interpretation on the scandal of the Overbury murder

---

22 See Lindley, 'Campion's *Lord Hay's Masque* and Anglo-Scottish union', *Huntington Library Quarterly* 43 (1979–80), 1–11.

23 On Chapman, see Lindley 'Courtly play', in Cruickshanks (ed.), *Stuart Courts*, 43–58. On Shirley, see Butler, 'Politics and the masque: *The Triumph of Peace*', *The Seventeenth Century* 2 (1987), 117–41.

24 Butler, 'Courtly negotiations', in Bevington and Holbrook (eds.), *The Politics of the Stuart Court Masque*, 28. (This essay gives a fine overview of the current state of masque criticism.)

trials, still in progress at the time,[25] and *Neptune's Triumph*, planned for 1624 though never performed, in dealing with Prince Charles's return from Spain without a bride, attempts desperately to reconcile very different perspectives upon the event.[26] Further complication could be introduced by the fact that the performers in a masque were appearing before an audience that knew them well. On some occasions the identity of particular masquers could become an important part of the meaning of the event – as when members of opposing factions danced together at the marriage masques for Frances Howard, or courtiers known to be uneasy with the king's policy participated in *Salmacida Spolia*'s assertion of the benefits of peaceful co-operation.[27] But at other times an audience would have been only too capable of measuring the distance between the heroic roles the masquers performed and their daily reality. Jonson himself recognised the gap that always threatened to appear when he wrote, in his 'An Epistle to Master John Selden':

> Though I confess (as every muse hath erred
> And mine not least) I have too oft preferred
> Man past their terms, and praised some names too much;
> But 'twas with purpose to have made them such.[28]

The poem may reflect directly upon the fact that Jonson himself was compelled to suppress all mention of the occasion of his masques for the two marriages of Frances Howard once she had been found guilty of plotting the murder of Sir Thomas Overbury, but it was precisely the potential for such a mismatch of courtier and role that a dramatist such as Middleton exploited and exaggerated in the grisly 'masques' which function as the climax of *The Revenger's Tragedy* and *Women Beware Women*. In many ways, then, the seamless surface of the printed record often conceals tensions, negotiations and ironies that would have been readily apparent to the original audience.

There is one final respect in which the familiar picture of the court masque as the celebration of a royalist ideology needs to be modified – for the masque provided a vocabulary that could be deployed in other places to other ends. When in *The Coleorton Masque* Sir Thomas Beaumont, a Leicestershire gentleman, celebrated the marriage of Sir William Seymour and the sister of the Earl of Essex, he deployed the familiar elements of the court masque to articulate a

25 Butler and Lindley, 'Restoring Astraea', *English Literary History* 61 (1994), 807–27.
26 See Butler, 'Courtly negotiations', 33–6.
27 See Butler, 'Politics and the masque: *Salmacida Spolia*', in Healy and Sawday (eds.), *Literature and the English Civil War*, 59–74.
28 *Ben Jonson*, ed. Donaldson, 331, lines 19–22.

critique of the decay of country hospitality. More significantly, John Milton, in composing *A Masque Presented at Ludlow Castle* (better known as *Comus*) for the official celebration of the Earl of Bridgewater's appointment as Lord President of the Council of the Marches, took this aristocratic, quasi-regal occasion to offer a critical perspective on many of the values of the court. In his 'reformed masque' (to borrow David Norbrook's term[29]) the defeat of Comus's vice is dependent upon heavenly grace, not upon the appearance of aristocratic masquers, and, whilst Milton incorporates the traditional elements of courtly entertainments in song and dance, their import is revised and refocused to celebrate an effortful and human virtue. As John Creaser puts it: 'Departing from courtly norms towards moral orthodoxy, Milton inserts human limitation into *Arcades* and *Comus*', but at the same time the children of the earl who were the principal performers (and had themselves already participated in masques at court) at the end 'lapse into the distinguished silence of masquers, and their function is to dance in triumph before their parents and the assembly in a culminating manifestation of aristocratic presence'.[30] That Milton, later one of the fiercest defenders of regicide, could yet find it possible to provide a masque for this aristocratic, vice-regal occasion indicates powerfully that, as Norbrook argues, 'puritan' objections to the court masque were not necessarily expressive of an opposition to the genre in itself, but to the uses to which it was, in their eyes, put.

In 1638 Davenant introduced *Luminalia* in these terms:

> The Queen commanded Inigo Jones, surveyor of her majesty's works, to make a new subject of a masque for herself, that with high and hearty invention might give occasion for variety of scenes, strange apparitions, songs, music, and dancing of several kinds, from whence doth result the true pleasure peculiar to our English masques, which by strangers and travelers of judgement are held to be as noble and ingenious as those of any other nations. (*IJ*, 706)

Without denying the aesthetic appeal to which Davenant bears witness, or downplaying the contribution of the genre to the evolution of theatrical practice, I would want to argue that the court masque is fascinating precisely because of the anxieties that bubble beneath its surface, anxieties which operate not only at the level of its explicit political address, but are endemic to its aesthetic attempt to incorporate and contain its diverse roots – in anarchic, seasonal celebration and feasting, panegyric and political advice – in a learned,

---

29 Norbrook, 'The reformation of the masque', in Lindley (ed.), *The Court Masque*, 94–110.
30 Creaser, '"The present aid of this occasion"', in Lindley (ed.), *The Court Masque*, 130.

elitist, fashionable yet ephemeral entertainment. In his 1631 preface to *Love's Triumph Through Callipolis* Jonson claimed that 'all representations, especially those of this nature in court, public spectacles, either have been or ought to be the mirror of man's life' (*IJ*, 405). It is the truthfulness of that mirror to the complexities of the culture of the Stuart court world which makes the masque worth studying.

16

Clowns, fools and knaves: stages in the evolution of acting

PETER THOMSON

Of the 800 performers traced by Edwin Nungezer for inclusion in his *Dictionary of Actors and of Other Persons Associated with the Public Representation of Plays in England before 1642* (1929), upwards of thirty can be identified as professional clowns or fools, but not one can be confidently said to have been both clown and fool. The first task of this essay is to distinguish between these two roles.

The clown

The word 'clown' is an Elizabethan importation to the English language. It came into currency because it usefully distinguished those who used it from those they used it about. 'Clowns' were rustic and therefore boorish, the polar opposites of the courtly sophisticates whose concern it was to establish anew a code of gentility for the great and the good in Elizabethan England.[1] It is in this sense, for instance, that Robert Greene uses the word in the opening stage direction to the third scene of *Friar Bacon and Friar Bungay* (c. 1589): 'Enter Margaret the faire Mayd of Fresingfield, with Thomas and Ione, and other clownes'; and it is in this sense that the mechanicals of *A Midsummer Night's Dream* are all clowns. In the Elizabethan theatre, though, such generic definitions are of less use to the performers than to the tireman who must costume them. The lively encounter between actor and audience on the platform stage begins with the recognition that, unique among clowns, Bottom is the Clown.

Distinct from the history of drama, the history of theatre is signposted by transcendent performers, and the first great artist of the English stage was a clown. Richard Tarlton (d.1588) was qualified to speak for the rustic immigrants to the great city of London because he was one himself. Biographical information is scanty and contradictory (he was a swineherd in Shropshire; he

---

1 The process of assimilation is comparable with that of the word 'hooligan', derived by the *Daily News* in 1898 from a notoriously rough Irish family in the East End of London.

was from Essex, where he learned the publican's trade; he was apprenticed to a water-carrier), but that is not surprising in the case of a man who was anecdotally mythologised during his own lifetime and in the decades immediately following his death. The probability is that Tarlton began his public life as a solo entertainer, and that it was only the coincident growth of professional theatre companies that turned him into a player. He owed his early reputation to his consummate skill as an improviser of responses, often in rhyming verse or sung, to taunts or challenges from members of his audience. From this developed the comic persona, subsequently exploited by playwrights in discrete episodes written for Tarlton's clown, of the hopelessly outwitted rustic who suddenly turns the tables on his tormentors. By the time this 'act' – easily adaptable into the kind of comic routines that *commedia dell'arte* performers termed *lazzi* – reached the public theatres, it had probably been polished in homelier environments. It is stated, in the posthumously published book of *Tarlton's Jests*, that he ran the Saba Tavern in Gracechurch Street and then an ordinary in Paternoster Row, and the implication is that customers were drawn by the vivid entertainment provided by the landlord. A conjectural biography would place this activity in the 1570s, before the first known reference to Tarlton as an actor,[2] but it should not be supposed that the move from tavern to playhouse was a leap into the unknown. David Wiles has argued that 'the basis of his theatrical technique was to recreate in the theatre the intimate atmosphere of the table-side, making spectators feel like participants',[3] though Wiles is careful to dissociate intimacy from cosiness. Tarlton was abrasive and adversarial, and any spectator who took him on was likely to experience intimacy as arm-wrestlers experience it.

It is the unlikely association of the clown and danger that I wish to emphasise. From the moment of his first entry onto the platform, Tarlton was as recognisably plebeian as the vociferous cobbler who bandies words with the tribunes in the opening scene of *Julius Caesar*. By genteel standards, for one thing, he was ugly: contemporaries remarked on his swine-face, squint and button nose, and there may have been a hint of a hunchback. As for his various costumes, they declared to a clothes-conscious audience both poverty and a quirky individuality. Despite his manifest adherence to an underclass, the clown is not temperamentally inclined to subservience, and some threat to hierarchy is implicit, even in fictional confrontations, when they are embodied in the presence of mixed-class spectators. Those in authority in Elizabethan

---

2 Nungezer dates this reference in *The Letter-Book of Gabriel Harvey* at c. 1579. See *A Dictionary of Actors*, 349.
3 Wiles, *Shakespeare's Clown*, 16.

England were understandably nervous of unruly assembly in the playhouses, and the immigrant Tarlton, notorious for his irreverence, was finely placed to make sympathetic contact with rebellious spirits among the groundlings. Whether or not such contact was made cannot, in the nature of things, be proved, but the portrait of Tarlton drawn in contemporary anecdotes, and inked in by the published *Jests*, is that of a fearless *provocateur* whose humour was often the shadow of his anger and sometimes spilled over into violence. Give to the displaced clown a weapon, as Shakespeare does to Jack Cade in the second part of *Henry VI*, and the outcome will be scenes of grotesquely mingled horror and humour.[4] Cade is a rustic oaf who runs amok. As a self-appointed Lord of Misrule – and Elizabethan audiences would certainly have recognised him as such – he carries a traditional metaphor of social inversion into rampant reality. Tarlton was not long dead when the *Henry VI* plays were staged at the Rose: in performance, Jack Cade resurrected him. This is not a fanciful point. Whether in truth or in legend, Tarlton was an untamed colossus, the most talked-about English actor before David Garrick. Robert Weimann has made the point that he was 'the first plebeian artist to achieve national recognition in England'.[5] Tarlton's weapon was ridicule, and it was his inherently oppositional stance that gave him his purchase on the popular imagination. The clown is nobody's fool.

We have few details of Tarlton's theatrical career. Andrew Gurr surmises that he may have been with Sussex's Men as early as 1575, when he was already a sufficient draw to attract an over-capacity audience to the mayoral hall in Bristol for the performance of a lost play called *The Red Knight*.[6] Thomas Radcliffe, third Earl of Sussex, was a valuable patron, whose office as lord chamberlain made him responsible for arranging entertainments at Elizabeth I's court. It is likely to have been Radcliffe who opened Tarlton's access to the queen. If he was already a player with Sussex's Men in 1575, he was not exclusively so, since contemporary anecdotes speak of his activities as a table-side entertainer at court banquets and as unofficial jester to Queen Elizabeth. When, in 1583, political opportunism led to the re-formation of a touring company of Queen's Men, Tarlton was a founder-member.[7] His persona as rustic clown must have been well established by then. It was, suggests Wiles, 'a response to London':

4 Edward Bond, in his speculative play about Shakespeare's last days, *Bingo*, provides Ben Jonson with a striking simile: 'Hate is like a clown armed with a knife' (34).
5 Weimann, *Shakespeare and the Popular Tradition in the Theater*, 186.
6 'The rush was so great that afterwards the hall's doors had to be repaired.' Gurr, *The Shakespearian Playing Companies*, 174.
7 For a lively account of the foundation of the Queen's Men, see the first two chapters of McMillin and MacLean, *The Queen's Men*.

As a surrogate Lord of Misrule, Tarlton the theatrical clown helped to foster in Londoners a new sense of community, shared values, and active participation in the making of a culture. His comedy cut across barriers of class, proving acceptable both at court and in the tavern, because most people could accept the proposition that beneath every human exterior there lurks a coarse anarchic peasant.[8]

The clown was not created out of nothing, of course. The precedent of the Vice in morality plays and interludes has been generally recognised. There is, though, an essential distinction. Whereas the Vice, however temporarily disruptive, is contained within a moral, homiletic frame, the clown is socially free-ranging. His self-awareness as a performer protects him from the constraints of the dramatic fiction. He has his eye on the audience, not the play. Here, too, there is danger: those who share the stage with him are at risk, and the playwrights had better swallow their pride and cherish their fee. We can see Tarlton at work in his first entrance as Derick in *The Famous Victories of Henry the Fifth* (c. 1587). The scene has opened with a passage of gossipy dialogue between a cobbler and a costermonger, the sort of inept members of the watch that Shakespeare would later parody in Dogberry and Verges. Derick enters precipitately, says 'Whoa! Whoa, there! Whoa, there!', and exits. The stage direction stipulates that he is 'roving' (i.e. looking around), evidently in search of a horse. Even on a flat, picture-frame stage, such an eye-blink appearance is an invitation to the actor to invent some comic business. On the platform stage, where an entrance at one stage door, a circuit of the platform, and an exit at the other stage door involves the covering of a fair distance, Tarlton must have had a field-day. He was a master of exits and entrances, anyway, but there is a further joke concealed in the terse text. Derick has been robbed, and he is looking for help. Tarlton as 'roving' Derick sees the audience, and registers it in his own inimitable way, but he fails to see the watch, the very people he is looking for. The true art of the clown is rarely discernible in the printed text.

Tarlton was the most famous, but by no means the only, clown in the Queen's Men. This was a popular company with a specific brief to carry the queen's good will to her subjects nationwide, and in popular entertainment, then as now, the clown is king. Tarlton's colleagues included the hungry clown John Adams, the improvising clown Robert Wilson, the athletic clown John Singer, the long-lived John Garland, and the versatile John Laneham. The company, then, was supremely equipped to crown the performance of

8 Wiles, *Shakespeare's Clown*, 23.

the day's play with any one of the numerous jigs in their repertoire. The jig is inappropriately neglected by students of the Elizabethan theatre. It was a short afterpiece incorporating song and dance, featuring the clowns, and generally involving them in sexual misadventures which called for risible cross-dressing. The very few surviving manuscripts (no jigs have survived in print: they belonged to the oral tradition which Tarlton sustained against the literary tide) share a taste for tolerant obscenity, and hint at the delight audiences took in scurrilous satire and the dramatic exploitation of local scandals. Wiles has observed how rarely the clown is provided any closure within the narrative of the play.[9] He had no need of dramatic completion since the theatrical finality of the jig lay ahead of him. Tarlton's jigs probably featured comic songs. It was his historical successor William Kemp, famous now as Shakespeare's clown but famous in his time as a solo artist, who specialised in dance.

His physical appearance has generally been part of the clown's comic armoury. Tarlton was evidently uncommonly ugly, and Kemp was probably uncommonly large. A fat man dancing daintily tends to provoke a mixture of admiration and laughter,[10] something on which Kemp relied to attract spectators for his nine-day dance from London to Norwich in February 1600. This eccentric publicity-stunt followed hard on, and may have been Kemp's response to, his abrupt severance from the Lord Chamberlain's Men, the brilliant company of which he had been a founder-member in 1594. His earliest known theatrical allegiance was to Robert Dudley, Earl of Leicester, at whose notoriously grandiose alternative court in the Netherlands he served intermittently as a kind of licensed jester between 1585 and 1588. Both there and subsequently his career reads restlessly. As a wandering clown on the continent, sometimes accompanied by a boy, he developed the non-verbal, physical skills for which later expatriate English clowns, like John Spencer and Robert Reynolds, would be justly celebrated abroad. This is a different kind of training from Tarlton's, and it was more likely mortal coincidence than forward planning that determined Kemp's succession as leading clown of the Elizabethan stage. On 3 September 1588 Tarlton died in Shoreditch, and early the next morning the Earl of Leicester died near Maidenhead. Without a patron, and with a ready-made reputation as a jig-maker, Kemp decided, or was persuaded, to join a company of players under the patronage of Ferdinando, Lord Strange,

9 Ibid., 53.
10 At Stratford in 1974, Barry Stanton played Lucio in the Royal Shakespeare Company's production of *Measure for Measure*. Stanton is big, but he established for Lucio a mincingly precise gait that was irresistibly startling.

and it was this company, after the sudden death of their patron in April 1594, that formed the nucleus of the Lord Chamberlain's Men.

To begin with, at least, Kemp was more crucial to the group's success than Shakespeare. The clown drew the crowds, not the playwright. It is a pity that we know so little for certain about their association. There is evidence that Shakespeare wrote the small part of Peter in *Romeo and Juliet*, and the more gratifying one of Dogberry in *Much Ado about Nothing*, with Kemp in mind. These blundering illiterates, struggling to master circumstances or language that are beyond them, hint at a persona for Kemp's rustic clown. The melancholy Launce of *The Two Gentlemen of Verona* and the put-upon Launcelot ('Launcelet' – little Launce – in one spelling) Gobbo of *The Merchant of Venice* are variations, rather than contradictions, of the theme. None of them is a team-player. Their 'stand-up' routines and double-acts scarcely impinge on the other performers of the play. If rehearsed at all, they could have been rehearsed in isolation. The clown's only significant relationship is with the spectators, who recognise the clever actor behind the character of a simpleton. Shakespeare knew what Kemp could do supremely: he would have seen him as the cobbler of Gotham in the celebrated inset 'merriment' of *A Knack to Know a Knave* (1592/3). But if, as has been persuasively argued,[11] Kemp created Bottom and Falstaff, we have to acknowledge a shift of enormous theatrical significance. The clown has been incorporated as a player. The problem is that, if Kemp had effectively accomplished that transition – and it is stretching credibility to argue that *A Midsummer Night's Dream* and the *Henry IV* plays succeeded in the theatre despite an ineffective Bottom and Falstaff – his sudden departure in 1599 becomes even more puzzling. The case remains open.

The conventional claim has been that the tide turned against the Tarltonian clown during the 1590s, as theatrical taste grew more refined. Kemp's fate is thus linked to the Chamberlain's Men's upmarket move to the Globe, and a corporate urge to break with the 'low' past. Texts employed to sustain the claim include Hamlet's advice to the players and Sir Philip Sidney's attack on plays that 'thrust in Clowns by head and shoulders, to play a part in majestical matters, with neither decency nor discretion',[12] but a fictional prince and a factual aristocrat are not natural spokesmen for popular taste, nor was the Globe the only playhouse in London. Jigs were still so fiercely patronised at the Fortune in 1612 that the Middlesex General Session of the Peace ordered their suppression, and it is by no means certain that the Chamberlain's Men

---

11 Not least by Wiles in *Shakespeare's Clown*, 116–35.
12 *The Prose Works of Philip Sidney*, ed. Feuillerat, III, 39.

used Kemp's defection as a pretext for abandoning them. Kemp himself, after a brief interlude on the continent, found a welcome with Worcester's Men and continued clowning; John Singer remained with the Admiral's Men at least until 1603; Thomas Greene made clowning capital out of his thinness with Queen Anne's Men at the Red Bull until his death in 1612; William Rowley, fat clown as well as playwright, remained active until 1625; and Andrew Cane and Timothy Reade maintained the tradition through to the 1642 closing of the theatres and beyond. In an often-forgotten sense, indeed, the clown outlasted the fool as the Jack Pudding of seventeenth-century drolls.

The clown is not a character. He embodies the essential truth that the real theatrical relationship is not between character and audience, but between actor and audience. The sophisticated argument is that the clown's popularity retarded the development of a fictionally sealed drama, dependent on the audience's willing suspension of disbelief. It is an argument derived more from a literary appreciation of great plays than from a concern with the physical circumstances of the Elizabethan public playhouses. As the actors at the new Globe have quickly discovered, improvising clowns are immensely useful in alerting a turbulent audience to the imminent beginning of the performance (the practice is akin to medieval 'whiffling'). Because they have licensed access to the real world of the theatre, and an often-disruptive view of the artificial world of the play, they link the enacted fiction to an actual community event. With an eye on Kemp and his successors, I find far-fetched Andrew Gurr's contention that 'by Tarlton's death the tragedians were recognised as the chief drawcard'.[13] It flies in the face of theatre history. But Gurr rightly points out the actorly shift, during the 1590s, from simple presentation to subtler personation. The dramatic 'character' was born in England before there was a word to describe it. We can trace it most clearly in Shakespeare. Whereas Richard III is almost the Tarlton-clown as king (Jack Cade with legitimacy on his side), in constant dialogue with the audience, the Brutus of *Julius Caesar* is the Burbage-actor, in troubled dialogue with himself. But literary critics make pure distinctions that sit awkwardly in the impure theatre. It may be that Shakespeare abandoned Kemp, and tried to bury Tarlton in *Hamlet*'s Yorick, but he needed his clown in order to present the truth as he observed it, as well as to make theatre as it must be made. Pompey, the pimp of *Measure for Measure*, is a part Tarlton could have played; the gravediggers of *Hamlet* are rustic clowns after Tarlton; Macbeth's Porter speaks Tarlton's language of the tavern. The clownish messenger who silences the musicians in *Othello*

13 Gurr, *Playgoing in Shakespeare's London*, 128.

Figure 34 A fool, from the chantry chapel of Bishop Thomas Bekynton in Wells Cathedral

plays briefly a role that Kemp had modelled in *Romeo and Juliet*, as does the worm-bearing clown in *Antony and Cleopatra*. I find it hard to believe that the Chamberlain's Men, even after they had evolved into the King's Men, were too purist to offer the players of these roles the reward of a jig.

The fool

Although the fool is culturally much older than the clown, he was a later arrival in the Elizabethan professional theatre. His contribution to seasonal celebrations, pastimes and parochial ceremonies is a central one: mock kings, boy bishops, players of May games and morris dancers need their fools. And he is present, also, in some of the events in the medieval church's ritual calendar, most prominently in his own dedicated feast.[14] The Feast of Fools followed hard on Christmas and, at least until the Pragmatic Sanction of 1438 ordered its cessation, it was regularly celebrated inside churches (see figure 34). There

14 For a lively account of the Feast of Fools, see Welsford, *The Fool*, 199f.

is some uncertainty about the effectiveness of the ban in England, though the feast was certainly sustained more spectacularly in France; nor can we confidently determine the intentions and impact of the characteristic inversion of priestly hierarchy and the burlesquing of the mass. One argument would claim that the spiritual authorities, like civic authorities up and down the land, licensed the letting-off of steam for a defined period because such occasional release serves the *status quo*. Human folly, having been pulled out of hiding and celebrated, could be more securely sequestered again. Another argument would find in carnivalesque challenges to established order evidence of the simmering anger of the suppressed masses. What is certain is that Christian exegetes felt the need to accommodate folly, and that there are powerful biblical reasons for that felt need, above all in the commanding prose of St Paul's letters to beleaguered church communities. Paul's delight in paradox affected the thinking of all the finest Renaissance writers, including, of course, the dramatists:

> the foolishness of God is wiser than men; and the weakness of God is stronger than men. For ye see your calling, brethren, how that not many wise men after the flesh, not many mighty, not many noble, are called: but God hath chosen the foolish things of the world to confound the wise; and God hath chosen the weak things of the world to confound the things which are mighty; and base things of the world, and things which are despised, hath God chosen, yea, and things which are not, to bring to nought things that are.[15]

The Pauline God, who had chosen to save the world by foolishness, endorsed the humanist propositions that all good men are fools for Christ, and that true wisdom is to know one's own foolishness.[16] It does not follow, of course, that all fools are good men; contradictory attitudes towards folly supply the tension that enlivens the figure of the fool on the Elizabethan stage. Psalms 14 and 53, in the Authorized Version of the Bible, both open with the bleak sentence, 'The fool hath said in his heart, There is no God', and proceed, in almost exact echo of each other, to condemn the human world as a sink of iniquity. Illustrated psalters regularly depict fools at the head of these psalms. Most of these are portraits of the fool as mental defective, an idiot trapped inside the capital 'D' of 'Dixit insipies in corde suo non est Deus', but court jesters, in parti-coloured suits with cap and bells, figure too. Most interesting of all, perhaps, is Jean Mallard's illustration (*c.* 1540) in Henry VIII's personal psalter

---

15 I Corinthians, 1: 25–8. The quotation is from the Authorised Version.
16 The classic Renaissance text is Erasmus's *Moriae Encomium*, written in 1509 and first published in 1511. It first appeared in English, as *The Praise of Folly*, in 1549.

patri **S** icut erat.

Figure 35 Henry VIII and his fool, from Henry VIII's personal psalter, written and decorated by David Mallard (c. 1540). Miniature for Psalm 52 shows Henry as David, playing a Welsh harp and Will Somer, Henry's fool

(see figure 35). Here, in the role of the angry psalmist King David, Henry fingers a Welsh harp, whilst his famous fool Will Somers stands in a significant pose of non-attention.[17]

It was presumably Mallard's intention to flatter Henry VIII, the wise king ignored at their peril by his foolish subjects. But the pairing of king and fool

17 Somers's costume is interesting. The stockings are vivid blue, there is no cap or bauble, and the 'coote of grene clothe with a hood to the same' corresponds to the one specified for him in the wardrobe account of 1535. The purse at his waist may be the 'velvet purse for W. Sommer' recorded in Thomas Cromwell's financial statement for January 1538.

has an ironic significance that would be fully realised in *King Lear*. The mentally defective 'natural' fool, like the king of divine right, is born so, not made so. Alone among Renaissance reachers and overreachers, they arrive in the world ready-made and cannot fashion themselves. The natural fool makes sporadic appearances in Elizabethan drama: Armin's study from the life of John in the Hospital in *The Two Maids of More-clacke* (1597/8); Morion in *The Valiant Welshman* (perhaps also by Armin), who strips himself to the traditional nakedness of the natural fool for love of the Fairy Queen; the immensely endearing Cuddy Banks in the multi-authored *The Witch of Edmonton* (1621), who combines elements of the rustic clown with his natural foolishness. Dimwits and gulls abound, of course: they people Jonsonian comedy, where they generally get what they deserve. But these are men (occasionally women) who create their own folly out of cupidity or obsession. The humiliation of monumental figures, like Morose in Jonson's *Epicoene* or Sir Giles Overreach in Massinger's *A New Way to Pay Old Debts*, aims to remind audiences of the proximity of worldly success and folly. The 'natural' household fool served a similar purpose: he invited humility in those who observed his defectiveness. But the natural fool, because he must be acted upon rather than active, is not a particularly useful element in dramaturgy. The theatrical innovation of the artificial fool, in the place previously occupied by the clown, is more clearly discernible in the work of Shakespeare than in that of his contemporaries, and the probable reason for that is the presence of Robert Armin among the Chamberlain's Men.

The artificial fool exists in pre-Shakespearian drama. The novice Shakespeare might have seen him in embryo in the Andrew of Robert Greene's *James the Fourth* (c. 1590). But Armin was well placed to bring his own ideas to the role. Having completed his apprenticeship as a goldsmith by the early 1590s, he joined Lord Chandos's Men as a player and set about gathering information about household fools while the company toured the country. His findings were published in book form in 1600, by which time he was a member of the Chamberlain's Men. *Fool upon Fool* is an anecdotal record of six sixteenth-century natural fools. Armin would later expand it into the more overtly philosophical *A Nest of Ninnies* (1608), but reflections on folly already inform the earlier version. Although he modelled his early career on Tarlton, Armin was very different from his mighty predecessor. Evidence suggests that he was very small, even dwarfish, and a counter-tenor, an opposite of the aggressively masculine Tarlton. Furthermore, his solo-act took him closer to the multiplicity of the quick-change artist than to the single-persona consistency of the clown. It is generally assumed that the title page of the 1609 quarto of *The*

Two Maids of More-clacke depicts Armin in the costume of John in the Hospital (see figure 36), but the play as he originally wrote it, perhaps for Chandos's Men, offered him more scope than that. Tutch, the artificial fool of the play, was Armin's part too; and Tutch, during the course of the action, disguises himself as a Welsh knight and as John in the Hospital. Attention is being openly drawn to Armin the performer. He is the natural fool, the artificial fool, the artificial fool imitating the natural fool, and all the time Armin. The historical likelihood is that Shakespeare, always intrigued by virtuosity, adapted the role of Touchstone that he had originally designed for Kemp, signalling the diminution of the Kemp line by giving the name of William to the bit-part rustic clown of *As You Like It*.

It is generally true that Armin's fool is more involved in the fictional world of the play than were the clowns of Tarlton and Kemp, but the involvement is strangely quizzical. The fool, like the clown, is aware of the audience, but he is aware of the dramatic action too, and this gives him a distance from the audience that the clown would not have relished. It is as if he is licensed both to represent and to criticise elements in a Christian society. (There is no fool in George Chapman's *All Fools* (1599) precisely because we are all fools: and Chapman's prologue insists that actors, because they pretend not to be themselves, are always on the cusp of folly.) Even when 'attached' (to master, mistress or household) the Armin fool scarcely belongs. He has come from nowhere, and generally he goes nowhere. He is almost 'nobody', in Pauline terms one of the 'things which are not'. The archetype here is Feste, whose involvement in the intrigues of *Twelfth Night* does nothing to make him a 'character'. He is not even, in the Jonsonian sense, a 'humour' or the possessor of a determinate temperament. The journeyman Elizabethan actor, learning his part from a scribal cue-script, could satisfy the basic demands of performance by coming to grips with the particular temperament inscribed in the words. Something different is required of Armin as Feste:

> He must observe their mood on whom he jests,
> The quality of persons, and the time,
> And, like the haggard, check at every feather
> That comes before his eye.   (3.1.60–3)

To judge from Feste, Armin was as capable of responding to other actors' leads as he was of seizing the attention in a song or drawing applause in the parsonical disguise of Sir Topas. There is a Feste-like invisibility about the historical jester James Lockwood, who travelled the country from Newcastle

THE
Hiftory of the two Maids of More-clacke,

VVith the life and fimple maner of IOHN
in the Hofpitall.

Played by the Children of the Kings
Maiefties Reuels.

VVritten by ROBERT ARMIN, feruant to the Kings
moft excellent Maieftie.

LONDON,
Printed by N.O. for *Thomas Archer,* and is to be fold at his
fhop in Popes-head Pallace, 1609.

Figure 36 Robert Armin, depicted on the title page of his *The History of the Two Maids of More-clacke* (1609)

and Nottingham to Folkestone and Barnstaple between 1541 and 1571, serving four monarchs, but leaving to posterity no inkling of his quality. Sir Francis Walsingham, Elizabeth I's spymaster, is known to have employed itinerant actors as 'invisible' observers and subsequent informants. The chameleon Feste spies for both Olivia and Orsino. Might Armin also have played the spying Duke of *Measure for Measure*? It is difficult to see another part for him in that play; and yet the mere speculation demonstrates Armin's distance from Kemp.

Apart from Touchstone, Feste, Lear's unnamed companion and, perhaps, Autolycus, Shakespeare's fools are less distinct among the *dramatis personae* than his clowns. This may tell us something about Armin's versatility as an actor, and it has certainly encouraged some retrospective guesses about casting. Wiles has him as Lavatch in *All's Well that Ends Well*, Thersites in *Troilus and Cressida*, Casca in *Julius Caesar*, Menenius in *Coriolanus*, Apemantus in *Timon of Athens*, Cloten in *Cymbeline* and Caliban in *The Tempest*. John Southworth, noting Armin's penchant for disguise, even challenges the assumption that he was the fool in *King Lear*, proposing the part of Edgar as a better alternative.[18] It is certainly in that play that the double-act of fool and king is displayed at its most poignant. Here, finally, is a fool who cannot detach himself from the dramatic fiction, and for whom, therefore, the audience is a lost resource. The scenes on the heath are Shakespeare's climactic portrait of folly. The king who has proved himself a fool is accompanied by a wise man pretending to be a natural fool and an artificial fool whose wisdom has been displaced by circumstance. There is no single Elizabethan acting style that can encompass the range of performance skills demanded. Elizabethan actors did not play the character, they played the scene.

The knave

Both clown and fool are specialised roles for adult actors, and it is unsurprising that they are generally absent from the plays written specifically for the boys' companies. That is not to say that adults never acted with the boys. Armin seems to have done so when *The Two Maids of More-clacke* was revived by the Children of the King's Revels,[19] and the citizen grocer and his wife in Francis Beaumont's *The Knight of the Burning Pestle* are necessarily adult roles. (The initial failure of this brilliant burlesque would be easily explained if boys

---

18 Southworth, *Fools and Jesters at the English Court*, 134.
19 See Wiles, *Shakespeare's Clown*, 142–3.

attempted these parts, and also that of the singing clown, Old Merrythought, in the first production.) The role the boys developed, and subsequently donated to the adult players, was that of the knave. ' How ready you are to play the knave', says Florimel to her page in John Day's *Humour out of Breath*.[20] In drama, the fool turns knave when he defies the wishes of his master/mistress. The aural association with the notoriously errant playing card is not accidental. It is confirmed in Armin's play when Sir William Vergir turns on Tutch with 'your a knave, they shuffle ye about, ile deale the cards and cut ye from the decke'.[21] There is a famous quip, ascribed to Tarlton, that similarly relies on the listeners' knowledge of card games. 'See', Tarlton is supposed to have said when observing Sir Walter Ralegh in intimate conversation with Elizabeth I, 'the knave commands the Queen'.[22] It is a property of the knave/jack in a pack of cards, as of the knave in folk narratives, to range from mere mischief to downright roguery. He may steal a trick or some tarts, serve as a surrogate joker, or betray secrets that lead to the death of the hero,[23] but there is usually a naivety in his behaviour that accords well with boyishness. Day's pubescent knaves (Florimel's page is paired with the boy of her destined husband, Aspero) are precocious quibblers:

FLORIMEL: Boy, dost know who that gentleman is?
PAGE: Gentle madam, no; but he is a man.
FLORIMEL: Believe me, boy, he is a proper man.
PAGE: Man is a proper name to man, and so he may be a proper man.
FLORIMEL: I love him, he's a very proper man.
PAGE: She loves him for his properties, and indeed many women love men
    only to make properties of them.[24]

This kind of punning cross-talk is typical of the games playwrights played with boy actors and their adult audiences. Prurience is the whole point. The boy who plays the knave *as if* he understands the full significance of his words piques the sexual curiosity of the auditors, and their laughter gratifies the boy. He apprehends even if he does not fully comprehend. In the private playhouses, the transaction between boys and audience was evidently a source of pleasure

20 *The Works of John Day*, ed. Bullen, 437.
21 *The Collected Works of Robert Armin*, DIV.
22 Nungezer, *A Dictionary of Actors*, 350. I have a particular fondness for the American Eugene
    Field's comment on Creston Clark's performance of King Lear: 'he played the King as
    though under the momentary apprehension that someone else was about to play the
    ace'.
23 The knave is vividly present in adult drama as early as Pedringano in Kyd's *The Spanish
    Tragedy*.
24 *Works of John Day*, 428.

to both, however tiresome it may be to the modern ear. And it is not, on the page, far distant from the quibbling of adult fools:

LUCREZIA: Well, Fool, what's thy latest?

FOOL: Aristotle's or Zeno's, Lady – 'tis neither latest nor last. For, marry, if the cobbler stuck to his last, then were his latest his last *in rebus ambulantibus*. Argal, I stick at nothing but cobble-stones, which, by the same token, are stuck to the road by men's fingers.

LUCREZIA: How many crows may nest in a grocer's jerkin?

FOOL: A full dozen at cock-crow, and something less under the dog-star by reason of the dew, which lies heavy on men taken by the scurvy.

LUCREZIA: Methinks the Fool is a fool.

FOOL: And therefore, by auricular deduction, am I own twin to the Lady Lucrezia!

(*Sings*)   When pears hang green on the garden wall
                    With a nid, and a nod, and a niddy-niddy-o
              Then prank you, lads and lasses all
                    With a yea and a nay and a niddy-o.
              But when the thrush flies out o' the frost
                    With a nid, (*etc*)
              'Tis time for loons to count the cost
                    With a yea (*etc*)

That is an excerpt from the pastiche Elizabethan play incorporated in Max Beerbohm's *'Savonarola' Brown* (1917), but it is disturbingly reminiscent of its models. It might almost be Feste talking to Olivia, or Autolycus to Perdita.

Autolycus embodies the transition of comic style from clown (which he is too knowing to be) to fool (which he is out of context to play) to knave. He is more openly knavish than the Boy and Page of *Humour out of Breath*, or most of the other characters who identify themselves as knaves.[25] The knave was not, of course, a suddenly invented replacement for the dying fool of Jacobean theatre. What is Puck if he is not a knave? What I am indicating may be no more than my own uncertainty about the placing of a company's leading 'funny man' in several of the better-known Jacobean and Caroline plays. Pompey has still the clown's detachment from the significant action of *Measure for Measure*, but no one has claimed Pompey for Armin. Lucio, who has the play's wittiest lines, is an out-and-out knave, possessed of the two key characteristics of the role: he is both confidant and self-interested schemer. Unlike the clown and the fool, the

---

25 One such is William Murley, the rebellious brewer of Dunstable in the surviving part of *Sir John Oldcastle*. It is in egregious roles like that of Murley that we can best recognise the demands made on comic actors, as distinct from clowns and fools, on the Elizabethan and Jacobean stage.

knave is fully engaged in the plot, and that engagement limits the range of his comedy. Feste incorporates his auditors; Lucio must alienate them. Is this a part for Armin? Lucio's humour has a dying fall; and the same might be said of all the roles Wiles has allotted to Armin in Jacobean Shakespeare. But the *locus classicus* of the knave is not Shakespearian. *The Changeling* (c. 1622) places knaves at the centre of both its plots, and the paralleling of their schemes is among the many disconcerting features of this Jacobean masterpiece. Middleton's co-author, fat William Rowley, was still active as a 'funny man' in any company he joined. Lollio, the would-be seducer in the madhouse plot, is his likeliest role. But it is the physically defective De Flores (clown-like in appearance; murderer, blackmailer, seducer in action) who stands in the service of Beatrice–Joanna where the fool used to stand. He serves her in order to 'service' her; and the play does nothing to conceal the crudely masculine / mechanistic connotations of that verb. The outcome is as grotesque as *Twelfth Night* would have been if Feste had deflowered Olivia. The actor of De Flores escapes from his destined role into the audience's nightmares.

I am proposing, in the shift from fool to knave, a downgrading of the philo-sophical significance of folly in Stuart London. In 1599, Jaques was open to instruction from the fool. In *The Winter's Tale*, written a decade later, the self-fashioned (and in that sense artificial) fools are Leontes and Polixenes. The clown of the play is a clown only insofar as he is a rustic simpleton. The knave Autolycus is lucky to escape with his life, and must, if taken seriously, threaten the restored order in Sicily much as the petty criminal Pistol threatens the new order of Henry V's England ('To England will I steal, and there I'll steal'). The accommodations of *The Winter's Tale* resolve the plot without quite promising a sturdy future. Supernatural grace has to be called into service, and knav-ery remains on the loose. It is not the case that Elizabethan drama routinely separated its clowns and fools from its knaves, nor that Jacobean drama rou-tinely replaced fools with knaves. There are knavish clowns and foolish knaves enough in both eras. My concern is to highlight shifts in the demands made on the comic actor during the early years of the English professional theatre. The knave who is neither fool nor clown, and rarely 'heavy' enough to be a villain, operates in a moral and social isolation that is more Jacobean than Elizabethan. Although his language may seek out laughter, he can no longer find his solace in the audience. His performance is under the same scrutiny as that of his fellow actors: he has lost the outlet of complicity. The impact of Ben Jonson is powerful here. His actors do not so much share folly *with* as expose folly *to* the audience. Foolishness has become shameful, and the Jacobean comedian must accommodate himself to satire.

17

Thomas Middleton's *A Game at Chess*: a case study

RICHARD DUTTON

Thomas Middleton's *A Game at Chess* was a phenomenon, being – by several criteria – the most successful play of the Tudor/Stuart era. It ran for nine consecutive days at the Globe, from 5–14 August 1624 (interrupted only by the standard prohibition against playing on Sunday 8 August), at a time when repertoires normally changed almost daily to provide fresh fare for playgoers. Even so, it played to packed houses. The indefatigable letter-writer John Chamberlain reported that it 'has been followed with extraordinary concourse, and frequented by all sorts of people old and young, rich and poor, masters and servants, papists and puritans, wise men et[c], churchmen and statesmen... and a world besides'.[1] John Holles also found daunting crowds when he rowed to the Globe: 'which house I found so thronged, that by scores they came away for want of place, though as yet little past one; nevertheless loath to check the appetite, which came so seldom to me (not having been in a playhouse these ten years) & such a dainty not every day to be found, I marched on, & heard the pasquin' (*Chess*, 198). The Spanish ambassador, Don Carlos Coloma, reported 'that there were more than 3000 persons there on the day that the audience was smallest' (*Chess*, 194), and it would have run even longer if he had not complained about it to King James, who then ordered the King's Men to cease playing altogether while the affair was investigated.

Interest in the play was so strong that Middleton, in conjunction with the King's Men's regular scrivener, Ralph Crane, set up a production line for manuscript copies; no less than six have survived, in a context where few manuscripts by professional dramatists of the era have survived at all, and in no other instance has more than one survived. In 1625 two separate

---

1 Quoted from the Revels Plays edition of *A Game at Chess*, ed. Howard-Hill, 205. All contemporary comment on the play is quoted from Appendix A (192–213), though silently modernised, and will henceforth be page-referenced (*Chess*) within the text. All references to the text of the play are also to this edition, unless otherwise specified.

Figure 37 Title page of first quarto Thomas Middleton's *A Game at Chess* (1624)

unauthorised editions were printed on the continent, based on distinctively different manuscripts, attesting to strong continuing interest.[2] To cap it all, the success and scandal of the play itself generated an unparalleled level of written comment by observers of the political scene, including foreign ambassadors and correspondents such as Chamberlain; these include a uniquely detailed eye witness account of a performance of the play by John Holles, Lord Haughton, sent to the disgraced royal favourite, the Earl of Somerset (*Chess*, 198–9).[3] In addition, because King James and his court were on progress in

---

2 These are usually known as Quarto 1 (*STC* 17882) and Quarto 3 (*STC* 17884). *STC* 17883 was simply a reprint of Quarto 1.
3 See Braunmuller, ' "To the Globe I rowed"', *English Literary Renaissance* 20 (1990), 340–56, and Howard-Hill, 'The unique eye-witness report of Middleton's *A Game at Chess*', *Review of English Studies*, n.s. 42 (1991), 168–78.

the midlands when the play was performed, an unusual amount of official correspondence about it has survived, as those at court liaised with members of the Privy Council who were still in London.

In short, everything about the play is so exceptional that it is difficult to know what precisely to make of it: what exactly made it so popular? Was it really so different from other plays of the period, and if so how? How are we to account for the fact that it generated so much official reaction after its performance when it had apparently not troubled the official censor, Sir Henry Herbert, Master of the Revels, beforehand? While we should not overlook the fact that this is one of the finest plays by one of the most skilled dramatists of the period (this is often sadly overshadowed by the scandal attaching to it), and that, as we shall see, the King's Men went to exceptional lengths to make it an effective stage-piece, it is inescapable that the answers to most of these questions are tied up with the politics of the period.

The play is a transparent commentary (filtered through the allegory of a chess game) on recent relations between England and Spain, about the Counter-Reformation ambitions of the Catholic church, and about the supposed involvement of Spain in the machinations of the most zealous of Catholic orders, the Jesuits. As everyone recognised, the Black Knight in the play represented Count Gondomar, who until 1622 had been Spanish ambassador in London; he was widely credited with undue influence over King James, both in encouraging his pacifist foreign policy and in promoting greater toleration for Catholics in England. Once that identification is secure, it follows that the Black House more generally represents the King of Spain and other agents of Roman Catholicism, while the White House largely represents James, his family and ministers. The final act of the play depicts the bizarre and ill-judged episode in 1623 when Prince Charles (the White Knight) and the Duke of Buckingham (immensely powerful favourite of the king, the White Duke) visited Spain, initially incognito. The intention of that expedition was to achieve a long-cherished goal of James's foreign policy, the marriage of Charles to the Spanish infanta; but negotiations went disastrously wrong and the pair returned empty-handed. In the play, it is construed entirely as a (successful) subterfuge to expose Spanish plotting.

This massaging of the facts indicates something of the care with which Middleton avoids openly criticising members of the White House, except the treacherous White King's Pawn (whose identity, as we shall see, is not easily pinned) and the double-turncoat Fat Bishop. Nevertheless, we may feel that it is remarkable that he was able to depict English royalty and their favourites so openly, and implicitly to discuss (if not actually criticise) their policies. Perhaps this in itself was sufficient to account for the play's popularity. Certainly people at the time felt the actors were taking a great risk. George Lowe reported that 'it is thought that it will be called in and the parties punished', while Sir Francis Nethersole assumed that 'they play no thing else, knowing their time cannot be long' and Holles likewise assumed that 'these gamesters must have a good retreat' – implying that they must have had someone important to hide behind (*Chess*, 193, 202, 199).

The modern debate about the play has largely revolved around the question of just how daring it was, and whether its domestic politics were in fact more charged than Middleton's apparent discretion would suggest. Margot Heinemann took the lead in designating *A Game at Chess* as a prime example of what she called 'oppositional drama', plays voicing a concerted, puritan-centred opposition to the policies of the Stuart government. She regarded the Earl of Pembroke, lord chamberlain, as a key figure in this opposition, especially in his resistance to the royal favourite, Buckingham; and since he was kinsman, patron and superior of Sir Henry Herbert, he would have been ideally placed to expedite a play which, for all its ostensible patriotism, she argued was antagonistic to the Stuart regime and its creature, Buckingham.[4] Albert Tricomi similarly saw the play as deeply critical of recent English policy, but resisted Heinemann's determination to find in the play 1620s parallels to modern, ideologically polarised party politics. He preferred in the term '*opposition drama*' to identify 'the work of playwrights . . . who were loyal to the idea of kingship as well as the king but who opposed, often vehemently, one or more major tenets of the crown's foreign or domestic policy and, commonly, the architects of those policies, James's and Charles's closest advisors'.[5] From this perspective, *A Game at Chess*, while inherently loyalist, is seen to be critical of the recently disgraced Earl of Middlesex (whom Tricomi equates with the White King's Pawn) but also of Buckingham's known vices and even of James's 'failure of leadership': 'Jubilant as its conclusion is, *A Game at Chess* attests to a peculiar English nationalism that cannot clearly identify the leaders who truly speak for England'.[6] While he argues that the play did 'threaten the Jacobean authorities'[7] he does not speculate about the censorship that allowed it to be staged nor, logically, does he suppose it had powerful sponsors.

But others have not been convinced either that the play was as daring or as critical as all that, or that a conspiracy is necessary to explain how it could have been staged. Key to this argument – variously advanced by Jerzy Limon,

4 Heinemann, *Puritanism and Theatre*, 166–9.
5 Tricomi, *Anticourt Drama in England*, 141.
6 Ibid., 148, 149.   7 Ibid., 144.

Thomas Cogswell and T. H. Howard-Hill[8] – is the 'moment' of the play, its precise timing. John Woolley confided at the time that 'such a thing was never before invented. And assuredly had so much been done last year, [the actors] had every man been hanged for it' (*Chess*, 193). That is, he recognised that policy had changed in a way that made the play much less contentious than it would have been only months before. When Charles and Buckingham set out for Spain they did so to cement an unpopular alliance between the leading Catholic and Protestant countries which would have set the seal on James's pacifist foreign policy. When they returned home safe – and with Charles unmarried – they sparked off unprecedented national rejoicing. By February 1624 Charles and Buckingham spoke openly in the House of Lords for war with Spain, and shortly thereafter Buckingham came to a tactical accommodation with his leading critic in the Privy Council, Pembroke. By June, when he issued his proclamation against Jesuits, it is clear that James had also reconciled himself to war with Spain.[9] In short, by the time the play was written, its anti-Spanish, anti-Jesuit message was offensive to no one who mattered and so closely mirrored national policy that there is no reason to wonder why Sir Henry Herbert should have licensed it normally, as he did on 12 June (*Chess*, 192). Limon still conceded that sponsorship might have been a factor: 'Because the play reveals striking congruity with the new ideology of "the war party" headed by the Duke of Buckingham and Prince Charles, it is therefore...plausible that these two sponsored the production'.[10] But Trevor Howard-Hill denies the need for special sponsorship, seeing the play as an uncritical celebration of a moment of common national purpose in its antipathy to Spain: 'This accounts for its popularity, its toleration by the authorities, and its initial approval by the censor.'[11]

It is perhaps not surprising that a play can give rise to such a wide variety of views. Each of these conclusions is based on at least four 'readings', which are properly distinct from each other but which inevitably overlap in suggestive ways: of the play text(s); of the relationship between text and performance;

---

8 Limon, *Dangerous Matter*; Cogswell, 'Thomas Middleton and the court', *Huntington Library Quarterly* 42 (1984), 273–88; Howard-Hill, 'Political interpretations of Middleton's *A Game at Chess*', *Year's Work in English Studies* 21 (1991), 274–85.
9 See Ruigh, *Parliament of 1624*, 244–5, 300.
10 Limon, *Dangerous Matter*, 98. The idea that Buckingham might have sponsored the play is not new, but Limon outlines a publishing, political and historical context which takes the suggestion beyond simple speculation. Yet, as both Heinemann and Tricomi point out, when the White Knight and Duke 'feign a little' (4.4.17) to entrap the Black House, the White Duke does admit to various vices, including womanising and vanity about his own figure, for which Buckingham was notorious.
11 Howard-Hill, *Middleton's 'Vulgar Pasquin'*, 108.

of processes of censorship and sponsorship; and of the politics of the national moment in mid 1624. Given the subjective slippage inherent in all of these, we should perhaps accept that objective conclusions are unattainable. What I propose to do here is to offer an account of the play from its inception, through aspects of its writing, to its performance, scrutiny by the authorities and beyond. I hope in the process to give some sense of the complexity of the evidence, and to make room for individual readers to engage in the debate.

We cannot know exactly when the play first took shape in Middleton's mind, but it can hardly have done so in anything like definitive form before the return of Charles and Buckingham from Spain (5 October 1623). We know that Herbert licensed the play on 12 June 1624, and since in the extensive later enquiries no one charged the actors with adding anything which was not 'allowed' it is reasonable to assume that Herbert saw something like the fullest versions of the play that have survived: the eye-witness account rendered by Holles tallies closely with these. Attempts have been made to pin the date and motive of composition more closely by reference to published work on which Middleton is known, or supposed, to have drawn; but nothing is really conclusive. He certainly drew on various recent anti-Spanish and anti-Catholic pamphlets, including Thomas Scott's *Vox Populi* (1620) and its *Second Part* (1624), John Reynolds's *Vox Coeli* (1624), Thomas Robinson's *The Anatomy of an English Nunnery in Lisbon* (1622), John Gee's *The Foot out of the Snare* (1624) and Thomas Goad's *The Friar's Chronicle* (1623). But none of these can really be shown to have given Middleton key elements of his plot or the shape of the play, which seem to have been his own invention. Many of them, including Scott's *The Second Part of Vox Populi*, perhaps published within a month of Herbert's licence, were mined for additional scandal to be associated with Gondomar/the Black Knight. But his stage figure is essentially sculpted from theatrical precedents such as Shakespeare's Richard III, Marlowe's Jew of Malta or Jonson's Volpone — ingenious villains in love with their own ingenuity, who forge an endearingly confidential relationship with the audience before succumbing to an inevitable nemesis.

Although it is clear, then, that Middleton was scanning the presses for useful material, this seems not to have had a bearing on the final stages of the play's composition. We can deduce this from the Archdall–Folger manuscript of the play. This is a copy in Crane's handwriting, which is actually dated by him to 13 August 1624 – one of the days of the play's performance. Yet it clearly reflects an early stage of composition: in particular, it lacks entirely the character of the Fat Bishop, it differs significantly from other texts in respect of the White King's Pawn, and it does not contain the flamboyant theatrical ending in which the members of the Black House are consigned to 'the bag'. Nevertheless, all the known sources on which Middleton drew can already be traced in the Archdall–Folger text.

Trevor Howard-Hill has argued that the late additions to the script, and especially the creation of the Fat Bishop, skewed Middleton's initial design away from essentially serious moral satire – centrally focused on a Jesuit plot to seduce the White Queen's Pawn – towards topical comedy. And he lays this at the door of the actors: 'There is no reason to doubt that this significant wrenching of the play from the playwright's fundamental conception was inspired by the theatrical company after Middleton had shown them his early script'.[12] The Fat Bishop represents Marc Antonio De Dominis, Archbishop of Spalato, a Catholic prelate who had ostentatiously converted to Anglicanism, then equally ostentatiously returned to Rome. As such he is a weather-vane in England's struggle with Roman Catholicism, but he had no links with Spain, Gondomar or the politics of 1623–4. The invention of a feud between the Fat Bishop and the Black Knight broadens the comedy of the latter's plotting, and Middleton makes the Fat Bishop the dominant figure in the consignment of the Black House to 'the bag' at the end, completely overshadowing the Black Knight (whose discomfiture we might have expected to be central) and making the final scene one of farce as much as moral vindication.

But is Howard-Hill right to lay these developments at the door of the actors, suggesting that their instinct for pleasing an audience cut across the author's more serious purpose? The invention of the Fat Bishop reunited Middleton with his old collaborator, William Rowley, who played the role.[13] The two men worked together on a number of plays as writers, most famously *The Changeling* (1622), where Rowley also played the fool role of Lollio, characteristically making comic capital out of his great physical bulk. He had done something similar in the roles of Plumporridge in Middleton's *Masque of Heroes* (1619) and the Fat Clown in his own *All's Lost by Lust* (c. 1620). The Fat Bishop is thus another modulation of a well-established and successful stage persona, and could as well derive from Middleton's past associations as from the instincts of the King's Men.

The business of the White King's Pawn is more complex, but instructively so. In Archdall–Folger his character is someone with pro-Jesuit leanings. The Black Knight scorns him as a 'Poor Jesuit ridden soul' (1.1.326) and leads him on with promises of a cardinal's 'red hat' (2.2.220). This apparently points to someone

12 Ibid., 70.
13 Although Rowley was a member of Prince Charles's Men, he intermittently performed with the King's Men from 1610.

like Sir Toby Matthew, a Jesuit convert who advocated restoration of the Catholic bishops in England and had been party to the marriage negotiations in Madrid. On the other hand, on the Pawn's first appearance the Black Knight calls out '*Curanda pecunia*' (1.1.308) – 'Watch out for your money.' This scarcely seems relevant to Matthew, but might well apply to Lionel Cranfield, Earl of Middlesex. As lord treasurer he had long opposed war with Spain on grounds of cost, had incurred Buckingham's displeasure when the duke's own policy changed in that direction, and paid the price, being accused of corruption in the House of Commons (15 April 1624) and convicted by the Lords (12 May). But Cranfield had no leanings towards Catholicism or the Jesuits. Yet when Middleton expanded the significance of the role he did so in ways that made the identification with Cranfield much more pronounced. He added these lines (the Pawn addressing the Black Knight):

> there shall nothing happen,
> Believe it, to extenuate your cause
> Or to oppress her friends, but I will strive
> To cross it with my counsel, purse and power,
> Keep all supplies back, both in means and men,
> That may raise strength against you.
>
> (1.1.216–21)

which could readily be interpreted as Cranfield's promise of anti-war counsel in the Privy Council; and these *in italics* (the White King's denunciation after his Pawn's treachery has been revealed):

> Has my goodness,
> Clemency, love, and favour gracious raised thee
> *From a condition next to popular labour,*
> *Took thee from all the dubitable hazards*
> *Of fortune, her most unsecure adventures,*
> And grafted thee into a branch of honour,
> And dost thou fall from the top-bough by the rottenness
> Of thy alone corruption, like a fruit
> That's over-ripened by the beams of favour?
>
> (3.1.263–70)

Lines which originally might have applied to any recipient of royal favour now clearly relate to someone who has risen from manual labour and trade to wealth and nobility: a rare trajectory which the one-time apprentice Cranfield had famously achieved.

So the White King's Pawn was always a rather mixed character – as it were, Matthew with a dash of Cranfield, who became predominantly Cranfield but without shedding Matthew characteristics. Yet when John Holles saw the character on stage he identified him with neither Cranfield nor Matthew, but John Digby, Earl of Bristol. Bristol had been resident ambassador in Madrid throughout the marriage negotiations, became Buckingham's scapegoat for the failure of that business, and was recalled in December 1623 to face impeachment for treason – a charge still hanging over him when the play was staged. Bristol neither had Jesuit leanings nor had risen from '*a condition next to popular labour*': Holles quoted those lines almost verbatim from performance, yet he still identified Bristol (who was a friend) from what he saw. Holles was neither a fool nor an inattentive observer, so unless the actors did something to prompt this identification, we should perhaps conclude that the White King's Pawn was perceived as an all-purpose traitor-figure, and that Holles only focused on Bristol because his was the case which most preoccupied him. Middleton perhaps worked on such ambiguity all along, calculating that this – along with the bland non-specificity of his handling of the Spanish expedition – would create a functional veiling acceptable to the Master of the Revels. The whole business should give pause today to anyone making over-easy assumptions about deciphering any facet of the play's allegory.

So Middleton shaped his play. But no surviving manuscript decisively gives us his last thoughts on it. One copy (Trinity College, Cambridge) is entirely in his own hand, but is quite careless in some respects and does not reflect his final thinking on the last scene; another (Bridgewater–Huntington) gives just the closing scenes in Middleton's hand, in something like definitive form, but is less satisfactory elsewhere. One of Crane's more elegant copies (British Library Lansdowne) reflects something close to the final version of the play, but is carefully edited as a reading text rather than as a record of performance and omits a whole scene – act 3 scene 2 in modern editions, a clown scene with great play on anal sexuality and on who 'firks' whom. Perhaps Crane omitted it on grounds of taste, or judged that it was essentially stage business which would not translate well on to the page. We may infer from Holles (who mentions a 'Spanish eunuch' and who found 'this vulgar pasquin' generally quite tasteless) that the scene was staged. But we do not have the copy that Herbert 'allowed', and for all the information we have on the play we are left guessing about many features of how it was actually staged in August 1624.

For example, we know that the action started with a conventional prologue and then an induction, involving Ignatius Loyola (founder of the Jesuits, d. 1556) and Envy. The play proper is then framed as Envy's 'dream', in response to Loyola's demand to know how his followers were prospering. Loyola has something of the shock value of Marlowe's Machevil, while the framing device resembles those of *The Spanish Tragedy* or *The Taming of the Shrew*. But was it presented, like Kyd's, on the upper stage, and did Loyola and Envy oversee the entire action? We have to look hard for answers. The Trinity manuscript begins with the direction: *Ignatius Loyola appearing, Error at his foot as asleep.* Does this suggest a discovery of some kind, a curtain being drawn back? Or an ingenious elevation from below the stage? *'Error at his foot'* makes the upper stage a less likely option, since the balustrade we believe the second Globe had there would have obscured it. Only Crane's BL Lansdowne text (the one least concerned with stage action) actually tells us that the characters left the stage at the end of the induction. But this is confirmed by Holles, who records that Loyola 'vanisheth, leaving his benediction over the work' (*Chess*, 199). Ambassador Coloma complicates matters, however. He did not personally see the play, but sent a detailed account of it to his superior in Madrid, the Conde-Duque Olivares (who appears in the play as the Black Duke) and this was presumably based on eye-witness accounts. In his version, 'when [Loyola] found himself again in the world, the first thing he did was to rape one of the female penitents' (*Chess*, 194). Nothing like this appears in any text. However, the Jesuit Black Bishop's Pawn does attempt to rape the White Queen's Pawn so it is not impossible that Coloma hazily records the actor playing Loyola doubling the part of the Black Bishop's Pawn, perhaps even partially retaining one identity in the other. There are many features of the play as a whole where we are left to piece together the possibilities in this way.

Another instance is the 'bag' into which all captured pieces are cast. It is often supposed that the bag was a hell-mouth, a gaping opening with fire and other marks of the devil, like that used for sinners in the old morality plays. Indeed, Coloma reported that 'he who acted the Prince of Wales heartily beat and kicked the "Count of Gondomar" into Hell, which consisted of a great hole and hideous figures' (*Chess*, 195). But Holles, who saw it for himself, put it somewhat differently: 'the Prince making a full discovery of all their knaveries, Olivares, Gondomar... are by the Prince putt... into the bag, & so the play ends' (*Chess*, 199). This is consonant with Middleton's text, where 'bag' always has the primary sense of the bag into which chess-pieces are retired when they are taken, with only a secondary suggestion of hell. This emphasis continues even in the last scene when (apparently for the first time) the members of the Black House are *physically* consigned to the 'bag'. So, in the moment of the White House's triumph, the White King declares:

'Tis their best course that so have lost their fame
To put their heads into the bag for shame.
[*The bag opens, the Black side in it.*]
And there behold: the bag, like hell-mouth, opens
To take her due.   (5.3.177–80)

That is, Middleton acknowledges the analogy with the old hell-mouth but distinguishes the witty variation of his own staging. A tent-like structure representing the bag was presumably erected on stage, perhaps over the central trap door by which the Black House may make their final exit. We could hardly expect the Spanish ambassador to appreciate the distinction: either version was a demeaning insult to his royal master. But it tells us something of the flavour of Middleton's satire, and helps to explain why the climax is dominated by the comic presence of the Fat Bishop, squashing all the other members of the Black House, rather than by the fall of the Black Knight.

Some other features of the staging are less ambiguous, especially those which contributed to the identification of the Black Knight. Chamberlain reported that the actors 'counterfeited his person to the life, with all his graces and faces, and had gotten (they say) a cast suit of his apparel for the purpose, with his litter' (*Chess*, 205). There is no other verification of the 'cast suit', though it is not improbable, but Holles confirms the litter: 'a representation of all our Spanish traffic, where Gondomar his litter, his open chair for the ease of that fistulated part, Spalato &ca, appeared upon the stage' (*Chess*, 198). Gondomar suffered cruelly from an anal fistula, the subject of much comic commentary by Middleton. He was carried around in a specially adapted litter, which must have been a familiar sight; and the actors acquired it for their performance. This was a late development, not being in Archdall–Folger. But all later versions add nine lines to the beginning of act 5 for what must, this late in the action, have been a *coup de théâtre*. As the stage direction in the Bridgewater–Huntington text has it: 'Enter the Black Knight in his litter, as passing in haste over the stage.'

Which left absolutely no room for ambiguity as to the identity of the Black Knight: not that there had been much before this. Repeated contemporary references to 'the play of Gondomar' confirm that the point was not lost. Holles and others had no difficulty, either, in identifying the Fat Bishop as 'Spalato'. This might be expected, since De Dominis was a portly figure, and the text makes no bones about discussing posts he had been given as a reward for his initial conversion from Rome, such as the mastership of the Savoy Hospital (2.2.36ff). The striking thing here is that this late addition is the only character, along with the Black Knight, to be so transparently identifiable, and to have been made unambiguously so by the actors. All the other 'identifications' have to be inferred, and there is little to suggest that the actors went out of their way to underscore them.[14] And since there was no actual overlap between the careers of Gondomar and De Dominis (both of whom had left England behind when the play was staged) these foregrounded identities to an extent obfuscate the details of the play's wider allegory, rather than bringing them into sharper focus.

For example, what should we make of the White Queen in a narrative dominated by Gondomar and De Dominis, and concluding with events fairly clearly located in 1623? She cannot in any literal sense 'be' Queen Anne, who had died in 1618, and so was not alive to lament the departure of the White Knight/Prince Charles for the Black House/Madrid, or to be nearly 'taken' by the Fat Bishop – events portrayed towards the end of act 4. Nor does it make any literal sense that the Black King should lust after the White Queen, as he does, if he 'is' Philip IV of Spain (only thirteen when she died and not crowned until 1621) and she Anne. Hence her character is usually taken to represent something rather more abstract, like the Church of England, to which – as its titular head – James I could be said to be married. In that sense, the Black King's lust, like the various assaults upon the White Queen's Pawn, could figure the designs of the Catholic powers on the Anglican church. Yet audiences would hardly have forgotten that Queen Anne had herself been a notable convert to Catholicism, so that the Fat Bishop's attempt to 'take' the White Queen on his own return to Rome could have made figurative (if not literal) sense as a commentary on the vulnerability of the English royal family to Catholic wiles. The instance of the White Queen graphically demonstrates why it is possible for critics like Heinemann and Howard-Hill to reach such antithetical conclusions about Middleton's attitude towards the English figures shadowed in the play. Are they virtuous characters who finally turn the tables on the ingenious villainy to which they have been subjected? Or are they weak, easily deluded and perhaps self-important characters, who must bear some responsibility for the danger in which 'the White House' finds itself? They are, in fact, both and neither: such is the functional ambiguity with which Middleton invests the play. Consider the White King's denunciation of his Pawn, quoted above: is this the righteous indignation of a just and betrayed king, or the belated self-justification of a man who should have observed earlier the calibre of those he promoted?

14 Coloma did report that 'the king of the blacks has easily been taken for our lord the King, because of his youth, dress, and other details' (*Chess*, 194).

Whatever contemporaries may have felt on this score, they did not record it for posterity. It is not an issue on which the official investigation concentrated. Albert Tricomi asks, 'Why did this play so threaten the Jacobean authorities?'.[15] But what evidence is there that it threatened them at all? None of them did anything to stop it until the Spanish ambassador complained, and this despite the fact that notable figures such as Sir Henry Wotton, Sir Albert Morton, Sir Benjamin Ruddier and Sir Thomas Lake (a former secretary of state, no less) had seen it (*Chess*, 205). As I have argued elsewhere, we need to look closely here at the circumstances in which Coloma complained.[16] There are numerous other instances of foreign ambassadors complaining about plays which traduced their nations, but Coloma was in an unusually difficult situation. Earlier in the year, he and his fellow envoy, the Marqués de la Hinosa, had been exposed in a plot to accuse Buckingham of planning to remove James from the throne, a matter which the English ambassador in Madrid was at that very time preparing to raise. Hinosa had been required ignominiously to leave the country, and Coloma worried whether he should also have left, fearing that he might be blamed for the disastrous direction Anglo-Spanish relations had taken in recent months. While England and Spain were clearly heading for war, diplomatic relations had not at this point been broken. And *A Game at Chess* conveniently restored to Coloma a fig-leaf of diplomatic dignity which the plotting had stripped him of.

When James responded to Coloma's complaint by writing (via his secretary of state, Sir Edward Conway) to the members of the Privy Council still in London, it is clear that he was aggrieved not only by the play but by its having been allowed to become such a diplomatic issue: 'His Majesty . . . wonders much . . . that the first notice thereof should be brought to him, by a foreign Ambassador, while so many Ministers of his owne are thereabouts and cannot but have heard about it' (*Chess*, 200). The play is less a threat than an embarrassment. But James is also quite specific about how the play is genuinely offensive: he 'remembers well there was a commandment and restraint given against the representing of any modern Christian kings in those stage-plays', a condition he believes to have been breached. He requires that the Privy Council 'presently call before you aswell the poet, that made the comedy, as the comedians that acted it . . . And then certify his Majesty what you find that comedy to be, in what points it is most offensive, by whom it was made, by whom licensed, and what course you thinke fittest to be held for the exemplary, and severe punishment of the present offenders'. That is, having told the

15 Tricomi, *Anticourt Drama in England*, 144.
16 See Dutton, *Licensing, Censorship and Authorship*.

Privy Council exactly why it was offensive and how remiss they themselves had been, James orders them to go through the proper motions of establishing blame with a view to 'exemplary, and severe punishment': an outcome which will leave Coloma without further grounds for complaint. In the meantime the King's Men are bound over with sureties and forbidden to play at all.

In their reply the Council neatly side-stepped all imputation of blame, which they redirected upon 'Sir Henry Herbert knight, Master of the Revells', by whom the actors' 'perfect copy' of the play had been 'seen and allowed ... under his owne hand, and subscribed in the last Page of the said booke' (*Chess*, 204). Under examination, the actors 'confidently protested, they added or varied from the same nothing at all', which other evidence suggests is true. So the Privy Council sent the licensed copy itself to the king, suggesting that he 'call Sir Henry Herbert before you to know a reason of his licensing thereof, who (as we are given to understand) is now attending at Court' (*Chess*, 205). They had failed, however, to examine the author, 'one Middleton, who shifting out of the way ... We have given warrant to a messenger for the apprehending of him'. This seemed to satisfy James, except that in Conway's next reply (27 August) the Council was specifically required to 'examine by whose direction, and application the personating of Gondomar, and others was done. And that being found out, that party, or parties to be severely punished. His Majesty being unwilling for one's sake, and only fault to punish the innocent or utterly to ruin the Company' (*Chess*, 206). Indeed, that same day Lord Chamberlain Pembroke also wrote to inform them 'That his Majesty now conceives the punishment [of the actors] is not satisfactory for that their insolency, yet such, as since it stops the current of their poor livelihood and maintenance without much prejudice they cannot longer undergo'. The King's Men were therefore to be allowed to resume playing, though not *A Game at Chess*. 'Yet notwithstanding that my Lordships proceed in their disquisition to find out the original root of this offence, whether it sprang from the poet, players, or both' (*Chess*, 207).

Although matters rumbled on, with Middleton's son, Edward, being re quired to attend when the father still could not be found, this was effectively the end of the affair. It is possible, though by no means certain, that Middleton was actually imprisoned, since verses exist which are said to be his petition to the king for release (*Chess*, 211–12). If so, this must have been because he was judged guilty of 'the original root of this offence' which was specifically 'the personating of Gondomar, and others' (and so by implication 'representing ... modern Christian kings') rather than the satirical content of the play as a whole. There is a parallel for this in Henry Herbert's later treatment of James

Shirley's *The Ball*, which he had licensed in the normal way, but then found 'there were divers personated so naturally, both of lords and others of the court, that I took it ill'.[17] He pursued this with Christopher Beeston, manager of the Queen's Men, who 'promised . . . that he would not suffer it to be done by the poet any more, who deserves to be punished; and the first that offends in this kind, of poets or players, shall be sure of public punishment'. Personations were multiply offensive, as an affront both to the persons concerned (especially to 'modern Christian kings' or their ministers) and also to the Master of the Revels, since they made a mockery of the licence he had granted in good faith. It stands to reason that everyone involved in 'personations' – authors and actors alike – would know what was going on. Yet Herbert and Beeston reached an understanding that the 'poet', Shirley, was responsible here, as the instigator: a comfortable understanding in that a guilty party could be identified for 'public punishment' without interrupting the normal business of the acting company and their licenser. The search, after *A Game at Chess*, for 'the original root of this offence' bears all the hallmarks of a similar understanding, though one involving a wider cast of authorities – including a foreign ambassador, to whose dignity protocol required that James and his ministers still paid public respect. But Coloma was recalled home within weeks of the performance of the play. If Middleton was indeed put in prison, it is difficult to see whose interests it would have served to keep him there after that.

17 Bawcutt (ed.), *The Control and Censorship of Caroline Drama*, 177.

18

The condition of the theatres in 1642

MARTIN BUTLER

The London theatres had been active for barely eight months of 1642 when their operations were peremptorily halted by order of Parliament. On 2 September, a directive was issued from Westminster commanding that performances of stage plays should cease forthwith:[1]

> Whereas the distressed Estate of Ireland, steeped in her own Blood, and the distracted Estate of England, threatened with a Cloud of Blood by a Civil War, call for all possible Means to appease and avert the Wrath of God, appearing in these Judgements; amongst which, Fasting and Prayer, having been often tried to be very effectual, have been lately and are still enjoined; and whereas Public Sports do not well agree with public Calamities, nor Public Stage-plays with the Seasons of Humiliation, this being an Exercise of sad and pious Solemnity, and the other being Spectacles of Pleasure, too commonly expressing lascivious Mirth and Levity: It is therefore thought fit, and Ordained, by the Lords and Commons in this Parliament assembled, That while these sad causes and set Times of Humiliation do continue, Public Stage Plays shall cease, and be forborne, instead of which are recommended to the People of this Land the profitable and seasonable considerations of Repentance, Reconciliation, and Peace with God, which probably may produce outward Peace and Prosperity, and bring again Times of Joy and Gladness to these Nations.

At around the same date, the Master of the Revels, Sir Henry Herbert, having licensed no new play since *The Irish Rebellion* on 8 June, wrote in his office book, 'Here ended my allowance of plays, for the war began in Aug. 1642'.[2] It would be another eighteen years before public performances of plays were again officially allowed in the capital.

The parliamentary order against stage plays has long been taken as marking the moment at which 'Elizabethan' drama effectively ended. By the time that conditions were restored under which London's theatres could once again

---

1 Firth and Rait (eds.), *Acts and Ordinances of the Interregnum*, I, 26–7.
2 Bawcutt, *The Control and Censorship of Caroline Drama*, 211.

open legally, the character of the drama that they hosted had completely altered. The arrival of actresses and the introduction of changeable scenery into the public theatres were only the most conspicuous signs that the plays that would be seen on the stages of 1660 would take forms radically different from those they had possessed before. September 1642 was thus a watershed in the history of English theatre, and marks a sharp discontinuity between two periods of drama. It has also frequently been regarded as a moment redolent with ideological symbolism, which brought to a head enmities that had long existed between the drama and those who were hostile to it on grounds of religion or morality. Not only was playing discontinued by order of Parliament, but the directive – with its emphasis on the need for fasting and prayer, and its assertion that 'lascivious mirth and levity' were ill-suited to times of 'sad and pious solemnity' – resonated with the discourse of puritan anti-theatricalism. Language such as this harked back to the 1570s, and the complaints made by preachers and city fathers that the building of permanent theatres in London was detrimental to civic order and morality. Such symbolism cannot easily be overlooked. The closure of the playhouses at the same moment that court and parliament went to war seems to signal once and for all that the fortunes of English Renaissance drama ultimately depended on the crown, and that only the king's presence at Whitehall had protected the drama from the enmity of puritanism. It seems to confirm that early Stuart theatre must always have been living on borrowed time.

Yet it is hard to know whether the playgoers who were deprived of their entertainment in 1642 saw parliament's order so clearly as a victory for puritanism, or imagined that stage plays would not again be legally available in London until 1660. London citizens were used to the playhouses being closed at moments of collective peril. They had been shut as security measures on the deaths of Queen Elizabeth and Prince Henry, and they were repeatedly closed, sometimes for months on end, during visitations of the plague, in order to limit the spread of infection. In fact, even had circumstances been more stable the playhouses would have closed at the end of August, for the weekly number of deaths due to plague passed at that moment through the forty mark, which was the ceiling that usually signalled the suspension of playing.[3] In normal times the theatres were also regularly shut during Lent, for the sake of the austerity of the season, and a similar motive is suggested in the directive's adjurations about 'set times of humiliation' and 'seasonable considerations of

---

3 Bentley, *The Jacobean and Caroline Stage*, II, 671; Gurr, *The Shakespearian Playing Companies*, 90.

repentance'. Such language linked the order's objectives with the acts of contrition which parliament was enjoining the whole nation to make at this time of uncertainty (in the contemporary mind plague and providential punishment were closely linked). Regular monthly fasts had been instituted on a national scale in January and, just a week before the ban on playing, parliament issued a further ordinance commanding that the fasts be more strictly observed.[4] Thus the theatres' closure belonged to an austerity drive that many at this moment felt to be desirable.

What was unclear in September was whether the ban on plays would be permanent, or whether it might be lifted once the upheavals generated by hostilities between king and parliament had subsided. Parliament's directive did not command the total suppression of plays but only their suspension 'while these sad causes and set times of humiliation do continue'. This form of words did not directly connote ideological hostility to drama as such, but linked the closure to the crisis caused by the political breakdown. It left open a possibility that playing might resume when the crisis ended, and the directive's closing prediction that 'Times of Joy and Gladness' would again be legitimate once peace was restored seems to imply as much. In other inhibitions issued by parliament in these years the possibility of a return to playing was implicit. When in January 1641 some MPs first mooted a closure, it was proposed to be only 'for a season';[5] in 1646 parliament awarded arrears of pay to the King's Men; and when in July 1647 the 1642 order was renewed, it was limited to a fixed term of six months. Matters changed with the much more severe decree of February 1648, issued in the context of the alarm caused by Charles's 'Engagement' with the Scots. This used language that more unambiguously expressed an attitude of moral and theological hostility to the theatre, and commanded that the playhouses themselves should be demolished. Subsequently several theatres were deliberately ruined, including the Salisbury Court and the Fortune; the Globe had already been pulled down in 1644. Still, the Blackfriars and the Hope were not demolished until 1655–6, and surreptitious playing at various venues continued on and off throughout the Interregnum. At the Restoration, some theatres, such as the Red Bull and the Drury Lane Cockpit / Phoenix, were still standing and were capable of being used for drama.

It is certainly the case that by the end of 1642 power had shifted decisively towards people who were opposed to plays on ideological grounds. In the provinces touring companies were increasingly meeting hostility from local

---

4 See Durston, ' "For the better humiliation of the people" ', *The Seventeenth Century* 7 (1992), 129–49.
5 Coates, Young and Snow (eds.), *The Private Journals of the Long Parliament*, i, 182.

mayors who regarded plays as disruptive to civic life, and many MPs sitting at Westminster saw them in similar terms. In February 1641, Alderman Isaac Pennington, one of the four members for the city, introduced into parliament a petition from the Blackfriars residents complaining that the playhouse in their neighbourhood was a disturbance to the locality and should be shut down. 'A good petition', echoed the Presbyterian Sir Simonds D'Ewes, 'Gods howse not so neare Divils'.[6] The Blackfriars residents, whose frequent protests against the playhouse on grounds of its inconvenience had borne no fruit with the Privy Council, must have hoped that the ears of the Commons would be more attuned to their grievances. Undoubtedly many MPs would have applauded the suppression of playing as one step towards the enforcement of greater moral and social discipline in the nation at large, along with maypoles, hobby-horses and Sunday dancing. In the 1640s and 50s parliament and the Westminster Assembly began a general assault on England's traditional festive culture, bringing forward social legislation designed to inculcate a process of moral renewal. In 1643 an order was made that Charles's *Book of Sports* – the proclamation that had sanctioned games and pastimes on Sundays – be burned. The next year maypoles were banned, and in 1647 Christmas, Easter and other holy days were abrogated by statute. In the 1650s, further legislation was passed that attempted to curb sexual promiscuity, swearing, drunkenness and sabbath-breaking. For many preachers and godly magistrates, the suspension of plays was one step in this larger reformation for which they were ambitious. Plays did not figure in their prescription for a properly ordered society.[7]

But it was by no means self-evident that parliament's establishment as a permanent presence at Westminster signalled in itself the beginning of the end for London's playhouses. Many MPs who arrived in November 1640 were gentlemen or representatives of the professional classes whose education and outlook predisposed them to take pleasure in theatre, and were connoisseurs rather than enemies of drama. For example, the moderate reformer Sir Edward Dering was an avid collector of playbooks, regularly attended plays when in London in the 1620s, and adapted Shakespeare for amateur performance on his Kent estate.[8] Another MP, the lawyer Bulstrode Whitelocke – later to be the

---

6 Bentley, *The Jacobean and Caroline Stage*, I, 64.
7 See Durston, 'Puritan rule and the failure of cultural revolution, 1645–1660', in Durston and Eales (eds.), *The Culture of English Puritanism, 1560–1700*, 210–34; Fletcher, *Reform in the Provinces*; Wrightson, 'The Puritan reformation of manners'; and Hutton, *The Rise and Fall of Merry England*, 200–26.
8 Lennam, 'Sir Edward Dering's collection of playbooks', *Shakespeare Quarterly* 16 (1965), 145–53; Williams and Evans (eds.), *'The History of King Henry the Fourth' as Revised by Sir Edward Dering*.

Republic's ambassador to Sweden and sit on Cromwell's Council of State – had in the 1630s been so well-known an habitué of the Blackfriars that the playhouse band struck up 'Whitelocke's coranto' whenever he appeared.[9] In the House of Lords, the Earl of Essex was a fervent supporter of parliament – his finest hour came as lord general of the parliamentary forces – but he had a long-standing taste for drama, his family having attended the Blackfriars in the 1630s and sponsored their own amateur theatricals.[10] Indeed, as lord chamberlain during 1641–2, Essex temporarily held ultimate control over the affairs of the playhouses and was responsible for the 1641 order protecting the King's Men against unauthorised printing of their plays. Such men, whose literary interests and theatregoing habits were as ingrained as their politics, were far from being a small minority, and some took advantage of their new status as semi-permanent Londoners to enjoy the capital's entertainments. In May 1641, Simonds D'Ewes was exasperated that afternoon sittings of the Commons were being disrupted because 'the greater parte' (so he claimed) of its members kept disappearing to 'Hide Park & playes & bowling grounds'.[11] In January 1642, Peter Legh, the member for Newton, Lancashire, died in a duel that had arisen from an argument in a playhouse, an event that provoked another parliamentary debate on plays, though no inhibition.[12] As opinion polarised, the more theatre-loving MPs typically sided with the crown, but their existence shows that support for parliament did not automatically translate into hostility towards drama. Members of the Commons were still visiting playhouses as late as 1649, when some were embarrassingly found amongst the audiences at illegal performances raided by the army as part of the preparations for Charles's execution.[13]

The immediate context of the suspension was the political upheaval of August 1642 – that extraordinary moment in national history, the greatest crisis that early modern England experienced. The events leading to this emergency were a litany of disasters in which the nation gradually inched towards military confrontation. The moderate reformation that many MPs had expected in 1641 had failed, for the unanimity of parliament collapsed under the pressure of

9 Bentley, *The Jacobean and Caroline Stage*, 1, 40.
10 Berry, 'The Globe bewitched and *El Hombre Fiel*', *Medieval and Renaissance Drama in England* 1 (1984), 211–30; Bentley, *The Jacobean and Caroline Stage*, v, 1270: Butler, *Theatre and Crisis*, 194.
11 Butler, *Theatre and Crisis*, 134.
12 Butler, 'Two playgoers, and the closing of the London theatres, 1642', *Theatre Research International* 9 (1984), 93–9.
13 Hotson, *The Commonwealth and Restoration Stage*, 41. Of course, such reports may have been put about because of their propaganda value, but the fact that people thought that some MPs might still be lovers of theatre is significant in itself.

religious disagreements. In November 1641 matters were galvanised by the rebellion in Ireland, which turned the situation into an international emergency
and created a crisis atmosphere. (This was the moment at which the lawyers of
the Middle Temple decided to suspend their usual Christmas revels, because
of 'the danger and troublesomeness of the times'.[14]) The ensuing months saw
Charles's disastrous attempt to regain the initiative by arresting the leaders
of the Commons and his subsequent departure from London, followed by
the struggle for control of the militia and the munitions stockpiled in the
ports. In the capital, the situation was deeply unstable, for the streets were
thronged with tumultuous crowds, barracking MPs and petitioning for redress
of grievances. For much of the time at Westminster a climate of turbulence and
intimidation prevailed, some of which seems to have been tacitly condoned
by parliament's leaders. Increasingly parliamentary ordinances became preoccupied with crisis measures, with the need to secure the home front and raise
troops for Ireland. The first domestic blood was shed at Manchester on 15 July,
and on 22 August Charles raised his standard at Nottingham, in effect declaring
war on his own parliament. In this context, the preamble to the directive on
playing, which stated that the inhibition was due to the distressed estates of
England and Ireland, was no empty form of words: it identified the order as a
response to an emergency more acute than anyone could have remembered.
Indeed, when the order was printed, it appeared as one of a pair, the other
being a declaration 'for the appeasing and quieting of all unlawful tumults and
insurrections in the several counties of England'.[15] Although the inhibition
pleased those who regarded plays as ungodly, its immediate impetus arose as
much from considerations of security as of morality.

It is evident that political uncertainties were starting to affect the theatres
well before parliament's order was issued. Only one play, Beaumont and
Fletcher's *The Scornful Lady*, was performed at court in the Christmas season 1641–2, a sharp reduction from the dozen or more that were typically
staged in earlier years. Court drama was about to disappear altogether, since
Charles abandoned Whitehall in January, not to return for another seven years.
On the professional stages, the number of new plays that were being produced
may already have been in decline. In 1642, only five plays were presented to
Herbert for licensing, in comparison with twelve in 1639 and eight in 1640 and
1641. This was, of course, an incomplete year, and some plays, notably Shirley's
The Court Secret, were being written when the inhibition fell. Still, fewer drama-
tists were around to do the writing, for natural and accidental wastage had

14 Hopwood and Martin (eds.), *Middle Temple Records*, II, 928.
15 Butler, *Theatre and Crisis*, 137.

significantly depleted the pool of playwrights. Massinger died in 1640, and Ford disappeared from the record about the same time. In spring 1641, Davenant and Suckling fell victim to events, for both became embroiled in the Army plot, a disastrously miscalculated attempt to intimidate parliament with force. This scheme's failure left Davenant in prison, and forced Suckling into exile in Paris, where he committed suicide shortly after. Some moves were afoot in London to close the gap these changes created, for on Massinger's death the King's Men persuaded Shirley to return from Dublin. Nonetheless, the loss of four significant playwrights in a matter of months was a serious blow to productivity. No less telling a sign of difficulties was the prologue to Shirley's *The Sisters*, performed at the Blackfriars in April 1642, which complains that attendance at the playhouse was down:[16]

> Does this look like a term? I cannot tell,
> Our poet thinks the whole town is not well,
> Has took some physic lately, and for fear
> Of catching cold dares not salute this air.
> But there's another reason, I hear say
> London is gone to York, 'tis a great way,
> Pox o'the proverb . . .

By saying 'London is gone to York', Shirley was drawing attention to Charles's absence from the capital, and his decision to make a temporary home in the north. Evidently he believed that the court's removal and the consequent attrition of the genteel London society from which the Blackfriars drew its spectators was responsible for declining audience numbers. It is unclear whether the other, less fashionable playhouses were experiencing similar problems, but they are unlikely to have been immune from the current disruptions.

Still, the difficulties that some playhouses were experiencing in spring 1642 have to be balanced against the legacy of relative social entrenchment that the playhouses had achieved under the early Stuarts. The London theatre was not the same marginal institution that had aroused puritan ire seventy years earlier, but now operated within a more settled commercial framework. Since 1630 the number of active playhouses had been stable at six, and although companies continued to move between venues, most were now firmly identified with one theatre or another, and their personnel remained relatively fixed. As Andrew Gurr has shown, under Charles the system of licensing companies was moving away from direct control by a royal patron to a more hands-off

---

16 Shirley, *Dramatic Works and Poems*, ed. Gifford and Dyce, v, 356.

and economically self-sufficient model.[17] Companies no longer needed the direct personal authorisation of royalty but were issued with annual licences by the Master of the Revels, and some, like the Red Bull company (which never acquired a patron), were known simply by the name of their playhouse. The turnover of plays had also become less frantic, and patterns of production were more regular. By the 1630s most theatres had stocks of tested favourites on which to draw, so fewer new scripts were needed, while the practice of staging a different play every day was beginning to be dislodged by that of mounting single plays for extended periods, sometimes for several weeks.[18] At the same time, the legitimacy of playgoing as a core social activity had become more established, as the fashionable theatres functioned increasingly as the haunts of London's incipient *beau monde*. Their geographical situation near the Inns of Court and the luxury housing developments of the future West End made them attractive meeting places for the gentlemen and wits who were gradually being drawn to London by its reputation as a social and entertainment centre. And plays themselves were becoming esteemed as serious literature and collectable objects, more playbooks being printed in the 1630s than in any previous decade. By 1642, one can identify the beginnings of a critical discourse about drama and an attitude of connoisseurship towards it that bespoke a new valorisation of theatre as an integral part of London's cultural and social life.

The wartime conditions of the 1640s rapidly brought this developing leisure industry to an end, but the theatres' commercial entrenchment gave them a momentum that lasted significantly beyond the king's departure from London. Although Charles left Whitehall for good on 10 January, Sir Henry Herbert went on licensing plays into the summer and the playhouses continued performing for another eight months. But, as the crisis intensified, this situation could not last: with king and parliament going to war and Whitehall's household system in disarray, the administrative structures by which the playhouses were regulated disappeared, and suspension hardened into suppression. Nonetheless, the trickle of surreptitious theatrical performances that can be traced beyond September 1642 demonstrates that the inhibition was never completely effective. Sir Humphrey Mildmay, whose account book provides important information about theatregoing in the 1630s, continued to see plays and rope-dancing down to November 1643.[19] Somehow the Fortune playhouse managed to open after the order, for in October 1643 their 'wanton and

---

17 *The Shakespearian Playing Companies*, 137.
18 Ibid., 85.
19 Bentley, *The Jacobean and Caroline Stage*, II, 680.

licentious plays' had to be put down by force.[20] And in January 1644, *The Actors' Remonstrance*, an appeal to parliament supposedly written by unemployed players, complained that although drama had been banned, puppet-shows and bear-baitings continued, and pleaded with parliament to correct this anomaly by rescinding the restraint on plays. Clearly, even at this late date some actors felt that the pool of potential playgoers remained significant, and hoped the suspension might be lifted. The times may have been unpropitious for drama, but the public appetite for plays was never entirely eradicated.

What would theatregoers of 1642 have encountered before stage plays ceased? Five companies were active, performing in six theatres. Of these, easily the most successful were the King's Men, whose operations since 1608 had been based at the Blackfriars playhouse within the city walls. The company of Shakespeare and Burbage, they had built up an enviable reputation. On Shakespeare's retirement, they retained Fletcher as house playwright; when Fletcher died, Massinger and Davenant became attached to them, and Shirley was recruited after Massinger's death. The King's Men were thus sustained across four decades by playwrights who managed to be both admired and unfailingly productive, and the 1641 order protecting their plays against unauthorised publication listed sixty-one current titles, over and above their many plays already in print. The quality of their acting was no less applauded, for after Burbage's death they acquired Joseph Taylor, who was perhaps the most admired tragic actor of his generation, and when the playhouses closed another youthful star, Stephen Hammerton, was rising. Undoubtedly a main reason for the King's Men's success was the stability of their operation over a long period. Unlike most other companies they were not controlled by an impresario, who from time to time might break up the troupe for strategic reasons or move them from theatre to theatre, but were led by a group of player–sharers whose stake in the operation was both financial and artistic. The consequence of that arrangement was the security and success they consistently achieved down to 1642.

The King's Men also had the greatest reputation for sophistication and status. As the premier company, they were most frequently invited to perform at court, and on four occasions Henrietta Maria herself attended the Blackfriars, twice with her nephew, the Palatine Prince. As one mark of favour, she presented the company with the costumes used in her court pastoral *The Shepherd's Paradise* (1633), a gesture repeated in 1638 by Sir John Suckling, who

---

20 Hotson, *The Commonwealth and Restoration Stage*, 17.

spent £400 on suits when they staged his play *Aglaura*. In the vogue for amateur plays that arose in the 1630s, the Blackfriars was the theatre of choice,
and the King's Men's repertoire came to feature plays by courtiers such as
Suckling, Carlell and Killigrew, that voiced the preoccupations and attitudes
of a relatively restricted elite. Although the Blackfriars was never a coterie,
it did attract spectators from the wealthiest and most powerful circles, and
maintained a very exclusive tone. Its auditorium became a favourite meeting
ground for the emerging Caroline high society, and on at least three occasions
duels broke out between prominent gentlemen jostling for position in the
social arena. Yet while the King's Men were the company whose repertoire
and clientele linked them most closely to the court, they did not unequivo-
cally echo its voice. In 1633, they ran into trouble with the church hierarchy
over remarks about religion in Jonson's *The Magnetic Lady*, and in 1638 Charles
himself ordered lines deleted from Massinger's *The King and the Subject* which
alluded to the current controversy over Ship Money.[21] Moreover, during the
summer months, when many of London's gentry returned to their estates,
the King's Men moved their operations from the small Blackfriars playhouse
to the Globe in Southwark, where they played to a larger audience for lower
prices. In his account of the London companies, Andrew Gurr has described
this twin-track arrangement as quixotic and uneconomic, since it reduced the
company's income by preventing them from renting out the Globe to other
troupes.[22] But it can be explained equally well as a mechanism by which the
King's Men exploited the shifting strengths of the London market, and adjusted
their output to the seasonal profile of their clientele. For all their prominence
in London's fashionable world, they managed to keep in touch with another,
more socially diverse, audience.

Gurr has argued that the King's Men's closeness to Whitehall meant that
they were particularly vulnerable in September 1642. Noting that some sharers
seem to have begun selling off stock immediately after the inhibition was
announced, he suggests that the company recognised at once that the ban was
final and fell apart rapidly.[23] Against this it can be remarked that, although in the
new climate the sharers sought to realise their cash early, the company network
held together for a surprisingly long time, and made several covert attempts
at reviving their activities. Ten King's Men players signed the dedication to

---

21 See Butler, 'Ecclesiastical censorship of early Stuart drama', *Modern Philology* 89 (1992),
   469–81; Dutton, ' "Discourse in the players, though no disobedience" ', *The Ben Jonson
   Journal* 5 (1998), 37–62; and Butler, *Theatre and Crisis*, 71–2.
22 *The Shakespearian Playing Companies*, 117–18.
23 Ibid., 385.

the 1647 Beaumont and Fletcher folio,[24] and in October 1647 it was reported that Blackfriars was being repaired with a view to renewed performances.[25] In January 1648 seven members contracted to repay a debt due to the widow of an eighth, and a surreptitious performance of the company play *Wit without Money* took place at the Red Bull in February. Ten months later several former King's Men were caught performing *The Bloody Brother* at the Drury Lane Cockpit, and had probably been established there for some time.[26] These signs of fugitive activity may be scattered, but they indicate that even at this late date the company had not disintegrated. Along with the other shadowy acting groups that resurfaced in these months, the remaining King's Men were ready to exploit a window of opportunity when one appeared.

In 1642, the principal competitors of the King's Men were the companies at the two other indoor playhouses, the King and Queen's Boys (also known as 'Beeston's Boys') at the Drury Lane Cockpit, and the Queen's Men, performing at the Salisbury Court. The Cockpit company was a new operation that was founded by the impresario Christopher Beeston during the plague closure of 1636–7, but the Cockpit itself had been established since 1617 as London's second most fashionable playhouse. Close to the Inns of Court and the developing West End, it was well placed to attract a quality audience, albeit one markedly less exclusive than the Blackfriars. As the theatre used by the Queen's Men during the years 1625–36, the Cockpit had forged good links to Whitehall: Charles and Henrietta Maria themselves attended a Drury Lane performance of Heywood's *Love's Mistress* in 1634. But unlike the Blackfriars, it never became home to courtly amateurs, and its repertoire mixed old favourites with some of the best new professional writing. Shirley, Heywood, Ford and Massinger supplied the backbone of the repertoire, and Cockpit audiences had a particular taste for plays that depicted everyday life in their familiar London environments. In Shirley's comedies *The Lady of Pleasure* and *Hyde Park*, and Nabbes's *Covent Garden* and *Tottenham Court*, the contemporary urban scene was explored in a quasi-realistic way, providing a mirror in which the manners and mores of metropolitan life could be sympathetically but caustically scrutinised. Yet the Cockpit repertoire also retained some surprisingly old favourites. Chettle's *Hoffman* was revived here *c.* 1631, and Marlowe's *Jew of Malta c.* 1633, Heywood's nostalgic Elizabethan fantasies, *The Fair Maid of the West* and *If You*

---

24 In 1652 Fletcher's *Wild Goose Chase* was printed for the benefit of the former King's Men actors, Taylor and Lowin.

25 Mentioned in *The Perfect Weekly Account* for 6–13 October 1647 (a reference for which I am grateful to Janet Clare).

26 Milhous and Hume, 'New light on English acting companies in 1646, 1648, and 1660', *Review of English Studies*, n.s. 42 (1991), 487–509.

Know Not Me, You Know Nobody, remained on the books. By the mid 1630s the Cockpit was known as the centre of a rich and diverse repertoire, one that appealed to tastes both current and nostalgic.

The Cockpit was essentially Beeston's operation, since he was both the leading member of the companies that played there, and the theatre's owner. He ran its activities like an autocrat, the troupe he founded in 1637 being aggressively managed and marketed. Beeston's Boys were a youthful group, in composition more like the boy companies from the early Jacobean period than the adult Caroline troupes. Beeston created them by dismissing the Queen's Men from his theatre and bringing together bright boys from rival companies, giving them a flying start with the plays he had accumulated. This was effectively the Queen's Men's repertoire, but when Beeston ejected the adults he kept possession of their scripts. When he died in 1638, his son William took over, and his style was no less entrepreneurial. He acquired Richard Brome as his house playwright, in a move which wrong-footed the rival Salisbury Court: not only was Brome the most politically adventurous dramatist of the period, but his recruitment broke his existing contract with the other theatre. Subsequently Beeston secured an order protecting his company's repertoire against performance by competitors, and he seems – uniquely on pre-Restoration professional stages – to have experimented with scenery.[27] He also pushed the company into political risk-taking, mounting in April 1640 a play that voiced offensive reflections on Charles's bungled military campaign against the Scots. I have argued elsewhere that this was Brome's *The Court Beggar*, which, besides satirising a crazed courtier who imagines himself taken prisoner in the north, attacks monopolists, projectors and court playwrights, and clearly echoes the concerns of the Short Parliament, then in session.[28] In a swift and determined response, the Master of the Revels closed down the theatre and sent Beeston and the leading actors to the Marshalsea – the only time in the Caroline period when a politically sensitive play led to imprisonments. Beeston was replaced as the company's governor with a safer pair of hands, Sir William Davenant, but by mid 1641 Davenant had fallen foul of the Army plot and Beeston was back in charge. Brome's *A Jovial Crew* (summer 1641), with its extraordinary depiction of a countryside heading into beggary, shows that the future Cockpit repertoire was unlikely to be shy of topicality.

---

27 Orrell, *The Theatres of Inigo Jones and John Webb*, 60–4.
28 Butler, *Theatre and Crisis*, 220–7. My identification is disputed by Nigel Bawcutt, who thinks the censored play was another text, now lost (*Control and Censorship*, 70–1). I can't believe Beeston would have simultaneously presented two outspoken plays on this sensitive subject, but if so, it makes his risk-taking all the more remarkable.

The remaining indoor playhouse, the Salisbury Court in Whitefriars, was the least secure of the three. This had only been playing since 1629, and its history was more disrupted, for the companies using it changed with unsettling frequency. Although its small size showed its builders wanted to create another exclusive venue, two of its three occupying companies, Prince Charles's Men and the King's Revels, were equally at home performing before citizen audiences in the old-style amphitheatre houses, and it never achieved a cachet to rival the Blackfriars. It is also difficult to define its repertoire, for relatively few plays can be confidently linked with it. Much of its core drama was produced by Brome, who in 1635 was contracted by the manager, Richard Heton, to act as house playwright. Although some of Brome's plays, such as *The Antipodes* and *The Sparagus Garden,* tapped into the vein of fashionable comedy that was a Cockpit speciality, his style was generally more robust and less deferential than that typical at other indoor theatres. Other plays seen here, such as Nathanael Richards's *Messalina* and Thomas Rawlins's *The Rebellion*, had an even more plebeian ethos, and there is evidence to suggest that the repertoire was extensively supplemented by revivals of Jacobean and Elizabethan plays.[29] Whatever the detail of this, it is clear that by 1642 the Salisbury Court was the main victim of the Beestons' canny tactics. The players occupying the theatre were the remnants of the Queen's Men ejected from the Cockpit in 1636, while Heton's ambitions were severely damaged in 1639 when Brome was poached. The company took Brome to law for breach of contract, and bitterly attacked the rival theatre in a 'praeludium' specially written for a revival of Thomas Goffe's *The Careless Shepherdess*. Beeston was forced to give *The Antipodes* back to Salisbury Court, but the few new plays Heton staged in the remaining months do not suggest his theatre was managing to develop a distinctive repertoire of its own.[30] Arguably, the Salisbury Court never successfully resolved the contradictions inherent in its situation, but always remained uncomfortably poised between serving the popular and fashionable ends of the theatrical market.

Since the Blackfriars, Cockpit and Salisbury Court mounted the greatest proportion of newly written plays, they look in 1642 like the most important venues. Yet too exclusive a concentration on the more select playhouses acknowledges only part of London's total theatrical activity, since two open-air amphitheatre playhouses were still functioning – the Fortune in Golding Lane and the Red Bull in Clerkenwell. These playhouses are almost invisible today

---

29 Butler, *Theatre and Crisis*, 184.
30 I develop these points in a forthcoming essay, 'Exit fighting', to be published in A. B. Farmer and A. Zucker (eds.), *Localizing Caroline Drama.*

since few new plays can be associated with them, and even fewer of the texts they did perform survive in print. They had acquired a reputation for attracting popular spectators with unsophisticated tastes, and playwrights with ambitions towards publication tended to place their output elsewhere. Nonetheless, even if the amphitheatres no longer commanded the same status they had held two generations before, the Prince's Men and Red Bull company still performed on a daily basis down to September 1642, playing to large audiences composed of a predominantly citizen clientele. Indeed, it seems likely that on any one day considerably more spectators visited the two amphitheatres than were present at all three of the indoor houses (a differential even greater in the summer, when the genteel audience went out of town and the King's Men moved to the Globe). If we measure significance in terms of numbers rather than esteem, the citizen venues were almost certainly well ahead.

It is evident that the Fortune and Red Bull repertories were dominated by nostalgia for Elizabethan forms. If the Cockpit and Salisbury Court performed some old plays alongside the new, the amphitheatres specialised in what Gurr calls 'drum-and-trumpet plays with wide-mouthed and loud-voiced players': plays involving action, spectacle, broad comedy, acting exaggerated to the point of rant, and popular social appeal.[31] The plays that can be associated with these venues include outsize pseudo-histories and chronicles of exotic adventure, like *Tamburlaine*, *Jugurtha* or *The Four Prentices of London*; wonder-plays of magic and the supernatural, such as *Dr Faustus* and John Kirke's *The Seven Champions of Christendom*; and tales of jolly roguery set amongst brothels and prisons, such as *The Knave in Grain* or Thomas Jordan's *The Walks of Islington and Hogsden*. It is tempting to dismiss amphitheatre taste as crude and undiscriminating, and their production values were indeed far removed from the refined drama of the fashionable theatres. However, the distinguishing feature of the Fortune and Red Bull repertories was not so much vulgarity as conservatism: their audiences enjoyed festive and celebratory performance styles against which the indoor playhouses, with their smaller, intimate auditoria, had generally turned their backs. Since these preferences held little attraction for the more select audiences, it meant that two strands of theatre were coexisting in 1642: the sophisticated literary drama associated with the indoor playhouses, and a tradition of popular performance which, though not highly rated, was still vigorous.

Quite what impact the Fortune and Red Bull had on London's cultural and political life it is hard to judge. Their audiences' backward-looking tastes and delight in exotic plots make the amphitheatres' contribution to the urban

---

31 *The Shakespearian Playing Companies*, 439.

scene appear less than dynamic: Kate McLuskie says they showed 'little evidence of a coherent counter-culture appealing to a lower-class social group'.[32] Yet in a reign when the crown lost public confidence by adopting a seemingly innovative and unpatriotic style of government, that very conservatism, with its nostalgia for time-honoured ways and a more heroic past, may have carried a political charge. Equally, the fantasies and prejudices on which this drama imaginatively played cannot have been without some counterpart in audience aspirations. At the very least, these playhouses fulfilled important functions as disseminators of news and popular political attitudes. If the Red Bull's lost play *The Irish Rebellion* (1642) was anything like Glapthorne's *Albertus Wallenstein* (Globe, 1639), it dramatised recent overseas events in a racily journalistic style. Some amphitheatre plays had topical commentary seeping into them, such as *The Whore New Vamped* (Red Bull, 1639), which was suppressed for its jokes about monopolies and the ecclesiastical courts. Other plays on remote subjects acquired topicality by virtue of oblique allusion: in 1639, during the first 'Bishops' War' in the north, the Fortune courted trouble by reviving *The Cardinal's Conspiracy* and *The Valiant Scot*. Such plays were only incidentally political and hardly added up to a coherent ideology, but, staged for the same city crowds who were calling on parliament to undo recent 'innovations' in church and state, they must have helped to inculcate wider expectations of change.

So although London theatre was showing signs of strain in the early months of 1642, it was far from being moribund, and its total range of activity was remarkably varied. In terms of status, the King's Men were the most prominent company, with their 'Cavalier' plays and intimate ties to Whitehall; nonetheless, the so-called 'love and honour' drama that was the Blackfriars staple was only one element within a more complicated profile. Other playhouses appealed to spectators with less courtly tastes, and the amphitheatres continued to provide venues for large and robust citizen audiences. 'Cavalier' plays may have led one end of the market, but the total picture was more complex, and during the final decade every company encountered some sort of trouble from the political or ecclesiastical authorities. It seems clear that by 1642 a process of gradual stratification had taken hold. Different playhouses were increasingly linked with different levels of the market, and a marked social divide had begun to emerge between the amphitheatres and the more sophisticated indoor playhouses, the effect of which appears in aesthetic differentiations between their

---

32 McLuskie, 'The plays and the playwrights', in Edwards *et al.*, *The Revels History of Drama in English*, IV: *1613–1660*, 168.

453

developing repertoires. However, the separations between these strands were far from absolute, for some companies bridged the incipiently diverging traditions. The King's Revels and Prince's Men moved between amphitheatre and indoor playhouses, and the King's Men worked both the Blackfriars and the Globe. Furthermore, the King's Men were organisationally a different kind of operation from the Cockpit and Salisbury Court companies. They were run in a relatively democratic way by a consortium of player–sharers, whereas the other two elite companies were essentially under the direction of the impresarios Beeston and Heton. The impresario system was the way of the future: when the theatres reopened in 1660, they were placed in the hands of a small managerial monopoly, with correspondingly greater power over their affairs. One can only speculate what the future directions of the two competing systems would have been had the Civil War not happened and the playhouses stayed open beyond 1642.

We can, finally, illustrate some of the functions performed by the drama at this moment by examining a typical text from the year. Brome claimed that *A Jovial Crew* was the last play to be performed, but the last to be written was Shirley's *The Court Secret*, which was still incomplete when the inhibition fell.[33] Intended for the Blackfriars, *The Court Secret* is a tragicomedy of politics and passion set in a fictional but contemporary Spanish court. Prince Carlo and Princess Maria of Spain are destined for arranged marriages with Isabella and Antonio of Portugal, but their desires run elsewhere. Carlo is in love with Clara, the daughter of Duke Mendoza, and Maria with Manuel, the son of Piracquo, an aristocrat who, unjustly exiled, has been conditionally allowed home through the mediation of the king's brother, Roderigo. However, it rapidly becomes apparent that Roderigo has his own self-serving reasons for desiring Piracquo's return, while Carlo and Maria's errant affections bring chaos. Their desires conflict with their politically arranged marriages, and their attentions are unwelcome to Clara and Manuel, who secretly love one another. This situation allows Shirley endless opportunities for encounters that display the conflicting claims of love, inheritance, obedience, discontent and ambition. By act 4, Manuel has apparently killed Carlo in a duel, and events have reached a seemingly inextricable tangle. The court is saved only by the discovery of the 'secret' at which its title hints: that Carlo and Manuel were exchanged at birth, making Manuel the real prince and Clara Carlo's sister.

33 References are to the text in Shirley, *Dramatic Works and Poems*, ed. Gifford and Dyce, vol. v.

This revelation clears the difficulties as if by magic, disclosing a pattern hidden behind the play which, once uncovered, makes its perplexingly frustrated passions fall miraculously into place.

With its elevated heroics amongst a courtly elite, its contrived structure of overlapping passions and its improbable conclusion, *The Court Secret* seems a typically 'Cavalier' play, yet this pejorative label simplifies the intricate ideological work that it performs. The play depicts an aristocratic community suffering from a variety of stresses, and organises its situations to foreground collisions between royalty and subjects which resonate with the concerns of 1642. Although the bulk of its conflicts happen in the horizontal plane – most episodes concern amorous rivalries between aristocrats of broadly similar age and status – the principal underlying faultline is vertical. The most significant structural divide falls between royalty and the rest, since the members of the royal family, whose desires and ambitions run athwart those of their subjects, are the main source of the plot's problems. Clara collides with Princess Maria over love of Manuel, Maria resists the king when he commands her to wed Antonio, Prince Carlo nearly destroys Manuel's loyalty by courting his mistress, Manuel is imprisoned for violence provoked by Antonio, and Piracquo is imperilled by the machinations of the king's brother. These conflicts, arising from the willingness of royal characters to pursue their own desires irrespective of their subjects' wishes, create dilemmas over obedience that put into play conflicting attitudes of patient submission and principled resistance. So while the action never directly alludes to contemporary events, Shirley thickens the romantic plot with an undercurrent of anxiety about the operations of royal power that is more than timely. Affairs of the heart are politicised by being focused on tensions between subjects and princes.

Shirley always presents his king with respect. A commanding but opaque figure, he is a cipher whose motives are allowed to remain diplomatically obscure. But the drama's divided attitudes towards his power are displaced onto his satellites, Carlo and Roderigo, who project opposed aspects of his regality. Carlo, the crown prince, is a figure of consummate duty. Though his desires create excruciating dilemmas of loyalty, he is governed by a neo-chivalric code that makes him punctilious about honour even when he is giving offence to his inferiors. Hence he adopts a disguise to provoke Manuel into a duel, because he needs to challenge him as an equal and knows loyalty will inhibit Manuel from fighting him in his own person. On the other side, the king's brother Roderigo is a self-serving machiavel, who pursues power for its own sake, regardless of right. The king's 'evil genius', he lives in a 'labyrinth' (p. 466) of stratagems designed to turn every event to his advantage, and he advises his brother to use his power ruthlessly. Any policy, he urges, is legitimate against dangerous subjects like Piracquo: 'Kings must act, / And not dispute their maxims' (p. 448). Carlo, by contrast, believes that the same principles apply in public and private. Rebuking the king for not keeping his word to Piracquo, he argues that rulers must observe the dictates of honour:

> This dishonourable
> Retreat will stagger all your people's faith:
> A king to break his sacred word will teach
> The great men to be safe without your service;
> Who will believe your smiles are snares to catch
> Their fortunes; and when once the crowd takes scent
> Of this, you leave yourself no oath to swear by.
>
> (p. 451)

This advice is both moral and pragmatic: monarchs have to keep their promises, since any slur on their probity will damage the basis of obedience. The attitudes of the king towards this sensitive subject are not disclosed, and because catastrophe is pre-empted by 'providence' (p. 513), the plot resolves without his views being tested. But it is difficult not to feel that the voices of his son and brother enable the play to remain in two minds about the sovereignty that he embodies. Carlo's replacement by Manuel allows loyalty to be preserved and the ethos of honourable kingship to be reaffirmed in the next generation, but the problem posed by Roderigo, of royal power untrammelled by responsibility, remains largely unsolved. Shirley's play respects monarchy but still worries over the doubts and dilemmas that attach to it.

The Court Secret exemplifies the complex cultural and ideological work that was being performed by the London theatres in 1642. Had it been staged, the Blackfriars spectators could scarcely have missed the resonance between its double vision over royalty and the inner contradictions with which they were increasingly preoccupied.[34] Simultaneously deferential towards monarchs and mistrustful about the nature of their power, the play struggles to reconcile the contemporary conflict of perceptions, seeking to render the divided experience of 1642 in a historically coherent form. Of course it is also a compensatory fantasy designed to discharge the anxieties that it arouses. The dangers of wilful princes and strained loyalties are dissolved by an ending in which everyone, amazingly, finds their desires falling into new happy patterns, and the message perceived by the servants is the need for reconciliation in court and state:

---

34 They might particularly have felt that the problems posed by Piracquo resembled the dilemmas that Charles had faced in 1641 over Strafford's attainder.

2ND GENTLEMAN: In my opinion, peace and wine and music
   Are more convenient for the natural body
   Than swords or guns.
1ST GENTLEMAN: And for the politic [body] too,
   If men were but so wise to like and cherish
   Their own estates.   (p. 465)

Yet the neatness of the ending is belied by the conflicting attitudes which the play has evoked and the contradictory perceptions between which it oscillates. Written at the exact moment when, offstage, ideological disagreements were escalating into political violence, *The Court Secret* tries to invent narrative shapes that make sense of the chaos of history. It voices its audience's divided loyalties, experiments with fictions in which their anxieties could be accommodated, and acts as an imaginative mechanism in which their collective identity could be reaffirmed. In doing so, it was fulfilling functions that must have been common to much London theatre at this moment: helping the audience towards an inward understanding of the crisis through which they were living, and managing the traumas of change.

19

Theatre and Commonwealth

JANET CLARE

The outbreak of civil war in 1642 and the subsequent establishment of a commonwealth or republic in 1649 are often assumed to have resulted in a virtual
hiatus in dramatic activity. On 2 September 1642, just nine days after Charles
I had raised his standard at Nottingham, it was decreed that public sports and
playgoing should be for the moment suspended.[1] In its attempt to eradicate
ungodly leisure pursuits, the Act could be interpreted as the triumph of the
puritan anti-theatrical view which through the decades since the establishment of professional theatre had been articulated in the writings of Stephen
Gosson, Philip Stubbes, William Rackin, William Prynne and others.[2] Indeed,
the wording of the Act, as do later ordinances against the theatre, recalls briefly
the familiar negative associations of theatricality. Nevertheless, the ordinance
is not as absolute as it may appear. It contains no reference to actual closure of
theatres and the qualification 'while these sad causes and set times of humiliation do continue' implies that the measures are temporary. The injunction is
less an expression of anti-theatrical polemic than a pragmatic expedient, im-
pelled by the exigencies of a country at war. As with Elizabethan regulation of
the theatre, it betrays the familiar apprehension of the potential in mass gatherings for riotous behaviour. Given the nature of the political crisis in 1642, the
decision to prohibit public theatre performance would seem unremarkable.

The context for all dramatic production during the ensuing years is that
of theatre censorship enshrined in the acts and ordinances of the Commonwealth. But the defiance of puritan social reform which is manifest in maypole
dancing and the preservation of traditional sports and festivals was also represented in the continuation of illicit theatre performance in which actors

---

1 Firth and Rait (eds.), *Acts and Ordinances of the Interregnum*, 1, 26–7. The Act is quoted at
the opening of Martin Butler's essay in this volume.
2 See Gosson, *The School of Abuse (1579)*, Stubbes, *The Anatomy of Abuses* (1583), *The Second Part
of the Anatomy of Abuses* (1583), Rankins, *A Mirror of Monsters* (1587), Prynne, *Histriomastix,
The Players Scourge* (1633).

and audiences colluded. Following the close of the first Civil War in 1646, the actors began to resume performance in overt challenge to the 1642 Act. Despite frequent raids by parliamentary troops, plays were performed surreptitiously at the private, indoor theatres, Salisbury Court and the Cockpit, and the outdoor, public theatres, the Fortune and the Red Bull. The newsbook *Perfect Occurrences*, for instance, reports on 6 October 1647 that bills were put up advertising a performance at Salisbury Court of Beaumont and Fletcher's *A King and No King*.[3] The performance was subsequently to be interrupted by the sheriffs of London, who found 'a great number of people, some young lords and other eminent persons'. Notices of subsequent performances were circulated by other means. *Perfect Occurrences* again records that on 3 February 1648 bills were thrown into gentlemen's coaches, advertising a production of Fletcher's *Wit without Money* at the Red Bull. On 5 February 1648, the diarist John Evelyn records seeing an unnamed tragicomedy at the Cockpit.[4] That such illicit playing continued was acknowledged in an ordinance of 11 February 1648 'for the utter suppression and abolishing of all stage plays and interludes, within the penalties to be inflicted on the actors and spectators therein expressed'. In its terms, this Act, which is considerably more expansive than the abrupt injunction of 1642, has resonances of Elizabethan regulation of players. The language of anti-theatrical prejudice is now enshrined in legislation. Reminiscent of earlier punitive injunctions, stage players and players of interludes are deemed rogues and are to be punished as such. The draconian sanctions of earlier legislation are reflected in the measures to be taken against the theatres. All playhouse galleries, seats and boxes are to be demolished; players who defy the ordinance are to be whipped and spectators fined five shillings. As with other social and cultural manifestations of the post-Civil War period, there is a reversion to Elizabethan attitudes: in the legislative evocation of the actor's marginalised social status, there is a reprise of Elizabethan ideology whereby players without aristocratic patent were condemned as rogues, vagabonds and sturdy beggars. That royalists regarded this as a parliamentary appropriation of Elizabethanism is suggested by a commentary in *Mercurius Anti-Pragmaticus* on the new legislation: 'They [the actors] are not only silenced, but branded with a name of infamy, rogues; but this word perhaps doth the less distaste them, on consideration that a famous Queen bestowed upon them the same epithet.'[5] Nevertheless, occasional advertisements for theatrical entertainments continued to appear in royalist newspapers or 'mercuries'. A notice for rope dancing

3 *Perfect Occurrences*, 1 October–8 October 1647, 281.
4 *Diary of John Evelyn*, ed. De Beer, I, 539.
5 *Mercurius Anti-Pragmaticus*, 28 October–4 November 1647, 2.

at the Red Bull in June 1653 concludes, 'there will also appear a merry conceited fellow which hath formerly given content. And you may come and
return with safety'.[6] The emphasis on rope dancing (on other occasions it was
sword dancing) rather than performance betokens the circumspect advertisement of plays. Moreover, the assurance that the audience could attend without
fear of arrest indicates a degree of acquiescence towards theatrical activity on
the part of the local authorities.

The actors were never completely silenced. Several, who had been affiliated
to the King's Men, Prince Charles's players and Beeston's Boys, based at the
Cockpit, continued to act in improvised companies. During the first Civil
War, players, including William Cooke and William Hall, who had formerly
belonged to Prince Charles's players, performed for the royal court in exile,
first at The Hague and then, probably, in Paris. But by the close of 1648 a
number of the players had returned to London and helped to constitute three
companies of shifting personnel which played intermittently at the surviving
theatres. In James Wright's account of the interruption in the winter of 1648–9
of a performance at the Cockpit of Fletcher and Massinger's *Rollo or the Bloody
Brother*, the cast included such celebrated Caroline actors as John Lowin and
Charles Hart.[7] Lowin had acted with the King's Men as early as 1604 and
Hart, who, according to Wright, had entered the profession acting women's
parts at Blackfriars, resumed his career at the Restoration as a member of the
King's Men now led by Thomas Killigrew. Indeed, as can be deduced from
pension claims later made by William Hall, another veteran of the company,
and Richard Baxter, the King's Men, or at least fragments of them, never
entirely ceased playing throughout the Commonwealth.[8]

Crucial to the survival of theatre was the availability or the adaptation of
theatrical space since the ordinances of the Commonwealth sought to suppress theatre simply by the destruction of its buildings. Although the King's
company had been deprived of its outdoor venue in 1644 when the Globe had
been dismantled and replaced by tenements, there were attempts to revive
playing at what had been their indoor house at Blackfriars.[9] According to the
parliamentary newsbook, *The Perfect Weekly Account*, attempted restorations
had begun in October 1647; the following week complaints were registered in
the Commons that 'stage-players were playing at public houses in the City'.[10]

6 *Mercurius Democritus*, 1 June–8 June 1653, 463.
7 Wright, *Historia Histrionica*, 7.
8 See Milhous and Hume, 'New light on English acting companies in 1646, 1648, and 1660',
   Review of English Studies 42 (1991), 487–509.
9 *The Perfect Weekly Account*, 6 October–13 October 1647, 22.
10 *A Perfect Diurnal of Some Passages in Parliament*, 18 October–25 October 1647, 1774.

Such overt defiance of the earlier prohibition no doubt prompted the passing of an ordinance later in the month for 'the better suppressing of stage plays', empowering the lord mayor and city of London justices of the peace 'to enter into all houses and other places . . . where stage plays, interludes, or other common plays are' and to call offending actors before the Sessions of the Peace where they were to be punished as rogues.[11] The active suppression of the stage, however, seems to have been more zealously undertaken by soldiers, in the form of raids on the playhouses, than by the presbyterian city leaders, opposed as they were to the power of the army and particularly its occupation of London in 1647. The most comprehensive raid on record is that which took place simultaneously at three theatres on 1 January 1649; the date suggests that the theatres were playing as part of traditional seasonal festivities. *The Kingdom's Weekly Intelligencer* reports a sweeping assault on those theatres still in operation:

> The soldiers seized on the players on their stages at Drury Lane, and at Salisbury Court. They went also to the Fortune in Golden Lane, but they found none there, but John Pudding dancing on the ropes, whom they took with them. In the meantime the players at the Red Bull, who had notice of it, made haste away, and were all gone before they came, and took away all their acting clothes with them. But at Salisbury Court they were taken on the stage the play being almost ended, and with many links and lighted torches they were carried to Whitehall with their players' clothes upon their backs. In the way they oftentimes took the crown from his head who acted the king, and in sport would oftentimes put it on again. Abraham had a black satin gown on, and before he came into the dirt, he was very neat in his white laced pumps. The people not expecting such a pageant looked and laughed at all the rest, and not knowing who he was, they asked, what had the Lady done? They made some resistance at the Cockpit in Drury Lane, which was the occasion that they were bereaved of their apparel, and were not so well used as those in Salisbury Court, who were more patient, and therefore at their releasement they had their clothes returned to them without the least diminution. After two days' confinement, they were ordered to put in bail, and to appear before the Lord Mayor to answer for what they have done unto the Law.[12]

This account is corroborated by a shorter item in *Perfect Occurrences*, which also includes an interesting detail about the composition of the audience at the Salisbury Court playhouse. The journal recounts that amongst the spectators were members who had been purged from parliament in December 1648 by

---

11 Firth and Rait (eds.), *Acts and Ordinances of the Interregnum*, 1, 1027.
12 *The Kingdom's Weekly Intelligencer*, 9 January–16 January 1649, 291.

the army under Colonel Pride for their willingness to negotiate with the king.[13] The parliamentary journal also clears up an ambiguity in the observation that it was the soldiers (and not the actors, as might be inferred from the account above) who participated in the derisive act of crowning and uncrowning the king. Here, in January 1649, the month of the regicide, the mock street pageant of deposition, in which the actors from Salisbury Court playhouse were forced to participate, presages the worst royalist fears. Kingship is exposed as an act. In a period when events, and individuals' experience of living through them, were repeatedly theatricalised as tragedy and tragicomedy, street onlookers were confused as to the nature of the spectacle they were watching, mistaking both the actor of female roles, Abraham Ivory, for his part and the nature of his transgression.

Shortly after this invasion of the London theatres, the ordinance against theatrical activity dating from the previous year was ruthlessly enforced, and the interiors of the Cockpit, Fortune and Salisbury Court were dismantled. On 6 August 1655 the Blackfriars was demolished, and, as had happened with the Globe, replaced by tenements. The players now had only the stage of the Red Bull on which to perform. That some kind of theatrical activity continued at this venue throughout the period is attested by records of Middlesex Sessions of the Peace in May 1659 when the Restoration actor Edward Shatterell, together with Anthony Turner, was bound over for 'the unlawful maintaining of stage plays and interludes at the Red Bull'. The actors had apparently collaborated with the parishioners of Clerkenwell by paying them not only twenty shillings a day for hire of the Red Bull but also money towards the relief of the poor and the repair of highways.[14]

Theatre, like other prohibited pastimes, went underground, as improvised stages were set up in private spaces. The wording of anti-theatre legislation acknowledges the performance of plays in private houses. William Davenant was eventually to inaugurate a theatrical revival by mounting theatrical productions in his own home, Rutland House, which was sanctioned by the Council of State. But before this, private performance remained covert. *Mercurius Democritus* reports, in March 1653, preparation for a performance of Thomas Killigrew's *Claricilla* at Charles Gibbon's tennis court in Vere Street, Clare Market, which was betrayed to the army by one of the players. The journal castigates the unnamed actor while also revealing that he had himself undertaken the production of a number of plays in his own home: 'An ill beast or

13 *Perfect Occurrences*, 29 December 1648–5 January 1649. See Worden, *The Rump Parliament*, 15, 23–6.
14 See Bentley, *The Jacobean and Caroline Stage*, II, 571.

rather bird (because the rest denied him a share of their profits) beshit his own nest, causing the poor actors to be routed by the soldiery, though he himself hath since the prohibition of plays had divers tragedies and comedies acted in his own home.' Outside London there is some evidence that drama continued to be performed in country houses, inns and fairs. The Cavendish sisters, daughters of the Duke of Newcastle and authors of *The Concealed Fancies*, may have acted in a performance at the family home of Welbeck Abbey before it was surrendered to parliamentary forces in November 1645.[15] In recently discovered archives at Castle Ashby is a manuscript collection of plays written by Cosmo Manuche, several dating from the 1650s and dedicated to James Compton, the third Earl of Northampton.[16] It would seem probable that the plays were performed before house guests at Castle Ashby. Dorothy Osborne certainly refers to such an occasion at Knowlton in Kent. Writing to William Temple in July 1654, Osborne tells him that she is in a house 'the most filled of any since the Ark', where she is to play – somewhat unwillingly – the title role in William Berkeley's *The Lost Lady*: 'They [the house guests] will have me act my part in a play, the Lost Lady it is, and I am she.'[17] How common such private performances were is difficult to know; but as royalist gentry withdrew from London to those estates which had not been sequestrated, it is highly probable that play production comprised part of their entertainment: a pastime which had the additional attraction of expressing opposition to the order of the Commonwealth.

Theatrical space could be created – as it long had been – within other buildings, especially in places which had earlier theatrical associations. There is an arresting account of an amateur performance of *Mucedorus* at an inn in the town of Witney in Oxfordshire in 1653 which had a disastrous outcome, in that overcrowding caused the collapse of the floor. The narrative appears as part of the prefatory material to three sermons published by a local preacher, John Rowe. The long preface, as with earlier anti-theatrical polemic, combines a theatrical and retributive idiom, registered in the title, *Tragi-Comedia Being a Brief Relation of the Strange and Wonderful hand of God discovered at Witney*. Rowe addresses the town's inhabitants, admonishing them not to contest 'the Almighty for setting you up as the public theatre whereon he would manifest his holiness, justice, and other attributes to the world'. As the language suggests, Rowe interpreted the event as a manifestation of divine disapproval of the abomination of stage playing. That the event occurred during a production

---

15 See Ceresano and Wynne-Davies (eds.), *Renaissance Drama by Women*, 127–30.
16 See Williams, 'The Castle Ashby manuscripts', *The Library*, 6th series, 2:4 (1960), 391–412.
17 See Moore Smith (ed.), *The Letters of Dorothy Osborne to William Temple*, 172–3.

of *Mucedorus* was not, in Rowe's providential interpretation, a coincidence, for this was a play which contained mocking references to puritanism. He reminds his reader that on the same day as the accident occurred, the townspeople and scholars of Oxford were keeping a fast. Implying the current anachronism of the term 'puritan', Rowe comments: 'How remarkable was this that some of them that were called Puritans in the days of old, had spent that very day in Oxford in fasting and prayer; and that the Lord by so eminent an hand should testify against such who were not only scoffers at Godly persons, but at religion itself.' Triumphantly, he concludes that 'the hand of God hath remarkably appeared against the actors and frequenters of stage plays'.

The following sermon rehearses all the anti-theatrical arguments associated with fundamental puritanism which were so brilliantly personified by Jonson forty years earlier in Zeal of the Land Busy in *Bartholomew Fair*. Stage plays are opposed to the word of God, which forbids idle conversation, jesting and unchaste looks, apparel and gestures. They are 'stuffed with scurrilous, filthy, unbecoming speeches, passages and gestures' and they defy the Deuteronomic injunction not to dress in women's attire. The entire piece resembles a parody of old anti-theatrical polemic. In its idiom the work recalls, and indeed cites from, *Theatre of God's Judgment* (1597), in which Thomas Beard had inveighed against the sins of dancing, singing and playing and warned of the retribution which befell those who pursued such dissolute activities. While attesting to the sustained popularity of provincial drama, Rowe's texts also reveal little change in the language and style of puritan hostility to dramatic practice.

The pamphlet play

With the collapse in 1641 of the Star Chamber and its powers over the regulation of printing, together with the diminished role of the Stationers' company,[18] printed drama became an effective medium for news, deploying the same sensational rumours, personal attacks, innuendo and exaggeration as the popular press. The displacement of the theatre by the pamphlet play is referred to in the Actors' Remonstrance of 1644, which includes amongst its catalogue of grievances the alleged degeneration of the art of playwriting: 'some of our ablest ordinary poets, instead of their annual stipends and beneficial second days, being for mere necessity compelled to get a living by writing contemptible penny pamphlets'. The writing of news dramas was thus seen as a viable, if vulgar, alternative to the composition of drama proper. Most of

18 See Siebert, *Freedom of the Press in England, 1476–1776*, 179–233.

the playlets were, of course, published anonymously, and the authors who can be identified, such as Samuel Sheppard and John Crouch, were editors of royalist weeklies. These 'contemptible penny pamphlets', as they are termed in the Actors' Remonstrance, were written as political polemic, while exploiting characters constructed on Jonsonian 'humours' and employing familiar stage motifs. Whether or not they were performed is open to question. Some evidence of performance is provided by the presentation of a play-within-a-play: Cosmo Manuche's *Loyal Lovers* (1652) contains an episode in which royalists stage a farce, in the vein of the pamphlet play, about the army preacher Hugh Peters. That the performance takes place in a private room of a tavern is some indication of one venue for the staging of political satire.

It is possible that the odd play was performed publicly at the Red Bull, and that others would have been performed as street theatre or entertainment at fairs, while the majority would have been enacted in taverns and private houses before a select audience. Many of the playlets show clear signs of having been conceived with performance in mind. The theatrical nature of the texts – notably in their detailed, often comic or farcical, stage directions, visual comedy and some quick-fire dialogue – makes it very probable that they were designed for impromptu acting. Indeed, the texts contain several oblique allusions to their performance. A number begin with a prologue which would have served to announce an extempore performance in the tavern or fair and thus command an audience. A covert allusion to performance, for example, is made in the prologue to the sequel of a pamphlet play of 1648, *The Second Part of Crafty Cromwell or Oliver in his Glory as King*. After anticipating their pleasure and applause at the representation of the army grandees and their rapid rise to and imagined fall from power, the prologue cautions the audience:

> I Iear then with candour; but be ruled by me,
> Speak not a word, what ere you hear or see,
> For this author, bid me to you say,
> He'd live, to see this played another day.
>
> (p. 2)

The address to the reader sustains the idea or the illusion of the play's secret performance. With mock hyperbole the author claims in his address to the 'readers of my former piece' that 'justly on the stage' he is castigating the crimes of the age and in so doing is courting danger.

The Disease of the House is a short prose drama with a verse prologue and epilogue. The former, designated 'His Prologue on the Stage', is spoken by John Capon. Capon is mentioned specifically in an advertisement in the royalist journal *Mercurius Democriticus* as appearing in an entertainment at the Red Bull which includes a display of rope, sword and country dancing.[19] The name was presumably a generic name like that of Jack Pudding, who had been found dancing on the ropes during the 1649 New Year's Day raid on the Red Bull. That Capon is alluded to as speaking the prologue of *The Disease of the House* suggests that the playlet was performed, possibly on the stage of the same theatre. Certainly the text, one of the shortest of the pamphlet plays, could easily be prepared for an impromptu performance.

The prologue to *1 New Market Fair or a Parliament Outcry of State Commodities* similarly creates an impression of performance. The prologue is 'sung by the cryer' and the stage direction for his entrance, bearing all the insignia of monarchy, is visually evocative: 'with a crown and sceptre, a carkanet of jewels, two or three suits, with some robes of state'. Mockingly, the prologue comments on the 'saint's market day' and recommends his audience to make a quick purchase and then watch the play:

> See but this play, and before you go away
> You'll say 'tis wondrous pretty.
> Welcome, welcome, with all my heart,
> For now the cryer must mind his part.
>
> (p. 3)

'Mind my part', in the sense of 'learning lines', would seem to be a tantalising allusion to the anticipated performance. The relationship between the written and performed texts of the pamphlet plays is a curious one. Typographically, the plays represent texts for the theatre, containing as they do the list of dramatis personae, prologues and epilogues, stage directions and details of scene locations. While performance of the pamphlet plays can only be conjectured from hints and allusions in the texts, the knowledge that illicit playing continued throughout the Civil War years and the years of the Republic lends the conjecture more substance. Amongst plays from the old repertoires, it is reasonable to surmise that the political satires were some of the plays performed illicitly at the public theatres. During the period, there was much emphasis on the publication of plays and it is often inferred that greater reading of dramatic texts became a substitute for performance.[20] By and large it must have been so, but, in the case of the popular pamphlet play, it seems unlikely that its audience comprised only the literate section of the male

---

19 See *Mercurius Democritus*, 2 March–9 March, 1653.
20 See Wright, 'The reading of plays during the puritan revolution', *Huntingdon Library Bulletin* 6 (1934), 73–108.

population. Certainly, performance would have ensured a wider reception for anti-parliamentary propaganda.

Dramatic forms: interludes, drolls and farces

The drama which proved most resilient to state opposition was that which had roots in popular pastime and non-commercial theatre: the interlude, jig or farce, or an entertainment which has been classified rather imprecisely as the droll, an abbreviation of 'drollery'. Droll, a post-Restoration term, as genre is somewhat misleading, since it has been used to incorporate such diverse dramatic forms as interludes, jigs, masques and plays in adapted and abridged form.

To add to the repertoire of jigs and interludes during the 1640s and 1650s, certain players seem to have begun to abridge popular Elizabethan and Jacobean plays which were subsequently termed drolls. Two miscellanies of drolls entitled *The Wits or Sport Upon Sport* were published at the Restoration: the first compiled by Henry Marsh in 1662, with a second enlarged edition by the bookseller Francis Kirkman in 1672; and *II Wits or Sport Upon Sport*, published by Kirkman in 1673. The title pages of both editions of *The Wits* claim social inclusiveness for the form: 'fitted for the pleasure and content of all persons, either in court, city, country, or camp'. Marsh recommends his collection not only to individuals, but for the purposes of recitation or extempore performance, an echo of earlier informal theatre practice. Both prefaces maintain that the drolls were performed during the Commonwealth. A specific reference to actual performance at the time of the Rump Parliament (1648–53) is found in Marsh's final line, 'Pray remember the Rump drolls, and for their sakes, your old servant, H. Marsh'. Kirkman's more discursive preface to *II Wits* refers to productions at Charing Cross and the Red Bull, and at fairs and inns. A small number of interludes, later incorporated into the Restoration anthologies of drolls, was, however, published in *c.* 1655 by the comedian and player Robert Cox, with the pieces advertised as having been performed on the stage of the Red Bull, the theatre with which Cox was associated. Cox was mentioned in the details of a raid in June 1653 on a surburban theatre – probably the Red Bull – occasioned by the betrayal of two fellow actors.[21] According to the report, Cox had been employed by the rope dancers 'to present a modest and harmless gig called Swabber'. *John Swabber the Seaman*, a comic farce of cuckoldry, is included in Cox's collection, which provides the only sure

---

21 See *Mercurius Democritus*, 22 June–29 June 1653, 467.

evidence of the nature of the Commonwealth interlude and of which pieces were actually performed.

The generic hybridity of the volume is apparent in Cox's full title: *Acteon and Diana: with a story of the nymph pastoral Oenone: followed by the several conceited humours of Bumpkin the Huntsman, Hobbinal the Shepherd, Singing Simpkin and John Swabber the Seaman*. *Singing Simpkin* is also included in Restoration anthologies, but it is almost certainly Elizabethan, indicating the continuity of jig, interlude and droll.[22] In the title piece, *Acteon and Diana*, as in *A Midsummer Night's Dream*, but in small compass, the mythic and popular coexist to comic effect. The interlude begins with the entrance of Bumpkin, 'chief dog-keeper' to Acteon, announcing that he is suffering from love-sickness and that he has 'a horrible mind to be in love', but he is scorned by the girls dancing around the maypole. Since maypole dancing had been condemned in an ordinance of 1644 as a 'heathenish vanity' and the raising of maypoles was forbidden, such dramatic imagery would seem intentionally provocative as well as sexually suggestive. The young women sing enticingly, 'Then to the Maypole come away, / For it is now a holiday.' Bumpkin reappears, telling them to take notice that he is in love 'with somebody'. In contrast to their earlier disdain, the women now hang about him and pull him down as he tries to extricate himself from these 'burrs'. The closure returns to the mythological as Acteon is pursued by his huntsmen and then borne away, while Diana dances with her nymphs. Within its brief confines, *Acteon and Diana* plays with the forms of rustic comedy and pastoral, while maintaining the cultural appeal of popular pastime.

Kirkman's second collection of twenty-seven drolls reveals a diversity of dramatic form. Some, like *Bottom the Weaver*, extracted from the rustic scenes of *A Midsummer Night's Dream*, are much longer than others; not all are humorous, some are abridgements from masques and some are little more than a short dialogue. If some of these pieces were performed during the 1650s – and we have only Kirkman's testimony – then it is possible to see how the drama of the Commonwealth reveals itself as both backward- and forward-looking. As a prime example of such dramatic hybridity, the droll appropriates the jig, the play-within-a-play and the moral interlude; but it can also be seen as the prototype of the burlesque drama associated with Thomas Duffet and the Shakespearian adaptations of Davenant and Dryden at the Restoration. Like the burlesque, the drolls were often derivative in their adaptation of

---

22 *Singing Simpkin* almost certainly dates back to the sixteenth century. On 21 October 1595, there was an entry in the Stationers' Register for 'a ballad called Kemp's New Jig betwixt a soldier and a miser and Sym the clown'. See Baskervill, *The Elizabethan Jig*, 238.

scenes from popular plays by Shakespeare. *The Bouncing Knight*, for example, included in Kirkman's second collection, is an amalgam of various scenes in *1 Henry IV* in which Falstaff appears. Thus, we move from the tavern scene (3.3), in which Falstaff accuses Mistress Quickly of rifling his pockets, to Falstaff's comic soliloquy about his abuse of recruitment ('I have misused the King's press damnably'), followed by his preposterous claim to have killed Hotspur. Such a redaction obviously depends on a folkloric appreciation of the character, divorced from any narrative framework. Other drolls in Kirkman's collection re-present scenes from plays by Jonson, Marston, Beaumont and Fletcher.

In a sense, Marsh and Kirkman created by their compilations a genre which was far from uniform in style or idiom. Marsh was not unaware of this, apologetically acknowledging in his preface that he has made of a fluid a solid body. By gathering extant Commonwealth and early Restoration drama and presenting it under the identity of a collection, the compilers imply homogeneity where there is only miscellany. Nevertheless, the prefaces of Marsh and Kirkman provide some evidence that abridgements and redactions of earlier Elizabethan and Jacobean plays, as well as jigs and reworkings of masques, continued to be performed during the years of the Civil Wars and the Republic.

Theatrical accommodations

In his tribute to Oliver Cromwell, *The idea of his Highness Oliver, late Lord Protector with certain brief reflections on his life*, published in 1659 after Cromwell's death, the priest, poet and playwright Richard Flecknoe had mused that 'men of Estates and Fortunes always comply with the present times and seek not (with hazard to make them worse) to better their conditions'. It was in this spirit that William Davenant, who was indebted to Flecknoe's ideas of a reformed stage, officially revived and produced drama governed by new theatrical aesthetics.

Flecknoe first made a bid to realign and reconstitute the drama by seeking the patronage of Lady Elizabeth Claypole, Cromwell's daughter. In dedicating *Love's Dominion* (1654) to Claypole, Flecknoe made a strong plea for the revival of drama, which is desired by 'the nobler and better sort'. The play was advertised as 'a dramatic piece full of excellent morality' and written as a pattern for the reformed stage. Suggesting a redefining of drama, Flecknoe claims that 'actions', 'opera' or works would all be more apt designations than 'plays'. A restored, reformed stage, he argues, should be welcomed by the dispensation of the Cromwellian protectorate and could, he suggests, be subject to moral censorship.

A similar line had been offered by Davenant in *A Proposition for the Advancement of Morality by a New Way of Entertainment of the People* (1653), presented to the Council of State, in which he argues the moral and socially educative advantages for the lower classes of a reformed stage, which he too suggests could be subjected to censorship.[23] Davenant advocates that the subject matter of the reformed drama would be heroic and the actions depicted would be inherently virtuous. His propositions were followed up three years later with a further apology for public entertainment in a letter to John Thurloe, Cromwell's secretary of state and occasional licenser of the press.[24] Here economic, pragmatic and ideological reasons are further offered to support a theatrical revival. The extent to which London had been impoverished by the absence of the court and its desertion by royalists enabled Davenant to argue that the gentry must be encouraged to reside in the City by the allure of 'pleasant assemblies', so that wealth can circulate. In contrast to the argument of his earlier document, Davenant emphasises that the clientele he now proposes to attract are the gentry. It is doubtful whether economic reasons alone could have persuaded the council to grant permission for what Davenant terms 'moral representations'. The clue to the eventual theatrical revival lies in the final paragraph of the letter, in which Davenant proposes his subject: 'If moral representations may be allowed . . . the first arguments may consist of the Spaniards' barbarous conquests in the West Indies and of their several cruelties there exercised upon the subjects of this nation: of which some use may be made.' The perceived political utility of the project, specifically in negative representations of Spain, an imperial rival, must have been a highly significant factor in the government's decision to sanction public performance.

Appropriately, the theatrical revival, in the private space of Rutland House, began with a debate about the nature of drama. There are two parts and two rhetorical exchanges to *The First Day's Entertainment*, whose very title draws attention to the novelty of the performance. The first debate is between Diogenes, the cynic philosopher who was alleged to have spent his life in a tub, and Aristophanes, the satiric playwright, and the second is set between a Frenchman and an Englishman. In the first dialogue Diogenes voices and possibly anticipates objections to recitative and scenic drama. Music is a deceitful art, leading to the 'evil of extremes' of feeling and transporting an audience 'beyond the regions of reason'. Scenes are deceptive of place and motion and,

23 See Jacob and Raylor, 'Opera and obedience', *The Seventeenth Century* 6:2 (1991), 205–50. The piece was published anonymously in 1653, but dated 1654.
24 See Firth, 'Sir William Davenant and the revival of drama during the Protectorate', *English Historical Review*, April 1903, 103–20.

argues Diogenes, may only inculcate the evil of deception in general. Aristophanes refutes such literalism with a reiteration of the therapeutic, moral and aesthetic refinement of drama. Music 'unites and recollects a broken and scattered mind; giving it sudden strength to resist the evils it hath long and strongly bred'. Pictorial representation, as in the uses of scenes, is 'the safest and shortest way to understanding'. The playwright dismisses Diogenes's claim that the tendency to use the remote past in dramatic representations makes their subject matter less credible by arguing that the past works with greater subtlety on the intelligence: predictably, the victory lies with Aristophanes, who defeats his antagonist by arguing that, since Diogenes is himself the worst representative of morality, he is justly afraid to be portrayed in the theatre. At the close of the dialogue, in a graphic rejection of anti-representational argument, Diogenes is forced to retreat to his tub.

Davenant, ever the entrepreneur, succeeded where Flecknoe failed, in gaining the Republic's sanction for the performance of his entertainments – three other pieces followed *The First Day's Entertainment* – but it was Flecknoe's continentally influenced theories of a scenic drama communicated in recitative music which influenced Davenant's work of the period. Flecknoe's *Ariadne Deserted by Theseus and Found and Courted by Bacchus*, published but not performed in 1654, set out in theory and action ideas for new stage practice. In his preface Flecknoe asserts that, in the course of travelling in Italy, he 'found that music I intended to introduce, exceedingly in vogue': that is, recitative music, which he claims has immense emotive power through its association with poetry. Again, there is no record of any performance of Flecknoe's final operatic entertainment, published in 1659, *The Marriage of Oceanus and Britannia*. Flecknoe's work, however, demands more elaborate stage effects than do Davenant's texts, and it is possible that restrictions on the scope of production rather than any official prohibition hindered its staging. Britannia herself appears in the second 'part' – Flecknoe avoids the masque term of 'entry' – reflecting on her present happiness in contrast to the recent miseries of the civil wars; nevertheless she orders Oceanus to desist from his pursuit of her until she has become 'the most renowned and opulent / Of all the isles with circling waves / You ever yet surrounded have'. In projecting imperial expansionism under Cromwell, Flecknoe is drawing on imagery of the Republic which had been mobilised earlier by Davenant.

The same celebration of 'Englishness', and in particular the nation's military and naval power, is central to Davenant's subsequent entertainments dating from the Protectorate: *The Siege of Rhodes*, *The Cruelty of the Spaniards in Peru* and *The History of Sir Francis Drake*. In theatrical form these dramas are the most innovatory works of the Republic; but, in adapting such nationalist themes as the apocryphal colonisation of Peru and Drake's plundering voyages to South America, Davenant produced a drama which harked back to Elizabethan foreign policy. This was, of course, a safe enough subject, and it was also one which had a unifying appeal. The Cromwellian protectorate spoke the language of Elizabethan expansionism. It had been a familiar theme of the news journals that, if the Stuarts had been Tudors, England would not have suffered the same religious, political and economic ills and would still have been recognised as a European power. When in 1628 the nephew of Francis Drake published *Sir Francis Drake Revived* – the source for *The History of Sir Francis Drake* – he called on his title page for 'this effeminate age' to follow 'his noble steps for gold and silver'.[25] In reviving such Elizabethan material and making a connection with Cromwellian foreign incursions, Davenant is contributing to the re-formation of an earlier English national identity in a guise which is compatible with the ideology of the Republic.

At the same time as depicting a military ethic, *The Siege of Rhodes*, the first of the narrative dramas, reveals a remarkable recovery of dramatic form, with the five entries closely resembling acts and the invented love plot between Alphonso and Ianthe complicating the historical action. Here, the debate between love and honour with which Alphonso wrestles refers back to the ideological conflicts in Davenant's pre-Civil War drama and adumbrates the concerns of later plays by John Dryden in particular. As is also the case with *The Cruelty of the Spaniards in Peru*, *The Siege of Rhodes* makes an appeal to both sides of the Civil Wars divide. It is the English who are represented – ahistorically – as the most valiant amongst the foreign soldiers in the defence of Rhodes. Yet through the characters of Alphonso and Ianthe, the drama is also an evocation of the codes of love, honour and loyalty associated with Charles I and Henrietta Maria.

The identification of *The Siege of Rhodes* with continental operatic practice is enhanced by the presence of the proscenium arch and by the use of changing scenes. The advertisement of the play, as a 'representation by the art of perspective in scenes', indicates the importance which Davenant attached to scenery as a medium for the drama. This had been a familiar feature in the production of court masques, although not in the public theatres. Scenes for *The Siege of Rhodes* were designed by John Webb, who was the nephew and pupil of Inigo Jones, Surveyor of the Works to James I and Charles I. Webb

25 'Sir Francis Drake revived', in Wright (ed.), *Documents Concerning English Voyages to the Spanish Main 1569–1580*, 245–326.

Figure 38 *The Siege of Rhodes* stage designs: side pieces (1656)

had worked with Jones on scenic devices for performances at the Cockpit in Drury Lane and at court, and he was thus well equipped to design shutters and relieve scenes for the small stage at Rutland House, which were later transferred to the Cockpit. Webb's drawings have survived and, together with Davenant's detailed descriptions of the scene at the opening of each entry, they enable us to reconstruct technically and pictorially the visual dimension of *The Siege of Rhodes*. The set comprised a frontispiece 15 centimetres back from the front of the stage, consisting of columns and a decorated frieze (see figure 38). This accommodated a curtain which, since the stage action was continuous, was raised and dropped only at the beginning and end of the performance. In comparison with the elaborate and sumptuous scene changes and machinery of the masque, the scenic devices for *The Siege of Rhodes* were simple. The three pairs of flat wings depicting a rocky coast remained fixed throughout the performance; only the back shutters, which ran on grooves, facilitated changes of scene. Three pictorial representations are described by Davenant and sketched by Webb (see figure 39): Rhodes in prosperity (entry one); Rhodes under siege (entries two, three and four); and an assault on the town at the English bulwark (entry five). In addition, when the back shutters

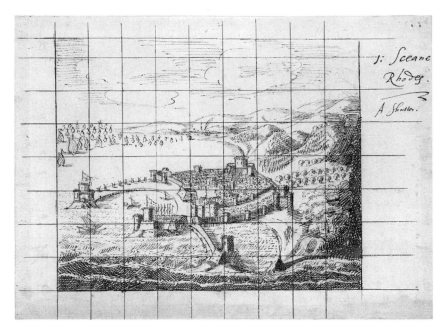

Figure 39 *The Siege of Rhodes* stage designs: shutters for Rhodes at peace (1656)

were opened, two relieve scenes depicting Solyman's pavilion and the building of the castle on Mount Philermus were displayed during the third and fourth entries respectively (see figure 40).

Webb was furnishing Davenant with generalised pictorial backgrounds.[26] The scenery served as a counterpoint to the plot, its purpose decorative rather than illusionistic. Davenant had defended the use of scenes in *The First Day's Entertainment* against Diogenes's claim that they were only 'useless visions of imagination' by arguing that, in functional terms, they provided the quickest route to an audience's understanding and that, aesthetically, they provided 'some variety of experience by a short journey of the sight'. The pictorial setting was thus a significant element in a drama which, in its concentration on moments of heroic crisis, could not afford to be rhetorically descriptive. Webb's scenes, apart from their aesthetic value, were important in conveying to the audience the quick turn of event and location.

The evident practical constraints on the first production of *The Siege of Rhodes* would have made it a kind of chamber work not unlike the early intimate performance of Monteverdi's *Orfeo*. Davenant ruefully acknowledged

26 See Southern, *Changeable Scenery*, 114.

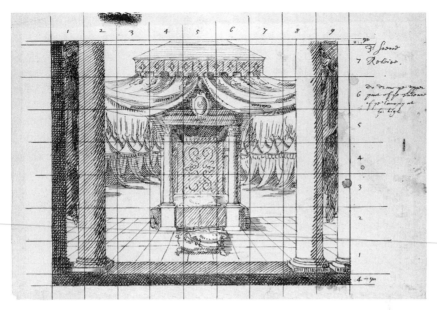

Figure 40 *The Siege of Rhodes* stage designs: Solyman's palace (1656)

in his address to the reader that, because of the small cast and confines of the Rutland House stage, he had been obliged to compress the drama 'to a small narration'. The strains of presenting narrative material so concisely are apparent at one moment at least in the drama. In the final entry, the Admiral refers to a letter written by Ianthe which has evoked feelings of deep remorse in Alphonso. This dramatic incident appears only in this one reference, and its brief inclusion indicates a tension between the imperatives of a compressed plot and the narrative demands of the unfolding drama.

The composite forms of *The Siege of Rhodes*, *The Cruelty of the Spaniards in Peru* and *The History of Sir Francis Drake* defy easy classification. No doubt their indistinct or novel generic identity allowed them to circumvent the prohibitions on the public performance of plays. In the correspondence about *The Siege of Rhodes* accompanying a copy of the work which Davenant sent to Bulstrode Whitelocke, a former Master of the Revels at the Inns of Court, and subsequently Cromwell's ambassador to Sweden, Davenant referred to his work as 'opera'.[27] But this is a loose and no doubt strategic use of the term, recalling Flecknoe's similar attempt to redefine drama, rather than an evocation of the specific Italianate form. It would have been indiscreet to refer to these

27 *The Diary of Bulstrode Whitelocke 1605–1675*, ed. Spalding, 449.

entertainments as masques, recalling associations with Stuart court culture; yet the Stationers' Register does describe *The Siege of Rhodes* as a masque, and manifestly the works do appropriate some of that genre's formal elements for distinct ideological purposes.[28]

The contributions during the Commonwealth of Davenant, and indirectly of Flecknoe, to such changes in theatre practice were far-reaching and cannot be over-estimated. Without doubt, the political had helped to define the aesthetics of drama, as the settlements of the 1650s stimulated its formal reinvention and the small-scale theatrical revival. It has been said that the execution of Charles I marked the end of the Renaissance. Despite the self-conscious allusion and appeal to Renaissance dramatic conventions and motifs, the drama of the English Commonwealth did indeed mark a decisive break with elements of the past. Scenic theatre had replaced the bare Renaissance stage and its fluent dramatic production. The appearance of Mrs Coleman as Ianthe in *The Siege of Rhodes* prepared audiences for the given of Restoration theatre: female impersonation of the woman's part. Blank verse was no longer the dominant verse medium. Conquest plays were to enjoy a vogue, and love and honour, however parodied, were to endure as themes in the plays of Dryden. In theatrical terms the period which was once regarded as a dramatic backwater provided the impetus for so much that was to follow. From the irreverent treatment of the Shakespearian text to the sensational political drama and satire of the Exclusion crisis to the opera of Purcell to the classical ethos of Nathaniel Lee, prototypes were developed in the years of the English Republic.

28 For the texts of the entertainments, see Janet Clare, *Drama of the English Republic, 1649–60*.

Works cited

Aaron, Melissa D., 'The Globe and *Henry V* as business document', *Studies in English Literature 1500–1900* 40:2 (2000), 277–92.

Aers, David (ed.), *Culture and History 1350–1600*, Detroit: Wayne State University Press, 1992.

Alexander, Sir William, *The Poetical Works of Sir William Alexander, Earl of Stirling*, ed. L. E. Kastner and H. B. Charlton, Edinburgh: A. Blackwood, 1921–9.

Anglo, S., *Spectacle, Pageantry, and Early Tudor Policy*, Oxford: Clarendon Press, 1969.

Armin, R., *The Collected Works of Robert Armin*, ed. John P. Feather, New York: Johnson Reprint Corporation, 1972.

Arnold, C. J., *Roman Britain to Saxon England: an Archaeological Study*, London: Croom Helm, 1984.

Astington, John, *English Court Theatre, 1558–1642*, Cambridge University Press, 1999.

Aston, Margaret, *The King's Bedpost: Reformation and Iconography in a Tudor Group Portrait*, Cambridge University Press, 1993

Axton, Marie, '*Ane Satyre of the Thrie Estaitis*: the first edition and its reception', in Gardner-Medwin and Williams (eds.), *A Day Festival*, 21–34.

Axton, Marie and Williams, Raymond (eds.), *English Drama: Forms and Development*, Cambridge University Press, 1977.

Axton, Richard, *European Drama of the Early Middle Ages*, London: Hutchinson & Co., 1974.

Axton, Richard, 'Folk play in Tudor interludes', in Axton and Williams (eds.), *English Drama: Forms and Development*, 1–23.

Badir, Patricia, ' "To allure vnto their loue": iconoclasm and striptease in Lewis Wager's *The Life and Repentaunce of Marie Magdalene*', *Theatre Journal* 51:1 (1999), 1–20.

Bakere, J. A., *The Cornish Ordinalia*, Cardiff: University of Wales Press, 1980.

Bakhtin, Mikhail, *The Dialogic Imagination*, trans. M. Holquist and C. Emerson, Austin: University of Texas Press, 1982.

Baldwin, Elizabeth, 'Rushbearings and maygames in the diocese of Chester before 1642', in Johnston and Hüsken (eds.), *English Parish Drama*.

Bale, John, *The Complete Plays of John Bale*, ed. Peter Happé, 2 vols., Cambridge: D. S. Brewer, 1985–6.

Barroll, Leeds, 'Inventing the Stuart masque', in Bevington and Holbrook (eds.), *The Politics of the Stuart Court Masque*, 121–43.

Barton, A., *Ben Jonson, Dramatist*, Cambridge University Press, 1984.

Baskervill, C. R., *The Elizabethan Jig*, New York: Dover, 1965.

Bawcutt, N. W. (ed.), *The Control and Censorship of Caroline Drama: the Records of Sir Henry Herbert, Master of the Revels 1623–73*, Oxford: Clarendon Press, 1996.

Bawcutt, N. W., 'Sir Henry Herbert and William Sands the puppeteer: some corrections', *REED Newsletter* 20:1 (1995), 17–19.

Bawcutt, Priscilla, '*Pamphilus de amore* "in Inglish toung" ', *Medium Aevum* 64:2 (1995), 264–72.

Beadle, Richard (ed.), *The Cambridge Companion to Medieval English Theatre*, Cambridge University Press, 1994.

Beadle, Richard (ed.), *The York Plays*, York Medieval Texts, Baltimore: Arnold, 1982.

Beckwith, Sarah, *Christ's Body: Identity, Culture and Society in Late Medieval Writings*, London: Routledge, 1993.

Benbow, Mark, 'Dutton and Goffe versus Broughton: a disputed contract for plays in the 1570s', *REED Newsletter* 2 (1981), 1–9.

Bentley, G. E., *The Jacobean and Caroline Stage*, 7 vols., Oxford: Clarendon Press, 1941–68.

Bentley, G. E., *The Profession of Dramatist in Shakespeare's Time, 1590–1642*, Princeton University Press, 1971.

Bentley, G. E., *The Profession of Player in Shakespeare's Time*, Princeton University Press, 1984.

Bergeron, David, 'Women as patrons of English Renaissance drama', in Lytle and Orgel (eds.), *Patronage in the Renaissance*, 274–90.

Berry, Herbert, *The Boar's Head Playhouse*, Washington: Folger Shakespeare Library, 1986.

Berry, Herbert (ed.), *The First Public Playhouse: the Theatre in Shoreditch 1576–1598*, Montreal: McGill–Queen's University Press, 1979.

Berry, Herbert, 'The Globe bewitched and *El Hombre Fiel*', *Medieval and Renaissance Drama in England* 1 (1984), 211–30.

Bevington, David, *Medieval Drama*, Boston: Houghton Mifflin Company, 1975.

Bevington, David, *Tudor Drama & Politics*, Cambridge, MA: Harvard University Press, 1968.

Bevington, D. and Holbrook, P. (eds.), *The Politics of the Stuart Court Masque*, Cambridge University Press, 1998.

Billington, Sandra, *Mock Kings in Medieval Society and Renaissance Drama*, Oxford: Clarendon Press, 1991.

Bishop, Tom, 'Tradition and novelty in the Jacobean masque', in Bevington and Holbrook (eds.), *The Politics of the Stuart Court Masque*, 88–120.

Blackstone, Mary, 'Patrons and Elizabethan dramatic companies', in C. E. McGee (ed.), *Elizabethan Theatre X*, Port Credit, Ontario: P. D. Meany, 1988, 112–32.

Blackley, F. D. and Hermansen, G. (eds.), *The Household Book of Queen Isabella of England for the Fifth Regnal Year of Edward II, 8th July 1311 to 7th July 1312*, Edmonton: University of Alberta Press, 1971.

Blayney, Peter, 'The Publication of Playbooks', in Cox and Kastan (eds.), *A New History of Early English Drama*, 383–422.

Blatt, Thora, *The Plays of John Bale: a Study of Ideas, Technique and Style*, Copenhagen: Gads Forlag, 1968.

Boas, Frederick, *University Drama in the Tudor Age*, Oxford University Press, 1914.

Bond, Edward, *Bingo*, London: Eyre Methuen, 1974.

Boose, Lynda E., 'Scolding bridles and bridling scolds: taming the woman's unruly member', *Shakespeare Quarterly* 42:2 (1991), 179–213.

Bordier, J.-P., *Le Jeu de la Passion: le message chrétien et le théâtre français (xiiie–xvie s.)*, Paris: H. Champion, 1998.

Bourgeault, Cynthia, 'Liturgical dramaturgy and modern production', in Campbell and Davidson (eds.), *The Fleury Playbook*, 144–60.

Bower, Walter, *Scotichronicon*, ed. D. E. R. Watt, 9 vols., Aberdeen University Press, 1987–8.

Bradley, David, *From Text to Performance in Elizabethan Theatre*, Cambridge University Press, 1992.

Braunmuller, A. R., ' "To the Globe I rowed": John Holles sees *A Game at Chess*', *English Literary Review* 20 (1990), 340–56.

Braunmuller, A. R. and Hattaway, Michael (eds.), *The Cambridge Companion to English Renaissance Drama*, Cambridge University Press, 1990.

Briggs, Asa, *A Social History of England*, London: Book Club Associates, 1983.

Briscoe, Marianne and Coldewey, John (eds.), *Contexts for Early English Drama*, Bloomington, IN: Indiana University Press, 1989.

Bristol, Michael, *Carnival and Theatre*, London: Methuen, 1985.

Brome, Richard, *A Jovial Crew*, ed. Ann Haaker, London: Edward Arnold, 1968.

Brooks, Douglas, *From Playhouse to Printing House*, Cambridge University Press, 2000.

Brown, Cedric C. (ed.), *Patronage, Politics and Literary Traditions in England: 1558–1658*, Detroit: Wayne State University Press, 1991.

Brown, C. and Marotti, A. (eds.), *Texts and Cultural Change in Early Modern England*, Basingstoke: Macmillan, 1997.

Brown, Keith, 'Historical context and *Henry V*', *Cahiers Elizabethaines* 29 (1986), 77–81.

Brownstein, O. L., 'A Record of London inn playhouses from c. 1565–1590', *Shakespeare Quarterly* 22 (1971), 17–24.

Brownstein, O. L., 'Why didn't Burbage lease the Beargarden? A conjecture in comparative architecture', in Berry (ed.), *The First Public Playhouse*, 81–96.

Bruster, Douglas, *Drama and the Market in the Age of Shakespeare*, Cambridge University Press, 1992.

Butler, Martin, 'Courtly negotiations', in Bevington and Holbrook (eds.), *The Politics of the Stuart Court Masque*, 20–40.

Butler, Martin, 'Ecclesiastical censorship of early Stuart drama: the case of Jonson's *The Magnetic Lady*', *Modern Philology* 89 (1992), 469–81.

Butler, Martin, 'Politics and the masque: *Salmacida Spolia*', in Healy and Sawday (eds.), *Literature and the English Civil War*, 59–74.

Butler, Martin, 'Politics and the masque: *The Triumph of Peace*', *The Seventeenth Century* 2 (1987), 117–41.

Butler, Martin, 'Reform or reverence? The politics of the Caroline masque', in Mulryne and Shewring (eds.), *Theatre and Government under the Early Stuarts*, 118–56.

Butler, Martin, *Theatre and Crisis, 1632–1642*, Cambridge University Press, 1984.

Butler, Martin, 'Two playgoers, and the closing of the London theatres, 1642', *Theatre Research International* 9 (1984), 93–9.

Butler, Martin and Lindley, David, 'Restoring Astraea: Jonson's masque for the fall of Somerset', *English Literary History* 61 (1994), 807–27.

Camden, William, *Annales*, trans. Thomas Browne, London, 1625.

Campbell, Thomas and Davidson, Clifford (eds.), *The Fleury Playbook: Essays and Studies*, Kalamazoo, MI: Western Michigan University Press, 1985.

Carnegie, David, 'Actors' parts and the "Play of Poore" ', *Harvard Library Bulletin* 30:1 (1982), 5–24.

Carpenter, Sarah, 'Early Scottish drama', in Jack (ed.), *The History of Scottish Literature*, I, 199–211.

Carson, Neil, *A Companion to Henslowe's Diary*, Cambridge University Press, 1988.

Cave, R. A., *Ben Jonson*, Basingstoke: Macmillan, 1991.

Cave, R. A., Schafer, E. and Woolland, B., *Ben Jonson and Theatre: Performance, Practice and Theory*, London: Routledge, 1999.

Cawley, A. C. (ed.), *The Wakefield Pageants in the Towneley Cycle*, Manchester University Press, 1958.

Ceresano, S. P., 'Philip Henslowe, Simon Forman, and the theatrical community of the 1590s', *Shakespeare Quarterly* 44 (1993), 145–58.

Ceresano, S. P. and Wynne-Davies, Marion, *Renaissance Drama by Women: Texts and Documents*, London: Routledge, 1996.

Chamberlain, John, *The Letters of John Chamberlain*, ed. Norman Egbert McClure, 2 vols., Philadelphia: American Philosophical Society, 1939.

Chambers, E. K., *The Elizabethan Stage*, 4 vols., Oxford: Clarendon Press, 1951.

Chambers, E. K., *The Medieval Stage*, 2 vols., Oxford University Press, 1903.

Chetwood, W. R., *A General History of the English Stage*, London, 1749.

Clare, Janet, *'Art Made Tongue-tied by Authority': Elizabethan and Jacobean Dramatic Censorship*, Manchester University Press, 1990.

Clare, Janet, 'The production and reception of Davenant's *Cruelty of the Spaniards in Peru*', *Modern Language Review* 89:4 (1994), 832–41.

Clare, Janet, *Drama of the English Republic, 1649–60*, Manchester University Press, 2002.

Clark, Peter and Slack, Paul (eds.), *Crisis and Order in English Towns, 1500–1700: Essays in Urban History*, London: Routledge and Kegan Paul, 1972.

Clegg, Cynthia Susan, *Press Censorship in Elizabethan England*, Cambridge University Press, 1998.

Coates, W. H., Young, A. S. and Snow, V. F. (eds.), *The Private Journals of the Long Parliament*, New Haven: Yale University Press, 1982.

Cogswell, Thomas, 'Thomas Middleton and the court, 1624: *A Game at Chess* in context', *Huntington Library Quarterly* 42 (1984), 273–88.

Coldewey, John C., 'The Digby plays and the Chelmsford records', *Research Opportunities in Renaissance Drama* 10 (1967), 103–21.

Coldewey, John C., 'The last rise and final demise of Essex town drama', *Modern Language Quarterly* 36:3 (1975), 239–60.

Coldewey, John C., 'Some aspects of the late medieval drama', in Briscoe and Coldewey (eds.) *Contexts for Early English Drama*, 77–101.

Coldewey, John C., 'The non-cycle plays and the East Anglian tradition', in Beadle (ed.), *The Cambridge Companion to Medieval English Theatre*, 189–210.

Collinson, Patrick, *From Iconoclasm to Iconophobia: the Cultural Impact of the Second English Reformation*, University of Reading Press, 1986.

Cook, Ann Jennalie, 'Audiences: investigation, interpretation, invention', in Cox and Kastan (eds.), *A New History of Early English Drama*, 305–20.

Corbin, Peter and Sedge, Douglas, *The Oldcastle Controversy*, Manchester University Press, 1991.

Cox, John and Kastan, David Scott (eds.), *A New History of Early English Drama*, New York: Columbia University Press, 1997.

Craik, T. W., *The Tudor Interlude*, Leicester University Press, 1958.

Creaser, John, ' "The present aid of this occasion": the setting of *Comus*', in Lindley (ed.), *The Court Masque*, 111–34.

Cruickshanks, Evelyn (ed.), *The Stuart Courts*, Stroud: Sutton, 2000.

Davidson, Clifford (ed.), *Fools and Folly*, Kalamazoo, MI: Medieval Institute Publications, 1996.

Davidson, Clifford (ed.), *Material Culture and Medieval Drama*, Kalamazoo, MI: Western Michigan University Press, 1999.

Davidson, Clifford (ed.), *The Saint Play in Medieval Europe*, Kalamazoo, MI: Western Michigan University Press, 1986.

Davidson, Clifford and Eljenholm, Ann (eds.), *Iconoclasm vs. Art and Drama*, Kalamazoo, MI: Medieval Institute Publications, 1989.

Davies, H. Neville, 'The limitations of festival: Christian IV's state visit to England in 1606', in Mulryne and Shewring (eds.), *Italian Renaissance Festivals and their European Influence*, 311–36.

Davis, Natalie Zemon, 'The sacred and the body social in sixteenth-century Lyon', *Past and Present* 90 (1981), 40–70.

Dawson, G. E. (ed.), *Records of Plays and Players in Kent, 1450–1642*, Malone Society Collections VII, Oxford University Press, 1965.

Day, John, *Works*, ed. A. H. Bullen, reprint, London: Holland Press, 1963.

De la Bédoyère, Guy, *Roman Towns in Britain*, London: B. T. Batsford, 1992.

Dekker, Thomas, *A Knight's Conjuring*, ed. Larry M. Robbins, The Hague: Mouton, 1974.

Dessen, Alan C. and Thomson, Leslie, *A Dictionary of Stage Directions in English Drama, 1580–1642*, Cambridge University Press, 1999.

A Diurnal of Remarkable Occurrents that have passed within the country of Scotland since the death of King James the Fourth till the year MDLXXV, Edinburgh: Bannatyne Club, 1833.

Dolan, Frances E., *Dangerous Familiars: Representation of Domestic Crime in England, 1550–1700*, Ithaca: Cornell University Press, 1994.

Dollimore, J. and Sinfield, A. (eds.), *Political Shakespeare*, Ithaca: Cornell University Press, 1985.

Douglas, Gavin, *The Shorter Poems*, ed. N. W. Bawcutt, Edinburgh, Scottish Text Society, 1967.

Dronke, Peter (ed. and trans.), *Nine Medieval Latin Plays*, Cambridge University Press, 1994.

Drumbl, Johan, *Quem Quaeritis? Teatro sacro dell'alto medioevo*, Rome: Bulzoni Editore, 1981.

Dunbar, William, *Poems*, ed. W. Mackay Mackenzie, London: Faber and Faber, 1932.

Dunbar, William, *Selected Poems*, ed. Priscilla Bawcutt, Harlow: Longman, 1996.

Durston, Christopher, ' "For the better humiliation of the people": public days of fasting and thanksgiving during the English revolution', *The Seventeenth Century* 7 (1992), 129–49.

Durston, Christopher, 'Puritan rule and the failure of cultural revolution, 1645–1660', in Durston and Eales (eds.), *The Culture of English Puritanism*, 210–34.

Durston, Christopher and Eales, Jacqueline (eds.), *The Culture of English Puritanism, 1560–1700*, Basingstoke: Macmillan, 1996.

Dutton, Richard, 'The birth of the author', in Brown and Marotti (eds.), *Texts and Cultural Change in Early Modern England*, 153–78.

Dutton, Richard, *Licensing, Censorship and Authorship: Buggeswords*, Basingstoke and New York: Palgrave, 2001.

Dutton, Richard, 'Censorship', in Cox and Kastan (eds.), *A New History of Early English Drama*, 287–304.

Dutton, Richard, ' "Discourse in the players, though no disobedience": Sir Henry Herbert's problems with the players and Archbishop Laud, 1632–34', *The Ben Jonson Journal* 5 (1998), 37–62.

Dutton, Richard, '*Hamlet, An Apology for Actors*, and the sign of the Globe', *Shakespeare Survey* 41 (1989), 35–43.

Dutton, Richard (ed.), *Jacobean Civic Pageants*, Keele University Press, 1995.

Dutton, Richard, *Mastering the Revels: the Regulation and Censorship of English Renaissance Drama*, Basingstoke: Macmillan, 1991.

Edmond, Mary, 'Pembroke's Men', *Review of English Studies*, n.s. 25 (1974), 129–36.

Edwards, Philip, *et al.* (eds.), *The Revels History of Drama in English*, vol. IV, London: Routledge, 1996.

Edwards, Warwick, 'Consort music', in Sadie (ed.), *The New Grove Dictionary of Music*, IV, 672–5.

Eliade, Mircea, *Cosmos and History: the Myth of the Eternal Return*, trans. W. R. Trask, New York: Harper, 1959.

Eliade, Mircea, *The Sacred and the Profane: the Nature of Religion*, trans. W. R. Trask, New York: Harper, 1961.

Elliott, Alison Goddard (ed. and trans.), *Seven Medieval Latin Comedies*, New York: Garland Publishing, 1984.

Elliott, Kenneth and Shire, Helen Mennie (eds.), *Music of Scotland 1500–1700*, Musica Britannica, vol. 15, London: Stainer and Bell, 1975, 141–7.

Emmerson, Richard, 'Contextualizing Performance: the Reception of the Chester *AntiChrist*', *Journal of Medieval and Early Modern Studies* 29 (1999), 89–119.

Emmison, Frederick, *Tudor Food and Pastimes*, London: Ernest Benn, 1964.

Evelyn, John, *Diary of John Evelyn*, ed. De Beer, 6 vols., Oxford: Clarendon Press, 1955.

Feuillerat, A. (ed.), *Documents Relating to the Revels at Court in the Time of King Edward VI and Queen Mary*, Louvain: A. Uystpruyst, 1914.

Firth, C. H., 'Sir William Davenant and the revival of drama during the Protectorate', *English Historical Review* (April 1903), 103–20.

Firth, C. H. and Rait, R. S. (eds.), *Acts and Ordinances of the Interregnum*, 3 vols., Cambridge, 1911.

Flanigan, C. Clifford, 'The liturgical context of the *quem queritis* trope', *Comparative Drama* 8 (1974), 45–62.

Fletcher, A., *Reform in the Provinces*, New Haven: Yale University Press, 1986.

Fletcher, Anthony and Stevenson, John (eds.), *Order and Disorder in Early Modern England*, Cambridge University Press, 1985.

Foakes, R. A, *Illustrations of the English Stage 1580–1642*, Stanford University Press, 1985.

Foakes, R. A. and Rickert, R. T. (eds.), *Henslowe's Diary*, Cambridge University Press, 1961.

Foxe, John, *Two Latin Comedies by John Foxe the Martyrologist*, ed. and trans. John Hazel Smith, Ithaca: Cornell University Press, 1973.

Fradenburg, Louise Olga, *City, Marriage, Tournament: Arts of Rule in Late Medieval Scotland*, Madison, WI: University of Wisconsin Press, 1991.

Gair, W. Reavley, *The Children of Paul's: the Story of a Theatre Company, 1553–1608*, Cambridge University Press, 1982.

Galloway, D. and Wasson, J. (eds.), *Records of Plays and Players in Norfolk and Suffolk, 1330–1642*, Malone Society Collections XI, Oxford University Press, 1980.

Gardiner, Samuel Rawson, *Documents Relating to the Proceedings against William Prynne in 1634 and 1637*, series 2, 18, London: Camden Society, 1878.

Gardner-Medwin, A. and Williams, J. H. (eds.), *A Day Festival*, Aberdeen University Press, 1990.

Gayton, Edmund, *Pleasant Notes upon Don Quixote*, London, 1656.

Geertz, Clifford, *The Interpretation of Cultures*, New York: Basic Books, 1973.

Geertz, Clifford, *Local Knowledge*, New York: Harper Collins, 1983.

George, David, 'Anti-Catholic plays, puppet shows, and horse-racing in Reformation Lancashire', *REED Newsletter* 19:1 (1994), 15–22.

Gibson, Gail McMurray, *The Theater of Devotion: East Anglian Drama and Society in the Late Middle Ages*, University of Chicago Press, 1989.

Gibson, James, ' "Interludum Passionis Domini": parish drama in medieval New Romney', in Johnston and Hüsken (eds.), *English Parish Drama*, 137–45.

Gibson, James, 'Stuart players in Kent: fact or fiction?', *REED Newsletter* 20.2 (1995), 1–13.

Gildersleeve, Virginia, *Government Regulation of the Elizabethan Drama*, New York: Burt Franklin, 1961.

Gordon, D. J., 'Poet and architect: the intellectual setting of the quarrel between Inigo Jones and Ben Jonson', in S. Orgel (ed.), *The Renaissance Imagination*, 77–101, Berkeley: University of California Press, 1975.

Graves, R. B., *Lighting the Shakespearean Stage 1576–1642*, Carbondale: Southern Illinois University Press, 1999.

Gray, Douglas, 'The royal entry in sixteenth-century Scotland', in Mapstone and Wood (eds.), *The Rose and the Thistle*, 10–37.

Greenblatt, Stephen, *Renaissance Self-Fashioning: From More to Shakespeare*, University of Chicago Press, 1980.

Greenfield, Peter H., 'Entertainments of Henry, Lord Berkeley, 1593–4 and 1600–05', *REED Newsletter* 8 (1983), 12–24.

Greenfield, Thelma, *The Induction in Elizabethan Drama*, Eugene: University of Oregon Books, 1969.

Greg, W. W. (ed.), *Henslowe Papers: Being Documents Supplementary to Henslowe's Diary*, London: A. H. Bullen, 1907.

Grose, Francis (comp.), 'The Earl of Northumberland's Household Book', *The Antiquarian Repertory*, vol. 4, London: E. Jeffery, 1809.

Gurr, Andrew, 'The bare island', *Shakespeare Survey* 47 (1994), 29–43.

Gurr, Andrew, 'Money or audiences: the choice of Shakespeare's Globe', *Theatre Notebook* 42 (1988), 3–14.

Gurr, Andrew, *Playgoing in Shakespeare's London*, Cambridge University Press, 1987.

Gurr, Andrew, *The Shakespearian Playing Companies*, Oxford: Clarendon Press, 1996.

Gurr, Andrew, *The Shakespearean Stage, 1574–1642*, 3rd edition, Cambridge University Press, 1992.

Gurr, Andrew, 'Why Captain Jamy in *Henry V?*', *Archiv* 226 (1989), 365–73.

Haaker, Ann, 'The plague, the theater, and the poet', *Renaissance Drama*, n.s. 1 (1968), 283–306.

Haigh, Christopher, *English Reformations: Religion, Politics, and Society under the Tudors*, Oxford University Press, 1993.

Hakluyt, R., *The Principall Navigations, Voyages and Discoveries of the English Nation*, Glasgow: James MacLehose and Sons, 1904.

Hall, Edward, *The Vnion of the Two Noble and Illustre Famelies of Lancastre and Yorke*, London: G. Woodfall, 1809.

Halpern, Richard, *The Poetics of Primitive Accumulation: English Renaissance Culture and the Genealogy of Capital*, Ithaca: Cornell University Press, 1991.

Happé, Peter, *John Bale*, London: Prentice Hall International, 1996.

Happé, Peter, 'The Protestant adaptation of the saint play', in Davidson (ed.), *The Saint Play in Medieval Europe*, 205–40.

Happé, Peter, 'Staging Folly in the early sixteenth century: Heywood, Lindsay and others', in Davidson (ed.), *Fools and Folly*, 73–111.

Happé, Peter and King, John N. (eds.), *The Vocacyon of Johan Bale*, Binghamton, NY: Renaissance English Text Society, 1990.

Hardison, O. B., *Christian Rite and Christian Drama in the Middle Ages*, Baltimore: Johns Hopkins University Press, 1965.

Harris, John Wesley, *Medieval Theatre in Context*, London: Routledge, 1992.

Hawkes, Terence (ed.), *Alternative Shakespeares*, vol. II, London: Routledge, 1996.

Hayes, Rosalind, 'Dorset church houses and the Drama', *Research Opportunities in Renaissance Drama* 31 (1992), 12–23.

Hayes, Rosalind 'Lot's wife or the burning of Sodom: the Tudor Corpus Christi play at Sherborne, Dorset', *Research Opportunities in Renaissance Drama* 33 (1994), 105.

Healy, Thomas and Sawday, Jonathan (eds.), *Literature and the English Civil War*, Cambridge University Press, 1990.

Heinemann, Margot, *Puritanism and Theatre: Middleton and Opposition Drama under the Early Stuarts*, Cambridge University Press, 1980.

Henderson, Diana E., 'The theater and domestic culture', in Cox and Kastan (eds.), *A New History of Early English Drama*, 173–194.

Heywood, Thomas, *An Apology for Actors from the edition of 1612,* ed. J. P. Collier, London: Shakespeare Society, 1841.

Higgins, Sydney (ed.), *European Medieval Drama 1998*, Camerino, Macerata: Università degli studi di Camerino, Centro linguistico di ateneo, 1999.

Hill-Vasquez, Heather, 'The possibilities of performance: a Reformation sponsorship for the Digby *Conversion of Saint Paul*', *REED Newsletter* 22 (1997), 2–20.

Honan, Park, *Shakespeare: a Life*, Oxford: Clarendon Press, 1999.

Honigmann, E. A. J., *Shakespeare: the 'Lost Years'*, Manchester University Press, 1985.

Honigmann, E. A. J. and Brock, Susan (eds.), *Playhouse Wills, 1558–1642*, Manchester University Press, 1993.

Hopwood, C. H. and Martin, C. T. (eds.), *Middle Temple Records*, London: Butterworth, 1904.

Hotson, L., *The Commonwealth and Restoration Stage*, Cambridge, MA: Harvard University Press, 1928.

Howard-Hill, T. H., 'The unique eye-witness report of Middleton's *A Game at Chess*', *Review of English Studies*, n.s. 42 (1991), 168–78.

Howard-Hill, T. H., 'Political interpretations of Middleton's *A Game at Chess*', *Yearbook of English Studies* 21 (1991), 274–85.

Howard-Hill, T. H., *Middleton's 'Vulgar Pasquin': Essays on 'A Game at Chess'*, Newark, Delaware: University of Delaware Press, 1995.

Hughes, Paul and Larkin, James (eds.), *Tudor Royal Proclamations*, 3 vols., New Haven: Yale University Press, 1964.

Hutton, Ronald, *The Rise and Fall of Merry England: the Ritual Year 1400–1700*, Oxford University Press, 1996.

Ingram, Martin, *Church Courts, Sex and Marriage, 1570–1640*, Cambridge University Press, 1990.

Ingram, R. W., '1579 and the decline of civic religious drama in Coventry', *Elizabethan Theatre VIII*, ed. G. R. Hibbard, Port Credit, Ontario: P. D. Meany, 1982, 114–28.

Ingram, R. W., ' "To find the players and all that longeth therto": notes on the production of medieval drama in Coventry', *The Elizabethan Theatre V*, Port Credit, Ontario: P. D. Meany, 1975, 17–44.

Ingram, William, *The Business of Playing: the Beginnings of Adult Professional Theatre in Elizabethan England*, Ithaca: Cornell University Press, 1992.

Ingram, William, 'The cost of touring', *Medieval and Renaissance Drama in England* 6 (1993), 58–9.

Ingram, William, 'The economics of playing', in Kastan (ed.), *A Companion to Shakespeare*, 313–27.

Ingram, William, 'The Theatre at Newington Butts', *Shakespeare Quarterly* 21 (1970), 385–98.

Jack, R. D. S. (ed.), *The History of Scottish Literature*, vol. 1 *Origins to 1660*, Aberdeen University Press, 1989.

Jack, R. D. S. and Rozendaal, P. (eds.), *The Mercat Anthology of Early Scottish Literature 1375–1707*, Edinburgh: Mercat Press, 1997.

Jacob, James R. and Raylor, Timothy, 'Opera and obedience: Thomas Hobbes and *A Proposition for Advancement of Moralitie* by Sir William Davenant', *The Seventeenth Century* 6:2 (1991), 205–50.

Jacquot, Jean, Konigson, Elie and Oddon, Marcel (eds.), *Dramaturgie et société: rapports entre l'œuvre théâtrale, son interprétation et son public aux XVIe et XVIIe siècles*, Paris: Editions du Centre National de la Recherche Scientifique, 1968.

James VI, King of Scotland, *New Poems by James I of England*, ed. Allan F. Westcott, New York: Columbia University Press, 1911.

James, Mervyn, 'Ritual, drama, and social body in the late medieval English town', *Past and Present* 98 (1983), 3–29.

Johnston, Alexandra F. and Hüsken, Wim (eds.), *Civic Ritual and Drama*, Amsterdam: Rodopi, 1997.

Johnston, Alexandra F. and Hüsken, Wim (eds.), *English Parish Drama*, Amsterdam: Rodopi, 1996.

Jones, Gareth, *A New History of Wales: the Gentry and the Elizabethan State*, Swansea: Christopher Davies, 1977.

Jones, Michael, *The End of Roman Britain*. Ithaca: Cornell University Press, 1996.

Jones, Robert C., 'Dangerous sport: the audience's engagement with vice in the moral interludes', *Renaissance Drama* 6 (1973), 45–64.

Ben Jonson, ed. Ian Donaldson, Oxford University Press, 1985.

Ben Jonson, ed. C. H. Herford and Percy and Evelyn Simpson, 11 vols. Oxford: Clarendon Press, 1925–52.

Jonson, Ben, *Eastward Ho!*, ed. R. W. Van Fossen, Manchester University Press, 1979.

Jonson, Ben, *Every Man in His Humour*, ed. J. W. Lever, Lincoln: University of Nebraska Press, 1971.

Jonson, Ben, *Sejanus*, ed. Philip J. Ayres, Manchester University Press, 1990.

Joughin, John J. (ed.), *Shakespeare and National Culture*, Manchester University Press, 1997.

Kastan, David Scott (ed.), *A Companion to Shakespeare*, Oxford: Blackwell, 1999.

Kenyon, Kathleen M., 'The Roman Theatre at Verulamium, St Albans', *Archaeologia* 84 (Second Series 34) (1935), 213–61.

King, John, *English Reformation Literature*, Princeton University Press, 1983.

King, John, *Tudor Royal Iconography: Literature and Art in the Age of Religious Crisis*, Princeton University Press, 1989.

King, Pamela, 'The York and Coventry mystery cycles: a comparative model of civic response to growth and recession', *REED Newsletter* 22 (1997), 20–6.

King, T. J., 'The staging of plays at the Phoenix in Drury Lane, 1617–42', *Theatre Notebook* 19 (1964–5), 146–66.

Kipling, G., *Enter the King: Theatre, Liturgy, and Ritual in the Medieval Civic Triumph*, Oxford: Clarendon Press, 1998.

Kirk, James (ed.), *Stirling Presbytery Records 1581–1587*, Edinburgh: Clark Constable, 1981.

Knowles, David, *Bare Ruined Choirs: the Dissolution of the English Monasteries*, Cambridge University Press, 1976.

Knutson, Roslyn, *The Repertory of Shakespeare's Company*, Fayetteville: University of Arkansas Press, 1991.

Kolve, V. A., *The Play Called Corpus Christi*, Stanford University Press, 1966.

Lancashire, Ian, *Dramatic Texts and Records of Britain: a Chronological Topography to 1558*, Cambridge University Press and University of Toronto Press, 1984.

Lancashire, Ian, 'Orders for Twelfth Day and Night circa 1515 in the Second Northumberland Household Book', *English Literary Renaissance* 10 (1980), 7–45.

Larkin, James F. and Hughes, Paul L. (eds.), *Stuart Royal Proclamations*, 2 vols., Oxford: Clarendon Press, 1983.

Lasocki, David, 'Professional recorder playing in England, 1500–1740', *Early Music* 10: 1 (1982), 23–28.

Lennam, T. N. S., 'Sir Edward Dering's collection of playbooks', *Shakespeare Quarterly* 16 (1965), 145–53.

Lewalski, Barbara, 'Milton's *Comus* and the politics of masquing', in Bevington and Holbrook (eds.), *The Politics of the Stuart Court Masque*, 296–320.

Lewalski, Barbara, 'Re-writing patriarchy and patronage: Margaret Clifford, Anne Clifford, and Aemilia Lanyer', in Brown (ed.), *Patronage, Politics and Literary Traditions in England*, 59–78.

Lewalski, Barbara, *Writing Women in Jacobean England*, Cambridge, MA: Harvard University Press, 1993.

Limon, Jerzy, *Dangerous Matter: English Drama and Politics in 1623/24*, Cambridge University Press, 1986.

Lindley, David, 'Campion's *Lord Hay's Masque* and Anglo-Scottish Union', *Huntington Library Quarterly* 43 (1979–80), 1–11.

Lindley, David (ed.), *The Court Masque*, Manchester University Press, 1984.

Lindley, David (ed.), *Court Masques*, Oxford University Press, 1995.

Lindley, David, 'Courtly play: the politics of Chapman's *The Memorable Masque*', in Cruickshanks (ed.), *Stuart Courts*, 43–58.

Lindley, David, 'The politics of music in the masque', in Bevington and Holbrook (eds.), *The Politics of the Stuart Court Masque*, 273–95.

Lindsay, Sir David, *Ane Satyre of the Thrie Estaitis*, ed. Roderick Lyall, Edinburgh: Canongate Publishing Ltd, 1989.

The Lisle Letters, ed. Muriel St Clare Byrne, 6 vols., University of Chicago Press, 1981.

Liversidge, Joan, *Britain in the Roman Empire*, New York: Frederick A. Praeger, 1968.

Loengard, Janet, 'An Elizabethan lawsuit: John Brayne, his carpenter, and the building of the Red Lion theatre', *Shakespeare Quarterly* 34 (1983), 298–310.

Long, William, ' "Precious Few": English manuscript playbooks', in Kastan (ed.), *A Companion to Shakespeare*, 414–33.

Long, William, 'Bookkeepers and playhouse manuscripts: a peek at the evidence', *Shakespeare Newsletter* 44:1 (1994), 3.

Loomba, Anita, 'Shakespeare and cultural difference', in Hawkes (ed.), *Alternative Shakespeares*, II, 164–91.

Luders, A. (ed.), *Statutes of the Realm*, 11 vols., London: George Eyre and Andrew Strahan, 1810–28.

Lynch, Michael, *Edinburgh and the Reformation*, Edinburgh: John Donald, 1981.

Lynch, Michael, 'Queen Mary's Triumph: the baptismal celebrations at Stirling in December 1566', *The Scottish Historical Review* 69:1 (1990), 1–21.

Lytle, Guy Fitch and Orgel, Stephen (eds.), *Patronage in the Renaissance*, Princeton University Press, 1981.

MacLaine, Allan H. (ed.), *The Christis Kirk Tradition: Scots Poems of Folk Festivity*, Glasgow: Association for Scottish Literary Studies, 1996.

MacLean, Sally-Beth, 'Players on tour: new evidence from Records of Early English Drama', in C. E. McGee (ed.), *Elizabethan Theatre X*, Port Credit, Ontario: P. D. Meany, 1988, 55–72.

MacLean, Sally-Beth, 'Reassessment of a popular pre-Reformation festival', in Twycross, *Festive Drama*, 233–41.

Maley, Willy, ' "This sceptred isle": Shakespeare and the British problem', in Joughin (ed.), *Shakespeare and National Culture*, 83–108.

Mapstone, Sally and Wood, Juliette (eds.), *The Rose and the Thistle: Essays on the Culture of Late Medieval and Renaissance Scotland*, East Linton: Tuckwell Press, 1998.

Masten, Jeffrey, 'Beaumont and/or Fletcher: collaboration and interpretation of Renaissance drama', *English Literary History* 59 (1992), 337–56.

Masten, Jeffrey, 'Playwrighting: authorship and collaboration', in Cox and Kastan (eds.), *A New History of Early English Drama*, 357–82.

Masten, Jeffrey, *Textual Intercourse: Collaboration, Authorship, and Sexualities in Renaissance Drama*, Cambridge University Press, 1997.

McClure, N. E. (ed.), *The Letters and Epigrams of Sir John Harington*, University of Philadelphia Press, 1930.

McDonald, Russ, *The Bedford Companion to Shakespeare: an Introduction with Documents*, Boston: Bedford Books, 1996.

McFarlane, I. D., *Buchanan*, London: Duckworth, 1981.

McGavin, John J., 'Robert III's "rough music": charivari and diplomacy in a medieval Scottish court', *The Scottish Historical Review* 74:2 (1995), 144–58.

McGavin, John, 'Drama in sixteenth-century Haddington', in Higgins (ed.), *European Medieval Drama*, I, 147–59.

McLuskie, Kathleen, *Dekker and Heywood: Professional Dramatists*, New York: St Martin's Press, 1994.

McLuskie, Kathleen, 'The patriarchal bard: feminist criticism and Shakespeare', in Dollimore and Sinfield (eds.), *Political Shakespeare*, 88–108.

McLuskie, Kathleen, 'The plays and the playwrights', in Edwards *et al.* (eds.), *The Revels History of Drama in English*, IV, 127–260.

McLuskie, K. and Dunsworth, F., 'Patronage and the economics of theatre', in Cox and Kastan (eds.), *A New History of Early English Drama*, 423–40.

McMillin, Scott, *The Elizabethan Theatre and 'The Book of Sir Thomas More'*, Ithaca: Cornell University Press, 1987.

McMillin, Scott, 'Professional playwrighting', in Kastan (ed.), *A Companion to Shakespeare*, 225–38.

McMillin, Scott, 'Sussex's Men in 1594: the evidence of *Titus Andronicus* and *The Jew of Malta*', *Theatre Survey* 32 (1991), 214–23.

McMillin, S. and MacLean, S., *The Queen's Men and their Plays*, Cambridge University Press, 1998.

Melville, James, *The Diary of Mr James Melville 1566–1601*, Edinburgh: Bannatyne Club, 1829.

Meredith, P., 'John Clerke's hand in the York Register', *Leeds Studies in English* 12 (1981), 245–71.

Middleton, Thomas, *A Game at Chess*, ed. T. H. Howard-Hill, Manchester University Press, 1993.

Middleton, Thomas, *The Second Maiden's Tragedy*, ed. A. B. Lancashire, Manchester University Press, 1978.

Milhous, Judith and Hume, Robert D., 'New light on English acting companies in 1646, 1648, and 1660', *Review of English Studies* 42 (1991), 487–509.

Mill, A. J., *Medieval Plays in Scotland*, St Andrews University Publications, 1927.

Mills, D., 'Chester's Midsummer Show: creation and adaptation', in Twycross (ed.), *Festive Drama*, 132–44.

Mills, D., *Re-Cycling the Cycle: the City of Chester and its Whitsun Plays*, University of Toronto Press, 1998.

Montgomerie, Alexander, *Poems*, ed. James Cranstoun, Edinburgh: William Blackwood & Sons, 1887.

Moore Smith, G. C. (ed.), *The Letters of Dorothy Osborne to William Temple*, Oxford: Clarendon Press, 1928.

Morse, David, *England's Time of Crisis: from Shakespeare to Milton: a Cultural History*, New York: St Martin's Press, 1989.

Muir, Lynette R., *Liturgy and Drama in the Anglo-Norman Adam*, Oxford: Basil Blackwell, 1973.

Mullaney, Steven, *The Place of the Stage: License, Play, and Power in Renaissance England*, University of Chicago Press, 1988.

Mullett, Charles F., *The Bubonic Plague and England*, Lexington: University of Kentucky Press, 1956.

Mulryne, J. R. and Shewring, Margaret (eds.), *Italian Renaissance Festivals and their European Influence*, Lampeter: Edwin Mellen Press, 1992.

Mulryne, J. R. and Shewring, Margaret (eds.), *Shakespeare's Globe Rebuilt*, Cambridge University Press, 1997.

Mulryne, J. R. and Shewring, Margaret (eds.), *Theatre of the English and Italian Renaissance*, Basingstoke: Macmillan, 1991.

Mulryne, J. R. and Shewring, Margaret (eds.), *Theatre and Government under the Early Stuarts*, Cambridge University Press, 1993.

Myers, Alec R. (ed.), *The Household Book of Edward IV: the Black Book and the Ordinance of 1478*, Manchester University Press, 1959.

Nashe, Thomas, *Works*, ed. Ronald B. McKerrow, II vols., Oxford: Blackwell, 1958.

Nelson, A. H., *Early Cambridge Theatres*, Cambridge University Press, 1994.

Nelson, A. H., *The Medieval English Stage: Corpus Christi Pageants and Plays*, University of Chicago Press, 1974.

Niblett, Rosalind, *Roman Hertfordshire*, Stanbridge, Dorset: Dovecote Press, 1995.

Nichols, J. G. (ed.), *Narratives of the Days of the Reformation*, London: Camden Society, 1859.

Nicoll, Allardyce, *British Drama: an Historical Survey from the Beginnings to the Present Time*, rev. edn., New York: Thomas Crowell, 1933.

Noomen, William, *Le Jeu d' Adam*, Paris: H. Champion, 1971.

Norbrook, David, 'The reformation of the masque', in Lindley (ed.), *The Court Masque*, 94–110.

Norland, Howard B., *Drama in Early Tudor Britain, 1485–1558*, Lincoln: University of Nebraska Press, 1995.

Nungezer, Edwin, *A Dictionary of Actors and other Persons associated with the Public Representation of Plays in England before 1642*, New Haven, CT: Greenwood Press, 1927.

O'Connell, Michael, *The Idolatrous Eye: Iconoclasm and Theater in Early Modern England*, Oxford University Press, 2000.

O'Connell, Michael, 'Vital cultural practices: Shakespeare and the mysteries', *Journal of Medieval and Early Modern Studies* 29 (1999), 149–68.

Orgel, S., *The Illusion of Power: Political Theater in the English Renaissance*, Berkeley: University of California Press, 1975.

Orgel, S., *Impersonations: the Performance of Gender in Shakespeare's England*, Cambridge University Press, 1996

Orgel, S., *The Jonsonian Masque*, Cambridge, MA: Harvard University Press, 1967.

Orgel, S., *The Renaissance Imagination*, Berkeley: University of California Press, 1975.

Orgel, Stephen and Strong, Roy (eds.), *Inigo Jones: the Theatre of the Stuart Court*, 2 vols., Berkeley: University of California Press, 1973.

Orlin, Lena Cowen, *Private Matters and Public Culture in Post-Reformation England*, Ithaca: Cornell University Press, 1994.

Orrell, John, 'The agent of Savoy at *The Somerset Masque*', *Review of English Studies* 28 (1977), 301–4.

Orrell, John, 'Designing the Globe', in Mulryne and Shewring (eds.), *Shakespeare's Globe Rebuilt*, 51–66.

Orrell, John, *The Theatres of Inigo Jones and John Webb*, Cambridge University Press, 1985.

Palmer, Barbara D., ' "Anye disguised persons": parish entertainment in West Yorkshire', in Johnston and Hüsken, *English Parish Drama*.

Patrick, David (ed.), *The Statutes of the Scottish Church 1225–1559*, Edinburgh: T. & A. Constable, 1907.

Patterson, Annabel, *Censorship and Interpretation: the Conditions of Writing and Reading in Early Modern England*, Madison, WI: University of Wisconsin Press, 1984.

Peacock, John, 'Ben Jonson's masques and Italian culture', in Mulryne and Shewring (eds.), *Theatre of the English and Italian Renaissance*, 73–92.

Peacock, John, 'Ben Jonson and the Italian festival books', in Mulryne and Shewring, *Italian Renaissance Festivals*, 271–88.

Peacock, John, *The Stage Designs of Inigo Jones: the European Context*, Cambridge University Press, 1995.

Pearsall Smith, L. (ed.), *The Life and Letters of Sir Henry Wotton*, 2 vols., Oxford: Clarendon Press, 1907.

Pendry, E., *Thomas Dekker*, London: Edward Arnold, 1967.

Peterkin, Alexander (ed.), *The Booke of the Universall Kirk of Scotland*, Edinburgh: Edinburgh Printing and Publishing Co., 1839.

Phythian-Adams, Charles, 'Ceremony and the citizen: the communal year at Coventry, 1450–1550', in Clark and Slack (eds.), *Crisis and Order in English Towns, 1500–1700*, 57–85.

Pitscottie, Robert Lindesay of, *The Historie and Cronicles of Scotland*, ed. A. E. J. G. Mackay, Edinburgh: William Blackwood & Sons, 1899.

Potter, Lois, 'The plays and playwrights: 1642–60', in Edwards *et al.* (eds.), *The Revels History of Drama in English*, IV, 261–304.

Raines, Robert, 'Thomas Drue's *The Duchess of Suffolk*: a critical old spelling edition', PhD thesis, University of Delaware, 1968.

Raman, Shankar, *Framing 'India': the Colonial Imaginary in Early Modern Culture*, Stanford University Press, 2001.

Rappaport, S. L., *Worlds within Worlds: Structures of Life in Sixteenth-Century London*, Cambridge University Press, 1989.

Rasmussen, Eric, 'Setting down what the clown spoke: improvisation, Hand B, and *The Book of Sir Thomas More*', *The Library* 13:2 (June 1991), 126–36.

Rasmussen, Eric, 'The revision of scripts', in Cox and Kastan (eds.), *A New History of Early English Drama*, 441–60.

Rastall, Richard, *The Heaven Singing: Music in Early English Religious Drama*, 2 vols., Cambridge: D. S. Brewer, 1996.

Ravelhofer, Barbara, ' "Virgin Wax" and "Hairy Men Monsters": unstable movement codes in the Stuart masque', in Bevington and Holbrook (eds.), *The Politics of the Stuart Court Masque*, 244–72

REED: Records of Early English Drama, University of Toronto Press

Bristol, ed. M. C. Pilkinton, 1997.

Cambridge, ed. A. H. Nelson, 2 vols., 1989.

Chester, ed. L. M. Clopper, 1979.

Coventry, ed. R. W. Ingram, 1981.

Cumberland, Westmorland, Gloucestershire, ed. A. Douglas and P. Greenfield, 1986.

Devon, ed. J. Wasson, 1986.

Herefordshire, Worcestershire, ed. D. N. Klausner, 1990.

Newcastle-upon-Tyne, ed. J. J. Anderson, 1982.

Norwich, 1540–1642, ed. D. Galloway, 1984.

Shropshire, ed. J. A. B. Somerset, 1994.

Somerset, ed. J. Stokes, 2 vols., 1995.

York, ed. A. F. Johnston and M. Rogerson, 2 vols., 1979.

The Resurrection of Our Lord, ed. J. Dover Wilson and Bertram Dobell, Oxford University Press, 1912.

Riggio, Milla Cozart, *The 'Wisdom' Symposium,* New York: AMS Press, 1986.

Robinson, Hastings (ed.), *The Zurich Letters*, Cambridge University Press, 1842.

Ross, D. James, *Musick Fyne: Robert Carver and the Art of Music in Sixteenth Century Scotland*, Edinburgh: Mercat Press, 1993.

Roston, Murray, *Biblical Drama in England from the Middle Ages to the Present Day*, London: Faber and Faber, 1968.

Ruigh, R. E., *Parliament of 1624*, Cambridge, MA. Harvard University Press, 1971.

Runnalls, G. A., *Les Mystères français imprimés*, Paris: H. Champion, 1999.

Rutter, Carol Chillington, *Documents of the Rose Playhouse,* Manchester University Press, 1984.

Rylance, Mark, 'Playing the Globe', in Mulryne and Shewring (eds.), *Shakespeare's Globe Rebuilt*, 169–76.

Sabol, A., *Four Hundred Songs and Dances from the Stuart Masque*, Hanover, NH: University Press of New England, 1982.

Sadie, Stanley (ed.), *The New Grove Dictionary of Music and Musicians*, 20 vols., London: Macmillan, 1980.

Sams, Eric, *The Real Shakespeare: Retrieving the Early Years, 1564–1594*, New Haven: Yale University Press, 1995.

Schell, E. and Shuchter, J. (eds.), *English Morality Plays and Moral Interludes*, New York: Holt, Rinehart and Winston, 1969.

Shakespeare, William, *Henry V*, ed. Andrew Gurr, Cambridge University Press, 1992.

Shakespeare, William, *Richard II*, ed. Andrew Gurr, Cambridge University Press, 1984.

Sharratt, P. and Walsh, P. G. (eds.), *George Buchanan Tragedies*, Edinburgh: Scottish Academic Press, 1983.

Shire, Helen Mennie, *Song, Dance and Poetry of the Court of Scotland under King James VI*, Cambridge University Press, 1969.

Shirley, James, *Dramatic Works and Poems*, ed. W. Gifford and A. Dyce, 6 vols., London: Murray, 1833.

Shirley, James, *The Bird in a Cage*, ed. F. F. Senescu, New York: Garland, 1980.

Shrewsbury, J. F. D., *A History of Bubonic Plague in the British Isles*, Cambridge University Press, 1970.

Sidney, Philip, *Prose Works*, ed. Albert Feuillerat, 4 vols., Cambridge University Press, 1963.

Siebert, Fred, *The Freedom of the Press in England, 1476–1776*, Urbana: University of Illinois Press, 1952.

Simon, Eckehard (ed.), *The Theatre of Medieval Europe*, Cambridge University Press, 1991.

Skura, Meredith, *Shakespeare the Actor and the Purposes of Playing*, University of Chicago Press, 1993.

Smoldon, William L., *The Music of the Medieval Church Dramas*, ed. Cynthia Bourgeault, Oxford University Press, 1980.

Smoldon, William L., 'The origins of the *quem quaeritis* trope and the Easter sepulchre music-drama, as demonstrated by their musical settings', in Sticca (ed.), *The Medieval Drama*, 121–54.

Somerset, J. A. B., ' "How chances it they travel?": provincial touring, playing places and the King's Men', *Shakespeare Survey* 47 (1994), 54–60.

Somerset, J. A. B., 'Local drama and playing places at Shrewsbury: new findings from the borough records', *Medieval and Renaissance Drama in England* 2 (1985), 1–32.

Soule, Lesley Wade, *Actor as Anti-Character: Dionysus, the Devil and the Boy Rosalind*, Westport, CT: Greenwood Press, 2000.

Southern, Richard, *Changeable Scenery: its Origin and Development in the British Theatre*, London: Faber and Faber, 1952.

Southern, Richard, *The Staging of Plays before Shakespeare*, London: Faber and Faber, 1973.

Southworth, J., *Fools and Jesters at the English Court*, Stroud: Sutton, 1998.

Spencer, T. J. B. and Wells, Stanley (eds.), *A Book of Masques*, Cambridge University Press, 1967.

Stevens, Martin, *Four Middle English Mystery Cycles*, Princeton University Press, 1987.

Stevens, M. and Cawley, A. C. (eds.), *The Towneley Plays*, 2 vols., Oxford University Press, 1994.

Sticca, Sandro, 'Christian drama and Christian liturgy', *Latomus* 26 (1967), 1025–34.

Sticca, Sandro (ed.), *The Medieval Drama*, Albany: State University of New York Press, 1972.

Streitberger, W. R., *Court Revels 1485–1559*, University of Toronto Press, 1994.

Streitberger, W. R., 'Devising the revels', *Early Theatre* 1 (1998) 55–74.

Streitberger, W. R., 'Financing court entertainments, 1509–1558', *Research Opportunities in Renaissance Drama* 27 (1984), 21–45.

Streitberger, W. R., 'Personnel and professionalization' in Cox and Kastan (eds.), *A New History of Early English Drama*, 337–56.

Strong, Roy, *Henry, Prince of Wales and England's Lost Renaissance*, London: Thames and Hudson, 1986.

Tacitus, *The Complete Works*, trans. A. J. Church and W. J. Brodribb, ed. M. Hadas, New York: Random House, 1942.

Tennenhouse, L. (ed.), *The Tudor Interludes: 'Nice Wanton' and 'Impatient Poverty'*, New York: Garland, 1984.

Tertullian, *The Writings of Septimus Florens Tertullianus*, trans. and ed. S. Thelwell, J. Kaye *et al.*, Edinburgh: T. & T. Clark, 1869.

Thomson, Peter, *Shakespeare's Professional Career*, Cambridge University Press, 1992.

Thomson, Peter, *Shakespeare's Theatre*, London: Routledge, 1992.

Thomson, T. and Innes, C. (eds.), *Acts of the Parliament of Scotland AD 1124 (–1707)*, 12 vols., Edinburgh, 1814–75.

Tittler, Robert, *Architecture and Power: the Town Hall and the English Urban Community c. 1500–1640*, Oxford: Clarendon Press, 1991.

Travis, Peter, 'The social body of the dramatic Christ in medieval England', *Acta* 13 (1987), 18–36.

Tricomi, Albert H., *Anticourt Drama in England 1603–1642*, Charlottesville: University of Virginia Press, 1989.

Tricomi, Albert H., 'The revised *Bussy D'Ambois* and *The Revenge of Bussy D'Ambois*: joint performance in thematic counterpoint', *English Language Notes* 9 (1972), 253–45.

Trussler, Simon, *Cambridge Illustrated History of British Theatre*, Cambridge University Press, 1994.

Twycross, Meg (ed.), *Festive Drama*, Cambridge: D. S. Brewer, 1996.

Tydeman, William (ed.), *The Medieval European Stage, 500–1550*, Cambridge University Press, 2001.

Tydeman, William (ed.), *The Theatre in the Middle Ages*, Cambridge University Press, 1978.

Underdown, David, 'The taming of the scold: the enforcement of patriarchal authority in early modern England', in Fletcher and Stevenson (eds.), *Order and Disorder in Early Modern England*, 116–136.

Veevers, Erica, *Images of Love and Religion: Queen Henrietta Maria and Court Entertainments*, Cambridge University Press, 1989.

Walker, Greg, *Plays of Persuasion: Drama and Politics at the Court of Henry VIII*, Cambridge University Press, 1991.

Walker, Greg, *The Politics of Performance in Early Renaissance Drama*, Cambridge University Press, 1998.

Walls, Peter, *Music in the English Courtly Masque 1604–1640*, Oxford University Press, 1996.

Wasson, John M., 'The English church as theatrical space', in Cox and Kastan (eds.), *A New History of Early English Drama*, 25–37.

Webster, John, 'An excellent actor', *Works*, ed. F. L. Lucas, 4 vols., London: Chatto & Windus, 1927, IV, 42–3.

Weimann, Robert, 'Le declin de la scène "indivisible" Elisabethaine: Beaumont, Fletcher et Heywood', in Jacquot, Konigson and Oddon (eds.), *Dramaturgie et société*, 814–27.

Weimann, Robert, *Shakespeare and the Popular Tradition in the Theater: Studies in the Social Dimension of Dramatic Form and Function*, Baltimore: Johns Hopkins University Press, 1978.

Welsford, Enid, *The Court Masque*, Cambridge University Press, 1927

Welsford, Enid, *The Fool*, London: Faber and Faber, 1935.

Werstine, Paul, 'Close contrivers: nameless collaborators in early modern plays', in A. L. Magnusson and C. E. McGee (eds.), *Elizabethan Theatre XV*, Toronto: P. D. Meaney, 2002.

Werstine, Paul, 'Plays in manuscript', in Cox and Kastan (eds.), *A New History of Early English Drama*, 481–98

Westfall, Suzanne R., 'The chapel: theatrical performances in early Tudor great households', *English Literary Renaissance* 18:2 (1988), 171–93.

Westfall, Suzanne R., *Patrons and Performance: Early Tudor Household Revels*, Oxford: Clarendon Press, 1990.

White, Martin, *Renaissance Drama in Action*, London: Routledge, 1998.

White, Paul Whitfield, ' "The actors are come hither": literary analogues of itinerant player troupe procedures', *Theatre Survey* (1989), 56–68.

White, Paul Whitfield, 'Reforming mysteries' end: a new look at Protestant intervention in English provincial drama', *Journal of Medieval and Early Modern Studies* 29 (1999), 121–48.

White, Paul Whitfield (ed.), *Reformation Biblical Drama in England*, New York: Garland, 1992.

White, Paul Whitfield, *Theatre and Reformation: Protestantism, Patronage, and Playing in Tudor England*, Cambridge University Press, 1993.

White, Paul Whitfield and Westfall, Suzanne (eds.), *Shakespeare and Theatrical Patronage in Early Modern England*, Cambridge University Press, 2002.

Whitelocke, Bulstrode, *Diary 1605–1675*, ed. Ruth Spalding, Oxford University Press, 1990.

Whitworth, C. W. (ed.), *Three Sixteenth-Century Comedies*, London: Ernest Benn, 1984.

Wickham, Glynne, *Early English Stages*, 3 vols., London: Routledge and Kegan Paul, 1959–80.

Wickham, Glynne, *Shakespeare's Dramatic Heritage*, London: Routledge and Kegan Paul, 1969.

Wickham, G., Berry, H. and Ingram, W. (eds.), *English Professional Theatre, 1530–1660*, Cambridge University Press, 2000.

Wiles, David, *Shakespeare's Clown*, Cambridge University Press, 1987.

Wiles, David, *The Early Plays of Robin Hood*, Cambridge: D. S. Brewer, 1981.

Williams, G. W. and Evans, G. B. (eds.), *'The History of King Henry the Fourth' as Revised by Sir Edward Dering*, Charlottesville: University Press of Virginia, 1974.

Williams, William P., 'The Castle Ashby manuscripts', *The Library* 2:4 (1960), 391–412.

Williamson, Eila, 'Drama and entertainment in Peebles in the fifteenth and sixteenth centuries', *Medieval English Theatre* 22 (2000), 127–44.

Wilson, Derek, *Sweet Robin: a Biography of Robert Dudley, Earl of Leicester 1533–1588*, London: Hamish Hamilton, 1981.

Wiseman, Susan, *Drama and Politics in the English Civil War*, Cambridge University Press, 1998.

Womack, Peter, *Ben Jonson*, Oxford: Blackwell, 1986.

Womack, Peter, 'Imagining communities: theatres and the English nation in the sixteenth century', in Aers (ed.), *Culture and History 1350–1600*, 91–145.

Worden, Blair, *The Rump Parliament 1648–1653*, Cambridge University Press, 1974.

Wright, Irene A. (ed.), *Documents Concerning English Voyages to the Spanish Main, 1569–1580*, London: Hakluyt Society, 1932.

Wright, James, *Historia Histrionica: an historical account of the English stage showing the ancient use, improvement, and perfection of dramatic representations in this nation*, London, 1699.

Wright, Louis B., 'The reading of plays during the puritan revolution', *Huntington Library Bulletin* 6 (1934), 73–112.

Wrightson, Keith, 'The puritan reformation of manners with special reference to the counties of Lancashire and Cheshire', unpublished PhD thesis, Cambridge, 1974.

Yachnin, Paul, 'The powerless theatre', *English Literary Renaissance* 21 (1991), 49–74.

Yachnin, Paul, *Stage-wrights: Jonson, Middleton, and the Making of Theatrical Value*, Philadelphia: University of Pennsylvania Press, 1997.

Yates, Frances, *The French Academies of the Sixteenth Century*, London: The Warburg Institute, 1947.

Young, Karl, *Drama of the Medieval Church*, 2 vols., Oxford: Clarendon Press, 1933.

Index

The page numbers in italic indicate illustrations.